PENGUIN CLASSICS

CHRISTINA ROSSETTI: THE COMPLETE POEMS

CHRISTINA ROSSETTI was born in London in 1830 to a literary and artistic family of Italian origin, and was educated at home. When she was sixteen, her grandfather printed a collection of her poems, convinced that they were worthy of publication. She became engaged in 1848 to James Collinson, an early member of the Pre-Raphaelite Brotherhood, of which her brothers Dante Gabriel and William Michael were among the founders. The engagement ended in 1850 on Collinson's conversion to Catholicism, which clashed with Christina's High Anglicanism. Her father retired in 1853 and Christina planned to open a day school to earn money. This plan was eventually abandoned because of ill-health, which required her to live quietly.

In 1850 several of her poems had been published under a pseudonym in her brothers' magazine, *The Germ*. More of her poems appeared in *Macmillan's Magazine* in 1861, of which 'Uphill' and 'A Birthday' received considerable critical praise. Christina went on to publish several collections of poetry, including *Goblin Market and Other Poems* (1862). She also published verse for children, including *Sing-Song: A Nursery Rhyme Book* (1872, illustrated by Arthur Hughes), short stories, prose works, including a commentary on the Apocalypse, and a number of devotional works. A devout Anglican, she was drawn to the Tractarian or Oxford Movement, and much of her writing was religious in theme, with a strong sense of spiritual yearning and melancholy. She also wrote about the frustrations and renunciation of love and in 1866 rejected a proposal of marriage from Charles Cayley, on the grounds that he was not a Christian. From then on she lived somewhat reclusively, although continuing to write and to meet her brothers' friends, whose circle included Whistler, Swinburne and Charles Dodgson (Lewis Carroll). She died in 1894.

R. W. CRUMP received her Ph.D. from the University of Texas at Austin in 1970 and has been a member of the Department of English at Louisiana State University for the past thirty years. Her publications include a variorum edition of Christina Rossetti's poems, an edition of Christina

Rossetti's *Maude: Prose and Verse* and a reference guide to the writings on Christina Rossetti.

BETTY S. FLOWERS is Professor of English and a member of the Academy of Distinguished Teachers at the University of Texas at Austin. She is a native Texan with degrees from the University of Texas and the University of London. Her publications include *Browning and the Modern Tradition* and *Extending the Shade* (poetry), and articles on Donald Barthelme, Adrienne Rich, Christina Rossetti, poetry therapy, writing, politics and myth, among other subjects. She has edited *Daughters and Fathers* (with Lynda Boose), as well as a number of television tie-in books and global scenarios.

CHRISTINA ROSSETTI

The Complete Poems

Text by R. W. CRUMP
Notes and Introduction by BETTY S. FLOWERS

PENGUIN BOOKS

PENGUIN BOOKS

Published by the Penguin Group
Penguin Books Ltd, 80 Strand, London WC2R ORL, England
Penguin Group (USA) Inc., 375 Hudson Street, New York, New York 10014, USA
Penguin Books Australia Ltd, 250 Camberwell Road, Camberwell, Victoria 3124, Australia
Penguin Books Canada Ltd, 10 Alcorn Avenue, Toronto, Ontario, Canada M4V 3B2
Penguin Books India (P) Ltd, 11 Community Centre, Panchsheel Park, New Delhi – 110 017, India
Penguin Group (NZ), cnr Airborne and Rosedale Roads, Albany, Auckland 1310, New Zealand
Penguin Books (South Africa) (Pty) Ltd, 24 Sturdee Avenue, Rosebank 2196, South Africa

Penguin Books Ltd, Registered Offices: 80 Strand, London WC2R ORL, England

www.penguin.com

First published 2001
Reprinted with corrections 2005
11

Texts copyright © Louisiana State University Press, 1979, 1986, 1990
Editorial material copyright © Betty S. Flowers, 2001, 2005
All rights reserved

The moral rights of the editors have been asserted

Set in 10/11 pt Monotype Baskerville
Typeset by Rowland Phototypesetting Ltd, Bury St Edmunds, Suffolk
Printed in Great Britain by Clays Ltd, St Ives plc

ISBN-13: 978-0-140-42366-2

www.greenpenguin.co.uk

CONTENTS

[DEVOTIONAL PIECES]

Poems Added in *Sing-Song:*
A Nursery Rhyme Book (1893)

Poems Added in *Poems*
(1888, 1890)

Verses (1893)

''OUT OF THE DEEP HAVE I CALLED UNTO THEE,
   O LORD''

CHRIST OUR ALL IN ALL

THE WORLD. SELF-DESTRUCTION

DIVERS WORLDS. TIME AND ETERNITY

IL ROSSEGGIAR DELL'ORIENTE

ACKNOWLEDGEMENTS

To R. W. Crump, the editor of *The Complete Poems of Christina Rossetti*, I owe thanks for the very existence of this book. Her splendid work over the years has been of enormous benefit to the community of Rossetti scholars.

The work and support of other Rossetti scholars have also been of immense importance to me, especially Antony H. Harrison, Nilda Jiménez, David A. Kent, Jerome J. McGann and Jan Marsh. I deeply appreciate Traci Andrighetti's admirable persistence in translating Rossetti's archaic and often idiosyncratic Italian, and the research assistance of D'Arcy Randall and Anais Spitzer.

The University Research Institute of the University of Texas at Austin provided a much appreciated semester's leave. Other forms of support were provided through the generosity of friends and family: Anthony Alofsin, Jim Autry, Philip Bobbitt, Jerome Bump, Elizabeth Cullingford, Alan Friedman, Linda Marable Jinks, Sanford Levinson, Carol MacKay, Rob Marable, Wayne Rebhorn, Mary Beth Rogers, Harriet Rubin, Tim Ruefli, John Stanning, Ellen Wartella and, especially, John, John Michael and Margaret Flowers.

To Paul Keegan at Penguin I owe much appreciation for patience and understanding; and to Lindeth Vasey I owe deepest thanks for the best close attention an editor could ever hope to receive. I'm also very grateful to the master editor, Christopher Ricks, whose keen eye and unfailing good sense are responsible for much of what I value in this work.

I would like to dedicate my work to my parents, Betty Lewis Marable and Paul Davis Marable, Jr.

Betty S. Flowers
University of Texas at Austin

INTRODUCTION

Christina Georgina Rossetti was born in London on 5 December 1830, the fourth child of an Italian poet in exile and an Italian-English mother. Her childhood home was both exotic and conventional – exotic in that it was enlivened by visiting Italian revolutionaries and writers, and conventional in that her mother Frances's teaching and example led Rossetti into an intense and lifelong devotion to Christianity.

Rossetti's bilingual household was also a lively home for the arts. Not only was Rossetti's father, Gabriele, a poet and translator, but her maternal grandfather was a translator, and her uncle was John Polidori, Byron's physician and author of *The Vampyre*. All the Rossetti children were encouraged to develop their artistic and scholarly talents. The oldest, Maria Francesca (b. 1827), published a commentary on Dante; Gabriel Charles Dante (later, Dante Gabriel) (b. 1828) became a poet and painter; and William Michael (b. 1829) became a critic, a biographer and an editor of the poems and letters of his more celebrated siblings.

In early childhood, Christina Rossetti was spirited and wilful, once ripping her arm with scissors in a fit of temper. But this story, which she told to her niece, provides a vivid contrast to the restrained and self-disciplined poet with the beautiful, melodious voice that William and other early biographers presented to the world. In spite of Rossetti's youthful temper tantrums, the picture that emerges from descriptions of her early childhood is a happy one, with its lively family life, including visits to her maternal grandfather in rural Holmer Green. The fields and orchards surrounding her grandfather's cottage, with their fruit trees and small animals, provided much of the natural imagery in her poems and short stories. But these idyllic country interludes lasted only until Rossetti was nine, when her grandfather moved to the city. There he set up a private press – and printed her first book of poems when she was sixteen – *Verses: Dedicated to Her Mother*.

From that volume to her last, all Rossetti's books of poetry were dedicated to her mother. Her first surviving poem is a birthday greeting to her mother. Like all the Rossetti children, Christina revered her mother. The letters among the four siblings reveal not only their affection for each other, even in disagreement, but their common bond in seeing that their mother was cared for. Rossetti's mother was her teacher, her nurse, her confidante and perhaps her best friend. In one of the many valentines she addressed to her mother, she expressed a 'lifelong love to this dear Saint of mine' ('A Valentine 1882').

The poems of Rossetti's adolescence include many short lyrics with themes of love and death as well as monologues based on characters from the Gothic novels of one of her favourite authors, Charles Maturin. The preoccupation with death that emerges in her earliest poetry is in part a reflection of the Romantic literature of writers like Maturin and Keats, whose poems were among her favourites throughout her life. But this theme was also no doubt linked to the ill health she began suffering in 1845. Her brother William reported that the family feared for her life during her youth, and many of her early manuscripts are written in the hand of her sister. The cause of Rossetti's illness during this time is not entirely clear, encompassing heart trouble, fainting fits, anaemia, and what appears to be a kind of nervous exhaustion.

Rossetti's frequent theme of love threatened by death is interwoven with another central theme: the vanity of youth and beauty given the inevitability of age and death. Allusions to the biblical verse 'Vanity of vanities . . . all is vanity' (Ecc. 1:2) occur over a dozen times in Rossetti's poetry, and the superiority of heavenly joys to earthly pleasures forms the implicit motif of poems throughout her career.

The spiritual devotion evident in Rossetti's life and work was unusually intense even in an age noted for its religious preoccupations. Like many others of her generation, Rossetti was influenced by the Oxford Movement, which aimed to revive the High Church traditions of the Anglican church, moving it closer to Catholic observances and rituals. Rossetti was deeply interested in many of the saints, observed fast days, followed the liturgical calendar, wrote a number of devotional prose books under the auspices of the Society for Promoting Christian Knowledge (SPCK) and lived an exemplary moral, almost nun-like existence, caring for her mother and aunts until late in her life. For many critics, this depth of devotion was a limiting factor, contributing, along with her ill health, to what they considered to be a 'morbid' strain in her poetry and constricting what might otherwise have been a string of *Goblin Markets* – richly imaginative, surprisingly sensual and innovative, informal verse.

But Rossetti's own view of her work differed from that of her more secular critics, including her brothers. One of her earliest ambitions was to write a really fine hymn. And the beauty of her lyricism, the perfect pitch and clarity of her line, the subtle effects of rhyme and rhythm owe much to the nakedness of feeling and simplicity of form to be found in the hymns she knew so well. Many of her lines weave together the rhythms of the Authorized Version (King James) of the Bible, and often she quotes entire verses, so that her lines resonate with overtones from centuries of associated meanings, even as they appear to move horizontally across a surface of lyric simplicity. In this, ironically, she was a harbinger of aestheticism, not in its insistence on art for art's sake but in its emphasis on the significance of the surface of things – a surface which she enriches by traditional, not psychological, associations. This makes her art iconic rather than psychological and calls for readings that pay attention to the interplay between allusions and emotion.

Such a reading could be given, for example to 'I Will Lift Up Mine Eyes Unto the Hills' ['When sick of life and all the world'], which echoes verses from Psalms, Revelation, John, Ecclesiastes, Proverbs, Isaiah and I John. These echoes create a virtual chorus of voices within Rossetti's own and turn what secular readers might experience as a kind of flat piety into a richly shaded emotional journey. The temptation to read Rossetti's verse as morbid or depressed must be tempered by these biblical allusions that speak of other realities beyond the merely personal reality of the moment.

In fact, the emotion of Rossetti's lines is almost always in dialogue with a meaning on another level that is partially created through allusions. The enacted emotion may be one of despair, for example; but the despair may be worded so as to echo a Bible verse that offers a promise of hope. While we feel the speaker's present sorrow, we know, because the allusion reminds us, that there is another reality larger than the sorrow we are feeling. For example, the Proverbs verse 'Hope deferred maketh the heart sick' (13:12) is echoed in at least sixteen of Rossetti's poems. On its face, the phrase 'hope deferred' alludes to disappointment and, perhaps, depression. But this phrase is shadowed by the second half of the verse, which Rossetti seldom quotes directly. The entire verse reads: 'Hope deferred maketh the heart sick: but when the desire cometh, it is a tree of life.' The importance of this second half of the verse is emphasized by Rossetti's comment in *Time Flies* that '[w]e feel or fancy ourselves quite at home in the first clause of this proverb,' but that, left to herself, she might never have caught the meaning of the second until someone pointed out that the tree of life was the cross 'which satisfied the world's heartsick hope' (pp. 80–81). The 'someone' who pointed this out, of course, was her mother.

While Rossetti lived a relatively quiet, even pious, life, it would be wrong to imagine her as living apart from the literary and political influences of her time. Her letters reveal her to be a witty woman with a teasing sense of humour. She wrote a number of poems based on contemporary political events and actively campaigned against cruelty to animals. She had many friends among writers, even contributing poems to a kind of women's artists' workshop, the Portfolio Society, although she did not attend its meetings. In addition, she had a wide correspondence and was very generous to aspiring writers. Poets ranging from Swinburne to Gerard Manley Hopkins admired her work. *Alice's Adventures in Wonderland* by Lewis Carroll (Charles Dodgson) owes a great deal to *Goblin Market*. And the picture of Rossetti as a pious recluse must be counterbalanced by the fact that she remained close to her two brothers all of her life, one of them, William, a free-thinking atheist, and the other, Dante Gabriel, an artist whose life was at least as lurid as hers was chaste. That they were her most trusted critics points to a largeness of spirit not usually associated with a religiously restricted sensibility.

In 1848, Rossetti's brothers, along with a number of other writers and painters, including William Holman Hunt and John Everett Millais, formed the 'Pre-Raphaelite Brotherhood', which admired early Italian painting, with its attention to detail. They were critical of Raphael (and of the nineteenth-century academy painting it was felt derived from him). The Pre-Raphaelites espoused fidelity to nature, creating works of art often characterized by implicit narratives and symbolic imagery. Rossetti, although a young woman and therefore excluded from the late-night meetings in Hunt's studio, nevertheless associated herself with their work, posing as a model for Hunt's *Light of the World* in 1852 and for several of her brother Gabriel's paintings during this period. Two of her early published poems appeared in the journal of the brotherhood, *The Germ*, in 1850.

One of its members was a young painter, James Collinson, who proposed to Rossetti in 1848. Rossetti at first refused because of Collinson's Catholicism, but when her suitor converted to Anglicanism, she accepted. Then two years later, Collinson returned to

Catholicism, and the engagement ended. Rossetti's next few years were marked by ill health, both of herself and of her father, who was forced to give up his job teaching Italian. She and her mother set up a day school in 1851 to help support the family, but the school failed. The next year, they set up another in Somerset, but had to return to London to care for Rossetti's father. After he died in 1854, Rossetti volunteered to join Florence Nightingale's expedition of nurses to aid the wounded in the Crimean War, but although her Aunt Eliza was accepted, Rossetti was turned down because of her youth and inexperience.

By the late 1850s, Rossetti was publishing short stories and poems in journals and had settled into a pattern of life that she maintained for the next decade: living with her mother and sister in William's household; writing and visiting with friends; sometimes visiting the seaside village of Hastings to improve her health; and, until the mid 1860s, working as a volunteer in a home for 'fallen' women. Twice during the 1860s she travelled to Europe with her mother and William.

While Rossetti's pattern of life seems quiet and uneventful, dramatic events were unfolding in the family around her. William broke his engagement to his fiancée of four years in the same year (1860) that Dante Gabriel married his long-time model and mistress, Elizabeth Siddal. Two years later, Siddal died of an overdose of laudanum, and Dante Gabriel buried the only copy of his poems with her. His 1869 exhumation of the manuscript, and the critical reaction to them as examples of 'the fleshly school of poetry' (from Robert Buchanan's article (1871)), as one outraged critic termed it, contributed to an emotional instability that he treated with addictive drugs. During all this time, Rossetti stayed close to her brother, carrying on a lively correspondence and visiting him in his house on Cheyne Walk. There is an evocative family portrait, taken by Charles Dodgson in 1863, showing the family in the garden, with Dante Gabriel and his mother playing chess while Maria sits on the steps, and Christina, leaning on the railing, looks on.

Rossetti's first publicly printed book of poetry, *Goblin Market and Other Poems*, was published in 1862 and proved to be very popular. A second edition followed three years later. Rossetti's second book of poems, *The Prince's Progress and Other Poems* (1866), was not as successful, although by this time she was achieving widespread recognition as a leading poet of the day. That Rossetti was deeply committed to her writing career is evident in her letters, many of which deal with publishing arrangements or function as conversations with her brothers about which poems to include in her books and how to revise them.

In 1866, Rossetti received a proposal of marriage from a reclusive Dante scholar and former pupil of her father, Charles Bagot Cayley. To judge from a series of love poems written in Italian (*Il Rosseggiar dell' Oriente*), which William found in her writing desk after her death, Rossetti loved Cayley very deeply. But she refused him, perhaps on religious grounds, since he was a religious sceptic.

The early 1870s were extremely difficult for Rossetti and her family. Dante Gabriel suffered an attack of dementia, and Rossetti was diagnosed as suffering from Graves' disease (exophthalmic bronchocele), a life-threatening thyroid condition that destroyed both her health and her beauty. Maria left the household to become an Anglican nun. And William married Lucy Brown, the daughter of the painter and family friend Ford Madox Brown – a happy event, but one that brought an outsider into the tightly knit Rossetti family constellation. During these difficult years, Rossetti published a book of short stories in Boston (*Commonplace*) and her popular book of children's rhymes, *Sing-Song: A Nursery Rhyme Book*. She also published a book of short stories for children, *Speaking Likenesses*, as well as the first of six books sponsored by the SPCK, *Annus Domini: A Prayer for Each Day of the Year, Founded on a Text of Holy Scripture*.

Although Rossetti's interest in children's rhymes and stories preceded the births of William and Lucy's five children, these nieces and nephews began to play an important role in her family life. Soon after the birth of the first, a growing tension between Lucy and Rossetti led to a change in living arrangements, with Rossetti, her mother and eventually her two aunts moving to a new home in Bloomsbury, where Rossetti lived for the rest of her life.

In 1875, Rossetti's first collected edition of poems appeared, both in England and the USA, followed in 1881 by a new book of poetry, *A Pageant and Other Poems*. During the ten years 1875–85, Rossetti enrolled in a course of lectures on Dante at University College London, and published four additional books of religious prose, *Seek and Find*, *Called to be Saints*, *Letter and Spirit* and *Time Flies*. Her discipline and dedication to both her art and her religion are evident in this outpouring of work despite the death of her sister Maria (1876), her first love James Collinson (1881), her brother Gabriel (1882), her infant nephew

Michael (1883), her beloved Charles Cayley (1883) and, in 1886, her mother.

Triumph and loss punctuated the last four years of Rossetti's life. In 1890, the second and enlarged collected edition of her poetry was published in England and the USA. Two years later, her monumental commentary on Revelation, *The Face of the Deep*, was published, followed in 1893 by *Verses*, which was made up of the poems collected from three of her religious books published by the SPCK. That same year, a new, illustrated edition of *Goblin Market* was published. Rossetti was by now so highly thought of that when Tennyson died in 1892, she was mentioned in literary circles as a possible candidate for poet laureate. But during these same four years, her sister-in-law, and the two aunts who had lived with her, died, and in 1892, Rossetti underwent surgery for breast cancer. She died, two years later, on 29 December.

Soon after her death, William began collecting her unpublished poems, which appeared in 1896 as *New Poems*. The next year, Rossetti's 1850 short story *Maude* appeared, and in 1904, William published what remained the standard edition of Rossetti's works for most of the century: *The Poetical Works of Christina Georgina Rossetti*.

Rossetti's life, publications and letters reveal her to be both ambitious and competitive. She was intensely aware of her role as a woman, tending to compare herself with other women writers, especially Elizabeth Barrett Browning. Although Barrett Browning was more avant-garde in her own day – eloping with a younger man, writing a verse novel, speaking out on political and social themes, coming forward on behalf of women – her poems seem dated when compared with those of Rossetti, many of whose lyrics have the power to startle us with their directness and clarity of expression – their 'trueness'. Though in her outer life, Rossetti chose to submit to the discipline of religion, her essential independence of spirit shines through her work. This independence is difficult to approach through standard close readings or psychoanalytically oriented biographical readings.

Early critics, strongly influenced by William's position of editorial and biographical authority, tended to read Rossetti's poetry through the prism of her unhappy love life. Her relationships with Collinson and Cayley both appear to have influenced the subject matter of much of her poetry, especially the poems of longing and thwarted love. But these relationships assumed a disproportionate influence in the reading of Rossetti's poetry, in part because they seemed to be among the few dramatic 'events' in her life and in part because the view of women that influenced early criticism made love relationships the key to any woman artist's life and work.

This view of women as reflected in the reading of the poems began to change with the advent of feminist literary criticism in the early 1970s. At first, Rossetti's poems, unlike Barrett Browning's *Aurora Leigh*, for example, seemed unpromising objects for feminist criticism. The exception was *Goblin Market*, which was read as a critique of economic exchange, as a commentary on the nature of desire, and in relation to consumerism, vampirism and anorexia, among other possibilities. Many of Rossetti's characteristic subjects – the dead woman, the betrayal of love, the superiority of other-worldly love to the satisfactions of this world – were re-read for their implicit strategies of resistance to authority as well as their conventional surfaces. At the same time that readings of Rossetti's poems were increasing in number and sophistication, important scholarly material was becoming available for the first time, most notably with new editions of Rossetti's works and letters.

Now, over a hundred years since her death, Rossetti is assuming a much more important place in the history of English poetry. The growing interest in her religious prose, the increased understanding of her relationship to earlier poets such as Dante, Milton, George Herbert and Keats, and the growing knowledge of her life occasioned by newly published biographies and letters all point to a renaissance in the study of Rossetti. The recontextualizing of Rossetti's poetry, to which this edition is intended as a contribution, will suggest to us new strategies for reading it – and perhaps a new understanding of the complex relations of tradition, talent and the life journey of an individual soul.

This edition

This Penguin edition is the first fully annotated collection of Christina Rossetti's poems. Although William Michael Rossetti's 1904 edition of *The Poetical Works of Christina Georgina Rossetti* was incomplete and, to some extent, unreliable, it remained the standard edition until the publication of R. W. Crump's three-volume edition (with textual notes and introductions) of *The Complete Poems of Christina Rossetti* (Louisiana State University Press, 1979–90). While Crump's edition provides a thoroughly reliable text, it lacks the useful information contained in William Rossetti's 'Notes' to many of the poems in his edition. And while his notes add a great deal to our understanding of the poems, they are limited in scope, and written for readers familiar with nineteenth-century terms and allusions.

This volume is intended to bring together the best features of both editions – William Rossetti's helpful contextual notes and Crump's text and textual information – and to provide, in addition, definitions, literal translations of all Rossetti's Italian poems, identifications of allusions, especially biblical and liturgical allusions, contextual material from her prose works, and contributions from letters, scholarly research and other sources, such as *The Book of Common Prayer*, that help illuminate Rossetti's poems.

Text

The text is Crump's, including her later corrections, which uses as copy-text the first English editions of Rossetti's poems, which she chose because they incorporate the numerous changes Rossetti and her brother Dante Gabriel made in the manuscript versions. Where the editions differ from the manuscript, Crump restores manuscript spellings, corrects typesetting errors and adopts manuscript line indentations, stanza breaks and punctuation. In addition, Crump incorporates some readings that appeared for the first time in the 1875 edition of *Goblin Market, The Prince's Progress, and Other Poems*. Thus, Crump's edition 'furnishes an eclectic text, which, unlike any single authoritative version, is based on a consideration of Christina's extant manuscripts, letters, editions, and individual printings of her poems in journals and anthologies' (I, 7). For poems that Rossetti did not include in her published collections, the basic text is identified in the headnote for each poem.

The order of the poems

The poems are printed in the order in which they appear in Crump's three-volume edition, beginning with Rossetti's published collections – *Goblin Market and Other Poems* (1862), *The Prince's Progress and Other Poems* (1866), *Sing-Song* (1872), *A Pageant and Other Poems* (1881) and *Verses* (1893). Within each collection, the poems are ordered as they were in the first edition, followed by the poems Rossetti added to subsequent editions. Next come poems published separately, usually in anthologies or periodicals, or in Rossetti's prose works. The final category is privately printed poems and those poems Rossetti chose not to print during her lifetime.

The notes

Information about sources of texts, publications, manuscripts and significant variants in published titles is taken from Crump's three-volume edition. To keep this volume to a manageable size, I have not included textual variants, with only a few exceptions. A full record of all textual matters can be found in Crump's three-volume edition.

In many instances, the biographical information in the annotations reflects William Rossetti's 'Notes' to the 1904 edition. In addition, I have attempted to identify words that may not be familiar to twenty-first-century readers, including those non-British readers who may not know some of the common British fruits, for example, or the landscape terms Rossetti mentions. For readers unfamiliar with the Bible, this first fully annotated edition reveals the great extent to which Rossetti calls on it, not only for her inspiration and subject matter, but also for many of her lines. Nilda Jiménez identifies most of these allusions in *The Bible and the Poetry of Christina Rossetti: A Concordance*, pointing out that Rossetti frequently alludes to verses in the Song of Solomon, Ecclesiastes and Revelation, and that the Bible passage Rossetti quotes most often is 'vanity of vanities; all is vanity' (Ecc. 1:2). Rossetti assumes her readers know biblical characters and verses, and the stories in which they are embedded – and her poems often depend on this knowledge for their effectiveness. In helping readers recreate a richer context for Rossetti's poems, I trust this edition will also encourage a fuller appreciation of the beauty and emotional complexity of her work.

TABLE OF DATES

June Dante Gabriel suffers attack of dementia.

1873   *July* William and Lucy Brown engaged.
       September Maria joins Anglican All Saints' Sisterhood and moves
       to convent.

1874   *Annus Domini: A Prayer for Each Day of the Year, Founded on a Text of
       Holy Scripture.*
       Speaking Likenesses (short stories for children).
       William marries Lucy Brown.

1875   *Goblin Market, The Prince's Progress, and Other Poems* (first collected
       edition).
       Birth of William and Lucy's first child, Olivia Rossetti.

1876   Death of Maria; CR, her two aunts and her mother move to 30
       Torrington Square in Bloomsbury.
       Poems published in Boston (new enlarged edition).

1877   Birth of William and Lucy's second child, Gabriel Arthur Rossetti.
       Enrols in a course of lectures on Dante's *Divine Comedy* at Univer-
       sity College London.

1879   *Seek and Find: A Double Series of Short Studies of the Benedicite* published
       by the Society for Promoting Christian Knowledge (SPCK).
       Birth of Helen Rossetti.

1881   *A Pageant and Other Poems* (also published in Boston).
       Called to be Saints: The Minor Festivals Devotionally Studied (SPCK).
       Birth of William and Lucy's twins, Michael and Mary Rossetti.
       Death of Collinson.

1882   *Poems* published in Boston.
       April Death of Dante Gabriel.

1883   *January* Death of William and Lucy's son Michael.
       Letter and Spirit: Notes on the Commandments (SPCK).
       December Death of Cayley.

1885   *Time Flies: A Reading Diary* (SPCK).

1886   *Time Flies* published in Boston.
       April Death of her mother.

1890   *Poems: New and Enlarged Edition* (second collected edition; also
       published in New York).
       Death of her Aunt Charlotte.

1892   *The Face of the Deep: A Devotional Commentary on the Apocalypse*
       (SPCK; also published in New York).
       Diagnosed with breast cancer and undergoes surgery.

1893   *Verses* (reprinted from *Called to be Saints, Time Flies* and *The Face
       of the Deep*; also published in New York).

Goblin Market republished, with illustrations by Laurence Housman.

Death of her Aunt Eliza.

1894 *April* Death of Lucy Rossetti.

29 December Dies.

1896 *New Poems, Hitherto Unpublished or Uncollected.*

1897 *Maude: A Story for Girls* (also published in Chicago).

1904 *The Poetical Works of Christina Georgina Rossetti, with Memoir and Notes by William Michael Rossetti.*

FURTHER READING

Editions

The Poetical Works of Christina Georgina Rossetti, with Memoir and Notes by William Michael Rossetti (Macmillan, 1904). The standard edition of Rossetti's poetry for over seventy-five years, until Crump's edition appeared. The notes are indispensable, in part because they reflect William's knowledge of Rossetti's life as well as her interactions with her brother Dante Gabriel, who sometimes influenced her writing. The 'Memoir' is the basis for all subsequent biographies of Rossetti. The edition, however, suffers from William's arbitrary re-arranging of poems – for example, removing lines from the middle of one poem and placing them in another, or breaking up a poem into several smaller ones. Some titles are his inventions.

The Complete Poems of Christina Rossetti: A Variorum Edition, ed. R. W. Crump, 3 vols. (Louisiana State University Press, 1979–90). An excellent scholarly edition, which supersedes, textually, the 1904 edition.

Christina Rossetti: Poems and Prose, ed. Jan Marsh (Everyman, 1994). A good selection of Rossetti's verse, including 226 of the over 1000 extant poems, along with some of the fiction, prose and correspondence, accompanied by notes on the texts.

Prose

Selected Prose of Christina Rossetti, ed. David A. Kent and P. G. Stanwood (St Martin's Press, 1998).

Bibliographies and Reference Works

William E. Fredeman, 'Christina Georgina Rossetti', in *Pre-Raphaelitism: A Bibliocritical Study* (Harvard University Press, 1965).
—, 'The Pre-Raphaelites. Christina Rossetti', in *The Victorian Poets: A*

Guide to Research, ed. Frederic E. Faverty, 2nd edn. (Harvard University Press, 1968).

R. W. Crump, *Christina Rossetti: A Reference Guide* (Hall, 1976). An annotated bibliography for publications up to 1973.

For works published after 1973, the best bibliographic sources are the annual bibliographies in *Victorian Poetry* and *Victorian Studies*, and the *MLA International Bibliography of Books and Articles on the Modern Languages and Literatures* (*PMLA Bibliography*), available online.

Letters

The most important collections are:

Rossetti Papers, 1862–1870, ed. William M. Rossetti (Scribner's, 1903). Includes letters by Rossetti, extracts from William's diary and comments on Rossetti's poems.

The Family Letters of Christina Georgina Rossetti, ed. William M. Rossetti (Brown, Langham, 1908). Does not include letters in *Rossetti Papers* or in Bell's biography; contains selections from William's diary, 1871–95, and from the diary Rossetti kept for her mother, 1881–6.

Three Rossettis: Unpublished Letters to and from Dante Gabriel, Christina, William, ed. Janet Camp Troxell (Harvard University Press, 1937).

The Rossetti–Macmillan Letters: Some 133 Unpublished Letters Written to Alexander Macmillan, F. S. Ellis, and Others, by Dante Gabriel, Christina, and William Michael Rossetti, 1861–1889, ed. Lona Mosk Packer (University of California Press, 1963).

The Collected Letters of Christina Rossetti, ed. Antony H. Harrison, Vol. I–III (of IV) (University Press of Virginia, 1997–).

Biographies

Over a dozen book-length biographies have been published. The most important early sources and later ones are:

Mackenzie Bell, *Christina Rossetti: A Biographical and Critical Study* (Hurst and Blackett, 1898). Includes primary materials given to Bell by William Rossetti.

William Michael Rossetti, 'Memoir', in *The Poetical Works of Christina Georgina Rossetti*, pp. xlv–lxxi. The basis for all subsequent biographical writings on Rossetti.

—, *Some Reminiscences*, 2 vols. (Brown, Langham, 1906).

Ellen A. Proctor, *A Brief Memoir of Christina G. Rossetti* (Society for Promoting Christian Knowledge, 1895). Includes preface by William Rossetti; especially revealing in relation to the last years of Rossetti's life.

Lona Mosk Packer, *Christina Rossetti* (University of California Press, 1963). A critical biography, but deeply flawed by its intriguing but ultimately unsound thesis: that the object of Rossetti's secret love and many love poems was William Bell Scott.

Jan Marsh, *Christina Rossetti: A Literary Biography* (Cape, 1994). The best biography to date.

Criticism

Significant general studies include the following (in chronological order):

Virginia Woolf, 'I am Christina Rossetti' (1930), in *Second Common Reader* (Harcourt, Brace, 1932).

C. M. Bowra, 'Christina Rossetti', in *The Romantic Imagination* (Cambridge, 1949).

Barbara Garlitz, 'Christina Rossetti's *Sing-Song* and Nineteenth-Century Children's Poetry', *Publications of the Modern Language Association* (1955), 539–43.

K. E. Janowitz, 'The Antipodes of Self: Three Poems by Christina Rossetti', *Victorian Poetry* 3 (1965), 261–3.

Winston Weathers, 'Christina Rossetti: The Sisterhood of Self', *Victorian Poetry* 3 (1965), 81–9.

Gisela Hönnighausen, 'Emblematic Tendencies in the Works of Christina Rossetti', *Victorian Poetry* 10 (1972), 1–15.

Lionel Stevenson, 'Christina Rossetti', in *The Pre-Raphaelite Poets* (University of North Carolina Press, 1972), pp. 78–122.

Theo Dombrowski, 'Dualism in the Poetry of Christina Rossetti', *Victorian Poetry* 14 (1976), 70–6.

Ralph A. Bellas, *Christina Rossetti* (Illinois State University, 1977). This contribution to Twayne's English Author Series is an overview of Rossetti's life and work.

Sandra Gilbert and Susan Gubar, 'The Aesthetics of Renunciation', in *The Madwoman in the Attic* (Yale, 1979), pp. 549–54, 564–75.

Nilda Jiménez, *The Bible and the Poetry of Christina Rossetti: A Concordance* (Greenwood Press, 1979).

Jerome J. McGann, 'Christina Rossetti's Poems: A New Edition and a Revaluation', *Victorian Studies* 23 (1980), 237–54.

—, 'The Religious Poetry of Christina Rossetti', *Critical Inquiry* 10 (1983), 133–41.

Joan Rees, 'Christina Rossetti: Poet', *Critical Quarterly* 26 (1984), 59–72.

Dolores Rosenblum, *Christina Rossetti: The Poetry of Endurance* (Southern Illinois University Press, 1986).

David A. Kent (ed.), *The Achievement of Christina Rossetti* (Cornell University Press, 1987).

Antony H. Harrison, *Christina Rossetti in Context* (University of North Carolina, 1988).

Katherine J. Mayberry, *Christina Rossetti and the Poetry of Discovery* (Louisiana State University Press, 1989).

Angela Leighton, 'Christina Rossetti', in *Victorian Women Poets: Writing Against the Heart* (University Press of Virginia, 1992), pp. 118–63.

Diane D'Amico, *Christina Rossetti: Faith, Gender, and Time* (Louisiana State University Press, 1999).

Mary Arseneau, Antony H. Harrison and Lorraine Janzen Kooistra (eds.), *The Culture of Christina Rossetti: Female Poetics and Victorian Context* (Ohio University Press, 1999).

Lynda Palazzo, *Christina Rossetti's Feminist Theology* (Palgrave, 2002).

Also see 'The Victorian Web' at *http://www.victorianweb.org/*; 'Victorian Web Sites' at *http://victorian.lang.nagoya-u.ac.jp/sites/links.html*; 'Victoria Research Web' at *http://victorianresearch.org/*; and 'Victorian Studies on the Web' at *http://www.victoriandatabase.com/*.

The Complete Poems

Goblin Market and Other Poems
(1862)

GOBLIN MARKET.

Morning and evening
Maids heard the goblins cry:
"Come buy our orchard fruits,
Come buy, come buy:
5   Apples and quinces,
Lemons and oranges,
Plump unpecked cherries,
Melons and raspberries,
Bloom-down-cheeked peaches,
10   Swart-headed mulberries,
Wild free-born cranberries,
Crab-apples, dewberries,
Pine-apples, blackberries,
Apricots, strawberries;—
15   All ripe together
In summer weather,—
Morns that pass by,
Fair eves that fly;
Come buy, come buy:
20   Our grapes fresh from the vine,
Pomegranates full and fine,
Dates and sharp bullaces,
Rare pears and greengages,
Damsons and bilberries,
25   Taste them and try:
Currants and gooseberries,
Bright-fire-like barberries,
Figs to fill your mouth,
Citrons from the South,

30   Sweet to tongue and sound to eye;
      Come buy, come buy."

      Evening by evening
      Among the brookside rushes,
      Laura bowed her head to hear,
35   Lizzie veiled her blushes:
      Crouching close together
      In the cooling weather,
      With clasping arms and cautioning lips,
      With tingling cheeks and finger tips.
40   "Lie close," Laura said,
      Pricking up her golden head:
      "We must not look at goblin men,
      We must not buy their fruits:
      Who knows upon what soil they fed
45   Their hungry thirsty roots?"
      "Come buy," call the goblins
      Hobbling down the glen.
      "Oh," cried Lizzie, "Laura, Laura,
      You should not peep at goblin men."
50   Lizzie covered up her eyes,
      Covered close lest they should look;
      Laura reared her glossy head,
      And whispered like the restless brook:
      "Look, Lizzie, look, Lizzie,
55   Down the glen tramp little men.
      One hauls a basket,
      One bears a plate,
      One lugs a golden dish
      Of many pounds weight.
60   How fair the vine must grow
      Whose grapes are so luscious;
      How warm the wind must blow
      Thro' those fruit bushes."
      "No," said Lizzie: "No, no, no;
65   Their offers should not charm us,
      Their evil gifts would harm us."
      She thrust a dimpled finger

In each ear, shut eyes and ran:
Curious Laura chose to linger
70   Wondering at each merchant man.
One had a cat's face,
One whisked a tail,
One tramped at a rat's pace,
One crawled like a snail,
75   One like a wombat prowled obtuse and furry,
One like a ratel tumbled hurry skurry.
She heard a voice like voice of doves
Cooing all together:
They sounded kind and full of loves
80   In the pleasant weather.

Laura stretched her gleaming neck
Like a rush-imbedded swan,
Like a lily from the beck,
Like a moonlit poplar branch,
85   Like a vessel at the launch
When its last restraint is gone.

Backwards up the mossy glen
Turned and trooped the goblin men,
With their shrill repeated cry,
90   "Come buy, come buy."
When they reached where Laura was
They stood stock still upon the moss,
Leering at each other,
Brother with queer brother;
95   Signalling each other,
Brother with sly brother.
One set his basket down,
One reared his plate;
One began to weave a crown
100   Of tendrils, leaves and rough nuts brown
(Men sell not such in any town);
One heaved the golden weight
Of dish and fruit to offer her:
"Come buy, come buy," was still their cry.

105   Laura stared but did not stir,
       Longed but had no money:
       The whisk-tailed merchant bade her taste
       In tones as smooth as honey,
       The cat-faced purr'd,
110   The rat-paced spoke a word
       Of welcome, and the snail-paced even was heard;
       One parrot-voiced and jolly
       Cried "Pretty Goblin" still for "Pretty Polly;"—
       One whistled like a bird.

115   But sweet-tooth Laura spoke in haste:
       "Good folk, I have no coin;
       To take were to purloin:
       I have no copper in my purse,
       I have no silver either,
120   And all my gold is on the furze
       That shakes in windy weather
       Above the rusty heather."
       "You have much gold upon your head,"
       They answered all together:
125   "Buy from us with a golden curl."
       She clipped a precious golden lock,
       She dropped a tear more rare than pearl,
       Then sucked their fruit globes fair or red:
       Sweeter than honey from the rock,
130   Stronger than man-rejoicing wine,
       Clearer than water flowed that juice;
       She never tasted such before,
       How should it cloy with length of use?
       She sucked and sucked and sucked the more
135   Fruits which that unknown orchard bore;
       She sucked until her lips were sore;
       Then flung the emptied rinds away
       But gathered up one kernel-stone,
       And knew not was it night or day
140   As she turned home alone.

       Lizzie met her at the gate
       Full of wise upbraidings:

"Dear, you should not stay so late,
Twilight is not good for maidens;
145 Should not loiter in the glen
In the haunts of goblin men.
Do you not remember Jeanie,
How she met them in the moonlight,
Took their gifts both choice and many,
150 Ate their fruits and wore their flowers
Plucked from bowers
Where summer ripens at all hours?
But ever in the noonlight
She pined and pined away;
155 Sought them by night and day,
Found them no more but dwindled and grew grey;
Then fell with the first snow,
While to this day no grass will grow
Where she lies low:
160 I planted daisies there a year ago
That never blow.
You should not loiter so."
"Nay, hush," said Laura:
"Nay, hush, my sister:
165 I ate and ate my fill,
Yet my mouth waters still;
Tomorrow night I will
Buy more:" and kissed her:
"Have done with sorrow;
170 I'll bring you plums tomorrow
Fresh on their mother twigs,
Cherries worth getting;
You cannot think what figs
My teeth have met in,
175 What melons icy-cold
Piled on a dish of gold
Too huge for me to hold,
What peaches with a velvet nap,
Pellucid grapes without one seed:
180 Odorous indeed must be the mead
Whereon they grow, and pure the wave they drink

With lilies at the brink,
And sugar-sweet their sap."

Golden head by golden head,
185 Like two pigeons in one nest
Folded in each other's wings,
They lay down in their curtained bed:
Like two blossoms on one stem,
Like two flakes of new-fall'n snow,
190 Like two wands of ivory
Tipped with gold for awful kings.
Moon and stars gazed in at them,
Wind sang to them lullaby,
Lumbering owls forbore to fly,
195 Not a bat flapped to and fro
Round their rest:
Cheek to cheek and breast to breast
Locked together in one nest.

Early in the morning
200 When the first cock crowed his warning,
Neat like bees, as sweet and busy,
Laura rose with Lizzie:
Fetched in honey, milked the cows,
Aired and set to rights the house,
205 Kneaded cakes of whitest wheat,
Cakes for dainty mouths to eat,
Next churned butter, whipped up cream,
Fed their poultry, sat and sewed;
Talked as modest maidens should:
210 Lizzie with an open heart,
Laura in an absent dream,
One content, one sick in part;
One warbling for the mere bright day's delight,
One longing for the night.

215 At length slow evening came:
They went with pitchers to the reedy brook;
Lizzie most placid in her look,
Laura most like a leaping flame.
They drew the gurgling water from its deep;

220   Lizzie plucked purple and rich golden flags,
     Then turning homewards said: "The sunset flushes
     Those furthest loftiest crags;
     Come, Laura, not another maiden lags,
     No wilful squirrel wags,
225   The beasts and birds are fast asleep."
     But Laura loitered still among the rushes
     And said the bank was steep.

     And said the hour was early still,
     The dew not fall'n, the wind not chill:
230   Listening ever, but not catching
     The customary cry,
     "Come buy, come buy,"
     With its iterated jingle
     Of sugar-baited words:
235   Not for all her watching
     Once discerning even one goblin
     Racing, whisking, tumbling, hobbling;
     Let alone the herds
     That used to tramp along the glen,
240   In groups or single,
     Of brisk fruit-merchant men.
     Till Lizzie urged, "O Laura, come;
     I hear the fruit-call but I dare not look:
     You should not loiter longer at this brook:
245   Come with me home.
     The stars rise, the moon bends her arc,
     Each glowworm winks her spark,
     Let us get home before the night grows dark:
     For clouds may gather
250   Tho' this is summer weather,
     Put out the lights and drench us thro';
     Then if we lost our way what should we do?"

     Laura turned cold as stone
     To find her sister heard that cry alone,
255   That goblin cry,
     "Come buy our fruits, come buy."
     Must she then buy no more such dainty fruit?

Must she no more such succous pasture find,
Gone deaf and blind?
260 Her tree of life drooped from the root:
She said not one word in her heart's sore ache;
But peering thro' the dimness, nought discerning,
Trudged home, her pitcher dripping all the way;
So crept to bed, and lay
265 Silent till Lizzie slept;
Then sat up in a passionate yearning,
And gnashed her teeth for baulked desire, and wept
As if her heart would break.

Day after day, night after night,
270 Laura kept watch in vain
In sullen silence of exceeding pain.
She never caught again the goblin cry:
"Come buy, come buy;"—
She never spied the goblin men
275 Hawking their fruits along the glen:
But when the noon waxed bright
Her hair grew thin and gray;
She dwindled, as the fair full moon doth turn
To swift decay and burn
280 Her fire away.

One day remembering her kernel-stone
She set it by a wall that faced the south;
Dewed it with tears, hoped for a root,
Watched for a waxing shoot,
285 But there came none;
It never saw the sun,
It never felt the trickling moisture run:
While with sunk eyes and faded mouth
She dreamed of melons, as a traveller sees
290 False waves in desert drouth
With shade of leaf-crowned trees,
And burns the thirstier in the sandful breeze.

She no more swept the house,
Tended the fowls or cows,

295   Fetched honey, kneaded cakes of wheat,
     Brought water from the brook:
     But sat down listless in the chimney-nook
     And would not eat.

     Tender Lizzie could not bear
300   To watch her sister's cankerous care
     Yet not to share.
     She night and morning
     Caught the goblins' cry:
     "Come buy our orchard fruits,
305   Come buy, come buy:"—
     Beside the brook, along the glen,
     She heard the tramp of goblin men,
     The voice and stir
     Poor Laura could not hear;
310   Longed to buy fruit to comfort her,
     But feared to pay too dear.
     She thought of Jeanie in her grave,
     Who should have been a bride;
     But who for joys brides hope to have
315   Fell sick and died
     In her gay prime,
     In earliest Winter time,
     With the first glazing rime,
     With the first snow-fall of crisp Winter time.

320   Till Laura dwindling
     Seemed knocking at Death's door:
     Then Lizzie weighed no more
     Better and worse;
     But put a silver penny in her purse,
325   Kissed Laura, crossed the heath with clumps of furze
     At twilight, halted by the brook:
     And for the first time in her life
     Began to listen and look.

     Laughed every goblin
330   When they spied her peeping:
     Came towards her hobbling,

Flying, running, leaping,
Puffing and blowing,
Chuckling, clapping, crowing,
335   Clucking and gobbling,
Mopping and mowing,
Full of airs and graces,
Pulling wry faces,
Demure grimaces,
340   Cat-like and rat-like,
Ratel- and wombat-like,
Snail-paced in a hurry,
Parrot-voiced and whistler,
Helter skelter, hurry skurry,
345   Chattering like magpies,
Fluttering like pigeons,
Gliding like fishes,—
Hugged her and kissed her,
Squeezed and caressed her:
350   Stretched up their dishes,
Panniers, and plates:
"Look at our apples
Russet and dun,
Bob at our cherries,
355   Bite at our peaches,
Citrons and dates,
Grapes for the asking,
Pears red with basking
Out in the sun,
360   Plums on their twigs;
Pluck them and suck them,
Pomegranates, figs."—

"Good folk," said Lizzie,
Mindful of Jeanie:
365   "Give me much and many:"—
Held out her apron,
Tossed them her penny.
"Nay, take a seat with us,
Honour and eat with us,"

370   They answered grinning:
      "Our feast is but beginning.
      Night yet is early,
      Warm and dew-pearly,
      Wakeful and starry:
375   Such fruits as these
      No man can carry;
      Half their bloom would fly,
      Half their dew would dry,
      Half their flavour would pass by.
380   Sit down and feast with us,
      Be welcome guest with us,
      Cheer you and rest with us."—
      "Thank you," said Lizzie: "But one waits
      At home alone for me:
385   So without further parleying,
      If you will not sell me any
      Of your fruits tho' much and many,
      Give me back my silver penny
      I tossed you for a fee."—
390   They began to scratch their pates,
      No longer wagging, purring,
      But visibly demurring,
      Grunting and snarling.
      One called her proud,
395   Cross-grained, uncivil;
      Their tones waxed loud,
      Their looks were evil.
      Lashing their tails
      They trod and hustled her,
400   Elbowed and jostled her,
      Clawed with their nails,
      Barking, mewing, hissing, mocking,
      Tore her gown and soiled her stocking,
      Twitched her hair out by the roots,
405   Stamped upon her tender feet,
      Held her hands and squeezed their fruits
      Against her mouth to make her eat.

White and golden Lizzie stood,
Like a lily in a flood,—
410 Like a rock of blue-veined stone
Lashed by tides obstreperously,—
Like a beacon left alone
In a hoary roaring sea,
Sending up a golden fire,—
415 Like a fruit-crowned orange-tree
White with blossoms honey-sweet
Sore beset by wasp and bee,—
Like a royal virgin town
Topped with gilded dome and spire
420 Close beleaguered by a fleet
Mad to tug her standard down.

One may lead a horse to water,
Twenty cannot make him drink.
Tho' the goblins cuffed and caught her,
425 Coaxed and fought her,
Bullied and besought her,
Scratched her, pinched her black as ink,
Kicked and knocked her,
Mauled and mocked her,
430 Lizzie uttered not a word;
Would not open lip from lip
Lest they should cram a mouthful in:
But laughed in heart to feel the drip
Of juice that syrupped all her face,
435 And lodged in dimples of her chin,
And streaked her neck which quaked like curd.
At last the evil people
Worn out by her resistance
Flung back her penny, kicked their fruit
440 Along whichever road they took,
Not leaving root or stone or shoot;
Some writhed into the ground,
Some dived into the brook
With ring and ripple,
445 Some scudded on the gale without a sound,
Some vanished in the distance.

In a smart, ache, tingle,
Lizzie went her way;
Knew not was it night or day;
450 Sprang up the bank, tore thro' the furze,
Threaded copse and dingle,
And heard her penny jingle
Bouncing in her purse,
Its bounce was music to her ear.
455 She ran and ran
As if she feared some goblin man
Dogged her with gibe or curse
Or something worse:
But not one goblin skurried after,
460 Nor was she pricked by fear;
The kind heart made her windy-paced
That urged her home quite out of breath with haste
And inward laughter.

She cried "Laura," up the garden,
465 "Did you miss me?
Come and kiss me.
Never mind my bruises,
Hug me, kiss me, suck my juices
Squeezed from goblin fruits for you,
470 Goblin pulp and goblin dew.
Eat me, drink me, love me;
Laura, make much of me:
For your sake I have braved the glen
And had to do with goblin merchant men."

475 Laura started from her chair,
Flung her arms up in the air,
Clutched her hair:
"Lizzie, Lizzie, have you tasted
For my sake the fruit forbidden?
480 Must your light like mine be hidden,
Your young life like mine be wasted,
Undone in mine undoing
And ruined in my ruin,
Thirsty, cankered, goblin-ridden?"—

485 She clung about her sister,
     Kissed and kissed and kissed her:
     Tears once again
     Refreshed her shrunken eyes,
     Dropping like rain
490 After long sultry drouth;
     Shaking with aguish fear, and pain,
     She kissed and kissed her with a hungry mouth.

     Her lips began to scorch,
     That juice was wormwood to her tongue,
495 She loathed the feast:
     Writhing as one possessed she leaped and sung,
     Rent all her robe, and wrung
     Her hands in lamentable haste,
     And beat her breast.
500 Her locks streamed like the torch
     Borne by a racer at full speed,
     Or like the mane of horses in their flight,
     Or like an eagle when she stems the light
     Straight toward the sun,
505 Or like a caged thing freed,
     Or like a flying flag when armies run.

     Swift fire spread thro' her veins, knocked at her heart,
     Met the fire smouldering there
     And overbore its lesser flame;
510 She gorged on bitterness without a name:
     Ah! fool, to choose such part
     Of soul-consuming care!
     Sense failed in the mortal strife:
     Like the watch-tower of a town
515 Which an earthquake shatters down,
     Like a lightning-stricken mast,
     Like a wind-uprooted tree
     Spun about,
     Like a foam-topped waterspout
520 Cast down headlong in the sea,
     She fell at last;

Pleasure past and anguish past,
Is it death or is it life?

Life out of death.
525 That night long Lizzie watched by her,
Counted her pulse's flagging stir,
Felt for her breath,
Held water to her lips, and cooled her face
With tears and fanning leaves:
530 But when the first birds chirped about their eaves,
And early reapers plodded to the place
Of golden sheaves,
And dew-wet grass
Bowed in the morning winds so brisk to pass,
535 And new buds with new day
Opened of cup-like lilies on the stream,
Laura awoke as from a dream,
Laughed in the innocent old way,
Hugged Lizzie but not twice or thrice;
540 Her gleaming locks showed not one thread of grey,
Her breath was sweet as May
And light danced in her eyes.

Days, weeks, months, years
Afterwards, when both were wives
545 With children of their own;
Their mother-hearts beset with fears,
Their lives bound up in tender lives;
Laura would call the little ones
And tell them of her early prime,
550 Those pleasant days long gone
Of not-returning time:
Would talk about the haunted glen,
The wicked, quaint fruit-merchant men,
Their fruits like honey to the throat
555 But poison in the blood;
(Men sell not such in any town:)
Would tell them how her sister stood
In deadly peril to do her good,

And win the fiery antidote:
560 Then joining hands to little hands
Would bid them cling together,
"For there is no friend like a sister
In calm or stormy weather;
To cheer one on the tedious way,
565 To fetch one if one goes astray,
To lift one if one totters down,
To strengthen whilst one stands."

IN THE ROUND TOWER AT JHANSI, JUNE 8, 1857.

A hundred, a thousand to one; even so;
    Not a hope in the world remained:
The swarming howling wretches below
    Gained and gained and gained.

5 Skene looked at his pale young wife:—
    "Is the time come?"—"The time is come!"—
Young, strong, and so full of life:
    The agony struck them dumb.

Close his arm about her now,
10   Close her cheek to his,
Close the pistol to her brow—
    God forgive them this!

"Will it hurt much?"—"No, mine own:
    I wish I could bear the pang for both."
15 "I wish I could bear the pang alone:
    Courage, dear, I am not loth."

Kiss and kiss: "It is not pain
    Thus to kiss and die.
One kiss more."—"And yet one again."—
20   "Good bye."—"Good bye."

**I retain this little poem, not as historically accurate, but as written and
published before I heard the supposed facts of its first verse contradicted.

DREAM-LAND.

Where sunless rivers weep
Their waves into the deep,
She sleeps a charmèd sleep:
   Awake her not.
5 Led by a single star,
She came from very far
To seek where shadows are
   Her pleasant lot.

She left the rosy morn,
10 She left the fields of corn,
For twilight cold and lorn
   And water springs.
Thro' sleep, as thro' a veil,
She sees the sky look pale,
15 And hears the nightingale
   That sadly sings.

Rest, rest, a perfect rest
Shed over brow and breast;
Her face is toward the west,
20   The purple land.
She cannot see the grain
Ripening on hill and plain;
She cannot feel the rain
   Upon her hand.

25 Rest, rest, for evermore
Upon a mossy shore;
Rest, rest at the heart's core
   Till time shall cease:
Sleep that no pain shall wake;
30 Night that no morn shall break,
Till joy shall overtake
   Her perfect peace.

AT HOME.

When I was dead, my spirit turned
    To seek the much frequented house:
I passed the door, and saw my friends
    Feasting beneath green orange boughs;
5 From hand to hand they pushed the wine,
    They sucked the pulp of plum and peach;
They sang, they jested, and they laughed,
      For each was loved of each.

I listened to their honest chat:
10   Said one: "Tomorrow we shall be
Plod plod along the featureless sands
    And coasting miles and miles of sea."
Said one: "Before the turn of tide
    We will achieve the eyrie-seat."
15 Said one: "Tomorrow shall be like
      Today, but much more sweet."

"Tomorrow," said they, strong with hope,
    And dwelt upon the pleasant way:
"Tomorrow," cried they one and all,
20   While no one spoke of yesterday.
Their life stood full at blessed noon;
    I, only I, had passed away:
"Tomorrow and today," they cried;
      I was of yesterday.

25 I shivered comfortless, but cast
    No chill across the tablecloth;
I all-forgotten shivered, sad
    To stay and yet to part how loth:
I passed from the familiar room,
30   I who from love had passed away,
Like the remembrance of a guest
      That tarrieth but a day.

A TRIAD.

Three sang of love together: one with
   Crimson, with cheeks and bosom in
Flushed to the yellow hair and finger ti[
   And one there sang who soft and sm[
5   Bloomed like a tinted hyacinth at a sh[
And one was blue with famine after love,
   Who like a harpstring snapped rang harsh and low
The burden of what those were singing of.
One shamed herself in love; one temperately
10   Grew gross in soulless love, a sluggish wife;
One famished died for love. Thus two of three
   Took death for love and won him after strife;
One droned in sweetness like a fattened bee:
   All on the threshold, yet all short of life.

LOVE FROM THE NORTH.

I had a love in soft south land,
   Beloved thro' April far in May;
He waited on my lightest breath,
   And never dared to say me nay.

5 He saddened if my cheer was sad,
   But gay he grew if I was gay;
We never differed on a hair,
   My yes his yes, my nay his nay.

The wedding hour was come, the aisles
10   Were flushed with sun and flowers that day;
I pacing balanced in my thoughts:
   "It's quite too late to think of nay."—

My bridegroom answered in his turn,
   Myself had almost answered "yea:"

:n thro' the flashing nave I heard
    A struggle and resounding "nay".

Bridemaids and bridegroom shrank in fear,
    But I stood high who stood at bay:
"And if I answer yea, fair Sir,
20   What man art thou to bar with nay?"

He was a strong man from the north,
    Light-locked, with eyes of dangerous grey:
"Put yea by for another time
    In which I will not say thee nay."

25 He took me in his strong white arms,
    He bore me on his horse away
O'er crag, morass, and hairbreadth pass,
    But never asked me yea or nay.

He made me fast with book and bell,
30   With links of love he makes me stay;
Till now I've neither heart nor power
    Nor will nor wish to say him nay.

WINTER RAIN.

Every valley drinks,
    Every dell and hollow:
Where the kind rain sinks and sinks,
    Green of Spring will follow.

5 Yet a lapse of weeks
    Buds will burst their edges,
Strip their wool-coats, glue-coats, streaks,
    In the woods and hedges;

Weave a bower of love
10   For birds to meet each other,
Weave a canopy above
    Nest and egg and mother.

But for fattening rain
  We should have no flowers,
15 Never a bud or leaf again
  But for soaking showers;

Never a mated bird
  In the rocking tree-tops,
Never indeed a flock or herd
20   To graze upon the lea-crops.

Lambs so woolly white,
  Sheep the sun-bright leas on,
They could have no grass to bite
  But for rain in season.

25 We should find no moss
  In the shadiest places,
Find no waving meadow grass
  Pied with broad-eyed daisies:

But miles of barren sand,
30   With never a son or daughter,
Not a lily on the land,
  Or lily on the water.

COUSIN KATE.

I was a cottage maiden
  Hardened by sun and air,
Contented with my cottage mates,
  Not mindful I was fair.
5 Why did a great lord find me out,
  And praise my flaxen hair?
Why did a great lord find me out
  To fill my heart with care?

He lured me to his palace home—
10   Woe's me for joy thereof—

To lead a shameless shameful life,
   His plaything and his love.
He wore me like a silken knot,
   He changed me like a glove;
15 So now I moan, an unclean thing,
   Who might have been a dove.

O Lady Kate, my cousin Kate,
   You grew more fair than I:
He saw you at your father's gate,
20   Chose you, and cast me by.
He watched your steps along the lane,
   Your work among the rye;
He lifted you from mean estate
   To sit with him on high.

25 Because you were so good and pure
   He bound you with his ring:
The neighbours call you good and pure,
   Call me an outcast thing.
Even so I sit and howl in dust,
30   You sit in gold and sing:
Now which of us has tenderer heart?
   You had the stronger wing.

O cousin Kate, my love was true,
   Your love was writ in sand:
35 If he had fooled not me but you,
   If you stood where I stand,
He'd not have won me with his love
   Nor bought me with his land;
I would have spit into his face
40   And not have taken his hand.

Yet I've a gift you have not got,
   And seem not like to get:
For all your clothes and wedding-ring
   I've little doubt you fret.
45 My fair-haired son, my shame, my pride,
   Cling closer, closer yet:
Your father would give lands for one
   To wear his coronet.

NOBLE SISTERS.

"Now did you mark a falcon,
   Sister dear, sister dear,
Flying toward my window
   In the morning cool and clear?
5   With jingling bells about her neck,
    But what beneath her wing?
It may have been a ribbon,
   Or it may have been a ring."—
      "I marked a falcon swooping
10   At the break of day:
        And for your love, my sister dove,
         I 'frayed the thief away."—

"Or did you spy a ruddy hound,
   Sister fair and tall,
15   Went snuffing round my garden bound,
    Or crouched by my bower wall?
With a silken leash about his neck;
   But in his mouth may be
A chain of gold and silver links,
20   Or a letter writ to me."—
      "I heard a hound, highborn sister,
        Stood baying at the moon:
        I rose and drove him from your wall
        Lest you should wake too soon."—

25   "Or did you meet a pretty page
    Sat swinging on the gate;
Sat whistling whistling like a bird,
   Or may be slept too late:
With eaglets broidered on his cap,
30   And eaglets on his glove?
If you had turned his pockets out,
   You had found some pledge of love."—
      "I met him at this daybreak,
        Scarce the east was red:
35   Lest the creaking gate should anger you,
        I packed him home to bed."—

"Oh patience, sister. Did you see
   A young man tall and strong,
Swift-footed to uphold the right
40   And to uproot the wrong,
Come home across the desolate sea
   To woo me for his wife?
And in his heart my heart is locked,
   And in his life my life."—
45   "I met a nameless man, sister,
       Who loitered round our door:
      I said: Her husband loves her much,
       And yet she loves him more."—

"Fie, sister, fie, a wicked lie,
50   A lie, a wicked lie,
I have none other love but him,
   Nor will have till I die.
And you have turned him from our door,
   And stabbed him with a lie:
55 I will go seek him thro' the world
   In sorrow till I die."—
      "Go seek in sorrow, sister,
       And find in sorrow too:
      If thus you shame our father's name
60   My curse go forth with you."

SPRING.

Frost-locked all the winter,
Seeds, and roots, and stones of fruits,
What shall make their sap ascend
That they may put forth shoots?
5 Tips of tender green,
Leaf, or blade, or sheath;
Telling of the hidden life
That breaks forth underneath,
Life nursed in its grave by Death.

10   Blows the thaw-wind pleasantly,
       Drips the soaking rain,
       By fits looks down the waking sun:
       Young grass springs on the plain;
       Young leaves clothe early hedgerow trees;
15   Seeds, and roots, and stones of fruits,
       Swollen with sap put forth their shoots;
       Curled-headed ferns sprout in the lane;
       Birds sing and pair again.

       There is no time like Spring,
20   When life's alive in everything,
       Before new nestlings sing,
       Before cleft swallows speed their journey back
       Along the trackless track—
       God guides their wing,
25   He spreads their table that they nothing lack,—
       Before the daisy grows a common flower,
       Before the sun has power
       To scorch the world up in his noontide hour.

       There is no time like Spring,
30   Like Spring that passes by;
       There is no life like Spring-life born to die,—
       Piercing the sod,
       Clothing the uncouth clod,
       Hatched in the nest,
35   Fledged on the windy bough,
       Strong on the wing:
       There is no time like Spring that passes by,
       Now newly born, and now
       Hastening to die.

THE LAMBS OF GRASMERE, 1860.

The upland flocks grew starved and thinned:
    Their shepherds scarce could feed the lambs

Whose milkless mothers butted them,
  Or who were orphaned of their dams.
5 The lambs athirst for mother's milk
  Filled all the place with piteous sounds:
Their mothers' bones made white for miles
  The pastureless wet pasture grounds.

Day after day, night after night,
10 From lamb to lamb the shepherds went,
With teapots for the bleating mouths
  Instead of nature's nourishment.
The little shivering gaping things
  Soon knew the step that brought them aid,
15 And fondled the protecting hand,
  And rubbed it with a woolly head.

Then, as the days waxed on to weeks,
  It was a pretty sight to see
These lambs with frisky heads and tails
20 Skipping and leaping on the lea,
Bleating in tender, trustful tones,
  Resting on rocky crag or mound,
And following the beloved feet
  That once had sought for them and found.

25 These very shepherds of their flocks,
  These loving lambs so meek to please,
Are worthy of recording words
  And honour in their due degrees:
So I might live a hundred years,
30 And roam from strand to foreign strand,
Yet not forget this flooded spring
  And scarce-saved lambs of Westmoreland.

A BIRTHDAY.

My heart is like a singing bird
  Whose nest is in a watered shoot;

My heart is like an apple tree
    Whose boughs are bent with thickset fruit;
5 My heart is like a rainbow shell
    That paddles in a halcyon sea;
My heart is gladder than all these
    Because my love is come to me.

Raise me a dais of silk and down;
10   Hang it with vair and purple dyes;
Carve it in doves and pomegranates,
    And peacocks with a hundred eyes;
Work it in gold and silver grapes,
    In leaves and silver fleurs-de-lys;
15 Because the birthday of my life
    Is come, my love is come to me.

REMEMBER.

Remember me when I am gone away,
    Gone far away into the silent land;
    When you can no more hold me by the hand,
Nor I half turn to go yet turning stay.
5 Remember me when no more day by day
    You tell me of our future that you planned:
    Only remember me; you understand
It will be late to counsel then or pray.
Yet if you should forget me for a while
10   And afterwards remember, do not grieve:
    For if the darkness and corruption leave
    A vestige of the thoughts that once I had,
Better by far you should forget and smile
    Than that you should remember and be sad.

AFTER DEATH.

The curtains were half drawn, the floor was swept
    And strewn with rushes, rosemary and may

Lay thick upon the bed on which I lay,
Where thro' the lattice ivy-shadows crept.
5 He leaned above me, thinking that I slept
   And could not hear him; but I heard him say:
   "Poor child, poor child:" and as he turned away
Came a deep silence, and I knew he wept.
He did not touch the shroud, or raise the fold
10   That hid my face, or take my hand in his,
      Or ruffle the smooth pillows for my head:
      He did not love me living; but once dead
   He pitied me; and very sweet it is
To know he still is warm tho' I am cold.

AN END.

Love, strong as Death, is dead.
Come, let us make his bed
Among the dying flowers:
A green turf at his head;
5 And a stone at his feet,
Whereon we may sit
In the quiet evening hours.

He was born in the Spring,
And died before the harvesting:
10 On the last warm Summer day
He left us; he would not stay
For Autumn twilight cold and gray.
Sit we by his grave, and sing
He is gone away.

15 To few chords and sad and low
Sing we so:
Be our eyes fixed on the grass
Shadow-veiled as the years pass,
While we think of all that was
20 In the long ago.

MY DREAM.

Hear now a curious dream I dreamed last night,
Each word whereof is weighed and sifted truth.

I stood beside Euphrates while it swelled
Like overflowing Jordan in its youth:
It waxed and coloured sensibly to sight,
Till out of myriad pregnant waves there welled
Young crocodiles, a gaunt blunt-featured crew,
Fresh-hatched perhaps and daubed with birthday dew.
The rest if I should tell, I fear my friend,
My closest friend would deem the facts untrue;
And therefore it were wisely left untold;
Yet if you will, why, hear it to the end.

Each crocodile was girt with massive gold
And polished stones that with their wearers grew:
But one there was who waxed beyond the rest,
Wore kinglier girdle and a kingly crown,
Whilst crowns and orbs and sceptres starred his breast.
All gleamed compact and green with scale on scale,
But special burnishment adorned his mail
And special terror weighed upon his frown;
His punier brethren quaked before his tail,
Broad as a rafter, potent as a flail.
So he grew lord and master of his kin:
But who shall tell the tale of all their woes?
An execrable appetite arose,
He battened on them, crunched, and sucked them in.
He knew no law, he feared no binding law,
But ground them with inexorable jaw:
The luscious fat distilled upon his chin,
Exuded from his nostrils and his eyes,
While still like hungry death he fed his maw;
Till every minor crocodile being dead
And buried too, himself gorged to the full,
He slept with breath oppressed and unstrung claw.
Oh marvel passing strange which next I saw:
In sleep he dwindled to the common size,

And all the empire faded from his coat.
Then from far off a wingèd vessel came,
Swift as a swallow, subtle as a flame:
40 I know not what it bore of freight or host,
But white it was as an avenging ghost.
It levelled strong Euphrates in its course;
Supreme yet weightless as an idle mote
It seemed to tame the waters without force
45 Till not a murmur swelled or billow beat:
Lo, as the purple shadow swept the sands,
The prudent crocodile rose on his feet
And shed appropriate tears and wrung his hands.

What can it mean? you ask. I answer not
50 For meaning, but myself must echo, What?
And tell it as I saw it on the spot.

SONG.

Oh roses for the flush of youth,
   And laurel for the perfect prime;
But pluck an ivy branch for me
      Grown old before my time.

5 Oh violets for the grave of youth,
   And bay for those dead in their prime;
Give me the withered leaves I chose
      Before in the old time.

THE HOUR AND THE GHOST.

BRIDE.
O love, love, hold me fast,
He draws me away from thee;
I cannot stem the blast,
Nor the cold strong sea:
5 Far away a light shines
Beyond the hills and pines;
It is lit for me.

BRIDEGROOM.

I have thee close, my dear,
No terror can come near;
10   Only far off the northern light shines clear.

GHOST.

Come with me, fair and false,
To our home, come home.
It is my voice that calls:
Once thou wast not afraid
15   When I woo'd, and said,
"Come, our nest is newly made"—
Now cross the tossing foam.

BRIDE.

Hold me one moment longer,
He taunts me with the past,
20   His clutch is waxing stronger,
Hold me fast, hold me fast.
He draws me from thy heart,
And I cannot withhold:
He bids my spirit depart
25   With him into the cold:—
Oh bitter vows of old!

BRIDEGROOM.

Lean on me, hide thine eyes:
Only ourselves, earth and skies,
Are present here: be wise.

GHOST.

30   Lean on me, come away,
I will guide and steady:
Come, for I will not stay:
Come, for house and bed are ready.
Ah, sure bed and house,
35   For better and worse, for life and death:
Goal won with shortened breath:
Come, crown our vows.

BRIDE.

One moment, one more word,
While my heart beats still,
40 While my breath is stirred
By my fainting will.
O friend forsake me not,
Forget not as I forgot:
But keep thy heart for me,
45 Keep thy faith true and bright;
Thro' the lone cold winter night
Perhaps I may come to thee.

BRIDEGROOM.

Nay peace, my darling, peace:
Let these dreams and terrors cease:
50 Who spoke of death or change or aught but ease?

GHOST.

O fair frail sin,
O poor harvest gathered in!
Thou shalt visit him again
To watch his heart grow cold;
55 To know the gnawing pain
I knew of old;
To see one much more fair
Fill up the vacant chair,
Fill his heart, his children bear:—
60 While thou and I together
In the outcast weather
Toss and howl and spin.

A SUMMER WISH.

Live all thy sweet life thro',
  Sweet Rose, dew-sprent,
Drop down thine evening dew
To gather it anew
5 When day is bright:

I fancy thou wast meant
Chiefly to give delight.

Sing in the silent sky,
    Glad soaring bird;
10 Sing out thy notes on high
To sunbeam straying by
Or passing cloud;
    Heedless if thou art heard
Sing thy full song aloud.

15 Oh that it were with me
    As with the flower;
Blooming on its own tree
For butterfly and bee
Its summer morns:
20   That I might bloom mine hour
A rose in spite of thorns.

Oh that my work were done
    As birds' that soar
Rejoicing in the sun:
25 That when my time is run
And daylight too,
    I so might rest once more
Cool with refreshing dew.

AN APPLE-GATHERING.

I plucked pink blossoms from mine apple tree
    And wore them all that evening in my hair:
Then in due season when I went to see
    I found no apples there.

5 With dangling basket all along the grass
    As I had come I went the selfsame track:
My neighbours mocked me while they saw me pass
    So empty-handed back.

Lilian and Lilias smiled in trudging by,
10   Their heaped-up basket teazed me like a jeer;

Sweet-voiced they sang beneath the sunset sky,
    Their mother's home was near.

Plump Gertrude passed me with her basket full,
    A stronger hand than hers helped it along;
15 A voice talked with her thro' the shadows cool
    More sweet to me than song.

Ah Willie, Willie, was my love less worth
    Than apples with their green leaves piled above?
I counted rosiest apples on the earth
20   Of far less worth than love.

So once it was with me you stooped to talk
    Laughing and listening in this very lane:
To think that by this way we used to walk
    We shall not walk again!

25 I let my neighbours pass me, ones and twos
    And groups; the latest said the night grew chill,
And hastened: but I loitered, while the dews
    Fell fast I loitered still.

SONG.

Two doves upon the selfsame branch,
    Two lilies on a single stem,
Two butterflies upon one flower:—
    Oh happy they who look on them.

5 Who look upon them hand in hand
    Flushed in the rosy summer light;
Who look upon them hand in hand
    And never give a thought to night.

MAUDE CLARE.

Out of the church she followed them
    With a lofty step and mien:

His bride was like a village maid,
    Maude Clare was like a queen.

5   "Son Thomas," his lady mother said,
    With smiles, almost with tears:
"May Nell and you but live as true
    As we have done for years;

"Your father thirty years ago
10   Had just your tale to tell;
But he was not so pale as you,
    Nor I so pale as Nell."

My lord was pale with inward strife,
    And Nell was pale with pride;
15   My lord gazed long on pale Maude Clare
    Or ever he kissed the bride.

"Lo, I have brought my gift, my lord,
    Have brought my gift," she said:
"To bless the hearth, to bless the board,
20   To bless the marriage-bed.

"Here's my half of the golden chain
    You wore about your neck,
That day we waded ankle-deep
    For lilies in the beck:

25   "Here's my half of the faded leaves
    We plucked from budding bough,
With feet amongst the lily leaves,—
    The lilies are budding now."

He strove to match her scorn with scorn,
30   He faltered in his place:
"Lady," he said,—"Maude Clare," he said,—
    "Maude Clare:"—and hid his face.

She turn'd to Nell: "My Lady Nell,
    I have a gift for you;
35   Tho', were it fruit, the bloom were gone,
    Or, were it flowers, the dew.

"Take my share of a fickle heart,
  Mine of a paltry love:
Take it or leave it as you will,
40   I wash my hands thereof."

"And what you leave," said Nell, "I'll take,
  And what you spurn, I'll wear;
For he's my lord for better and worse,
  And him I love, Maude Clare.

45 "Yea, tho' you're taller by the head,
  More wise, and much more fair;
I'll love him till he loves me best,
  Me best of all, Maude Clare."

ECHO.

Come to me in the silence of the night;
  Come in the speaking silence of a dream;
Come with soft rounded cheeks and eyes as bright
  As sunlight on a stream;
5   Come back in tears,
O memory, hope, love of finished years.

Oh dream how sweet, too sweet, too bitter sweet,
  Whose wakening should have been in Paradise,
Where souls brimfull of love abide and meet;
10   Where thirsting longing eyes
    Watch the slow door
That opening, letting in, lets out no more.

Yet come to me in dreams, that I may live
  My very life again tho' cold in death:
15 Come back to me in dreams, that I may give
  Pulse for pulse, breath for breath:
    Speak low, lean low,
As long ago, my love, how long ago.

WINTER: MY SECRET.

I tell my secret? No indeed, not I:
Perhaps some day, who knows?
But not today; it froze, and blows, and snows,
And you're too curious: fie!
5   You want to hear it? well:
Only, my secret's mine, and I won't tell.

Or, after all, perhaps there's none:
Suppose there is no secret after all,
But only just my fun.
10 Today's a nipping day, a biting day;
In which one wants a shawl,
A veil, a cloak, and other wraps:
I cannot ope to every one who taps,
And let the draughts come whistling thro' my hall;
15 Come bounding and surrounding me,
Come buffeting, astounding me,
Nipping and clipping thro' my wraps and all.
I wear my mask for warmth: who ever shows
His nose to Russian snows
20 To be pecked at by every wind that blows?
You would not peck? I thank you for good will,
Believe, but leave that truth untested still.

Spring's an expansive time: yet I don't trust
March with its peck of dust,
25 Nor April with its rainbow-crowned brief showers,
Nor even May, whose flowers
One frost may wither thro' the sunless hours.

Perhaps some languid summer day,
When drowsy birds sing less and less,
30 And golden fruit is ripening to excess,
If there's not too much sun nor too much cloud,
And the warm wind is neither still nor loud,
Perhaps my secret I may say,
Or you may guess.

ANOTHER SPRING.

If I might see another Spring
    I'd not plant summer flowers and wait:
I'd have my crocuses at once,
My leafless pink mezereons,
5   My chill-veined snowdrops, choicer yet
        My white or azure violet,
Leaf-nested primrose; anything
        To blow at once, not late.

If I might see another Spring
10   I'd listen to the daylight birds
That build their nests and pair and sing,
Nor wait for mateless nightingale;
        I'd listen to the lusty herds,
        The ewes with lambs as white as snow,
15   I'd find out music in the hail
        And all the winds that blow.

If I might see another Spring—
        Oh stinging comment on my past
That all my past results in "if"—
20   If I might see another Spring
I'd laugh today, today is brief;
I would not wait for anything:
        I'd use today that cannot last,
            Be glad today and sing.

A PEAL OF BELLS.

Strike the bells wantonly,
    Tinkle tinkle well;
Bring me wine, bring me flowers,
    Ring the silver bell.
5   All my lamps burn scented oil,
        Hung on laden orange trees,

Whose shadowed foliage is the foil
    To golden lamps and oranges.
Heap my golden plates with fruit,
10   Golden fruit, fresh-plucked and ripe;
    Strike the bells and breathe the pipe;
Shut out showers from summer hours—
Silence that complaining lute—
    Shut out thinking, shut out pain,
15   From hours that cannot come again.

Strike the bells solemnly,
    Ding dong deep:
My friend is passing to his bed,
    Fast asleep;
20   There's plaited linen round his head,
    While foremost go his feet—
His feet that cannot carry him.
My feast's a show, my lights are dim;
    Be still, your music is not sweet,—
25   There is no music more for him:
    His lights are out, his feast is done;
His bowl that sparkled to the brim
Is drained, is broken, cannot hold;
My blood is chill, his blood is cold;
30   His death is full, and mine begun.

FATA MORGANA.

A blue-eyed phantom far before
    Is laughing, leaping toward the sun:
Like lead I chase it evermore,
    I pant and run.

5   It breaks the sunlight bound on bound:
    Goes singing as it leaps along
To sheep-bells with a dreamy sound
    A dreamy song.

I laugh, it is so brisk and gay;
10   It is so far before, I weep:
I hope I shall lie down some day,
        Lie down and sleep.

"NO, THANK YOU, JOHN."

I never said I loved you, John:
    Why will you teaze me day by day,
And wax a weariness to think upon
    With always "do" and "pray"?

5   You know I never loved you, John;
    No fault of mine made me your toast:
Why will you haunt me with a face as wan
    As shows an hour-old ghost?

I dare say Meg or Moll would take
10   Pity upon you, if you'd ask:
And pray don't remain single for my sake
    Who can't perform that task.

I have no heart?—Perhaps I have not;
    But then you're mad to take offence
15 That I don't give you what I have not got:
    Use your own common sense.

Let bygones be bygones:
    Don't call me false, who owed not to be true:
I'd rather answer "No" to fifty Johns
20   Than answer "Yes" to you.

Let's mar our pleasant days no more,
    Song-birds of passage, days of youth:
Catch at today, forget the days before:
    I'll wink at your untruth.

25 Let us strike hands as hearty friends;
    No more, no less; and friendship's good:

Only don't keep in view ulterior ends,
    And points not understood

In open treaty. Rise above
30   Quibbles and shuffling off and on:
Here's friendship for you if you like; but love,—
    No, thank you, John.

MAY.

I cannot tell you how it was;
But this I know: it came to pass
Upon a bright and breezy day
When May was young; ah pleasant May!
5 As yet the poppies were not born
Between the blades of tender corn;
The last eggs had not hatched as yet,
Nor any bird foregone its mate.

I cannot tell you what it was;
10 But this I know: it did but pass.
It passed away with sunny May,
With all sweet things it passed away,
And left me old, and cold, and grey.

A PAUSE OF THOUGHT.

I looked for that which is not, nor can be,
    And hope deferred made my heart sick in truth:
    But years must pass before a hope of youth
      Is resigned utterly.

5 I watched and waited with a steadfast will:
    And though the object seemed to flee away

That I so longed for, ever day by day
    I watched and waited still.

Sometimes I said: This thing shall be no more;
10   My expectation wearies and shall cease;
    I will resign it now and be at peace:
        Yet never gave it o'er.

Sometimes I said: It is an empty name
    I long for; to a name why should I give
15   The peace of all the days I have to live?—
        Yet gave it all the same.

Alas, thou foolish one! alike unfit
    For healthy joy and salutary pain:
    Thou knowest the chase useless, and again
20   Turnest to follow it.

TWILIGHT CALM.

    Oh pleasant eventide!
    Clouds on the western side
Grow grey and greyer hiding the warm sun:
The bees and birds, their happy labours done,
5   Seek their close nests and bide.

    Screened in the leafy wood
    The stock-doves sit and brood:
The very squirrel leaps from bough to bough
But lazily; pauses; and settles now
10   Where once he stored his food.

    One by one the flowers close,
    Lily and dewy rose
Shutting their tender petals from the moon:
The grasshoppers are still; but not so soon
15   Are still the noisy crows.

The dormouse squats and eats
Choice little dainty bits
Beneath the spreading roots of a broad lime;
Nibbling his fill he stops from time to time
20   And listens where he sits.

From far the lowings come
Of cattle driven home:
From farther still the wind brings fitfully
The vast continual murmur of the sea,
25   Now loud, now almost dumb.

The gnats whirl in the air,
The evening gnats; and there
The owl opes broad his eyes and wings to sail
For prey; the bat wakes; and the shell-less snail
30   Comes forth, clammy and bare.

Hark! that's the nightingale,
Telling the selfsame tale
Her song told when this ancient earth was young:
So echoes answered when her song was sung
35   In the first wooded vale.

We call it love and pain
The passion of her strain;
And yet we little understand or know:
Why should it not be rather joy that so
40   Throbs in each throbbing vein?

In separate herds the deer
Lie; here the bucks, and here
The does, and by its mother sleeps the fawn:
Through all the hours of night until the dawn
45   They sleep, forgetting fear.

The hare sleeps where it lies,
With wary half-closed eyes;
The cock has ceased to crow, the hen to cluck:
Only the fox is out, some heedless duck
50   Or chicken to surprise.

Remote, each single star
Comes out, till there they are
All shining brightly: how the dews fall damp!
While close at hand the glow-worm lights her lamp
55   Or twinkles from afar.

But evening now is done
As much as if the sun
Day-giving had arisen in the East:
For night has come; and the great calm has ceased,
60   The quiet sands have run.

WIFE TO HUSBAND.

Pardon the faults in me,
    For the love of years ago:
        Good bye.
I must drift across the sea,
5   I must sink into the snow,
        I must die.

You can bask in this sun,
    You can drink wine, and eat:
        Good bye.
10 I must gird myself and run,
    Tho' with unready feet:
        I must die.

Blank sea to sail upon,
    Cold bed to sleep in:
15   Good bye.
While you clasp, I must be gone
    For all your weeping:
        I must die.

A kiss for one friend,
20   And a word for two,—
        Good bye:—

A lock that you must send,
  A kindness you must do:
    I must die.

25 Not a word for you,
  Not a lock or kiss,
    Good bye.
We, one, must part in two;
  Verily death is this:
30   I must die.

THREE SEASONS.

"A cup for hope!" she said,
In springtime ere the bloom was old:
The crimson wine was poor and cold
  By her mouth's richer red.

5 "A cup for love!" how low,
How soft the words; and all the while
Her blush was rippling with a smile
  Like summer after snow.

"A cup for memory!"
10 Cold cup that one must drain alone:
While autumn winds are up and moan
  Across the barren sea.

Hope, memory, love:
Hope for fair morn, and love for day,
15 And memory for the evening grey
  And solitary dove.

MIRAGE.

The hope I dreamed of was a dream,
  Was but a dream; and now I wake

Exceeding comfortless, and worn, and old,
    For a dream's sake.

5   I hang my harp upon a tree,
    A weeping willow in a lake;
I hang my silenced harp there, wrung and snapt
    For a dream's sake.

Lie still, lie still, my breaking heart;
10   My silent heart, lie still and break:
Life, and the world, and mine own self, are changed
    For a dream's sake.

SHUT OUT.

The door was shut. I looked between
    Its iron bars; and saw it lie,
    My garden, mine, beneath the sky,
Pied with all flowers bedewed and green:

5   From bough to bough the song-birds crossed,
    From flower to flower the moths and bees;
    With all its nests and stately trees
It had been mine, and it was lost.

A shadowless spirit kept the gate,
10   Blank and unchanging like the grave.
    I peering thro' said: "Let me have
Some buds to cheer my outcast state."

He answered not. "Or give me, then,
    But one small twig from shrub or tree;
15   And bid my home remember me
Until I come to it again."

The spirit was silent; but he took
    Mortar and stone to build a wall;
    He left no loophole great or small
20   Thro' which my straining eyes might look:

So now I sit here quite alone
  Blinded with tears; nor grieve for that,
  For nought is left worth looking at
Since my delightful land is gone.

25 A violet bed is budding near,
    Wherein a lark has made her nest:
    And good they are, but not the best;
And dear they are, but not so dear.

SOUND SLEEP.

Some are laughing, some are weeping;
She is sleeping, only sleeping.
Round her rest wild flowers are creeping;
There the wind is heaping, heaping
5 Sweetest sweets of Summer's keeping,
By the corn fields ripe for reaping.

There are lilies, and there blushes
The deep rose, and there the thrushes
Sing till latest sunlight flushes
10 In the west; a fresh wind brushes
Thro' the leaves while evening hushes.

There by day the lark is singing
And the grass and weeds are springing;
There by night the bat is winging;
15 There for ever winds are bringing
Far-off chimes of church-bells ringing.

Night and morning, noon and even,
Their sound fills her dreams with Heaven:
The long strife at length is striven:
20 Till her grave-bands shall be riven,
Such is the good portion given
To her soul at rest and shriven.

SONG.

She sat and sang alway
  By the green margin of a stream,
Watching the fishes leap and play
  Beneath the glad sunbeam.

5   I sat and wept alway
    Beneath the moon's most shadowy beam,
Watching the blossoms of the May
    Weep leaves into the stream.

I wept for memory;
10   She sang for hope that is so fair:
My tears were swallowed by the sea;
    Her songs died on the air.

SONG.

When I am dead, my dearest,
  Sing no sad songs for me;
Plant thou no roses at my head,
  Nor shady cypress tree:
5 Be the green grass above me
  With showers and dewdrops wet;
And if thou wilt, remember,
  And if thou wilt, forget.

I shall not see the shadows,
10   I shall not feel the rain;
I shall not hear the nightingale
  Sing on, as if in pain:
And dreaming through the twilight
  That doth not rise nor set,
15 Haply I may remember,
  And haply may forget.

DEAD BEFORE DEATH.

Ah! changed and cold, how changed and very cold!
   With stiffened smiling lips and cold calm eyes:
   Changed, yet the same; much knowing, little wise;
This was the promise of the days of old!
5 Grown hard and stubborn in the ancient mould,
   Grown rigid in the sham of lifelong lies:
   We hoped for better things as years would rise,
But it is over as a tale once told.
All fallen the blossom that no fruitage bore,
10   All lost the present and the future time,
All lost, all lost, the lapse that went before:
So lost till death shut-to the opened door,
   So lost from chime to everlasting chime,
So cold and lost for ever evermore.

BITTER FOR SWEET.

Summer is gone with all its roses,
   Its sun and perfumes and sweet flowers,
   Its warm air and refreshing showers:
     And even Autumn closes.

5 Yea, Autumn's chilly self is going,
   And Winter comes which is yet colder;
   Each day the hoar-frost waxes bolder,
     And the last buds cease blowing.

SISTER MAUDE.

Who told my mother of my shame,
   Who told my father of my dear?

Oh who but Maude, my sister Maude,
   Who lurked to spy and peer.

5   Cold he lies, as cold as stone,
   With his clotted curls about his face:
The comeliest corpse in all the world
   And worthy of a queen's embrace.

You might have spared his soul, sister,
10   Have spared my soul, your own soul too:
Though I had not been born at all,
   He'd never have looked at you.

My father may sleep in Paradise,
   My mother at Heaven-gate:
15   But sister Maude shall get no sleep
   Either early or late.

My father may wear a golden gown,
   My mother a crown may win;
If my dear and I knocked at Heaven-gate
20   Perhaps they'd let us in:
But sister Maude, oh sister Maude,
   Bide *you* with death and sin.

REST.

O Earth, lie heavily upon her eyes;
   Seal her sweet eyes weary of watching, Earth;
   Lie close around her; leave no room for mirth
With its harsh laughter, nor for sound of sighs.
5   She hath no questions, she hath no replies,
   Hushed in and curtained with a blessèd dearth
   Of all that irked her from the hour of birth;
With stillness that is almost Paradise.
Darkness more clear than noon-day holdeth her,
10   Silence more musical than any song;
Even her very heart has ceased to stir:

Until the morning of Eternity
Her rest shall not begin nor end, but be;
   And when she wakes she will not think it long.

THE FIRST SPRING DAY.

I wonder if the sap is stirring yet,
If wintry birds are dreaming of a mate,
If frozen snowdrops feel as yet the sun
And crocus fires are kindling one by one:
5   Sing, robin, sing;
I still am sore in doubt concerning Spring.

I wonder if the springtide of this year
Will bring another Spring both lost and dear;
If heart and spirit will find out their Spring,
10 Or if the world alone will bud and sing:
     Sing, hope, to me;
Sweet notes, my hope, soft notes for memory.

The sap will surely quicken soon or late,
The tardiest bird will twitter to a mate;
15 So Spring must dawn again with warmth and bloom,
Or in this world, or in the world to come:
     Sing, voice of Spring,
Till I too blossom and rejoice and sing.

THE CONVENT THRESHOLD.

There's blood between us, love, my love,
There's father's blood, there's brother's blood;
And blood's a bar I cannot pass:
I choose the stairs that mount above,
5 Stair after golden skyward stair,

To city and to sea of glass.
My lily feet are soiled with mud,
With scarlet mud which tells a tale
Of hope that was, of guilt that was,
10   Of love that shall not yet avail;
Alas, my heart, if I could bare
My heart, this selfsame stain is there:
I seek the sea of glass and fire
To wash the spot, to burn the snare;
15   Lo, stairs are meant to lift us higher:
Mount with me, mount the kindled stair.

Your eyes look earthward, mine look up.
I see the far-off city grand,
Beyond the hills a watered land,
20   Beyond the gulf a gleaming strand
Of mansions where the righteous sup;
Who sleep at ease among their trees,
Or wake to sing a cadenced hymn
With Cherubim and Seraphim;
25   They bore the Cross, they drained the cup,
Racked, roasted, crushed, wrenched limb from limb,
They the offscouring of the world:
The heaven of starry heavens unfurled,
The sun before their face is dim.

30   You looking earthward, what see you?
Milk-white, wine-flushed among the vines,
Up and down leaping, to and fro,
Most glad, most full, made strong with wines,
Blooming as peaches pearled with dew,
35   Their golden windy hair afloat,
Love-music warbling in their throat,
Young men and women come and go.

You linger, yet the time is short:
Flee for your life, gird up your strength
40   To flee; the shadows stretched at length
Show that day wanes, that night draws nigh;
Flee to the mountain, tarry not.

Is this a time for smile and sigh,
For songs among the secret trees
45 Where sudden blue birds nest and sport?
The time is short and yet you stay:
Today while it is called today
Kneel, wrestle, knock, do violence, pray;
Today is short, tomorrow nigh:
50 Why will you die? why will you die?

You sinned with me a pleasant sin:
Repent with me, for I repent.
Woe's me the lore I must unlearn!
Woe's me that easy way we went,
55 So rugged when I would return!
How long until my sleep begin,
How long shall stretch these nights and days?
Surely, clean Angels cry, she prays;
She laves her soul with tedious tears:
60 How long must stretch these years and years?

I turn from you my cheeks and eyes,
My hair which you shall see no more—
Alas for joy that went before,
For joy that dies, for love that dies.
65 Only my lips still turn to you,
My livid lips that cry, Repent.
Oh weary life, Oh weary Lent,
Oh weary time whose stars are few.

How should I rest in Paradise,
70 Or sit on steps of heaven alone?
If Saints and Angels spoke of love
Should I not answer from my throne:
Have pity upon me, ye my friends,
For I have heard the sound thereof:
75 Should I not turn with yearning eyes,
Turn earthwards with a pitiful pang?
Oh save me from a pang in heaven.
By all the gifts we took and gave,
Repent, repent, and be forgiven:

80   This life is long, but yet it ends;
     Repent and purge your soul and save:
     No gladder song the morning stars
     Upon their birthday morning sang
     Than Angels sing when one repents.

85   I tell you what I dreamed last night:
     A spirit with transfigured face
     Fire-footed clomb an infinite space.
     I heard his hundred pinions clang,
     Heaven-bells rejoicing rang and rang,
90   Heaven-air was thrilled with subtle scents,
     Worlds spun upon their rushing cars:
     He mounted shrieking: "Give me light."
     Still light was poured on him, more light;
     Angels, Archangels he outstripped
95   Exultant in exceeding might,
     And trod the skirts of Cherubim.
     Still "Give me light," he shrieked; and dipped
     His thirsty face, and drank a sea,
     Athirst with thirst it could not slake.
100 I saw him, drunk with knowledge, take
     From aching brows the aureole crown—
     His locks writhed like a cloven snake—
     He left his throne to grovel down
     And lick the dust of Seraphs' feet:
105 For what is knowledge duly weighed?
     Knowledge is strong, but love is sweet;
     Yea all the progress he had made
     Was but to learn that all is small
     Save love, for love is all in all.

110 I tell you what I dreamed last night:
     It was not dark, it was not light,
     Cold dews had drenched my plenteous hair
     Thro' clay; you came to seek me there.
     And "Do you dream of me?" you said.
115 My heart was dust that used to leap
     To you; I answered half asleep:
     "My pillow is damp, my sheets are red,

There's a leaden tester to my bee
Find you a warmer playfellow,
120 A warmer pillow for your head,
A kinder love to love than mine."
You wrung your hands; while I like l
Crushed downwards thro' the sodden
You smote your hands but not in mirth,
125 And reeled but were not drunk with win

For all night long I dreamed of you:
I woke and prayed against my will,
Then slept to dream of you again.
At length I rose and knelt and prayed:
130 I cannot write the words I said,
My words were slow, my tears were few;
But thro' the dark my silence spoke
Like thunder. When this morning broke,
My face was pinched, my hair was grey,
135 And frozen blood was on the sill
Where stifling in my struggle I lay.

If now you saw me you would say:
Where is the face I used to love?
And I would answer: Gone before;
140 It tarries veiled in paradise.
When once the morning star shall rise,
When earth with shadow flees away
And we stand safe within the door,
Then you shall lift the veil thereof.
145 Look up, rise up: for far above
Our palms are grown, our place is set;
There we shall meet as once we met
And love with old familiar love.

UP-HILL.

Does the road wind up-hill all the way?
  Yes, to the very end.

e day's journey take the whole long day?
rom morn to night, my friend.

But is there for the night a resting-place?
   A roof for when the slow dark hours begin.
May not the darkness hide it from my face?
   You cannot miss that inn.

Shall I meet other wayfarers at night?
10   Those who have gone before.
Then must I knock, or call when just in sight?
   They will not keep you standing at that door.

Shall I find comfort, travel-sore and weak?
   Of labour you shall find the sum.
15 Will there be beds for me and all who seek?
   Yea, beds for all who come.

"THE LOVE OF CHRIST WHICH PASSETH KNOWLEDGE."

I bore with thee long weary days and nights,
   Through many pangs of heart, through many tears;
I bore with thee, thy hardness, coldness, slights,
   For three and thirty years.

5 Who else had dared for thee what I have dared?
   I plunged the depth most deep from bliss above;
I not My flesh, I not My spirit spared:
   Give thou Me love for love.

For thee I thirsted in the daily drouth,
10   For thee I trembled in the nightly frost:
Much sweeter thou than honey to My mouth:
   Why wilt thou still be lost?

I bore thee on My shoulders and rejoiced:
   Men only marked upon My shoulders borne
15 The branding cross; and shouted hungry-voiced,
   Or wagged their heads in scorn.

Thee did nails grave upon My hands, thy name
　　Did thorns for frontlets stamp between Mine eyes:
I, Holy One, put on thy guilt and shame;
20　　　　I, God, Priest, Sacrifice.

A thief upon My right hand and My left;
　　Six hours alone, athirst, in misery:
At length in death one smote My heart and cleft
　　　　A hiding-place for thee.

25　Nailed to the racking cross, than bed of down
　　More dear, whereon to stretch Myself and sleep:
So did I win a kingdom,—share My crown;
　　　　A harvest,—come and reap.

"A BRUISED REED SHALL HE NOT BREAK."

I will accept thy will to do and be,
　　Thy hatred and intolerance of sin,
　　Thy will at least to love, that burns within
　　　　And thirsteth after Me:
5　So will I render fruitful, blessing still
　　The germs and small beginnings in thy heart,
　　Because thy will cleaves to the better part.—
　　　　Alas, I cannot will.

Dost not thou will, poor soul? Yet I receive
10　　The inner unseen longings of the soul,
　　I guide them turning towards Me; I control
　　　　And charm hearts till they grieve:
If thou desire, it yet shall come to pass,
　　Tho' thou but wish indeed to choose My love;
15　For I have power in earth and heaven above.—
　　　　I cannot wish, alas!

What, neither choose nor wish to choose? and yet
　　I still must strive to win thee and constrain:
　　For thee I hung upon the cross in pain,
20　　　　How then can I forget?

If thou as yet dost neither love, nor hate,
  Nor choose, nor wish,—resign thyself, be still
  Till I infuse love, hatred, longing, will.—
    I do not deprecate.

A BETTER RESURRECTION.

I have no wit, no words, no tears;
  My heart within me like a stone
Is numbed too much for hopes or fears;
  Look right, look left, I dwell alone;
5 I lift mine eyes, but dimmed with grief
  No everlasting hills I see;
My life is in the falling leaf:
    O Jesus, quicken me.

My life is like a faded leaf,
10 My harvest dwindled to a husk;
Truly my life is void and brief
  And tedious in the barren dusk;
My life is like a frozen thing,
  No bud nor greenness can I see:
15 Yet rise it shall—the sap of Spring;
    O Jesus, rise in me.

My life is like a broken bowl,
  A broken bowl that cannot hold
One drop of water for my soul
20 Or cordial in the searching cold;
Cast in the fire the perished thing,
  Melt and remould it, till it be
A royal cup for Him my King:
    O Jesus, drink of me.

ADVENT.

This Advent moon shines cold and clear,
  These Advent nights are long;

Our lamps have burned year after year
  And still their flame is strong.
5 "Watchman, what of the night?" we cry
  Heart-sick with hope deferred:
"No speaking signs are in the sky,"
  Is still the watchman's word.

The Porter watches at the gate,
10 The servants watch within;
The watch is long betimes and late,
  The prize is slow to win.
"Watchman, what of the night?" but still
  His answer sounds the same:
15 "No daybreak tops the utmost hill,
  Nor pale our lamps of flame."

One to another hear them speak
  The patient virgins wise:
"Surely He is not far to seek"—
20 "All night we watch and rise."
"The days are evil looking back,
  The coming days are dim;
Yet count we not His promise slack,
  But watch and wait for Him."

25 One with another, soul with soul,
  They kindle fire from fire:
"Friends watch us who have touched the goal."
  "They urge us, come up higher."
"With them shall rest our waysore feet,
30 With them is built our home,
With Christ."—"They sweet, but He most sweet,
  Sweeter than honeycomb."

There no more parting, no more pain,
  The distant ones brought near,
35 The lost so long are found again,
  Long lost but longer dear:
Eye hath not seen, ear hath not heard,
  Nor heart conceived that rest,
With them our good things long deferred,
40 With Jesus Christ our Best.

We weep because the night is long,
    We laugh for day shall rise,
We sing a slow contented song
    And knock at Paradise.
45 Weeping we hold Him fast, Who wept
    For us, we hold Him fast;
And will not let Him go except
    He bless us first or last.

Weeping we hold Him fast tonight;
50   We will not let Him go
Till daybreak smite our wearied sight
    And summer smite the snow:
Then figs shall bud, and dove with dove
    Shall coo the livelong day;
55 Then He shall say, "Arise, My love,
    My fair one, come away."

THE THREE ENEMIES.

THE FLESH.
"Sweet, thou art pale."
        "More pale to see,
Christ hung upon the cruel tree
And bore His Father's wrath for me."

5 "Sweet, thou art sad."
        "Beneath a rod
More heavy, Christ for my sake trod
The winepress of the wrath of God."

"Sweet, thou art weary."
10   "Not so Christ:
Whose mighty love of me sufficed
For Strength, Salvation, Eucharist."

"Sweet, thou art footsore."
        "If I bleed,

15   His feet have bled: yea, in my need
      His Heart once bled for mine indeed."

THE WORLD.

    "Sweet, thou art young."
            "So He was young
    Who for my sake in silence hung
20   Upon the Cross with Passion wrung."

    "Look, thou art fair."
            "He was more fair
    Than men, Who deigned for me to wear
    A visage marred beyond compare."

25   "And thou hast riches."
            "Daily bread:
    All else is His; Who living, dead,
    For me lacked where to lay His Head."

    "And life is sweet."
30   "It was not so
    To Him, Whose Cup did overflow
    With mine unutterable woe."

THE DEVIL.

    "Thou drinkest deep."
            "When Christ would sup
35   He drained the dregs from out my cup:
    So how should I be lifted up?"

    "Thou shalt win Glory."
            "In the skies,
    Lord Jesus, cover up mine eyes
40   Lest they should look on vanities."

    "Thou shalt have Knowledge."
            "Helpless dust,
    In Thee, O Lord, I put my trust:
    Answer Thou for me, Wise and Just."

45   "And Might."—
            "Get thee behind me. Lord,

Who hast redeemed and not abhorred
My soul, oh keep it by Thy Word."

ONE CERTAINTY.

Vanity of vanities, the Preacher saith,
   All things are vanity. The eye and ear
   Cannot be filled with what they see and hear.
Like early dew, or like the sudden breath
5 Of wind, or like the grass that withereth,
   Is man, tossed to and fro by hope and fear:
   So little joy hath he, so little cheer,
Till all things end in the long dust of death.
Today is still the same as yesterday,
10 Tomorrow also even as one of them;
And there is nothing new under the sun:
Until the ancient race of Time be run,
   The old thorns shall grow out of the old stem,
And morning shall be cold and twilight grey.

CHRISTIAN AND JEW.
A DIALOGUE.

"Oh happy happy land!
Angels like rushes stand
   About the wells of light."—
   "Alas, I have not eyes for this fair sight:
5 Hold fast my hand."—

"As in a soft wind, they
Bend all one blessed way,
   Each bowed in his own glory, star with star."—
   "I cannot see so far,
10 Here shadows are."—

"White-winged the cherubim,
Yet whiter seraphim,
 Glow white with intense fire of love."—
"Mine eyes are dim:
15 I look in vain above,
And miss their hymn."—

"Angels, Archangels cry
One to other ceaselessly
 (I hear them sing)
20 One 'Holy, Holy, Holy' to their King."—
"I do not hear them, I."—

"Joy to thee, Paradise,—
 Garden and goal and nest!
Made green for wearied eyes;
25 Much softer than the breast
Of mother-dove clad in a rainbow's dyes.

"All precious souls are there
 Most safe, elect by grace,
 All tears are wiped for ever from their face:
30 Untired in prayer
 They wait and praise
 Hidden for a little space.

"Boughs of the Living Vine
They spread in summer shine
35 Green leaf with leaf:
Sap of the Royal Vine it stirs like wine
 In all both less and chief.

"Sing to the Lord,
 All spirits of all flesh, sing;
40 For He hath not abhorred
Our low estate nor scorn'd our offering:
 Shout to our King."—

"But Zion said:
 My Lord forgetteth me.
45 Lo, she hath made her bed
 In dust; forsaken weepeth she
 Where alien rivers swell the sea.

"She laid her body as the ground,
    Her tender body as the ground to those
50 Who passed; her harpstrings cannot sound
In a strange land; discrowned
    She sits, and drunk with woes."—

"O drunken not with wine,
    Whose sins and sorrows have fulfilled the sum,—
55   Be not afraid, arise, be no more dumb;
Arise, shine,
    For thy light is come."—

"Can these bones live?"—
                    "God knows:
60 The prophet saw such clothed with flesh and skin,
A wind blew on them and life entered in,
They shook and rose.
    Hasten the time, O Lord, blot out their sin,
    Let life begin."

SWEET DEATH.

The sweetest blossoms die.
    And so it was that, going day by day
    Unto the Church to praise and pray,
And crossing the green churchyard thoughtfully,
5   I saw how on the graves the flowers
    Shed their fresh leaves in showers,
And how their perfume rose up to the sky
    Before it passed away.

The youngest blossoms die.
10   They die and fall and nourish the rich earth
    From which they lately had their birth;
Sweet life, but sweeter death that passeth by
    And is as though it had not been:—
    All colours turn to green;

15   The bright hues vanish and the odours fly,
      The grass hath lasting worth.

And youth and beauty die.
    So be it, O my God, Thou God of truth:
    Better than beauty and than youth
20   Are Saints and Angels, a glad company;
      And Thou, O Lord, our Rest and Ease,
      Art better far than these.
Why should we shrink from our full harvest? why
    Prefer to glean with Ruth?

SYMBOLS.

I watched a rosebud very long
    Brought on by dew and sun and shower,
    Waiting to see the perfect flower:
Then, when I thought it should be strong,
5   It opened at the matin hour
      And fell at evensong.

I watched a nest from day to day,
    A green nest full of pleasant shade,
    Wherein three speckled eggs were laid:
10   But when they should have hatched in May,
    The two old birds had grown afraid
      Or tired, and flew away.

Then in my wrath I broke the bough
    That I had tended so with care,
15   Hoping its scent should fill the air;
I crushed the eggs, not heeding how
    Their ancient promise had been fair:
      I would have vengeance now.

But the dead branch spoke from the sod,
20   And the eggs answered me again:
    Because we failed dost thou complain?

Is thy wrath just? And what if God,
    Who waiteth for thy fruits in vain,
        Should also take the rod?

"CONSIDER THE LILIES OF THE FIELD."

Flowers preach to us if we will hear:—
The rose saith in the dewy morn:
I am most fair;
Yet all my loveliness is born
5   Upon a thorn.
The poppy saith amid the corn:
Let but my scarlet head appear
And I am held in scorn;
Yet juice of subtle virtue lies
10 Within my cup of curious dyes.
The lilies say: Behold how we
Preach without words of purity.
The violets whisper from the shade
Which their own leaves have made:
15 Men scent our fragrance on the air,
Yet take no heed
Of humble lessons we would read.

But not alone the fairest flowers:
The merest grass
20 Along the roadside where we pass,
Lichen and moss and sturdy weed,
Tell of His love who sends the dew,
The rain and sunshine too,
To nourish one small seed.

THE WORLD.

By day she wooes me, soft, exceeding fair:
    But all night as the moon so changeth she;
    Loathsome and foul with hideous leprosy

And subtle serpents gliding in her hair.
5 By day she wooes me to the outer air,
        Ripe fruits, sweet flowers, and full satiety:
        But thro' the night, a beast she grins at me,
A very monster void of love and prayer.
By day she stands a lie: by night she stands
10   In all the naked horror of the truth
With pushing horns and clawed and clutching hands.
Is this a friend indeed; that I should sell
        My soul to her, give her my life and youth,
Till my feet, cloven too, take hold on hell?

A TESTIMONY.

I said of laughter: it is vain.
        Of mirth I said: what profits it?
        Therefore I found a book, and writ
Therein how ease and also pain,
5 How health and sickness, every one
Is vanity beneath the sun

Man walks in a vain shadow; he
        Disquieteth himself in vain.
        The things that were shall be again:
10 The rivers do not fill the sea,
But turn back to their secret source;
The winds too turn upon their course.

Our treasures moth and rust corrupt,
        Or thieves break thro' and steal, or they
15   Make themselves wings and fly away.
One man made merry as he supped,
Nor guessed how when that night grew dim
His soul would be required of him.

We build our houses on the sand
20   Comely withoutside and within;
        But when the winds and rains begin

To beat on them, they cannot stand:
They perish, quickly overthrown,
Loose from the very basement stone.

25 All things are vanity, I said:
        Yea vanity of vanities.
        The rich man dies; and the poor dies:
    The worm feeds sweetly on the dead.
    Whate'er thou lackest, keep this trust:
30 All in the end shall have but dust:

    The one inheritance, which best
        And worst alike shall find and share:
        The wicked cease from troubling there,
    And there the weary be at rest;
35 There all the wisdom of the wise
    Is vanity of vanities.

    Man flourishes as a green leaf,
        And as a leaf doth pass away;
        Or as a shade that cannot stay
40 And leaves no track, his course is brief:
    Yet man doth hope and fear and plan
    Till he is dead:—oh foolish man!

    Our eyes cannot be satisfied
        With seeing, nor our ears be filled
45   With hearing: yet we plant and build
    And buy and make our borders wide;
    We gather wealth, we gather care,
    But know not who shall be our heir.

    Why should we hasten to arise
50   So early, and so late take rest?
        Our labour is not good; our best
    Hopes fade; our heart is stayed on lies:
    Verily, we sow wind; and we
    Shall reap the whirlwind, verily.

55 He who hath little shall not lack;
        He who hath plenty shall decay:
        Our fathers went; we pass away;

Our children follow on our track:
  So generations fail, and so
60 They are renewed and come and go.

The earth is fattened with our dead;
  She swallows more and doth not cease:
  Therefore her wine and oil increase
And her sheaves are not numberèd;
65 Therefore her plants are green, and all
  Her pleasant trees lusty and tall.

Therefore the maidens cease to sing,
  And the young men are very sad;
  Therefore the sowing is not glad,
70 And mournful is the harvesting.
Of high and low, of great and small,
Vanity is the lot of all.

A King dwelt in Jerusalem;
  He was the wisest man on earth;
75   He had all riches from his birth,
And pleasures till he tired of them;
Then, having tested all things, he
Witnessed that all are vanity.

SLEEP AT SEA.

Sound the deep waters:—
  Who shall sound that deep?—
Too short the plummet
  And the watchmen sleep.
5 Some dream of effort
  Up a toilsome steep;
Some dream of pasture grounds
  For harmless sheep.

White shapes flit to and fro
10   From mast to mast;

They feel the distant tempest
   That nears them fast:
Great rocks are straight ahead,
   Great shoals not past;
15 They shout to one another
   Upon the blast.

Oh soft the streams drop music
   Between the hills,
And musical the birds' nests
20   Beside those rills:
The nests are types of home
   Love-hidden from ills,
The nests are types of spirits
   Love-music fills.

25 So dream the sleepers,
   Each man in his place;
The lightning shows the smile
   Upon each face:
The ship is driving, driving,
30   It drives apace:
And sleepers smile, and spirits
   Bewail their case.

The lightning glares and reddens
   Across the skies;
35 It seems but sunset
   To those sleeping eyes.
When did the sun go down
   On such a wise?
From such a sunset
40   When shall day arise?

"Wake," call the spirits:
   But to heedless ears;
They have forgotten sorrows
   And hopes and fears;
45 They have forgotten perils
   And smiles and tears;

Their dream has held them long,
  Long years and years.

"Wake," call the spirits again:
50   But it would take
A louder summons
  To bid them awake.
Some dream of pleasure
  For another's sake;
55 Some dream, forgetful
  Of a lifelong ache.

One by one slowly,
  Ah how sad and slow—
Wailing and praying
60   The spirits rise and go:
Clear stainless spirits
  White as white as snow;
Pale spirits, wailing
  For an overthrow.

65 One by one flitting,
  Like a mournful bird
Whose song is tired at last
  For no mate heard.
The loving voice is silent,
70   The useless word;
One by one flitting
  Sick with hope deferred.

Driving and driving,
  The ship drives amain:
75 While swift from mast to mast
  Shapes flit again,
Flit silent as the silence
  Where men lie slain;
Their shadow cast upon the sails
80   Is like a stain.

No voice to call the sleepers,
  No hand to raise:

They sleep to death in dreaming
   Of length of days.
85 Vanity of vanities,
   The Preacher says:
Vanity is the end
   Of all their ways.

FROM HOUSE TO HOME.

The first was like a dream thro' summer heat,
   The second like a tedious numbing swoon,
While the half-frozen pulses lagged to beat
   Beneath a winter moon.

5 "But," says my friend, "what was this thing and where?"
   It was a pleasure-place within my soul;
An earthly paradise supremely fair
   That lured me from the goal.

The first part was a tissue of hugged lies;
10   The second was its ruin fraught with pain:
Why raise the fair delusion to the skies
   But to be dashed again?

My castle stood of white transparent glass
   Glittering and frail with many a fretted spire,
15 But when the summer sunset came to pass
   It kindled into fire.

My pleasaunce was an undulating green,
   Stately with trees whose shadows slept below,
With glimpses of smooth garden-beds between
20   Like flame or sky or snow.

Swift squirrels on the pastures took their ease,
   With leaping lambs safe from the unfeared knife;
All singing-birds rejoicing in those trees
   Fulfilled their careless life.

25 Wood-pigeons cooed there, stockdoves nestled there,

My trees were full of songs and flowers and fruit,
Their branches spread a city to the air
    And mice lodged in their root.

My heath lay farther off, where lizards lived
30   In strange metallic mail, just spied and gone;
Like darted lightnings here and there perceived
    But no where dwelt upon.

Frogs and fat toads were there to hop or plod
    And propagate in peace, an uncouth crew,
35 Where velvet-headed rushes rustling nod
    And spill the morning dew.

All caterpillars throve beneath my rule,
    With snails and slugs in corners out of sight;
I never marred the curious sudden stool
40   That perfects in a night.

Safe in his excavated gallery
    The burrowing mole groped on from year to year;
No harmless hedgehog curled because of me
    His prickly back for fear.

45 Ofttimes one like an angel walked with me,
    With spirit-discerning eyes like flames of fire,
But deep as the unfathomed endless sea
    Fulfilling my desire:

And sometimes like a snowdrift he was fair,
50   And sometimes like a sunset glorious red,
And sometimes he had wings to scale the air
    With aureole round his head.

We sang our songs together by the way,
    Calls and recalls and echoes of delight;
55 So communed we together all the day,
    And so in dreams by night.

I have no words to tell what way we walked,
    What unforgotten path now closed and sealed;
I have no words to tell all things we talked,
60   All things that he revealed:

This only can I tell: that hour by hour
    I waxed more feastful, lifted up and glad;
I felt no thorn-prick when I plucked a flower,
        Felt not my friend was sad.

65 "Tomorrow," once I said to him with smiles:
    "Tonight," he answered gravely and was dumb,
But pointed out the stones that numbered miles
        And miles and miles to come.

"Not so," I said: "tomorrow shall be sweet;
70   Tonight is not so sweet as coming days."
Then first I saw that he had turned his feet,
        Had turned from me his face:

Running and flying miles and miles he went,
    But once looked back to beckon with his hand
75 And cry: "Come home, O love, from banishment:
        Come to the distant land."—

That night destroyed me like an avalanche;
    One night turned all my summer back to snow:
Next morning not a bird upon my branch,
80   Not a lamb woke below;

No bird, no lamb, no living breathing thing;
    No squirrel scampered on my breezy lawn,
No mouse lodged by his hoard: all joys took wing
        And fled before that dawn.

85 Azure and sun were starved from heaven above,
    No dew had fallen but biting frost lay hoar:
O love, I knew that I should meet my love,
        Should find my love no more.

"My love no more," I muttered, stunned with pain:
90   I shed no tear, I wrung no passionate hand,
Till something whispered: "You shall meet again,
        Meet in a distant land."

Then with a cry like famine I arose,
    I lit my candle, searched from room to room,
95 Searched up and down; a war of winds that froze
        Swept thro' the blank of gloom.

I searched day after day, night after night;
   Scant change there came to me of night or day:
"No more," I wailed, "no more:" and trimmed my light,
100   And gnashed but did not pray,

Until my heart broke and my spirit broke:
   Upon the frost-bound floor I stumbled, fell,
And moaned: "It is enough: withhold the stroke.
    Farewell, O love, farewell."

105 Then life swooned from me. And I heard the song
   Of spheres and spirits rejoicing over me:
One cried: "Our sister, she hath suffered long "—
    One answered: "Make her see "—

One cried: "Oh blessed she who no more pain,
110   Who no more disappointment shall receive "—
One answered: "Not so: she must live again;
    Strengthen thou her to live."

So while I lay entranced a curtain seemed
   To shrivel with crackling from before my face;
115 Across mine eyes a waxing radiance beamed
    And showed a certain place.

I saw a vision of a woman, where
   Night and new morning strive for domination;
Incomparably pale, and almost fair,
120   And sad beyond expression.

Her eyes were like some fire-enshrining gem,
   Were stately like the stars, and yet were tender;
Her figure charmed me like a windy stem
    Quivering and drooped and slender.

125 I stood upon the outer barren ground,
   She stood on inner ground that budded flowers;
While circling in their never-slackening round
    Danced by the mystic hours.

But every flower was lifted on a thorn,
130   And every thorn shot upright from its sands
To gall her feet; hoarse laughter pealed in scorn
    With cruel clapping hands.

She bled and wept, yet did not shrink; her strength
    Was strung up until daybreak of delight:
135 She measured measureless sorrow toward its length,
    And breadth, and depth, and height.

Then marked I how a chain sustained her form,
    A chain of living links not made nor riven:
It stretched sheer up thro' lightning, wind, and storm,
140   And anchored fast in heaven.

One cried: "How long? yet founded on the Rock
    She shall do battle, suffer, and attain "—
One answered: "Faith quakes in the tempest shock:
    Strengthen her soul again."

145 I saw a cup sent down and come to her
    Brim full of loathing and of bitterness:
She drank with livid lips that seemed to stir
    The depth, not make it less.

But as she drank I spied a hand distil
150   New wine and virgin honey; making it
First bitter-sweet, then sweet indeed, until
    She tasted only sweet.

Her lips and cheeks waxed rosy-fresh and young;
    Drinking she sang: "My soul shall nothing want;"
155 And drank anew: while soft a song was sung,
    A mystical slow chant.

One cried: "The wounds are faithful of a friend:
    The wilderness shall blossom as a rose "—
One answered: "Rend the veil, declare the end,
160   Strengthen her ere she goes."

Then earth and heaven were rolled up like a scroll;
    Time and space, change and death, had passed away;
Weight, number, measure, each had reached its whole;
    The day had come, that day.

165 Multitudes—multitudes—stood up in bliss,
    Made equal to the angels, glorious, fair;
With harps, palms, wedding-garments, kiss of peace,
    And crowned and haloed hair.

They sang a song, a new song in the height,
170   Harping with harps to Him Who is Strong and True:
They drank new wine, their eyes saw with new light,
          Lo, all things were made new.

Tier beyond tier they rose and rose and rose
     So high that it was dreadful, flames with flames:
175 No man could number them, no tongue disclose
          Their secret sacred names.

As tho' one pulse stirred all, one rush of blood
     Fed all, one breath swept thro' them myriad-voiced,
They struck their harps, cast down their crowns, they stood
180   And worshipped and rejoiced.

Each face looked one way like a moon new-lit,
     Each face looked one way towards its Sun of Love;
Drank love and bathed in love and mirrored it
          And knew no end thereof.

185 Glory touched glory on each blessed head,
     Hands locked dear hands never to sunder more:
These were the new-begotten from the dead
          Whom the great birthday bore.

Heart answered heart, soul answered soul at rest,
190   Double against each other, filled, sufficed:
All loving, loved of all; but loving best
          And best beloved of Christ.

I saw that one who lost her love in pain,
     Who trod on thorns, who drank the loathsome cup;
195 The lost in night, in day was found again;
          The fallen was lifted up.

They stood together in the blessed noon,
     They sang together thro' the length of days;
Each loving face bent Sunwards like a moon
200   New-lit with love and praise.

Therefore, O friend, I would not if I might
     Rebuild my house of lies, wherein I joyed
One time to dwell: my soul shall walk in white,
          Cast down but not destroyed.

205   Therefore in patience I possess my soul;
    Yea, therefore as a flint I set my face,
To pluck down, to build up again the whole—
    But in a distant place.

These thorns are sharp, yet I can tread on them;
210   This cup is loathsome, yet He makes it sweet:
My face is steadfast toward Jerusalem,
    My heart remembers it.

I lift the hanging hands, the feeble knees—
    I, precious more than seven times molten gold—
215 Until the day when from His storehouses
    God shall bring new and old;

Beauty for ashes, oil of joy for grief,
    Garment of praise for spirit of heaviness:
Altho' today I fade as doth a leaf,
220   I languish and grow less.

Altho' today He prunes my twigs with pain,
    Yet doth His blood nourish and warm my root:
Tomorrow I shall put forth buds again
    And clothe myself with fruit.

225 Altho' today I walk in tedious ways,
    Today His staff is turned into a rod,
Yet will I wait for Him the appointed days
    And stay upon my God.

OLD AND NEW YEAR DITTIES.

1.

New Year met me somewhat sad:
    Old Year leaves me tired,
Stripped of favourite things I had,
    Baulked of much desired:
5 Yet farther on my road today
God willing, farther on my way.

New Year coming on apace
   What have you to give me?
Bring you scathe, or bring you grace,
Face me with an honest face;
   You shall not deceive me:
Be it good or ill, be it what you will,
It needs shall help me on my road,
My rugged way to heaven, please God.

2.

Watch with me, men, women, and children dear,
You whom I love, for whom I hope and fear,
Watch with me this last vigil of the year.
Some hug their business, some their pleasure scheme;
Some seize the vacant hour to sleep or dream;
Heart locked in heart some kneel and watch apart.

Watch with me, blessed spirits, who delight
All thro' the holy night to walk in white,
Or take your ease after the long-drawn fight.
I know not if they watch with me: I know
They count this eve of resurrection slow,
And cry, "How long?" with urgent utterance strong.

Watch with me, Jesus, in my loneliness:
Tho' others say me nay, yet say Thou yes;
Tho' others pass me by, stop Thou to bless.
Yea, Thou dost stop with me this vigil night;
Tonight of pain, tomorrow of delight:
I, Love, am Thine; Thou, Lord my God, art mine.

3.

Passing away, saith the World, passing away:
Chances, beauty and youth sapped day by day:
Thy life never continueth in one stay.
Is the eye waxen dim, is the dark hair changing to grey
That hath won neither laurel nor bay?
I shall clothe myself in Spring and bud in May:
Thou, root-stricken, shalt not rebuild thy decay
On my bosom for aye.
Then I answered: Yea.

10   Passing away, saith my Soul, passing away:
      With its burden of fear and hope, of labour and play;
      Hearken what the past doth witness and say:
      Rust in thy gold, a moth is in thine array,
      A canker is in thy bud, thy leaf must decay.
15   At midnight, at cockcrow, at morning, one certain day
      Lo the bridegroom shall come and shall not delay:
      Watch thou and pray.
      Then I answered: Yea.

      Passing away, saith my God, passing away:
20   Winter passeth after the long delay:
      New grapes on the vine, new figs on the tender spray,
      Turtle calleth turtle in Heaven's May.
      Tho' I tarry, wait for Me, trust Me, watch and pray.
      Arise, come away, night is past and lo it is day,
25   My love, My sister, My spouse, thou shalt hear Me say.
      Then I answered: Yea.

AMEN.

      It is over. What is over?
        Nay, how much is over truly:
      Harvest days we toiled to sow for;
        Now the sheaves are gathered newly,
5   Now the wheat is garnered duly.

      It is finished. What is finished?
        Much is finished known or unknown:
      Lives are finished; time diminished;
        Was the fallow field left unsown?
10   Will these buds be always unblown?

      It suffices. What suffices?
        All suffices reckoned rightly:

Spring shall bloom where now the ice is,
　Roses make the bramble sightly,
15　　And the quickening sun shine brightly,
　　And the latter wind blow lightly,
And my garden teem with spices.

The Prince's Progress and Other Poems
(1866)

THE PRINCE'S PROGRESS.

Till all sweet gums and juices flow,
Till the blossom of blossoms blow,
The long hours go and come and go,
   The bride she sleepeth, waketh, sleepeth,
Waiting for one whose coming is slow:—
     Hark! the bride weepeth.

"How long shall I wait, come heat come rime?"—
"Till the strong Prince comes, who must come in time"
(Her women say), "there's a mountain to climb,
   A river to ford. Sleep, dream and sleep:
Sleep" (they say): "we've muffled the chime,
     Better dream than weep."

In his world-end palace the strong Prince sat,
Taking his ease on cushion and mat,
Close at hand lay his staff and his hat.
   "When wilt thou start? the bride waits, O youth."—
"Now the moon's at full; I tarried for that,
     Now I start in truth.

"But tell me first, true voice of my doom,
Of my veiled bride in her maiden bloom;
Keeps she watch thro' glare and thro' gloom,
   Watch for me asleep and awake?"—
"Spell-bound she watches in one white room,
     And is patient for thy sake.

"By her head lilies and rosebuds grow;
The lilies droop, will the rosebuds blow?

The silver slim lilies hang the head low;
   Their stream is scanty, their sunshine rare;
Let the sun blaze out, and let the stream flow,
30   They will blossom and wax fair.

"Red and white poppies grow at her feet,
The blood-red wait for sweet summer heat,
Wrapped in bud-coats hairy and neat;
   But the white buds swell, one day they will burst,
35 Will open their death-cups drowsy and sweet—
      Which will open the first?"

Then a hundred sad voices lifted a wail,
And a hundred glad voices piped on the gale:
"Time is short, life is short," they took up the tale:
40 "Life is sweet, love is sweet, use today while you may;
Love is sweet, and tomorrow may fail;
      Love is sweet, use today."

While the song swept by, beseeching and meek,
Up rose the Prince with a flush on his cheek,
45 Up he rose to stir and to seek,
   Going forth in the joy of his strength;
Strong of limb if of purpose weak,
      Starting at length.

Forth he set in the breezy morn,
50 Across green fields of nodding corn,
As goodly a Prince as ever was born,
   Carolling with the carolling lark;—
Sure his bride will be won and worn,
      Ere fall of the dark.

55 So light his step, so merry his smile,
A milkmaid loitered beside a stile,
Set down her pail and rested awhile,
   A wave-haired milkmaid, rosy and white;
The Prince, who had journeyed at least a mile,
60   Grew athirst at the sight.

"Will you give me a morning draught?"—
"You're kindly welcome," she said, and laughed.

He lifted the pail, new milk he quaffed;
  Then wiping his curly black beard like silk:
65 "Whitest cow that ever was calved
    Surely gave you this milk."

Was it milk now, or was it cream?
Was she a maid, or an evil dream?
Her eyes began to glitter and gleam;
70 He would have gone, but he stayed instead;
Green they gleamed as he looked in them:
    "Give me my fee," she said.—

"I will give you a jewel of gold."—
"Not so; gold is heavy and cold."—
75 "I will give you a velvet fold
    Of foreign work your beauty to deck."—
"Better I like my kerchief rolled
    Light and white round my neck."—

"Nay," cried he, "but fix your own fee."—
80 She laughed, "You may give the full moon to me;
Or else sit under this apple-tree
  Here for one idle day by my side;
After that I'll let you go free,
    And the world is wide."

85 Loth to stay, yet to leave her slack,
He half turned away, then he quite turned back:
For courtesy's sake he could not lack
  To redeem his own royal pledge;
Ahead too the windy heaven lowered black
90   With a fire-cloven edge.

So he stretched his length in the apple-tree shade,
Lay and laughed and talked to the maid,
Who twisted her hair in a cunning braid
  And writhed it in shining serpent-coils,
95 And held him a day and night fast laid
    In her subtle toils.

At the death of night and the birth of day,
When the owl left off his sober play,

And the bat hung himself out of the way,
100   Woke the song of mavis and merle,
And heaven put off its hodden grey
        For mother-o'-pearl.

Peeped up daisies here and there,
Here, there, and everywhere;
105   Rose a hopeful lark in the air,
        Spreading out towards the sun his breast;
While the moon set solemn and fair
        Away in the West.

"Up, up, up," called the watchman lark,
110   In his clear réveillée: "Hearken, oh hark!
Press to the high goal, fly to the mark.
        Up, O sluggard, new morn is born;
If still asleep when the night falls dark,
        Thou must wait a second morn."

115   "Up, up, up," sad glad voices swelled:
"So the tree falls and lies as it's felled.
Be thy bands loosed, O sleeper, long held
        In sweet sleep whose end is not sweet.
Be the slackness girt and the softness quelled
120   And the slowness fleet."

Off he set. The grass grew rare,
A blight lurked in the darkening air,
The very moss grew hueless and spare,
        The last daisy stood all astunt;
125   Behind his back the soil lay bare,
        But barer in front.

A land of chasm and rent, a land
Of rugged blackness on either hand:
If water trickled its track was tanned
130   With an edge of rust to the chink;
If one stamped on stone or on sand
        It returned a clink.

A lifeless land, a loveless land,
Without lair or nest on either hand:

135   Only scorpions jerked in the sand,
     Black as black iron, or dusty pale;
From point to point sheer rock was manned
     By scorpions in mail.

A land of neither life nor death,
140   Where no man buildeth or fashioneth,
Where none draws living or dying breath;
     No man cometh or goeth there,
No man doeth, seeketh, saith,
     In the stagnant air.

145   Some old volcanic upset must
Have rent the crust and blackened the crust;
Wrenched and ribbed it beneath its dust
     Above earth's molten centre at seethe,
Heaved and heaped it by huge upthrust
150   Of fire beneath.

Untrodden before, untrodden since:
Tedious land for a social Prince;
Halting, he scanned the outs and ins,
     Endless, labyrinthine, grim,
155   Of the solitude that made him wince,
     Laying wait for him.

By bulging rock and gaping cleft,
Even of half mere daylight reft,
Rueful he peered to right and left,
160   Muttering in his altered mood:
"The fate is hard that weaves my weft,
     Tho' my lot be good."

Dim the changes of day to night,
Of night scarce dark to day not bright.
165   Still his road wound towards the right,
     Still he went, and still he went,
Till one night he spied a light,
     In his discontent.

Out it flashed from a yawn-mouthed cave,
170   Like a red-hot eye from a grave.

No man stood there of whom to crave
   Rest for wayfarer plodding by:
Tho' the tenant were churl or knave
   The Prince might try.

175 In he passed and tarried not,
Groping his way from spot to spot,
Towards where the cavern flare glowed hot:—
   An old, old mortal, cramped and double,
Was peering into a seething-pot,
180   In a world of trouble.

The veriest atomy he looked,
With grimy fingers clutching and crooked,
Tight skin, a nose all bony and hooked,
   And a shaking, sharp, suspicious way;
185 Blinking, his eyes had scarcely brooked
   The light of day.

Stared the Prince, for the sight was new;
Stared, but asked without more ado:
"May a weary traveller lodge with you,
190   Old father, here in your lair?
In your country the inns seem few,
   And scanty the fare."

The head turned not to hear him speak;
The old voice whistled as thro' a leak
195 (Out it came in a quavering squeak):
   "Work for wage is a bargain fit:
If there's aught of mine that you seek
   You must work for it.

"Buried alive from light and air
200 This year is the hundredth year,
I feed my fire with a sleepless care,
   Watching my potion wane or wax:
Elixir of Life is simmering there,
   And but one thing lacks.

205 "If you're fain to lodge here with me,
Take that pair of bellows you see—

Too heavy for my old hands they be—
　　Take the bellows and puff and puff:
When the steam curls rosy and free
210　　　　The broth's boiled enough.

"Then take your choice of all I have;
I will give you life if you crave.
Already I'm mildewed for the grave,
　　So first myself I must drink my fill:
215　But all the rest may be yours, to save
　　　　Whomever you will."

"Done," quoth the Prince, and the bargain stood.
First he piled on resinous wood,
Next plied the bellows in hopeful mood;
220　　　Thinking, "My love and I will live.
If I tarry, why life is good,
　　　　And she may forgive."

The pot began to bubble and boil;
The old man cast in essence and oil,
225　He stirred all up with a triple coil
　　Of gold and silver and iron wire,
Dredged in a pinch of virgin soil,
　　　　And fed the fire.

But still the steam curled watery white;
230　Night turned to day and day to night;
One thing lacked, by his feeble sight
　　Unseen, unguessed by his feeble mind:
Life might miss him, but Death the blight
　　　　Was sure to find.

235　So when the hundredth year was full
The thread was cut and finished the school.
Death snapped the old worn-out tool,
　　Snapped him short while he stood and stirred
(Tho' stiff he stood as a stiff-necked mule)
240　　　With never a word.

Thus at length the old crab was nipped.
The dead hand slipped, the dead finger dipped

In the broth as the dead man slipped,—
  That same instant, a rosy red
245 Flushed the steam, and quivered and clipped
  Round the dead old head.

The last ingredient was supplied
(Unless the dead man mistook or lied).
Up started the Prince, he cast aside
250 The bellows plied thro' the tedious trial,
Made sure that his host had died,
  And filled a phial.

"One night's rest," thought the Prince: "This done,
Forth I speed with the rising sun:
255 With the morrow I rise and run,
  Come what will of wind or of weather.
This draught of Life when my Bride is won
  We'll drink together."

Thus the dead man stayed in his grave,
260 Self-chosen, the dead man in his cave;
There he stayed, were he fool or knave,
  Or honest seeker who had not found:
While the Prince outside was prompt to crave
  Sleep on the ground.

265 "If she watches, go bid her sleep;
Bid her sleep, for the road is steep:
He can sleep who holdeth her cheap,
  Sleep and wake and sleep again.
Let him sow, one day he shall reap,
270 Let him sow the grain.

"When there blows a sweet garden rose,
Let it bloom and wither if no man knows:
But if one knows when the sweet thing blows,
  Knows, and lets it open and drop,
275 If but a nettle his garden grows
  He hath earned the crop."

Thro' his sleep the summons rang,
Into his ears it sobbed and it sang.

Slow he woke with a drowsy pang,
280   Shook himself without much debate,
Turned where he saw green branches hang,
    Started tho' late.

For the black land was travelled o'er,
He should see the grim land no more.
285 A flowering country stretched before
    His face when the lovely day came back:
He hugged the phial of Life he bore,
    And resumed his track.

By willow courses he took his path,
290 Spied what a nest the kingfisher hath,
Marked the fields green to aftermath,
    Marked where the red-brown field-mouse ran,
Loitered awhile for a deep-stream bath,
    Yawned for a fellow-man.

295 Up on the hills not a soul in view,
In the vale not many nor few;
Leaves, still leaves, and nothing new.
    It's oh for a second maiden, at least,
To bear the flagon, and taste it too,
300   And flavour the feast.

Lagging he moved, and apt to swerve;
Lazy of limb, but quick of nerve.
At length the water-bed took a curve,
    The deep river swept its bankside bare;
305 Waters streamed from the hill-reserve—
    Waters here, waters there.

High above, and deep below,
Bursting, bubbling, swelling the flow,
Like hill-torrents after the snow,—
310   Bubbling, gurgling, in whirling strife,
Swaying, sweeping, to and fro,—
    He must swim for his life.

Which way?—which way?—his eyes grew dim
With the dizzying whirl—which way to swim?

315 The thunderous downshoot deafened him;
    Half he choked in the lashing spray:
Life is sweet, and the grave is grim—
    Which way?—which way?

A flash of light, a shout from the strand:
320 "This way—this way; here lies the land!"
His phial clutched in one drowning hand;
    He catches—misses—catches a rope;
His feet slip on the slipping sand:
    Is there life?—is there hope?

325 Just saved, without pulse or breath,—
Scarcely saved from the gulp of death;
Laid where a willow shadoweth—
    Laid where a swelling turf is smooth.
(O Bride! but the Bridegroom lingereth
330   For all thy sweet youth.)

Kind hands do and undo,
Kind voices whisper and coo:
"I will chafe his hands"—"And I"—"And you
    Raise his head, put his hair aside."
335 (If many laugh, one well may rue:
    Sleep on, thou Bride.)

So the Prince was tended with care:
One wrung foul ooze from his clustered hair;
Two chafed his hands, and did not spare;
340   But one propped his head that drooped awry:
Till his eyes oped, and at unaware
    They met eye to eye.

Oh a moon face in a shadowy place,
And a light touch and a winsome grace,
345 And a thrilling tender voice which says:
    "Safe from waters that seek the sea—
Cold waters by rugged ways—
    Safe with me."

While overhead bird whistles to bird,
350 And round about plays a gamesome herd:

"Safe with us"—some take up the word—
   "Safe with us, dear lord and friend:
All the sweeter if long deferred
      Is rest in the end."

355   Had he stayed to weigh and to scan,
He had been more or less than a man:
He did what a young man can,
      Spoke of toil and an arduous way—
Toil tomorrow, while golden ran
360   The sands of today.

Slip past, slip fast,
Uncounted hours from first to last,
Many hours till the last is past,
      Many hours dwindling to one—
365   One hour whose die is cast,
         One last hour gone.

Come, gone—gone for ever—
Gone as an unreturning river—
Gone as to death the merriest liver—
370   Gone as the year at the dying fall—
Tomorrow, today, yesterday, never—
         Gone once for all.

Came at length the starting-day,
With last words, and last, last words to say,
375   With bodiless cries from far away—
      Chiding wailing voices that rang
Like a trumpet-call to the tug and fray;
         And thus they sang:

"Is there life?—the lamp burns low;
380   Is there hope?—the coming is slow:
The promise promised so long ago,
      The long promise, has not been kept.
Does she live?—does she die?—she slumbers so
         Who so oft has wept.

385   "Does she live?—does she die?—she languisheth
As a lily drooping to death,

As a drought-worn bird with failing breath,
   As a lovely vine without a stay,
As a tree whereof the owner saith,
390   'Hew it down today.'"

Stung by that word the Prince was fain
To start on his tedious road again.
He crossed the stream where a ford was plain,
   He clomb the opposite bank tho' steep,
395 And swore to himself to strain and attain
     Ere he tasted sleep.

Huge before him a mountain frowned
With foot of rock on the valley ground,
And head with snows incessant crowned,
400   And a cloud mantle about its strength,
And a path which the wild goat hath not found
     In its breadth and length.

But he was strong to do and dare:
If a host had withstood him there,
405 He had braved a host with little care
    In his lusty youth and his pride,
Tough to grapple tho' weak to snare.
     He comes, O Bride.

Up he went where the goat scarce clings,
410 Up where the eagle folds her wings,
Past the green line of living things,
    Where the sun cannot warm the cold,—
Up he went as a flame enrings
     Where there seems no hold.

415 Up a fissure barren and black,
Till the eagles tired upon his track,
And the clouds were left behind his back,
    Up till the utmost peak was past.
Then he gasped for breath and his strength fell slack;
420   He paused at last.

Before his face a valley spread
Where fatness laughed, wine, oil, and bread,

Where all fruit-trees their sweetness shed,
   Where all birds made love to their kind,
425 Where jewels twinkled, and gold lay red
    And not hard to find.

Midway down the mountain side
(On its green slope the path was wide)
Stood a house for a royal bride,
430   Built all of changing opal stone,
The royal palace, till now descried
    In his dreams alone.

Less bold than in days of yore,
Doubting now tho' never before,
435 Doubting he goes and lags the more:
   Is the time late? does the day grow dim?
Rose, will she open the crimson core
    Of her heart to him?

Above his head a tangle glows
440 Of wine-red roses, blushes, snows,
Closed buds and buds that unclose,
   Leaves, and moss, and prickles too;
His hand shook as he plucked a rose,
    And the rose dropped dew.

445 Take heart of grace! the potion of Life
May go far to woo him a wife:
If she frown, yet a lover's strife
   Lightly raised can be laid again:
A hasty word is never the knife
450   To cut love in twain.

Far away stretched the royal land,
Fed by dew, by a spice-wind fanned:
Light labour more, and his foot would stand
   On the threshold, all labour done;
455 Easy pleasure laid at his hand,
    And the dear Bride won.

His slackening steps pause at the gate—
Does she wake or sleep?—the time is late—

Does she sleep now, or watch and wait?
460   She has watched, she has waited long,
Watching athwart the golden grate
        With a patient song.

Fling the golden portals wide,
The Bridegroom comes to his promised Bride;
465 Draw the gold-stiff curtains aside,
        Let them look on each other's face,
She in her meekness, he in his pride—
        Day wears apace.

Day is over, the day that wore.
470 What is this that comes thro' the door,
The face covered, the feet before?
        This that coming takes his breath;
This Bride not seen, to be seen no more
        Save of Bridegroom Death?

475 Veiled figures carrying her
Sweep by yet make no stir;
There is a smell of spice and myrrh,
        A bride-chant burdened with one name;
The bride-song rises steadier
480   Than the torches' flame:

"Too late for love, too late for joy,
        Too late, too late!
You loitered on the road too long,
        You trifled at the gate:
485 The enchanted dove upon her branch
        Died without a mate;
The enchanted princess in her tower
        Slept, died, behind the grate;
Her heart was starving all this while
490   You made it wait.

"Ten years ago, five years ago,
        One year ago,
Even then you had arrived in time,
        Tho' somewhat slow;

495 Then you had known her living face
 Which now you cannot know:
The frozen fountain would have leaped,
 The buds gone on to blow,
The warm south wind would have awaked
500 To melt the snow.

"Is she fair now as she lies?
 Once she was fair;
Meet queen for any kingly king,
 With gold-dust on her hair.
505 Now these are poppies in her locks,
 White poppies she must wear;
Must wear a veil to shroud her face
 And the want graven there:
Or is the hunger fed at length,
510 Cast off the care?

"We never saw her with a smile
 Or with a frown;
Her bed seemed never soft to her,
 Tho' tossed of down;
515 She little heeded what she wore,
 Kirtle, or wreath, or gown;
We think her white brows often ached
 Beneath her crown,
Till silvery hairs showed in her locks
520 That used to be so brown.

"We never heard her speak in haste:
 Her tones were sweet,
And modulated just so much
 As it was meet:
525 Her heart sat silent thro' the noise
 And concourse of the street.
There was no hurry in her hands,
 No hurry in her feet;
There was no bliss drew nigh to her,
530 That she might run to greet.

"You should have wept her yesterday,
   Wasting upon her bed:
But wherefore should you weep today
   That she is dead?
535 Lo, we who love weep not today,
   But crown her royal head.
Let be these poppies that we strew,
   Your roses are too red:
Let be these poppies, not for you
540   Cut down and spread."

MAIDEN-SONG.

Long ago and long ago,
   And long ago still,
There dwelt three merry maidens
   Upon a distant hill.
5 One was tall Meggan,
   And one was dainty May,
But one was fair Margaret,
   More fair than I can say,
Long ago and long ago.

10 When Meggan plucked the thorny rose,
   And when May pulled the brier,
Half the birds would swoop to see,
   Half the beasts draw nigher;
Half the fishes of the streams
15   Would dart up to admire:
But when Margaret plucked a flag-flower,
   Or poppy hot aflame,
All the beasts and all the birds
   And all the fishes came
20 To her hand more soft than snow.

Strawberry leaves and May-dew
   In brisk morning air,

Strawberry leaves and May-dew
  Make maidens fair.
25 "I go for strawberry leaves,"
  Meggan said one day:
"Fair Margaret can bide at home,
  But you come with me, May;
Up the hill and down the hill,
30 Along the winding way
You and I are used to go."

So these two fair sisters
  Went with innocent will
Up the hill and down again,
35 And round the homestead hill:
While the fairest sat at home,
  Margaret like a queen,
Like a blush-rose, like the moon
  In her heavenly sheen,
40 Fragrant-breathed as milky cow
  Or field of blossoming bean,
Graceful as an ivy bough
  Born to cling and lean;
Thus she sat to sing and sew.

45 When she raised her lustrous eyes
  A beast peeped at the door;
When she downward cast her eyes
  A fish gasped on the floor;
When she turned away her eyes
50 A bird perched on the sill,
Warbling out its heart of love,
  Warbling warbling still,
With pathetic pleadings low.

Light-foot May with Meggan
55 Sought the choicest spot,
Clothed with thyme-alternate grass:
  Then, while day waxed hot,
Sat at ease to play and rest,
  A gracious rest and play;

60   The loveliest maidens near or far,
         When Margaret was away,
     Who sat at home to sing and sew.

     Sun-glow flushed their comely cheeks,
         Wind-play tossed their hair,
65   Creeping things among the grass
         Stroked them here and there;
     Meggan piped a merry note,
         A fitful wayward lay,
     While shrill as bird on topmost twig
70   Piped merry May;
     Honey-smooth the double flow.

     Sped a herdsman from the vale,
         Mounting like a flame,
     All on fire to hear and see,
75   With floating locks he came.
     Looked neither north nor south,
         Neither east nor west,
     But sat him down at Meggan's feet
         As love-bird on his nest,
80   And wooed her with a silent awe,
         With trouble not expressed;
     She sang the tears into his eyes,
         The heart out of his breast:
     So he loved her, listening so.

85   She sang the heart out of his breast,
         The words out of his tongue;
     Hand and foot and pulse he paused
         Till her song was sung.
     Then he spoke up from his place
90   Simple words and true:
     "Scanty goods have I to give,
         Scanty skill to woo;
     But I have a will to work,
         And a heart for you:
95   Bid me stay or bid me go."

Then Meggan mused within herself:
　　"Better be first with him,
Than dwell where fairer Margaret sits,
　　Who shines my brightness dim,
100　For ever second where she sits,
　　　However fair I be:
I will be lady of his love,
　　And he shall worship me;
I will be lady of his herds
105　　And stoop to his degree,
At home where kids and fatlings grow."

Sped a shepherd from the height
　　Headlong down to look,
(White lambs followed, lured by love
110　　Of their shepherd's crook):
He turned neither east nor west,
　　Neither north nor south,
But knelt right down to May, for love
　　Of her sweet-singing mouth;
115　Forgot his flocks, his panting flocks
　　　In parching hill-side drouth;
Forgot himself for weal or woe.

Trilled her song and swelled her song
　　With maiden coy caprice
120　In a labyrinth of throbs,
　　　Pauses, cadences;
Clear-noted as a dropping brook,
　　Soft-noted like the bees,
Wild-noted as the shivering wind
125　　Forlorn thro' forest trees:
Love-noted like the wood-pigeon
　　Who hides herself for love,
Yet cannot keep her secret safe,
　　But cooes and cooes thereof:
130　Thus the notes rang loud or low.

He hung breathless on her breath;
　　Speechless, who listened well;

Could not speak or think or wish
   Till silence broke the spell.
135 Then he spoke, and spread his hands,
   Pointing here and there:
"See my sheep and see the lambs,
   Twin lambs which they bare.
All myself I offer you,
140   All my flocks and care,
Your sweet song hath moved me so."

In her fluttered heart young May
   Mused a dubious while:
"If he loves me as he says"—
145   Her lips curved with a smile:
"Where Margaret shines like the sun
   I shine but like a moon;
If sister Meggan makes her choice
   I can make mine as soon;
150 At cockcrow we were sister-maids,
   We may be brides at noon."
Said Meggan, "Yes;" May said not "No."

Fair Margaret stayed alone at home,
   Awhile she sang her song,
155 Awhile sat silent, then she thought:
   "My sisters loiter long."
That sultry noon had waned away,
   Shadows had waxen great:
"Surely," she thought within herself,
160   "My sisters loiter late."
She rose, and peered out at the door,
   With patient heart to wait,
And heard a distant nightingale
   Complaining of its mate;
165 Then down the garden slope she walked,
   Down to the garden gate,
Leaned on the rail and waited so.

The slope was lightened by her eyes
   Like summer lightning fair,

170 Like rising of the haloed moon
    Lightened her glimmering hair,
While her face lightened like the sun
    Whose dawn is rosy white.
Thus crowned with maiden majesty
175   She peered into the night,
Looked up the hill and down the hill,
    To left hand and to right,
Flashing like fire-flies to and fro.

Waiting thus in weariness
180   She marked the nightingale
Telling, if any one would heed,
    Its old complaining tale.
Then lifted she her voice and sang,
    Answering the bird:
185 Then lifted she her voice and sang,
    Such notes were never heard
From any bird where Spring's in blow.

The king of all that country
    Coursing far, coursing near,
190 Curbed his amber-bitted steed,
    Coursed amain to hear;
All his princes in his train,
    Squire, and knight, and peer,
With his crown upon his head,
195   His sceptre in his hand,
Down he fell at Margaret's knees
    Lord king of all that land,
To her highness bending low.

Every beast and bird and fish
200   Came mustering to the sound,
Every man and every maid
    From miles of country round:
Meggan on her herdsman's arm,
    With her shepherd May,
205 Flocks and herds trooped at their heels
    Along the hill-side way;

No foot too feeble for the ascent,
   Not any head too grey;
Some were swift and none were slow.

210 So Margaret sang her sisters home
   In their marriage mirth;
Sang free birds out of the sky,
   Beasts along the earth,
Sang up fishes of the deep—
215   All breathing things that move
Sang from far and sang from near
   To her lovely love;
Sang together friend and foe;

Sang a golden-bearded king
220   Straightway to her feet,
Sang him silent where he knelt
   In eager anguish sweet.
But when the clear voice died away,
   When longest echoes died,
225 He stood up like a royal man
   And claimed her for his bride.
So three maids were wooed and won
   In a brief May-tide,
Long ago and long ago.

JESSIE CAMERON.

"Jessie, Jessie Cameron,
   Hear me but this once," quoth he.
"Good luck go with you, neighbour's son,
   But I'm no mate for you," quoth she.
5 Day was verging toward the night
   There beside the moaning sea,
Dimness overtook the light
   There where the breakers be.

"O Jessie, Jessie Cameron,
10　　I have loved you long and true."—
"Good luck go with you, neighbour's son,
　　But I'm no mate for you."

She was a careless, fearless girl,
　　And made her answer plain,
15　Outspoken she to earl or churl,
　　Kindhearted in the main,
But somewhat heedless with her tongue
　　And apt at causing pain;
A mirthful maiden she and young,
20　　Most fair for bliss or bane.
"Oh long ago I told you so,
　　I tell you so today:
Go you your way, and let me go
　　Just my own free way."

25　The sea swept in with moan and foam
　　Quickening the stretch of sand;
They stood almost in sight of home;
　　He strove to take her hand.
"Oh can't you take your answer then,
30　　And won't you understand?
For me you're not the man of men,
　　I've other plans are planned.
You're good for Madge, or good for Cis,
　　Or good for Kate, may be:
35　But what's to me the good of this
　　While you're not good for me?"

They stood together on the beach,
　　They two alone,
And louder waxed his urgent speech,
40　　His patience almost gone:
"Oh say but one kind word to me,
　　Jessie, Jessie Cameron."—
"I'd be too proud to beg," quoth she,
　　And pride was in her tone.

45 And pride was in her lifted head,
  And in her angry eye,
And in her foot, which might have fled,
  But would not fly.

Some say that he had gipsy blood,
50   That in his heart was guile:
Yet he had gone thro' fire and flood
  Only to win her smile.
Some say his grandam was a witch,
  A black witch from beyond the Nile,
55 Who kept an image in a niche
  And talked with it the while.
And by her hut far down the lane
  Some say they would not pass at night,
Lest they should hear an unked strain
60   Or see an unked sight.

Alas for Jessie Cameron!—
  The sea crept moaning, moaning nigher:
She should have hastened to begone,—
  The sea swept higher, breaking by her:
65 She should have hastened to her home
  While yet the west was flushed with fire,
But now her feet are in the foam,
  The sea-foam sweeping higher.
O mother, linger at your door,
70   And light your lamp to make it plain;
But Jessie she comes home no more,
  No more again.

They stood together on the strand,
  They only each by each;
75 Home, her home, was close at hand,
  Utterly out of reach.
Her mother in the chimney nook
  Heard a startled sea-gull screech,
But never turned her head to look
80   Towards the darkening beach:
Neighbours here and neighbours there
  Heard one scream, as if a bird

Shrilly screaming cleft the air:—
   That was all they heard.

85 Jessie she comes home no more,
   Comes home never;
Her lover's step sounds at his door
   No more for ever.
And boats may search upon the sea
90   And search along the river,
But none know where the bodies be:
   Sea-winds that shiver,
Sea-birds that breast the blast,
   Sea-waves swelling,
95 Keep the secret first and last
   Of their dwelling.

Whether the tide so hemmed them round
   With its pitiless flow,
That when they would have gone they found
100   No way to go;
Whether she scorned him to the last
   With words flung to and fro,
Or clung to him when hope was past,
   None will ever know:
105 Whether he helped or hindered her,
   Threw up his life or lost it well,
The troubled sea for all its stir
   Finds no voice to tell.

Only watchers by the dying
110   Have thought they heard one pray
Wordless, urgent; and replying
   One seem to say him nay:
And watchers by the dead have heard
   A windy swell from miles away,
115 With sobs and screams, but not a word
   Distinct for them to say:
And watchers out at sea have caught
   Glimpse of a pale gleam here or there,
Come and gone as quick as thought,
120   Which might be hand or hair.

SPRING QUIET.

Gone were but the Winter,
   Come were but the Spring,
I would go to a covert
   Where the birds sing;

5   Where in the whitethorn
   Singeth a thrush,
And a robin sings
   In the holly-bush.

Full of fresh scents
10   Are the budding boughs
Arching high over
   A cool green house:

Full of sweet scents,
   And whispering air
15 Which sayeth softly:
   "We spread no snare;

"Here dwell in safety,
   Here dwell alone,
With a clear stream
20   And a mossy stone.

"Here the sun shineth
   Most shadily;
Here is heard an echo
   Of the far sea,
25   Tho' far off it be."

THE POOR GHOST.

"Oh whence do you come, my dear friend, to me,
With your golden hair all fallen below your knee,
And your face as white as snowdrops on the lea,
And your voice as hollow as the hollow sea?"

5   "From the other world I come back to you,
    My locks are uncurled with dripping drenching dew.
    You know the old, whilst I know the new:
    But tomorrow you shall know this too."

    "Oh not tomorrow into the dark, I pray;
10 Oh not tomorrow, too soon to go away:
    Here I feel warm and well-content and gay:
    Give me another year, another day."

    "Am I so changed in a day and a night
    That mine own only love shrinks from me with fright,
15 Is fain to turn away to left or right
    And cover up his eyes from the sight?"

    "Indeed I loved you, my chosen friend,
    I loved you for life, but life has an end;
    Thro' sickness I was ready to tend:
20 But death mars all, which we cannot mend.

    "Indeed I loved you; I love you yet
    If you will stay where your bed is set,
    Where I have planted a violet
    Which the wind waves, which the dew makes wet."

25 "Life is gone, then love too is gone,
    It was a reed that I leant upon:
    Never doubt I will leave you alone
    And not wake you rattling bone with bone.

    "I go home alone to my bed,
30 Dug deep at the foot and deep at the head,
    Roofed in with a load of lead,
    Warm enough for the forgotten dead.

    "But why did your tears soak thro' the clay,
    And why did your sobs wake me where I lay?
35 I was away, far enough away:
    Let me sleep now till the Judgment Day."

A PORTRAIT.

I.

She gave up beauty in her tender youth,
 Gave all her hope and joy and pleasant ways;
 She covered up her eyes lest they should gaze
On vanity, and chose the bitter truth.
5 Harsh towards herself, towards others full of ruth,
 Servant of servants, little known to praise,
 Long prayers and fasts trenched on her nights and days:
She schooled herself to sights and sounds uncouth
That with the poor and stricken she might make
10 A home, until the least of all sufficed
Her wants; her own self learned she to forsake,
Counting all earthly gain but hurt and loss.
So with calm will she chose and bore the cross
 And hated all for love of Jesus Christ.

II.

15 They knelt in silent anguish by her bed,
 And could not weep; but calmly there she lay;
 All pain had left her; and the sun's last ray
Shone through upon her, warming into red
The shady curtains. In her heart she said:
20 "Heaven opens; I leave these and go away;
 The Bridegroom calls,—shall the Bride seek to stay?"
Then low upon her breast she bowed her head.
O lily flower, O gem of priceless worth,
 O dove with patient voice and patient eyes,
25 O fruitful vine amid a land of dearth,
 O maid replete with loving purities,
Thou bowedst down thy head with friends on earth
 To raise it with the saints in Paradise.

DREAM-LOVE.

Young Love lies sleeping
    In May-time of the year,
Among the lilies,
    Lapped in the tender light:
5 White lambs come grazing,
    White doves come building there;
And round about him
    The May-bushes are white.

Soft moss the pillow
10   For oh, a softer cheek;
Broad leaves cast shadow
    Upon the heavy eyes:
There winds and waters
    Grow lulled and scarcely speak;
15 There twilight lingers
    The longest in the skies.

Young Love lies dreaming;
    But who shall tell the dream?
A perfect sunlight
20   On rustling forest tips;
Or perfect moonlight
    Upon a rippling stream;
Or perfect silence,
    Or song of cherished lips.

25 Burn odours round him
    To fill the drowsy air;
Weave silent dances
    Around him to and fro;
For oh, in waking
30   The sights are not so fair,
And song and silence
    Are not like these below.

Young Love lies dreaming
    Till summer days are gone,—

35 Dreaming and drowsing
       Away to perfect sleep:
    He sees the beauty
       Sun hath not looked upon,
    And tastes the fountain
40   Unutterably deep.

    Him perfect music
       Doth hush unto his rest,
    And thro' the pauses
       The perfect silence calms:
45 Oh poor the voices
       Of earth from east to west,
    And poor earth's stillness
       Between her stately palms.

    Young Love lies drowsing
50   Away to poppied death;
    Cool shadows deepen
       Across the sleeping face:
    So fails the summer
       With warm, delicious breath;
55 And what hath autumn
       To give us in its place?

    Draw close the curtains
       Of branched evergreen;
    Change cannot touch them
60   With fading fingers sere:
    Here the first violets
       Perhaps will bud unseen,
    And a dove, may be,
       Return to nestle here.

TWICE.

    I took my heart in my hand
       (O my love, O my love),

I said: Let me fall or stand,
   Let me live or die,
5 But this once hear me speak—
   (O my love, O my love)—
Yet a woman's words are weak;
   You should speak, not I.

You took my heart in your hand
10   With a friendly smile,
With a critical eye you scanned,
   Then set it down,
And said: It is still unripe,
   Better wait awhile;
15 Wait while the skylarks pipe,
   Till the corn grows brown.

As you set it down it broke—
   Broke, but I did not wince;
I smiled at the speech you spoke,
20   At your judgment that I heard:
But I have not often smiled
   Since then, nor questioned since,
Nor cared for corn-flowers wild,
   Nor sung with the singing bird.

25 I take my heart in my hand,
   O my God, O my God,
My broken heart in my hand:
   Thou hast seen, judge Thou.
My hope was written on sand,
30   O my God, O my God;
Now let Thy judgment stand—
   Yea, judge me now.

This contemned of a man,
   This marred one heedless day,
35 This heart take Thou to scan
   Both within and without:
Refine with fire its gold,
   Purge Thou its dross away—
Yea hold it in Thy hold,
40   Whence none can pluck it out.

I take my heart in my hand—
  I shall not die, but live—
Before Thy face I stand;
  I, for Thou callest such:
45 All that I have I bring,
  All that I am I give,
Smile Thou and I shall sing,
  But shall not question much.

SONGS IN A CORNFIELD.

    A song in a cornfield
      Where corn begins to fall,
    Where reapers are reaping,
      Reaping one, reaping all.
5   Sing pretty Lettice,
      Sing Rachel, sing May;
    Only Marian cannot sing
      While her sweetheart's away.

    Where is he gone to
10   And why does he stay?
    He came across the green sea
      But for a day,
    Across the deep green sea
      To help with the hay.
15   His hair was curly yellow
      And his eyes were grey,
    He laughed a merry laugh
      And said a sweet say.
    Where is he gone to
20   That he comes not home?
    Today or tomorrow
      He surely will come.
    Let him haste to joy
      Lest he lag for sorrow,

25   For one weeps today
           Who'll not weep tomorrow:
         Today she must weep
           For gnawing sorrow,
         Tonight she may sleep
30   And not wake tomorrow.

         May sang with Rachel
           In the waxing warm weather,
         Lettice sang with them,
           They sang all together:—

35   "Take the wheat in your arm
           Whilst day is broad above,
         Take the wheat to your bosom,
           But not a false false love.
         Out in the fields
40   Summer heat gloweth,
         Out in the fields
           Summer wind bloweth,
         Out in the fields
           Summer friend showeth,
45   Out in the fields
           Summer wheat groweth:
         But in the winter
           When summer heat is dead
         And summer wind has veered
50   And summer friend has fled,
          Only summer wheat remaineth,
           White cakes and bread.
         Take the wheat, clasp the wheat
           That's food for maid and dove;
55   Take the wheat to your bosom,
           But not a false false love."

     A silence of full noontide heat
        Grew on them at their toil:
     The farmer's dog woke up from sleep,
60   The green snake hid her coil
     Where grass stood thickest: bird and beast
        Sought shadows as they could,

The reaping men and women paused
  And sat down where they stood;
65 They ate and drank and were refreshed,
  For rest from toil is good.

While the reapers took their ease,
  Their sickles lying by,
Rachel sang a second strain,
70 And singing seemed to sigh:—

  "There goes the swallow—
  Could we but follow!
    Hasty swallow stay,
    Point us out the way;
75 Look back swallow, turn back swallow, stop swallow.

  "There went the swallow—
  Too late to follow:
    Lost our note of way,
    Lost our chance today;
80 Good bye swallow, sunny swallow, wise swallow.

  "After the swallow
  All sweet things follow:
    All things go their way,
    Only we must stay,
85 Must not follow; good bye swallow, good swallow."

Then listless Marian raised her head
  Among the nodding sheaves;
Her voice was sweeter than that voice;
  She sang like one who grieves:
90 Her voice was sweeter than its wont
  Among the nodding sheaves;
All wondered while they heard her sing
  Like one who hopes and grieves:—

  "Deeper than the hail can smite,
95 Deeper than the frost can bite,
  Deep asleep thro' day and night,
    Our delight.

"Now thy sleep no pang can break,
No tomorrow bid thee wake,
100 Not our sobs who sit and ache
    For thy sake.

"Is it dark or light below?
Oh but is it cold like snow?
Dost thou feel the green things grow
105   Fast or slow?

"Is it warm or cold beneath,
Oh but is it cold like death?
Cold like death, without a breath,
    Cold like death?"

110 If he comes today
    He will find her weeping;
If he comes tomorrow
    He will find her sleeping;
If he comes the next day
115   He'll not find her at all,
He may tear his curling hair,
    Beat his breast and call.

A YEAR'S WINDFALLS.

On the wind of January
    Down flits the snow,
Travelling from the frozen North
    As cold as it can blow.
5 Poor robin redbreast,
    Look where he comes;
Let him in to feel your fire,
    And toss him of your crumbs.

On the wind in February
10   Snowflakes float still,
Half inclined to turn to rain,
    Nipping, dripping, chill.
Then the thaws swell the streams,
    And swollen rivers swell the sea:—
15   If the winter ever ends
    How pleasant it will be.

In the wind of windy March
    The catkins drop down,
Curly, caterpillar-like,
20   Curious green and brown.
With concourse of nest-building birds
    And leaf-buds by the way,
We begin to think of flowers
    And life and nuts some day.

25   With the gusts of April
    Rich fruit-tree blossoms fall,
On the hedged-in orchard-green,
    From the southern wall.
Apple trees and pear trees
30   Shed petals white or pink,
Plum trees and peach trees;
    While sharp showers sink and sink.

Little brings the May breeze
    Beside pure scent of flowers,
35   While all things wax and nothing wanes
    In lengthening daylight hours.
Across the hyacinth beds
    The wind lags warm and sweet,
Across the hawthorn tops,
40   Across the blades of wheat.

In the wind of sunny June
    Thrives the red-rose crop,
Every day fresh blossoms blow
    While the first leaves drop;

45   White rose and yellow rose
      And moss rose choice to find,
    And the cottage cabbage rose
      Not one whit behind.

    On the blast of scorched July
50   Drives the pelting hail,
    From thunderous lightning-clouds, that blot
      Blue heaven grown lurid-pale.
    Weedy waves are tossed ashore,
      Sea-things strange to sight
55   Gasp upon the barren shore
      And fade away in light.

    In the parching August wind
      Cornfields bow the head,
    Sheltered in round valley depths,
60   On low hills outspread.
    Early leaves drop loitering down
      Weightless on the breeze,
    Firstfruits of the year's decay
      From the withering trees.

65   In brisk wind of September
      The heavy-headed fruits
    Shake upon their bending boughs
      And drop from the shoots;
    Some glow golden in the sun,
70   Some show green and streaked,
    Some set forth a purple bloom,
      Some blush rosy-cheeked.

    In strong blast of October
      At the equinox,
75   Stirred up in his hollow bed
      Broad ocean rocks;
    Plunge the ships on his bosom,
      Leaps and plunges the foam,—
    It's oh! for mothers' sons at sea,
80   That they were safe at home.

In slack wind of November
   The fog forms and shifts;
All the world comes out again
   When the fog lifts.
85 Loosened from their sapless twigs
   Leaves drop with every gust;
Drifting, rustling, out of sight
   In the damp or dust.

Last of all, December,
90   The year's sands nearly run,
Speeds on the shortest day,
   Curtails the sun;
With its bleak raw wind
   Lays the last leaves low,
95 Brings back the nightly frosts,
   Brings back the snow.

THE QUEEN OF HEARTS.

How comes it, Flora, that, whenever we
Play cards together, you invariably,
   However the pack parts,
   Still hold the Queen of Hearts?

5 I've scanned you with a scrutinizing gaze,
Resolved to fathom these your secret ways:
   But, sift them as I will,
   Your ways are secret still.

I cut and shuffle; shuffle, cut, again;
10 But all my cutting, shuffling, proves in vain:
   Vain hope, vain forethought too;
   That Queen still falls to you.

I dropped her once, prepense; but, ere the deal
Was dealt, your instinct seemed her loss to feel:
15   "There should be one card more,"
   You said, and searched the floor.

I cheated once; I made a private notch
In Heart-Queen's back, and kept a lynx-eyed watch;
    Yet such another back
20   Deceived me in the pack:

The Queen of Clubs assumed by arts unknown
An imitative dint that seemed my own;
    This notch, not of my doing,
    Misled me to my ruin.

25 It baffles me to puzzle out the clue,
Which must be skill, or craft, or luck in you:
    Unless, indeed, it be
    Natural affinity.

ONE DAY.

I will tell you when they met:
In the limpid days of Spring;
Elder boughs were budding yet,
Oaken boughs looked wintry still,
5 But primrose and veined violet
In the mossful turf were set,
While meeting birds made haste to sing
And build with right good will.

I will tell you when they parted:
10 When plenteous Autumn sheaves were brown,
Then they parted heavy-hearted;
The full rejoicing sun looked down
As grand as in the days before;
Only they had lost a crown;
15 Only to them those days of yore
Could come back nevermore.

When shall they meet? I cannot tell,
Indeed, when they shall meet again,
Except some day in Paradise:
20 For this they wait, one waits in pain.

Beyond the sea of death love lies
For ever, yesterday, today;
Angels shall ask them, "Is it well?"
And they shall answer, "Yea."

A BIRD'S-EYE VIEW.

"Croak, croak, croak,"
Thus the Raven spoke,
Perched on his crooked tree
As hoarse as hoarse could be.
5 Shun him and fear him,
Lest the Bridegroom hear him;
Scout him and rout him
With his ominous eye about him.

Yet, "Croak, croak, croak,"
10 Still tolled from the oak;
From that fatal black bird,
Whether heard or unheard:
"O ship upon the high seas,
Freighted with lives and spices,
15 Sink, O ship," croaked the Raven:
"Let the Bride mount to heaven."

In a far foreign land
Upon the wave-edged sand,
Some friends gaze wistfully
20 Across the glittering sea.
"If we could clasp our sister,"
Three say, "now we have missed her!"
"If we could kiss our daughter!"
Two sigh across the water.

25 Oh the ship sails fast
With silken flags at the mast,
And the home-wind blows soft;

But a Raven sits aloft,
Chuckling and choking,
30   Croaking, croaking, croaking:—
Let the beacon-fire blaze higher;
Bridegroom, watch; the Bride draws nigher.

On a sloped sandy beach,
Which the spring-tide billows reach,
35   Stand a watchful throng
Who have hoped and waited long:
"Fie on this ship, that tarries
With the priceless freight it carries.
The time seems long and longer:
40   O languid wind, wax stronger;"—

Whilst the Raven perched at east
Still croaks and does not cease,
One monotonous note
Tolled from his iron throat:
45   "No father, no mother,
But I have a sable brother:
He sees where ocean flows to,
And he knows what he knows too."

A day and a night
50   They kept watch worn and white;
A night and a day
For the swift ship on its way:
For the Bride and her maidens
—Clear chimes the bridal cadence—
55   For the tall ship that never
Hove in sight for ever.

On either shore, some
Stand in grief loud or dumb
As the dreadful dread
60   Grows certain tho' unsaid.
For laughter there is weeping,
And waking instead of sleeping,
And a desperate sorrow
Morrow after morrow.

65   Oh who knows the truth,
How she perished in her youth,
And like a queen went down
Pale in her royal crown:
How she went up to glory
70   From the sea-foam chill and hoary,
From the sea-depth black and riven
To the calm that is in Heaven?

They went down, all the crew,
The silks and spices too,
75   The great ones and the small,
One and all, one and all.
Was it thro' stress of weather,
Quicksands, rocks, or all together?
Only the Raven knows this,
80   And he will not disclose this.—

After a day and a year
The bridal bells chime clear;
After a year and a day
The Bridegroom is brave and gay:
85   Love is sound, faith is rotten;
The old Bride is forgotten:—
Two ominous Ravens only
Remember, black and lonely.

LIGHT LOVE.

"Oh sad thy lot before I came,
   But sadder when I go;
My presence but a flash of flame,
   A transitory glow
5   Between two barren wastes like snow.
What wilt thou do when I am gone,
   Where wilt thou rest, my dear?

For cold thy bed to rest upon,
  And cold the falling year
10   Whose withered leaves are lost and sere."

She hushed the baby at her breast,
  She rocked it on her knee:
"And I will rest my lonely rest,
  Warmed with the thought of thee,
15   Rest lulled to rest by memory."
She hushed the baby with her kiss,
  She hushed it with her breast:
"Is death so sadder much than this—
  Sure death that builds a nest
20   For those who elsewhere cannot rest?"

"Oh sad thy note, my mateless dove,
  With tender nestling cold;
But hast thou ne'er another love
  Left from the days of old,
25   To build thy nest of silk and gold,
To warm thy paleness to a blush
  When I am far away—
To warm thy coldness to a flush,
  And turn thee back to May,
30   And turn thy twilight back to day?"

She did not answer him again,
  But leaned her face aside,
Wrung with the pang of shame and pain,
  And sore with wounded pride:
35   He knew his very soul had lied.
She strained his baby in her arms,
  His baby to her heart:
"Even let it go, the love that harms:
  We twain will never part;
40   Mine own, his own, how dear thou art."

"Now never teaze me, tender-eyed,
  Sigh-voiced," he said in scorn:
"For nigh at hand there blooms a bride,
  My bride before the morn;
45   Ripe-blooming she, as thou forlorn.

Ripe-blooming she, my rose, my peach;
  She wooes me day and night:
I watch her tremble in my reach;
  She reddens, my delight;
50   She ripens, reddens in my sight."

"And is she like a sunlit rose?
  Am I like withered leaves?
Haste where thy spicèd garden blows:
  But in bare Autumn eves
55   Wilt thou have store of harvest sheaves?
Thou leavest love, true love behind,
  To seek a love as true;
Go, seek in haste: but wilt thou find?
  Change new again for new;
60   Pluck up, enjoy—yea, trample too.

"Alas for her, poor faded rose,
  Alas for her, like me,
Cast down and trampled in the snows."
  "Like thee? nay, not like thee:
65   She leans, but from a guarded tree.
Farewell, and dream as long ago,
  Before we ever met:
Farewell; my swift-paced horse seems slow."
  She raised her eyes, not wet
70   But hard, to Heaven: "Does God forget?"

ON THE WING.

Once in a dream (for once I dreamed of you)
  We stood together in an open field;
  Above our heads two swift-winged pigeons wheeled,
Sporting at ease and courting full in view.
5 When loftier still a broadening darkness flew,
  Down-swooping, and a ravenous hawk revealed;
  Too weak to fight, to fond to fly, they yield;
So farewell life and love and pleasures new.

Then as their plumes fell fluttering to the ground,
10   Their snow-white plumage flecked with crimson drops,
        I wept, and thought I turned towards you to weep:
        But you were gone; while rustling hedgerow tops
Bent in a wind which bore to me a sound
        Of far-off piteous bleat of lambs and sheep.

A RING POSY.

Jess and Jill are pretty girls,
    Plump and well to do,
In a cloud of windy curls:
    Yet I know who
5   Loves me more than curls or pearls.

I'm not pretty, not a bit;
    Thin and sallow-pale;
When I trudge along the street
    I don't need a veil:
10   Yet I have one fancy hit.

Jess and Jill can trill and sing
    With a flute-like voice,
Dance as light as bird on wing,
    Laugh for careless joys:
15   Yet it's I who wear the ring.

Jess and Jill will mate some day,
    Surely, surely;
Ripen on to June thro' May,
While the sun shines make their hay,
20   Slacken steps demurely:
Yet even there I lead the way.

BEAUTY IS VAIN.

While roses are so red,
    While lilies are so white,

Shall a woman exalt her face
　　Because it gives delight?
5 She's not so sweet as a rose,
　　A lily's straighter than she,
And if she were as red or white
　　She'd be but one of three.

Whether she flush in love's summer
10 　　Or in its winter grow pale,
Whether she flaunt her beauty
　　Or hide it away in a veil,
Be she red or white,
　　And stand she erect or bowed,
15 Time will win the race he runs with her
　　And hide her away in a shroud.

MAGGIE A LADY.

You must not call me Maggie, you must not call me Dear,
　　For I'm Lady of the Manor now stately to see;
And if there comes a babe, as there may some happy year,
　　'Twill be little lord or lady at my knee.

5 Oh but what ails you, my sailor cousin Phil,
　　That you shake and turn white like a cockcrow ghost?
You're as white as I turned once down by the mill,
　　When one told me you and ship and crew were lost:

Philip my playfellow, when we were boy and girl
10 　　(It was the Miller's Nancy told it to me),
Philip with the merry life in lip and curl,
　　Philip my playfellow drowned in the sea!

I thought I should have fainted, but I did not faint;
　　I stood stunned at the moment, scarcely sad,
15 Till I raised my wail of desolate complaint
　　For you, my cousin, brother, all I had.

They said I looked so pale—some say so fair—
    My lord stopped in passing to soothe me back to life:
I know I missed a ringlet from my hair
20   Next morning; and now I am his wife.

Look at my gown, Philip, and look at my ring,
    I'm all crimson and gold from top to toe:
All day long I sit in the sun and sing,
    Where in the sun red roses blush and blow.

25 And I'm the rose of roses, says my lord;
    And to him I'm more than the sun in the sky,
While I hold him fast with the golden cord
    Of a curl, with the eyelash of an eye.

His mother said "fie," and his sisters cried "shame,"
30   His highborn ladies cried "shame" from their place:
They said "fie" when they only heard my name,
    But fell silent when they saw my face.

Am I so fair, Philip? Philip, did you think
    I was so fair when we played boy and girl,
35 Where blue forget-me-nots bloomed on the brink
    Of our stream which the mill-wheel sent awhirl?

If I was fair then sure I'm fairer now,
    Sitting where a score of servants stand,
With a coronet on high days for my brow
40   And almost a sceptre for my hand.

You're but a sailor, Philip, weatherbeaten brown,
    A stranger on land and at home on the sea,
Coasting as best you may from town to town:
    Coasting along do you often think of me?

45 I'm a great lady in a sheltered bower,
    With hands grown white thro' having nought to do:
Yet sometimes I think of you hour after hour
    Till I nigh wish myself a child with you.

WHAT WOULD I GIVE?

What would I give for a heart of flesh to warm me thro',
Instead of this heart of stone ice-cold whatever I do;
Hard and cold and small, of all hearts the worst of all.

What would I give for words, if only words would come;
5   But now in its misery my spirit has fallen dumb:
O merry friends, go your way, I have never a word to say.

What would I give for tears, not smiles but scalding tears,
To wash the black mark clean, and to thaw the frost of years,
To wash the stain ingrain and to make me clean again.

THE BOURNE.

Underneath the growing grass,
    Underneath the living flowers,
    Deeper than the sound of showers:
    There we shall not count the hours
5   By the shadows as they pass.

Youth and health will be but vain,
    Beauty reckoned of no worth:
    There a very little girth
    Can hold round what once the earth
10   Seemed too narrow to contain.

SUMMER.

Winter is cold-hearted,
    Spring is yea and nay,
Autumn is a weathercock
    Blown every way:
5   Summer days for me
When every leaf is on its tree;

When Robin's not a beggar,
    And Jenny Wren's a bride,
And larks hang singing, singing, singing,
10   Over the wheat-fields wide,
    And anchored lilies ride,
And the pendulum spider
    Swings from side to side,

And blue-black beetles transact business,
15   And gnats fly in a host,
And furry caterpillars hasten
    That no time be lost,
And moths grow fat and thrive,
And ladybirds arrive.

20 Before green apples blush,
    Before green nuts embrown,
Why, one day in the country
    Is worth a month in town;
    Is worth a day and a year
25 Of the dusty, musty, lag-last fashion
    That days drone elsewhere.

AUTUMN.

    I dwell alone—I dwell alone, alone,
    Whilst full my river flows down to the sea,
        Gilded with flashing boats
        That bring no friend to me:
5   O love-songs, gurgling from a hundred throats,
        O love-pangs, let me be.

    Fair fall the freighted boats which gold and stone
        And spices bear to sea:
    Slim, gleaming maidens swell their mellow notes,
10   Love-promising, entreating—
            Ah! sweet, but fleeting—
    Beneath the shivering, snow-white sails.
    Hush! the wind flags and fails—

Hush! they will lie becalmed in sight of strand—
15   Sight of my strand, where I do dwell alone;
Their songs wake singing echoes in my land—
    They cannot hear me moan.

One latest, solitary swallow flies
    Across the sea, rough autumn-tempest tost,
20   Poor bird, shall it be lost?
Dropped down into this uncongenial sea,
    With no kind eyes
    To watch it while it dies,
    Unguessed, uncared for, free:
25   Set free at last,
    The short pang past,
In sleep, in death, in dreamless sleep locked fast.

Mine avenue is all a growth of oaks,
    Some rent by thunder strokes,
30 Some rustling leaves and acorns in the breeze;
    Fair fall my fertile trees,
That rear their goodly heads, and live at ease.

A spider's web blocks all mine avenue;
    He catches down and foolish painted flies,
35   That spider wary and wise.
Each morn it hangs a rainbow strung with dew
    Betwixt boughs green with sap,
    So fair, few creatures guess it is a trap:
    I will not mar the web,
40 Tho' sad I am to see the small lives ebb.

It shakes—my trees shake—for a wind is roused
    In cavern where it housed:
    Each white and quivering sail,
    Of boats among the water leaves
45 Hollows and strains in the full-throated gale:
    Each maiden sings again—
Each languid maiden, whom the calm
Had lulled to sleep with rest and spice and balm.
    Miles down my river to the sea
50   They float and wane,
    Long miles away from me.

Perhaps they say: "She grieves,
    Uplifted, like a beacon, on her tower."
    Perhaps they say: "One hour
55 More, and we dance among the golden sheaves."
    Perhaps they say: "One hour
        More, and we stand,
        Face to face, hand in hand;
Make haste, O slack gale, to the looked-for land!"

60   My trees are not in flower,
    I have no bower,
    And gusty creaks my tower,
And lonesome, very lonesome, is my strand.

THE GHOST'S PETITION.

"There's a footstep coming; look out and see."—
    "The leaves are falling, the wind is calling;
No one cometh across the lea."—

"There's a footstep coming; O sister, look."—
5   "The ripple flashes, the white foam dashes;
No one cometh across the brook."—

"But he promised that he would come:
    Tonight, tomorrow, in joy or sorrow,
He must keep his word, and must come home.

10 "For he promised that he would come:
    His word was given; from earth or heaven,
He must keep his word, and must come home.

"Go to sleep, my sweet sister Jane;
    You can slumber, who need not number
15 Hour after hour, in doubt and pain.

"I shall sit here awhile, and watch;
    Listening, hoping, for one hand groping
In deep shadow to find the latch."

After the dark, and before the light,
20   One lay sleeping; and one sat weeping,
Who had watched and wept the weary night.

After the night, and before the day,
    One lay sleeping; and one sat weeping—
Watching, weeping for one away.

25   There came a footstep climbing the stair;
    Some one standing out on the landing
Shook the door like a puff of air—

Shook the door and in he passed.
    Did he enter? In the room centre
30   Stood her husband: the door shut fast.

"O Robin, but you are cold—
    Chilled with the night-dew: so lily-white you
Look like a stray lamb from our fold.

"O Robin, but you are late:
35   Come and sit near me—sit here and cheer me."—
(Blue the flame burnt in the grate.)

"Lay not down your head on my breast:
    I cannot hold you, kind wife, nor fold you
In the shelter that you love best.

40   "Feel not after my clasping hand:
    I am but a shadow, come from the meadow
Where many lie, but no tree can stand.

"We are trees which have shed their leaves:
    Our heads lie low there, but no tears flow there;
45   Only I grieve for my wife who grieves.

"I could rest if you would not moan
    Hour after hour; I have no power
To shut my ears where I lie alone.

"I could rest if you would not cry;
50   But there's no sleeping while you sit weeping—
Watching, weeping so bitterly."—

"Woe's me! woe's me! for this I have heard.
    Oh night of sorrow!—oh black tomorrow!
Is it thus that you keep your word?

55 "O you who used so to shelter me
    Warm from the least wind—why, now the east wind
Is warmer than you, whom I quake to see.

"O my husband of flesh and blood,
    For whom my mother I left, and brother,
60 And all I had, accounting it good,

"What do you do there, underground,
    In the dark hollow? I'm fain to follow.
What do you do there?—what have you found?"—

"What I do there I must not tell:
65   But I have plenty: kind wife, content ye:
It is well with us—it is well.

"Tender hand hath made our nest;
    Our fear is ended, our hope is blended
With present pleasure, and we have rest."—

70 "Oh but Robin, I'm fain to come,
    If your present days are so pleasant;
For my days are so wearisome.

"Yet I'll dry my tears for your sake:
    Why should I tease you, who cannot please you
75 Any more with the pains I take?"

MEMORY.

I

I nursed it in my bosom while it lived,
    I hid it in my heart when it was dead;
In joy I sat alone, even so I grieved
    Alone and nothing said.

5 I shut the door to face the naked truth,
      I stood alone—I faced the truth alone,
   Stripped bare of self-regard or forms or ruth
         Till first and last were shown.

   I took the perfect balances and weighed;
10   No shaking of my hand disturbed the poise;
   Weighed, found it wanting: not a word I said,
         But silent made my choice.

   None know the choice I made; I make it still.
      None know the choice I made and broke my heart,
15 Breaking mine idol: I have braced my will
         Once, chosen for once my part.

   I broke it at a blow, I laid it cold,
      Crushed in my deep heart where it used to live.
   My heart dies inch by inch; the time grows old,
20   Grows old in which I grieve.

                    II

   I have a room whereinto no one enters
      Save I myself alone:
      There sits a blessed memory on a throne,
   There my life centres;

25 While winter comes and goes—oh tedious comer!—
      And while its nip-wind blows;
      While bloom the bloodless lily and warm rose
   Of lavish summer.

   If any should force entrance he might see there
30   One buried yet not dead,
      Before whose face I no more bow my head
   Or bend my knee there;

   But often in my worn life's autumn weather
      I watch there with clear eyes,
35   And think how it will be in Paradise
   When we're together.

A ROYAL PRINCESS.

I, a princess, king-descended, decked with jewels, gilded,
    drest,
Would rather be a peasant with her baby at her breast,
For all I shine so like the sun, and am purple like the west.

Two and two my guards behind, two and two before,
5 Two and two on either hand, they guard me evermore;
Me, poor dove that must not coo—eagle that must not soar.

All my fountains cast up perfumes, all my gardens grow
Scented woods and foreign spices, with all flowers in blow
That are costly, out of season as the seasons go.

10 All my walls are lost in mirrors, whereupon I trace
Self to right hand, self to left hand, self in every place,
Self-same solitary figure, self-same seeking face.

Then I have an ivory chair high to sit upon,
Almost like my father's chair, which is an ivory throne;
15 There I sit uplift and upright, there I sit alone.

Alone by day, alone by night, alone days without end;
My father and my mother give me treasures, search and
    spend—
O my father! O my mother! have you ne'er a friend?

As I am a lofty princess, so my father is
20 A lofty king, accomplished in all kingly subtilties,
Holding in his strong right hand world-kingdoms' balances.

He has quarrelled with his neighbours, he has scourged his
    foes;
Vassal counts and princes follow where his pennon goes,
Long-descended valiant lords whom the vulture knows,

25 On whose track the vulture swoops, when they ride in state
To break the strength of armies and topple down the great:
Each of these my courteous servant, none of these my mate.

My father counting up his strength sets down with equal pen
So many head of cattle, head of horses, head of men;
30   These for slaughter, these for labour, with the how and when.

Some to work on roads, canals; some to man his ships;
Some to smart in mines beneath sharp overseers' whips;
Some to trap fur-beasts in lands where utmost winter nips.

Once it came into my heart and whelmed me like a flood,
35   That these too are men and women, human flesh and blood;
Men with hearts and men with souls, tho' trodden down like
         mud.

Our feasting was not glad that night, our music was not gay;
On my mother's graceful head I marked a thread of grey,
My father frowning at the fare seemed every dish to weigh.

40   I sat beside them sole princess in my exalted place,
My ladies and my gentlemen stood by me on the dais:
A mirror showed me I look old and haggard in the face;

It showed me that my ladies all are fair to gaze upon,
Plump, plenteous-haired, to every one love's secret lore is
         known,
45   They laugh by day, they sleep by night; ah, me, what is a
         throne?

The singing men and women sang that night as usual,
The dancers danced in pairs and sets, but music had a fall,
A melancholy windy fall as at a funeral.

Amid the toss of torches to my chamber back we swept;
50   My ladies loosed my golden chain; meantime I could have
         wept
To think of some in galling chains whether they waked or
         slept.

I took my bath of scented milk, delicately waited on,
They burned sweet things for my delight, cedar and
         cinnamon,
They lit my shaded silver lamp, and left me there alone.

55   A day went by, a week went by. One day I heard it said:
"Men are clamouring, women, children, clamouring to be
      fed;
Men like famished dogs are howling in the streets for bread."

So two whispered by my door, not thinking I could hear,
Vulgar naked truth, ungarnished for a royal ear;
60   Fit for cooping in the background, not to stalk so near.

But I strained my utmost sense to catch this truth, and mark:
"There are families out grazing like cattle in the park."
"A pair of peasants must be saved, even if we build an ark."

A merry jest, a merry laugh, each strolled upon his way;
65   One was my page, a lad I reared and bore with day by day;
One was my youngest maid, as sweet and white as cream in
      May.

Other footsteps followed softly with a weightier tramp;
Voices said: "Picked soldiers have been summoned from the
      camp,
To quell these base-born ruffians who make free to howl and
      stamp."

70   "Howl and stamp?" one answered: "They made free to hurl a
      stone
At the minister's state coach, well aimed and stoutly thrown."
"There's work then for the soldiers, for this rank crop must
      be mown."

"One I saw, a poor old fool with ashes on his head,
Whimpering because a girl had snatched his crust of bread:
75   Then he dropped; when some one raised him, it turned out
      he was dead."

"After us the deluge," was retorted with a laugh:
"If bread's the staff of life, they must walk without a staff."
"While I've a loaf they're welcome to my blessing and the
      chaff."

These passed. "The king:" stand up. Said my father with a
      smile:

80   "Daughter mine, your mother comes to sit with you awhile,
       She's sad today, and who but you her sadness can beguile?"

       He too left me. Shall I touch my harp now while I wait,—
       (I hear them doubling guard below before our palace gate)—
       Or shall I work the last gold stitch into my veil of state;

85   Or shall my woman stand and read some unimpassioned
                 scene,
       There's music of a lulling sort in words that pause between;
       Or shall she merely fan me while I wait here for the queen?

       Again I caught my father's voice in sharp word of command:
       "Charge!" a clash of steel: "Charge again, the rebels stand.
90   Smite and spare not, hand to hand; smite and spare not, hand
                 to hand."

       There swelled a tumult at the gate, high voices waxing higher;
       A flash of red reflected light lit the cathedral spire;
       I heard a cry for faggots, then I heard a yell for fire.

       "Sit and roast there with your meat, sit and bake there with
                 your bread,
95   You who sat to see us starve," one shrieking woman said:
       "Sit on your throne and roast with your crown upon your
                 head."

       Nay, this thing will I do, while my mother tarrieth,
       I will take my fine spun gold, but not to sew therewith,
       I will take my gold and gems, and rainbow fan and wreath;

100   With a ransom in my lap, a king's ransom in my hand,
       I will go down to this people, will stand face to face, will stand
       Where they curse king, queen, and princess of this cursed
                 land.

       They shall take all to buy them bread, take all I have to give;
       I, if I perish, perish; they today shall eat and live;
105   I, if I perish, perish; that's the goal I half conceive:

       Once to speak before the world, rend bare my heart and show
       The lesson I have learned, which is death, is life, to know.
       I, if I perish, perish; in the name of God I go.

SHALL I FORGET?

Shall I forget on this side of the grave?
I promise nothing: you must wait and see
    Patient and brave.
(O my soul, watch with him and he with me.)

5   Shall I forget in peace of Paradise?
I promise nothing: follow, friend, and see
    Faithful and wise.
(O my soul, lead the way he walks with me.)

VANITY OF VANITIES.

Ah woe is me for pleasure that is vain,
    Ah woe is me for glory that is past:
    Pleasure that bringeth sorrow at the last,
Glory that at the last bringeth no gain!
5   So saith the sinking heart; and so again
    It shall say till the mighty angel-blast
    Is blown, making the sun and moon aghast,
And showering down the stars like sudden rain.
And evermore men shall go fearfully
10   Bending beneath their weight of heaviness;
    And ancient men shall lie down wearily,
    And strong men shall rise up in weariness;
Yea, even the young shall answer sighingly,
    Saying one to another: How vain it is!

L. E. L.
"Whose heart was breaking for a little love."

Downstairs I laugh, I sport and jest with all:
    But in my solitary room above

I turn my face in silence to the wall;
  My heart is breaking for a little love.
5   Tho' winter frosts are done,
        And birds pair every one,
And leaves peep out, for springtide is begun.

I feel no spring, while spring is wellnigh blown,
  I find no nest, while nests are in the grove:
10 Woe's me for mine own heart that dwells alone,
    My heart that breaketh for a little love.
        While golden in the sun
        Rivulets rise and run,
While lilies bud, for springtide is begun.

15 All love, are loved, save only I; their hearts
    Beat warm with love and joy, beat full thereof:
They cannot guess, who play the pleasant parts,
    My heart is breaking for a little love.
        While beehives wake and whirr,
20   And rabbit thins his fur,
In living spring that sets the world astir.

I deck myself with silks and jewelry,
  I plume myself like any mated dove:
They praise my rustling show, and never see
25   My heart is breaking for a little love.
        While sprouts green lavender
        With rosemary and myrrh,
For in quick spring the sap is all astir.

Perhaps some saints in glory guess the truth,
30   Perhaps some angels read it as they move,
And cry one to another full of ruth,
    "Her heart is breaking for a little love."
        Tho' other things have birth,
        And leap and sing for mirth,
35 When springtime wakes and clothes and feeds the earth.

Yet saith a saint: "Take patience for thy scathe;"
  Yet saith an angel: "Wait, for thou shalt prove
True best is last, true life is born of death,
  O thou, heart-broken for a little love.

40   Then love shall fill thy girth,
        And love make fat thy dearth,
When new spring builds new heaven and clean new earth."

LIFE AND DEATH.

Life is not sweet. One day it will be sweet
        To shut our eyes and die:
Nor feel the wild flowers blow, nor birds dart by
        With flitting butterfly,
5   Nor grass grow long above our heads and feet,
    Nor hear the happy lark that soars sky high,
    Nor sigh that spring is fleet and summer fleet,
        Nor mark the waxing wheat,
    Nor know who sits in our accustomed seat.

10 Life is not good. One day it will be good
        To die, then live again;
    To sleep meanwhile: so not to feel the wane
    Of shrunk leaves dropping in the wood,
    Nor hear the foamy lashing of the main,
15 Nor mark the blackened bean-fields, nor where stood
        Rich ranks of golden grain
    Only dead refuse stubble clothe the plain:
    Asleep from risk, asleep from pain.

BIRD OR BEAST?

Did any bird come flying
    After Adam and Eve,
When the door was shut against them
    And they sat down to grieve?

5   I think not Eve's peacock
         Splendid to see,
     And I think not Adam's eagle;
         But a dove may be.

     Did any beast come pushing
10   Thro' the thorny hedge
     Into the thorny thistly world
         Out from Eden's edge?

     I think not a lion
         Tho' his strength is such;
15   But an innocent loving lamb
         May have done as much.

     If the dove preached from her bough
         And the lamb from his sod,
     The lamb and the dove
20   Were preachers sent from God.

     EVE.

     "While I sit at the door
     Sick to gaze within
     Mine eye weepeth sore
     For sorrow and sin:
5   As a tree my sin stands
     To darken all lands;
     Death is the fruit it bore.

     "How have Eden bowers grown
     Without Adam to bend them!
10   How have Eden flowers blown
     Squandering their sweet breath
     Without me to tend them!
     The Tree of Life was ours,
     Tree twelvefold-fruited,

15   Most lofty tree that flowers,
        Most deeply rooted:
        I chose the tree of death.

        "Hadst thou but said me nay,
        Adam, my brother,
20   I might have pined away;
        I, but none other:
        God might have let thee stay
        Safe in our garden,
        By putting me away
25   Beyond all pardon.

        "I, Eve, sad mother
        Of all who must live,
        I, not another,
        Plucked bitterest fruit to give
30   My friend, husband, lover;—
        O wanton eyes, run over;
        Who but I should grieve?—
        Cain hath slain his brother:
        Of all who must die mother,
35   Miserable Eve!"

        Thus she sat weeping,
        Thus Eve our mother,
        Where one lay sleeping
        Slain by his brother.
40   Greatest and least
        Each piteous beast
        To hear her voice
        Forgot his joys
        And set aside his feast.

45   The mouse paused in his walk
        And dropped his wheaten stalk;
        Grave cattle wagged their heads
        In rumination;
        The eagle gave a cry
50   From his cloud station;

Larks on thyme beds
Forbore to mount or sing;
Bees drooped upon the wing;
The raven perched on high
55 Forgot his ration;
The conies in their rock,
A feeble nation,
Quaked sympathetical;
The mocking-bird left off to mock;
60 Huge camels knelt as if
In deprecation;
The kind hart's tears were falling;
Chattered the wistful stork;
Dove-voices with a dying fall
65 Cooed desolation
Answering grief by grief.

Only the serpent in the dust
Wriggling and crawling,
Grinned an evil grin and thrust
70 His tongue out with its fork.

GROWN AND FLOWN.

I loved my love from green of Spring
    Until sere Autumn's fall;
But now that leaves are withering
    How should one love at all?
5   One heart's too small
For hunger, cold, love, everything.

I loved my love on sunny days
    Until late Summer's wane;
But now that frost begins to glaze
10   How should one love again?
    Nay, love and pain
Walk wide apart in diverse ways.

I loved my love—alas to see
    That this should be, alas!
15 I thought that this could scarcely be,
    Yet has it come to pass:
    Sweet sweet love was,
Now bitter bitter grown to me.

A FARM WALK.

The year stood at its equinox
    And bluff the North was blowing,
A bleat of lambs came from the flocks,
    Green hardy things were growing;
5 I met a maid with shining locks
    Where milky kine were lowing.

She wore a kerchief on her neck,
    Her bare arm showed its dimple,
Her apron spread without a speck,
10   Her air was frank and simple.

She milked into a wooden pail
    And sang a country ditty,
An innocent fond lovers' tale,
    That was not wise nor witty,
15 Pathetically rustical,
    Too pointless for the city.

She kept in time without a beat
    As true as church-bell ringers,
Unless she tapped time with her feet,
20   Or squeezed it with her fingers;
Her clear unstudied notes were sweet
    As many a practised singer's.

I stood a minute out of sight,
    Stood silent for a minute
25 To eye the pail, and creamy white
    The frothing milk within it;

To eye the comely milking maid
  Herself so fresh and creamy:
"Good day to you," at last I said;
30   She turned her head to see me:
"Good day," she said with lifted head;
  Her eyes looked soft and dreamy,

And all the while she milked and milked
  The grave cow heavy-laden:
35 I've seen grand ladies plumed and silked,
  But not a sweeter maiden;

But not a sweeter fresher maid
  Than this in homely cotton
Whose pleasant face and silky braid
40   I have not yet forgotten.

Seven springs have passed since then, as I
  Count with a sober sorrow;
Seven springs have come and passed me by,
  And spring sets in tomorrow.

45 I've half a mind to shake myself
  Free just for once from London,
To set my work upon the shelf
  And leave it done or undone;

To run down by the early train,
50   Whirl down with shriek and whistle,
And feel the bluff North blow again,
  And mark the sprouting thistle
Set up on waste patch of the lane
  Its green and tender bristle,

55 And spy the scarce-blown violet banks,
  Crisp primrose leaves and others,
And watch the lambs leap at their pranks
  And butt their patient mothers.

Alas, one point in all my plan
60   My serious thoughts demur to:
Seven years have passed for maid and man,
  Seven years have passed for her too;

Perhaps my rose is overblown,
  Not rosy or too rosy;
65 Perhaps in farmhouse of her own
  Some husband keeps her cosy,
Where I should show a face unknown.
  Good bye, my wayside posy.

SOMEWHERE OR OTHER.

Somewhere or other there must surely be
  The face not seen, the voice not heard,
The heart that not yet—never yet—ah me!
  Made answer to my word.

5 Somewhere or other, may be near or far;
  Past land and sea, clean out of sight;
Beyond the wandering moon, beyond the star
  That tracks her night by night.

Somewhere or other, may be far or near;
10 With just a wall, a hedge, between;
With just the last leaves of the dying year
  Fallen on a turf grown green.

A CHILL.

What can lambkins do
  All the keen night thro'?
Nestle by their woolly mother
  The careful ewe.

5 What can nestlings do
  In the nightly dew?
Sleep beneath their mother's wing
  Till day breaks anew.

If in field or tree
10   There might only be
Such a warm soft sleeping-place
     Found for me!

CHILD'S TALK IN APRIL.

I wish you were a pleasant wren,
    And I your small accepted mate;
How we'd look down on toilsome men!
    We'd rise and go to bed at eight
5   Or it may be not quite so late.

Then you should see the nest I'd build,
    The wondrous nest for you and me;
The outside rough perhaps, but filled
    With wool and down: ah, you should see
10   The cosy nest that it would be.

We'd have our change of hope and fear,
    Small quarrels, reconcilements sweet:
I'd perch by you to chirp and cheer,
    Or hop about on active feet
15   And fetch you dainty bits to eat.

We'd be so happy by the day,
    So safe and happy thro' the night,
We both should feel, and I should say,
    It's all one season of delight,
20   And we'll make merry whilst we may.

Perhaps some day there'd be an egg
    When spring had blossomed from the snow:
I'd stand triumphant on one leg;
    Like chanticleer I'd almost crow
25   To let our little neighbours know.

Next you should sit and I would sing
Thro' lengthening days of sunny spring;
   Till, if you wearied of the task,
I'd sit; and you should spread your wing
30   From bough to bough; I'd sit and bask.

Fancy the breaking of the shell,
   The chirp, the chickens wet and bare,
The untried proud paternal swell;
   And you with housewife-matron air
35   Enacting choicer bills of fare.

Fancy the embryo coats of down,
   The gradual feathers soft and sleek;
Till clothed and strong from tail to crown,
   With virgin warblings in their beak,
40   They too go forth to soar and seek.

So would it last an April thro'
And early summer fresh with dew:
   Then should we part and live as twain,
Love-time would bring me back to you
45   And build our happy nest again.

GONE FOR EVER.

O happy rose-bud blooming
   Upon thy parent tree,
Nay, thou art too presuming;
For soon the earth entombing
5   Thy faded charms shall be,
And the chill damp consuming.

O happy skylark springing
   Up to the broad blue sky,
Too fearless in thy winging,
10 Too gladsome in thy singing,
   Thou also soon shalt lie
Where no sweet notes are ringing.

And through life's shine and shower
   We shall have joy and pain;
15 But in the summer bower,
And at the morning hour,
   We still shall look in vain
For the same bird and flower.

"THE INIQUITY OF THE FATHERS
UPON THE CHILDREN"

Oh the rose of keenest thorn!
One hidden summer morn
Under the rose I was born.

I do not guess his name
5 Who wrought my Mother's shame,
And gave me life forlorn,
But my Mother, Mother, Mother,
I know her from all other.
My Mother pale and mild,
10 Fair as ever was seen,
She was but scarce sixteen,
Little more than a child,
When I was born
To work her scorn.
15 With secret bitter throes,
In a passion of secret woes,
She bore me under the rose.

One who my Mother nursed
Took me from the first:—
20 "O nurse, let me look upon
This babe that costs so dear;
Tomorrow she will be gone:
Other mothers may keep
Their babes awake and asleep,
25 But I must not keep her here."—
Whether I know or guess,
I know this not the less.

So I was sent away
That none might spy the truth:
30 And my childhood waxed to youth
And I left off childish play.
I never cared to play
With the village boys and girls;
And I think they thought me proud,
35 I found so little to say
And kept so from the crowd:
But I had the longest curls
And I had the largest eyes,
And my teeth were small like pearls;
40 The girls might flout and scout me,
But the boys would hang about me
In sheepish mooning wise.

Our one-street village stood
A long mile from the town,
45 A mile of windy down
And bleak one-sided wood,
With not a single house.
Our town itself was small,
With just the common shops,
50 And throve in its small way.
Our neighbouring gentry reared
The good old-fashioned crops,
And made old-fashioned boasts
Of what John Bull would do
55 If Frenchman Frog appeared,
And drank old-fashioned toasts,
And made old-fashioned bows
To my Lady at the Hall.

My Lady at the Hall
60 Is grander than they all:
Hers is the oldest name
In all the neighbourhood;
But the race must die with her
Tho' she's a lofty dame,
65 For she's unmarried still.

Poor people say she's good
And has an open hand
As any in the land,
And she's the comforter
70   Of many sick and sad;
My nurse once said to me
That everything she had
Came of my Lady's bounty:
"Tho' she's greatest in the county
75   She's humble to the poor,
No beggar seeks her door
But finds help presently.
I pray both night and day
For her, and you must pray:
80   But she'll never feel distress
If needy folk can bless."

I was a little maid
When here we came to live
From somewhere by the sea.
85   Men spoke a foreign tongue
There where we used to be
When I was merry and young,
Too young to feel afraid;
The fisher-folk would give
90   A kind strange word to me,
There by the foreign sea:
I don't know where it was,
But I remember still
Our cottage on a hill,
95   And fields of flowering grass
On that fair foreign shore.

I liked my old home best,
But this was pleasant too:
So here we made our nest
100 And here I grew.
And now and then my Lady
In riding past our door
Would nod to Nurse and speak,
Or stoop and pat my cheek;

105   And I was always ready
       To hold the field-gate wide
       For my Lady to go thro';
       My Lady in her veil
       So seldom put aside,
110   My Lady grave and pale.

       I often sat to wonder
       Who might my parents be,
       For I knew of something under
       My simple-seeming state.
115   Nurse never talked to me
       Of mother or of father,
       But watched me early and late
       With kind suspicious cares:
       Or not suspicious, rather
120   Anxious, as if she knew
       Some secret I might gather
       And smart for unawares.
       Thus I grew.

       But Nurse waxed old and grey,
125   Bent and weak with years.
       There came a certain day
       That she lay upon her bed
       Shaking her palsied head,
       With words she gasped to say
130   Which had to stay unsaid.
       Then with a jerking hand
       Held out so piteously
       She gave a ring to me
       Of gold wrought curiously,
135   A ring which she had worn
       Since the day that I was born,
       She once had said to me:
       I slipped it on my finger;
       Her eyes were keen to linger
140   On my hand that slipped it on;
       Then she sighed one rattling sigh
       And stared on with sightless eyes:—
       The one who loved me was gone.

How long I stayed alone
145 With the corpse, I never knew,
For I fainted dead as stone:
When I came to life once more
I was down upon the floor,
With neighbours making ado
150 To bring me back to life.
I heard the sexton's wife
Say: "Up, my lad, and run
To tell it at the Hall;
She was my Lady's nurse,
155 And done can't be undone.
I'll watch by this poor lamb.
I guess my Lady's purse
Is always open to such:
I'd run up on my crutch
160 A cripple as I am,"
(For cramps had vexed her much)
"Rather than this dear heart
Lack one to take her part."

For days day after day
165 On my weary bed I lay
Wishing the time would pass;
Oh, so wishing that I was
Likely to pass away:
For the one friend whom I knew
170 Was dead, I knew no other,
Neither father nor mother;
And I, what should I do?

One day the sexton's wife
Said: "Rouse yourself, my dear:
175 My Lady has driven down
From the Hall into the town,
And we think she's coming here.
Cheer up, for life is life."

But I would not look or speak,
180 Would not cheer up at all.

My tears were like to fall,
So I turned round to the wall
And hid my hollow cheek
Making as if I slept,
185 As silent as a stone,
And no one knew I wept.
What was my Lady to me,
The grand lady from the Hall?
She might come, or stay away,
190 I was sick at heart that day:
The whole world seemed to be
Nothing, just nothing to me,
For aught that I could see.

Yet I listened where I lay:
195 A bustle came below,
A clear voice said: "I know;
I will see her first alone,
It may be less of a shock
If she's so weak today:"—
200 A light hand turned the lock,
A light step crossed the floor,
One sat beside my bed:
But never a word she said.

For me, my shyness grew
205 Each moment more and more:
So I said never a word
And neither looked nor stirred;
I think she must have heard
My heart go pit-a-pat:
210 Thus I lay, my Lady sat,
More than a mortal hour—
(I counted one and two
By the house-clock while I lay):
I seemed to have no power
215 To think of a thing to say,
Or do what I ought to do,
Or rouse myself to a choice.

At last she said: "Margaret,
Won't you even look at me?"
220   A something in her voice
Forced my tears to fall at last,
Forced sobs from me thick and fast;
Something not of the past,
Yet stirring memory;
225   A something new, and yet
Not new, too sweet to last,
Which I never can forget.

I turned and stared at her:
Her cheek showed hollow-pale;
230   Her hair like mine was fair,
A wonderful fall of hair
That screened her like a veil;
But her height was statelier,
Her eyes had depth more deep;
235   I think they must have had
Always a something sad,
Unless they were asleep.

While I stared, my Lady took
My hand in her spare hand
240   Jewelled and soft and grand,
And looked with a long long look
Of hunger in my face;
As if she tried to trace
Features she ought to know,
245   And half hoped, half feared, to find.
Whatever was in her mind
She heaved a sigh at last,
And began to talk to me.

"Your nurse was my dear nurse,
250   And her nursling's dear," said she:
"No one told me a word
Of her getting worse and worse,
Till her poor life was past"
(Here my Lady's tears dropped fast):

255   "I might have been with her,
     I might have promised and heard,
     But she had no comforter.
     She might have told me much
     Which now I shall never know,
260   Never never shall know."
     She sat by me sobbing so,
     And seemed so woe-begone,
     That I laid one hand upon
     Hers with a timid touch,
265   Scarce thinking what I did,
     Not knowing what to say:
     That moment her face was hid
     In the pillow close by mine,
     Her arm was flung over me,
270   She hugged me, sobbing so
     As if her heart would break,
     And kissed me where I lay.

     After this she often came
     To bring me fruit or wine,
275   Or sometimes hothouse flowers.
     And at nights I lay awake
     Often and often thinking
     What to do for her sake.
     Wet or dry it was the same:
280   She would come in at all hours,
     Set me eating and drinking
     And say I must grow strong;
     At last the day seemed long
     And home seemed scarcely home
285   If she did not come.

     Well, I grew strong again:
     In time of primroses,
     I went to pluck them in the lane;
     In time of nestling birds,
290   I heard them chirping round the house;
     And all the herds
     Were out at grass when I grew strong,

And days were waxen long,
And there was work for bees
295 Among the May-bush boughs,
And I had shot up tall,
And life felt after all
Pleasant, and not so long
When I grew strong.

300 I was going to the Hall
To be my Lady's maid:
"Her little friend," she said to me,
"Almost her child,"
She said and smiled
305 Sighing painfully;
Blushing, with a second flush
As if she blushed to blush.

Friend, servant, child: just this
My standing at the Hall;
310 The other servants call me "Miss,"
My Lady calls me "Margaret,"
With her clear voice musical.
She never chides when I forget
This or that; she never chides.

315 Except when people come to stay,
(And that's not often) at the Hall,
I sit with her all day
And ride out when she rides.
She sings to me and makes me sing;
320 Sometimes I read to her,
Sometimes we merely sit and talk.
She noticed once my ring
And made me tell its history:
That evening in our garden walk
325 She said she should infer
The ring had been my father's first,
Then my mother's, given for me
To the nurse who nursed
My mother in her misery,

330   That so quite certainly
      Some one might know me, who . . .
      Then she was silent, and I too.

      I hate when people come:
      The women speak and stare
335   And mean to be so civil.
      This one will stroke my hair,
      That one will pat my cheek
      And praise my Lady's kindness,
      Expecting me to speak;
340   I like the proud ones best
      Who sit as struck with blindness,
      As if I wasn't there.
      But if any gentleman
      Is staying at the Hall
345   (Tho' few come prying here),
      My Lady seems to fear
      Some downright dreadful evil,
      And makes me keep my room
      As closely as she can:
350   So I hate when people come,
      It is so troublesome.
      In spite of all her care,
      Sometimes to keep alive
      I sometimes do contrive
355   To get out in the grounds
      For a whiff of wholesome air,
      Under the rose you know:
      It's charming to break bounds,
      Stolen waters are sweet,
360   And what's the good of feet
      If for days they mustn't go?
      Give me a longer tether,
      Or I may break from it.

      Now I have eyes and ears
365   And just some little wit:
      "Almost my Lady's child;"

I recollect she smiled,
Sighed and blushed together;
Then her story of the ring
370 Sounds not improbable,
She told it me so well
It seemed the actual thing:—
Oh, keep your counsel close,
But I guess under the rose,
375 In long past summer weather
When the world was blossoming,
And the rose upon its thorn:
I guess not who he was
Flawed honour like a glass
380 And made my life forlorn,
But my Mother, Mother, Mother,
Oh, I know her from all other.

My Lady, you might trust
Your daughter with your fame.
385 Trust me, I would not shame
Our honourable name,
For I have noble blood
Tho' I was bred in dust
And brought up in the mud.
390 I will not press my claim,
Just leave me where you will:
But you might trust your daughter,
For blood is thicker than water
And you're my mother still.

395 So my Lady holds her own
With condescending grace,
And fills her lofty place
With an untroubled face
As a queen may fill a throne.
400 While I could hint a tale—
(But then I am her child)—
Would make her quail;
Would set her in the dust,
Lorn with no comforter,

405 Her glorious hair defiled
     And ashes on her cheek:
     The decent world would thrust
     Its finger out at her,
     Not much displeased I think
410 To make a nine days' stir;
     The decent world would sink
     Its voice to speak of her.

     Now this is what I mean
     To do, no more, no less:
415 Never to speak, or show
     Bare sign of what I know.
     Let the blot pass unseen;
     Yea, let her never guess
     I hold the tangled clue
420 She huddles out of view.
     Friend, servant, almost child,
     So be it and nothing more
     On this side of the grave.
     Mother, in Paradise,
425 You'll see with clearer eyes;
     Perhaps in this world even
     When you are like to die
     And face to face with Heaven
     You'll drop for once the lie:
430 But you must drop the mask, not I.

     My Lady promises
     Two hundred pounds with me
     Whenever I may wed
     A man she can approve:
435 And since besides her bounty
     I'm fairest in the county
     (For so I've heard it said,
     Tho' I don't vouch for this),
     Her promised pounds may move
440 Some honest man to see
     My virtues and my beauties;
     Perhaps the rising grazier,

Or temperance publican,
May claim my wifely duties.
445 Meanwhile I wait their leisure
And grace-bestowing pleasure,
I wait the happy man;
But if I hold my head
And pitch my expectations
450 Just higher than their level,
They must fall back on patience:
I may not mean to wed,
Yet I'll be civil.

Now sometimes in a dream
455 My heart goes out of me
To build and scheme,
Till I sob after things that seem
So pleasant in a dream:
A home such as I see
460 My blessed neighbours live in
With father and with mother,
All proud of one another,
Named by one common name
From baby in the bud
465 To full-blown workman father;
It's little short of Heaven.
I'd give my gentle blood
To wash my special shame
And drown my private grudge;
470 I'd toil and moil much rather
The dingiest cottage drudge
Whose mother need not blush,
Than live here like a lady
And see my Mother flush
475 And hear her voice unsteady
Sometimes, yet never dare
Ask to share her care.

Of course the servants sneer
Behind my back at me;
480 Of course the village girls,

Who envy me my curls
And gowns and idleness,
Take comfort in a jeer;
Of course the ladies guess
485 Just so much of my history
As points the emphatic stress
With which they laud my Lady;
The gentlemen who catch
A casual glimpse of me
490 And turn again to see,
Their valets on the watch
To speak a word with me,
All know and sting me wild;
Till I am almost ready
495 To wish that I were dead,
No faces more to see,
No more words to be said,
My Mother safe at last
Disburdened of her child,
500 And the past past.

"All equal before God"—
Our Rector has it so,
And sundry sleepers nod:
It may be so; I know
505 All are not equal here,
And when the sleepers wake
They make a difference.
"All equal in the grave"—
That shows an obvious sense:
510 Yet something which I crave
Not death itself brings near;
How should death half atone
For all my past; or make
The name I bear my own?

515 I love my dear old Nurse
Who loved me without gains;
I love my mistress even,
Friend, Mother, what you will:

But I could almost curse
520 My Father for his pains;
And sometimes at my prayer
Kneeling in sight of Heaven
I almost curse him still:
Why did he set his snare
525 To catch at unaware
My Mother's foolish youth;
Load me with shame that's hers,
And her with something worse,
A lifelong lie for truth?

530 I think my mind is fixed
On one point and made up:
To accept my lot unmixed;
Never to drug the cup
But drink it by myself.
535 I'll not be wooed for pelf;
I'll not blot out my shame
With any man's good name;
But nameless as I stand,
My hand is my own hand,
540 And nameless as I came
I go to the dark land.

"All equal in the grave"—
I bide my time till then:
"All equal before God"—
545 Today I feel His rod,
Tomorrow He may save:
                Amen.

DESPISED AND REJECTED.

My sun has set, I dwell
In darkness as a dead man out of sight;
And none remains, not one, that I should tell
To him mine evil plight
5 This bitter night.

I will make fast my door
That hollow friends may trouble me no more.

"Friend, open to Me."—Who is this that calls?
Nay, I am deaf as are my walls:
10 Cease crying, for I will not hear
Thy cry of hope or fear.
Others were dear,
Others forsook me: what art thou indeed
That I should heed
15 Thy lamentable need?
Hungry should feed,
Or stranger lodge thee here?

"Friend, My Feet bleed.
Open thy door to Me and comfort Me."
20 I will not open, trouble me no more.
Go on thy way footsore,
I will not rise and open unto thee.

"Then is it nothing to thee? Open, see
Who stands to plead with thee.
25 Open, lest I should pass thee by, and thou
One day entreat My Face
And howl for grace,
And I be deaf as thou art now.
Open to Me."

30 Then I cried out upon him: Cease,
Leave me in peace:
Fear not that I should crave
Aught thou mayst have.
Leave me in peace, yea trouble me no more,
35 Lest I arise and chase thee from my door.
What, shall I not be let
Alone, that thou dost vex me yet?

But all night long that voice spake urgently:
"Open to Me."
40 Still harping in mine ears:
"Rise, let Me in."

Pleading with tears:
"Open to Me that I may come to thee."
While the dew dropped, while the dark hours were cold
45 "My Feet bleed, see My Face,
See My Hands bleed that bring thee grace,
My Heart doth bleed for thee,
Open to Me."

So till the break of day:
50 Then died away
That voice, in silence as of sorrow;
Then footsteps echoing like a sigh
Passed me by,
Lingering footsteps slow to pass.
55 On the morrow
I saw upon the grass
Each footprint marked in blood, and on my door
The mark of blood for evermore.

LONG BARREN.

Thou who didst hang upon a barren tree,
My God, for me;
   Tho' I till now be barren, now at length,
   Lord, give me strength
5 To bring forth fruit to Thee.

Thou who didst bear for me the crown of thorn,
Spitting and scorn;
   Tho' I till now have put forth thorns, yet now
   Strengthen me Thou
10 That better fruit be borne.

Thou Rose of Sharon, Cedar of broad roots,
Vine of sweet fruits,
   Thou Lily of the vale with fadeless leaf,
   Of thousands Chief,
15 Feed Thou my feeble shoots.

IF ONLY.

If I might only love my God and die!
  But now He bids me love Him and live on,
  Now when the bloom of all my life is gone,
The pleasant half of life has quite gone by.
5 My tree of hope is lopped that spread so high;
  And I forget how Summer glowed and shone,
  While Autumn grips me with its fingers wan,
And frets me with its fitful windy sigh.
When Autumn passes then must Winter numb,
10 And Winter may not pass a weary while,
    But when it passes Spring shall flower again:
  And in that Spring who weepeth now shall smile,
    Yea, they shall wax who now are on the wane,
Yea, they shall sing for love when Christ shall come.

DOST THOU NOT CARE?

I love and love not: Lord, it breaks my heart
  To love and not to love.
Thou veiled within Thy glory, gone apart
  Into Thy shrine, which is above,
5 Dost Thou not love me, Lord, or care
  For this mine ill?—
I love thee here or there,
  I will accept thy broken heart, lie still.

Lord, it was well with me in time gone by
10 That cometh not again,
When I was fresh and cheerful, who but I?
  I fresh, I cheerful: worn with pain
Now, out of sight and out of heart;
  O Lord, how long?—
15 *I watch thee as thou art,*
  I will accept thy fainting heart, be strong.

"Lie still," "be strong," today; but, Lord, tomorrow,
   What of tomorrow, Lord?
Shall there be rest from toil, be truce from sorrow,
20   Be living green upon the sward
Now but a barren grave to me,
   Be joy for sorrow?—
Did I not die for thee?
   Do I not live for thee? leave Me tomorrow.

WEARY IN WELL-DOING.

I would have gone; God bade me stay:
   I would have worked; God bade me rest.
He broke my will from day to day,
   He read my yearnings unexpressed
5   And said them nay.

Now I would stay; God bids me go:
   Now I would rest; God bids me work.
He breaks my heart tossed to and fro,
   My soul is wrung with doubts that lurk
10   And vex it so.

I go, Lord, where Thou sendest me;
   Day after day I plod and moil:
But, Christ my God, when will it be
   That I may let alone my toil
15   And rest with Thee?

MARTYRS' SONG.

We meet in joy, tho' we part in sorrow;
We part tonight, but we meet tomorrow.

Be it flood or blood the path that's trod,
All the same it leads home to God:
5   Be it furnace-fire voluminous,
One like God's Son will walk with us.

What are these that glow from afar,
These that lean over the golden bar,
Strong as the lion, pure as the dove,
10   With open arms and hearts of love?
They the blessed ones gone before,
They the blessed for evermore.
Out of great tribulation they went
Home to their home of Heaven-content;
15   Thro' flood, or blood, or furnace-fire,
To the rest that fulfils desire.

What are these that fly as a cloud,
With flashing heads and faces bowed,
In their mouths a victorious psalm,
20   In their hands a robe and a palm?
Welcoming angels these that shine,
Your own angel, and yours, and mine;
Who have hedged us both day and night
On the left hand and on the right,
25   Who have watched us both night and day
Because the devil keeps watch to slay.

Light above light, and Bliss beyond bliss,
Whom words cannot utter, lo, Who is This?
As a King with many crowns He stands,
30   And our names are graven upon His hands;
As a Priest, with God-uplifted eyes,
He offers for us His Sacrifice;
As the Lamb of God for sinners slain,
That we too may live He lives again;
35   As our Champion behold Him stand,
Strong to save us, at God's Right Hand.

God the Father give us grace
To walk in the light of Jesus' Face.

God the Son give us a part
40 In the hiding-place of Jesus' Heart:
God the Spirit so hold us up
That we may drink of Jesus' cup.

Death is short and life is long;
Satan is strong, but Christ more strong.
45 At His Word, Who hath led us hither,
The Red Sea must part hither and thither.
At His Word, Who goes before us too,
Jordan must cleave to let us thro'.

Yet one pang searching and sore,
50 And then Heaven for evermore;
Yet one moment awful and dark,
Then safety within the Veil and the Ark;
Yet one effort by Christ His grace,
Then Christ for ever face to face.

55 God the Father we will adore,
In Jesus' Name, now and evermore:
God the Son we will love and thank
In this flood and on the farther bank:
God the Holy Ghost we will praise,
60 In Jesus' Name, thro' endless days:
God Almighty, God Three in One,
God Almighty, God alone.

AFTER THIS THE JUDGMENT.

As eager homebound traveller to the goal,
    Or steadfast seeker on an unsearched main,
Or martyr panting for an aureole,
    My fellow-pilgrims pass me, and attain
5 That hidden mansion of perpetual peace
    Where keen desire and hope dwell free from pain:

That gate stands open of perennial ease;
   I view the glory till I partly long,
Yet lack the fire of love which quickens these.
10   O passing Angel, speed me with a song,
A melody of heaven to reach my heart
   And rouse me to the race and make me strong;
Till in such music I take up my part
   Swelling those Hallelujahs full of rest,
15   One, tenfold, hundredfold, with heavenly art,
   Fulfilling north and south and east and west,
Thousand, ten thousandfold, innumerable,
   All blent in one yet each one manifest;
Each one distinguished and beloved as well
20   As if no second voice in earth or heaven
Were lifted up the Love of God to tell.
   Ah, Love of God, which Thine Own Self hast given
To me most poor, and made me rich in love,
   Love that dost pass the tenfold seven times seven,
25   Draw Thou mine eyes, draw Thou my heart above,
   My treasure and my heart store Thou in Thee,
Brood over me with yearnings of a dove;
   Be Husband, Brother, closest Friend to me;
Love me as very mother loves her son,
30   Her sucking firstborn fondled on her knee:
Yea, more than mother loves her little one;
   For, earthly, even a mother may forget
And feel no pity for its piteous moan;
   But Thou, O Love of God, remember yet,
35   Thro' the dry desert, thro' the waterflood
   (Life, death), until the Great White Throne is set.
If now I am sick in chewing the bitter cud
   Of sweet past sin, tho' solaced by Thy grace
And ofttimes strengthened by Thy Flesh and Blood,
40   How shall I then stand up before Thy face
When from Thine eyes repentance shall be hid
   And utmost Justice stand in Mercy's place:
When every sin I thought or spoke or did
   Shall meet me at the inexorable bar,

45   And there be no man standing in the mid
     To plead for me; while star fallen after star
With heaven and earth are like a ripened shock,
     And all time's mighty works and wonders are
Consumed as in a moment; when no rock
50   Remains to fall on me, no tree to hide,
But I stand all creation's gazing-stock,
     Exposed and comfortless on every side,
Placed trembling in the final balances
     Whose poise this hour, this moment, must be tried?—
55 Ah Love of God, if greater love than this
     Hath no man, that a man die for his friend,
And if such love of love Thine Own Love is,
     Plead with Thyself, with me, before the end;
Redeem me from the irrevocable past;
60   Pitch Thou Thy Presence round me to defend;
Yea seek with piercèd feet, yea hold me fast
     With piercèd hands whose wounds were made by love;
Not what I am, remember what Thou wast
     When darkness hid from Thee Thy heavens above,
65 And sin Thy Father's Face, while Thou didst drink
     The bitter cup of death, didst taste thereof
For every man; while Thou wast nigh to sink
     Beneath the intense intolerable rod,
Grown sick of love; not what I am, but think
70   Thy Life then ransomed mine, my God, my God.

GOOD FRIDAY.

Am I a stone and not a sheep
     That I can stand, O Christ, beneath Thy Cross,
     To number drop by drop Thy Blood's slow loss,
And yet not weep?

5　　Not so those women loved
　　　　Who with exceeding grief lamented Thee;
　　　　Not so fallen Peter weeping bitterly;
　　Not so the thief was moved;

　　Not so the Sun and Moon
10　　　Which hid their faces in a starless sky,
　　A horror of great darkness at broad noon—
　　　　I, only I.

　　Yet give not o'er,
　　　　But seek Thy sheep, true Shepherd of the flock;
15　Greater than Moses, turn and look once more
　　　　And smite a rock.

THE LOWEST PLACE.

Give me the lowest place: not that I dare
　　Ask for that lowest place, but Thou hast died
That I might live and share
　　Thy glory by Thy side.

5　Give me the lowest place: or if for me
　　That lowest place too high, make one more low
Where I may sit and see
　　My God and love Thee so.

Poems Added in *Goblin Market,
The Prince's Progress and Other Poems*
(1875)

BY THE SEA.

Why does the sea moan evermore?
  Shut out from heaven it makes its moan,
It frets against the boundary shore;
  All earth's full rivers cannot fill
5   The sea, that drinking thirsteth still.

Sheer miracles of loveliness
  Lie hid in its unlooked-on bed:
Anemones, salt, passionless,
  Blow flower-like; just enough alive
10   To blow and multiply and thrive.

Shells quaint with curve, or spot, or spike,
  Encrusted live things argus-eyed,
All fair alike, yet all unlike,
  Are born without a pang, and die
15   Without a pang, and so pass by.

FROM SUNSET TO STAR RISE.

Go from me, summer friends, and tarry not:
  I am no summer friend, but wintry cold,
  A silly sheep benighted from the fold,
A sluggard with a thorn-choked garden plot.
5 Take counsel, sever from my lot your lot,
  Dwell in your pleasant places, hoard your gold;
  Lest you with me should shiver on the wold,
Athirst and hungering on a barren spot.

For I have hedged me with a thorny hedge,
10   I live alone, I look to die alone:
Yet sometimes when a wind sighs through the sedge
    Ghosts of my buried years and friends come back,
My heart goes sighing after swallows flown
    On sometime summer's unreturning track.

DAYS OF VANITY.

    A dream that waketh,
    Bubble that breaketh,
Song whose burden sigheth,
    A passing breath,
5   Smoke that vanisheth,—
Such is life that dieth.

    A flower that fadeth,
    Fruit the tree sheddeth,
Trackless bird that flieth,
10   Summer time brief,
    Falling of the leaf,—
Such is life that dieth.

    A scent exhaling,
    Snow waters failing,
15 Morning dew that drieth,
    A windy blast,
    Lengthening shadows cast,—
Such is life that dieth.

    A scanty measure,
20   Rust-eaten treasure,
Spending that nought buyeth,
    Moth on the wing,
    Toil unprofiting,—
Such is life that dieth.

25 Morrow by morrow
  Sorrow breeds sorrow,
For this my song sigheth;
  From day to night
  We lapse out of sight,—
30 Such is life that dieth.

ONCE FOR ALL.
(MARGARET.)

I said: This is a beautiful fresh rose.
  I said: I will delight me with its scent;
  Will watch its lovely curve of languishment,
Will watch its leaves unclose, its heart unclose.
5 I said: Old earth has put away her snows,
  All living things make merry to their bent,
  A flower is come for every flower that went
In autumn, the sun glows, the south wind blows.
So walking in a garden of delight
10 I came upon one sheltered shadowed nook
Where broad leaf shadows veiled the day with night,
  And there lay snow unmelted by the sun:—
I answered: Take who will the path I took,
  Winter nips once for all; love is but one.

ENRICA, 1865.

She came among us from the South
  And made the North her home awhile;
  Our dimness brightened in her smile,
Our tongue grew sweeter in her mouth.

5   We chilled beside her liberal glow,
           She dwarfed us by her ampler scale,
           Her full-blown blossom made us pale,
       She summer-like and we like snow.

       We Englishwomen, trim, correct,
10   All minted in the selfsame mould,
           Warm-hearted but of semblance cold,
       All-courteous out of self-respect.

       She woman in her natural grace,
           Less trammelled she by lore of school,
15   Courteous by nature not by rule,
       Warm-hearted and of cordial face.

       So for awhile she made her home
           Among us in the rigid North,
           She who from Italy came forth
20   And scaled the Alps and crossed the foam.

       But if she found us like our sea,
           Of aspect colourless and chill,
           Rock-girt; like it she found us still
       Deep at our deepest, strong and free.

AUTUMN VIOLETS.

       Keep love for youth, and violets for the spring:
           Or if these bloom when worn-out autumn grieves,
           Let them lie hid in double shade of leaves,
       Their own, and others dropped down withering;
5   For violets suit when home birds build and sing,
           Not when the outbound bird a passage cleaves;
           Not with dry stubble of mown harvest sheaves,
       But when the green world buds to blossoming.
       Keep violets for the spring, and love for youth,
10   Love that should dwell with beauty, mirth, and hope:
               Or if a later sadder love be born,

Let this not look for grace beyond its scope,
But give itself, nor plead for answering truth—
   A grateful Ruth tho' gleaning scanty corn.

A DIRGE.

Why were you born when the snow was falling?
You should have come to the cuckoo's calling,
Or when grapes are green in the cluster,
Or, at least, when lithe swallows muster
     For their far off flying
     From summer dying.

Why did you die when the lambs were cropping?
You should have died at the apples' dropping,
When the grasshopper comes to trouble,
And the wheat-fields are sodden stubble,
     And all winds go sighing
     For sweet things dying.

"THEY DESIRE A BETTER COUNTRY."

I.

I would not if I could undo my past,
   Tho' for its sake my future is a blank;
   My past for which I have myself to thank,
For all its faults and follies first and last.
I would not cast anew the lot once cast,
   Or launch a second ship for one that sank,
   Or drug with sweets the bitterness I drank,
Or break by feasting my perpetual fast.
I would not if I could: for much more dear
   Is one remembrance than a hundred joys,
   More than a thousand hopes in jubilee;

Dearer the music of one tearful voice
  That unforgotten calls and calls to me,
"Follow me here, rise up, and follow here."

II.

15 What seekest thou, far in the unknown land?
  In hope I follow joy gone on before;
  In hope and fear persistent more and more,
As the dry desert lengthens out its sand.
Whilst day and night I carry in my hand
20   The golden key to ope the golden door
  Of golden home; yet mine eye weepeth sore,
For long the journey is that makes no stand.
And who is this that veiled doth walk with thee?
  Lo, this is Love that walketh at my right;
25   One exile holds us both, and we are bound
  To selfsame home-joys in the land of light.
Weeping thou walkest with him; weepeth he?—
  Some sobbing weep, some weep and make no sound.

III.

A dimness of a glory glimmers here
30   Thro' veils and distance from the space remote,
  A faintest far vibration of a note
Reaches to us and seems to bring us near;
Causing our face to glow with braver cheer,
  Making the serried mist to stand afloat,
35   Subduing languor with an antidote,
And strengthening love almost to cast out fear:
Till for one moment golden city walls
  Rise looming on us, golden walls of home,
Light of our eyes until the darkness falls;
40   Then thro' the outer darkness burdensome
I hear again the tender voice that calls,
  "Follow me hither, follow, rise, and come."

A GREEN CORNFIELD.

"And singing still dost soar and
    soaring ever singest."

The earth was green, the sky was blue:
    I saw and heard one sunny morn
A skylark hang between the two,
    A singing speck above the corn;

5   A stage below, in gay accord,
       White butterflies danced on the wing,
And still the singing skylark soared
       And silent sank and soared to sing.

The cornfield stretched a tender green
10   To right and left beside my walks;
I knew he had a nest unseen
    Somewhere among the million stalks:

And as I paused to hear his song
    While swift the sunny moments slid,
15   Perhaps his mate sat listening long,
       And listened longer than I did.

A BRIDE SONG.

Thro' the vales to my love!
    To the happy small nest of home
Green from basement to roof;
    Where the honey-bees come
5   To the window-sill flowers,
       And dive from above,
Safe from the spider that weaves
    Her warp and her woof
In some outermost leaves.

10 Thro' the vales to my love!
        In sweet April hours
        All rainbows and showers,
    While dove answers dove,—
        In beautiful May,
15 When the orchards are tender
        And frothing with flowers,—
        In opulent June,
    When the wheat stands up slender
        By sweet-smelling hay,
20 And half the sun's splendour
        Descends to the moon.

    Thro' the vales to my love!
        Where the turf is so soft to the feet
        And the thyme makes it sweet,
25 And the stately foxglove
        Hangs silent its exquisite bells;
        And where water wells
    The greenness grows greener,
        And bulrushes stand
30 Round a lily to screen her.

    Nevertheless, if this land,
        Like a garden to smell and to sight,
    Were turned to a desert of sand;
        Stripped bare of delight,
35   All its best gone to worst,
    For my feet no repose,
        No water to comfort my thirst,
    And heaven like a furnace above,—
        The desert would be
40   As gushing of waters to me,
    The wilderness be as a rose,
        If it led me to thee,
        O my love.

CONFLUENTS.

As rivers seek the sea,
  Much more deep than they,
So my soul seeks thee
  Far away:
5 As running rivers moan
On their course alone,
  So I moan
  Left alone.

As the delicate rose
10   To the sun's sweet strength
Doth herself unclose,
  Breadth and length;
So spreads my heart to thee
Unveiled utterly,
15   I to thee
  Utterly.

As morning dew exhales
  Sunwards pure and free,
So my spirit fails
20   After thee:
As dew leaves not a trace
On the green earth's face;
  I, no trace
  On thy face.

25 Its goal the river knows,
  Dewdrops find a way,
Sunlight cheers the rose
  In her day:
Shall I, lone sorrow past,
30 Find thee at the last?
  Sorrow past,
  Thee at last?

THE LOWEST ROOM.

Like flowers sequestered from the sun
    And wind of summer, day by day
I dwindled paler, whilst my hair
    Showed the first tinge of grey.

5 "Oh what is life, that we should live?
    Or what is death, that we must die?
A bursting bubble is our life:
    I also, what am I?"

"What is your grief? now tell me, sweet,
10   That I may grieve," my sister said;
And stayed a white embroidering hand
    And raised a golden head:

Her tresses showed a richer mass,
    Her eyes looked softer than my own,
15 Her figure had a statelier height,
    Her voice a tenderer tone.

"Some must be second and not first;
    All cannot be the first of all:
Is not this, too, but vanity?
20   I stumble like to fall.

"So yesterday I read the acts
    Of Hector and each clangorous king
With wrathful great Aeacides:—
    Old Homer leaves a sting."

25 The comely face looked up again,
    The deft hand lingered on the thread:
"Sweet, tell me what is Homer's sting,
    Old Homer's sting?" she said.

"He stirs my sluggish pulse like wine,
30   He melts me like the wind of spice,
Strong as strong Ajax' red right hand,
    And grand like Juno's eyes.

"I cannot melt the sons of men,
    I cannot fire and tempest-toss:—
35 Besides, those days were golden days,
      Whilst these are days of dross."

She laughed a feminine low laugh,
    Yet did not stay her dexterous hand:
"Now tell me of those days," she said,
40   "When time ran golden sand."

"Then men were men of might and right,
    Sheer might, at least, and weighty swords;
Then men in open blood and fire
      Bore witness to their words,

45 "Crest-rearing kings with whistling spears;
    But if these shivered in the shock
They wrenched up hundred-rooted trees,
      Or hurled the effacing rock.

"Then hand to hand, then foot to foot,
    Stern to the death-grip grappling then,
Who ever thought of gunpowder
      Amongst these men of men?

"They knew whose hand struck home the death,
    They knew who broke but would not bend,
55 Could venerate an equal foe
      And scorn a laggard friend.

"Calm in the utmost stress of doom,
    Devout toward adverse powers above,
They hated with intenser hate
60   And loved with fuller love.

"Then heavenly beauty could allay
    As heavenly beauty stirred the strife:
By them a slave was worshipped more
      Than is by us a wife."

65 She laughed again, my sister laughed;
    Made answer o'er the laboured cloth:
"I rather would be one of us
      Than wife, or slave, or both."

"Oh better then be slave or wife
70   Than fritter now blank life away:
Then night had holiness of night,
     And day was sacred day.

"The princess laboured at her loom,
   Mistress and handmaiden alike;
75 Beneath their needles grew the field
     With warriors armed to strike.

"Or, look again, dim Dian's face
   Gleamed perfect thro' the attendant night;
Were such not better than those holes
80   Amid that waste of white?

"A shame it is, our aimless life:
   I rather from my heart would feed
From silver dish in gilded stall
   With wheat and wine the steed—

85 "The faithful steed that bore my lord
   In safety thro' the hostile land,
The faithful steed that arched his neck
     To fondle with my hand."

Her needle erred; a moment's pause,
90   A moment's patience, all was well.
Then she: "But just suppose the horse,
     Suppose the rider fell?

"Then captive in an alien house,
   Hungering on exile's bitter bread,—
95 They happy, they who won the lot
     Of sacrifice," she said.

Speaking she faltered, while her look
   Showed forth her passion like a glass:
With hand suspended, kindling eye,
100   Flushed cheek, how fair she was!

"Ah well, be those the days of dross;
   This, if you will, the age of gold:
Yet had those days a spark of warmth,
     While these are somewhat cold—

105   "Are somewhat mean and cold and slow,
     Are stunted from heroic growth:
  We gain but little when we prove
     The worthlessness of both."

  "But life is in our hands," she said:
110   "In our own hands for gain or loss:
  Shall not the Sevenfold Sacred Fire
     Suffice to purge our dross?

  "Too short a century of dreams,
     One day of work sufficient length:
115   Why should not you, why should not I
     Attain heroic strength?

  "Our life is given us as a blank;
     Ourselves must make it blest or curst:
  Who dooms me I shall only be
120   The second, not the first?

  "Learn from old Homer, if you will,
     Such wisdom as his books have said:
  In one the acts of Ajax shine,
     In one of Diomed.

125   "Honoured all heroes whose high deeds
     Thro' life, thro' death, enlarge their span:
  Only Achilles in his rage
     And sloth is less than man."

  "Achilles only less than man?
130   He less than man who, half a god,
  Discomfited all Greece with rest,
     Cowed Ilion with a nod?

  "He offered vengeance, lifelong grief
     To one dear ghost, uncounted price:
135   Beasts, Trojans, adverse gods, himself,
     Heaped up the sacrifice.

  "Self-immolated to his friend,
     Shrined in world's wonder, Homer's page,
  Is this the man, the less than men
140   Of this degenerate age?"

"Gross from his acorns, tusky boar
 Does memorable acts like his;
So for her snared offended young
  Bleeds the swart lioness."

145 But here she paused; our eyes had met,
 And I was whitening with the jeer;
She rose: "I went too far," she said;
  Spoke low: "Forgive me, dear.

"To me our days seem pleasant days,
150 Our home a haven of pure content;
Forgive me if I said too much,
  So much more than I meant.

"Homer, tho' greater than his gods,
 With rough-hewn virtues was suffced
155 And rough-hewn men: but what are such
  To us who learn of Christ?"

The much-moved pathos of her voice,
 Her almost tearful eyes, her cheek
Grown pale, confessed the strength of love
160   Which only made her speak:

For mild she was, of few soft words,
 Most gentle, easy to be led,
Content to listen when I spoke
  And reverence what I said;

165 I elder sister by six years;
 Not half so glad, or wise, or good:
Her words rebuked my secret self
  And shamed me where I stood.

She never guessed her words reproved
170 A silent envy nursed within,
A selfish, souring discontent
  Pride-born, the devil's sin.

I smiled, half bitter, half in jest:
 "The wisest man of all the wise
175 Left for his summary of life
  'Vanity of vanities.'

"Beneath the sun there's nothing new:
 Men flow, men ebb, mankind flows on:
If I am wearied of my life,
180 Why so was Solomon.

"Vanity of vanities he preached
 Of all he found, of all he sought:
Vanity of vanities, the gist
  Of all the words he taught.

185 "This in the wisdom of the world,
 In Homer's page, in all, we find:
As the sea is not filled, so yearns
  Man's universal mind.

"This Homer felt, who gave his men
190 With glory but a transient state:
His very Jove could not reverse
  Irrevocable fate.

"Uncertain all their lot save this—
 Who wins must lose, who lives must die:
195 All trodden out into the dark
  Alike, all vanity."

She scarcely answered when I paused,
 But rather to herself said: "One
Is here," low-voiced and loving, "Yea,
200 Greater than Solomon."

So both were silent, she and I:
 She laid her work aside, and went
Into the garden-walks, like spring,
  All gracious with content;

205 A little graver than her wont,
 Because her words had fretted me;
Not warbling quite her merriest tune
  Bird-like from tree to tree.

I chose a book to read and dream:
210 Yet half the while with furtive eyes
Marked how she made her choice of flowers
  Intuitively wise,

And ranged them with instinctive taste
  Which all my books had failed to teach;
215 Fresh rose herself, and daintier
    Than blossom of the peach.

By birthright higher than myself,
  Tho' nestling of the selfsame nest:
No fault of hers, no fault of mine,
220   But stubborn to digest.

I watched her, till my book unmarked
  Slid noiseless to the velvet floor;
Till all the opulent summer-world
  Looked poorer than before.

225 Just then her busy fingers ceased,
    Her fluttered colour went and came;
I knew whose step was on the walk,
    Whose voice would name her name.

    *   *   *   *   *

Well, twenty years have passed since then:
230   My sister now, a stately wife
Still fair, looks back in peace and sees
    The longer half of life—

The longer half of prosperous life,   .
  With little grief, or fear, or fret:
235 She, loved and loving long ago,
    Is loved and loving yet.

A husband honourable, brave,
  Is her main wealth in all the world:
And next to him one like herself,
240   One daughter golden-curled;

Fair image of her own fair youth,
  As beautiful and as serene,
With almost such another love
  As her own love has been.

245 Yet, tho' of world-wide charity,
        And in her home most tender dove,
    Her treasure and her heart are stored
        In the home-land of love:

    She thrives, God's blessed husbandry;
250   Most like a vine which full of fruit
    Doth cling and lean and climb toward heaven
        While earth still binds its root.

    I sit and watch my sister's face:
        How little altered since the hours
255 When she, a kind, light-hearted girl,
        Gathered her garden flowers;

    Her song just mellowed by regret
        For having teased me with her talk;
    Then all-forgetful as she heard
260   One step upon the walk.

    While I? I sat alone and watched;
        My lot in life, to live alone
    In mine own world of interests,
        Much felt but little shown.

265 Not to be first: how hard to learn
        That lifelong lesson of the past;
    Line graven on line and stroke on stroke;
        But, thank God, learned at last.

    So now in patience I possess
270   My soul year after tedious year,
    Content to take the lowest place,
        The place assigned me here.

    Yet sometimes, when I feel my strength
        Most weak, and life most burdensome,
275 I lift mine eyes up to the hills
        From whence my help shall come:

    Yea, sometimes still I lift my heart
        To the Archangelic trumpet-burst,
    When all deep secrets shall be shown,
280   And many last be first.

DEAD HOPE.

Hope new born one pleasant morn
   Died at even;
Hope dead lives nevermore,
   No, not in heaven.

5   If his shroud were but a cloud
     To weep itself away;
Or were he buried underground
     To sprout some day!
But dead and gone is dead and gone
10   Vainly wept upon.

Nought we place above his face
     To mark the spot,
But it shows a barren place
     In our lot.
15   Hope has birth no more on earth
     Morn or even;
Hope dead lives nevermore,
     No, not in heaven.

A DAUGHTER OF EVE.

A fool I was to sleep at noon,
   And wake when night is chilly
Beneath the comfortless cold moon;
A fool to pluck my rose too soon,
5   A fool to snap my lily.

My garden-plot I have not kept;
   Faded and all-forsaken,
I weep as I have never wept:
Oh it was summer when I slept,
10   It's winter now I waken.

Talk what you please of future Spring
   And sun-warmed sweet tomorrow:—
Stripped bare of hope and everything,
No more to laugh, no more to sing,
15   I sit alone with sorrow.

SONG.

Oh what comes over the sea,
   Shoals and quicksands past;
And what comes home to me,
   Sailing slow, sailing fast?

5   A wind comes over the sea
   With a moan in its blast;
But nothing comes home to me,
   Sailing slow, sailing fast.

Let me be, let me be,
10   For my lot is cast:
Land or sea all's one to me,
   And sail it slow or fast.

VENUS'S LOOKING-GLASS.

I marked where lovely Venus and her court
   With song and dance and merry laugh went by;
   Weightless, their wingless feet seemed made to fly,
Bound from the ground and in mid air to sport.
5 Left far behind I heard the dolphins snort,
   Tracking their goddess with a wistful eye,
   Around whose head white doves rose, wheeling high
Or low, and cooed after their tender sort.

All this I saw in Spring. Thro' Summer heat
10　　I saw the lovely Queen of Love no more.
　　　　But when flushed Autumn thro' the woodlands went
I spied sweet Venus walk amid the wheat:
　　Whom seeing, every harvester gave o'er
　　　His toil, and laughed and hoped and was content.

LOVE LIES BLEEDING.

Love that is dead and buried, yesterday
　　Out of his grave rose up before my face;
　　No recognition in his look, no trace
Of memory in his eyes dust-dimmed and grey.
5　　While I, remembering, found no word to say,
　　But felt my quickened heart leap in its place;
　　Caught afterglow, thrown back from long-set days,
Caught echoes of all music passed away.
Was this indeed to meet?—I mind me yet
10　　In youth we met when hope and love were quick,
　　　We parted with hope dead, but love alive:
　　I mind me how we parted then heart-sick,
　　　Remembering, loving, hopeless, weak to strive:—
Was this to meet? Not so, we have not met.

BIRD RAPTURES.

The sunrise wakes the lark to sing,
　　The moonrise wakes the nightingale.
Come darkness, moonrise, everything
　　That is so silent, sweet, and pale,
5　　Come, so ye wake the nightingale.

Make haste to mount, thou wistful moon,
    Make haste to wake the nightingale:
Let silence set the world in tune
    To hearken to that wordless tale
10   Which warbles from the nightingale.

O herald skylark, stay thy flight
    One moment, for a nightingale
Floods us with sorrow and delight.
    Tomorrow thou shalt hoist the sail;
15 Leave us tonight the nightingale.

MY FRIEND.

Two days ago with dancing glancing hair,
    With living lips and eyes:
    Now pale, dumb, blind, she lies;
So pale, yet still so fair.

5   We have not left her yet, not yet alone;
    But soon must leave her where
    She will not miss our care,
Bone of our bone.

Weep not; O friends, we should not weep:
10   Our friend of friends lies full of rest;
    No sorrow rankles in her breast,
Fallen fast asleep.

She sleeps below,
    She wakes and laughs above:
15   Today, as she walked, let us walk in love;
Tomorrow follow so.

TWILIGHT NIGHT.

I

We met, hand to hand,
  We clasped hands close and fast,
As close as oak and ivy stand;
  But it is past:
5   Come day, come night, day comes at last.

We loosed hand from hand,
  We parted face from face;
Each went his way to his own land
  At his own pace,
10   Each went to fill his separate place.

If we should meet one day,
  If both should not forget,
We shall clasp hands the accustomed way,
  As when we met
15   So long ago, as I remember yet.

II

Where my heart is (wherever that may be)
  Might I but follow!
If you fly thither over heath and lea,
  O honey-seeking bee,
20   O careless swallow,
Bid some for whom I watch keep watch for me.

Alas! that we must dwell, my heart and I,
  So far asunder.
Hours wax to days, and days and days creep by;
25 I watch with wistful eye,
    I wait and wonder:
When will that day draw nigh—that hour draw nigh?

Not yesterday, and not, I think, today;
  Perhaps tomorrow.
30 Day after day "tomorrow" thus I say:
I watched so yesterday
  In hope and sorrow,
Again today I watch the accustomed way.

A BIRD SONG.

It's a year almost that I have not seen her:
Oh last summer green things were greener,
Brambles fewer, the blue sky bluer.

It's surely summer, for there's a swallow:
5   Come one swallow, his mate will follow,
The bird-race quicken and wheel and thicken.

Oh happy swallow whose mate will follow
O'er height, o'er hollow! I'd be a swallow
To build this weather one nest together.

A SMILE AND A SIGH.

A smile because the nights are short!
   And every morning brings such pleasure
Of sweet love-making, harmless sport:
   Love that makes and finds its treasure;
5   Love, treasure without measure.

A sigh because the days are long!
   Long long these days that pass in sighing,
A burden saddens every song:
   While time lags which should be flying,
10   We live who would be dying.

AMOR MUNDI.

"Oh where are you going with your love-locks flowing
   On the west wind blowing along this valley track?"
"The downhill path is easy, come with me an it please ye,
   We shall escape the uphill by never turning back."

5   So they two went together in glowing August weather,
      The honey-breathing heather lay to their left and right;
    And dear she was to doat on, her swift feet seemed to float on
      The air like soft twin pigeons too sportive to alight.

    "Oh what is that in heaven where grey cloud-flakes are seven,
10   Where blackest clouds hang riven just at the rainy skirt?"
    "Oh that's a meteor sent us, a message dumb, portentous,
      An undeciphered solemn signal of help or hurt."

    "Oh what is that glides quickly where velvet flowers grow
          thickly,
      Their scent comes rich and sickly?"—"A scaled and hooded
          worm."
15   "Oh what's that in the hollow, so pale I quake to follow?"
      "Oh that's a thin dead body which waits the eternal term."

    "Turn again, O my sweetest,—turn again, false and fleetest:
      This beaten way thou beatest I fear is hell's own track."
    "Nay, too steep for hill-mounting; nay, too late for
          cost-counting:
20   This downhill path is easy, but there's no turning back."

THE GERMAN-FRENCH CAMPAIGN.
1870–1871.

    These two pieces, written during the suspense
of a great nation's agony, aim at expressing
human sympathy, not political bias.

1.
"THY BROTHER'S BLOOD CRIETH."

All her corn-fields rippled in the sunshine,
    All her lovely vines, sweets-laden, bowed;
Yet some weeks to harvest and to vintage:
    When, as one man's hand, a cloud
5 Rose and spread, and, blackening, burst asunder
      In rain and fire and thunder.

Is there nought to reap in the day of harvest?
　　Hath the vine in her day no fruit to yield?
Yea, men tread the press, but not for sweetness,
10　　And they reap a red crop from the field.
Build barns, ye reapers, garner all aright,
　　　Tho' your souls be called tonight.

A cry of tears goes up from blackened homesteads,
　　A cry of blood goes up from reeking earth:
15　Tears and blood have a cry that pierces Heaven
　　Thro' all its Hallelujah swells of mirth;
God hears their cry, and tho' He tarry, yet
　　　He doth not forget.

Mournful Mother, prone in dust weeping
20　　Who shall comfort thee for those who are not?
As thou didst, men do to thee; and heap the measure,
　　And heat the furnace sevenfold hot:
As thou once, now these to thee—who pitieth thee
　　　From sea to sea?

25　O thou King, terrible in strength, and building
　　Thy strong future on thy past!
Tho' he drink the last, the King of Sheshach,
　　Yet he shall drink at the last.
Art thou greater than great Babylon,
30　　　Which lies overthrown?

Take heed, ye unwise among the people;
　　O ye fools, when will ye understand?—
He that planted the ear shall He not hear,
　　Nor He smite who formed the hand?
35　"Vengeance is Mine, is Mine," thus saith the Lord:—
　　　O Man, put up thy sword.

2.
"TODAY FOR ME."

She sitteth still who used to dance,
She weepeth sore and more and more:—
Let us sit with thee weeping sore,
40　　　O fair France.

She trembleth as the days advance
Who used to be so light of heart:—
We in thy trembling bear a part,
    Sister France.

45   Her eyes shine tearful as they glance:
"Who shall give back my slaughtered sons?
"Bind up," she saith, "my wounded ones."—
    Alas, France!

She struggles in a deathly trance,
50   As in a dream her pulses stir,
She hears the nations calling her,
    "France, France, France."

Thou people of the lifted lance,
Forbear her tears, forbear her blood:
55   Roll back, roll back, thy whelming flood,
    Back from France.

Eye not her loveliness askance,
Forge not for her a galling chain;
Leave her at peace to bloom again,
60   Vine-clad France.

A time there is for change and chance,
A time for passing of the cup:
And One abides can yet bind up
    Broken France.

65   A time there is for change and chance:
Who next shall drink the trembling cup,
Wring out its dregs and suck them up
    After France?

A CHRISTMAS CAROL.

In the bleak mid-winter
    Frosty wind made moan,

Earth stood hard as iron,
   Water like a stone;
5 Snow had fallen, snow on snow,
   Snow on snow,
In the bleak mid-winter
   Long ago.

Our God, Heaven cannot hold Him
10   Nor earth sustain;
Heaven and earth shall flee away
   When He comes to reign:
In the bleak mid-winter
   A stable-place sufficed
15 The Lord God Almighty
   Jesus Christ.

Enough for Him whom cherubim
   Worship night and day,
A breastful of milk
20   And a mangerful of hay;
Enough for Him whom angels
   Fall down before,
The ox and ass and camel
   Which adore.

25 Angels and archangels
   May have gathered there,
Cherubim and seraphim
   Throng'd the air,
But only His mother
30   In her maiden bliss
Worshipped the Beloved
   With a kiss.

What can I give Him,
   Poor as I am?
35 If I were a shepherd
   I would bring a lamb,
If I were a wise man
   I would do my part,—
Yet what I can I give Him,
40   Give my heart.

CONSIDER.

    Consider
The lilies of the field whose bloom is brief:—
      We are as they;
      Like them we fade away,
5   As doth a leaf.

    Consider
The sparrows of the air of small account:
      Our God doth view
Whether they fall or mount,—
10   He guards us too.

    Consider
The lilies that do neither spin nor toil,
      Yet are most fair:—
      What profits all this care
15 And all this coil?

    Consider
The birds that have no barn nor harvest-weeks;
      God gives them food:—
Much more our Father seeks
20   To do us good.

BY THE WATERS OF BABYLON.
B.C. 570.

Here, where I dwell, I waste to skin and bone;
   The curse is come upon me, and I waste
   In penal torment powerless to atone.
The curse is come on me, which makes no haste
5   And doth not tarry, crushing both the proud
   Hard man and him the sinner double-faced.
Look not upon me, for my soul is bowed
   Within me, as my body in this mire;
   My soul crawls dumb-struck, sore bestead and cowed.

10   As Sodom and Gomorrah scourged by fire,
            As Jericho before God's trumpet-peal,
            So we the elect ones perish in His ire.
        Vainly we gird on sackcloth, vainly kneel
            With famished faces toward Jerusalem:
15   His heart is shut against us not to feel,
        His ears against our cry He shutteth them,
            His hand He shorteneth that He will not save,
            His law is loud against us to condemn:
        And we, as unclean bodies in the grave
20   Inheriting corruption and the dark,
            Are outcast from His presence which we crave.
        Our Mercy hath departed from His Ark,
            Our Glory hath departed from His rest,
            Our Shield hath left us naked as a mark
25   Unto all pitiless eyes made manifest.
            Our very Father hath forsaken us,
            Our God hath cast us from Him: we oppress'd
        Unto our foes are even marvellous,
            A hissing and a butt for pointing hands,
30   Whilst God Almighty hunts and grinds us thus;
        For He hath scattered us in alien lands,
            Our priests, our princes, our anointed king,
            And bound us hand and foot with brazen bands.
        Here while I sit my painful heart takes wing
35   Home to the home-land I may see no more,
            Where milk and honey flow, where waters spring
        And fail not, where I dwelt in days of yore
            Under my fig-tree and my fruitful vine,
            There where my parents dwelt at ease before:
40   Now strangers press the olives that are mine,
            Reap all the corners of my harvest-field,
            And make their fat hearts wanton with my wine;
        To them my trees, to them my gardens yield
            Their sweets and spices and their tender green,
45   O'er them in noontide heat outspread their shield.
        Yet these are they whose fathers had not been
            Housed with my dogs, whom hip and thigh we smote
            And with their blood washed their pollutions clean,

Purging the land which spewed them from its throat;
50   Their daughters took we for a pleasant prey,
       Choice tender ones on whom the fathers doat.
Now they in turn have led our own away;
       Our daughters and our sisters and our wives
       Sore weeping as they weep who curse the day,
55 To live, remote from help, dishonoured lives,
       Soothing their drunken masters with a song,
       Or dancing in their golden tinkling gyves:
Accurst if they remember thro' the long
       Estrangement of their exile, twice accursed
60   If they forget and join the accursèd throng.
How doth my heart that is so wrung not burst
       When I remember that my way was plain,
       And that God's candle lit me at the first,
Whilst now I grope in darkness, grope in vain,
65   Desiring but to find Him Who is lost,
       To find Him once again, but once again!
His wrath came on us to the uttermost,
       His covenanted and most righteous wrath:
       Yet this is He of Whom we made our boast,
70 Who lit the Fiery Pillar in our path,
       Who swept the Red Sea dry before our feet,
       Who in His jealousy smote kings, and hath
Sworn once to David: One shall fill thy seat
       Born of thy body, as the sun and moon
75   'Stablished for aye in sovereignty complete.
O Lord, remember David, and that soon.
       The Glory hath departed, Ichabod!
       Yet now, before our sun grow dark at noon,
Before we come to nought beneath Thy rod,
80   Before we go down quick into the pit,
       Remember us for good, O God, our God:—
Thy Name will I remember, praising it,
       Tho' Thou forget me, tho' Thou hide Thy face,
       And blot me from the Book which Thou hast writ;
85 Thy Name will I remember in my praise
       And call to mind Thy faithfulness of old,
Tho' as a weaver Thou cut off my days
       And end me as a tale ends that is told.

PARADISE.

Once in a dream I saw the flowers
　　That bud and bloom in Paradise;
　　More fair they are than waking eyes
Have seen in all this world of ours.
5　And faint the perfume-bearing rose,
　　And faint the lily on its stem,
And faint the perfect violet
　　　Compared with them.

I heard the songs of Paradise:
10　Each bird sat singing in his place;
　　A tender song so full of grace
It soared like incense to the skies.
Each bird sat singing to his mate
　　Soft cooing notes among the trees:
15　The nightingale herself were cold
　　　To such as these.

I saw the fourfold River flow,
　　And deep it was, with golden sand;
　　It flowed between a mossy land
20　With murmured music grave and low.
It hath refreshment for all thirst,
　　For fainting spirits strength and rest;
Earth holds not such a draught as this
　　　From east to west.

25　The Tree of Life stood budding there,
　　Abundant with its twelvefold fruits;
　　Eternal sap sustains its roots,
Its shadowing branches fill the air.
Its leaves are healing for the world,
30　Its fruit the hungry world can feed,
Sweeter than honey to the taste
　　　And balm indeed.

I saw the gate called Beautiful;
　　And looked, but scarce could look within;
35　I saw the golden streets begin,
And outskirts of the glassy pool.

Oh harps, oh crowns of plenteous stars,
   Oh green palm branches many-leaved—
Eye hath not seen, nor ear hath heard,
40   Nor heart conceived.

I hope to see these things again,
   But not as once in dreams by night;
   To see them with my very sight,
And touch and handle and attain:
45 To have all Heaven beneath my feet
   For narrow way that once they trod;
To have my part with all the saints,
    And with my God.

MOTHER COUNTRY.

Oh what is that country
   And where can it be,
Not mine own country,
   But dearer far to me?
5 Yet mine own country,
   If I one day may see
Its spices and cedars,
   Its gold and ivory.

As I lie dreaming
10   It rises, that land;
There rises before me
   Its green golden strand,
With the bowing cedars
   And the shining sand;
15 It sparkles and flashes
   Like a shaken brand.

Do angels lean nearer
   While I lie and long?
I see their soft plumage
20   And catch their windy song,

Like the rise of a high tide
  Sweeping full and strong;
I mark the outskirts
  Of their reverend throng.

25 Oh what is a king here,
  Or what is a boor?
Here all starve together,
  All dwarfed and poor;
Here Death's hand knocketh
30   At door after door,
He thins the dancers
  From the festal floor.

Oh what is a handmaid,
  Or what is a queen?
35 All must lie down together.
  Where the turf is green,
The foulest face hidden,
  The fairest not seen;
Gone as if never
40   They had breathed or been.

Gone from sweet sunshine
  Underneath the sod,
Turned from warm flesh and blood
  To senseless clod,
45 Gone as if never
  They had toiled or trod,
Gone out of sight of all
  Except our God.

Shut into silence
50   From the accustomed song,
Shut into solitude
  From all earth's throng,
Run down tho' swift of foot,
  Thrust down tho' strong;
55 Life made an end of
  Seemed it short or long.

Life made an end of,
   Life but just begun,
Life finished yesterday,
60   Its last sand run;
Life new-born with the morrow,
   Fresh as the sun:
While done is done for ever;
   Undone, undone.

65 And if that life is life,
   This is but a breath,
The passage of a dream
   And the shadow of death;
But a vain shadow
70   If one considereth;
Vanity of vanities,
   As the Preacher saith.

"I WILL LIFT UP MINE EYES UNTO THE HILLS."

I am pale with sick desire,
   For my heart is far away
From this world's fitful fire
   And this world's waning day;
5 In a dream it overleaps
   A world of tedious ills
To where the sunshine sleeps
   On the everlasting hills.—
   Say the Saints: There Angels ease us
10   Glorified and white.
   They say: We rest in Jesus,
   Where is not day nor night.

My soul saith: I have sought
   For a home that is not gained,
15 I have spent yet nothing bought,
   Have laboured but not attained;

My pride strove to mount and grow,
   And hath but dwindled down;
My love sought love, and lo!
20   Hath not attained its crown.—
     Say the Saints: Fresh souls increase us,
       None languish or recede.
     They say: We love our Jesus,
       And He loves us indeed.

25 I cannot rise above,
     I cannot rest beneath,
I cannot find out love,
     Or escape from death;
Dear hopes and joys gone by
30   Still mock me with a name;
My best beloved die
     And I cannot die with them.—
     Say the Saints: No deaths decrease us,
       Where our rest is glorious.
35   They say: We live in Jesus,
       Who once died for us.

O my soul, she beats her wings
     And pants to fly away
Up to immortal things
40   In the heavenly day:
Yet she flags and almost faints;
     Can such be meant for me?—
Come and see, say the Saints.
     Saith Jesus: Come and see.
45   Say the Saints: His pleasures please us
       Before God and the Lamb.
     Come and taste My sweets, saith Jesus:
       Be with Me where I am.

"THE MASTER IS COME, AND CALLETH FOR THEE."

Who calleth?—Thy Father calleth,
  Run, O Daughter, to wait on Him:
He Who chasteneth but for a season
  Trims thy lamp that it burn not dim.

5 Who calleth?—Thy Master calleth,
  Sit, Disciple, and learn of Him:
He Who teacheth wisdom of Angels
  Makes thee wise as the Cherubim.

Who calleth?—Thy Monarch calleth,
10 Rise, O Subject, and follow Him:
He is stronger than Death or Devil,
  Fear not thou if the foe be grim.

Who calleth?—Thy Lord God calleth,
  Fall, O Creature, adoring Him:
15 He is jealous, thy God Almighty,
  Count not dear to thee life or limb.

Who calleth?—Thy Bridegroom calleth,
  Soar, O Bride, with the Seraphim:
He Who loves thee as no man loveth,
20 Bids thee give up thy heart to Him.

WHO SHALL DELIVER ME?

God strengthen me to bear myself;
That heaviest weight of all to bear,
Inalienable weight of care.

All others are outside myself;
5 I lock my door and bar them out,
The turmoil, tedium, gad-about.

I lock my door upon myself,
And bar them out; but who shall wall
Self from myself, most loathed of all?

10   If I could once lay down myself,
      And start self-purged upon the race
      That all must run! Death runs apace.

      If I could set aside myself,
      And start with lightened heart upon
15   The road by all men overgone!

      God harden me against myself,
      This coward with pathetic voice
      Who craves for ease, and rest, and joys:

      Myself, arch-traitor to myself;
20   My hollowest friend, my deadliest foe,
      My clog whatever road I go.

      Yet One there is can curb myself,
      Can roll the strangling load from me,
      Break off the yoke and set me free.

"WHEN MY HEART IS VEXED, I WILL COMPLAIN."

      "O Lord, how canst Thou say Thou lovest me?
        Me whom Thou settest in a barren land,
        Hungry and thirsty on the burning sand,
      Hungry and thirsty where no waters be
5   Nor shadows of date-bearing tree:—
      O Lord, how canst Thou say Thou lovest me?"

      "I came from Edom by as parched a track,
        As rough a track beneath My bleeding feet.
        I came from Edom seeking thee, and sweet
10   I counted bitterness; I turned not back
      But counted life as death, and trod
      The winepress all alone: and I am God."

      "Yet, Lord, how canst Thou say Thou lovest me?
        For Thou art strong to comfort: and could I
15   But comfort one I love, who, like to die,

Lifts feeble hands and eyes that fail to see
In one last prayer for comfort—nay,
I could not stand aside or turn away."

"Alas! thou knowest that for thee I died,
20   For thee I thirsted with the dying thirst;
     I, Blessed, for thy sake was counted cursed,
In sight of men and angels crucified:
All this and more I bore to prove
My love, and wilt thou yet mistrust My love?"

25   "Lord, I am fain to think Thou lovest me,
     For Thou art all in all and I am Thine,
     And lo! Thy love is better than new wine,
And I am sick of love in loving Thee.
But dost Thou love me? speak and save,
30   For jealousy is cruel as the grave."

"Nay, if thy love is not an empty breath
     My love is as thine own, deep answers deep.
     Peace, peace: I give to My beloved sleep,
Not death but sleep, for love is strong as death:
35   Take patience; sweet thy sleep shall be,
Yea, thou shalt wake in Paradise with Me."

AFTER COMMUNION.

Why should I call Thee Lord, Who art my God?
     Why should I call Thee Friend, Who art my Love?
     Or King, Who art my very Spouse above?
Or call Thy Sceptre on my heart Thy rod?
5   Lo, now Thy banner over me is love,
All heaven flies open to me at Thy nod:
For Thou hast lit Thy flame in me a clod,
     Made me a nest for dwelling of Thy Dove.
     What wilt Thou call me in our home above,
10   Who now hast called me friend? how will it be
          When Thou for good wine settest forth the best?

Now Thou dost bid me come and sup with Thee,
    Now Thou dost make me lean upon Thy breast:
How will it be with me in time of love?

SAINTS AND ANGELS.

It's oh in Paradise that I fain would be,
    Away from earth and weariness and all beside:
Earth is too full of loss with its dividing sea,
    But Paradise upbuilds the bower for the bride.

5   Where flowers are yet in bud while the boughs are green,
    I would get quit of earth and get robed for heaven;
Putting on my raiment white within the screen,
    Putting on my crown of gold whose gems are seven.

Fair is the fourfold river that maketh no moan,
10   Fair are the trees fruit-bearing of the wood,
Fair are the gold and bdellium and the onyx stone,
    And I know the gold of that land is good.

O my love, my dove, lift up your eyes
    Toward the eastern gate like an opening rose;
15   You and I who parted will meet in Paradise,
    Pass within and sing when the gates unclose.

This life is but the passage of a day,
    This life is but a pang and all is over,
But in the life to come which fades not away
20   Every love shall abide and every lover.

He who wore out pleasure and mastered all lore,
    Solomon wrote "Vanity of vanities:"
Down to death, of all that went before
    In his mighty long life, the record is this.

25   With loves by the hundred, wealth beyond measure,
    Is this he who wrote "Vanity of vanities"?
Yea, "Vanity of vanities" he saith of pleasure,
    And of all he learned set his seal to this.

Yet we love and faint not, for our love is one,
30   And we hope and flag not, for our hope is sure,
Altho' there be nothing new beneath the sun
    And no help for life and for death no cure.

The road to death is life, the gate of life is death,
    We who wake shall sleep, we shall wax who wane;
35 Let us not vex our souls for stoppage of a breath,
    The fall of a river that turneth not again.

Be the road short, and be the gate near,—
    Shall a short road tire, a strait gate appal?
The loves that meet in Paradise shall cast out fear,
40   And Paradise hath room for you and me and all.

A ROSE PLANT IN JERICHO.

At morn I plucked a rose and gave it Thee,
    A rose of joy and happy love and peace,
      A rose with scarce a thorn:
      But in the chillness of a second morn
5   My rose bush drooped, and all its gay increase
Was but one thorn that wounded me.

I plucked the thorn and offered it to Thee;
    And for my thorn Thou gavest love and peace,
      Not joy this mortal morn:
10   If Thou hast given much treasure for a thorn,
    Wilt Thou not give me for my rose increase
Of gladness, and all sweets to me?

My thorny rose, my love and pain, to Thee
    I offer; and I set my heart in peace,
15   And rest upon my thorn:
      For verily I think tomorrow morn
    Shall bring me Paradise, my gift's increase,
Yea, give Thy very Self to me.

Sing-Song: A Nursery Rhyme Book (1872)

RHYMES
DEDICATED
WITHOUT PERMISSION
TO
THE BABY
WHO
SUGGESTED
THEM

Angels at the foot,
   And Angels at the head,
And like a curly little lamb
   My pretty babe in bed.

Love me,—I love you,
   Love me, my baby;
Sing it high, sing it low,
   Sing it as may be.
5 Mother's arms under you,
   Her eyes above you;
Sing it high, sing it low,
   Love me,—I love you.

My baby has a father and a mother,
   Rich little baby!
Fatherless, motherless, I know another
   Forlorn as may be:
5   Poor little baby!

Our little baby fell asleep,
  And may not wake again
For days and days, and weeks and weeks;
  But then he'll wake again,
5 And come with his own pretty look,
  And kiss Mamma again.

"Kookoorookoo! kookoorookoo!"
  Crows the cock before the morn;
"Kikirikee! kikirikee!"
  Roses in the east are born.

5 "Kookoorookoo! kookoorookoo!"
  Early birds begin their singing;
"Kikirikee! kikirikee!"
  The day, the day, the day is springing.

  Baby cry—
  Oh fie!—
At the physic in the cup:
  Gulp it twice
5 And gulp it thrice,
Baby gulp it up.

Eight o'clock;
The postman's knock!
Five letters for Papa;
  One for Lou,
5 And none for you,
And three for dear Mamma.

Bread and milk for breakfast,
  And woollen frocks to wear,
And a crumb for robin redbreast
  On the cold days of the year.

There's snow on the fields,
   And cold in the cottage,
While I sit in the chimney nook
   Supping hot pottage.

5   My clothes are soft and warm,
      Fold upon fold,
But I'm so sorry for the poor
      Out in the cold.

Dead in the cold, a song-singing thrush,
Dead at the foot of a snowberry bush,—
Weave him a coffin of rush,
Dig him a grave where the soft mosses grow,
5   Raise him a tombstone of snow.

I dug and dug amongst the snow,
And thought the flowers would never grow;
I dug and dug amongst the sand,
And still no green thing came to hand.

5   Melt, O snow! the warm winds blow
To thaw the flowers and melt the snow;
But all the winds from every land
Will rear no blossom from the sand.

A city plum is not a plum;
A dumb-bell is no bell, though dumb;
A party rat is not a rat;
A sailor's cat is not a cat;
5   A soldier's frog is not a frog;
A captain's log is not a log.

Your brother has a falcon,
   Your sister has a flower;
But what is left for mannikin,
   Born within an hour?

5 I'll nurse you on my knee, my knee,
  My own little son;
I'll rock you, rock you, in my arms,
  My least little one.

Hear what the mournful linnets say:
 "We built our nest compact and warm,
But cruel boys came round our way
 And took our summerhouse by storm.

5 "They crushed the eggs so neatly laid;
  So now we sit with drooping wing,
And watch the ruin they have made,
  Too late to build, too sad to sing."

A baby's cradle with no baby in it,
 A baby's grave where autumn leaves drop sere;
The sweet soul gathered home to Paradise,
 The body waiting here.

Hop-o'-my-thumb and little Jack Horner,
 What do you mean by tearing and fighting?
Sturdy dog Trot close round the corner,
 I never caught him growling and biting.

Hope is like a harebell trembling from its birth,
Love is like a rose the joy of all the earth;
Faith is like a lily lifted high and white,
Love is like a lovely rose the world's delight;
5 Harebells and sweet lilies show a thornless growth,
But the rose with all its thorns excels them both.

O wind, why do you never rest,
 Wandering, whistling to and fro,

Bringing rain out of the west,
From the dim north bringing snow?

Crying, my little one, footsore and weary?
Fall asleep, pretty one, warm on my shoulder:
I must tramp on through the winter night dreary,
While the snow falls on me colder and colder.

5   You are my one, and I have not another;
Sleep soft, my darling, my trouble and treasure;
Sleep warm and soft in the arms of your mother,
Dreaming of pretty things, dreaming of pleasure.

Growing in the vale
By the uplands hilly,
Growing straight and frail,
Lady Daffadowndilly.

5   In a golden crown,
And a scant green gown
While the spring blows chilly,
Lady Daffadown,
Sweet Daffadowndilly.

A linnet in a gilded cage,—
A linnet on a bough,—
In frosty winter one might doubt
Which bird is luckier now.

5   But let the trees burst out in leaf,
And nests be on the bough,
Which linnet is the luckier bird,
Oh who could doubt it now?

Wrens and robins in the hedge,
Wrens and robins here and there;

Building, perching, pecking, fluttering,
    Everywhere!

My baby has a mottled fist,
    My baby has a neck in creases;
My baby kisses and is kissed,
    For he's the very thing for kisses.

Why did baby die,
Making Father sigh,
Mother cry?

Flowers, that bloom to die,
5   Make no reply
Of "why?"
But bow and die.

If all were rain and never sun,
    No bow could span the hill;
If all were sun and never rain,
    There'd be no rainbow still.

O wind, where have you been,
    That you blow so sweet?
Among the violets
    Which blossom at your feet.
5   The honeysuckle waits
    For Summer and for heat.
But violets in the chilly Spring
    Make the turf so sweet.

On the grassy banks
Lambkins at their pranks;
Woolly sisters, woolly brothers

    Jumping off their feet
5 While their woolly mothers
     Watch by them and bleat.

Rushes in a watery place,
  And reeds in a hollow;
A soaring skylark in the sky,
  A darting swallow;
5 And where pale blossom used to hang
    Ripe fruit to follow.

Minnie and Mattie
  And fat little May,
Out in the country,
  Spending a day.

5 Such a bright day,
    With the sun glowing,
And the trees half in leaf,
    And the grass growing.

Pinky white pigling
10 Squeals through his snout,
Woolly white lambkin
  Frisks all about.

Cluck! cluck! the nursing hen
  Summons her folk,—
15 Ducklings all downy soft
    Yellow as yolk.

Cluck! cluck! the mother hen
  Summons her chickens
To peck the dainty bits
20 Found in her pickings.

Minnie and Mattie
  And May carry posies,
Half of sweet violets,
  Half of primroses.

25   Give the sun time enough,
            Glowing and glowing,
        He'll rouse the roses
            And bring them blowing.

        Don't wait for roses
30   Losing today,
        O Minnie, Mattie,
            And wise little May.

        Violets and primroses
            Blossom today
35   For Minnie and Mattie
            And fat little May.

        Heartsease in my garden bed,
            With sweetwilliam white and red,
        Honeysuckle on my wall:—
            Heartsease blossoms in my heart
5   When sweet William comes to call,
            But it withers when we part,
        And the honey-trumpets fall.

        If I were a Queen,
            What would I do?
        I'd make you King,
            And I'd wait on you.

5   If I were a King,
            What would I do?
        I'd make you Queen,
            For I'd marry you.

        What are heavy? sea-sand and sorrow:
        What are brief? today and tomorrow:
        What are frail? Spring blossoms and youth:
        What are deep? the ocean and truth.

There is but one May in the year,
   And sometimes May is wet and cold;
There is but one May in the year
   Before the year grows old.

5   Yet though it be the chilliest May,
   With least of sun and most of showers,
Its wind and dew, its night and day,
   Bring up the flowers.

The summer nights are short
   Where northern days are long:
For hours and hours lark after lark
   Trills out his song.

5   The summer days are short
   Where southern nights are long:
Yet short the night when nightingales
   Trill out their song.

The days are clear,
   Day after day,
When April's here,
   That leads to May,
5   And June
Must follow soon:
   Stay, June, stay!—
If only we could stop the moon
And June!

Twist me a crown of wind-flowers;
   That I may fly away
To hear the singers at their song,
   And players at their play.

5   Put on your crown of wind-flowers:
   But whither would you go?

Beyond the surging of the sea
   And the storms that blow.

Alas! your crown of wind-flowers
10   Can never make you fly:
I twist them in a crown today,
   And tonight they die.

Brown and furry
Caterpillar in a hurry,
Take your walk
To the shady leaf, or stalk,
5   Or what not,
Which may be the chosen spot.
No toad spy you,
Hovering bird of prey pass by you;
Spin and die,
10   To live again a butterfly.

A toadstool comes up in a night,—
   Learn the lesson, little folk:—
An oak grows on a hundred years,
   But then it is an oak.

A pocket handkerchief to hem—
   Oh dear, oh dear, oh dear!
How many stitches it will take
   Before it's done, I fear.

5   Yet set a stitch and then a stitch,
   And stitch and stitch away,
Till stitch by stitch the hem is done—
   And after work is play!

If a pig wore a wig,
   What could we say?

Treat him as a gentleman,
  And say "Good day."

5 If his tail chanced to fail,
  What could we do?—
Send him to the tailoress
  To get one new.

Seldom "can't,"
  Seldom "don't;"
Never "shan't,"
  Never "won't."

1 and 1 are 2—
  That's for me and you.

2 and 2 are 4—
  That's a couple more.

5 3 and 3 are 6
  Barley-sugar sticks.

4 and 4 are 8
  Tumblers at the gate.

5 and 5 are 10
10 Bluff seafaring men.

6 and 6 are 12
  Garden lads who delve.

7 and 7 are 14
  Young men bent on sporting.

15 8 and 8 are 16
  Pills the doctor's mixing.

9 and 9 are 18
  Passengers kept waiting.

10 and 10 are 20
20 Roses—pleasant plenty!

11 and 11 are 22
Sums for brother George to do.

12 and 12 are 24
Pretty pictures, and no more.

How many seconds in a minute?
Sixty, and no more in it.

How many minutes in an hour?
Sixty for sun and shower.

5   How many hours in a day?
Twenty-four for work and play.

How many days in a week?
Seven both to hear and speak.

How many weeks in a month?
10   Four, as the swift moon runn'th.

How many months in a year?
Twelve the almanack makes clear.

How many years in an age?
One hundred says the sage.

15   How many ages in time?
No one knows the rhyme.

What will you give me for my pound?
Full twenty shillings round.
What will you give me for my shilling?
Twelve pence to give I'm willing.
5   What will you give me for my penny?
Four farthings, just so many.

January cold desolate;
February all dripping wet;
March wind ranges;
April changes;

5   Birds sing in tune
       To flowers of May,
    And sunny June
       Brings longest day;
    In scorched July
10   The storm-clouds fly
    Lightning torn;
    August bears corn,
    September fruit;
    In rough October
15   Earth must disrobe her;
    Stars fall and shoot
    In keen November;
    And night is long
    And cold is strong
20   In bleak December.

    What is pink? a rose is pink
    By the fountain's brink.
    What is red? a poppy's red
    In its barley bed.
5   What is blue? the sky is blue
    Where the clouds float thro'.
    What is white? a swan is white
    Sailing in the light.
    What is yellow? pears are yellow,
10   Rich and ripe and mellow.
    What is green? the grass is green,
    With small flowers between.
    What is violet? clouds are violet
    In the summer twilight.
15   What is orange? why, an orange,
    Just an orange!

    Mother shake the cherry-tree,
       Susan catch a cherry;

Oh how funny that will be,
   Let's be merry!

5   One for brother, one for sister,
    Two for mother more,
Six for father, hot and tired,
    Knocking at the door.

A pin has a head, but has no hair;
A clock has a face, but no mouth there;
Needles have eyes, but they cannot see;
A fly has a trunk without lock or key;
5   A timepiece may lose, but cannot win;
A corn-field dimples without a chin;
A hill has no leg, but has a foot;
A wine-glass a stem, but not a root;
A watch has hands, but no thumb or finger;
10 A boot has a tongue, but is no singer;
Rivers run, though they have no feet;
A saw has teeth, but it does not eat;
Ash-trees have keys, yet never a lock;
And baby crows, without being a cock.

Hopping frog, hop here and be seen,
   I'll not pelt you with stick or stone:
Your cap is laced and your coat is green;
   Good bye, we'll let each other alone.

5   Plodding toad, plod here and be looked at,
You the finger of scorn is crooked at:
But though you're lumpish, you're harmless too;
You won't hurt me, and I won't hurt you.

Where innocent bright-eyed daisies are,
   With blades of grass between,
Each daisy stands up like a star
   Out of a sky of green.

The city mouse lives in a house;—
  The garden mouse lives in a bower,
He's friendly with the frogs and toads,
  And sees the pretty plants in flower.

5 The city mouse eats bread and cheese;—
  The garden mouse eats what he can;
We will not grudge him seeds and stalks,
  Poor little timid furry man.

What does the donkey bray about?
What does the pig grunt through his snout?
What does the goose mean by a hiss?
Oh, Nurse, if you can tell me this,
5 I'll give you such a kiss.

The cockatoo calls "cockatoo,"
The magpie chatters "how d'ye do?"
The jackdaw bids me "go away,"
Cuckoo cries "cuckoo" half the day:
10 What do the others say?

Three plum buns
  To eat here at the stile
In the clover meadow,
  For we have walked a mile.

5 One for you, and one for me,
  And one left over:
Give it to the boy who shouts
  To scare sheep from the clover.

A motherless soft lambkin
  Alone upon a hill;
No mother's fleece to shelter him
  And wrap him from the cold:—
5 I'll run to him and comfort him,
  I'll fetch him, that I will;

I'll care for him and feed him
  Until he's strong and bold.

Dancing on the hill-tops,
  Singing in the valleys,
Laughing with the echoes,
  Merry little Alice.
5 Playing games with lambkins
  In the flowering valleys,
Gathering pretty posies,
  Helpful little Alice.

If her father's cottage
10 Turned into a palace,
And he owned the hill-tops
  And the flowering valleys,
She'd be none the happier,
  Happy little Alice.

When fishes set umbrellas up
  If the rain-drops run,
Lizards will want their parasols
  To shade them from the sun.

The peacock has a score of eyes,
  With which he cannot see;
The cod-fish has a silent sound,
  However that may be;
5 No dandelions tell the time,
  Although they turn to clocks;
Cat's-cradle does not hold the cat,
  Nor foxglove fit the fox.

Pussy has a whiskered face,
Kitty has such pretty ways;

Doggie scampers when I call,
And has a heart to love us all.

The dog lies in his kennel,
  And Puss purrs on the rug,
And baby perches on my knee
  For me to love and hug.
5 Pat the dog and stroke the cat,
  Each in its degree;
And cuddle and kiss my baby,
  And baby kiss me.

If hope grew on a bush,
  And joy grew on a tree,
What a nosegay for the plucking
  There would be!
5 But oh! in windy autumn,
  When frail flowers wither,
What should we do for hope and joy,
  Fading together?

I planted a hand
  And there came up a palm,
I planted a heart
  And there came up balm.
5 Then I planted a wish,
  But there sprang a thorn,
While heaven frowned with thunder
  And earth sighed forlorn.

Under the ivy bush
  One sits sighing,
And under the willow tree
  One sits crying:—

5   Under the ivy bush
    Cease from your sighing,
But under the willow tree
    Lie down a-dying.

There is one that has a head without an eye,
    And there's one that has an eye without a head:
You may find the answer if you try;
      And when all is said,
5   Half the answer hangs upon a thread!

If a mouse could fly,
    Or if a crow could swim,
Or if a sprat could walk and talk,
    I'd like to be like him.
5   If a mouse could fly,
    He might fly away;
Or if a crow could swim,
    It might turn him grey;
Or if a sprat could walk and talk,
10   What would he find to say?

Sing me a song—
    What shall I sing?—
Three merry sisters
    Dancing in a ring,
5   Light and fleet upon their feet
    As birds upon the wing.

Tell me a tale—
    What shall I tell?—
Two mournful sisters,
10   And a tolling knell,
Tolling ding and tolling dong,
    Ding dong bell.

The lily has an air,
  And the snowdrop a grace,
And the sweetpea a way,
  And the heartsease a face,—
5 Yet there's nothing like the rose
    When she blows.

Margaret has a milking-pail,
  And she rises early;
Thomas has a threshing-flail,
    And he's up betimes.

5 Sometimes crossing through the grass
  Where the dew lies pearly,
They say "Good morrow" as they pass
    By the leafy limes.

In the meadow—what in the meadow?
Bluebells, buttercups, meadowsweet,
And fairy rings for the children's feet
    In the meadow.

5   In the garden—what in the garden?
Jacob's-ladder and Solomon's-seal,
And Love-lies-bleeding beside All-heal
    In the garden.

A frisky lamb
And a frisky child
Playing their pranks
  In a cowslip meadow:
5 The sky all blue
And the air all mild
And the fields all sun
  And the lanes half shadow.

Mix a pancake,
Stir a pancake,
  Pop it in the pan;
Fry the pancake,
5 Toss the pancake,—
  Catch it if you can.

The wind has such a rainy sound
  Moaning through the town,
The sea has such a windy sound,—
  Will the ships go down?

5 The apples in the orchard
  Tumble from their tree.—
Oh will the ships go down, go down,
  In the windy sea?

Three little children
  On the wide wide earth,
Motherless children—
  Cared for from their birth
5   By tender Angels.

Three little children
  On the wide wide sea,
Motherless children—
  Safe as safe can be
10   With guardian Angels.

Fly away, fly away over the sea,
  Sun-loving swallow, for summer is done;
Come again, come again, come back to me,
  Bringing the summer and bringing the sun.

Minnie bakes oaten cakes,
  Minnie brews ale,

All because her Johnny's coming
    Home from sea.
5 And she glows like a rose,
    Who was so pale,
And "Are you sure the church clock goes?"
    Says she.

A white hen sitting
    On white eggs three:
Next, three speckled chickens
    As plump as plump can be.
5 An owl, and a hawk,
    And a bat come to see:
But chicks beneath their mother's wing
    Squat safe as safe can be.

Currants on a bush,
    And figs upon a stem,
And cherries on a bending bough,
    And Ned to gather them.

I have but one rose in the world,
    And my one rose stands a-drooping:
Oh when my single rose is dead
    There'll be but thorns for stooping.

Rosy maiden Winifred,
With a milkpail on her head,
Tripping through the corn,
    While the dew lies on the wheat
5   In the sunny morn.
Scarlet shepherd's-weatherglass
    Spreads wide open at her feet
      As they pass;

Cornflowers give their almond smell
10   While she brushes by,
    And a lark sings from the sky
        "All is well."

When the cows come home the milk is coming,
Honey's made while the bees are humming;
Duck and drake on the rushy lake,
And the deer live safe in the breezy brake;
5 And timid, funny, brisk little bunny,
Winks his nose and sits all sunny.

Roses blushing red and white,
    For delight;
Honeysuckle wreaths above,
    For love;
5 Dim sweet-scented heliotrope,
    For hope;
Shining lilies tall and straight,
    For royal state;
Dusky pansies, let them be
10   For memory;
With violets of fragrant breath,
    For death.

"Ding a ding,"
The sweet bells sing,
And say:
"Come, all be gay"
5 For a wedding day.

"Dong a dong,"
The bells sigh long,
And call:
"Weep one, weep all"
10 For a funeral.

A ring upon her finger,
   Walks the bride,
With the bridegroom tall and handsome
   At her side.

5   A veil upon her forehead,
   Walks the bride,
With the bridegroom proud and merry
   At her side.

Fling flowers beneath the footsteps
10   Of the bride;
Fling flowers before the bridegroom
   At her side.

"Ferry me across the water,
   Do, boatman, do."
"If you've a penny in your purse
   I'll ferry you."

5   "I have a penny in my purse,
   And my eyes are blue;
So ferry me across the water,
   Do, boatman, do."

"Step into my ferry-boat,
10   Be they black or blue,
And for the penny in your purse
   I'll ferry you."

When a mounting skylark sings
   In the sunlit summer morn,
I know that heaven is up on high,
   And on earth are fields of corn.

5   But when a nightingale sings
   In the moonlit summer even,
I know not if earth is merely earth,
   Only that heaven is heaven.

Who has seen the wind?
  Neither I nor you:
But when the leaves hang trembling
  The wind is passing thro'.

5   Who has seen the wind?
  Neither you nor I:
But when the trees bow down their heads
  The wind is passing by.

The horses of the sea
  Rear a foaming crest,
But the horses of the land
  Serve us the best.

5   The horses of the land
  Munch corn and clover,
While the foaming sea-horses
  Toss and turn over.

O sailor, come ashore,
  What have you brought for me?
Red coral, white coral,
  Coral from the sea.

5   I did not dig it from the ground,
  Nor pluck it from a tree;
Feeble insects made it
  In the stormy sea.

A diamond or a coal?
  A diamond, if you please:
Who cares about a clumsy coal
  Beneath the summer trees?

5   A diamond or a coal?
  A coal, sir, if you please:
One comes to care about the coal
  What time the waters freeze.

An emerald is as green as grass;
    A ruby red as blood;
A sapphire shines as blue as heaven;
    A flint lies in the mud.

5 A diamond is a brilliant stone,
    To catch the world's desire;
An opal holds a fiery spark;
    But a flint holds fire.

Boats sail on the rivers,
    And ships sail on the seas;
But clouds that sail across the sky
    Are prettier far than these.

5 There are bridges on the rivers,
    As pretty as you please;
But the bow that bridges heaven,
    And overtops the trees,
And builds a road from earth to sky,
10   Is prettier far than these.

The lily has a smooth stalk,
    Will never hurt your hand;
But the rose upon her briar
    Is lady of the land.

5 There's sweetness in an apple tree,
    And profit in the corn;
But lady of all beauty
    Is a rose upon a thorn.

When with moss and honey
10   She tips her bending briar,
And half unfolds her glowing heart,
    She sets the world on fire.

Hurt no living thing:
    Ladybird, nor butterfly,

Nor moth with dusty wing,
   Nor cricket chirping cheerily,
5 Nor grasshopper so light of leap,
   Nor dancing gnat, nor beetle fat,
Nor harmless worms that creep.

I caught a little ladybird
   That flies far away;
I caught a little lady wife
   That is both staid and gay.

5 Come back, my scarlet ladybird,
   Back from far away;
I weary of my dolly wife,
   My wife that cannot play.

She's such a senseless wooden thing
10   She stares the livelong day;
Her wig of gold is stiff and cold
   And cannot change to grey.

All the bells were ringing
And all the birds were singing,
When Molly sat down crying
   For her broken doll:
5   O you silly Moll!
Sobbing and sighing
   For a broken doll,
When all the bells are ringing,
And all the birds are singing.

Wee wee husband,
   Give me some money,
I have no comfits,
   And I have no honey.

5 Wee wee wifie,
   I have no money,

Milk, nor meat, nor bread to eat,
  Comfits, nor honey.

I have a little husband
  And he is gone to sea,
The winds that whistle round his ship
  Fly home to me.
5 The winds that sigh about me
    Return again to him;
So I would fly, if only I
  Were light of limb.

The dear old woman in the lane
  Is sick and sore with pains and aches,
We'll go to her this afternoon,
  And take her tea and eggs and cakes.
5 We'll stop to make the kettle boil,
    And brew some tea, and set the tray,
And poach an egg, and toast a cake,
  And wheel her chair round, if we may.

Swift and sure the swallow,
  Slow and sure the snail:
Slow and sure may miss his way,
  Swift and sure may fail.

"I dreamt I caught a little owl
  And the bird was blue—"

"But you may hunt for ever
And not find such an one."

5 "I dreamt I set a sunflower,
    And red as blood it grew—"

"But such a sunflower never
Bloomed beneath the sun."

What does the bee do?
   Bring home honey.
And what does Father do?
   Bring home money.
5   And what does Mother do?
     Lay out the money.
And what does baby do?
   Eat up the honey.

I have a Poll parrot,
   And Poll is my doll,
And my nurse is Polly,
   And my sister Poll.

5   "Polly!" cried Polly,
"Don't tear Polly dolly"—
While softhearted Poll
Trembled for the doll.

A house of cards
   Is neat and small:
Shake the table,
   It must fall.

5   Find the Court cards
     One by one;
Raise it, roof it,—
   Now it's done:—
Shake the table!
10   That's the fun.

The rose with such a bonny blush,
   What has the rose to blush about?
If it's the sun that makes her flush,
   What's in the sun to flush about?

The rose that blushes rosy red,
  She must hang her head;
The lily that blows spotless white,
  She may stand upright.

Oh fair to see
Bloom-laden cherry tree,
  Arrayed in sunny white;
  An April day's delight,
5 Oh fair to see!

Oh fair to see
Fruit-laden cherry tree,
  With balls of shining red
  Decking a leafy head,
10 Oh fair to see!

Clever little Willie wee,
  Bright eyed, blue eyed little fellow;
Merry little Margery
  With her hair all yellow.

5 Little Willie in his heart
  Is a sailor on the sea,
And he often cons a chart
  With sister Margery.

The peach tree on the southern wall
  Has basked so long beneath the sun,
Her score of peaches great and small
  Bloom rosy, every one.

5 A peach for brothers, one for each,
  A peach for you and a peach for me;
But the biggest, rosiest, downiest peach
  For Grandmamma with her tea.

A rose has thorns as well as honey,
I'll not have her for love or money;
An iris grows so straight and fine,
That she shall be no friend of mine;
5   Snowdrops like the snow would chill me;
Nightshade would caress and kill me;
Crocus like a spear would fright me;
Dragon's-mouth might bark or bite me;
Convolvulus but blooms to die;
10   A wind-flower suggests a sigh;
Love-lies-bleeding makes me sad;
And poppy-juice would drive me mad:—
But give me holly, bold and jolly,
Honest, prickly, shining holly;
15   Pluck me holly leaf and berry
For the day when I make merry.

Is the moon tired? she looks so pale
Within her misty veil:
She scales the sky from east to west,
And takes no rest.

5   Before the coming of the night
The moon shows papery white;
Before the dawning of the day
She fades away.

If stars dropped out of heaven,
    And if flowers took their place,
The sky would still look very fair,
    And fair earth's face.

5   Winged Angels might fly down to us
    To pluck the stars,
But we could only long for flowers
    Beyond the cloudy bars.

"Goodbye in fear, goodbye in sorrow,
   Goodbye, and all in vain,
Never to meet again, my dear—"
   "Never to part again."
5 "Goodbye today, goodbye tomorrow,
   Goodbye till earth shall wane,
Never to meet again, my dear—"
   "Never to part again."

If the sun could tell us half
   That he hears and sees,
Sometimes he would make us laugh,
   Sometimes make us cry:
5 Think of all the birds that make
   Homes among the trees;
Think of cruel boys who take
   Bird that cannot fly.

If the moon came from heaven,
   Talking all the way,
What could she have to tell us,
   And what could she say?
5 "I've seen a hundred pretty things,
   And seen a hundred gay;
But only think: I peep by night
   And do not peep by day!"

O Lady Moon, your horns point toward the east:
         Shine, be increased;
O Lady Moon, your horns point toward the west:
         Wane, be at rest.

What do the stars do
   Up in the sky,

Higher than the wind can blow,
   Or the clouds can fly?

5   Each star in its own glory
     Circles, circles still;
As it was lit to shine and set,
     And do its Maker's Will.

Motherless baby and babyless mother,
Bring them together to love one another.

Crimson curtains round my mother's bed,
     Silken soft as may be;
Cool white curtains round about my bed,
     For I am but a baby.

Baby lies so fast asleep
     That we cannot wake her:
Will the Angels clad in white
     Fly from heaven to take her?

5   Baby lies so fast asleep
     That no pain can grieve her;
Put a snowdrop in her hand,
     Kiss her once and leave her.

I know a baby, such a baby,—
     Round blue eyes and cheeks of pink,
Such an elbow furrowed with dimples,
     Such a wrist where creases sink.

5   "Cuddle and love me, cuddle and love me"
     Crows the mouth of coral pink:
Oh the bald head, and oh the sweet lips,
     And oh the sleepy eyes that wink!

> Lullaby, oh lullaby!
> Flowers are closed and lambs are sleeping;
> > Lullaby, oh lullaby!
> Stars are up, the moon is peeping;
5 > > Lullaby, oh lullaby!
> While the birds are silence keeping,
> > (Lullaby, oh lullaby!)
> Sleep, my baby, fall a-sleeping,
> > Lullaby, oh lullaby!

Lie a-bed,
Sleepy head,
Shut up eyes, bo-peep;
Till daybreak
5 Never wake:—
Baby, sleep.

Poems Added in *Sing-Song:*
A Nursery Rhyme Book
(1893)

Brownie, Brownie, let down your milk
White as swansdown and smooth as silk,
Fresh as dew and pure as snow:
For I know where the cowslips blow,
5 And you shall have a cowslip wreath
No sweeter scented than your breath.

Stroke a flint, and there is nothing to admire:
Strike a flint, and forthwith flash out sparks of fire.

I am a King,
    Or an Emperor rather,
I wear crown-imperial
    And prince's-feather;
5 Golden-rod is the sceptre
    I wield and wag,
And a broad purple flag flower
    Waves for my flag.

Elder the pithy
10   With old-man and sage,
These are my councillors
    Green in old age;
Lords-and-ladies in silence
    Stand round me and wait,
15 While gay ragged-robin
    Makes bows at my gate.

Playing at bob cherry
   Tom and Nell and Hugh:
Cherry bob! cherry bob!
   There's a bob for you.

5   Tom bobs a cherry
   For gaping snapping Hugh,
While curly-pated Nelly
   Snaps at it too.

Look, look, look—
10   Oh what a sight to see!
The wind is playing cherry bob
   With the cherry tree.

Blind from my birth,
Where flowers are springing
I sit on earth
All dark.
5   Hark! hark!
A lark is singing,
His notes are all for me,
For me his mirth:—
Till some day I shall see
10   Beautiful flowers
And birds in bowers
Where all Joy Bells are ringing.

A Pageant and Other Poems (1881)

Sonnets are full of love, and this my tome
  Has many sonnets: so here now shall be
  One sonnet more, a love sonnet, from me
To her whose heart is my heart's quiet home,
5   To my first Love, my Mother, on whose knee
I learnt love-lore that is not troublesome;
  Whose service is my special dignity,
And she my loadstar while I go and come.
And so because you love me, and because
10   I love you, Mother, I have woven a wreath
    Of rhymes wherewith to crown your honoured name:
    In you not fourscore years can dim the flame
Of love, whose blessed glow transcends the laws
    Of time and change and mortal life and death.

THE KEY-NOTE.

Where are the songs I used to know,
  Where are the notes I used to sing?
  I have forgotten everything
I used to know so long ago;
5 Summer has followed after Spring;
  Now Autumn is so shrunk and sere,
  I scarcely think a sadder thing
  Can be the Winter of my year.

Yet Robin sings thro' Winter's rest,
10   When bushes put their berries on;
    While they their ruddy jewels don,
He sings out of a ruddy breast;

The hips and haws and ruddy breast
　　Make one spot warm where snowflakes lie,
15 They break and cheer the unlovely rest
　　Of Winter's pause—and why not I?

THE MONTHS:
A PAGEANT.

PERSONIFICATIONS.

Boys.	*Girls.*
JANUARY.	FEBRUARY.
MARCH.	APRIL.
JULY.	MAY.
AUGUST.	JUNE.
OCTOBER.	SEPTEMBER.
DECEMBER.	NOVEMBER.

ROBIN REDBREASTS; LAMBS AND SHEEP; NIGHTINGALE AND
NESTLINGS.

Various Flowers, Fruits, etc.

Scene: A COTTAGE WITH ITS GROUNDS.

[A room in a large comfortable cottage; a fire burning on the
　hearth; a table on which the breakfast things have been left
　standing. January discovered seated by the fire.]

　JANUARY.

Cold the day and cold the drifted snow,
Dim the day until the cold dark night.

　　　　　　　　　　　　　　　　　　[Stirs the fire.

Crackle, sparkle, faggot; embers glow:
Some one may be plodding thro' the snow
5 Longing for a light,
For the light that you and I can show.
If no one else should come,
Here Robin Redbreast's welcome to a crumb,
And never troublesome:
10 Robin, why don't you come and fetch your crumb?

Here's butter for my hunch of bread,
    And sugar for your crumb;
Here's room upon the hearthrug,
    If you'll only come.

15 In your scarlet waistcoat,
    With your keen bright eye,
Where are you loitering?
    Wings were made to fly!

Make haste to breakfast,
20   Come and fetch your crumb,
For I'm as glad to see you
    As you are glad to come.

[Two Robin Redbreasts are seen tapping with their beaks at the lattice, which January opens. The birds flutter in, hop about the floor, and peck up the crumbs and sugar thrown to them. They have scarcely finished their meal, when a knock is heard at the door. January hangs a guard in front of the fire, and opens to February, who appears with a bunch of snowdrops in her hand.]

JANUARY.
Good-morrow, sister.

FEBRUARY.
                  Brother, joy to you!
25 I've brought some snowdrops; only just a few,
But quite enough to prove the world awake,
Cheerful and hopeful in the frosty dew
    And for the pale sun's sake.

[She hands a few of her snowdrops to January, who retires into the background. While February stands arranging the remaining snowdrops in a glass of water on the window-sill, a soft butting and bleating are heard outside. She opens the door, and sees one foremost lamb, with other sheep and lambs bleating and crowding towards her.]

FEBRUARY.

O you, you little wonder, come—come in,
30   You wonderful, you woolly soft white lamb:
You panting mother ewe, come too,
And lead that tottering twin
Safe in:
Bring all your bleating kith and kin,
35   Except the horny ram.

[February opens a second door in the background, and
    the little flock files thro' into a warm and sheltered
    compartment out of sight.]

The lambkin tottering in its walk
    With just a fleece to wear;
The snowdrop drooping on its stalk
    So slender,—
40   Snowdrop and lamb, a pretty pair,
Braving the cold for our delight,
    Both white,
    Both tender.

[A rattling of doors and windows; branches seen without,
    tossing violently to and fro.]

How the doors rattle, and the branches sway!
45   Here's brother March comes whirling on his way
With winds that eddy and sing:—

[She turns the handle of the door, which bursts open, and
    discloses March hastening up, both hands full of violets
    and anemones.]

FEBRUARY.

Come, show me what you bring;
For I have said my say, fulfilled my day,
And must away.

MARCH.

[Stopping short on the threshold.]

50   I blow an arouse
        Thro' the world's wide house
    To quicken the torpid earth:
        Grappling I fling
        Each feeble thing,
55 But bring strong life to the birth.
        I wrestle and frown,
        And topple down;
    I wrench, I rend, I uproot;
        Yet the violet
60   Is born where I set
    The sole of my flying foot,

[Hands violets and anemones to February, who retires into the
    background.]

        And in my wake
        Frail windflowers quake,
    And the catkins promise fruit.
65   I drive ocean ashore
        With rush and roar,
    And he cannot say me nay:
        My harpstrings all
        Are the forests tall,
70 Making music when I play.
        And as others perforce,
        So I on my course
    Run and needs must run,
        With sap on the mount
75   And buds past count
    And rivers and clouds and sun,
        With seasons and breath
        And time and death
    And all that has yet begun.

[Before March has done speaking, a voice is heard
    approaching accompanied by a twittering of birds. April
    comes along singing, and stands outside and out of sight
    to finish her song.]

APRIL.

[Outside.]

80   Pretty little three
        Sparrows in a tree,
            Light upon the wing;
            Tho' you cannot sing
            You can chirp of Spring:
85   Chirp of Spring to me,
        Sparrows, from your tree.

        Never mind the showers,
        Chirp about the flowers
            While you build a nest:
90   Straws from east and west,
            Feathers from your breast,
        Make the snuggest bowers
        In a world of flowers.

        You must dart away
95   From the chosen spray,
            You intrusive third
            Extra little bird;
            Join the unwedded herd!
        These have done with play,
100   And must work today.

APRIL.

[Appearing at the open door.]

Good-morrow and good-bye: if others fly,
Of all the flying months you're the most flying.

MARCH.

You're hope and sweetness, April.

APRIL.

Birth means dying,

105 As wings and wind mean flying;
So you and I and all things fly or die;
And sometimes I sit sighing to think of dying.
But meanwhile I've a rainbow in my showers,
And a lapful of flowers,
110 And these dear nestlings aged three hours;
And here's their mother sitting,
Their father's merely flitting
To find their breakfast somewhere in my bowers.

[As she speaks April shows March her apron full of flowers
   and nest full of birds. March wanders away into the grounds.
   April, without entering the cottage, hangs over the hungry
   nestlings watching them.]

APRIL.

What beaks you have, you funny things,
115   What voices shrill and weak;
Who'd think that anything that sings
    Could sing thro' such a beak?
Yet you'll be nightingales one day,
    And charm the country side,
120 When I'm away and far away
    And May is queen and bride.

[May arrives unperceived by April, and gives her a kiss. April
   starts and looks round.]

APRIL.

Ah May, good-morrow May, and so good-bye.

MAY.

That's just your way, sweet April, smile and sigh:
Your sorrow's half in fun,

125   Begun and done
       And turned to joy while twenty seconds run.
       I've gathered flowers all as I came along,
       At every step a flower
       Fed by your last bright shower,—

       [She divides an armful of all sorts of flowers with April, who
          strolls away thro' the garden.]

       MAY.

130   And gathering flowers I listened to the song
       Of every bird in bower.

              The world and I are far too full of bliss
              To think or plan or toil or care;
                 The sun is waxing strong,
135   The days are waxing long,
                    And all that is,
                       Is fair.

              Here are my buds of lily and of rose,
              And here's my namesake blossom may;
140   And from a watery spot
                 See here forget-me-not,
                    With all that blows
                       Today.

              Hark to my linnets from the hedges green,
145   Blackbird and lark and thrush and dove,
                 And every nightingale
                 And cuckoo tells its tale,
                    And all they mean
                       Is love.

       [June appears at the further end of the garden, coming
          slowly towards May, who, seeing her, exclaims]

       MAY.

150   Surely you're come too early, sister June.

JUNE.

Indeed I feel as if I came too soon
To round your young May moon
And set the world a-gasping at my noon.
Yet come I must. So here are strawberries
155 Sun-flushed and sweet, as many as you please;
And here are full-blown roses by the score,
More roses, and yet more.

[May, eating strawberries, withdraws among the flower beds.]

JUNE.

The sun does all my long day's work for me,
    Raises and ripens everything;
160 I need but sit beneath a leafy tree
        And watch and sing.

            [Seats herself in the shadow of a laburnum.

Or if I'm lulled by note of bird and bee,
    Or lulled by noontide's silence deep,
I need but nestle down beneath my tree
165   And drop asleep.

[June falls asleep; and is not awakened by the voice of July,
    who behind the scenes is heard half singing, half calling.]

JULY.

[Behind the scenes.]

Blue flags, yellow flags, flags all freckled,
Which will you take? yellow, blue, speckled!
Take which you will, speckled, blue, yellow,
Each in its way has not a fellow.

[Enter July, a basket of many-coloured irises slung upon his
    shoulders, a bunch of ripe grass in one hand, and a plate
    piled full of peaches balanced upon the other. He steals up
    to June, and tickles her with the grass. She wakes.]

JUNE.

170   What, here already?

JULY.

                        Nay, my tryst is kept;
The longest day slipped by you while you slept.
I've brought you one curved pyramid of bloom,

                              [Hands her the plate.

Not flowers but peaches, gathered where the bees,
175   As downy, bask and boom
In sunshine and in gloom of trees.
But get you in, a storm is at my heels;
The whirlwind whistles and wheels,
Lightning flashes and thunder peals,
180   Flying and following hard upon my heels.

            [June takes shelter in a thickly-woven arbour.]

JULY.

            The roar of a storm sweeps up
                From the east to the lurid west,
            The darkening sky, like a cup,
                Is filled with rain to the brink;
185   The sky is purple and fire,
                Blackness and noise and unrest;
            The earth, parched with desire,
                Opens her mouth to drink.

            Send forth thy thunder and fire,
190   Turn over thy brimming cup,
            O sky, appease the desire
                Of earth in her parched unrest;
            Pour out drink to her thrist,
                Her famishing life lift up;
195   Make thyself fair as at first,
                With a rainbow for thy crest.

Have done with thunder and fire,
    O sky with the rainbow crest;
O earth, have done with desire,
200   Drink, and drink deep, and rest.

[Enter August, carrying a sheaf made up of different kinds of
    grain.]

JULY.

Hail, brother August, flushed and warm
And scatheless from my storm.
Your hands are full of corn, I see,
As full as hands can be:
205 And earth and air both smell as sweet as balm
In their recovered calm,
And that they owe to me.

        [July retires into a shrubbery.]

AUGUST.

Wheat sways heavy, oats are airy,
    Barley bows a graceful head,
210 Short and small shoots up canary,
    Each of these is some one's bread;
Bread for man or bread for beast,
    Or at very least
    A bird's savoury feast.

215 Men are brethren of each other,
    One in flesh and one in food;
And a sort of foster brother
    Is the litter, or the brood,
Of that folk in fur or feather,
220   Who, with men together,
    Breast the wind and weather.

[August descries September toiling across the lawn.]

AUGUST.

My harvest home is ended; and I spy
September drawing nigh
With the first thought of Autumn in her eye,
225   And the first sigh
Of Autumn wind among her locks that fly.

[September arrives, carrying upon her head a basket heaped
    high with fruit.]

SEPTEMBER.

Unload me, brother. I have brought a few
Plums and these pears for you,
A dozen kinds of apples, one or two
230   Melons, some figs all bursting thro'
Their skins, and pearled with dew
These damsons violet-blue.

[While September is speaking, August lifts the basket to the
    ground, selects various fruits, and withdraws slowly along
    the gravel walk, eating a pear as he goes.]

SEPTEMBER.

      My song is half a sigh
      Because my green leaves die;
235 Sweet are my fruits, but all my leaves are dying;
          And well may Autumn sigh,
            And well may I
      Who watch the sere leaves flying.

      My leaves that fade and fall,
240   I note you one and all;
      I call you, and the Autumn wind is calling,
          Lamenting for your fall,
            And for the pall
      You spread on earth in falling.

245 And here's a song of flowers to suit such hours:
A song of the last lilies, the last flowers,
Amid my withering bowers.

In the sunny garden bed
  Lilies look so pale,
250   Lilies droop the head
  In the shady grassy vale;
If all alike they pine
In shade and in shine,
If everywhere they grieve,
255   Where will lilies live?

[October enters briskly, some leafy twigs bearing different
    sorts of nuts in one hand, and a long ripe hop-bine trailing
    after him from the other. A dahlia is stuck in his bottonhole.]

OCTOBER.

Nay, cheer up sister. Life is not quite over,
Even if the year has done with corn and clover,
With flowers and leaves; besides, in fact it's true,
Some leaves remain and some flowers too,
260 For me and you.
Now see my crops:

               [Offering his produce to September.

         I've brought you nuts and hops;
And when the leaf drops, why, the walnut drops.

[October wreaths the hop-bine about September's neck, and
    gives her the nut twigs. They enter the cottage together, but
    without shutting the door. She steps into the background:
    he advances to the hearth, removes the guard, stirs up the
    smouldering fire, and arranges several chestnuts ready to
    roast.]

OCTOBER.

Crack your first nut and light your first fire,
265   Roast your first chestnut crisp on the bar;
Make the logs sparkle, stir the blaze higher,
    Logs are cheery as sun or as star,
    Logs we can find wherever we are.

Spring one soft day will open the leaves,
270   `Spring one bright day will lure back the flowers;
Never fancy my whistling wind grieves,
    Never fancy I've tears in my showers;
    Dance, nights and days! and dance on, my hours!

                  [Sees November approaching.

OCTOBER.

Here comes my youngest sister, looking dim
275 And grim,
With dismal ways.
What cheer, November?

NOVEMBER.

[Entering and shutting the door.]

Nought have I to bring
Tramping a-chill and shivering,
280 Except these pine-cones for a blaze,—
Except a fog which follows,
And stuffs up all the hollows,—
Except a hoar frost here and there,—
Except some shooting stars
285 Which dart their luminous cars
Trackless and noiseless thro' the keen night air.

[October, shrugging his shoulders, withdraws into the
    background, while November throws her pine cones
    on the fire, and sits down listlessly.]

NOVEMBER.

    The earth lies fast asleep, grown tired
      Of all that's high or deep;
    There's nought desired and nought required
290   Save a sleep.

    I rock the cradle of the earth,
      I lull her with a sigh;

> And know that she will wake to mirth
>> By and by.

[Thro' the window December is seen running and leaping in
the direction of the door. He knocks.]

NOVEMBER.

[Calls out without rising.]

295 Ah, here's my youngest brother come at last:
Come in, December.

[He opens the door and enters, loaded with evergreens in
berry, etc.]

NOVEMBER.

>> Come, and shut the door,
> For now it's snowing fast;
> It snows, and will snow more and more;
300 Don't let it drift in on the floor.
> But you, you're all aglow; how can you be
> Rosy and warm and smiling in the cold?

DECEMBER.

> Nay, no closed doors for me,
> But open doors and open hearts and glee
305 To welcome young and old.
>> Dimmest and brightest month am I;
> My short days end, my lengthening days begin;
> What matters more or less sun in the sky,
>> When all is sun within?

>> [He begins making a wreath as he sings.

310 > Ivy and privet dark as night,
> I weave with hips and haws a cheerful show,
> And holly for a beauty and delight,
>> And milky mistletoe.

      While high above them all I set
315 Yew twigs and Christmas roses pure and pale;
      Then Spring her snowdrop and her violet
          May keep, so sweet and frail;

      May keep each merry singing bird,
      Of all her happy birds that singing build:
320 For I've a carol which some shepherds heard
          Once in a wintry field.

     [While December concludes his song all the other Months
        troop in from the garden, or advance out of the background.
        The Twelve join hands in a circle, and begin dancing round
        to a stately measure as the Curtain falls.]

PASTIME.

A boat amid the ripples, drifting, rocking,
     Two idle people, without pause or aim;
While in the ominous west there gathers darkness
     Flushed with flame.

5 A haycock in a hayfield backing, lapping,
     Two drowsy people pillowed round about;
While in the ominous west across the darkness
     Flame leaps out.

Better a wrecked life than a life so aimless,
10   Better a wrecked life than a life so soft;
The ominous west glooms thundering, with its fire
     Lit aloft.

"ITALIA, IO TI SALUTO!"

To come back from the sweet South, to the North
     Where I was born, bred, look to die;
Come back to do my day's work in its day,
        Play out my play—
5   Amen, amen, say I.

To see no more the country half my own,
　　Nor hear the half familiar speech,
Amen, I say; I turn to that bleak North
　　　　Whence I came forth—
10　　The South lies out of reach.

But when our swallows fly back to the South,
　　To the sweet South, to the sweet South,
The tears may come again into my eyes
　　　　On the old wise,
15　　And the sweet name to my mouth.

MIRRORS OF LIFE AND DEATH.

The mystery of Life, the mystery
Of Death, I see
Darkly as in a glass;
Their shadows pass,
5　And talk with me.

As the flush of a Morning Sky,
As a Morning Sky colourless—
Each yields its measure of light
To a wet world or a dry;
10　Each fares thro' day to night
With equal pace,
And then each one
Is done.

As the Sun with glory and grace
15　In his face,
Benignantly hot,
Graciously radiant and keen,
Ready to rise and to run,—
Not without spot,
20　Not even the Sun.

As the Moon
On the wax, on the wane,
With night for her noon;

            Vanishing soon,
25   To appear again.

            As Roses that droop
            Half warm, half chill, in the languid May,
            And breathe out a scent
            Sweet and faint;
30   Till the wind gives one swoop
            To scatter their beauty away.

            As Lilies a multitude,
            One dipping, one rising, one sinking,
            On rippling waters, clear blue
35   And pure for their drinking;
            One new dead, and one opened anew,
            And all good.

            As a cankered pale Flower,
            With death for a dower,
40   Each hour of its life half dead;
            With death for a crown
            Weighing down
            Its head.

            As an Eagle, half strength and half grace,
45   Most potent to face
            Unwinking the splendour of light;
            Harrying the East and the West,
            Soaring aloft from our sight;
            Yet one day or one night dropped to rest,
50   On the low common earth
            Of his birth.

            As a Dove,
            Not alone,
            In a world of her own
55   Full of fluttering soft noises
            And tender sweet voices
            Of love.

            As a Mouse
            Keeping house

60   In the fork of a tree,
     With nuts in a crevice,
     And an acorn or two;
     What cares he
     For blossoming boughs,
65   Or the song-singing bevies
     Of birds in their glee,
     Scarlet, or golden, or blue?

     As a Mole grubbing underground;
     When it comes to the light
70   It grubs its way back again,
     Feeling no bias of fur
     To hamper it in its stir,
     Scant of pleasure and pain,
     Sinking itself out of sight
75   Without sound.

     As Waters that drop and drop,
     Weariness without end,
     That drop and never stop,
     Wear that nothing can mend,
80   Till one day they drop—
     Stop—
     And there's an end,
     And matters mend.

     As Trees, beneath whose skin
85   We mark not the sap begin
     To swell and rise,
     Till the whole bursts out in green:
     We mark the falling leaves
     When the wide world grieves
90   And sighs.

     As a Forest on fire,
     Where maddened creatures desire
     Wet mud or wings
     Beyond all those things
95   Which could assuage desire
     On this side the flaming fire.

As Wind with a sob and sigh
To which there comes no reply
But a rustle and shiver
100 From rushes of the river;
As Wind with a desolate moan,
Moaning on alone.

As a Desert all sand,
Blank, neither water nor land
105 For solace, or dwelling, or culture,
Where the storms and the wild creatures howl;
Given over to lion and vulture,
To ostrich, and jackal, and owl:
Yet somewhere an oasis lies;
110 There waters arise
To nourish one seedling of balm,
Perhaps, or one palm.

As the Sea,
Murmuring, shifting, swaying;
115 One time sunnily playing,
One time wrecking and slaying;
In whichever mood it be,
Worst or best,
Never at rest.

120 As still Waters and deep,
As shallow Waters that brawl,
As rapid Waters that leap
To their fall.

As Music, as Colour, as Shape,
125 Keys of rapture and pain
Turning in vain
In a lock which turns not again,
While breaths and moments escape.

As Spring, all bloom and desire;
130 As Summer, all gift and fire;
As Autumn, a dying glow;
As Winter, with nought to show:

Winter which lays its dead all out of sight,
All clothed in white,
135   All waiting for the long-awaited light.

A BALLAD OF BODING.

There are sleeping dreams and waking dreams;
What seems is not always as it seems.

I looked out of my window in the sweet new morning,
And there I saw three barges of manifold adorning
5   Went sailing toward the East:
The first had sails like fire,
The next like glittering wire,
But sackcloth were the sails of the least;
And all the crews made music, and two had spread a
         feast.

10   The first choir breathed in flutes,
And fingered soft guitars;
The second won from lutes
Harmonious chords and jars,
With drums for stormy bars:
15   But the third was all of harpers and scarlet trumpeters;
Notes of triumph, then
An alarm again,
As for onset, as for victory, rallies, stirs,
Peace at last and glory to the vanquishers.

20   The first barge showed for figurehead a Love with wings;
The second showed for figurehead a Worm with stings;
The third, a Lily tangled to a Rose which clings.
The first bore for freight gold and spice and down;
The second bore a sword, a sceptre, and a crown;
25   The third, a heap of earth gone to dust and brown.
Winged Love meseemed like Folly in the face;
Stinged Worm meseemed loathly in his place;
Lily and Rose were flowers of grace.

Merry went the revel of the fire-sailed crew,
30   Singing, feasting, dancing to and fro:
Pleasures ever changing, ever graceful, ever new;
Sighs, but scarce of woe;
All the sighing
Wooed such sweet replying;
35   All the sighing, sweet and low,
Used to come and go
For more pleasure, merely so.
Yet at intervals some one grew tired
Of everything desired,
40   And sank, I knew not whither, in sorry plight,
Out of sight.

The second crew seemed ever
Wider-visioned, graver,
More distinct of purpose, more sustained of will;
45   With heads erect and proud,
And voices sometimes loud;
With endless tacking, counter-tacking,
All things grasping, all things lacking,
It would seem;
50   Ever shifting helm, or sail, or shroud,
Drifting on as in a dream.
Hoarding to their utmost bent,
Feasting to their fill,
Yet gnawed by discontent,
55   Envy, hatred, malice, on their road they went.
Their freight was not a treasure,
Their music not a pleasure;
The sword flashed, cleaving thro' their bands,
Sceptre and crown changed hands.

60   The third crew as they went
Seemed mostly different;
They toiled in rowing, for to them the wind was contrary,
As all the world might see.
They laboured at the oar,
65   While on their heads they bore
The fiery stress of sunshine more and more.

They laboured at the oar hand-sore,
Till rain went splashing,
And spray went dashing,
70 Down on them, and up on them, more and more.
Their sails were patched and rent,
Their masts were bent,
In peril of their lives they worked and went.
For them no feast was spread,
75 No soft luxurious bed
Scented and white,
No crown or sceptre hung in sight;
In weariness and painfulness,
In thirst and sore distress,
80 They rowed and steered from left to right
With all their might.
Their trumpeters and harpers round about
Incessantly played out,
And sometimes they made answer with a shout;
85 But oftener they groaned or wept,
And seldom paused to eat, and seldom slept.
I wept for pity watching them, but more
I wept heart-sore
Once and again to see
90 Some weary man plunge overboard, and swim
To Love or Worm ship floating buoyantly:
And there all welcomed him.

The ships steered each apart and seemed to scorn each
    other,
Yet all the crews were interchangeable;
95 Now one man, now another,
—Like bloodless spectres some, some flushed by health,—
Changed openly, or changed by stealth,
Scaling a slippery side, and scaled it well.
The most left Love ship, hauling wealth
100 Up Worm ship's side;
While some few hollow-eyed
Left either for the sack-sailed boat;
But this, tho' not remote,

Was worst to mount, and whoso left it once
105 Scarce ever came again,
But seemed to loathe his erst companions,
And wish and work them bane.

Then I knew (I know not how) there lurked quicksands
                    full of dread,
Rocks and reefs and whirlpools in the water bed,
110 Whence a waterspout
Instantaneously leaped out,
Roaring as it reared its head.
Soon I spied a something dim,
Many-handed, grim,
115 That went flitting to and fro the first and second ship;
It puffed their sails full out
With puffs of smoky breath
From a smouldering lip,
And cleared the waterspout
120 Which reeled roaring round about
Threatening death.
With a horny hand it steered,
And a horn appeared
On its sneering head upreared
125 Haughty and high
Against the blackening lowering sky.
With a hoof it swayed the waves;
They opened here and there,
Till I spied deep ocean graves
130 Full of skeletons
That were men and women once
Foul or fair;
Full of things that creep
And fester in the deep
135 And never breathe the clean life-nurturing air.

The third bark held aloof
From the Monster with the hoof,
Despite his urgent beck,
And fraught with guile
140 Abominable his smile;

Till I saw him take a flying leap on to that deck.
Then full of awe,
With these same eyes I saw
His head incredible retract its horn
145   Rounding like babe's new born,
While silvery phosphorescence played
About his dis-horned head.
The sneer smoothed from his lip,
He beamed blandly on the ship;
150   All winds sank to a moan,
All waves to a monotone
(For all these seemed his realm),
While he laid a strong caressing hand upon the helm.

Then a cry well nigh of despair
155   Shrieked to heaven, a clamour of desperate prayer.
The harpers harped no more,
While the trumpeters sounded sore,
An alarm to wake the dead from their bed:
To the rescue, to the rescue, now or never,
160   To the rescue, O ye living, O ye dead,
Or no more help or hope for ever!—
The planks strained as tho' they must part asunder,
The masts bent as tho' they must dip under,
And the winds and the waves at length
165   Girt up their strength,
And the depths were laid bare,
And heaven flashed fire and volleyed thunder
Thro' the rain-choked air,
And sea and sky seemed to kiss
170   In the horror and the hiss
Of the whole world shuddering everywhere.

Lo! a Flyer swooping down
With wings to span the globe,
And splendour for his robe
175   And splendour for his crown.
He lighted on the helm with a foot of fire,
And spun the Monster overboard:
And that monstrous thing abhorred,

Gnashing with balked desire,
180 Wriggled like a worm infirm
     Up the Worm
     Of the loathly figurehead.
     There he crouched and gnashed;
     And his head re-horned, and gashed
185 From the other's grapple, dripped bloody red.

     I saw that thing accurst
     Wreak his worst
     On the first and second crew:
     Some with baited hook
190 He angled for and took,
     Some dragged overboard in a net he threw,
     Some he did to death
     With hoof or horn or blasting breath.

     I heard a voice of wailing
195 Where the ships went sailing,
     A sorrowful voice prevailing
     Above the sound of the sea,
     Above the singers' voices,
     And musical merry noises;
200 All songs had turned to sighing,
     The light was failing,
     The day was dying—
     Ah me,.
     That such a sorrow should be!

205 There was sorrow on the sea and sorrow on the land
     When Love ship went down by the bottomless quicksand
     To its grave in the bitter wave.
     There was sorrow on the sea and sorrow on the land
     When Worm ship went to pieces on the rock-bound
               strand,
210 And the bitter wave was its grave.
     But land and sea waxed hoary
     In whiteness of a glory
     Never told in story
     Nor seen by mortal eye,
215 When the third ship crossed the bar

Where whirls and breakers are,
And steered into the splendours of the sky;
That third bark and that least
Which had never seemed to feast,
220 Yet kept high festival above sun and moon and star.

YET A LITTLE WHILE.

I dreamed and did not seek: today I seek
    Who can no longer dream;
But now am all behindhand, waxen weak,
    And dazed amid so many things that gleam
5   Yet are not what they seem.

I dreamed and did not work: today I work
    Kept wide awake by care
And loss, and perils dimly guessed to lurk;
    I work and reap not, while my life goes bare
10   And void in wintry air.

I hope indeed; but hope itself is fear
    Viewed on the sunny side;
I hope, and disregard the world that's here,
    The prizes drawn, the sweet things that betide;
15   I hope, and I abide.

HE AND SHE.

"Should one of us remember,
    And one of us forget,
I wish I knew what each will do—
    But who can tell as yet?"

5 "Should one of us remember,
    And one of us forget,
I promise you what I will do—
And I'm content to wait for you,
    And not be sure as yet."

MONNA INNOMINATA.
A Sonnet Of Sonnets.

Beatrice, immortalized by "altissimo poeta . . . cotanto amante"; Laura, celebrated by a great tho' an inferior bard,— have alike paid the exceptional penalty of exceptional honour, and have come down to us resplendent with charms, but (at least, to my apprehension) scant of attractiveness.

These heroines of world-wide fame were preceded by a bevy of unnamed ladies "donne innominate" sung by a school of less conspicuous poets; and in that land and that period which gave simultaneous birth to Catholics, to Albigenses, and to Troubadours, one can imagine many a lady as sharing her lover's poetic aptitude, while the barrier between them might be one held sacred by both, yet not such as to render mutual love incompatible with mutual honour.

Had such a lady spoken for herself, the portrait left us might have appeared more tender, if less dignified, than any drawn even by a devoted friend. Or had the Great Poetess of our own day and nation only been unhappy instead of happy, her circumstances would have invited her to bequeath to us, in lieu of the "Portuguese Sonnets," an inimitable "donna innominata" drawn not from fancy but from feeling, and worthy to occupy a niche beside Beatrice and Laura.

1.

"Lo dì che han detto a' dolci amici addio."—Dante.
"Amor, con quanto sforzo oggi mi vinci!"—Petrarca.

Come back to me, who wait and watch for you:—
    Or come not yet, for it is over then,
    And long it is before you come again,
So far between my pleasures are and few.
5 While, when you come not, what I do I do
    Thinking "Now when he comes," my sweetest "when:"
    For one man is my world of all the men
This wide world holds; O love, my world is you.
Howbeit, to meet you grows almost a pang
10   Because the pang of parting comes so soon;

My hope hangs waning, waxing, like a moon
 Between the heavenly days on which we meet:
Ah me, but where are now the songs I sang
 When life was sweet because you called them sweet?

2.

"Era già l'ora che volge il desio."—DANTE.
"Ricorro al tempo ch'io vi vidi prima."—PETRARCA.

I wish I could remember that first day,
 First hour, first moment of your meeting me,
 If bright or dim the season, it might be
Summer or Winter for aught I can say;
5 So unrecorded did it slip away,
 So blind was I to see and to foresee,
 So dull to mark the budding of my tree
That would not blossom yet for many a May.
If only I could recollect it, such
10 A day of days! I let it come and go
 As traceless as a thaw of bygone snow;
It seemed to mean so little, meant so much;
If only now I could recall that touch,
 First touch of hand in hand—Did one but know!

3.

"O ombre vane, fuor che ne l'aspetto!"—DANTE.
"Immaginata guida la conduce."—PETRARCA.

I dream of you to wake: would that I might
 Dream of you and not wake but slumber on;
 Nor find with dreams the dear companion gone,
As Summer ended Summer birds take flight.
5 In happy dreams I hold you full in sight,
 I blush again who waking look so wan;
 Brighter than sunniest day that ever shone,
In happy dreams your smile makes day of night.
Thus only in a dream we are at one,
10 Thus only in a dream we give and take
 The faith that maketh rich who take or give;

If thus to sleep is sweeter than to wake,
    To die were surely sweeter than to live,
Tho' there be nothing new beneath the sun.

4.

"Poca favilla gran fiamma seconda."—DANTE.
"Ogni altra cosa, ogni pensier va fore,
  E sol ivi con voi rimansi amore."—PETRARCA.

I loved you first: but afterwards your love
    Outsoaring mine, sang such a loftier song
As drowned the friendly cooings of my dove.
    Which owes the other most? my love was long,
5   And yours one moment seemed to wax more strong;
I loved and guessed at you, you construed me
And loved me for what might or might not be—
    Nay, weights and measures do us both a wrong.
For verily love knows not "mine" or "thine;"
10   With separate "I" and "thou" free love has done,
      For one is both and both are one in love:
Rich love knows nought of "thine that is not mine;"
    Both have the strength and both the length thereof,
    Both of us, of the love which makes us one.

5.

"Amor che a nulla amato amar perdona."—DANTE.
"Amor m'addusse in sì gioiosa spene."—PETRARCA.

O my heart's heart, and you who are to me
    More than myself myself, God be with you,
    Keep you in strong obedience leal and true
To Him whose noble service setteth free,
5   Give you all good we see or can foresee,
    Make your joys many and your sorrows few,
    Bless you in what you bear and what you do,
Yea, perfect you as He would have you be.
So much for you; but what for me, dear friend?
10   To love you without stint and all I can

Today, tomorrow, world without an end;
    To love you much and yet to love you more,
    As Jordan at his flood sweeps either shore;
Since woman is the helpmeet made for man.

6.

"Or puoi la quantitate
Comprender de l'amor che a te mi scalda."—DANTE.
"Non vo'che da tal nodo amor mi scioglia."—PETRARCA.

Trust me, I have not earned your dear rebuke,
    I love, as you would have me, God the most;
    Would lose not Him, but you, must one be lost,
Nor with Lot's wife cast back a faithless look
5   Unready to forego what I forsook;
    This say I, having counted up the cost,
    This, tho' I be the feeblest of God's host,
The sorriest sheep Christ shepherds with His crook.
Yet while I love my God the most, I deem
10   That I can never love you overmuch;
    I love Him more, so let me love you too;
    Yea, as I apprehend it, love is such
I cannot love you if I love not Him,
    I cannot love Him if I love not you.

7.

"Qui primavera sempre ed ogni frutto."—DANTE.
"Ragionando con meco ed io con lui."—PETRARCA.

"Love me, for I love you"—and answer me,
    "Love me, for I love you"—so shall we stand
    As happy equals in the flowering land
Of love, that knows not a dividing sea.
5   Love builds the house on rock and not on sand,
    Love laughs what while the winds rave desperately;
    And who hath found love's citadel unmanned?
    And who hath held in bonds love's liberty?
My heart's a coward tho' my words are brave—

10   We meet so seldom, yet we surely part
            So often; there's a problem for your art!
                Still I find comfort in his Book, who saith,
        Tho' jealousy be cruel as the grave,
            And death be strong, yet love is strong as death.

            8.

            "Come dicesse a Dio: D'altro non calme."—DANTE.
            "Spero trovar pietà non che perdono."—PETRARCA.

        "I, if I perish, perish"—Esther spake:
            And bride of life or death she made her fair
            In all the lustre of her perfumed hair
        And smiles that kindle longing but to slake.
5   She put on pomp of loveliness, to take
            Her husband thro' his eyes at unaware;
            She spread abroad her beauty for a snare,
        Harmless as doves and subtle as a snake.
        She trapped him with one mesh of silken hair,
10   She vanquished him by wisdom of her wit,
                And built her people's house that it should stand:—
                If I might take my life so in my hand,
        And for my love to Love put up my prayer,
            And for love's sake by Love be granted it!

            9.

            "O dignitosa coscienza e netta!"—DANTE.
            "Spirto più acceso di virtuti ardenti."—PETRARCA.

        Thinking of you, and all that was, and all
            That might have been and now can never be,
            I feel your honoured excellence, and see
        Myself unworthy of the happier call:
5   For woe is me who walk so apt to fall,
            So apt to shrink afraid, so apt to flee,
            Apt to lie down and die (ah, woe is me!)
        Faithless and hopeless turning to the wall.
        And yet not hopeless quite nor faithless quite,

10   Because not loveless; love may toil all night,
            But take at morning; wrestle till the break
                Of day, but then wield power with God and man:—
            So take I heart of grace as best I can,
        Ready to spend and be spent for your sake.

                    10.

            "Con miglior corso e con migliore stella."—DANTE.
            "La vita fugge e non s'arresta un' ora."—PETRARCA.

        Time flies, hope flags, life plies a wearied wing;
            Death following hard on life gains ground apace;
            Faith runs with each and rears an eager face,
        Outruns the rest, makes light of everything,
5   Spurns earth, and still finds breath to pray and sing;
            While love ahead of all uplifts his praise,
            Still asks for grace and still gives thanks for grace,
        Content with all day brings and night will bring.
        Life wanes; and when love folds his wings above
10   Tired hope, and less we feel his conscious pulse,
                Let us go fall asleep, dear friend, in peace:
                A little while, and age and sorrow cease;
            A little while, and life reborn annuls
        Loss and decay and death, and all is love.

                    11.

            "Vien dietro a me e lascia dir le genti."—DANTE.
            "Contando i casi della vita nostra."—PETRARCA.

        Many in aftertimes will say of you
            "He loved her"—while of me what will they say?
            Not that I loved you more than just in play,
        For fashion's sake as idle women do.
5   Even let them prate; who know not what we knew
            Of love and parting in exceeding pain,
            Of parting hopeless here to meet again,
        Hopeless on earth, and heaven is out of view.
        But by my heart of love laid bare to you,

10   My love that you can make not void nor vain,
    Love that foregoes you but to claim anew
            Beyond this passage of the gate of death,
    I charge you at the Judgment make it plain
            My love of you was life and not a breath.

        12.

        "Amor, che ne la mente mi ragiona."—DANTE.
        "Amor vien nel bel viso di costei."—PETRARCA.

    If there be any one can take my place
        And make you happy whom I grieve to grieve,
        Think not that I can grudge it, but believe
    I do commend you to that nobler grace,
5   That readier wit than mine, that sweeter face;
        Yea, since your riches make me rich, conceive
        I too am crowned, while bridal crowns I weave,
    And thread the bridal dance with jocund pace.
    For if I did not love you, it might be
10   That I should grudge you some one dear delight;
            But since the heart is yours that was mine own,
        Your pleasure is my pleasure, right my right,
    Your honourable freedom makes me free,
            And you companioned I am not alone.

        13.

        "E drizzeremo glí occhi al Primo Amore."—DANTE.
        "Ma trovo peso non da le mie braccia."—PETRARCA.

    If I could trust mine own self with your fate,
        Shall I not rather trust it in God's hand?
        Without Whose Will one lily doth not stand,
    Nor sparrow fall at his appointed date;
5   Who numbereth the innumerable sand,
    Who weighs the wind and water with a weight,
    To Whom the world is neither small nor great,
        Whose knowledge foreknew every plan we planned.
    Searching my heart for all that touches you,
10   I find there only love and love's goodwill

Helpless to help and impotent to do,
 Of understanding dull, of sight most dim;
 And therefore I commend you back to Him
Whose love your love's capacity can fill.

14.

"E la Sua Volontade è nostra pace."—DANTE.
"Sol con questi pensier, con altre chiome."—PETRARCA.

Youth gone, and beauty gone if ever there
 Dwelt beauty in so poor a face as this;
 Youth gone and beauty, what remains of bliss?
I will not bind fresh roses in my hair,
5 To shame a cheek at best but little fair,—
 Leave youth his roses, who can bear a thorn,—
I will not seek for blossoms anywhere,
 Except such common flowers as blow with corn.
Youth gone and beauty gone, what doth remain?
10 The longing of a heart pent up forlorn,
 A silent heart whose silence loves and longs;
 The silence of a heart which sang its songs
While youth and beauty made a summer morn,
Silence of love that cannot sing again.

"LUSCIOUS AND SORROWFUL."

Beautiful, tender, wasting away for sorrow;
Thus today; and how shall it be with thee tomorrow?
 Beautiful, tender—what else?
  A hope tells.

5 Beautiful, tender, keeping the jubilee
In the land of home together, past death and sea;
 No more change or death, no more
  Salt sea-shore.

DE PROFUNDIS.

Oh why is heaven built so far,
    Oh why is earth set so remote?
I cannot reach the nearest star
    That hangs afloat.

5   I would not care to reach the moon,
    One round monotonous of change;
Yet even she repeats her tune
    Beyond my range.

I never watch the scattered fire
10   Of stars, or sun's far-trailing train,
But all my heart is one desire,
    And all in vain:

For I am bound with fleshly bands,
    Joy, beauty, lie beyond my scope;
15 I strain my heart, I stretch my hands,
    And catch at hope.

TEMPUS FUGIT.

Lovely Spring,
A brief sweet thing,
Is swift on the wing;
Gracious Summer,
5   A slow sweet comer,
Hastens past;
Autumn while sweet
Is all incomplete
With a moaning blast,—
10 Nothing can last,
Can be cleaved unto,
Can be dwelt upon;
It is hurried thro',
It is come and gone,
15 Undone it cannot be done,
It is ever to do,

Ever old, ever new,
Ever waxing old
And lapsing to Winter cold.

GOLDEN GLORIES.

The buttercup is like a golden cup,
　　The marigold is like a golden frill,
The daisy with a golden eye looks up,
　　And golden spreads the flag beside the rill,
5　　　And gay and golden nods the daffodil,
The gorsey common swells a golden sea,
　　The cowslip hangs a head of golden tips,
And golden drips the honey which the bee
　　Sucks from sweet hearts of flowers and stores and sips.

JOHNNY.
Founded On An Anecdote Of The First French
Revolution.

Johnny had a golden head
　　Like a golden mop in blow,
Right and left his curls would spread
　　In a glory and a glow,
5　　And they framed his honest face
Like stray sunbeams out of place.

Long and thick, they half could hide
　　How threadbare his patched jacket hung;
They used to be his Mother's pride;
10　　She praised them with a tender tongue,
And stroked them with a loving finger
That smoothed and stroked and loved to linger.

On a doorstep Johnny sat,
　　Up and down the street looked he;
15　Johnny did not own a hat,
　　Hot or cold tho' days might be;

Johnny did not own a boot
To cover up his muddy foot.

Johnny's face was pale and thin,
20   Pale with hunger and with crying;
For his Mother lay within,
        Talked and tossed and seemed a-dying,
While Johnny racked his brains to think
How to get her help and drink,

25   Get her physic, get her tea,
        Get her bread and something nice;
Not a penny piece had he,
        And scarce a shilling might suffice;
No wonder that his soul was sad,
30   When not one penny piece he had.

As he sat there thinking, moping,
        Because his Mother's wants were many,
Wishing much but scarcely hoping
        To earn a shilling or a penny,
35   A friendly neighbour passed him by
And questioned him: Why did he cry?

Alas! his trouble soon was told:
        He did not cry for cold or hunger,
Tho' he was hungry both and cold;
40   He only felt more weak and younger,
Because he wished so to be old
And apt at earning pence or gold.

Kindly that neighbour was, but poor,
        Scant coin had he to give or lend;
45   And well he guessed there needed more
        Than pence or shillings to befriend
The helpless woman in her strait,
So much loved, yet so desolate.

One way he saw, and only one:
50   He would—he could not—give the advice,
And yet he must: the widow's son
        Had curls of gold would fetch their price;

Long curls which might be clipped, and sold
For silver, or perhaps for gold.

55 Our Johnny, when he understood
    Which shop it was that purchased hair,
Ran off as briskly as he could,
    And in a trice stood cropped and bare,
Too short of hair to fill a locket,
60 But jingling money in his pocket.

Precious money—tea and bread,
    Physic, ease, for Mother dear,
Better than a golden head:
    Yet our hero dropped one tear
65 When he spied himself close shorn,
Barer much than lamb new born.

His Mother throve upon the money,
    Ate and revived and kissed her son:
But oh! when she perceived her Johnny,
70   And understood what he had done
All and only for her sake,
She sobbed as if her heart must break.

"HOLLOW-SOUNDING AND MYSTERIOUS."

There's no replying
To the Wind's sighing,
Telling, foretelling,
Dying, undying,
5 Dwindling and swelling,
Complaining, droning,
Whistling and moaning,
Ever beginning,
Ending, repeating,
10 Hinting and dinning,
Lagging and fleeting—
We've no replying
Living or dying
To the Wind's sighing.

15   What are you telling,
        Variable Wind-tone?
        What would be teaching,
        O sinking, swelling,
        Desolate Wind-moan?
20   Ever for ever
        Teaching and preaching,
        Never, ah never
        Making us wiser—
        The earliest riser
25   Catches no meaning,
        The last who hearkens
        Garners no gleaning
        Of wisdom's treasure,
        While the world darkens:—
30   Living or dying,
        In pain, in pleasure,
        We've no replying
        To wordless flying
        Wind's sighing.

MAIDEN MAY.

        Maiden May sat in her bower,
        In her blush rose bower in flower,
                Sweet of scent;
        Sat and dreamed away an hour,
5   Half content, half uncontent.

        "Why should rose blossoms be born,
        Tender blossoms, on a thorn
                Tho' so sweet?
        Never a thorn besets the corn
10   Scentless in its strength complete.

        "Why are roses all so frail,
        At the mercy of a gale,
                Of a breath?

Yet so sweet and perfect pale,
15   Still so sweet in life and death."

Maiden May sat in her bower,
In her blush rose bower in flower,
        Where a linnet
Made one bristling branch the tower
20   For her nest and young ones in it.

"Gay and clear the linnet trills;
Yet the skylark only, thrills
        Heaven and earth
When he breasts the height, and fills
25   Height and depth with song and mirth.

"Nightingales which yield to night
Solitary strange delight,
        Reign alone:
But the lark for all his height
30   Fills no solitary throne;

"While he sings, a hundred sing;
Wing their flight below his wing
        Yet in flight;
Each a lovely joyful thing
35   To the measure of its delight.

"Why then should a lark be reckoned
One alone, without a second
        Near his throne?
He in skyward flight unslackened,
40   In his music, not alone."

Maiden May sat in her bower;
Her own face was like a flower
        Of the prime,
Half in sunshine, half in shower,
45   In the year's most tender time.

Her own thoughts in silent song
Musically flowed along,
        Wise, unwise,

Wistful, wondering, weak or strong:
50   As brook shallows sink or rise.

Other thoughts another day,
Maiden May, will surge and sway
        Round your heart;
Wake, and plead, and turn at bay,
55   Wisdom part, and folly part.

Time not far remote will borrow
Other joys, another sorrow,
        All for you;
Not today, and yet tomorrow
60   Reasoning false and reasoning true.

Wherefore greatest? Wherefore least?
Hearts that starve and hearts that feast?
        You and I?
Stammering Oracles have ceased,
65   And the whole earth stands at "why?"

Underneath all things that be
Lies an unsolved mystery;
        Over all
Spreads a veil impenetrably,
70   Spreads a dense unlifted pall.

Mystery of mysteries:
This creation hears and sees
        High and low—
Vanity of vanities:
75   *This* we test and *this* we know.

Maiden May, the days of flowering
Nurse you now in sweet embowering,
        Sunny days;
Bright with rainbows all the showering,
80   Bright with blossoms all the ways.

Close the inlet of your bower,
Close it close with thorn and flower,
        Maiden May;
Lengthen out the shortening hour,—
85   Morrows are not as today.

Stay today which wanes too soon,
Stay the sun and stay the moon,
      Stay your youth;
Bask you in the actual noon,
90   Rest you in the present truth.

Let today suffice today:
For itself tomorrow may
      Fetch its loss,
Aim and stumble, say its say,
95   Watch and pray and bear its cross.

TILL TOMORROW.

Long have I longed, till I am tired
      Of longing and desire;
Farewell my points in vain desired,
      My dying fire;
5 Farewell all things that die and fail and tire.

Springtide and youth and useless pleasure
      And all my useless scheming,
My hopes of unattainable treasure,
      Dreams not worth dreaming,
10 Glow-worms that gleam but yield no warmth in gleaming,

Farewell all shows that fade in showing:
      My wish and joy stand over
Until tomorrow; Heaven is glowing
      Thro' cloudy cover,
15 Beyond all clouds loves me my Heavenly Lover.

DEATH-WATCHES.

The Spring spreads one green lap of flowers
      Which Autumn buries at the fall,
No chilling showers of Autumn hours
      Can stay them or recall;

5   Winds sing a dirge, while earth lays out of sight
     Her garment of delight.

     The cloven East brings forth the sun,
         The cloven West doth bury him
     What time his gorgeous race is run
10   And all the world grows dim;
     A funeral moon is lit in heaven's hollow,
     And pale the star-lights follow.

TOUCHING "NEVER."

Because you never yet have loved me, dear,
    Think you you never can nor ever will?
    Surely while life remains hope lingers still,
Hope the last blossom of life's dying year.
5   Because the season and mine age grow sere,
    Shall never Spring bring forth her daffodil,
    Shall never sweeter Summer feast her fill
Of roses with the nightingales they hear?
If you had loved me, I not loving you,
10   If you had urged me with the tender plea
Of what our unknown years to come might do
(Eternal years, if Time should count too few),
    I would have owned the point you pressed on me,
Was possible, or probable, or true.

BRANDONS BOTH.

Oh fair Milly Brandon, a young maid, a fair maid!
    All her curls are yellow and her eyes are blue,
And her cheeks were rosy red till a secret care made
    Hollow whiteness of their brightness as a care will do.

5   Still she tends her flowers, but not as in the old days,
    Still she sings her songs, but not the songs of old:
If now it be high Summer her days seem brief and cold
        days,
    If now it be high Summer her nights are long and cold.

If you have a secret keep it, pure maid Milly;
10   Life is filled with troubles and the world with scorn;
And pity without love is at best times hard and chilly,
    Chilling sore and stinging sore a heart forlorn.

Walter Brandon, do you guess Milly Brandon's secret?
    Many things you know, but not everything,
15   With your locks like raven's plumage, and eyes like an egret,
    And a laugh that is music, and such a voice to sing.

Nelly Knollys, she is fair, but she is not fairer
    Than fairest Milly Brandon was before she turned so
       pale:
Oh, but Nelly's dearer if she be not rarer,
20   She need not keep a secret or blush behind a veil.

Beyond the first green hills, beyond the nearest valleys,
    Nelly dwells at home beneath her mother's eyes:
Her home is neat and homely, not a cot and not a palace,
    Just the home where love sets up his happiest
       memories.

25   Milly has no mother; and sad beyond another
    Is she whose blessed mother is vanished out of call:
Truly comfort beyond comfort is stored up in a Mother
    Who bears with all, and hopes thro' all, and loves us all.

Where peacocks nod and flaunt up and down the terrace,
30   Furling and unfurling their scores of sightless eyes,
To and fro among the leaves and buds and flowers and
      berries
    Maiden Milly strolls and pauses, smiles and sighs.

On the hedged-in terrace of her father's palace
    She may stroll and muse alone, may smile or sigh alone,
35   Letting thoughts and eyes go wandering over hills and
      valleys
    Today her father's, and one day to be all her own.

If her thoughts go coursing down lowlands and up
      highlands,
    It is because the startled game are leaping from their
      lair;

If her thoughts dart homeward to the reedy river islands,
40   It is because the waterfowl rise startled here or there.

At length a footfall on the steps: she turns, composed and
              steady,
       All the long-descended greatness of her father's house
Lifting up her head; and there stands Walter keen and
              ready
       For hunting or for hawking, a flush upon his brows.

45   "Good-morrow, fair cousin." "Good-morrow, fairest
              cousin:
       The sun has started on his course, and I must start
              today.
If you have done me one good turn you've done me many
              a dozen,
       And I shall often think of you, think of you away."

"Over hill and hollow what quarry will you follow,
50   Or what fish will you angle for beside the river's edge?
There's cloud upon the hill-top and there's mist deep
              down the hollow,
       And fog among the rushes and the rustling sedge."

"I shall speed well enough be it hunting or hawking,
       Or casting a bait toward the shyest daintiest fin.
55   But I kiss your hands, my cousin; I must not loiter
              talking,
       For nothing comes of nothing, and I'm fain to seek and
              win."

"Here's a thorny rose: will you wear it an hour,
       Till the petals drop apart still fresh and pink and sweet?
Till the petals drop from the drooping perished flower,
60   And only the graceless thorns are left of it."

"Nay, I have another rose sprung in another garden,
       Another rose which sweetens all the world for me.
Be you a tenderer mistress and be you a warier warden
       Of your rose, as sweet as mine, and full as fair to see."

65   "Nay, a bud once plucked there is no reviving,
       Nor is it worth your wearing now, nor worth indeed my
              own;

The dead to the dead, and the living to the living.
　　It's time I go within, for it's time now you were gone."

"Good-bye, Milly Brandon, I shall not forget you,
70　　Tho' it be good-bye between us for ever from today;
I could almost wish today that I had never met you,
　　And I'm true to you in this one word that I say."

"Good-bye, Walter. I can guess which thornless rose you
　　　covet;
　　Long may it bloom and prolong its sunny morn:
75　Yet as for my one thorny rose, I do not cease to love it,
　　And if it is no more a flower I love it as a thorn."

A LIFE'S PARALLELS.

Never on this side of the grave again,
　　On this side of the river,
On this side of the garner of the grain,
　　　　Never,—

5　Ever while time flows on and on and on,
　　That narrow noiseless river,
Ever while corn bows heavy-headed, wan,
　　　　Ever,—

Never despairing, often fainting, rueing,
10　　But looking back, ah never!
Faint yet pursuing, faint yet still pursuing
　　　　Ever.

AT LAST.

Many have sung of love a root of bane:
　　While to my mind a root of balm it is,
　　For love at length breeds love; sufficient bliss
For life and death and rising up again.
5　Surely when light of Heaven makes all things plain,
　　Love will grow plain with all its mysteries;
　　Nor shall we need to fetch from over seas

Wisdom or wealth or pleasure safe from pain.
Love in our borders, love within our heart,
10 Love all in all, we then shall bide at rest,
Ended for ever life's unending quest,
Ended for ever effort, change and fear:
Love all in all;—no more that better part
Purchased, but at the cost of all things here.

GOLDEN SILENCES.

There is silence that saith, "Ah me!"
There is silence that nothing saith;
One the silence of life forlorn,
One the silence of death;
5 One is, and the other shall be.

One we know and have known for long,
One we know not, but we shall know,
All we who have ever been born;
Even so, be it so,—
10 There is silence, despite a song.

Sowing day is a silent day,
Resting night is a silent night;
But whoso reaps the ripened corn
Shall shout in his delight,
15 While silences vanish away.

IN THE WILLOW SHADE.

I sat beneath a willow tree,
Where water falls and calls;
While fancies upon fancies solaced me,
Some true, and some were false.

5 Who set their heart upon a hope
That never comes to pass,
Droop in the end like fading heliotrope
The sun's wan looking-glass.

Who set their will upon a whim
10   Clung to thro' good and ill,
Are wrecked alike whether they sink or swim,
    Or hit or miss their will.

All things are vain that wax and wane,
    For which we waste our breath;
15   Love only doth not wane and is not vain,
    Love only outlives death.

A singing lark rose toward the sky,
    Circling he sang amain;
He sang, a speck scarce visible sky-high,
20   And then he sank again.

A second like a sunlit spark
    Flashed singing up his track;
But never overtook that foremost lark,
    And songless fluttered back.

25   A hovering melody of birds
    Haunted the air above;
They clearly sang contentment without words,
    And youth and joy and love.

O silvery weeping willow tree
30   With all leaves shivering,
Have you no purpose but to shadow me
    Beside this rippled spring?

On this first fleeting day of Spring,
    For Winter is gone by,
35   And every bird on every quivering wing
    Floats in a sunny sky;

On this first Summer-like soft day,
    While sunshine steeps the air,
And every cloud has gat itself away,
40   And birds sing everywhere.

Have you no purpose in the world
    But thus to shadow me
With all your tender drooping twigs unfurled,
    O weeping willow tree?

45 With all your tremulous leaves outspread
    Betwixt me and the sun,
While here I loiter on a mossy bed
    With half my work undone;

My work undone, that should be done
50   At once with all my might;
For after the long day and lingering sun
    Comes the unworking night.

This day is lapsing on its way,
    Is lapsing out of sight;
55 And after all the chances of the day
    Comes the resourceless night.

The weeping willow shook its head
    And stretched its shadow long;
The west grew crimson, the sun smouldered red,
60   The birds forbore a song.

Slow wind sighed thro' the willow leaves,
    The ripple made a moan,
The world drooped murmuring like a thing that grieves;
    And then I felt alone.

65 I rose to go, and felt the chill,
    And shivered as I went;
Yet shivering wondered, and I wonder still,
    What more that willow meant;

That silvery weeping willow tree
70   With all leaves shivering,
Which spent one long day overshadowing me
    Beside a spring in Spring.

FLUTTERED WINGS.

The splendour of the kindling day,
    The splendour of the setting sun,
These move my soul to wend its way,
    And have done
5 With all we grasp and toil amongst and say.

The paling roses of a cloud,
  The fading bow that arches space,
These woo my fancy toward my shroud;
    Toward the place
10 Of faces veiled, and heads discrowned and bowed.

The nation of the steadfast stars,
  The wandering star whose blaze is brief,
These make me beat against the bars
    Of my grief;
15 My tedious grief, twin to the life it mars.

O fretted heart tossed to and fro,
  So fain to flee, so fain to rest!
All glories that are high or low,
    East or west,
20 Grow dim to thee who art so fain to go.

A FISHER-WIFE.

The soonest mended, nothing said;
  And help may rise from east or west;
But my two hands are lumps of lead,
  My heart sits leaden in my breast.

5 O north wind swoop not from the north,
    O south wind linger in the south,
Oh come not raving raging forth,
    To bring my heart into my mouth;

For I've a husband out at sea,
10   Afloat on feeble planks of wood;
He does not know what fear may be;
    I would have told him if I could.

I would have locked him in my arms,
    I would have hid him in my heart;
15 For oh! the waves are fraught with harms,
    And he and I so far apart.

WHAT'S IN A NAME?

Why has Spring one syllable less
Than any its fellow season?
There may be some other reason,
And I'm merely making a guess;
5   But surely it hoards such wealth
Of happiness, hope and health,
Sunshine and musical sound,
It may spare a foot from its name
Yet all the same
10   Superabound.

Soft-named Summer,
Most welcome comer,
Brings almost everything
Over which we dream or sing
15   Or sigh;
But then summer wends its way,
Tomorrow,—today,—
Good-bye!

Autumn,—the slow name lingers,
20   While we likewise flag;
It silences many singers;
Its slow days drag,
Yet hasten at speed
To leave us in chilly need
25   For Winter to strip indeed.

In all-lack Winter,
Dull of sense and of sound,
We huddle and shiver
Beside our splinter
30   Of crackling pine,
Snow in sky and snow on ground.
Winter and cold
Can't last for ever!
Today, tomorrow, the sun will shine;
35   When we are old,
But some still are young,

Singing the song
Which others have sung,
Ringing the bells
40   Which others have rung,—
Even so!
We ourselves, who else?
We ourselves long
Long ago.

MARIANA.

Not for me marring or making,
Not for me giving or taking;
    I love my Love and he loves not me,
I love my Love and my heart is breaking.

5   Sweet is Spring in its lovely showing,
Sweet the violet veiled in blowing,
    Sweet it is to love and be loved;
Ah, sweet knowledge beyond my knowing!

Who sighs for love sighs but for pleasure,
10   Who wastes for love hoards up a treasure;
    Sweet to be loved and take no count,
Sweet it is to love without measure.

Sweet my Love whom I loved to try for,
Sweet my Love whom I love and sigh for,
15   Will you once love me and sigh for me,
You my Love whom I love and die for?

MEMENTO MORI.

Poor the pleasure
Doled out by measure,
Sweet tho' it be, while brief
As falling of the leaf;
5   Poor is pleasure
By weight and measure.

Sweet the sorrow
Which ends tomorrow;
Sharp tho' it be and sore,
10   It ends for evermore:
Zest of sorrow,
What ends tomorrow.

"ONE FOOT ON SEA, AND ONE ON SHORE."

"Oh tell me once and tell me twice
    And tell me thrice to make it plain,
When we who part this weary day,
    When we who part shall meet again."

5   "When windflowers blossom on the sea
    And fishes skim along the plain,
Then we who part this weary day,
    Then you and I shall meet again."

"Yet tell me once before we part,
10   Why need we part who part in pain?
If flowers must blossom on the sea,
    Why, we shall never meet again.

"My cheeks are paler than a rose,
    My tears are salter than the main,
15 My heart is like a lump of ice
    If we must never meet again."

"Oh weep or laugh, but let me be,
    And live or die, for all's in vain;
For life's in vain since we must part,
20   And parting must not meet again

"Till windflowers blossom on the sea
    And fishes skim along the plain;
Pale rose of roses let me be,
    Your breaking heart breaks mine again."

BUDS AND BABIES.

A million buds are born that never blow,
 That sweet with promise lift a pretty head
 To blush and wither on a barren bed
  And leave no fruit to show.

5 Sweet, unfulfilled. Yet have I understood
  One joy, by their fragility made plain:
  Nothing was ever beautiful in vain,
   Or all in vain was good.

BOY JOHNNY.

"If you'll busk you as a bride
 And make ready,
It's I will wed you with a ring,
 O fair lady."

5 "Shall I busk me as a bride,
  I so bonny,
For you to wed me with a ring,
  O boy Johnny?"

"When you've busked you as a bride
10 And made ready,
Who else is there to marry you,
 O fair lady?"

"I will find my lover out,
 I so bonny,
15 And you shall bear my wedding-train,
 O boy Johnny."

FREAKS OF FASHION.

Such a hubbub in the nests,
 Such a bustle and squeak!

Nestlings, guiltless of a feather,
   Learning just to speak,
5 Ask—"And how about the fashions?"
   From a cavernous beak.

Perched on bushes, perched on hedges,
   Perched on firm hahas,
Perched on anything that holds them,
10   Gay papas and grave mammas
Teach the knowledge-thirsty nestlings:
   Hear the gay papas.

Robin says: "A scarlet waistcoat
   Will be all the wear,
15 Snug, and also cheerful-looking
   For the frostiest air,
Comfortable for the chest too
   When one comes to plume and pair."

"Neat gray hoods will be in vogue,"
20   Quoth a Jackdaw: "Glossy gray,
Setting close, yet setting easy,
   Nothing fly-away;
Suited to our misty mornings,
   À la negligée."

25 Flushing salmon, flushing sulphur,
   Haughty Cockatoos
Answer—"Hoods may do for mornings,
   But for evenings choose
High head-dresses, curved like crescents,
30   Such as well-bred persons use."

"Top-knots, yes; yet more essential
   Still, a train or tail,"
Screamed the Peacock: "Gemmed and lustrous,
   Not too stiff, and not too frail;
35 Those are best which rearrange as
   Fans, and spread or trail."

Spoke the Swan, entrenched behind
   An inimitable neck:

"After all, there's nothing sweeter
40 For the lawn or lake
Than simple white, if fine and flaky
And absolutely free from speck."

"Yellow," hinted a Canary,
"Warmer, not less *distingué*."
45 "Peach colour," put in a Lory,
"Cannot look *outré*."
"All the colours are in fashion,
And are right," the Parrots say.

"Very well. But do contrast
50 Tints harmonious,"
Piped a Blackbird, justly proud
Of bill aurigerous;
"Half the world may learn a lesson
As to that from us."

55 Then a Stork took up the word:
"Aim at height and *chic*:
Not high heels, they're common; somehow,
Stilted legs, not thick,
Nor yet thin:" he just glanced downward
60 And snapped to his beak.

Here a rustling and a whirring,
As of fans outspread,
Hinted that mammas felt anxious
Lest the next thing said
65 Might prove less than quite judicious,
Or even underbred.

So a mother Auk resumed
The broken thread of speech:
"Let colours sort themselves, my dears,
70 Yellow, or red, or peach;
The main points, as it seems to me,
We mothers have to teach,

"Are form and texture, elegance,
An air reserved, sublime;

75   The mode of wearing what we wear
            With due regard to month and clime.
        But now, let's all compose ourselves,
            It's almost breakfast-time."

        A hubbub, a squeak, a bustle!
80   Who cares to chatter or sing
        With delightful breakfast coming?
            Yet they whisper under the wing:
        "So we may wear whatever we like,
            Anything, everything!"

AN OCTOBER GARDEN.

        In my Autumn garden I was fain
            To mourn among my scattered roses;
            Alas for that last rosebud which uncloses
        To Autumn's languid sun and rain
5   When all the world is on the wane!
            Which has not felt the sweet constraint of June,
            Nor heard the nightingale in tune.

        Broad-faced asters by my garden walk,
            You are but coarse compared with roses:
10   More choice, more dear that rosebud which uncloses
        Faint-scented, pinched, upon its stalk,
        That least and last which cold winds balk;
            A rose it is tho' least and last of all,
            A rose to me tho' at the fall.

"SUMMER IS ENDED."

        To think that this meaningless thing was ever a rose,
                Scentless, colourless, *this*!
            Will it ever be thus (who knows?)
                    Thus with our bliss,
5   If we wait till the close?

Tho' we care not to wait for the end, there comes the end
    Sooner, later, at last,
  Which nothing can mar, nothing mend:
    An end locked fast,
10   Bent we cannot re-bend.

PASSING AND GLASSING.

    All things that pass
    Are woman's looking-glass;
They show her how her bloom must fade,
  And she herself be laid
5 With withered roses in the shade;
    With withered roses and the fallen peach,
    Unlovely, out of reach
      Of summer joy that was.

    All things that pass
10   Are woman's tiring-glass;
The faded lavender is sweet,
Sweet the dead violet
Culled and laid by and cared for yet;
    The dried-up violets and dried lavender
15   Still sweet, may comfort her,
      Nor need she cry Alas!

    All things that pass
    Are wisdom's looking-glass;
Being full of hope and fear, and still
20 Brimful of good or ill,
According to our work and will;
    For there is nothing new beneath the sun;
    Our doings have been done,
      And that which shall be was.

"I WILL ARISE."

Weary and weak,—accept my weariness;
   Weary and weak and downcast in my soul,
With hope growing less and less,
   And with the goal
5   Distant and dim,—accept my sore distress.
I thought to reach the goal so long ago,
   At outset of the race I dreamed of rest,
Not knowing what now I know
   Of breathless haste,
10   Of long-drawn straining effort across the waste.

One only thing I knew, Thy love of me;
   One only thing I know, Thy sacred same
Love of me full and free,
   A craving flame
15   Of selfless love of me which burns in Thee.
How can I think of Thee, and yet grow chill;
   Of Thee, and yet grow cold and nigh to death?
Re-energize my will,
   Rebuild my faith;
20   I will arise and run, Thou giving me breath.

I will arise, repenting and in pain;
   I will arise, and smite upon my breast
And turn to Thee again;
   Thou choosest best,
25   Lead me along the road Thou makest plain.
Lead me a little way, and carry me
   A little way, and hearken to my sighs,
And store my tears with Thee,
   And deign replies
30   To feeble prayers;—O Lord, I will arise.

A PRODIGAL SON.

Does that lamp still burn in my Father's house,
   Which he kindled the night I went away?

I turned once beneath the cedar boughs,
    And marked it gleam with a golden ray;
5   Did he think to light me home some day?

Hungry here with the crunching swine,
    Hungry harvest have I to reap;
In a dream I count my Father's kine,
    I hear the tinkling bells of his sheep,
10   I watch his lambs that browse and leap.

There is plenty of bread at home,
    His servants have bread enough and to spare;
The purple wine-fat froths with foam,
    Oil and spices make sweet the air,
15   While I perish hungry and bare.

Rich and blessed those servants, rather
    Than I who see not my Father's face!
I will arise and go to my Father:—
    "Fallen from sonship, beggared of grace,
20   Grant me, Father, a servant's place."

SOEUR LOUISE DE LA MISÉRICORDE.
(1674.)

I have desired, and I have been desired;
    But now the days are over of desire,
    Now dust and dying embers mock my fire;
Where is the hire for which my life was hired?
5   Oh vanity of vanities, desire!

Longing and love, pangs of a perished pleasure,
    Longing and love, a disenkindled fire,
    And memory a bottomless gulf of mire,
And love a fount of tears outrunning measure;
10   Oh vanity of vanities, desire!

Now from my heart, love's deathbed, trickles, trickles,
    Drop by drop slowly, drop by drop of fire,
    The dross of life, of love, of spent desire;

Alas, my rose of life gone all to prickles,—
15   Oh vanity of vanities, desire!

Oh vanity of vanities, desire;
    Stunting my hope which might have strained up higher,
    Turning my garden plot to barren mire;
Oh death-struck love, oh disenkindled fire,
20   Oh vanity of vanities, desire!

AN "IMMURATA" SISTER.

Life flows down to death; we cannot bind
    That current that it should not flee:
Life flows down to death, as rivers find
    The inevitable sea.

5   Men work and think, but women feel;
    And so (for I'm a woman, I)
    And so I should be glad to die
And cease from impotence of zeal,
And cease from hope, and cease from dread,
10   And cease from yearnings without gain,
    And cease from all this world of pain,
And be at peace among the dead.

Hearts that die, by death renew their youth,
    Lightened of this life that doubts and dies;
15   Silent and contented, while the Truth
    Unveiled makes them wise.

Why should I seek and never find
    That something which I have not had?
    Fair and unutterably sad
20   The world hath sought time out of mind;
The world hath sought and I have sought,—
    Ah, empty world and empty I!
    For we have spent our strength for nought,
And soon it will be time to die.

25 Sparks fly upward toward their fount of fire,
　　Kindling, flashing, hovering:—
　Kindle, flash, my soul; mount higher and higher,
　　Thou whole burnt-offering!

"IF THOU SAYEST, BEHOLD, WE KNEW IT NOT."
　　—Proverbs xxiv. 11, 12.

1.

I have done I know not what,—what have I done?
　　My brother's blood, my brother's soul, doth cry:
　　And I find no defence, find no reply,
No courage more to run this race I run
5 Not knowing what I have done, have left undone;
　　Ah me, these awful unknown hours that fly
　　Fruitless it may be, fleeting fruitless by
Rank with death-savour underneath the sun.
For what avails it that I did not know
10　　The deed I did? what profits me the plea
That had I known I had not wronged him so?
　　　Lord Jesus Christ, my God, him pity Thou;
　　Lord, if it may be, pity also me:
　　　In judgment pity, and in death, and now.

2.

Thou Who hast borne all burdens, bear our load,
　　Bear Thou our load whatever load it be;
　　Our guilt, our shame, our helpless misery,
Bear Thou Who only canst, O God my God.
5　　Seek us and find us, for we cannot Thee
Or seek or find or hold or cleave unto:
We cannot do or undo; Lord, undo
　　Our self-undoing, for Thine is the key
Of all we are not tho' we might have been.
10　　Dear Lord, if ever mercy moved Thy mind,
　　If so be love of us can move Thee yet,

If still the nail-prints in Thy Hands are seen,
    Remember us,—yea, how shouldst Thou forget?
    Remember us for good, and seek, and find.

3.

Each soul I might have succoured, may have slain,
    All souls shall face me at the last Appeal,
    That great last moment poised for woe or weal,
That final moment for man's bliss or bane.
5 Vanity of vanities, yea all is vain
    Which then will not avail or help or heal:
    Disfeatured faces, worn-out knees that kneel,
Will more avail than strength or beauty then.
Lord, by Thy Passion,—when Thy Face was marred
10 In sight of earth and hell tumultuous,
    And Thy heart failed in Thee like melting wax,
And Thy Blood dropped more precious than the nard,—
    Lord, for Thy sake, not our's, supply our lacks,
    For Thine own sake, not our's, Christ, pity us.

THE THREAD OF LIFE.

1.

The irresponsive silence of the land,
    The irresponsive sounding of the sea,
    Speak both one message of one sense to me:—
Aloof, aloof, we stand aloof, so stand
5 Thou too aloof bound with the flawless band
    Of inner solitude; we bind not thee;
    But who from thy self-chain shall set thee free?
What heart shall touch thy heart? what hand thy hand?—
And I am sometimes proud and sometimes meek,
10 And sometimes I remember days of old
When fellowship seemed not so far to seek
    And all the world and I seemed much less cold,
    And at the rainbow's foot lay surely gold,
And hope felt strong and life itself not weak.

2.

Thus am I mine own prison. Everything
   Around me free and sunny and at ease:
   Or if in shadow, in a shade of trees
Which the sun kisses, where the gay birds sing
5 And where all winds make various murmuring;
   Where bees are found, with honey for the bees;
   Where sounds are music, and where silences
Are music of an unlike fashioning.
Then gaze I at the merrymaking crew,
10 And smile a moment and a moment sigh
Thinking: Why can I not rejoice with you?
   But soon I put the foolish fancy by:
I am not what I have nor what I do;
   But what I was I am, I am even I.

3.

Therefore myself is that one only thing
   I hold to use or waste, to keep or give;
   My sole possession every day I live,
And still mine own despite Time's winnowing.
5 Ever mine own, while moons and seasons bring
   From crudeness ripeness mellow and sanative;
   Ever mine own, till Death shall ply his sieve;
And still mine own, when saints break grave and sing.
And this myself as king unto my King
10 I give, to Him Who gave Himself for me;
Who gives Himself to me, and bids me sing
   A sweet new song of His redeemed set free;
He bids me sing: O death, where is thy sting?
   And sing: O grave, where is thy victory?

AN OLD-WORLD THICKET.

. . . "Una selva oscura."—DANTE.

Awake or sleeping (for I know not which)
   I was or was not mazed within a wood

Where every mother-bird brought up her brood
  Safe in some leafy niche
5   Of oak or ash, of cypress or of beech,

Of silvery aspen trembling delicately,
  Of plane or warmer-tinted sycomore,
  Of elm that dies in secret from the core,
    Of ivy weak and free,
10   Of pines, of all green lofty things that be.

Such birds they seemed as challenged each desire;
  Like spots of azure heaven upon the wing,
  Like downy emeralds that alight and sing,
    Like actual coals on fire,
15   Like anything they seemed, and everything.

Such mirth they made, such warblings and such chat
  With tongue of music in a well-tuned beak,
  They seemed to speak more wisdom than we speak,
    To make our music flat
20   And all our subtlest reasonings wild or weak.

Their meat was nought but flowers like butterflies,
  With berries coral-coloured or like gold;
  Their drink was only dew, which blossoms hold
    Deep where the honey lies;
25   Their wings and tails were lit by sparkling eyes.

The shade wherein they revelled was a shade
  That danced and twinkled to the unseen sun;
  Branches and leaves cast shadows one by one,
    And all their shadows swayed
30   In breaths of air that rustled and that played.

A sound of waters neither rose nor sank,
  And spread a sense of freshness through the air;
  It seemed not here or there, but everywhere,
    As if the whole earth drank,
35   Root fathom deep and strawberry on its bank.

But I who saw such things as I have said,
  Was overdone with utter weariness;
  And walked in care, as one whom fears oppress
    Because above his head

40   Death hangs, or damage, or the dearth of bread.

Each sore defeat of my defeated life
    Faced and outfaced me in that bitter hour;
    And turned to yearning palsy all my power,
        And all my peace to strife,
45   Self stabbing self with keen lack-pity knife.

Sweetness of beauty moved me to despair,
    Stung me to anger by its mere content,
    Made me all lonely on that way I went,
        Piled care upon my care,
50   Brimmed full my cup, and stripped me empty and bare:

For all that was but showed what all was not,
    But gave clear proof of what might never be;
    Making more destitute my poverty,
        And yet more blank my lot,
55   And me much sadder by its jubilee.

Therefore I sat me down: for wherefore walk?
    And closed mine eyes: for wherefore see or hear?
    Alas, I had no shutter to mine ear,
        And could not shun the talk
60   Of all rejoicing creatures far or near.

Without my will I hearkened and I heard
    (Asleep or waking, for I know not which),
    Till note by note the music changed its pitch;
        Bird ceased to answer bird,
65   And every wind sighed softly if it stirred.

The drip of widening waters seemed to weep,
    All fountains sobbed and gurgled as they sprang,
    Somewhere a cataract cried out in its leap
        Sheer down a headlong steep;
70   High over all cloud-thunders gave a clang.

Such universal sound of lamentation
    I heard and felt, fain not to feel or hear;
    Nought else there seemed but anguish far and near;
        Nought else but all creation
75   Moaning and groaning wrung by pain or fear,

Shuddering in the misery of its doom:
    My heart then rose a rebel against light,
    Scouring all earth and heaven and depth and height,
        Ingathering wrath and gloom,
80   Ingathering wrath to wrath and night to night.

Ah me, the bitterness of such revolt,
    All impotent, all hateful, and all hate,
That kicks and breaks itself against the bolt
        Of an imprisoning fate,
85   And vainly shakes, and cannot shake the gate.

Agony to agony, deep called to deep,
    Out of the deep I called of my desire;
    My strength was weakness and my heart was fire;
        Mine eyes that would not weep
90 Or sleep, scaled height and depth, and could not sleep;

The eyes, I mean, of my rebellious soul,
    For still my bodily eyes were closed and dark:
    A random thing I seemed without a mark,
        Racing without a goal,
95   Adrift upon life's sea without an ark.

More leaden than the actual self of lead
    Outer and inner darkness weighed on me.
    The tide of anger ebbed. Then fierce and free
        Surged full above my head
100   The moaning tide of helpless misery.

Why should I breathe, whose breath was but a sigh?
    Why should I live, who drew such painful breath?
Oh weary work, the unanswerable why!—
        Yet I, why should I die,
105   Who had no hope in life, no hope in death?

Grasses and mosses and the fallen leaf
    Make peaceful bed for an indefinite term;
    But underneath the grass there gnaws a worm—
        Haply, there gnaws a grief—
110 Both, haply always; not, as now, so brief.

The pleasure I remember, it is past;
    The pain I feel, is passing passing by;

Thus all the world is passing, and thus I:
　　All things that cannot last
115　Have grown familiar, and are born to die.

And being familiar, have so long been borne
　　That habit trains us not to break but bend:
Mourning grows natural to us who mourn
　　In foresight of an end,
120　But that which ends not who shall brave or mend?

Surely the ripe fruits tremble on their bough,
　　They cling and linger trembling till they drop:
I, trembling, cling to dying life; for how
　　Face the perpetual Now?
125　Birthless and deathless, void of start or stop,

Void of repentance, void of hope and fear,
　　Of possibility, alternative,
　　Of all that ever made us bear to live
　　From night to morning here,
130　Of promise even which has no gift to give.

The wood, and every creature of the wood,
　　Seemed mourning with me in an undertone;
Soft scattered chirpings and a windy moan,
　　Trees rustling where they stood
135　And shivered, showed compassion for my mood.

Rage to despair; and now despair had turned
　　Back to self-pity and mere weariness,
With yearnings like a smouldering fire that burned,
　　And might grow more or less,
140　And might die out or wax to white excess.

Without, within me, music seemed to be;
　　Something not music, yet most musical,
Silence and sound in heavenly harmony;
　　At length a pattering fall
145　Of feet, a bell, and bleatings, broke through all.

Then I looked up. The wood lay in a glow
　　From golden sunset and from ruddy sky;
　　The sun had stooped to earth though once so high;
　　Had stooped to earth, in slow

150 Warm dying loveliness brought near and low.

Each water drop made answer to the light,
  Lit up a spark and showed the sun his face;
  Soft purple shadows paved the grassy space
    And crept from height to height,
155 From height to loftier height crept up apace.

While opposite the sun a gazing moon
  Put on his glory for her coronet,
Kindling her luminous coldness to its noon,
  As his great splendour set;
160 One only star made up her train as yet.

Each twig was tipped with gold, each leaf was edged
  And veined with gold from the gold-flooded west;
Each mother-bird, and mate-bird, and unfledged
  Nestling, and curious nest,
165 Displayed a gilded moss or beak or breast.

And filing peacefully between the trees,
  Having the moon behind them, and the sun
Full in their meek mild faces, walked at ease
  A homeward flock, at peace
170 With one another and with every one.

A patriarchal ram with tinkling bell
  Led all his kin; sometimes one browsing sheep
  Hung back a moment, or one lamb would leap
    And frolic in a dell;
175 Yet still they kept together, journeying well,

And bleating, one or other, many or few,
  Journeying together toward the sunlit west;
  Mild face by face, and woolly breast by breast,
    Patient, sun-brightened too,
180 Still journeying toward the sunset and their rest.

"ALL THY WORKS PRAISE THEE, O LORD."
A PROCESSIONAL OF CREATION.

ALL.

I all-creation sing my song of praise
To God Who made me and vouchsafes my days,
And sends me forth by multitudinous ways.

SERAPH.

I, like my Brethren, burn eternally
5   With love of Him Who is Love, and loveth me;
The Holy, Holy, Holy Unity.

CHERUB.

I, with my Brethren, gaze eternally
On Him Who is Wisdom, and Who knoweth me;
The Holy, Holy, Holy Trinity.

ALL ANGELS.

10   We rule, we serve, we work, we store His treasure,
Whose vessels are we brimmed with strength and
           pleasure;
Our joys fulfil, yea, overfill our measure.

HEAVENS.

We float before the Presence Infinite,
We cluster round the Throne in our delight,
15   Revolving and rejoicing in God's sight.

FIRMAMENT.

I, blue and beautiful, and framed of air,
At sunrise and at sunset grow most fair;
His glory by my glories I declare.

POWERS.

We Powers are powers because He makes us strong;
20 Wherefore we roll all rolling orbs along,
We move all moving things, and sing our song.

SUN.

I blaze to Him in mine engarlanding
Of rays, I flame His whole burnt-offering,
While as a bridegroom I rejoice and sing.

MOON.

25 I follow, and am fair, and do His Will;
Thro' all my changes I am faithful still,
Full-orbed or strait His mandate to fulfil.

STARS.

We Star-hosts numerous, innumerous,
Throng space with energy untumultuous,
30 And work His Will Whose eye beholdeth us.

GALAXIES AND NEBULAE.

No thing is far or near; and therefore we
Float neither far nor near; but where we be
Weave dances round the Throne perpetually.

COMETS AND METEORS.

Our lights dart here and there, whirl to and fro,
35 We flash and vanish, we die down and glow;
All doing His Will Who bids us do it so.

SHOWERS.

We give ourselves; and be we great or small,
Thus are we made like Him Who giveth all,
Like Him Whose gracious pleasure bids us fall.

DEWS.

40   We give ourselves in silent secret ways,
Spending and spent in silence full of grace;
And thus are made like God, and show His praise.

WINDS.

We sift the air and winnow all the earth;
And God Who poised our weights and weighs our worth
45   Accepts the worship of our solemn mirth.

FIRE.

My power and strength are His Who fashioned me,
Ordained me image of His Jealousy,
Forged me His weapon fierce exceedingly.

HEAT.

I glow unto His glory, and do good:
50   I glow, and bring to life both bud and brood;
I glow, and ripen harvest-crops for food.

WINTER AND SUMMER.

Our wealth and joys and beauties celebrate
His wealth of beauty Who sustains our state,
Before Whose changelessness we alternate.

SPRING AND AUTUMN.

55   I hope,—
          And I remember,—
                    We give place
Either to other with contented grace,
Acceptable and lovely all our days.

FROST.

60   I make the unstable stable, binding fast
The world of waters prone to ripple past:
Thus praise I God, Whose mercies I forecast.

COLD.

I rouse and goad the slothful apt to nod,
I stir and urge the laggards with my rod:
65   My praise is not of men, yet I praise God.

SNOW.

My whiteness shadoweth Him Who is most fair,
All spotless: yea, my whiteness which I wear
Exalts His Purity beyond compare.

VAPOURS.

We darken sun and moon, and blot the day,
70   The good Will of our Maker to obey:
Till to the glory of God we pass away.

NIGHT.

Moon and all stars I don for diadem
To make me fair: I cast myself and them
Before His feet, Who knows us gem from gem.

DAY.

75   I shout before Him in my plentitude
Of light and warmth, of hope and wealth and food;
Ascribing all good to the Only Good.

LIGHT AND DARKNESS.

I am God's dwelling-place,—

                    And also I

80   Make His pavilion,—
                              Lo, we bide and fly
       Exulting in the Will of God Most High.

LIGHTNING AND THUNDER.

We indivisible flash forth His Fame,
We thunder forth the glory of His Name,
85   In harmony of resonance and flame.

CLOUDS.

Sweet is our store, exhaled from sea or river:
We wear a rainbow, praising God the Giver
Because His mercy is for ever and ever.

EARTH.

I rest in Him rejoicing: resting so
90   And so rejoicing, in that I am low;
Yet known of Him, and following on to know.

MOUNTAINS.

Our heights which laud Him, sink abased before
Him higher than the highest evermore:
God higher than the highest we adore.

HILLS.

95   We green-tops praise Him, and we fruitful heads,
Whereon the sunshine and the dew He sheds:
We green-tops praise Him, rising from our beds.

GREEN THINGS.

We all green things, we blossoms bright or dim,
Trees, bushes, brushwood, corn and grasses slim,
100   We lift our many-favoured lauds to Him.

ROSE,—LILY,—VIOLET.

I praise Him on my thorn which I adorn,—
And I, amid my world of thistle and thorn,—
And I, within my veil where I am born.

APPLE,—CITRON,—POMEGRANATE.

We Apple-blossom, Citron, Pomegranate,
105　We clothed of God without our toil and fret,
We offer fatness where His Throne is set.

VINE,—CEDAR,—PALM.

I proffer Him my sweetness, who am sweet,—
I bow my strength in fragrance at His feet,—
I wave myself before His Judgment Seat.

MEDICINAL HERBS.

110　I bring refreshment,—
　　　　　　　　　　　　I bring ease and calm,—
I lavish strength and healing,—
　　　　　　　　　　　　　I am balm,—
We work His pitiful Will and chant our psalm.

A SPRING.

115　Clear my pure fountain, clear and pure my rill,
My fountain and mine outflow deep and still,
I set His semblance forth and do His Will.

SEA.

Today I praise God with a sparkling face,
My thousand thousand waves all uttering praise:
120　Tomorrow I commit me to His Grace.

FLOODS.

We spring and swell meandering to and fro,
From height to depth, from depth to depth we flow,
We fertilize the world, and praise Him so.

WHALES AND SEA MAMMALS.

We Whales and Monsters gambol in His sight
125 Rejoicing every day and every night,
Safe in the tender keeping of His Might.

FISHES.

Our fashions and our colours and our speeds
Set forth His praise Who framed us and Who feeds,
Who knows our number and regards our needs.

BIRDS.

130 Winged Angels of this visible world, we fly
To sing God's praises in the lofty sky;
We scale the height to praise our Lord most High.

EAGLE AND DOVE.

I the sun-gazing Eagle,—
                                    I the Dove
135 With plumes of softness and a note of love,—
We praise by divers gifts One God above.

BEASTS AND CATTLE.

We forest Beasts,—
                              We Beasts of hill or cave,—
We border-loving Creatures of the wave,—
140 We praise our King with voices deep and grave.

SMALL ANIMALS.

God forms us weak and small, but pours out all
We need, and notes us while we stand or fall:
Wherefore we praise Him, weak and safe and small.

LAMB.

I praise my loving Lord, Who maketh me
145 His type by harmless sweet simplicity:
Yet He the Lamb of lambs incomparably.

LION.

I praise the Lion of the Royal Race,
Strongest in fight and swiftest in the chase:
With all my might I leap and lavish praise.

ALL MEN.

150 All creatures sing around us, and we sing:
We bring our own selves as our offering,
Our very selves we render to our King.

ISRAEL.

Flock of our Shepherd's pasture and His fold,
Purchased and well-beloved from days of old,
155 We tell His praise which still remains untold.

PRIESTS.

We free-will Shepherds tend His sheep and feed;
We follow Him while caring for their need;
We follow praising Him, and them we lead.

SERVANTS OF GOD.

We love God, for He loves us; we are free
160 In serving Him, who serve Him willingly:
As kings we reign, and praise His Majesty.

HOLY AND HUMBLE PERSONS.

All humble souls He calls and sanctifies;
All holy souls He calls to make them wise;
Accepting all, His free-will sacrifice.

BABES.

165　He maketh me,—
　　　　　　And me,—
　　　　　　　　　　And me,—
　　　　　　　　　　　　　To be
His blessed little ones around His knee,
170　Who praise Him by mere love confidingly.

WOMEN.

God makes our service love, and makes our wage
Love: so we wend on patient pilgrimage,
Extolling Him by love from age to age.

MEN.

God gives us power to rule: He gives us power
175　To rule ourselves, and prune the exuberant flower
Of youth, and worship Him hour after hour.

SPIRITS AND SOULS—

Lo, in the hidden world we chant our chant
To Him Who fills us that we nothing want,
To Him Whose bounty leaves our craving scant.

OF BABES—

180　With milky mouths we praise God, from the breast
Called home betimes to rest the perfect rest,
By love and joy fulfilling His behest.

OF WOMEN—

We praise His Will which made us what He would,
His Will which fashioned us and called us good,
185   His Will our plenary beatitude.

OF MEN.

We praise His Will Who bore with us so long,
Who out of weakness wrought us swift and strong,
Champions of right and putters-down of wrong.

ALL.

Let everything that hath or hath not breath,
190   Let days and endless days, let life and death,
Praise God, praise God, praise God, His creature saith.

LATER LIFE: A DOUBLE SONNET OF SONNETS.

1.

Before the mountains were brought forth, before
    Earth and the world were made, then God was God:
And God will still be God, when flames shall roar
    Round earth and heaven dissolving at His nod:
5   And this God is our God, even while His rod
Of righteous wrath falls on us smiting sore:
And this God is our God for evermore
    Thro' life, thro' death, while clod returns to clod.
For tho' He slay us we will trust in Him;
10   We will flock home to Him by divers ways:
        Yea, tho' He slay us we will vaunt His praise,
Serving and loving with the Cherubim,
Watching and loving with the Seraphim,
    Our very selves His praise thro' endless days.

2.

Rend hearts and rend not garments for our sins;
   Gird sackcloth not on body but on soul;
   Grovel in dust with faces toward the goal
Nor won, nor neared: he only laughs who wins.
5   Not neared the goal, the race too late begins;
   All left undone, we have yet to do the whole;
   The sun is hurrying west and toward the pole
Where darkness waits for earth with all her kins.
Let us today while it is called today
10   Set out, if utmost speed may yet avail—
   The shadows lengthen and the light grows pale:
     For who thro' darkness and the shadow of death,
Darkness that may be felt, shall find a way,
   Blind-eyed, deaf-eared, and choked with failing
     breath?

3.

Thou Who didst make and knowest whereof we are
     made,
   Oh bear in mind our dust and nothingness,
   Our wordless tearless dumbness of distress:
Bear Thou in mind the burden Thou hast laid
5   Upon us, and our feebleness unstayed
   Except Thou stay us: for the long long race
   Which stretches far and far before our face
Thou knowest,—remember Thou whereof we are made.
If making makes us Thine then Thine we are,
10   And if redemption we are twice Thine own:
If once Thou didst come down from heaven afar
     To seek us and to find us, how not save?
   Comfort us, save us, leave us not alone,
     Thou Who didst die our death and fill our grave.

4.

So tired am I, so weary of today,
   So unrefreshed from foregone weariness,

So overburdened by foreseen distress,
So lagging and so stumbling on my way,
5   I scarce can rouse myself to watch or pray,
    To hope, or aim, or toil for more or less,—
    Ah, always less and less, even while I press
Forward and toil and aim as best I may.
Half-starved of soul and heartsick utterly,
10   Yet lift I up my heart and soul and eyes
    (Which fail in looking upward) toward the prize:
Me, Lord, Thou seest tho' I see not Thee;
    Me now, as once the Thief in Paradise,
Even me, O Lord my Lord, remember me.

5.

Lord, Thou Thyself art Love and only Thou;
    Yet I who am not love would fain love Thee;
    But Thou alone being Love canst furnish me
With that same love my heart is craving now.
5   Allow my plea! for if Thou disallow,
    No second fountain can I find but Thee;
    No second hope or help is left to me,
No second anything, but only Thou.
O Love accept, according my request;
10   O Love exhaust, fulfilling my desire:
    Uphold me with the strength that cannot tire,
Nerve me to labour till Thou bid me rest,
    Kindle my fire from Thine unkindled fire,
And charm the willing heart from out my breast.

6.

We lack, yet cannot fix upon the lack:
    Not this, nor that; yet somewhat, certainly.
    We see the things we do not yearn to see
Around us: and what see we glancing back?
5   Lost hopes that leave our hearts upon the rack,
    Hopes that were never ours yet seemed to be,
    For which we steered on life's salt stormy sea

Braving the sunstroke and the frozen pack.
If thus to look behind is all in vain,
10   And all in vain to look to left or right,
Why face we not our future once again,
Launching with hardier hearts across the main,
    Straining dim eyes to catch the invisible sight,
And strong to bear ourselves in patient pain?

7.

To love and to remember; that is good:
    To love and to forget; that is not well:
    To lapse from love to hatred; that is hell
And death and torment, rightly understood.
5 Soul dazed by love and sorrow, cheer thy mood;
    More blest art thou than mortal tongue can tell:
    Ring not thy funeral but thy marriage bell,
And salt with hope thy life's insipid food.
Love is the goal, love is the way we wend,
10   Love is our parallel unending line
        Whose only perfect Parallel is Christ,
Beginning not begun, End without end:
        For He Who hath the Heart of God sufficed,
    Can satisfy all hearts,—yea, thine and mine.

8.

We feel and see with different hearts and eyes:—
    Ah Christ, if all our hearts could meet in Thee
    How well it were for them and well for me,
Our hearts Thy dear accepted sacrifice.
5 Thou, only Life of hearts and Light of eyes,
    Our life, our light, if once we turn to Thee,
    So be it, O Lord, to them and so to me;
Be all alike Thine own dear sacrifice.
Thou Who by death hast ransomed us from death,
10   Thyself God's sole well-pleasing Sacrifice,
        Thine only sacred Self I plead with Thee:
        Make Thou it well for them and well for me

That Thou hast given us souls and wills and breath,
  And hearts to love Thee, and to see Thee eyes.

9.

Star Sirius and the Pole Star dwell afar
  Beyond the drawings each of other's strength:
  One blazes thro' the brief bright summer's length
Lavishing life-heat from a flaming car;
5   While one unchangeable upon a throne
  Broods o'er the frozen heart of earth alone,
Content to reign the bright particular star
  Of some who wander or of some who groan.
They own no drawings each of other's strength,
10   Nor vibrate in a visible sympathy,
    Nor veer along their courses each toward each:
  Yet are their orbits pitched in harmony
Of one dear heaven, across whose depth and length
    Mayhap they talk together without speech.

10.

Tread softly! all the earth is holy ground.
  It may be, could we look with seeing eyes,
  This spot we stand on is a Paradise
Where dead have come to life and lost been found,
5 Where Faith has triumphed, Martyrdom been crowned,
  Where fools have foiled the wisdom of the wise;
  From this same spot the dust of saints may rise,
And the King's prisoners come to light unbound.
O earth, earth, earth, hear thou thy Maker's Word:
10   "Thy dead thou shalt give up, nor hide thy slain"—
  Some who went weeping forth shall come again
    Rejoicing from the east or from the west,
As doves fly to their windows, love's own bird
    Contented and desirous to the nest.[1]

[1]"Quali colombe dal disio chiamate
Con l'ali aperte e ferme al dolce nido
Volan per l'aer dal voler portate."
                              DANTE.

11.

Lifelong our stumbles, lifelong our regret,
   Lifelong our efforts failing and renewed,
   While lifelong is our witness, "God is good:"
Who bore with us till now, bears with us yet,
5   Who still remembers and will not forget,
   Who gives us light and warmth and daily food;
   And gracious promises half understood,
And glories half unveiled, whereon to set
Our heart of hearts and eyes of our desire;
10   Uplifting us to longing and to love,
Luring us upward from this world of mire,
   Urging us to press on and mount above
   Ourselves and all we have had experience of,
Mounting to Him in love's perpetual fire.

12.

A dream there is wherein we are fain to scream,
   While struggling with ourselves we cannot speak:
   And much of all our waking life, as weak
And misconceived, eludes us like the dream.
5   For half life's seemings are not what they seem,
   And vain the laughs we laugh, the shrieks we shriek;
   Yea, all is vain that mars the settled meek
Contented quiet of our daily theme.
When I was young I deemed that sweets are sweet:
10   But now I deem some searching bitters are
   Sweeter than sweets, and more refreshing far,
     And to be relished more, and more desired,
And more to be pursued on eager feet,
     On feet untired, and still on feet tho' tired.

13.

Shame is a shadow cast by sin: yet shame
   Itself may be a glory and a grace,
   Refashioning the sin-disfashioned face;
A nobler bruit than hollow-sounded fame,

5   A new-lit lustre on a tarnished name,
        One virtue pent within an evil place,
        Strength for the fight, and swiftness for the race,
    A stinging salve, a life-requickening flame.
    A salve so searching we may scarcely live,
10   A flame so fierce it seems that we must die,
            An actual cautery thrust into the heart:
            Nevertheless, men die not of such smart;
    And shame gives back what nothing else can give,
        Man to himself,—then sets him up on high.

        14.

    When Adam and when Eve left Paradise
        Did they love on and cling together still,
        Forgiving one another all that ill
    The twain had wrought on such a different wise?
5   She propped upon his strength, and he in guise
        Of lover tho' of lord, girt to fulfil
        Their term of life and die when God should will;
    Lie down and sleep, and having slept arise.
    Boast not against us, O our enemy!
10   Today we fall, but we shall rise again;
    We grope today, tomorrow we shall see:
            What is today that we should fear today?
            A morrow cometh which shall sweep away
    Thee and thy realm of change and death and pain.

        15.

    Let woman fear to teach and bear to learn,
        Remembering the first woman's first mistake.
        Eve had for pupil the inquiring snake,
    Whose doubts she answered on a great concern;
5   But he the tables so contrived to turn,
        It next was his to give and her's to take;
        Till man deemed poison sweet for her sweet sake,
    And fired a train by which the world must burn.
    Did Adam love his Eve from first to last?

10   I think so; as we love who works us ill,
And wounds us to the quick, yet loves us still.
Love pardons the unpardonable past:
Love in a dominant embrace holds fast
    His frailer self, and saves without her will.

16.

Our teachers teach that one and one make two:
    Later, Love rules that one and one make one:
    Abstruse the problems! neither need we shun,
But skilfully to each should yield its due.
5   The narrower total seems to suit the few,
    The wider total suits the common run;
    Each obvious in its sphere like moon or sun;
Both provable by me, and both by you.
Befogged and witless, in a wordy maze
10   A groping stroll perhaps may do us good;
    If cloyed we are with much we have understood,
If tired of half our dusty world and ways,
    If sick of fasting, and if sick of food;—
And how about these long still-lengthening days?

17.

Something this foggy day, a something which
    Is neither of this fog nor of today,
    Has set me dreaming of the winds that play
Past certain cliffs, along one certain beach,
5   And turn the topmost edge of waves to spray:
    Ah pleasant pebbly strand so far away,
So out of reach while quite within my reach,
    As out of reach as India or Cathay!
I am sick of where I am and where I am not,
10   I am sick of foresight and of memory,
    I am sick of all I have and all I see,
    I am sick of self, and there is nothing new;
Oh weary impatient patience of my lot!—
    Thus with myself: how fares it, Friends, with you?

18.

So late in Autumn half the world's asleep,
    And half the wakeful world looks pinched and pale;
    For dampness now, not freshness, rides the gale;
And cold and colourless comes ashore the deep
5   With tides that bluster or with tides that creep;
    Now veiled uncouthness wears an uncouth veil
    Of fog, not sultry haze; and blight and bale
Have done their worst, and leaves rot on the heap.
So late in Autumn one forgets the Spring,
10   Forgets the Summer with its opulence,
The callow birds that long have found a wing,
    The swallows that more lately gat them hence:
Will anything like Spring, will anything
    Like Summer, rouse one day the slumbering sense?

19.

Here now is Winter. Winter, after all,
    Is not so drear as was my boding dream
    While Autumn gleamed its latest watery gleam
On sapless leafage too inert to fall.
5   Still leaves and berries clothe my garden wall
    Where ivy thrives on scantiest sunny beam;
    Still here a bud and there a blossom seem
Hopeful, and robin still is musical.
Leaves, flowers and fruit and one delightful song
10   Remain; these days are short, but now the nights
    Intense and long, hang out their utmost lights;
Such starry nights are long, yet not too long;
Frost nips the weak, while strengthening still the strong
    Against that day when Spring sets all to rights.

20.

A hundred thousand birds salute the day:—
    One solitary bird salutes the night:
Its mellow grieving wiles our grief away,
    And tunes our weary watches to delight;

5   It seems to sing the thoughts we cannot say,
          To know and sing them, and to set them right;
      Until we feel once more that May is May,
          And hope some buds may bloom without a blight.
      This solitary bird outweighs, outvies,
10   The hundred thousand merry-making birds
      Whose innocent warblings yet might make us wise
      Would we but follow when they bid us rise,
          Would we but set their notes of praise to words
      And launch our hearts up with them to the skies.

                    21.

      A host of things I take on trust: I take
          The nightingales on trust, for few and far
          Between those actual summer moments are
      When I have heard what melody they make.
5   So chanced it once at Como on the Lake:
          But all things, then, waxed musical; each star
          Sang on its course, each breeze sang on its car,
      All harmonies sang to senses wide awake.
      All things in tune, myself not out of tune,
10   Those nightingales were nightingales indeed:
          Yet truly an owl had satisfied my need,
      And wrought a rapture underneath that moon,
          Or simple sparrow chirping from a reed;
      For June that night glowed like a doubled June.

                    22.

      The mountains in their overwhelming might
          Moved me to sadness when I saw them first,
      And afterwards they moved me to delight;
          Struck harmonies from silent chords which burst
5   Out into song, a song by memory nursed;
      For ever unrenewed by touch or sight
      Sleeps the keen magic of each day or night,
          In pleasure and in wonder then immersed.
      All Switzerland behind us on the ascent,

10   All Italy before us we plunged down
           St. Gothard, garden of forget-me-not:
              Yet why should such a flower choose such a spot?
      Could we forget that way which once we went
           Tho' not one flower had bloomed to weave its crown?

              23.

      Beyond the seas we know, stretch seas unknown
           Blue and bright-coloured for our dim and green;
           Beyond the lands we see, stretch lands unseen
      With many-tinted tangle overgrown;
5   And icebound seas there are like seas of stone,
           Serenely stormless as death lies serene;
           And lifeless tracts of sand, which intervene
      Betwixt the lands where living flowers are blown.
      This dead and living world befits our case
10   Who live and die: we live in wearied hope,
      We die in hope not dead; we run a race
      Today, and find no present halting-place;
           All things we see lie far within our scope,
      And still we peer beyond with craving face.

              24.

      The wise do send their hearts before them to
           Dear blessed Heaven, despite the veil between;
           The foolish nurse their hearts within the screen
      Of this familiar world, where all we do
5   Or have is old, for there is nothing new:
           Yet elder far that world we have not seen;
           God's Presence antedates what else hath been:
      Many the foolish seem, the wise seem few.
      Oh foolishest fond folly of a heart
10   Divided, neither here nor there at rest!
              That hankers after Heaven, but clings to earth;
              That neither here nor there knows thorough mirth,
      Half-choosing, wholly missing, the good part:—
           Oh fool among the foolish, in thy quest.

25.

When we consider what this life we lead
   Is not, and is: how full of toil and pain,
   How blank of rest and of substantial gain,
Beset by hunger earth can never feed,
And propping half our hearts upon a reed;
   We cease to mourn lost treasures, mourned in vain,
   Lost treasures we are fain and yet not fain
To fetch back for a solace of our need.
For who that feel this burden and this strain,
   This wide vacuity of hope and heart,
Would bring their cherished well-beloved again:
   To bleed with them and wince beneath the smart,
To have with stinted bliss such lavish bane,
   To hold in lieu of all so poor a part?

26.

This Life is full of numbness and of balk,
   Of haltingness and baffled short-coming,
   Of promise unfulfilled, of everything
That is puffed vanity and empty talk:
Its very bud hangs cankered on the stalk,
   Its very song-bird trails a broken wing,
   Its very Spring is not indeed like Spring,
But sighs like Autumn round an aimless walk.
This Life we live is dead for all its breath;
   Death's self it is, set off on pilgrimage,
   Travelling with tottering steps the first short stage:
     The second stage is one mere desert dust
     Where Death sits veiled amid creation's rust:—
Unveil thy face, O Death who art not Death.

27.

I have dreamed of Death:—what will it be to die
   Not in a dream, but in the literal truth
   With all Death's adjuncts ghastly and uncouth,

The pang that is the last and the last sigh?
5   Too dulled, it may be, for a last good-bye,
Too comfortless for any one to soothe,
A helpless charmless spectacle of ruth
Thro' long last hours, so long while yet they fly.
So long to those who hopeless in their fear
10   Watch the slow breath and look for what they dread:
While I supine with ears that cease to hear,
With eyes that glaze, with heart pulse running down
(Alas! no saint rejoicing on her bed),
May miss the goal at last, may miss a crown.

28.

In life our absent friend is far away:
But death may bring our friend exceeding near,
Show him familiar faces long so dear
And lead him back in reach of words we say.
5   He only cannot utter yea or nay
In any voice accustomed to our ear;
He only cannot make his face appear
And turn the sun back on our shadowed day.
The dead may be around us, dear and dead;
10   The unforgotten dearest dead may be
Watching us with unslumbering eyes and heart;
Brimful of words which cannot yet be said,
Brimful of knowledge they may not impart,
Brimful of love for you and love for me.

"FOR THINE OWN SAKE, O MY GOD."

Wearied of sinning, wearied of repentance,
Wearied of self, I turn, my God, to Thee;
To Thee, my Judge, on Whose all-righteous sentence
Hangs mine eternity:
5   I turn to Thee, I plead Thyself with Thee,—
Be pitiful to me.

Wearied I loathe myself, I loathe my sinning,
 My stains, my festering sores, my misery:
Thou the Beginning, Thou ere my beginning
10 Didst see and didst foresee
Me miserable, me sinful, ruined me,—
  I plead Thyself with Thee.

I plead Thyself with Thee Who art my Maker,
 Regard Thy handiwork that cries to Thee;
15 I plead Thyself with Thee Who wast partaker
  Of mine infirmity,
Love made Thee what Thou art, the love of me,—
  I plead Thyself with Thee.

UNTIL THE DAY BREAK.

When will the day bring its pleasure?
 When will the night bring its rest?
Reaper and gleaner and thresher
 Peer toward the east and the west:—
5 The Sower He knoweth, and He knoweth best.

Meteors flash forth and expire,
 Northern lights kindle and pale;
These are the days of desire,
 Of eyes looking upward that fail;
10 Vanishing days as a finishing tale.

Bows down the crop in its glory
 Tenfold, fiftyfold, hundredfold;
The millet is ripened and hoary,
 The wheat ears are ripened to gold:—
15 Why keep us waiting in dimness and cold?

The Lord of the harvest, He knoweth
 Who knoweth the first and the last:
The Sower Who patiently soweth,
 He scanneth the present and past:
20 He saith, "What thou hast, what remaineth, hold fast."

Yet, Lord, o'er Thy toil-wearied weepers
    The storm-clouds hang muttering and frown:
On threshers and gleaners and reapers,
    O Lord of the harvest, look down;
25   Oh for the harvest, the shout, and the crown!

"Not so," saith the Lord of the reapers,
    The Lord of the first and the last:
"O My toilers, My weary, My weepers,
    What ye have, what remaineth, hold fast.
30   Hide in My heart till the vengeance be past."

"OF HIM THAT WAS READY TO PERISH."

Lord, I am waiting, weeping, watching for Thee:
    My youth and hope lie by me buried and dead,
    My wandering love hath not where to lay its head
      Except Thou say "Come to Me."

5 My noon is ended, abolished from life and light,
    My noon is ended, ended and done away,
    My sun went down in the hours that still were day,
      And my lingering day is night.

How long, O Lord, how long in my desperate pain
10   Shall I weep and watch, shall I weep and long for
      Thee?
    Is Thy grace ended, Thy love cut off from me?
      How long shall I long in vain?

O God Who before the beginning hast seen the end,
    Who hast made me flesh and blood, not frost and not
      fire,
15   Who hast filled me full of needs and love and desire
      And a heart that craves a friend,

Who hast said "Come to Me and I will give thee rest,"
    Who hast said "Take on thee My yoke and learn of Me,"
    Who calledst a little child to come to Thee,
20   And pillowedst John on Thy breast;

Who spak'st to women that followed Thee sorrowing,
   Bidding them weep for themselves and weep for their
      own;
   Who didst welcome the outlaw adoring Thee all alone,
    And plight Thy word as a King,—

25 By Thy love of these and of all that ever shall be,
   By Thy love of these and of all the born and unborn,
   Turn Thy gracious eyes on me and think no scorn
    Of me, not even of me.

Beside Thy Cross I hang on my cross in shame,
30   My wounds, weakness, extremity cry to Thee:
   Bid me also to Paradise, also me
    For the glory of Thy Name.

"BEHOLD THE MAN!"

Shall Christ hang on the Cross, and we not look?
   Heaven, earth and hell stood gazing at the first,
   While Christ for long-cursed man was counted cursed;
Christ, God and Man, Whom God the Father strook
5 And shamed and sifted and one while forsook:—
   Cry shame upon our bodies we have nursed
   In sweets, our souls in pride, our spirits immersed
In wilfulness, our steps run all acrook.
Cry shame upon us! for He bore our shame
10   In agony, and we look on at ease
With neither hearts on flame nor cheeks on flame:
   What hast thou, what have I, to do with peace?
Not to send peace but send a sword He came,
   And fire and fasts and tearful night-watches.

THE DESCENT FROM THE CROSS.

Is this the Face that thrills with awe
   Seraphs who veil their face above?

Is this the Face without a flaw,
   The Face that is the Face of Love?
5 Yea, this defaced, a lifeless clod,
   Hath all creation's love sufficed,
Hath satisfied the love of God,
   This Face the Face of Jesus Christ.

"IT IS FINISHED."

Dear Lord, let me recount to Thee
Some of the great things Thou hast done
   For me, even me
   Thy little one.

5 It was not I that cared for Thee,—
But Thou didst set Thy heart upon
   Me, even me
   Thy little one.

And therefore was it sweet to Thee
10 To leave Thy Majesty and Throne,
   And grow like me
   A Little One,

A swaddled Baby on the knee
Of a dear Mother of Thine own,
15   Quite weak like me
   Thy little one.

Thou didst assume my misery,
And reap the harvest I had sown,
   Comforting me
20   Thy little one.

Jerusalem and Galilee,—
Thy love embraced not those alone,
   But also me
   Thy little one.

25 Thy unblemished Body on the Tree
Was bared and broken to atone
  For me, for me
  Thy little one.

Thou lovedst me upon the Tree,—
30 Still me, hid by the ponderous stone,—
  Me always,—me
  Thy little one.

And love of me arose with Thee
When death and hell lay overthrown:
35   Thou lovedst me
  Thy little one.

And love of me went up with Thee
To sit upon Thy Father's Throne:
  Thou lovest me
40   Thy little one.

Lord, as Thou me, so would I Thee
Love in pure love's communion,
  For Thou lov'st me
  Thy little one:

45 Which love of me bring back with Thee
To Judgment when the Trump is blown,
  Still loving me
  Thy little one.

AN EASTER CAROL.

  Spring bursts today,
For Christ is risen and all the earth's at play.

  Flash forth, thou Sun,
The rain is over and gone, its work is done.

5   Winter is past,
Sweet Spring is come at last, is come at last.

          Bud, Fig and Vine,
Bud, Olive, fat with fruit and oil and wine.

          Break forth this morn
10   In roses, thou but yesterday a Thorn.

          Uplift thy head,
O pure white Lily thro' the Winter dead.

          Beside your dams
Leap and rejoice, you merry-making Lambs.

15   All Herds and Flocks
Rejoice, all Beasts of thickets and of rocks.

          Sing, Creatures, sing,
Angels and Men and Birds and everything,

          All notes of Doves
20   Fill all our world: this is the time of loves.

"BEHOLD A SHAKING."

1.

Man rising to the doom that shall not err,—
   Which hath most dread: the arouse of all or each;
   All kindreds of all nations of all speech,
Or one by one of *him* and *him* and *her*?
5   While dust reanimate begins to stir
   Here, there, beyond, beyond, reach beyond reach;
   While every wave refashions on the beach
Alive or dead-in-life some seafarer.
Now meeting doth not join or parting part;
10   True meeting and true parting wait till then,
     When whoso meet are joined for evermore,
Face answering face and heart at rest in heart:—
     God bring us all rejoicing to the shore
   Of happy Heaven, His sheep home to the pen.

2.

Blessed that flock safe penned in Paradise;
   Blessed this flock which tramps in weary ways;
   All form one flock, God's flock; all yield Him praise
By joy or pain, still tending toward the prize.
5 Joy speaks in praises there, and sings and flies
   Where no night is, exulting all its days;
   Here, pain finds solace, for, behold, it prays;
In both love lives the life that never dies.
Here life is the beginning of our death,
10   And death the starting-point whence life ensues;
    Surely our life is death, our death is life:
    Nor need we lay to heart our peace or strife,
But calm in faith and patience breathe the breath
   God gave, to take again when He shall choose.

ALL SAINTS.

They are flocking from the East
And the West,
They are flocking from the North
And the South,
5 Every moment setting forth
From realm of snake or lion,
Swamp or sand,
Ice or burning;
Greatest and least,
10 Palm in hand
And praise in mouth,
They are flocking up the path
To their rest,
Up the path that hath
15 No returning.

Up the steeps of Zion
They are mounting,
Coming, coming,
Throngs beyond man's counting;

20   With a sound
      Like innumerable bees
      Swarming, humming
      Where flowering trees
      Many tinted,
25   Many scented,
      All alike abound
      With honey,—
      With a swell
      Like a blast upswaying unrestrainable
30   From a shadowed dell
      To the hill-tops sunny,—
      With a thunder
      Like the ocean when in strength
      Breadth and length
35   It sets to shore;
      More and more
      Waves on waves redoubled pour
      Leaping flashing to the shore
      (Unlike the under
40   Drain of ebb that loseth ground
      For all its roar).

      They are thronging
      From the East and West,
      From the North and South,
45   Saints are thronging, loving, longing,
      To their land
      Of rest,
      Palm in hand
      And praise in mouth.

"TAKE CARE OF HIM."

"Thou whom I love, for whom I died,
    Lovest thou Me, My bride?"—
Low on my knees I love Thee, Lord,
    Believed in and adored.

5 "That I love thee the proof is plain:
 How dost thou love again?"—
In prayer, in toil, in earthly loss,
 In a long-carried cross.

"Yea, thou dost love: yet one adept
10   Brings more for Me to accept."—
I mould my will to match with Thine,
 My wishes I resign.

"Thou givest much: then give the whole
 For solace of My soul."—
15 More would I give, if I could get:
 But, Lord, what lack I yet?

"In Me thou lovest Me: I call
 Thee to love Me in all."—
Brim full my heart, dear Lord, that so
20   My love may overflow.

"Love Me in sinners and in saints,
 In each who needs or faints."—
Lord, I will love Thee as I can
 In every brother man.

25 "All sore, all crippled, all who ache,
 Tend all for My dear sake."—
All for Thy sake, Lord: I will see
 In every sufferer Thee.

"So I at last, upon My Throne
30   Of glory, Judge alone,
So I at last will say to thee:
 Thou diddest it to Me."

A MARTYR.
THE VIGIL OF THE FEAST.

Inner not outer, without gnash of teeth
 Or weeping, save quiet sobs of some who pray
 And feel the Everlasting Arms beneath,—

Blackness of darkness this, but not for aye;
5   Darkness that even in gathering fleeteth fast,
    Blackness of blackest darkness close to day.
Lord Jesus, thro' Thy darkened pillar cast,
    Thy gracious eyes all-seeing cast on me
    Until this tyranny be overpast.
10 Me, Lord, remember who remember Thee,
    And cleave to Thee, and see Thee without sight,
    And choose Thee still in dire extremity,
And in this darkness worship Thee my Light,
    And Thee my Life adore in shadow of death,
15   Thee loved by day, and still beloved by night.
It is the Voice of my Beloved that saith:
    "I am the Way, the Truth, the Life, I go
    Whither that soul knows well that followeth"—
O Lord, I follow, little as I know;
20   At this eleventh hour I rise and take
    My life into my hand, and follow so,
With tears and heart-misgivings and heart-ache;
    Thy feeblest follower, yet Thy follower
    Indomitable for Thine only sake.
25 Tonight I gird my will afresh, and stir
    My strength, and brace my heart to do and dare,
    Marvelling: Will tomorrow wake the whirr
Of the great rending wheel, or from his lair
    Startle the jubilant lion in his rage,
30   Or clench the headsman's hand within my hair,
Or kindle fire to speed my pilgrimage,
    Chariot of fire and horses of sheer fire
    Whirling me home to heaven by one fierce stage?—
Thy Will I will, I Thy desire desire;
35   Let not the waters close above my head,
    Uphold me that I sink not in this mire:
For flesh and blood are frail and sore afraid;
    And young I am, unsatisfied and young,
    With memories, hopes, with cravings all unfed,
40 My song half sung, its sweetest notes unsung,
    All plans cut short, all possibilities,
    Because my cord of life is soon unstrung.

Was I a careless woman set at ease
   That this so bitter cup is brimmed for me?
45   Had mine own vintage settled on the lees?
A word, a puff of smoke, would set me free;
   A word, a puff of smoke, over and gone: . . .
   Howbeit, whom have I, Lord, in heaven but Thee?
Yea, only Thee my choice is fixed upon
50   In heaven or earth, eternity or time:—
   Lord, hold me fast, Lord, leave me not alone,
Thy silly heartless dove that sees the lime
   Yet almost flutters to the tempting bough:
   Cover me, hide me, pluck me from this crime.
55 A word, a puff of smoke, would save me now: . . .
   But who, my God, would save me in the day
   Of Thy fierce anger? only Saviour Thou.
Preoccupy my heart, and turn away
   And cover up mine eyes from frantic fear,
60   And stop mine ears lest I be driven astray:
For one stands ever dinning in mine ear
   How my gray Father withers in the blight
   Of love for me, who cruel am and dear;
And how my Mother thro' this lingering night
65   Until the day, sits tearless in her woe,
   Loathing for love of me the happy light
Which brings to pass a concourse and a show
   To glut the hungry faces merciless,
   The thousand faces swaying to and fro,
70 Feasting on me unveiled in helplessness
   Alone,—yet not alone: Lord, stand by me
   As once by lonely Paul in his distress.
As blossoms to the sun I turn to Thee;
   Thy dove turns to her window, think no scorn;
75   As one dove to an ark on shoreless sea,
To Thee I turn mine eyes, my heart forlorn;
   Put forth Thy scarred right Hand, kind Lord, take hold
   Of me Thine all-forsaken dove who mourn:
For Thou hast loved me since the days of old,
80   And I love Thee Whom loving I will love
   Thro' life's short fever-fits of heat and cold;

Thy Name will I extol and sing thereof,
   Will flee for refuge to Thy Blessed Name.
   Lord, look upon me from Thy bliss above:
85 Look down on me, who shrink from all the shame
   And pangs and desolation of my death,
   Wrenched piecemeal or devoured or set on flame,
While all the world around me holds its breath
   With eyes glued on me for a gazing-stock,
90   Pitiless eyes, while no man pitieth.
The floods are risen, I stagger in their shock,
   My heart reels and is faint, I fail, I faint:
   My God, set Thou me up upon the rock,
Thou Who didst long ago Thyself acquaint
95   With death, our death; Thou Who didst long ago
   Pour forth Thy soul for sinner and for saint.
Bear me in mind, whom no one else will know;
   Thou Whom Thy friends forsook, take Thou my part,
   Of all forsaken in mine overthrow;
100 Carry me in Thy bosom, in Thy heart,
   Carry me out of darkness into light,
   Tomorrow make me see Thee as Thou art.
Lover and friend Thou hidest from my sight:—
   Alas, alas, mine earthly love, alas,
105   For whom I thought to don the garments white
And white wreath of a bride, this rugged pass
   Hath utterly divorced me from thy care;
   Yea, I am to thee as a shattered glass
Worthless, with no more beauty lodging there,
110   Abhorred, lest I involve thee in my doom:
   For sweet are sunshine and this upper air,
And life and youth are sweet, and give us room
   For all most sweetest sweetnesses we taste:
   Dear, what hast thou in common with a tomb?
115 I bow my head in silence, I make haste
   Alone, I make haste out into the dark,
   My life and youth and hope all run to waste.
Is this my body cold and stiff and stark,
   Ashes made ashes, earth becoming earth,
120   Is this a prize for man to make his mark?

Am I that very I who laughed in mirth
   A while ago, a little little while,
   Yet all the while a-dying since my birth?
Now am I tired, too tired to strive or smile;
125   I sit alone, my mouth is in the dust:
   Look Thou upon me, Lord, for I am vile.
In Thee is all my hope, is all my trust,
   On Thee I centre all my self that dies,
   And self that dies not with its mortal crust,
130 But sleeps and wakes, and in the end will rise
   With hymns and hallelujahs on its lips,
   Thee loving with the love that satisfies.
As once in Thine unutterable eclipse
   The sun and moon grew dark for sympathy,
135   And earth cowered quaking underneath the drips
Of Thy slow Blood priceless exceedingly,
   So now a little spare me, and show forth
   Some pity, O my God, some pity of me.
If trouble comes not from the south or north,
140   But meted to us by Thy tender hand,
   Let me not in Thine eyes be nothing worth:
Behold me where in agony I stand,
   Behold me no man caring for my soul,
   And take me to Thee in the far-off land,
145 Shorten the race and lift me to the goal.

WHY?

Lord, if I love Thee and Thou lovest me,
   Why need I any more these toilsome days;
   Why should I not run singing up Thy ways
Straight into heaven, to rest myself with Thee?
5   What need remains of death-pang yet to be,
   If all my soul is quickened in Thy praise;
   If all my heart loves Thee, what need the amaze,
Struggle and dimness of an agony?—
Bride whom I love, if thou too lovest Me,

10   Thou needs must choose My Likeness for thy dower:
            So wilt thou toil in patience, and abide
          Hungering and thirsting for that blessed hour
        When I My Likeness shall behold in thee,
            And thou therein shalt waken satisfied.

"LOVE IS STRONG AS DEATH."

"I have not sought Thee, I have not found Thee,
    I have not thirsted for Thee:
And now cold billows of death surround me,
Buffeting billows of death astound me,—
5   Wilt Thou look upon, wilt Thou see
        Thy perishing me?"

"Yea, I have sought thee, yea, I have found thee,
    Yea, I have thirsted for thee,
Yea, long ago with love's bands I bound thee:
10   Now the Everlasting Arms surround thee,—
        Thro' death's darkness I look and see
        And clasp thee to Me."

Poems Added in *Poems*
(1888, 1890)

Poems Added in Poems
1858, 1860

BIRCHINGTON CHURCHYARD.

A lowly hill which overlooks a flat,
   Half sea, half country side;
   A flat-shored sea of low-voiced creeping tide
Over a chalky weedy mat.

5   A hill of hillocks, flowery and kept green
   Round Crosses raised for hope,
   With many-tinted sunsets where the slope
Faces the lingering western sheen.

A lowly hope, a height that is but low,
10   While Time sets solemnly,
   While the tide rises of Eternity,
Silent and neither swift nor slow.

ONE SEA-SIDE GRAVE.

Unmindful of the roses,
   Unmindful of the thorn,
A reaper tired reposes
   Among his gathered corn:
5   So might I, till the morn!

Cold as the cold Decembers,
   Past as the days that set,
While only one remembers
   And all the rest forget,—
10   But one remembers yet.

BROTHER BRUIN.

A dancing Bear grotesque and funny
Earned for his master heaps of money,
Gruff yet good-natured, fond of honey,
And cheerful if the day was sunny.
5   Past hedge and ditch, past pond and wood
He tramped, and on some common stood;
There cottage children circling gaily,
He in their midmost footed daily.
Pandean pipes and drum and muzzle
10 Were quite enough his brain to puzzle:
But like a philosophic bear
He let alone extraneous care
And danced contented anywhere.

Still, year on year, and wear and tear,
15 Age even the gruffest bluffest bear.
A day came when he scarce could prance,
And when his master looked askance
On dancing Bear who would not dance.
To looks succeeded blows; hard blows
20 Battered his ears and poor old nose.
From bluff and gruff he waxed curmudgeon;
He danced indeed, but danced in dudgeon,
Capered in fury fast and faster:—
Ah, could he once but hug his master
25 And perish in one joint disaster!
But deafness, blindness, weakness growing,
Not fury's self could keep him going.
One dark day when the snow was snowing
His cup was brimmed to overflowing:
30 He tottered, toppled on one side,
Growled once, and shook his head, and died.
The master kicked and struck in vain,
The weary drudge had distanced pain
And never now would wince again.
35 The master growled: he might have howled
Or coaxed—that slave's last growl was growled.

So gnawed by rancour and chagrin
One thing remained: he sold the skin.

What next the man did is not worth
40 Your notice or my setting forth,
But hearken what befell at last.
His idle working days gone past,
And not one friend and not one penny
Stored up (if ever he had any
45 Friends: but his coppers had been many),
All doors stood shut against him, but
The workhouse door which cannot shut.
There he droned on—a grim old sinner
Toothless and grumbling for his dinner,
50 Unpitied quite, uncared for much
(The ratepayers not favouring such),
Hungry and gaunt, with time to spare:
Perhaps the hungry gaunt old Bear
Danced back, a haunting memory.
55 Indeed I hope so: for you see
If once the hard old heart relented
The hard old man may have repented.

"A HELPMEET FOR HIM."

Woman was made for man's delight;
    Charm, O woman, be not afraid!
His shadow by day, his moon by night,
    Woman was made.

5 Her strength with weakness is overlaid;
    Meek compliances veil her might;
Him she stays, by whom she is stayed.

World-wide champion of truth and right,
    Hope in gloom and in danger aid,
10 Tender and faithful, ruddy and white,
    Woman was made.

A SONG OF FLIGHT.

While we slumber and sleep
The sun leaps up from the deep
—Daylight born at the leap!—
Rapid, dominant, free,
5   Athirst to bathe in the uttermost sea.

While we linger at play
—If the year would stand at May!—
Winds are up and away
Over land, over sea,
10   To their goal wherever their goal may be.

It is time to arise,
To race for the promised prize,
—The Sun flies, the Wind flies—
We are strong, we are free,
15   And home lies beyond the stars and the sea.

A WINTRY SONNET.

A Robin said: The Spring will never come,
    And I shall never care to build again.
A Rosebush said: These frosts are wearisome,
    My sap will never stir for sun or rain.
5   The half Moon said: These nights are fogged and slow,
    I neither care to wax nor care to wane.
The Ocean said: I thirst from long ago,
    Because earth's rivers cannot fill the main.—
When Springtime came, red Robin built a nest,
10   And trilled a lover's song in sheer delight.
    Gray hoarfrost vanished, and the Rose with might
    Clothed her in leaves and buds of crimson core.
The dim Moon brightened. Ocean sunned his crest,
    Dimpled his blue, yet thirsted evermore.

RESURGAM.

From depth to height, from height to loftier height,
   The climber sets his foot and sets his face,
   Tracks lingering sunbeams to their halting-place,
And counts the last pulsations of the light.
5 Strenuous thro' day and unsurprised by night
   He runs a race with Time and wins the race,
   Emptied and stripped of all save only Grace,
Will, Love, a threefold panoply of might.
Darkness descends for light he toiled to seek:
10 He stumbles on the darkened mountain-head,
   Left breathless in the unbreathable thin air,
   Made freeman of the living and the dead:—
He wots not he has topped the topmost peak,
   But the returning sun will find him there.

TODAY'S BURDEN.

"Arise, depart, for this is not your rest."—
   Oh burden of all burdens, still to arise
   And still depart, nor rest in any wise!
Rolling, still rolling thus to east from west
5 Earth journeys on her immemorial quest,
   Whom a moon chases in no different guise:
   Thus stars pursue their courses, and thus flies
The sun, and thus all creatures manifest.
Unrest the common heritage, the ban
10 Flung broadcast on all humankind, on all
   Who live; for living, all are bound to die:
That which is old, we know that it is man:
   These have no rest who sit and dream and sigh,
   Nor have those rest who wrestle and who fall.

"THERE IS A BUDDING MORROW IN MIDNIGHT."

Wintry boughs against a wintry sky;
    Yet the sky is partly blue
        And the clouds are partly bright:—
Who can tell but sap is mounting high
5   Out of sight,
Ready to burst through?

Winter is the mother-nurse of Spring,
    Lovely for her daughter's sake,
        Not unlovely for her own:
10 For a future buds in everything;
        Grown, or blown,
Or about to break.

EXULTATE DEO.

Many a flower hath perfume for its dower,
    And many a bird a song,
And harmless lambs milkwhite beside their dams
    Frolic along;
5 Perfume and song and whiteness offering praise
    In humble, peaceful ways.

Man's high degree hath will and memory,
    Affection and desire,
By loftier ways he mounts of prayer and praise;
10   Fire unto fire,
Deep unto deep responsive, height to height,
    Until he walk in white.

A HOPE CAROL.

A night was near, a day was near,
    Between a day and night
I heard sweet voices calling clear,
    Calling me:

5 I heard a whirr of wing on wing,
  But could not see the sight;
I long to see my birds that sing,
  I long to see.

Below the stars, beyond the moon,
10 Between the night and day
I heard a rising falling tune
  Calling me:
I long to see the pipes and strings
  Whereon such minstrels play;
15 I long to see each face that sings,
  I long to see.

Today or may be not today,
  Tonight or not tonight,
All voices that command or pray
20 Calling me,
Shall kindle in my soul such fire
  And in my eyes such light
That I shall see that heart's desire
  I long to see.

CHRISTMAS CAROLS.

1.

Whoso hears a chiming for Christmas at the nighest,
  Hears a sound like Angels chanting in their glee,
Hears a sound like palm boughs waving in the highest,
  Hears a sound like ripple of a crystal sea.

5 Sweeter than a prayer-bell for a saint in dying,
  Sweeter than a death-bell for a saint at rest,
Music struck in Heaven with earth's faint replying
  "Life is good, and death is good, for Christ is Best."

2.

A holy, heavenly chime
Rings fulness in of time,
And on His Mother's breast
Our Lord God ever-Blest
5   Is laid a Babe at rest.

Stoop, Spirits unused to stoop,
Swoop, Angels, flying swoop,
Adoring as you gaze,
Uplifting hymns of praise:—
10   "Grace to the Full of Grace!"

The cave is cold and strait
To hold the angelic state:
More strait it is, more cold,
To foster and infold
15   Its Maker one hour old.

Thrilled thro' with awestruck love,
Meek Angels poised above,
To see their God, look down:
"What, is there never a Crown
20   For Him in swaddled gown?

"How comes He soft and weak
With such a tender cheek,
With such a soft small hand?—
The very Hand which spann'd
25   Heaven when its girth was plann'd.

"How comes He with a voice
Which is but baby-noise?—
That Voice which spake with might
—'Let there be light'—and light
30   Sprang out before our sight.

"What need hath He of flesh
Made flawless now afresh?
What need of human heart?—
Heart that must bleed and smart
35   Choosing the better part.

"But see: His gracious smile
Dismisses us a while
To serve Him in His kin.
Haste we, make haste, begin
40   To fetch His brethren in."

Like stars they flash and shoot,
The Shepherds they salute:
"Glory to God" they sing:
"Good news of peace we bring,
45   For Christ is born a King."

3.

Lo! newborn Jesus
    Soft and weak and small,
Wrapped in baby's bands
By His Mother's hands,
5   Lord God of all.

Lord God of Mary,
    Whom His Lips caress
While He rocks to rest
On her milky breast
10   In helplessness.

Lord God of shepherds
    Flocking through the cold,
Flocking through the dark
To the only Ark,
15   The only Fold.

Lord God of all things
    Be they near or far,
Be they high or low;
Lord of storm and snow,
20   Angel and star.

Lord God of all men,—
    My Lord and my God!
Thou who lovest me,
Keep me close to Thee
25   By staff and rod.

Lo! newborn Jesus
   Loving great and small,
Love's free Sacrifice,
Opening Arms and Eyes
30   To one and all.

A CANDLEMAS DIALOGUE.

"Love brought Me down: and cannot love make thee
Carol for joy to Me?
Hear cheerful robin carol from his tree,
Who owes not half to Me
5 I won for thee."

"Yea, Lord, I hear his carol's wordless voice;
And well may he rejoice
Who hath not heard of death's discordant noise.
So might I too rejoice
10 With such a voice."

"True, thou hast compassed death: but hast not thou
The tree of life's own bough?
Am I not Life and Resurrection now?
My Cross balm-bearing bough
15 For such as thou."

"Ah me, Thy Cross!—but that seems far away;
Thy Cradle-song today
I too would raise and worship Thee and pray:
Not empty, Lord, today
20 Send me away."

"If thou wilt not go empty, spend thy store;
And I will give thee more,
Yea, make thee ten times richer than before.
Give more and give yet more
25 Out of thy store."

"Because Thou givest me Thyself, I will
Thy blessed word fulfil,
Give with both hands, and hoard by giving still:
Thy pleasure to fulfil,
30   And work Thy Will."

MARY MAGDALENE AND THE OTHER MARY.
A SONG FOR ALL MARIES.

Our Master lies asleep and is at rest:
    His Heart has ceased to bleed, His Eye to weep:
The sun ashamed has dropt down in the west:
    Our Master lies asleep.

5   Now we are they who weep, and trembling keep
Vigil, with wrung heart in a sighing breast,
    While slow time creeps, and slow the shadows creep.

Renew Thy youth, as eagle from the nest;
    O Master, who hast sown, arise to reap:—
10 No cock-crow yet, no flush on eastern crest:
    Our Master lies asleep.

PATIENCE OF HOPE.

The flowers that bloom in sun and shade
    And glitter in the dew,
    The flowers must fade.
The birds that build their nest and sing
5   When lovely Spring is new,
        Must soon take wing.

The sun that rises in his strength
    To wake and warm the world,
        Must set at length.
10 The sea that overflows the shore
    With billows frothed and curled,
        Must ebb once more.

All come and go, all wax and wane,
   O Lord, save only Thou
15   Who dost remain
The Same to all eternity.
   All things which fail us now
        We trust to Thee.

Verses (1893)

"OUT OF THE DEEP
HAVE I CALLED UNTO THEE,
O LORD."

Alone Lord God, in Whom our trust and peace,
   Our love and our desire, glow bright with hope;
   Lift us above this transitory scope
Of earth, these pleasures that begin and cease,
5 This moon which wanes, these seasons which decrease:
   We turn to Thee; as on an eastern slope
   Wheat feels the dawn beneath night's lingering cope,
Bending and stretching sunward ere it sees.
Alone Lord God, we see not yet we know;
10 By love we dwell with patience and desire,
    And loving so and so desiring pray;
    Thy will be done in earth as heaven today;
As yesterday it was, tomorrow so;
   Love offering love on love's self-feeding fire.

Seven vials hold Thy wrath: but what can hold
   Thy mercy save Thine own Infinitude
   Boundlessly overflowing with all good,
All lovingkindness, all delights untold?
5 Thy Love, of each created love the mould;
   Thyself, of all the empty plenitude;
   Heard of at Ephrata, found in the Wood,
For ever One, the Same, and Manifold.

Lord, give us grace to tremble with that dove
10   Which Ark-bound winged its solitary way
      And overpast the Deluge in a day,
           Whom Noah's hand pulled in and comforted:
For we who much more hang upon Thy Love
      Behold its shadow in the deed he did.

"Where neither rust nor moth doth corrupt."

Nerve us with patience, Lord, to toil or rest,
    Toiling at rest on our allotted level;
      Unsnared, unscared by world or flesh or devil,
Fulfilling the good Will of Thy behest:
5   Not careful here to hoard, not here to revel;
But waiting for our treasure and our zest
Beyond the fading splendour of the west,
      Beyond this deathstruck life and deathlier evil.
Not with the sparrow building here a house:
10   But with the swallow tabernacling so
      As still to poise alert to rise and go
           On eager wings with wing-outspeeding wills
Beyond earth's gourds and past her almond boughs,
      Past utmost bound of the everlasting hills.

"As the sparks fly upwards."

Lord, grant us wills to trust Thee with such aim
    Of hope and passionate craving of desire,
      That we may mount aspiring, and aspire
Still while we mount; rejoicing in Thy Name
5   Yesterday, this day, day by day the Same:
      So sparks fly upward scaling heaven by fire,
      Still mount and still attain not, yet draw nigher
While they have being to their fountain flame.

  To saints who mount, the bottomless abyss
10   Is as mere nothing, they have set their face
    Onward and upward toward that blessèd place
     Where man rejoices with his God, and soul
  With soul, in the unutterable kiss
    Of peace for every victor at the goal.

  Lord, make us all love all: that when we meet
   Even myriads of earth's myriads at Thy Bar,
   We may be glad as all true lovers are
  Who having parted count reunion sweet.
5   Safe gathered home around Thy blessèd Feet,
    Come home by different roads from near or far,
    Whether by whirlwind or by flaming car,
  From pangs or sleep, safe folded round Thy seat.
  Oh, if our brother's blood cry out at us,
10   How shall we meet Thee Who hast loved us all,
    Thee Whom we never loved, not loving him?
    The unloving cannot chant with Seraphim,
  Bear harp of gold or palm victorious,
   Or face the Vision Beatifical.

  O Lord, I am ashamed to seek Thy Face
   As tho' I loved Thee as Thy saints love Thee:
   Yet turn from those Thy lovers, look on me,
  Disgrace me not with uttermost disgrace;
5   But pour on me ungracious, pour Thy grace
    To purge my heart and bid my will go free,
    Till I too taste Thy hidden Sweetness, see
  Thy hidden Beauty in the holy place.
  O Thou Who callest sinners to repent,
10   Call me Thy sinner unto penitence,
    For many sins grant me the greater love:
    Set me above the waterfloods, above
  Devil and shifting world and fleshly sense,
   Thy Mercy's all-amazing monument.

It is not death, O Christ, to die for Thee:
　　Nor is that silence of a silent land
　　Which speaks Thy praise so all may understand:
Darkness of death makes Thy dear lovers see
5　Thyself Who Wast and Art and Art to Be;
　　Thyself, more lovely than the lovely band
　　Of saints who worship Thee on either hand,
Loving and loved thro' all eternity.
Death is not death, and therefore do I hope:
10　Nor silence silence; and I therefore sing
　　　A very humble hopeful quiet psalm,
　　Searching my heart-field for an offering;
A handful of sun-courting heliotrope,
　　　Of myrrh a bundle, and a little balm.

Lord, grant us eyes to see and ears to hear,
　　And souls to love and minds to understand,
　　And steadfast faces toward the Holy Land,
And confidence of hope, and filial fear,
5　And citizenship where Thy saints appear
　　Before Thee heart in heart and hand in hand,
　　And Alleluias where their chanting band
As waters and as thunders fill the sphere.
Lord, grant us what Thou wilt, and what Thou wilt
10　Deny, and fold us in Thy peaceful fold:
　　　Not as the world gives, give to us Thine own:
Inbuild us where Jerusalem is built
　　With walls of jasper and with streets of gold,
　　　And Thou Thyself, Lord Christ, for Corner Stone.

"Cried out with Tears."

Lord, I believe, help Thou mine unbelief:
　　Lord, I repent, help mine impenitence:
　　Hide not Thy Face from me, nor spurn me hence,
Nor utterly despise me in my grief;

5   Nor say me nay, who worship with the thief
        Bemoaning my so long lost innocence:—
        Ah me! my penitence a fresh offence,
    Too tardy and too tepid and too brief.
    Lord, must I perish, I who look to Thee?
10   Look Thou upon me, bid me live, not die;
            Say "Come," say not "Depart," tho' Thou art just:
            Yea, Lord, be mindful how out of the dust
        I look to Thee while Thou dost look on me,
            Thou Face to face with me and Eye to eye.

    O Lord, on Whom we gaze and dare not gaze,
        Increase our faith that gazing we may see,
        And seeing love, and loving worship Thee
    Thro' all our days, our long and lengthening days.
5   O Lord, accessible to prayer and praise,
        Kind Lord, Companion of the two or three,
        Good Lord, be gracious to all men and me,
    Lighten our darkness and amend our ways.
    Call up our hearts to Thee, that where Thou art
10   Our treasure and our heart may dwell at one:
            Then let the pallid moon pursue her sun,
        So long as it shall please Thee, far apart,—
            Yet art Thou with us, Thou to Whom we run,
    We hand in hand with Thee and heart in heart.

"I will come and heal him."

    O Lord God, hear the silence of each soul,
        Its cry unutterable of ruth and shame,
        Its voicelessness of self-contempt and blame:
    Nor suffer harp and palm and aureole
5   Of multitudes who praise Thee at the goal,
        To set aside Thy poor and blind and lame;
        Nor blazing Seraphs utterly to outflame
    The spark that flies up from each earthly coal.

My price Thy priceless Blood; and therefore I
10   Price of Thy priceless Blood am precious so
     That good things love me in their love of Thee:
    I comprehend not why Thou lovedst me
    With Thy so mighty Love; but this I know,
No man hath greater love than thus to die.

Ah Lord, Lord, if my heart were right with Thine
   As Thine with mine, then should I rest resigned
    Awaiting knowledge with a quiet mind
Because of heavenly wisdom's anodyne.
5 Then would Thy Love be more to me than wine,
   Then should I seek being sure at length to find,
    Then should I trust to Thee all humankind
Because Thy Love of them is more than mine.
Then should I stir up hope and comfort me
10   Remembering Thy Cradle and Thy Cross;
    How Heaven to Thee without us had been loss,
     How Heaven with us is Thy one only Heaven,
Heaven shared with us thro' all eternity,
     With us long sought, long loved, and much forgiven.

"The gold of that land is good."

I long for joy, O Lord, I long for gold,
   I long for all Thou profferest to me,
I long for the unimagined manifold
   Abundance laid up in Thy treasury.
5   I long for pearls, but not from mundane sea;
I long for palms, but not from earthly mould;
   Yet in all else I long for, long for Thee,
Thyself to hear and worship and behold.
For Thee, beyond the splendour of that day
10   Where all is day and is not any night;
    For Thee, beyond refreshment of that rest
   To which tired saints press on for its delight:—

Or if not thus for Thee, yet Thee I pray
    To make me long so till Thou make me blest.

Weigh all my faults and follies righteously,
    Omissions and commissions, sin on sin;
    Make deep the scale, O Lord, to weigh them in;
Yea, set the Accuser vulture-eyed to see
5 All loads ingathered which belong to me:
    That so in life the judgement may begin,
    And Angels learn how hard it is to win
One solitary sinful soul to Thee.
I have no merits for a counterpoise:
10 Oh vanity my work and hastening day,
What can I answer to the accusing voice?
    Lord, drop Thou in the counterscale alone
    One Drop from Thine own Heart, and overweigh
    My guilt, my folly, even my heart of stone.

Lord, grant me grace to love Thee in my pain,
    Thro' all my disappointment love Thee still,
    Thy love my strong foundation and my hill,
Tho' I be such as cometh not again,
5 A fading leaf, a spark upon the wane:
    So evermore do Thou Thy perfect Will
    Beloved thro' all my good, thro' all mine ill,
Beloved tho' all my love beside be vain.
If thus I love Thee, how wilt Thou love me,
10 Thou Who art greater than my heart? (Amen!)
    Wilt Thou bestow a part, withhold a part?
The longing of my heart cries out to Thee,
    The hungering thirsting longing of my heart:
    What I forewent wilt Thou not grant me then?

Lord, make me one with Thine own faithful ones,
    Thy Saints who love Thee and are loved by Thee;
    Till the day break and till the shadows flee,

At one with them in alms and orisons;
5   At one with him who toils and him who runs,
        And him who yearns for union yet to be;
        At one with all who throng the crystal sea
And wait the setting of our moons and suns.
Ah, my beloved ones gone on before,
10   Who looked not back with hand upon the plough!
          If beautiful to me while still in sight,
        How beautiful must be your aspects now;
          Your unknown, well-known aspects in that light
Which clouds shall never cloud for evermore.

"Light of Light."

O Christ our Light, Whom even in darkness we
      (So we look up) discern and gaze upon,
      O Christ, Thou loveliest Light that ever shone,
Thou Light of Light, Fount of all lights that be,
5   Grant us clear vision of Thy Light to see,
        Tho' other lights elude us, or begone
        Into the secret of oblivion,
Or gleam in places higher than man's degree.
Who looks on Thee looks full on his desire,
10   Who looks on Thee looks full on Very Love:
          Looking, he answers well, "What lack I yet?"
His heat and cold wait not on earthly fire,
        His wealth is not of earth to lose or get;
        Earth reels, but he has stored his store above.

CHRIST OUR ALL IN ALL.

"The ransomed of the Lord."

Thy lovely saints do bring Thee love,
      Incense and joy and gold;

Fair star with star, fair dove with dove,
   Beloved by Thee of old.
5 I, Master, neither star nor dove,
   Have brought Thee sins and tears;
Yet I too bring a little love
   Amid my flaws and fears.
A trembling love that faints and fails
10   Yet still is love of Thee,
A wondering love that hopes and hails
   Thy boundless Love of me;
Love kindling faith and pure desire,
   Love following on to bliss,
15 A spark, O Jesu, from Thy fire,
   A drop from Thine abyss.

Lord, we are rivers running to Thy sea,
Our waves and ripples all derived from Thee:
A nothing we should have, a nothing be,
   Except for Thee.

5 Sweet are the waters of Thy shoreless sea,
Make sweet our waters that make haste to Thee;
Pour in Thy sweetness, that ourselves may be
   Sweetness to Thee.

"An exceeding bitter cry."

Contempt and pangs and haunting fears—
   Too late for hope, too late for ease,
     Too late for rising from the dead;
   Too late, too late to bend my knees,
5   Or bow my head,
Or weep, or ask for tears.

Hark! . . . One I hear Who calls to me:
   "Give Me thy thorn and grief and scorn,
    Give Me thy ruin and regret.

10 Press on thro' darkness toward the morn:
  One loves thee yet:
Have I forgotten thee?"

Lord, Who art Thou? Lord, is it Thou
 My Lord and God Lord Jesus Christ?
15 How said I that I sat alone
 And desolate and unsufficed?
  Surely a stone
Would raise Thy praises now!

O Lord, when Thou didst call me, didst Thou know
 My heart disheartened thro' and thro',
 Still hankering after Egypt full in view
Where cucumbers and melons grow?
5   —"Yea, I knew."—

But, Lord, when Thou didst choose me, didst Thou know
 How marred I was and withered too,
 Nor rose for sweetness nor for virtue rue,
Timid and rash, hasty and slow?
10   —"Yea, I knew."—

My Lord, when Thou didst love me, didst Thou know
 How weak my efforts were, how few,
 Tepid to love and impotent to do,
Envious to reap while slack to sow?
15   —"Yea, I knew."—

Good Lord, Who knowest what I cannot know
 And dare not know, my false, my true,
 My new, my old; Good Lord, arise and do
If loving Thou hast known me so.
20   —"Yea, I knew."—

"Thou, God, seest me."

Ah me, that I should be
Exposed and open evermore to Thee!—
 "Nay, shrink not from My light,

And I will make thee glorious in My sight
5   With the overcoming Shulamite."—
Yea, Lord, Thou moulding me.

. . . Without a hiding-place
To hide me from the terrors of Thy Face.—
    "Thy hiding-place is here
10   In Mine own heart, wherefore the Roman spear
    For thy sake I accounted dear."—
My Jesus! King of Grace.

. . . Without a veil, to give
Whiteness before Thy Face that I might live.—
15   "Am I too poor to dress
    Thee in My royal robe of righteousness?
    Challenge and prove My Love's excess."—
Give, Lord, I will receive.

. . . Without a pool wherein
20   To wash my piteous self and make me clean.—
    "My Blood hath washed away
    Thy guilt, and still I wash thee day by day:
    Only take heed to trust and pray."—
Lord, help me to begin.

Lord Jesus, who would think that I am Thine?
    Ah, who would think
Who sees me ready to turn back or sink,
    That Thou art mine?
5 I cannot hold Thee fast tho' Thou art mine:
    Hold Thou me fast,
So earth shall know at last and heaven at last
    That I am Thine.

"The Name of Jesus."

Jesus, Lord God from all eternity,
    Whom love of us brought down to shame,

  I plead Thy Life with Thee,
   I plead Thy Death, I plead Thy Name.

5 Jesus, Lord God of every living soul,
   Thy Love exceeds its uttered fame,
  Thy Will can make us whole,
   I plead Thyself, I plead Thy Name.

  Lord God of Hosts, most Holy and most High,
   What made Thee tell Thy Name of Love to me?
  What made Thee live our life? what made Thee die?
   "My love of thee."

5 I pitched so low, Thou so exceeding high,
   What was it made Thee stoop to look at me
  While flawless sons of God stood wondering by?
   "My love of thee."

  What is there which can lift me up on high
10 That we may dwell together, Thou with me,
  When sin and death and suffering are gone by?
   "My love of thee."

  O Lord, what is that best thing hid on high
   Which makes heaven heaven as Thou hast promised
    me,
15 Yea, makes it Christ to live and gain to die?
   "My love of thee."

  Lord, what have I that I may offer Thee?
  Look, Lord, I pray Thee, and see.—

  What is it thou hast got?
  Nay, child, what is it thou hast not?
5 Thou hast all gifts that I have given to thee:
  Offer them all to Me,
  The great ones and the small,
  I will accept them one and all.—

  I have a will, good Lord, but it is marred;
10 A heart both crushed and hard:

Not such as these the gift
Clean-handed lovely saints uplift.—

Nay, child, but wilt thou judge for Me?
I crave not thine, but thee.—

15   Ah, Lord, Who lovest me!
Such as I have now give I Thee.

If I should say "my heart is in my home,"
I turn away from that high halidom
    Where Jesus sits: for nowhere else
    But with its treasure dwells
5   The heart: this Truth and this experience tells.

If I should say "my heart is in a grave,"
I turn away from Jesus risen to save:
    I slight that death He died for me;
    I, too, deny to see
10   His beauty and desirability.

O Lord, Whose Heart is deeper than my heart,
Draw mine to Thine to worship where Thou art;
    For Thine own glory join the twain
    Never to part again,
15   Nor to have lived nor to have died in vain.

Leaf from leaf Christ knows;
Himself the Lily and the Rose:

Sheep from sheep Christ tells;
Himself the Shepherd, no one else:

5   Star and star He names,
Himself outblazing all their flames:

Dove by dove, He calls
To set each on the golden walls:

Drop by drop, He counts
10   The flood of ocean as it mounts:

Grain by grain, His hand
Numbers the innumerable sand.

Lord, I lift to Thee
In peace what is and what shall be:

15   Lord, in peace I trust
To Thee all spirits and all dust.

Lord, carry me.—Nay, but I grant thee strength
To walk and work thy way to Heaven at length.—

Lord, why then am I weak?—Because I give
Power to the weak, and bid the dying live.—

5   Lord, I am tired.—He hath not much desired
The goal, who at the starting-point is tired.—

Lord, dost Thou know?—I know what is in man;
What the flesh can, and what the spirit can.—

Lord, dost Thou care?—Yea, for thy gain or loss
10   So much I cared, it brought Me to the Cross.—

Lord, I believe; help Thou mine unbelief.—
Good is the word; but rise, for life is brief.

The follower is not greater than the Chief:
Follow thou Me along My way of grief.

Lord, I am here.—But, child, I look for thee
    Elsewhere and nearer Me.—
Lord, that way moans a wide insatiate sea:
    How can I come to Thee?—
5   Set foot upon the water, test and see
    If thou canst come to Me.—
Couldst Thou not send a boat to carry me,
    Or dolphin swimming free?—
Nay, boat nor fish if thy will faileth thee:
10   For My Will too is free.—
O Lord, I am afraid.—Take hold on Me:
    I am stronger than the sea.—

Save, Lord, I perish.—I have hold of thee,
    I made and rule the sea,
15 I bring thee to the haven where thou wouldst be.

New creatures; the Creator still the Same
    For ever and for ever: therefore we
    Win hope from God's unsearchable decree
And glorify His still unchanging Name.
5 We too are still the same: and still our claim,
    Our trust, our stay, is Jesus, none but He:
    He still the Same regards us, and still we
Mount toward Him in old love's accustomed flame.
We know Thy wounded Hands: and Thou dost know
10   Our praying hands, our hands that clasp and cling
To hold Thee fast and not to let Thee go.
      All else be new then, Lord, as Thou hast said:
      Since it is Thou, we dare not be afraid,
    Our King of old and still our Self-same King.

"King of kings and Lord of lords."

Is this that Name as ointment poured forth
    For which the virgins love Thee; King of kings
    And Lord of lords? All Seraphs clad in wings;
All Cherubs and all Wheels which south and north,
5 Which east and west turn not in going forth;
    All many-semblanced ordered Spirits, as rings
    Of rainbow in unwonted fashionings,
Might answer, Yes. But we from south and north,
From east and west, a feeble folk who came
10   By desert ways in quest of land unseen,
    A promised land of pasture ever green
      And ever springing ever singing wave,
Know best Thy Name of Jesus: Blessed Name,
    Man's life and resurrection from the grave.

Thy Name, O Christ, as incense streaming forth
   Sweetens our names before God's Holy Face;
Luring us from the south and from the north
    Unto the sacred place.

5   In Thee God's promise is Amen and Yea.
    What art Thou to us? Prize of every lot,
Shepherd and Door, our Life and Truth and Way:—
    Nay, Lord, what art Thou not?

"The Good Shepherd."

O Shepherd with the bleeding Feet,
   Good Shepherd with the pleading Voice,
    What seekest Thou from hill to hill?
Sweet were the valley pastures, sweet
5   The sound of flocks that bleat their joys,
    And eat and drink at will.
Is one worth seeking, when Thou hast of Thine
    Ninety and nine?—

How should I stay My bleeding Feet,
10   How should I hush My pleading Voice?
    I Who chose death and clomb a hill,
Accounting gall and wormwood sweet,
   That hundredfold might bud My joys
    For love's sake and good will.
15 I seek My one, for all there bide of Mine
    Ninety and nine.

"Rejoice with Me."

Little Lamb, who lost thee?—
   I myself, none other.—
Little Lamb, who found thee?—
   Jesus, Shepherd, Brother.
5 Ah, Lord, what I cost Thee!
   Canst Thou still desire?—

Still Mine arms surround thee,
　　Still I lift thee higher,
　　Draw thee nigher.

Shall not the Judge of all the earth do right?
　　Yea, Lord, altho' Thou say me nay:
Shall not His Will be to me life and light?
　　Yea, Lord, altho' Thou slay.

5　Yet, Lord, remembering turn and sift and see,
　　Remember tho' Thou sift me thro',
Remember my desire, remember me,
　　Remember, Lord, and do.

Me and my gift: kind Lord, behold,
　　Be not extreme to test or sift;
Thy Love can turn to fire and gold
　　Me and my gift.

5　　Myself and mine to Thee I lift:
Gather us to Thee from the cold
　　Dead outer world where dead things drift.

If much were mine, then manifold
　　Should be the offering of my thrift:
10　I am but poor, yet love makes bold
　　Me and my gift.

"He cannot deny Himself."

Love still is Love, and doeth all things well,
Whether He show me heaven or hell
　　　　Or earth in her decay
　　　　Passing away
5　　　　On a day.

Love still is Love, tho' He should say, "Depart,"
And break my incorrigible heart,
    And set me out of sight
    Widowed of light
10   In the night.

Love still is Love, is Love, if He should say,
"Come," on that uttermost dread day;
    "Come," unto very me,
    "Come where I be,
15   Come and see."

Love still is Love, whatever comes to pass:
O Only Love, make me Thy glass,
    Thy pleasure to fulfil
    By loving still
20   Come what will.

"Slain from the foundation of the world."

Slain for man, slain for me, O Lamb of God, look down;
    Loving to the end look down, behold and see:
Turn Thine Eyes of pity, turn not on us Thy frown,
    O Lamb of God, slain for man, slain for me.

5 Mark the wrestling, mark the race for indeed a crown;
    Mark our chariots how we drive them heavily;
Mark the foe upon our track blasting thundering down,
    O Lamb of God, slain for man, slain for me.

Set as a Cloudy Pillar against them Thy frown,
10   Thy Face of Light toward us gracious utterly;
Help granting, hope granting, until Thou grant a crown,
    O Lamb of God, slain for man, slain for me.

Lord Jesu, Thou art sweetness to my soul:
    I to myself am bitterness:

Regard my fainting struggle toward the goal,
  Regard my manifold distress,
5   O Sweet Jesu.

Thou art Thyself my goal, O Lord my King:
  Stretch forth Thy hand to save my soul:
What matters more or less of journeying?
    While I touch Thee I touch my goal,
10   O Sweet Jesu.

I, Lord, Thy foolish sinner low and small,
Lack all.
His heart too high was set
Who asked, What lack I yet?
5 Woe's me at my most woeful pass!
I, Lord, who scarcely dare adore,
Weep sore:
Steeped in this rotten world I fear to rot.
Alas! what lack I not?
10 Alas! alas for me! alas
More and yet more!—

Nay, stand up on thy feet, betaking thee
To Me.
Bring fear; but much more bring
15 Hope to thy patient King:
What, is My pleasure in thy death?
I loved that youth who little knew
The true
Width of his want, yet worshipped with goodwill:
20 So love I thee, and still
Prolong thy day of grace and breath.
Rise up and do.—

Lord, let me know mine end, and certify
When I
25 Shall die and have to stand
Helpless on Either Hand,
Cut off, cut off, my day of grace.—
Not so: for what is that to thee?

    I see
30 The measure and the number of thy day:
    Keep patience, tho' I slay;
    Keep patience till thou see My Face.
    Follow thou Me.

"Because He first loved us."

    I was hungry, and Thou feddest me;
      Yea, Thou gavest drink to slake my thirst:
    O Lord, what love gift can I offer Thee
        Who hast loved me first?—

5 Feed My hungry brethren for My sake;
      Give them drink, for love of them and Me:
    Love them as I loved thee, when Bread I brake
        In pure love of thee.—

    Yea, Lord, I will serve them by Thy grace;
10   Love Thee, seek Thee, in them; wait and pray:
    Yet would I love Thyself, Lord, face to face,
        Heart to heart, one day.—

    Let today fulfil its daily task,
      Fill thy heart and hand to them and Me:
15 Tomorrow thou shalt ask, and shalt not ask
        Half I keep for thee.

    Lord, hast Thou so loved us, and will not we
      Love Thee with heart and mind and strength and soul,
      Desiring Thee beyond our glorious goal,
    Beyond the heaven of heavens desiring Thee?
5 Each saint, all saints cry out: Yea me, yea me,
      Thou hast desired beyond an aureole,
      Beyond Thy many Crowns, beyond the whole
    Ninety and nine unwandering family.
    Souls in green pastures of the watered land,

10   Faint pilgrim souls wayfaring thro' the sand,
       Abide with Thee and in Thee are at rest:
       Yet evermore, kind Lord, renew Thy quest
    After new wanderers; such as once Thy Hand
       Gathered, Thy Shoulders bore, Thy Heart caressed.

    As the dove which found no rest
       For the sole of her foot, flew back
    To the ark her only nest
       And found safety there;
5   Because Noah put forth his hand,
       Drew her in from ruin and wrack,
    And was more to her than the land
       And the air:

    So my spirit, like that dove,
10   Fleeth away to an ark
    Where dwelleth a Heart of Love,
       A Hand pierced to save,
    Tho' the sun and the moon should fail,
       Tho' the stars drop into the dark,
15   And my body lay itself pale
       In a grave.

"Thou art Fairer than the children of men."

    A rose, a lily, and the Face of Christ
       Have all our hearts sufficed:
    For He is Rose of Sharon nobly born,
       Our Rose without a thorn;
5   And He is Lily of the Valley, He
       Most sweet in purity.
    But when we come to name Him as He is,
       Godhead, Perfection, Bliss,
    All tongues fall silent, while pure hearts alone
10   Complete their orison.

"As the Apple Tree among the trees of the wood."

As one red rose in a garden where all other roses are
  white
 Blossoms alone in its glory, crowned all alone
In a solitude of own sweetness and fragrance of own
  delight,
 With loveliness not another's and thorns its own;
5 As one ruddy sun amid million orbs comely and
  colourless,
 Among all others, above all others is known;
As it were alone in the garden, alone in the heavenly
  place,
 Chief and centre of all, in fellowship yet alone.

None other Lamb, none other Name,
 None other Hope in heaven or earth or sea,
None other Hiding-place from guilt and shame,
 None beside Thee.

5 My faith burns low, my hope burns low,
 Only my heart's desire cries out in me
By the deep thunder of its want and woe,
 Cries out to Thee.

Lord, Thou art Life tho' I be dead,
10 Love's Fire Thou art however cold I be:
Nor heaven have I, nor place to lay my head,
 Nor home, but Thee.

"Thy Friend and thy Father's Friend forget not."

Friends, I commend to you the narrow way:
 Not because I, please God, will walk therein,
 But rather for the Love Feast of that day,
The exceeding prize which whoso will may win.
5 Earth is half spent and rotting at the core,
 Here hollow death's heads mock us with a grin,

Here heartiest laughter leaves us tired and sore.
   Men heap up pleasures and enlarge desire,
   Outlive desire, and famished evermore
10 Consume themselves within the undying fire.
   Yet not for this God made us: not for this
   Christ sought us far and near to draw us nigher,
Sought us and found and paid our penalties.
   If one could answer "Nay" to God's command,
15   Who shall say "Nay" when Christ pleads all He is
For us, and holds us with a wounded Hand?

"Surely He hath borne our griefs."

Christ's Heart was wrung for me, if mine is sore;
   And if my feet are weary, His have bled;
   He had no place wherein to lay His Head;
If I am burdened, He was burdened more.
5 The cup I drink, He drank of long before;
   He felt the unuttered anguish which I dread;
   He hungered Who the hungry thousands fed,
And thirsted Who the world's refreshment bore.
   If grief be such a looking-glass as shows
10   Christ's Face and man's in some sort made alike,
    Then grief is pleasure with a subtle taste:
    Wherefore should any fret or faint or haste?
Grief is not grievous to a soul that knows
   Christ comes,—and listens for that hour to strike.

"They toil not, neither do they spin."

Clother of the lily, Feeder of the sparrow,
   Father of the fatherless, dear Lord,
Tho' Thou set me as a mark against Thine arrow,
   As a prey unto Thy sword,
5 As a ploughed up field beneath Thy harrow,
   As a captive in Thy cord,
Let that cord be love; and some day make my narrow
   Hallowed bed according to Thy Word.   Amen.

Darkness and light are both alike to Thee:
   Therefore to Thee I lift my darkened face;
Upward I look with eyes that fail to see,
   Athirst for future light and present grace.
5   I trust the Hand of Love I scarcely trace.
With breath that fails I cry, Remember me:
   Add breath to breath, so I may run my race
That where Thou art there may Thy servant be.
For Thou art gulf and fountain of my love,
10   I unreturning torrent to Thy sea,
      Yea, Thou the measureless ocean for my rill:
      Seeking I find, and finding seek Thee still:
And oh! that I had wings as hath a dove,
   Then would I flee away to rest with Thee.

"And now why tarriest thou?"

Lord, grant us grace to mount by steps of grace
   From grace to grace nearer, my God, to Thee;
     Not tarrying for tomorrow,
     Lest we lie down in sorrow
5   And never see
Unveiled Thy Face.

Life is a vapour vanishing in haste;
   Life is a day whose sun grows pale to set;
     Life is a stint and sorrow,
10   One day and not the morrow;
   Precious, while yet
It runs to waste.

Lord, strengthen us; lest fainting by the way
   We come not to Thee, we who come from far;
15   Lord, bring us to that morrow
     Which makes an end of sorrow,
   Where all saints are
On holyday.

Where all the saints rest who have heard Thy call,
20   Have risen and striven and now rejoice in rest:
      Call us too home from sorrow
      To rest in Thee tomorrow;
    In Thee our Best,
In Thee our All.

Have I not striven, my God, and watched and prayed?
    Have I not wrestled in mine agony?
    Wherefore still turn Thy Face of Grace from me?
Is Thine Arm shortened that Thou canst not aid?
5   Thy silence breaks my heart: speak tho' to upbraid,
    For Thy rebuke yet bids us follow Thee.
    I grope and grasp not; gaze, but cannot see.
When out of sight and reach my bed is made,
And piteous men and women cease to blame
10   Whispering and wistful of my gain or loss;
    Thou Who for my sake once didst feel the Cross,
      Lord, wilt Thou turn and look upon me then,
And in Thy Glory bring to nought my shame,
    Confessing me to angels and to men?

"God is our Hope and Strength."

Tempest and terror below; but Christ the Almighty
      above.
  Tho' the depth of the deep overflow, tho' fire run
      along on the ground,
Tho' all billows and flames make a noise,—and where
      is an Ark for the dove?—
  Tho' sorrows rejoice against joys, and death and
      destruction abound:
5   Yet Jesus abolisheth death, and Jesus Who loves us we
      love;

His dead are renewed with a breath, His lost are the
    sought and the found.

Thy wanderers call and recall, Thy dead men lift out of
    the ground;
    O Jesus, Who lovest us all, stoop low from Thy Glory
      above:
Where sin hath abounded make grace to abound and to
    superabound,
10   Till we gaze on Thee face unto Face, and respond to
      Thee love unto Love.

Day and night the Accuser makes no pause,
Day and night protest the Righteous Laws,
Good and Evil witness to man's flaws;
Man the culprit, man's the ruined cause,
5   Man midway to death's devouring jaws
    And the worm that gnaws.

Day and night our Jesus makes no pause,
Pleads His own fulfilment of all laws,
Veils with His Perfections mortal flaws,
10   Clears the culprit, pleads the desperate cause,
Plucks the dead from death's devouring jaws
    And the worm that gnaws.

O mine enemy
Rejoice not over me!
    Jesus waiteth to be gracious:
      I will yet arise,
5   Mounting free and far,
Past sun and star,
    To a house prepared and spacious
      In the skies.

Lord, for Thine own sake
10   Kindle my heart and break;
    Make mine anguish efficacious
      Wedded to Thine own:

Be not Thy dear pain,
Thy Love in vain,
15   Thou Who waitest to be gracious
       On Thy Throne.

Lord, dost Thou look on me, and will not I
    Launch out my heart to Heaven to look on Thee?
    Here if one loved me I should turn to see,
And often think on him and often sigh,
5   And by a tender friendship make reply
    To love gratuitous poured forth on me,
    And nurse a hope of happy days to be,
And mean "until we meet" in each good-bye.
Lord, Thou dost look and love is in Thine Eyes,
10   Thy Heart is set upon me day and night,
    Thou stoopest low to set me far above:
O Lord, that I may love Thee make me wise;
    That I may see and love Thee grant me sight;
    And give me love that I may give Thee love.

"Peace I leave with you."

Tumult and turmoil, trouble and toil,
    Yet peace withal in a painful heart;
Never a grudge and never a broil,
    And ever the better part.

5   O my King and my heart's own choice,
    Stretch Thy Hand to Thy fluttering dove;
Teach me, call to me with Thy Voice,
    Wrap me up in Thy Love.

O Christ our All in each, our All in all!
    Others have this or that, a love, a friend,
    A trusted teacher, a long worked for end:

But what to me were Peter or were Paul
5 Without Thee? fame or friend if such might be?
   Thee wholly will I love, Thee wholly seek,
Follow Thy foot-track, hearken for Thy call.
  O Christ mine All in all, my flesh is weak,
  A trembling fawning tyrant unto me:
10 Turn, look upon me, let me hear Thee speak:
  Tho' bitter billows of Thine utmost sea
Swathe me, and darkness build around its wall,
Yet will I rise, Thou lifting when I fall,
  And if Thou hold me fast, yet cleave to Thee.

Because Thy Love hath sought me,
  All mine is Thine and Thine is mine:
Because Thy Blood hath bought me,
  I will not be mine own but Thine.

5 I lift my heart to Thy Heart,
  Thy Heart sole resting-place for mine:
Shall Thy Heart crave for my heart,
  And shall not mine crave back for Thine?

Thy fainting spouse, yet still Thy spouse;
  Thy trembling dove, yet still Thy dove;
Thine own by mutual vows,
  By mutual love.

5 Recall Thy vows, if not her vows;
  Recall Thy Love, if not her love:
For weak she is, Thy spouse,
  And tired, Thy dove.

"Like as the hart desireth the water brooks."

My heart is yearning:
  Behold my yearning heart,

    And lean low to satisfy
      Its lonely beseeching cry,
5   For Thou its fulness art.

Turn, as once turning
    Thou didst behold Thy Saint
      In deadly extremity;
      Didst look, and win back to Thee
10   His will frighted and faint.

Kindle my burning
    From Thine unkindled Fire;
      Fill me with gifts and with grace
      That I may behold Thy Face,
15   For Thee I desire.

My heart is yearning,
    Yearning and thrilling thro'
      For Thy Love mine own of old,
      For Thy Love unknown, untold,
20   Ever old, ever new.

"That where I am, there ye may be also."

How know I that it looms lovely that land I have never
        seen,
With morning-glories and heartsease and unexampled
        green,
With neither heat nor cold in the balm-redolent air?
    Some of this, not all, I know; but this is so;
5   Christ is there.

How know I that blessedness befalls who dwell in
        Paradise,
The outwearied hearts refreshing, rekindling the
        worn-out eyes,
All souls singing, seeing, rejoicing everywhere?
    Nay, much more than this I know; for this is so;
10   Christ is there.

O Lord Christ, Whom having not seen I love and desire
    to love,
O Lord Christ, Who lookest on me uncomely yet still Thy
    dove,
Take me to Thee in Paradise, Thine own made fair;
  For whatever else I know, this thing is so;
15   Thou art there.

"Judge not according to the appearance."

Lord, purge our eyes to see
Within the seed a tree,
  Within the glowing egg a bird,
    Within the shroud a butterfly:

5 Till taught by such, we see
Beyond all creatures Thee,
  And hearken for Thy tender word,
    And hear it, "Fear not: it is I."

My God, wilt Thou accept, and will not we
  Give aught to Thee?
The kept we lose, the offered we retain
  Or find again.

5 Yet if our gift were lost, we well might lose
  All for Thy use:
Well lost for Thee, Whose Love is all for us
  Gratuitous.

A chill blank world. Yet over the utmost sea
The light of a coming dawn is rising to me,
  No more than a paler shade of darkness as yet;
While I lift my heart, O Lord, my heart unto Thee
5   Who hast not forgotten me, yea, Who wilt not forget.

Forget not Thy sorrowful servant, O Lord my God,
Weak as I cry, faint as I cry underneath Thy rod,

Soon to lie dumb before Thee a body devoid of breath,
Dust to dust, ashes to ashes, a sod to the sod:
10   Forget not my life, O my Lord, forget not my death.

"The Chiefest among ten thousand."

O Jesu, better than Thy gifts
    Art Thou Thine only Self to us!
Palm branch its triumph, harp uplifts
    Its triumph-note melodious:
5   But what are such to such as we?
O Jesu, better than Thy saints
    Art Thou Thine only Self to us!
The heart faints and the spirit faints
    For only Thee all-Glorious,
10   For Thee, O only Lord, for Thee.

SOME FEASTS AND FASTS.

ADVENT SUNDAY.

Behold, the Bridegroom cometh: go ye out
With lighted lamps and garlands round about
To meet Him in a rapture with a shout.

It may be at the midnight, black as pitch,
5   Earth shall cast up her poor, cast up her rich.

It may be at the crowing of the cock
Earth shall upheave her depth, uproot her rock.

For lo, the Bridegroom fetcheth home the Bride:
His Hands are Hands she knows, she knows His Side.

10   Like pure Rebekah at the appointed place,
Veiled, she unveils her face to meet His Face.

Like great Queen Esther in her triumphing,
She triumphs in the Presence of her King.

His Eyes are as a Dove's, and she's Dove-eyed;
15   He knows His lovely mirror, sister, Bride.

He speaks with Dove-voice of exceeding love,
And she with love-voice of an answering Dove.

Behold, the Bridegroom cometh: go we out
With lamps ablaze and garlands round about
20   To meet Him in a rapture with a shout.

ADVENT.

Earth grown old, yet still so green,
        Deep beneath her crust of cold
Nurses fire unfelt, unseen:
        Earth grown old.

5   We who live are quickly told:
Millions more lie hid between
        Inner swathings of her fold.

When will fire break up her screen?
        When will life burst thro' her mould?
10   Earth, earth, earth, thy cold is keen,
        Earth grown old.

Sooner or later: yet at last
The Jordan must be past;

It may be he will overflow
His banks the day we go;

5   It may be that his cloven deep
Will stand up on a heap.

Sooner or later: yet one day
We all must pass that way;

Each man, each woman, humbled, pale,
10   Pass veiled within the veil;

Child, parent, bride, companion,
Alone, alone, alone.

For none a ransom can be paid,
A suretyship be made:

15   I, bent by mine own burden, must
Enter my house of dust;

I, rated to the full amount,
Must render mine account.

When earth and sea shall empty all
20   Their graves of great and small;

When earth wrapped in a fiery flood
Shall no more hide her blood;

When mysteries shall be revealed;
All secrets be unsealed;

25   When things of night, when things of shame,
Shall find at last a name,

Pealed for a hissing and a curse
Throughout the universe:

Then Awful Judge, most Awful God,
30   Then cause to bud Thy rod,

To bloom with blossoms, and to give
Almonds; yea, bid us live.

I plead Thyself with Thee, I plead
Thee in our utter need:

35   Jesus, most Merciful of Men,
Show mercy on us then;

Lord God of Mercy and of men,
Show mercy on us then.

CHRISTMAS EVE.

Christmas hath a darkness
   Brighter than the blazing noon,

Christmas hath a chillness
   Warmer than the heat of June,
5 Christmas hath a beauty
   Lovelier than the world can show:
For Christmas bringeth Jesus,
   Brought for us so low.

Earth, strike up your music,
10   Birds that sing and bells that ring;
Heaven hath answering music
   For all Angels soon to sing:
Earth, put on your whitest
   Bridal robe of spotless snow:
15 For Christmas bringeth Jesus,
   Brought for us so low.

CHRISTMAS DAY.

A baby is a harmless thing
   And wins our hearts with one accord,
And Flower of Babies was their King,
   Jesus Christ our Lord:
5 Lily of lilies He
Upon His Mother's knee;
Rose of roses, soon to be
Crowned with thorns on leafless tree.

A lamb is innocent and mild
10   And merry on the soft green sod;
And Jesus Christ, the Undefiled,
   Is the Lamb of God:
Only spotless He
Upon His Mother's knee;
15 White and ruddy, soon to be
Sacrificed for you and me.

Nay, lamb is not so sweet a word,
   Nor lily half so pure a name;
Another name our hearts hath stirred,
20   Kindling them to flame:

"Jesus" certainly
Is music and melody:
Heart with heart in harmony
Carol we and worship we.

CHRISTMASTIDE.

Love came down at Christmas,
    Love all lovely, Love Divine;
Love was born at Christmas,
    Star and Angels gave the sign.

5   Worship we the Godhead,
    Love Incarnate, Love Divine;
Worship we our Jesus:
    But wherewith for sacred sign?

Love shall be our token,
10   Love be yours and love be mine,
Love to God and all men,
    Love for plea and gift and sign.

ST. JOHN, APOSTLE.

Earth cannot bar flame from ascending,
Hell cannot bind light from descending,
Death cannot finish life never ending.

Eagle and sun gaze at each other,
5   Eagle at sun, brother at Brother,
Loving in peace and joy one another.

O St. John, with chains for thy wages,
Strong thy rock where the storm-blast rages,
Rock of refuge, the Rock of Ages.

10   Rome hath passed with her awful voice,
Earth is passing with all her joys,
Heaven shall pass away with a noise.

So from us all follies that please us,
So from us all falsehoods that ease us,—
15   Only all saints abide with their Jesus.

Jesus, in love looking down hither,
Jesus, by love draw us up thither,
That we in Thee may abide together.

"Beloved, let us love one another," says St. John,
    Eagle of eagles calling from above:
Words of strong nourishment for life to feed upon,
    "Beloved, let us love."

5   Voice of an eagle, yea, Voice of the Dove:
If we may love, winter is past and gone;
    Publish we, praise we, for lo! it is enough.

More sunny than sunshine that ever yet shone,
    Sweetener of the bitter, smoother of the rough,
10   Highest lesson of all lessons for all to con,
    "Beloved, let us love."

HOLY INNOCENTS.

They scarcely waked before they slept,
    They scarcely wept before they laughed;
    They drank indeed death's bitter draught,
But all its bitterest dregs were kept
5   And drained by Mothers while they wept.

From Heaven the speechless Infants speak:
    Weep not (they say), our Mothers dear,
    For swords nor sorrows come not here.
Now we are strong who were so weak,
10   And all is ours we could not seek.

We bloom among the blooming flowers,
    We sing among the singing birds;
    Wisdom we have who wanted words:

Here morning knows not evening hours,
15 All's rainbow here without the showers.

And softer than our Mother's breast,
　　And closer than our Mother's arm,
　　Is here the Love that keeps us warm
And broods above our happy nest.
20 Dear Mothers, come: for Heaven is best.

Unspotted lambs to follow the one Lamb,
　　Unspotted doves to wait on the one Dove;
To whom Love saith, "Be with Me where I am,"
　　And lo! their answer unto Love is love.

5 For tho' I know not any note they know,
　　Nor know one word of all their song above,
I know Love speaks to them, and even so
　　I know the answer unto Love is love.

EPIPHANY.

"Lord Babe, if Thou art He
We sought for patiently,
Where is Thy court?
Hither may prophecy and star resort;
5 Men heed not their report."—
　　"Bow down and worship, righteous man:
　　This Infant of a span
　　Is He man sought for since the world began!"—
"Then, Lord, accept my gold, too base a thing
10 For Thee, of all kings King."—

"Lord Babe, despite Thy youth
I hold Thee of a truth
Both Good and Great:
But wherefore dost Thou keep so mean a state,
15 Low-lying desolate?"—
　　"Bow down and worship, righteous seer:

The Lord our God is here
Approachable, Who bids us all draw near."—
"Wherefore to Thee I offer frankincense,
20   Thou Sole Omnipotence."—

"But I have only brought
Myrrh; no wise afterthought
Instructed me
To gather pearls or gems, or choice to see
25   Coral or ivory."—
        "Not least thine offering proves thee wise:
        For myrrh means sacrifice,
        And He that lives, this Same is He that dies."—
"Then here is myrrh: alas! yea, woe is me
30   That myrrh befitteth Thee."—

Myrrh, frankincense, and gold:
And lo! from wintry fold
Good-will doth bring
A Lamb, the innocent likeness of this King
35   Whom stars and seraphs sing:
        And lo! the bird of love, a Dove
        Flutters and coos above:
        And Dove and Lamb and Babe agree in love:—
Come all mankind, come all creation hither,
40   Come, worship Christ together.

EPIPHANYTIDE.

Trembling before Thee we fall down to adore Thee,
    Shamefaced and trembling we lift our eyes to Thee:
O First and with the last! annul our ruined past,
    Rebuild us to Thy glory, set us free
5   From sin and from sorrow to fall down and worship
            Thee.

Full of pity view us, stretch Thy sceptre to us,
    Bid us live that we may give ourselves to Thee:

O faithful Lord and True! stand up for us and do,
   Make us lovely, make us new, set us free—
10   Heart and soul and spirit—to bring all and worship
      Thee.

SEPTUAGESIMA.
"So run that ye may obtain."

One step more, and the race is ended;
   One word more, and the lesson's done;
One toil more, and a long rest follows
     At set of sun.

5   Who would fail, for one step withholden?
   Who would fail, for one word unsaid?
Who would fail, for a pause too early?
     Sound sleep the dead.

One step more, and the goal receives us;
10   One word more, and life's task is done;
One toil more, and the Cross is carried
     And sets the sun.

SEXAGESIMA.
"Cursed is the ground for thy sake."

Yet earth was very good in days of old,
   And earth is lovely still:
Still for the sacred flock she spreads the fold,
   For Sion rears the hill.

5   Mother she is, and cradle of our race,
   A depth where treasures lie,
The broad foundation of a holy place,
   Man's step to scale the sky.

She spreads the harvest-field which Angels reap,
10   And lo! the crop is white;
She spreads God's Acre where the happy sleep
   All night that is not night.

Earth may not pass till heaven shall pass away,
    Nor heaven may be renewed
15   Except with earth: and once more in that day
        Earth shall be very good.

That Eden of earth's sunrise cannot vie
With Paradise beyond her sunset sky
        Hidden on high.

Four rivers watered Eden in her bliss,
5   But Paradise hath One which perfect is
        In sweetnesses.

Eden had gold, but Paradise hath gold
Like unto glass of splendours manifold
        Tongue hath not told.

10   Eden had sun and moon to make her bright;
But Paradise hath God and Lamb for light,
        And hath no night.

Unspotted innocence was Eden's best;
Great Paradise shows God's fulfilled behest,
15   Triumph and rest.

Hail, Eve and Adam, source of death and shame!
New life has sprung from death, and Jesu's Name
        Clothes you with fame.

Hail Adam, and hail Eve! your children rise
20   And call you blessed, in their glad surmise
        Of Paradise.

QUINQUAGESIMA.

Love is alone the worthy law of love:
    All other laws have presupposed a taint:
    Love is the law from kindled saint to saint,
From lamb to lamb, from dove to answering dove.

5   Love is the motive of all things that move
      Harmonious by free will without constraint:
      Love learns and teaches: love shall man acquaint
With all he lacks, which all his lack is love.
Because Love is the fountain, I discern
10   The stream as love: for what but love should flow
      From fountain Love? not bitter from the sweet!
      I ignorant, have I laid claim to know?
        Oh, teach me, Love, such knowledge as is meet
For one to know who is fain to love and learn.

      Piteous my rhyme is
What while I muse of love and pain,
Of love misspent, of love in vain,
Of love that is not loved again:
5   And is this all then?
      As long as time is,
Love loveth. Time is but a span,
The dalliance space of dying man:
And is this all immortals can?
10   The gain were small then.

      Love loves for ever,
And finds a sort of joy in pain,
And gives with nought to take again,
And loves too well to end in vain:
15   Is the gain small then?
      Love laughs at "never,"
Outlives our life, exceeds the span
Appointed to mere mortal man:
All which love is and does and can
20   Is all in all then.

ASH WEDNESDAY.

My God, my God, have mercy on my sin,
For it is great; and if I should begin

To tell it all, the day would be too small
   To tell it in.
5 My God, Thou wilt have mercy on my sin
For Thy Love's sake: yea, if I should begin
To tell This all, the day would be too small
   To tell it in.

Good Lord, today
I scarce find breath to say:
 Scourge, but receive me.
For stripes are hard to bear, but worse
5 Thy intolerable curse;
 So do not leave me.

Good Lord, lean down
In pity, tho' Thou frown;
 Smite, but retrieve me:
10 For so Thou hold me up to stand
And kiss Thy smiting hand,
 It less will grieve me.

LENT.

It is good to be last not first,
 Pending the present distress;
It is good to hunger and thirst,
 So it be for righteousness.
5 It is good to spend and be spent,
 It is good to watch and to pray:
Life and Death make a goodly Lent
 So it leads us to Easter Day.

EMBERTIDE.

I saw a Saint.—How canst thou tell that he
 Thou sawest was a Saint?—

I saw one like to Christ so luminously
  By patient deeds of love, his mortal taint
5 Seemed made his groundwork for humility.

And when he marked me downcast utterly
  Where foul I sat and faint,
Then more than ever Christ-like kindled he;
  And welcomed me as I had been a saint,
10 Tenderly stooping low to comfort me.

Christ bade him, "Do thou likewise." Wherefore he
  Waxed zealous to acquaint
His soul with sin and sorrow, if so be
  He might retrieve some latent saint:—
15 "Lo, I, with the child God hath given to me!"

MID-LENT.

Is any grieved or tired? Yea, by God's Will:
  Surely God's Will alone is good and best:
  O weary man, in weariness take rest,
O hungry man, by hunger feast thy fill.
5 Discern thy good beneath a mask of ill,
  Or build of loneliness thy secret nest:
  At noon take heart, being mindful of the west,
At night wake hope, for dawn advances still.
At night wake hope. Poor soul, in such sore need
10   Of wakening and of girding up anew,
  Hast thou that hope which fainting doth pursue?
    No saint but hath pursued and hath been faint;
Bid love wake hope, for both thy steps shall speed,
    Still faint yet still pursuing, O thou saint.

PASSIONTIDE.

It is the greatness of Thy love, dear Lord, that we
    would celebrate
  With sevenfold powers.

Our love at best is cold and poor, at best unseemly
      for Thy state,
    This best of ours.
5 Creatures that die, we yet are such as Thine own hands
      deigned to create:
    We frail as flowers,
We bitter bondslaves ransomed at a price incomparably
      great
    To grace Heaven's bowers.

Thou callest: "Come at once"—and still Thou callest
      us: "Come late, tho' late"—
10   (The moments fly)—
"Come, every one that thirsteth, come"—"Come prove
      Me, knocking at My gate"—
    (Some souls draw nigh!)—
"Come thou who waiting seekest Me"—"Come thou for
      whom I seek and wait"—
    (Why will we die?)—
15 "Come and repent: come and amend: come joy the joys
      unsatiate"—
    —(Christ passeth by . . .)—
    Lord, pass not by—I come—and I—and I.
      Amen.

PALM SUNDAY.
"He treadeth the winepress of the fierceness and wrath of Almighty God."

I lift mine eyes, and see
Thee, tender Lord, in pain upon the tree,
Athirst for my sake and athirst for me.

"Yea, look upon Me there,
5 Compassed with thorns and bleeding everywhere,
For thy sake bearing all, and glad to bear."

I lift my heart to pray:
Thou Who didst love me all that darkened day,
Wilt Thou not love me to the end alway?

10   "Yea, thee My wandering sheep,
      Yea, thee My scarlet sinner slow to weep,
      Come to Me, I will love thee and will keep."

      Yet am I racked with fear:
      Behold the unending outer darkness drear,
15   Behold the gulf unbridgeable and near!

      "Nay, fix thy heart, thine eyes,
      Thy hope upon My boundless sacrifice:
      Will I lose lightly one so dear-bought prize?"

      Ah, Lord; it is not Thou,
20   Thou that wilt fail; yet woe is me, for how
      Shall I endure who half am failing now?

      "Nay, weld thy resolute will
      To Mine: glance not aside for good or ill:
      I love thee; trust Me still and love Me still."

25   Yet Thou Thyself hast said,
      When Thou shalt sift the living from the dead
      Some must depart shamed and uncomforted.

      "Judge not before that day:
      Trust Me with all thy heart, even tho' I slay:
30   Trust Me in love, trust on, love on, and pray."

MONDAY IN HOLY WEEK.
"The Voice of my Beloved."

      Once I ached for thy dear sake:
      Wilt thou cause Me now to ache?
      Once I bled for thee in pain:
      Wilt thou rend My Heart again?
5   Crown of thorns and shameful tree,
      Bitter death I bore for thee,
      Bore My Cross to carry thee,
      And wilt thou have nought of Me?

TUESDAY IN HOLY WEEK.

By Thy long-drawn anguish to atone,
Jesus Christ, show mercy on Thine own:
Jesus Christ, show mercy and atone
Not for other sake except Thine own.

5   Thou Who thirsting on the Cross didst see
All mankind and all I love and me,
Still from Heaven look down in love and see
All mankind and all I love and me.

WEDNESDAY IN HOLY WEEK.

Man's life is death. Yet Christ endured to live,
    Preaching and teaching, toiling to and fro,
Few men accepting what He yearned to give,
    Few men with eyes to know
5   His Face, that Face of Love He stooped to show.

Man's death is life. For Christ endured to die
    In slow unuttered weariness of pain,
A curse and an astonishment, passed by,
    Pointed at, mocked again
10   By men for whom He shed His Blood—in vain?

MAUNDY THURSDAY.
"And the Vine said . . . Should I leave my wine, which cheereth God and
man, and go to be promoted over the trees?"

The great Vine left its glory to reign as Forest King.
"Nay," quoth the lofty forest trees, "we will not have this
            thing;
We will not have this supple one enring us with its ring.
Lo, from immemorial time our might towers shadowing:
5   Not we were born to curve and droop, not we to climb
            and cling:

We buffet back the buffeting wind, tough to its buffeting:
We screen great beasts, the wild fowl build in our heads
     and sing,
Every bird of every feather from off our tops takes wing:
I a king, and thou a king, and what king shall be our
     king?"

10   Nevertheless the great Vine stooped to be the Forest King,
While the forest swayed and murmured like seas that are
     tempesting:
Stooped and drooped with thousand tendrils in thirsty
     languishing;
Bowed to earth and lay on earth for earth's replenishing;
Put off sweetness, tasted bitterness, endured time's
     fashioning;
15   Put off life and put on death: and lo! it was all to bring
All its fellows down to a death which hath lost the sting,
All its fellows up to a life in endless triumphing,—
I a king, and thou a king, and this King to be our King.

GOOD FRIDAY MORNING.
"Bearing His Cross."

Up Thy Hill of Sorrows
    Thou all alone,
Jesus, man's Redeemer,
    Climbing to a Throne:
5   Thro' the world triumphant,
    Thro' the Church in pain,
Which think to look upon Thee
    No more again.

Upon my hill of sorrows
10   I, Lord, with Thee,
Cheered, upheld, yea, carried,
    If a need should be:
Cheered, upheld, yea, carried,
    Never left alone,
15   Carried in Thy heart of hearts
    To a throne.

GOOD FRIDAY.

Lord Jesus Christ, grown faint upon the Cross,
   A sorrow beyond sorrow in Thy look,
     The unutterable craving for my soul;
      Thy love of me sufficed
5 To load upon Thee and make good my loss
   In face of darkened heaven and earth that shook:—
     In face of earth and heaven, take Thou my whole
      Heart, O Lord Jesus Christ.

GOOD FRIDAY EVENING.
"Bring forth the Spear."

No Cherub's heart or hand for us might ache,
   No Seraph's heart of fire had half sufficed:
Thine own were pierced and broken for our sake,
     O Jesus Christ.

5 Therefore we love Thee with our faint good-will,
   We crave to love Thee not as heretofore,
To love Thee much, to love Thee more, and still
     More and yet more.

"A bundle of myrrh is my Well-beloved unto me."

Thy Cross cruciferous doth flower in all
   And every cross, dear Lord, assigned to us:
Ours lowly-statured crosses; Thine how tall,
     Thy Cross cruciferous.

5   Thy Cross alone life-giving, glorious:
For love of Thine, souls love their own when small,
   Easy and light, or great and ponderous.

Since deep calls deep, Lord, hearken when we call;
   When cross calls Cross racking and emulous:—
10 Remember us with him who shared Thy gall,
     Thy Cross cruciferous.

EASTER EVEN.

The tempest over and gone, the calm begun,
   Lo, "it is finished" and the Strong Man sleeps:
All stars keep vigil watching for the sun,
    The moon her vigil keeps.

5   A garden full of silence and of dew
    Beside a virgin cave and entrance stone:
Surely a garden full of Angels too,
    Wondering, on watch, alone.

They who cry "Holy, Holy, Holy," still
10   Veiling their faces round God's Throne above,
May well keep vigil on this heavenly hill
    And cry their cry of love,

Adoring God in His new mystery
    Of Love more deep than hell, more strong than death;
15 Until the day break and the shadows flee,
    The Shaking and the Breath.

Our Church Palms are budding willow twigs.

While Christ lay dead the widowed world
    Wore willow green for hope undone:
Till, when bright Easter dews impearled
    The chilly burial earth,
5   All north and south, all east and west,
    Flushed rosy in the arising sun;
Hope laughed, and Faith resumed her rest,
    And Love remembered mirth.

EASTER DAY.

Words cannot utter
    Christ His returning:
Mankind, keep jubilee,
    Strip off your mourning,

5   Crown you with garlands,
           Set your lamps burning.

       Speech is left speechless;
           Set you to singing,
       Fling your hearts open wide,
10   Set your bells ringing:
       Christ the Chief Reaper
           Comes, His sheaf bringing.

       Earth wakes her song-birds,
           Puts on her flowers,
15   Leads out her lambkins,
           Builds up her bowers:
       This is man's spousal day,
           Christ's day and ours.

EASTER MONDAY.

       Out in the rain a world is growing green,
           On half the trees quick buds are seen
               Where glued-up buds have been.
       Out in the rain God's Acre stretches green,
5   Its harvest quick tho' still unseen:
               For there the Life hath been.

       If Christ hath died His brethren well may die,
           Sing in the gate of death, lay by
               This life without a sigh:
10   For Christ hath died and good it is to die;
           To sleep whenso He lays us by,
               Then wake without a sigh.

       Yea, Christ hath died, yea, Christ is risen again:
           Wherefore both life and death grow plain
15   To us who wax and wane;
       For Christ Who rose shall die no more again:
           Amen: till He makes all things plain
               Let us wax on and wane.

EASTER TUESDAY.

"Together with my dead body shall they arise."
    Shall my dead body arise? then amen and yea
On track of a home beyond the uttermost skies
    Together with my dead body shall they.

5   We know the way: thank God Who hath showed us the
         way!
    Jesus Christ our Way to beautiful Paradise,
Jesus Christ the Same for ever, the Same today.

Five Virgins replenish with oil their lamps, being wise,
    Five Virgins awaiting the Bridegroom watch and pray:
10   And if I one day spring from my grave to the prize,
    Together with my dead body shall they.

ROGATIONTIDE.

Who scatters tares shall reap no wheat,
But go hungry while others eat.

Who sows the wind shall not reap grain;
The sown wind whirleth back again.

5   What God opens must open be,
Tho' man pile the sand of the sea.

What God shuts is opened no more,
Tho' man weary himself to find the door.

ASCENSION EVE.

O Lord Almighty, Who hast formed us weak,
    With us whom Thou hast formed deal fatherly;
Be found of us whom Thou hast deigned to seek,
    Be found that we the more may seek for Thee;
5   Lord, speak and grant us ears to hear Thee speak;
    Lord, come to us and grant us eyes to see;

Lord, make us meek, for Thou Thyself art meek;
    Lord, Thou art Love, fill us with charity.
O Thou the Life of living and of dead,
10   Who givest more the more Thyself hast given,
        Suffice us as Thy saints Thou hast sufficed;
That beautified, replenished, comforted,
    Still gazing off from earth and up at heaven
        We may pursue Thy steps, Lord Jesus Christ.

ASCENSION DAY.
"A Cloud received Him out of their sight."

When Christ went up to Heaven the Apostles stayed
    Gazing at Heaven with souls and wills on fire,
Their hearts on flight along the track He made,
        Winged by desire.

5   Their silence spake: "Lord, why not follow Thee?
    Home is not home without Thy Blessed Face,
Life is not life. Remember, Lord, and see,
        Look back, embrace.

"Earth is one desert waste of banishment,
10   Life is one long-drawn anguish of decay.
Where Thou wert wont to go we also went:
        Why not today?"

Nevertheless a cloud cut off their gaze:
    They tarry to build up Jerusalem,
15   Watching for Him, while thro' the appointed days
        He watches them.

They do His Will, and doing it rejoice,
    Patiently glad to spend and to be spent:
Still He speaks to them, still they hear His Voice
20   And are content.

For as a cloud received Him from their sight,
    So with a cloud will He return ere long:
Therefore they stand on guard by day, by night,
        Strenuous and strong.

25   They do, they dare, they beyond seven times seven
        Forgive, they cry God's mighty word aloud:
     Yet sometimes haply lift tired eyes to Heaven—
            "Is that His cloud?"

WHITSUN EVE.

"As many as I love."—Ah, Lord, Who lovest all,
     If thus it is with Thee why sit remote above,
Beholding from afar, stumbling and marred and small,
        So many Thou dost love?

5   Whom sin and sorrow make their worn reluctant thrall;
        Who fain would flee away but lack the wings of dove;
     Who long for love and rest; who look to Thee, and call
            To Thee for rest and love.

WHITSUN DAY.
"When the Day of Pentecost was fully come."

At sound as of rushing wind, and sight as of fire,
     Lo! flesh and blood made spirit and fiery flame,
     Ambassadors in Christ's and the Father's Name,
        To woo back a world's desire.

5   These men chose death for their life and shame for their
                boast,
        For fear courage, for doubt intuition of faith,
     Chose love that is strong as death and stronger than
                death
            In the power of the Holy Ghost.

WHITSUN MONDAY.
"A pure River of Water of Life."

We know not a voice of that River,
     If vocal or silent it be,
Where for ever and ever and ever
        It flows to no sea.

5   More deep than the seas is that River,
        More full than their manifold tides,
    Where for ever and ever and ever
            It flows and abides.

    Pure gold is the bed of that River
10   (The gold of that land is the best),
    Where for ever and ever and ever
            It flows on at rest.

    Oh goodly the banks of that River,
        Oh goodly the fruits that they bear,
15   Where for ever and ever and ever
            It flows and is fair.

    For lo! on each bank of that River
        The Tree of Life life-giving grows,
    Where for ever and ever and ever
20   The Pure River flows.

WHITSUN TUESDAY.

Lord Jesus Christ, our Wisdom and our Rest,
    Who wisely dost reveal and wisely hide,
    Grant us such grace in wisdom to abide
According to Thy Will whose Will is best.
5   Contented with Thine uttermost behest,
    Too sweet for envy and too high for pride;
    All simple-souled, dove-hearted and dove-eyed,
Soft-voiced, and satisfied in humble nest.
Wondering at the bounty of Thy Love
10   Which gives us wings of silver and of gold;
    Wings folded close, yet ready to unfold
        When Thou shalt say, "Winter is past and gone:"
When Thou shalt say, "Spouse, sister, love and dove,
        Come hither, sit with Me upon My Throne."

TRINITY SUNDAY.

My God, Thyself being Love Thy heart is love,
    And love Thy Will and love Thy Word to us,
    Whether Thou show us depths calamitous
Or heights and flights of rapturous peace above.
5   O Christ the Lamb, O Holy Ghost the Dove,
    Reveal the Almighty Father unto us;
    That we may tread Thy courts felicitous,
Loving Who loves us, for our God is Love.
Lo, if our God be Love thro' heaven's long day,
10   Love is He thro' our mortal pilgrimage,
    Love was He thro' all aeons that are told.
    We change, but Thou remainest; for Thine age
    Is, Was, and Is to come, nor new nor old;
We change, but Thou remainest; yea and yea!

CONVERSION OF ST. PAUL.

O blessed Paul elect to grace,
    Arise and wash away thy sin,
Anoint thy head and wash thy face,
    Thy gracious course begin.
5   To start thee on thy outrunning race
Christ shows the splendour of His Face:
What will that Face of splendour be
When at the goal He welcomes thee?

In weariness and painfulness St. Paul
    Served God and pleased Him: after-saints no less
Can wait on and can please Him, one and all
    In weariness and painfulness,

5   By faith and hope triumphant thro' distress:
Not with the rankling service of a thrall;
    But even as loving children trust and bless,

    Weep and rejoice, answering their Father's call,
      Work with tired hands, and forward upward press
10 On sore tired feet still rising when they fall,
      In weariness and painfulness.

VIGIL OF THE PRESENTATION.

Long and dark the nights, dim and short the days,
Mounting weary heights on our weary ways,
    Thee our God we praise.
Scaling heavenly heights by unearthly ways,
5 Thee our God we praise all our nights and days,
    Thee our God we praise.

FEAST OF THE PRESENTATION.

O Firstfruits of our grain,
Infant and Lamb appointed to be slain,
A Virgin and two doves were all Thy train,
With one old man for state,
5 When Thou didst enter first Thy Father's gate.

Since then Thy train hath been
Freeman and bondman, bishop, king and queen,
With flaming candles and with garlands green:
Oh happy all who wait
10 One day or thousand days around Thy gate.

And these have offered Thee,
Beside their hearts, great stores for charity,
Gold, frankincense and myrrh; if such may be
For savour or for state
15 Within the threshold of Thy golden gate.

Then snowdrops and my heart
I'll bring, to find those blacker than Thou art:
Yet, loving Lord, accept us in good part;
And give me grace to wait
20 A bruised reed bowed low before Thy gate.

THE PURIFICATION OF ST. MARY THE VIRGIN.

Purity born of a Maid:
Was such a Virgin defiled?
Nay, by no shade of a shade.
She offered her gift of pure love,
5   A dove with a fair fellow-dove.
She offered her Innocent Child
The Essence and Author of Love;
The Lamb that indwelt by the Dove
Was spotless and holy and mild;
10   More pure than all other,
More pure than His Mother,
Her God and Redeemer and Child.

VIGIL OF THE ANNUNCIATION.

All weareth, all wasteth,
All flitteth, all hasteth,
All of flesh and time:—
Sound, sweet heavenly chime,
5   Ring in the unutterable eternal prime.

Man hopeth, man feareth,
Man droopeth:—Christ cheereth,
Compassing release,
Comforting with peace,
10   Promising rest where strife and anguish cease.

Saints waking, saints sleeping,
Rest well in safe keeping;
Well they rest today
While they watch and pray,—
15   But their tomorrow's rest what tongue shall say?

FEAST OF THE ANNUNCIATION.

Whereto shall we liken this Blessed Mary Virgin,
Fruitful shoot from Jesse's root graciously emerging?
Lily we might call her, but Christ alone is white;
Rose delicious, but that Jesus is the one Delight;
5   Flower of women, but her Firstborn is mankind's one
           flower:
He the Sun lights up all moons thro' their radiant hour.
"Blessed among women, highly favoured," thus
Glorious Gabriel hailed her, teaching words to us:
Whom devoutly copying we too cry "All hail!"
10   Echoing on the music of glorious Gabriel.

Herself a rose, who bore the Rose,
   She bore the Rose and felt its thorn.
   All Loveliness new-born
Took on her bosom its repose,
5   And slept and woke there night and morn.

Lily herself, she bore the one
   Fair Lily; sweeter, whiter, far
   Than she or others are:
The Sun of Righteousness her Son,
10   She was His morning star.

She gracious, He essential Grace,
   He was the Fountain, she the rill:
   Her goodness to fulfil
And gladness, with proportioned pace
15   He led her steps thro' good and ill.

Christ's mirror she of grace and love,
   Of beauty and of life and death:
   By hope and love and faith
Transfigured to His Likeness, "Dove,
20   Spouse, Sister, Mother," Jesus saith.

ST. MARK.

Once like a broken bow Mark sprang aside:
Yet grace recalled him to a worthier course,
To feeble hands and knees increasing force,
    Till God was magnified.

5   And now a strong Evangelist, St. Mark
Hath for his sign a Lion in his strength;
And thro' the stormy water's breadth and length
    He helps to steer God's Ark.

Thus calls he sinners to be penitents,
10   He kindles penitents to high desire,
He mounts before them to the sphere of saints,
    And bids them come up higher.

ST. BARNABAS.

"Now when we had discovered Cyprus, we left it on the left hand."—
Acts xxi. 3.
"We sailed under Cyprus, because the winds were contrary."—*Acts* xxvii. 4.

St. Barnabas, with John his sister's son,
    Set sail for Cyprus; leaving in their wake
    That chosen Vessel, who for Jesus' sake
Proclaimed the Gentiles and the Jews at one.
5   Divided while united, each must run
    His mighty course not hell should overtake;
    And pressing toward the mark must own the ache
Of love, and sigh for heaven not yet begun.
For saints in life-long exile yearn to touch
10   Warm human hands, and commune face to face;
     But these we know not ever met again:
Yet once St. Paul at distance overmuch
     Just sighted Cyprus; and once more in vain
     Neared it and passed;—not there his landing-place.

VIGIL OF ST. PETER.

O Jesu, gone so far apart
   Only my heart can follow Thee,
That look which pierced St. Peter's heart
    Turn now on me.

5   Thou Who dost search me thro' and thro'
   And mark the crooked ways I went,
Look on me, Lord, and make me too
    Thy penitent.

ST. PETER.

"Launch out into the deep," Christ spake of old
   To Peter: and he launched into the deep;
   Strengthened should tempest wake which lay asleep,
Strengthened to suffer heat or suffer cold.
5   Thus, in Christ's Prescience: patient to behold
   A fall, a rise, a scaling Heaven's high steep;
   Prescience of Love, which deigned to overleap
The mire of human errors manifold.
Lord, Lover of Thy Peter, and of him
10   Beloved with craving of a humbled heart
    Which eighteen hundred years have satisfied;
Hath he his throne among Thy Seraphim
   Who love? or sits he on a throne apart,
    Unique, near Thee, to love Thee human-eyed?

St. Peter once: "Lord, dost Thou wash my feet?"—
   Much more I say: Lord, dost Thou stand and knock
   At my closed heart more rugged than a rock,
Bolted and barred, for Thy soft touch unmeet,
5   Nor garnished nor in any wise made sweet?
   Owls roost within and dancing satyrs mock.
   Lord, I have heard the crowing of the cock

And have not wept: ah, Lord, Thou knowest it.
Yet still I hear Thee knocking, still I hear:
10 "Open to Me, look on Me eye to eye,
        That I may wring thy heart and make it whole;
And teach thee love because I hold thee dear,
        And sup with thee in gladness soul with soul,
        And sup with thee in glory by and by."

I followed Thee, my God, I followed Thee
        To see the end:
I turned back flying from Gethsemane,
Turned back on flying steps to see
5   Thy Face, my God, my Friend.

Even fleeing from Thee my heart clave to Thee:
        I turned perforce
Constrained, yea chained by love which maketh free;
I turned perforce, and silently
10   Followed along Thy course.

Lord, didst Thou know that I was following Thee?
        I weak and small
Yet Thy true lover, mean tho' I must be,
Sinning and sorrowing—didst Thou see?
15   O Lord, Thou sawest all.

I thought I had been strong to die for Thee;
        I disbelieved
Thy word of warning spoken patiently:
My heart cried, "That be far from me,"
20   Till Thy bruised heart I grieved.

Once I had urged: "Lord, this be far from Thee:"—
        Rebel to light,
It needed first that Thou shouldst die for me
Or ever I could plumb and see
25   Love's lovely depth and height.

Alas that I should trust myself, not Thee;
        Not trust Thy word:
I faithless slumberer in Gethsemane,

Blinded and rash; who instantly
30   Put trust, but in a sword.

Ah Lord, if even at the last in Thee
    I had put faith,
I might even at the last have counselled me,
And not have heaped up cruelty
35   To sting Thee in Thy death.

Alas for me, who bore to think on Thee
    And yet to lie:
While Thou, O Lord, didst bear to look on me
Goaded by fear to blasphemy,
40   And break my heart and die.

No balm I find in Gilead, yet in Thee
    Nailed to Thy palm
I find a balm that wrings and comforts me:
Balm wrung from Thee by agony,
45   My balm, mine only balm.

Oh blessed John who standeth close to Thee,
    With Magdalene,
And Thine own Mother praying silently,
Yea, blessed above women she,
50   Now blessed even as then.

And blessed the scorned thief who hangs by Thee,
    Whose thirsting mouth
Thirsts for Thee more than water, whose eyes see,
Whose lips confess in ecstasy
55   Nor feel their parching drouth.

Like as the hart the water-brooks I Thee
    Desire, my hands
I stretch to Thee; O kind Lord, pity me:
Lord, I have wept, wept bitterly,
60   I driest of dry lands.

Lord, I am standing far far off from Thee;
    Yet is my heart
Hanging with Thee upon the accursed tree;
The nails, the thorns, pierce Thee and me:
65   My God, I claim my part

Scarce in Thy throne and kingdom; yet with Thee
   In shame, in loss,
In Thy forsaking, in Thine agony:
Love crucified, behold even me,
70   Me also bear Thy cross.

VIGIL OF ST. BARTHOLOMEW.

Lord, to Thine own grant watchful hearts and eyes;
   Hearts strung to prayer, awake while eyelids sleep;
   Eyes patient till the end to watch and weep.
So will sleep nourish power to wake and rise
5   With Virgins who keep vigil and are wise,
    To sow among all sowers who shall reap,
    From out man's deep to call Thy vaster deep,
And tread the uphill track to Paradise.
Sweet souls! so patient that they make no moan,
10   So calm on journey that they seem at rest,
      So rapt in prayer that half they dwell in heaven
      Thankful for all withheld and all things given;
    So lit by love that Christ shines manifest
Transfiguring their aspects to His own.

ST. BARTHOLOMEW.

He bore an agony whereof the name
   Hath turned his fellows pale:
But what if God should call us to the same,
   Should call, and we should fail?

5   Nor earth nor sea could swallow up our shame,
    Nor darkness draw a veil:
For he endured that agony whose name
    Hath made his fellows quail.

ST. MICHAEL AND ALL ANGELS.
"Ye that excel in strength."

Service and strength, God's Angels and Archangels;
   His Seraphs fires, and lamps His Cherubim:
Glory to God from highest and from lowest,
   Glory to God in everlasting hymn
5   From all His creatures.

Princes that serve, and Powers that work His pleasure,
   Heights that soar to'ard Him, Depths that sink to'ard
      Him;
Flames fire out-flaming, chill beside His Essence;
   Insight all-probing, save where scant and dim
10   To'ard its Creator.

Sacred and free exultant in God's pleasure,
   His Will their solace, thus they wait on Him;
And shout their shout of ecstasy eternal,
   And trim their splendours that they burn not dim
15   To'ard their Creator.

Wherefore with Angels, wherefore with Archangels,
   With lofty Cherubs, loftier Seraphim,
We laud and magnify our God Almighty,
   And veil our faces rendering love to Him
20   With all His creatures.

VIGIL OF ALL SAINTS.

Up, my drowsing eyes!
   Up, my sinking heart!
Up to Jesus Christ arise!
   Claim your part
5 In all raptures of the skies.

Yet a little while,
   Yet a little way,
Saints shall reap and rest and smile
   All the day.
10 Up! let's trudge another mile.

ALL SAINTS.

As grains of sand, as stars, as drops of dew,
 Numbered and treasured by the Almighty Hand,
 The Saints triumphant throng that holy land
Where all things and Jerusalem are new.
5 We know not half they sing or half they do,
 But this we know, they rest and understand;
 While like a conflagration freshly fanned
Their love glows upward, outward, thro' and thro'.
Lo! like a stream of incense launched on flame
10 Fresh Saints stream up from death to life above,
 To shine among those others and rejoice:
What matters tribulation whence they came?
 All love and only love can find a voice
Where God makes glad His Saints, for God is Love.

ALL SAINTS: MARTYRS.

Once slain for Him Who first was slain for them,
 Now made alive in Him for evermore,
 All luminous and lovely in their gore
With no more buffeting winds or tides to stem
5 The Martyrs look for New Jerusalem;
 And cry "How long?" remembering all they bore,
 "How long?" with heart and eyes sent on before
Toward consummated throne and diadem.
"How long?" White robes are given to their desire;
10 "How long?" deep rest that is and is to be;
 With a great promise of the oncoming host,
Loves to their love and fires to flank their fire:
 So rest they, worshipping incessantly
 One God, the Father, Son, and Holy Ghost.

"I gave a sweet smell."

Saints are like roses when they flush rarest,
Saints are like lilies when they bloom fairest,
    Saints are like violets sweetest of their kind:
      Bear in mind
5   This today. Then tomorrow:
All like roses rarer than the rarest,
All like lilies fairer than the fairest,
    All like violets sweeter than we know.
      Be it so.
10   Tomorrow blots out sorrow.

Hark! the Alleluias of the great salvation
  Still beginning, never ending, still begin,
The thunder of an endless adoration:
Open ye the gates, that the righteous nation
5 Which have kept the truth may enter in.

Roll ye back, ye pearls, on your twelvefold station:
  No more deaths to die, no more fights to win!
Lift your heads, ye gates, that the righteous nation
Led by the Great Captain of their sole salvation,
10 Having kept the truth, may enter in.

A SONG FOR THE LEAST OF ALL SAINTS.

    Love is the key of life and death,
      Of hidden heavenly mystery:
    Of all Christ is, of all He saith,
      Love is the key.

5   As three times to His Saint He saith,
      He saith to me, He saith to thee,
    Breathing His Grace-conferring Breath:
      "Lovest thou Me?"

Ah, Lord, I have such feeble faith,
10   Such feeble hope to comfort me:
But love it is, is strong as death,
          And I love Thee.

SUNDAY BEFORE ADVENT.

The end of all things is at hand. We all
    Stand in the balance trembling as we stand;
Or if not trembling, tottering to a fall.
    The end of all things is at hand.
5   O hearts of men, covet the unending land!
O hearts of men, covet the musical,
    Sweet, never-ending waters of that strand!

While Earth shows poor, a slippery rolling ball,
    And Hell looms vast, a gulf unplumbed, unspanned,
10 And Heaven flings wide its gates to great and small,
    The end of all things is at hand.

GIFTS AND GRACES.

Love loveth Thee, and wisdom loveth Thee:
    The love that loveth Thee sits satisfied;
    Wisdom that loveth Thee grows million-eyed,
Learning what was, and is, and is to be.
5   Wisdom and love are glad of all they see;
    Their heart is deep, their hope is not denied;
    They rock at rest on time's unresting tide,
And wait to rest thro' long eternity.
Wisdom and love and rest, each holy soul
10   Hath these today while day is only night:
    What shall souls have when morning brings to light
        Love, wisdom, rest, God's treasure stored above?
Palm shall they have, and harp and aureole,
    Wisdom, rest, love—and lo! the whole is love.

Lord, give me love that I may love Thee much,
   Yea, give me love that I may love Thee more,
   And all for love may worship and adore
And touch Thee with love's consecrated touch.
5   I halt today; be love my cheerful crutch,
   My feet to plod, some day my wings to soar:
   Some day; but, Lord, not any day before
Thou call me perfect, having made me such.
This is a day of love, a day of sorrow,
10   Love tempering sorrow to a sort of bliss;
      A day that shortens while we call it long:
A longer day of love will dawn tomorrow,
   A longer, brighter, lovelier day than this,
      Endless, all love, no sorrow, but a song.

"As a king, ... unto the King."

Love doth so grace and dignify
   That beggars treat as king with king
Before the Throne of God most High:
Love recognises love's own cry,
5   And stoops to take love's offering.

A loving heart, tho' soiled and bruised;
   A kindling heart, tho' cold before;
Who ever came and was refused
By Love? Do, Lord, as Thou art used
10   To do, and make me love Thee more.

O ye who love today,
Turn away
From Patience with her silver ray:
   For Patience shows a twilight face,
5   Like a half-lighted moon
   When daylight dies apace.

But ye who love tomorrow
Beg or borrow

Today some bitterness of sorrow:
10 For Patience shows a lustrous face,
        In depth of night her noon;
    Then to her sun gives place.

Life that was born today
Must make no stay,
    But tend to end
As blossom-bloom of May.
5   O Lord, confirm my root,
Train up my shoot,
    To live and give
Harvest of wholesome fruit.

Life that was born to die ,
10 Sets heart on high,
        And counts and mounts
Steep stages of the sky.
Two things, Lord, I desire
And I require;
15   Love's name, and flame
To wrap my soul in fire.

Life that was born to love
Sends heart above
        Both cloud and shroud,
20 And broods a peaceful dove.
Two things I ask of Thee;
Deny not me;
        Eyesight and light
Thy Blessed Face to see.

"Perfect Love casteth out Fear."

Lord, give me blessed fear,
    And much more blessed love
That fearing I may love Thee here
    And be Thy harmless dove:

5   Until Thou cast out fear,
        Until Thou perfect love,
     Until Thou end mine exile here
        And fetch Thee home Thy dove.

     Hope is the counterpoise of fear
     While night enthralls us here.

     Fear hath a startled eye that holds a tear:
     Hope hath an upward glance, for dawn draws near
5   With sunshine and with cheer.
     Fear gazing earthwards spies a bier;
     And sets herself to rear
     A lamentable tomb where leaves drop sere,
     Bleaching to congruous skeletons austere:
10   Hope chants a funeral hymn most sweet and clear,
     And seems true chanticleer
     Of resurrection and of all things dear
     In the oncoming endless year.

     Fear ballasts hope, hope buoys up fear,
15   And both befit us here.

"Subject to like Passions as we are."

     Whoso hath anguish is not dead in sin,
        Whoso hath pangs of utterless desire.
        Like as in smouldering flax which harbours fire,—
     Red heat of conflagration may begin,
5   Melt that hard heart, burn out the dross within,
        Permeate with glory the new man entire,
        Crown him with fire, mould for his hands a lyre
     Of fiery strings to sound with those who win.
     Anguish is anguish, yet potential bliss,
10   Pangs of desire are birth-throes of delight;
        Those citizens felt such who walk in white,
     And meet, but no more sunder, with a kiss;

Who fathom still unfathomed mysteries,
  And love, adore, rejoice, with all their might.

Experience bows a sweet contented face,
  Still setting to her seal that God is true:
  Beneath the sun, she knows, is nothing new;
All things that go return with measured pace,
5   Winds, rivers, man's still recommencing race:—
  While Hope beyond earth's circle strains her view,
  Past sun and moon, and rain and rainbow too,
Enamoured of unseen eternal grace.
Experience saith, "My God doth all things well:"
10   And for the morrow taketh little care,
    Such peace and patience garrison her soul:—
    While Hope, who never yet hath eyed the goal,
  With arms flung forth, and backward floating hair,
Touches, embraces, hugs the invisible.

"Charity never Faileth."

Such is Love, it comforts in extremity,
  Tho' a tempest rage around and rage above,
Tempest beyond tempest, far as eye can see:
  Such is Love,
5   That it simply heeds its mourning inward Dove;
Dove which craves contented for a home to be
  Set amid the myrtles or an olive grove.

Dove-eyed Love contemplates the Twelve-fruited Tree,
  Marks the bowing palms which worship as they move;
10 Simply sayeth, simply prayeth, "All for me!"
    Such is Love.

"The Greatest of these is Charity."

A moon impoverished amid stars curtailed,
   A sun of its exuberant lustre shorn,
   A transient morning that is scarcely morn,
A lingering night in double dimness veiled.—
5 Our hands are slackened and our strength has failed:
   We born to darkness, wherefore were we born?
   No ripening more for olive, grape, or corn:
Faith faints, hope faints, even love himself has paled.
Nay! love lifts up a face like any rose
10 Flushing and sweet above a thorny stem,
Softly protesting that the way he knows;
   And as for faith and hope, will carry them
   Safe to the gate of New Jerusalem,
Where light shines full and where the palm-tree blows.

All beneath the sun hasteth,
All that hath begun wasteth;
Earth-notes change in tune
With the changeful moon,
5 Which waneth
While earth's chant complaineth.

Plumbs the deep, Fear descending;
Scales the steep, Hope ascending;
Faith betwixt the twain
10 Plies both goad and rein,
Half fearing,
All hopeful, day is nearing.

If thou be dead, forgive and thou shalt live;
   If thou hast sinned, forgive and be forgiven;
God waiteth to be gracious and forgive,
     And open heaven.

5 Set not thy will to die and not to live;
   Set not thy face as flint refusing heaven;

Thou fool, set not thy heart on hell: forgive
    And be forgiven.

"Let Patience have her perfect work."

Can man rejoice who lives in hourly fear?
  Can man make haste who toils beneath a load?
  Can man feel rest who has no fixed abode?
All he lays hold of, or can see or hear,
5   Is passing by, is prompt to disappear,
    Is doomed, foredoomed, continueth in no stay:
    This day he breathes in is his latter day,
This year of time is this world's latter year.
Thus in himself is he most miserable:
10   Out of himself, Lord, lift him up to Thee,
    Out of himself and all these worlds that flee;
      Hold him in patience underneath the rod,
Anchor his hope beyond life's ebb and swell,
    Perfect his patience in the love of God.

Patience must dwell with Love, for Love and Sorrow
    Have pitched their tent together here:
Love all alone will build a house tomorrow,
    And sorrow not be near.

5 Today for Love's sake hope, still hope, in sorrow,
    Rest in her shade and hold her dear:
Today she nurses thee; and lo! tomorrow
    Love only will be near.

"Let everything that hath breath praise the Lord."

All that we see rejoices in the sunshine,
  All that we hear makes merry in the Spring:
God grant us such a mind to be glad after our kind,
    And to sing
5   His praises evermore for everything.

Much that we see must vanish with the sunshine,
    Sweet Spring must fail, and fail the choir of Spring:
But Wisdom shall burn on when the lesser lights
        are gone,
        And shall sing
10   God's praises evermore for everything.

What is the beginning? Love. What the course? Love still.
What the goal? The goal is Love on the happy hill.
Is there nothing then but Love, search we sky or earth?
There is nothing out of Love hath perpetual worth:
5   All things flag but only Love, all things fail or flee;
There is nothing left but Love worthy you and me.

        Lord, make me pure:
Only the pure shall see Thee as Thou art
        And shall endure.
        Lord, bring me low;
5   For Thou wert lowly in Thy blessed heart:
        Lord, keep me so.

Love, to be love, must walk Thy way
        And work Thy Will;
        Or if Thou say, "Lie still,"
Lie still and pray.

5   Love, Thine own Bride, with all her might
        Will follow Thee,
        And till the shadows flee
Keep Thee in sight.

Love will not mar her peaceful face
10   With cares undue,
        Faithless and hopeless too
And out of place.

Love, knowing Thou much more art Love,
        Will sun her grief,

15   And pluck her myrtle-leaf,
And be Thy dove.

Love here hath vast beatitude:
        What shall be hers
        Where there is no more curse,
20   But all is good?

Lord, I am feeble and of mean account:
Thou Who dost condescend as well as mount,
        Stoop Thou Thyself to me
        And grant me grace to hear and grace to see.

5   Lord, if Thou grant me grace to hear and see
Thy very Self Who stoopest thus to me,
        I make but slight account
        Of aught beside wherein to sink or mount.

Tune me, O Lord, into one harmony
        With Thee, one full responsive vibrant chord;
Unto Thy praise all love and melody,
        Tune me, O Lord.

5   Thus need I flee nor death, nor fire, nor sword:
A little while these be, then cease to be,
        And sent by Thee not these should be abhorred.

Devil and world, gird me with strength to flee,
        To flee the flesh, and arm me with Thy word:
10   As Thy Heart is to my heart, unto Thee
        Tune me, O Lord.

"They shall be as white as snow."

Whiteness most white. Ah, to be clean again
        In mine own sight and God's most holy sight!
To reach thro' any flood or fire of pain
        Whiteness most white:

5   To learn to hate the wrong and love the right
       Even while I walk thro' shadows that are vain,
         Descending thro' vain shadows into night.

       Lord, not today: yet some day bliss for bane
         Give me, for mortal frailty give me might,
10   Give innocence for guilt, and for my stain
         Whiteness most white.

           Thy lilies drink the dew,
       Thy lambs the rill, and I will drink them too;
           For those in purity
       And innocence are types, dear Lord, of Thee.
5   The fragrant lily flower
       Bows and fulfils Thy Will its lifelong hour;
           The lamb at rest and play
       Fulfils Thy Will in gladness all the day;
           They leave tomorrow's cares
10   Until the morrow, what it brings it bears.
           And I, Lord, would be such;
       Not high or great or anxious overmuch,
           But pure and temperate,
       Earnest to do Thy Will betimes and late,
15   Fragrant with love and praise
       And innocence thro' all my appointed days;
           Thy lily I would be,
       Spotless and sweet, Thy lamb to follow Thee.

"When I was in trouble I called upon the Lord."

       A burdened heart that bleeds and bears
         And hopes and waits in pain,
       And faints beneath its fears and cares,
         Yet hopes again:

5   Wilt Thou accept the heart I bring,
         O gracious Lord and kind,

To ease it of a torturing sting,
   And staunch and bind?

Alas, if Thou wilt none of this,
10   None else have I to give:
Look Thou upon it as it is,
   Accept, relieve.

Or if Thou wilt not yet relieve,
   Be not extreme to sift:
15 Accept a faltering will to give,
   Itself Thy gift.

Grant us such grace that we may work Thy Will
   And speak Thy words and walk before Thy Face,
Profound and calm, like waters deep and still:
   Grant us such grace.

5   Not hastening and not loitering in our pace
For gloomiest valley or for sultriest hill,
   Content and fearless on our downward race.

As rivers seek a sea they cannot fill
   But are themselves filled full in its embrace,
10 Absorbed, at rest, each river and each rill:
   Grant us such grace.

"Who hath despised the day of small things?"

As violets so be I recluse and sweet,
   Cheerful as daisies unaccounted rare,
Still sunward-gazing from a lowly seat,
   Still sweetening wintry air.

5 While half-awakened Spring lags incomplete,
   While lofty forest trees tower bleak and bare,
Daisies and violets own remotest heat
   And bloom and make them fair.

"Do this, and he doeth it."

Content to come, content to go,
   Content to wrestle or to race,
Content to know or not to know,
    Each in his place;

5   Lord, grant us grace to love Thee so
    That glad of heart and glad of face
At last we may sit, high or low,
    Each in his place;

Where pleasures flow as rivers flow,
10   And loss has left no barren trace,
And all that are, are perfect so,
    Each in his place.

"That no man take thy Crown."

Be faithful unto death. Christ proffers thee
   Crown of a life that draws immortal breath:
To thee He saith, yea, and He saith to me,
   "Be faithful unto death."

5   To every living soul that same He saith,
   "Be faithful":—whatsoever else we be,
   Let us be faithful, challenging His faith.

Tho' trouble storm around us like the sea,
   Tho' hell surge up to scare us and to scathe,
10 Tho' heaven and earth betake themselves to flee,
   "Be faithful unto death."

"Ye are come unto Mount Sion."

Fear, Faith, and Hope have sent their hearts above:
   Prudence, Obedience, and Humility
   Climb at their call, all scaling heaven toward Love.

Fear hath least grace but great expediency;
5   Faith and Humility show grave and strong;
          Prudence and Hope mount balanced equally.
Obedience marches marshalling their throng,
     Goes first, goes last, to left hand or to right;
     And all the six uplift a pilgrim's song.
10 By day they rest not, nor they rest by night:
     While Love within them, with them, over them,
     Weans them and woos them from the dark to light.
Each plies for staff not reed with broken stem,
     But olive branch in pledge of patient peace;
15   Till Love being theirs in New Jerusalem,
Transfigure them to Love, and so they cease.
     Love is the sole beatitude above:
     All other graces, to their vast increase
Of glory, look on Love and mirror Love.

"Sit down in the lowest room."

Lord, give me grace
To take the lowest place;
Nor even desire,
Unless it be Thy Will, to go up higher.

5   Except by grace,
I fail of lowest place;
Except desire
Sit low, it aims awry to go up higher.

"Lord, it is good for us to be here."

Grant us, O Lord, that patience and that faith:
     Faith's patience imperturbable in Thee,
     Hope's patience till the long-drawn shadows flee,
Love's patience unresentful of all scathe.
5   Verily we need patience breath by breath:
     Patience while faith holds up her glass to see,
     While hope toils yoked in fear's copartnery,

And love goes softly on the way to death.
How gracious and how perfecting a grace
10   Must patience be on which those others wait:
Faith with suspended rapture in her face,
    Hope pale and careful hand in hand with fear,
Love—ah, good love who would not antedate
    God's Will, but saith, Good is it to be here.

Lord, grant us grace to rest upon Thy word,
    To rest in hope until we see Thy Face;
To rest thro' toil unruffled and unstirred,
    Lord, grant us grace.

5   This burden and this heat wear on apace:
Night comes, when sweeter than night's singing bird
    Will swell the silence of our ended race.

Ah, songs which flesh and blood have never heard
    And cannot hear, songs of the silent place
10 Where rest remains! Lord, slake our hope deferred,
    Lord, grant us grace.

THE WORLD.
SELF-DESTRUCTION.

"A vain Shadow."

The world,—what a world, ah me!
    Mouldy, worm-eaten, grey:
Vain as a leaf from a tree,
    As a fading day,
5   As veriest vanity,
    As the froth and the spray
Of the hollow-billowed sea,
As what was and shall not be,
    As what is and passes away.

"Lord, save us, we perish."

O Lord, seek us, O Lord, find us
    In Thy patient care;
Be Thy Love before, behind us,
    Round us, everywhere:
5   Lest the god of this world blind us,
    Lest he speak us fair,
Lest he forge a chain to bind us,
    Lest he bait a snare.
Turn not from us, call to mind us,
10   Find, embrace us, bear;
Be Thy Love before, behind us,
    Round us, everywhere.

What is this above thy head,
    O Man?—
The World, all overspread
With pearls and golden rays
5   And gems ablaze;
A sight which day and night
    Fills an eye's span.

What is this beneath thy feet,
    O Saint?—
10   The World, a nauseous sweet
Puffed up and perishing;
A hollow thing,
A lie, a vanity,
    Tinsel and paint.

15   What is she while time is time,
    O Man?—
In a perpetual prime
Beauty and youth she hath;
And her footpath
20   Breeds flowers thro' dancing hours
    Since time began.

While time lengthens what is she,
　　O Saint?—
Nought: yea, all men shall see
25　How she is nought at all,
When her death-pall
Of fire ends their desire
　　And brands her taint.

Ah, poor Man, befooled and slow
30　　And faint!
Ah, poorest Man, if so
Thou turn thy back on bliss
And choose amiss!
For thou art choosing now:
35　　Sinner,—or Saint.

Babylon the Great.

Foul is she and ill-favoured, set askew:
　　Gaze not upon her till thou dream her fair,
　　Lest she should mesh thee in her wanton hair,
Adept in arts grown old yet ever new.
5　Her heart lusts not for love, but thro' and thro'
　　For blood, as spotted panther lusts in lair;
　　No wine is in her cup, but filth is there
Unutterable, with plagues hid out of view.
Gaze not upon her, for her dancing whirl
10　　Turns giddy the fixed gazer presently:
　　Gaze not upon her, lest thou be as she
　　　When, at the far end of her long desire,
Her scarlet vest and gold and gem and pearl
　　　And she amid her pomp are set on fire.

"Standing afar off for the fear of her torment."

Is this the end? is there no end but this?
   Yea, none beside:
   No other end for pride
And foulness and besottedness.

5   Hath she no friend? hath she no clinging friend?
    Nay, none at all;
    Who stare upon her fall
Quake for themselves with hair on end.

Will she be done away? vanish away?
10   Yea, like a dream;
   Yea, like the shades that seem
Somewhat, and lo! are nought by day.

Alas for her amid man's helpless moan,
   Alas for her!
15   She hath no comforter:
In solitude of fire she sits alone.

"O Lucifer, Son of the Morning!"

Oh fallen star! a darkened light,
   A glory hurtled from its car,
Self-blasted from the holy height:
    Oh fallen star!

5   Fallen beyond earth's utmost bar,
Beyond return, beyond far sight
   Of outmost glimmering nebular.

Now blackness, which once walked in white;
   Now death, whose life once glowed afar;
10   Oh son of dawn that loved the night,
    Oh fallen star!

Alas, alas! for the self-destroyed
   Vanish as images from a glass,
Sink down and die down by hope unbuoyed:—
   Alas, alas!

5   Who shall stay their ruinous mass?
Besotted, reckless, possessed, decoyed,
   They hurry to the dolorous pass.

Saints fall a-weeping who would have joyed,
   Sore they weep for a glory that was,
10   For a fulness emptied into the void,
     Alas, alas!

As froth on the face of the deep,
   As foam on the crest of the sea,
As dreams at the waking of sleep,
   As gourd of a day and a night,
5   As harvest that no man shall reap,
   As vintage that never shall be,
   Is hope if it cling not aright,
     O my God, unto Thee.

"Where their worm dieth not, and the fire is not quenched."

In tempest and storm blackness of darkness for ever,
   A fire unextinguished, a worm's indestructible swarm;
Where no hope shall ever be more, and love shall be
       never,
     In tempest and storm;
5   Where the form of all things is fashionless, void of all
       form;
Where from death that severeth all, the soul cannot sever
     In tempest and storm.

Toll, bell, toll. For hope is flying
    Sighing from the earthbound soul:
Life is sighing, life is dying:
    Toll, bell, toll.

5   Gropes in its own grave the mole
Wedding darkness, undescrying,
    Tending to no different goal.

Self-slain soul, in vain thy sighing:
    Self-slain, who should make thee whole?
10   Vain the clamour of thy crying:
    Toll, bell, toll.

DIVERS WORLDS. TIME AND ETERNITY.

Earth has clear call of daily bells,
    A chancel-vault of gloom and star,
    A rapture where the anthems are,
A thunder when the organ swells:
5   Alas, man's daily life—what else?—
Is out of tune with daily bells.

While Paradise accords the chimes
    Of Earth and Heaven, its patient pause
    Is rest fulfilling music's laws.
10 Saints sit and gaze, where oftentimes
Precursive flush of morning climbs
And air vibrates with coming chimes.

"Escape to the Mountain."

I peered within, and saw a world of sin;
    Upward, and saw a world of righteousness;
Downward, and saw darkness and flame begin
    Which no man can express.

5   I girt me up, I gat me up to flee
  From face of darkness and devouring flame:
And fled I had, but guilt is loading me
   With dust of death and shame.

Yet still the light of righteousness beams pure,
10 Beams to me from the world of far-off day:—
Lord, Who hast called them happy that endure,
   Lord, make me such as they.

I lift mine eyes to see: earth vanisheth.
  I lift up wistful eyes and bend my knee:
Trembling, bowed down, and face to face with Death,
  I lift mine eyes to see.

5 Lo, what I see is Death that shadows me:
Yet whilst I, seeing, draw a shuddering breath,
  Death like a mist grows rare perceptibly.

Beyond the darkness light, beyond the scathe
  Healing, beyond the Cross a palm-branch tree,
10 Beyond Death Life, on evidence of faith:
  I lift mine eyes to see.

"Yet a little while."

Heaven is not far, tho' far the sky
  Overarching earth and main.
It takes not long to live and die,
  Die, revive, and rise again.
5 Not long: how long? Oh, long re-echoing song!
O Lord, how long?

"Behold, it was very good."

All things are fair, if we had eyes to see
  How first God made them goodly everywhere:

And goodly still in Paradise they be,—
   All things are fair.

5   O Lord, the solemn heavens Thy praise declare;
The multi-fashioned saints bring praise to Thee,
   As doves fly home and cast away their care.

As doves on divers branches of their tree,
   Perched high or low, sit all contented there
10 Not mourning any more; in each degree
   All things are fair.

"Whatsoever is right, that shall ye receive."

When all the overwork of life
   Is finished once, and fallen asleep
We shrink no more beneath the knife,
   But having sown prepare to reap;
5 Delivered from the crossway rough,
   Delivered from the thorny scourge,
   Delivered from the tossing surge,
Then shall we find—(please God!)—it is enough?

Not in this world of hope deferred,
10   This world of perishable stuff;
Eye hath not seen, nor ear hath heard,
   Nor heart conceived that full "enough":
Here moans the separating sea,
   Here harvests fail, here breaks the heart;
15   There God shall join and no man part,
All one in Christ, so one—(please God!)—with me.

This near-at-hand land breeds pain by measure:
That far-away land overflows with treasure
     Of heaped-up good pleasure.

Our land that we see is befouled by evil:
5 The land that we see not makes mirth and revel,
     Far from death and devil.

This land hath for music sobbing and sighing:
That land hath soft speech and sweet soft replying
    Of all loves undying.

10 This land hath for pastime errors and follies:
That land hath unending unflagging solace
    Of full-chanted "Holies."

Up and away, call the Angels to us;
Come to our home where no foes pursue us,
15   And no tears bedew us;

Where that which riseth sets again never,
Where that which springeth flows in a river
    For ever and ever;

Where harvest justifies labour of sowing,
20 Where that which budded comes to the blowing
    Sweet beyond your knowing.

Come and laugh with us, sing in our singing;
Come, yearn no more, but rest in your clinging.
    See what we are bringing;

25 Crowns like our own crowns, robes for your wearing;
For love of you we kiss them in bearing,
    All good with you sharing:

Over you gladdening, in you delighting;
Come from your famine, your failure, your fighting;
30   Come to full wrong-righting.

Come, where all balm is garnered to ease you;
Come, where all beauty is spread out to please you;
    Come, gaze upon Jesu.

"Was Thy Wrath against the Sea?"

The sea laments with unappeasable
   Hankering wail of loss,
     Lifting its hands on high and passing by
      Out of the lovely light:

5   No foambow any more may crest that swell
       Of clamorous waves which toss;
          Lifting its hands on high it passes by
           From light into the night.
    Peace, peace, thou sea! God's wisdom worketh well,
10   Assigns it crown or cross:
          Lift we all hands on high, and passing by
           Attest: God doeth right.

"And there was no more Sea."

Voices from above and from beneath,
    Voices of creation near and far,
Voices out of life and out of death,
      Out of measureless space,
5   Sun, moon, star,
        In oneness of contentment offering praise.

Heaven and earth and sea jubilant,
    Jubilant all things that dwell therein;
Filled to fullest overflow they chant,
10   Still roll onward, swell,
      Still begin,
        Never flagging praise interminable.

Thou who must fall silent in a while,
    Chant thy sweetest, gladdest, best, at once;
15   Sun thyself today, keep peace and smile;
      By love upward send
      Orisons,
        Accounting love thy lot and love thine end.

Roses on a brier,
    Pearls from out the bitter sea,
Such is earth's desire
    However pure it be.

5   Neither bud nor brier,
           Neither pearl nor brine for me:
       Be stilled, my long desire;
           There shall be no more sea.

       Be stilled, my passionate heart;
10   Old earth shall end, new earth shall be:
       Be still, and earn thy part
           Where shall be no more sea.

       We are of those who tremble at Thy word;
           Who faltering walk in darkness toward our close
       Of mortal life, by terrors curbed and spurred:
           We are of those.

5   We journey to that land which no man knows
       Who any more can make his voice be heard
           Above the clamour of our wants and woes.

       Not ours the hearts Thy loftiest love hath stirred,
           Not such as we Thy lily and Thy rose:—
10   Yet, Hope of those who hope with hope deferred,
           We are of those.

"Awake, thou that sleepest."

       The night is far spent, the day is at hand:
           Let us therefore cast off the works of darkness,
               And let us put on the armour of light.
           Night for the dead in their stiffness and starkness!
5   Day for the living who mount in their might
       Out of their graves to the beautiful land.

       Far, far away lies the beautiful land:
           Mount on wide wings of exceeding desire,
               Mount, look not back, mount to life and to light,
10   Mount by the gleam of your lamps all on fire
               Up from the dead men and up from the night.
       The night is far spent, the day is at hand.

We know not when, we know not where,
　　We know not what that world will be;
But this we know: it will be fair
　　　　To see.

5　　With heart athirst and thirsty face
　　We know and know not what shall be:
Christ Jesus bring us of His grace
　　　　To see.

Christ Jesus bring us of His grace,
10　　Beyond all prayers our hope can pray,
One day to see Him face to Face,
　　　　One day.

"I will lift up mine eyes unto the Hills."

When sick of life and all the world—
How sick of all desire but Thee!—
I lift mine eyes up to the hills,
　　Eyes of my heart that see,
5　I see beyond all death and ills
Refreshing green for heart and eyes,
The golden streets and gateways pearled,
　　The trees of Paradise.

"There is a time for all things," saith
10　The Word of Truth, Thyself the Word;
And many things Thou reasonest of:
　　A time for hope deferred,
But time is now for grief and fears;
A time for life, but now is death;
15　Oh, when shall be the time of love
　　When Thou shalt wipe our tears?

Then the new Heavens and Earth shall be
Where righteousness shall dwell indeed;
There shall be no more blight, nor need,
20　　Nor barrier of the sea;

No sun and moon alternating,
For God shall be the Light thereof;
No sorrow more, no death, no sting,
   For God Who reigns is Love.

"Then whose shall those things be?"

Oh what is earth, that we should build
Our houses here, and seek concealed
Poor treasure, and add field to field,
And heap to heap, and store to store,
5 Still grasping more and seeking more,
While step by step Death nears the door?

"His Banner over me was Love."

In that world we weary to attain,
   Love's furled banner floats at large unfurled:
There is no more doubt and no more pain
   In that world.

5   There are gems and gold and inlets pearled;
There the verdure fadeth not again;
   There no clinging tendrils droop uncurled.

Here incessant tides stir up the main,
   Stormy miry depths aloft are hurled:
10 There is no more sea, or storm, or stain,
   In that world.

Beloved, yield thy time to God, for He
   Will make eternity thy recompense;
Give all thy substance for His Love, and be
   Beatified past earth's experience.
5 Serve Him in bonds, until He set thee free;
   Serve Him in dust, until He lift thee thence;

Till death be swallowed up in victory
 When the great trumpet sounds to bid thee hence.
Shall setting day win day that will not set?
10 Poor price wert thou to spend thyself for Christ,
  Had not His wealth thy poverty sufficed:
   Yet since He makes His garden of thy clod,
Water thy lily, rose, or violet,
  And offer up thy sweetness unto God.

Time seems not short:
 If so I call to mind
 Its vast prerogative to loose or bind,
And bear and strike amort
5 All humankind.

Time seems not long:
 If I peer out and see
 Sphere within sphere, time in eternity,
And hear the alternate song
10 Cry endlessly.

Time greatly short,
 O time so briefly long,
 Yea, time sole battle-ground of right and wrong:
Art thou a time for sport
15 And for a song?

The half moon shows a face of plaintive sweetness
 Ready and poised to wax or wane;
A fire of pale desire in incompleteness,
 Tending to pleasure or to pain:—
5 Lo, while we gaze she rolleth on in fleetness
 To perfect loss or perfect gain.

Half bitterness we know, we know half sweetness;
 This world is all on wax, on wane:
When shall completeness round time's incompleteness,
10 Fulfilling joy, fulfilling pain?—

Lo, while we ask, life rolleth on in fleetness
    To finished loss or finished gain.

"As the Doves to their windows."

They throng from the east and the west,
    The north and the south, with a song;
To golden abodes of their rest
    They throng.

5   Eternity stretches out long:
Time, brief at its worst or its best,
    Will quit them of ruin and wrong.

A rainbow aloft for their crest,
    A palm for their weakness made strong!
10 As doves breast all winds to their nest,
    They throng.

Oh knell of a passing time,
Will it never cease to chime?
Oh stir of the tedious sea,
Will it never cease to be?
5 Yea, when night and when day,
Moon and sun, pass away.

Surely the sun burns low,
The moon makes ready to go,
Broad ocean ripples to waste,
10 Time is running in haste,
Night is numbered, and day
Numbered to pass away.

Time passeth away with its pleasure and pain,
    Its garlands of cypress and bay,
With wealth and with want, with a balm and a bane,
    Time passeth away.

5   Eternity cometh to stay,
   Eternity stayeth to go not again;
     Eternity barring the way,

Arresting all courses of planet or main,
    Arresting who plan or who pray,
10   Arresting creation: while grand in its wane
     Time passeth away.

"The Earth shall tremble at the Look of Him."

Tremble, thou earth, at the Presence of the Lord
   Whose Will conceived thee and brought thee to the birth,
Always, everywhere, thy Lord to be adored:
   Tremble, thou earth.

5   Wilt thou laugh time away in music and mirth?
Time hath days of pestilence, hath days of a sword,
   Hath days of hunger and thirst in desolate dearth.

Till eternity wake up the multicord
   Thrilled harp of heaven, and breathe full its organ's
     girth
10   For joy of heaven and infinite reward,
   Tremble, thou earth.

Time lengthening, in the lengthening seemeth long:
   But ended Time will seem a little space,
   A little while from morn to evensong,
A little while that ran a rapid race;
5   A little while, when once Eternity
   Denies proportion to the other's pace.
Eternity to be and be and be,
   Ever beginning, never ending still,
   Still undiminished far as thought can see;
10   Farther than thought can see, by dint of will
   Strung up and strained and shooting like a star
   Past utmost bound of everlasting hill:

Eternity unswaddled, without bar,
    Finishing sequence in its awful sum;
15   Eternity still rolling forth its car,
Eternity still here and still to come.

"All Flesh is Grass."

So brief a life, and then an endless life
    Or endless death;
So brief a life, then endless peace or strife:
    Whoso considereth
5   How man but like a flower
    Or shoot of grass
Blooms an hour,
    Well may sigh "Alas!"

So brief a life, and then an endless grief
10   Or endless joy;
So brief a life, then ruin or relief:
    What solace, what annoy
Of Time needs dwelling on?
    It is, it was,
15 It is done,
    While we sigh "Alas!"

Yet saints are singing in a happy hope
    Forecasting pleasure,
Bright eyes of faith enlarging all their scope;
20   Saints love beyond Time's measure:
Where love is, there is bliss
    That will not pass;
Where love is,
    Dies away "Alas!"

Heaven's chimes are slow, but sure to strike at last:
    Earth's sands are slow, but surely dropping thro':
    And much we have to suffer, much to do,
        Before the time be past.

5   Chimes that keep time are neither slow nor fast:
      Not many are the numbered sands nor few:
      A time to suffer, and a time to do,
        And then the time is past.

"There remaineth therefore a Rest to the People of God."

    Rest remains when all is done,
      Work and vigil, prayer and fast,
      All fulfilled from first to last,
      All the length of time gone past
5   And eternity begun!

    Fear and hope and chastening rod
      Urge us on the narrow way:
      Bear we now as best we may
      Heat and burden of today,
10   Struggling, panting up to God.

    Parting after parting,
      Sore loss and gnawing pain:
    Meeting grows half a sorrow
      Because of parting again.
5   When shall the day break
      That these things shall not be?
    When shall new earth be ours
      Without a sea,
    And time that is not time
10   But eternity?

    To meet, worth living for;
      Worth dying for, to meet;
    To meet, worth parting for,
      Bitter forgot in sweet:
15   To meet, worth parting before
      Never to part more.

"They put their trust in Thee, and were not confounded."

I.

Together once, but never more
    While Time and Death run out their runs:
Tho' sundered now as shore from shore,
    Together once.

5   Nor rising suns, nor setting suns,
Nor life renewed which springtide bore,
    Make one again Death's sundered ones.

Eternity holds rest in store,
    Holds hope of long reunions:
10   But holds it what they hungered for
    Together once?

II.

Whatso it be, howso it be, Amen.
    Blessed it is, believing, not to see.
Now God knows all that is; and we shall, then,
    Whatso it be.

5   God's Will is best for man whose will is free.
God's Will is better to us, yea, than ten
    Desires whereof He holds and weighs the key.

Amid her household cares He guides the wren,
    He guards the shifty mouse from poverty;
10   He knows all wants, allots each where and when,
    Whatso it be.

Short is time, and only time is bleak;
    Gauge the exceeding height thou hast to climb:
Long eternity is nigh to seek:
    Short is time.

5   Time is shortening with the wintry rime:
Pray and watch and pray, girt up and meek;
    Praying, watching, praying, chime by chime.

Pray by silence if thou canst not speak:
    Time is shortening; pray on till the prime:
10   Time is shortening; soul, fulfil thy week:
    Short is time.

For Each.

My harvest is done, its promise is ended,
    Weak and watery sets the sun,
Day and night in one mist are blended,
    My harvest is done.

5   Long while running, how short when run,
Time to eternity has descended,
    Timeless eternity has begun.

Was it the narrow way that I wended?
    Snares and pits was it mine to shun?
10   The scythe has fallen, so long suspended,
    My harvest is done.

For All.

Man's harvest is past, his summer is ended,
    Hope and fear are finished at last,
Day hath descended, night hath ascended,
    Man's harvest is past.

5   Time is fled that fleeted so fast:
All the unmended remains unmended,
    The perfect, perfect: all lots are cast.

Waiting till earth and ocean be rended,
    Waiting for call of the trumpet blast,
10   Each soul at goal of that way it wended,—
    Man's harvest is past.

NEW JERUSALEM AND ITS CITIZENS.

"The Holy City, New Jerusalem."

Jerusalem is built of gold,
   Of crystal, pearl, and gem:
Oh fair thy lustres manifold,
   Thou fair Jerusalem!
5   Thy citizens who walk in white
Have nought to do with day or night,
And drink the river of delight.

Jerusalem makes melody
   For simple joy of heart;
10   An organ of full compass she,
   One-tuned thro' every part:
While not to day or night belong
Her matins and her evensong,
The one thanksgiving of her throng.

15   Jerusalem a garden is,
   A garden of delight;
Leaf, flower, and fruit make fair her trees,
   Which see not day or night:
Beside her River clear and calm
20   The Tree of Life grows with the Palm,
For triumph and for food and balm.

Jerusalem, where song nor gem
   Nor fruit nor waters cease,
God bring us to Jerusalem,
25   God bring us home in peace;
The strong who stand, the weak who fall,
The first and last, the great and small,
Home one by one, home one and all.

When wickedness is broken as a tree
   Paradise comes to light, ah holy land!

Whence death has vanished like a shifting sand,
And barrenness is banished with the sea.
5   Its bulwarks are salvation fully manned,
    All gems it hath for glad variety,
    And pearls for pureness radiant glimmeringly,
And gold for grandeur where all good is grand.
An inner ring of saints meets linked above,
10   And linked of angels is an outer ring;
      For voice of waters or for thunders' voice
      Lo! harps and songs wherewith all saints rejoice,
    And all the trembling there of any string
Is but a trembling of enraptured love.

Jerusalem of fire
  And gold and pearl and gem,
Saints flock to fill thy choir,
  Jerusalem.

5   Lo, thrones thou hast for them;
Desirous they desire
  Thy harp, thy diadem,

Thy bridal white attire,
  A palm-branch from thy stem:
10 Thy holiness their hire,
  Jerusalem.

"She shall be brought unto the King."

The King's Daughter is all glorious within,
  Her clothing of wrought gold sets forth her bliss;
Where the endless choruses of heaven begin
  The King's Daughter is;

5   Perfect her notes in the perfect harmonies;
With tears wiped away, no conscience of sin,
  Loss forgotten and sorrowful memories;

Alight with Cherubin, afire with Seraphin,
    Lily for pureness, rose for charities,
10 With joy won and with joy evermore to win,
    The King's Daughter is.

Who is this that cometh up not alone
    From the fiery-flying-serpent wilderness,
Leaning upon her own Beloved One:
    Who is this?
5   Lo, the King of kings' daughter, a high princess,
Going home as bride to her Husband's Throne,
    Virgin queen in perfected loveliness.

Her eyes a dove's eyes and her voice a dove's moan,
    She shows like a full moon for heavenliness:
10 Eager saints and angels ask in heaven's zone,
    Who is this?

Who sits with the King in His Throne? Not a slave but a
    Bride,
    With this King of all Greatness and Grace Who reigns
        not alone;
His Glory her glory, where glorious she glows at His side
    Who sits with the King in His Throne.

5   She came from dim uttermost depths which no Angel
        hath known,
Leviathan's whirlpool and Dragon's dominion worldwide,
    From the frost or the fire to Paradisiacal zone.

Lo, she is fair as a dove, silvery, golden, dove-eyed:
    Lo, Dragon laments and Death laments, for their prey
        is flown:
10 She dwells in the Vision of Peace, and her peace shall
        abide
    Who sits with the King in His Throne.

Antipas.

Hidden from the darkness of our mortal sight,
Hidden in the Paradise of lovely light,
Hidden in God's Presence, worshipped face to face,
Hidden in the sanctuary of Christ's embrace.
5   Up, O Wills! to track him home among the bless'd;
Up, O Hearts! to know him in the joy of rest;
Where no darkness more shall hide him from our sight,
Where we shall be love with love, and light with light,
Worshipping our God together face to face,
10   Wishless in the sanctuary of Christ's embrace.

"Beautiful for situation."

A lovely city in a lovely land,
    Whose citizens are lovely, and whose King
    Is Very Love; to Whom all Angels sing;
To Whom all saints sing crowned, their sacred band
5   Saluting Love with palm-branch in their hand:
    Thither all doves on gold or silver wing
    Flock home thro' agate windows glistering
Set wide, and where pearl gates wide open stand.
A bower of roses is not half so sweet,
10   A cave of diamonds doth not glitter so,
    Nor Lebanon is fruitful set thereby:
    And thither thou, beloved, and thither I
May set our heart and set our face and go,
Faint yet pursuing, home on tireless feet.

Lord, by what inconceivable dim road
    Thou leadest man on footsore pilgrimage!
    Weariness is his rest from stage to stage,
Brief halting-places are his sole abode.

5   Onward he fares thro' rivers overflowed,
         Thro' deserts where all doleful creatures rage;
         Onward from year to year, from age to age,
     He groans and totters onward with his load.
     Behold how inconceivable his way;
10   How tenfold inconceivable the goal,
             His goal of hope deferred, his promised peace:
                 Yea, but behold him sitting down at ease,
             Refreshed in body and refreshed in soul,
     At rest from labour on the Sabbath Day.

"As cold waters to a thirsty soul, so is good news
from a far country."

     "Golden haired, lily white,
         Will you pluck me lilies?
     Or will you show me where they grow,
         Show where the limpid rill is?
5   But is your hair of gold or light,
         And is your foot of flake or fire,
     And have you wings rolled up from sight
         And songs to slake desire?"

     "I pluck fresh flowers of Paradise,
10   Lilies and roses red,
     A bending sceptre for my hand,
         A crown to crown my head.
     I sing my songs, I pluck my flowers
         Sweet-scented from their fragrant trees;
15   I sing, we sing, amid the bowers
         And gather palm-branches."

     "Is there a path to Heaven
         My stumbling foot may tread?
     And will you show that way to go,
20   That bower and blossom bed?"
     "The path to Heaven is steep and straight
         And scorched, but ends in shade of trees,

Where yet a while we sing and wait
   And gather palm-branches."

Cast down but not destroyed, chastened not slain:
   Thy Saints have lived that life, but how can I?
   I, who thro' dread of death do daily die
By daily foretaste of an unfelt pain.
5   Lo, I depart who shall not come again;
   Lo, as a shadow I am flitting by;
   As a leaf trembling, as a wheel I fly,
While death flies faster and my flight is vain.
Chastened not slain, cast down but not destroyed:—
10   If thus Thy Saints have struggled home to peace,
    Why should not I take heart to be as they?
    They too pent passions in a house of clay,
   Fear and desire, and pangs and ecstasies;
Yea, thus they joyed who now are overjoyed.

Lift up thine eyes to seek the invisible:
   Stir up thy heart to choose the still unseen:
   Strain up thy hope in glad perpetual green
To scale the exceeding height where all saints dwell.
5   —Saints, it is well with you?—Yea, it is well.—
   Where they have reaped, by faith kneel thou to glean:
   Because they stooped so low to reap, they lean
Now over golden harps unspeakable.
   —But thou purblind and deafened, knowest thou
10   Those glorious beauties unexperienced
    By ear or eye or by heart hitherto?—
I know Whom I have trusted: wherefore now
   All amiable, accessible tho' fenced,
    Golden Jerusalem floats full in view.

"Love is strong as Death."

As flames that consume the mountains, as winds that
    coerce the sea,
    Thy men of renown show forth Thy might in the clutch
      of death:
Down they go into silence, yet the Trump of the Jubilee
    Swells not Thy praise as swells it the breathless pause of
      their breath.

5   What is the flame of their fire, if so I may catch the flame;
    What the strength of their strength, if also I may wax
      strong?
The flaming fire of their strength is the love of Jesu's
    Name,
    In Whom their death is life, their silence utters a song.

"Let them rejoice in their beds."

Crimson as the rubies, crimson as the roses,
    Crimson as the sinking sun,
Singing on his crimsoned bed each saint reposes,
    Fought his fight, his battle won;
5   Till the rosy east the day of days discloses,
    All his work, save waiting, done.

Far above the stars, while underneath the daisies,
    Resting, for his race is run,
Unto Thee his heart each quiet saint upraises,
10   God the Father, Spirit, Son;
Unto Thee his heart, unto Thee his praises,
    O Lord God, the Three in One.

Slain in their high places: fallen on rest
    Where the eternal peace lights up their faces,
In God's sacred acre breast to breast:—
    Slain in their high places.

5   From all tribes, all families, all races,
  Gathered home together; east or west
    Sending home its tale of gifts and graces.

  Twine, oh twine, heaven's amaranth for their crest,
    Raise their praise while home their triumph paces;
10   Kings by their own King of kings confessed,
    Slain in their high places.

"What hath God wrought!"

The shout of a King is among them. One day may I be
Of that perfect communion of lovers contented and free
In the land that is very far off, and far off from the sea.

The shout of the King is among them. One King and one
      song,
5   One thunder of manifold voices harmonious and strong,
One King and one love, and one shout of one worshipping
      throng.

"Before the Throne, and before the Lamb."

As the voice of many waters all saints sing as one,
  As the voice of an unclouded thundering;
Unswayed by the changing moon and unswayed by the sun,
  As the voice of many waters all saints sing.

5   Circling round the rainbow of their perfect ring,
Twelve thousand times twelve thousand voices in unison
  Swell the triumph, swell the praise of Christ the King.

Where raiment is white of blood-steeped linen slowly spun,
  Where crowns are golden of Love's own largessing,
10   Where eternally the ecstasy is but begun,
  As the voice of many waters all saints sing.

"He shall go no more out."

Once within, within for evermore:
　　There the long beatitudes begin:
Overflows the still unwasting store,
　　Once within.

5　　　Left without are death and doubt and sin;
All man wrestled with and all he bore,
　　Man who saved his life, skin after skin.

Blow the trumpet-blast unheard before,
　　Shout the unheard-of shout for these who win,
10　These, who cast their crowns on Heaven's high floor
　　Once within.

Yea, blessed and holy is he that hath part in the First
　　　Resurrection!
　　We mark well his bulwarks, we set up his tokens, we
　　　gaze, even we,
On this lustre of God and of Christ, this creature of
　　flawless perfection:
　　Yea, blessed and holy is he.

5　　　But what? an offscouring of earth, a wreck from the
　　　turbulent sea,
A bloodstone unflinchingly hewn for the Temple's eternal
　　erection,
　　One scattered and peeled, one sifted and chastened
　　　and scourged and set free?

Yea, this is that worshipful stone of the Wise Master
　　Builder's election,
　　Yea, this is that King and that Priest where all Hallows
　　　bow down the knee,
10　Yea, this man set nigh to the Throne is Jonathan of David's
　　　delection,
　　　Yea, blessed and holy is he.

The joy of Saints, like incense turned to fire
   In golden censers, soars acceptable;
   And high their heavenly hallelujahs swell
Desirous still with still-fulfilled desire.
5   Sweet thrill the harpstrings of the heavenly choir,
   Most sweet their voice while love is all they tell;
   Where love is all in all, and all is well
Because their work is love and love their hire.
All robed in white and all with palm in hand,
10   Crowns too they have of gold and thrones of gold;
   The street is golden which their feet have trod,
Or on a sea of glass and fire they stand:
   And none of them is young, and none is old,
   Except as perfect by the Will of God.

What are these lovely ones, yea, what are these?
   Lo, these are they who for pure love of Christ
Stripped off the trammels of soft silken ease,
   Beggaring themselves betimes, to be sufficed
5   Throughout heaven's one eternal day of peace:
   By golden streets, thro' gates of pearl unpriced,
They entered on the joys that will not cease,
   And found again all firstfruits sacrificed.
And wherefore have you harps, and wherefore palms,
10   And wherefore crowns, O ye who walk in white?
Because our happy hearts are chanting psalms,
   Endless Te Deum for the ended fight;
While thro' the everlasting lapse of calms
   We cast our crowns before the Lamb our Might.

"The General Assembly and Church of the Firstborn."

Bring me to see, Lord, bring me yet to see
   Those nations of Thy glory and Thy grace
   Who splendid in Thy splendour worship Thee.

Light in all eyes, content in every face,
5   Raptures and voices one while manifold,
        Love and are well-beloved the ransomed race:—
Great mitred priests, great kings in crowns of gold,
        Patriarchs who head the army of their sons,
        Matrons and mothers by their own extolled,
10   Wise and most harmless holy little ones,
        Virgins who, making merry, lead the dance,
        Full-breathed victorious racers from all runs,
Home-comers out of every change and chance,
        Hermits restored to social neighbourhood,
15   Aspects which reproduce One Countenance,
Life-losers with their losses all made good,
        All blessed hungry and athirst sufficed,
        All who bore crosses round the Holy Rood,
Friends, brethren, sisters, of Lord Jesus Christ.

"Every one that is perfect shall be as his master."

How can one man, how can all men,
    How can we be like St. Paul,
Like St. John, or like St. Peter,
    Like the least of all
5   Blessed Saints? for we are small.

Love can make us like St. Peter,
    Love can make us like St. Paul,
Love can make us like the blessed
    Bosom friend of all,
10   Great St. John, tho' we are small.

Love which clings and trusts and worships,
    Love which rises from a fall,
Love which, prompting glad obedience,
    Labours most of all,
15   Love makes great the great and small.

"As dying, and behold we live!"
    So live the Saints while time is flying;
Make all they make, give all they give,
    As dying;

5   Bear all they bear without replying;
They grieve as tho' they did not grieve,
    Uplifting praise with prayer and sighing.

Patient thro' life's long-drawn reprieve,
    Aloof from strife, at peace from crying,
10   The morrow to its day they leave,
    As dying.

"So great a cloud of Witnesses."

I think of the saints I have known, and lift up mine eyes
To the far-away home of beautiful Paradise,
Where the song of saints gives voice to an undividing sea
On whose plain their feet stand firm while they keep their
         jubilee.
5   As the sound of waters their voice, as the sound of
         thunderings,
While they all at once rejoice, while all sing and while
         each one sings;
Where more saints flock in, and more, and yet more, and
         again yet more,
And not one turns back to depart thro' the open
         entrance-door.

O sights of our lovely earth, O sound of our earthly sea,
10   Speak to me of Paradise, of all blessed saints to me:
Or keep silence touching them, and speak to my heart
         alone
Of the Saint of saints, the King of kings, the Lamb on the
         Throne.

Our Mothers, lovely women pitiful;
   Our Sisters, gracious in their life and death;
   To us each unforgotten memory saith:
"Learn as we learned in life's sufficient school,
5 Work as we worked in patience of our rule,
   Walk as we walked, much less by sight than faith,
   Hope as we hoped, despite our slips and scathe,
Fearful in joy and confident in dule."
I know not if they see us or can see;
10 But if they see us in our painful day,
   How looking back to earth from Paradise
   Do tears not gather in those loving eyes?—
Ah, happy eyes! whose tears are wiped away
Whether or not you bear to look on me.

Safe where I cannot lie yet,
   Safe where I hope to lie too,
Safe from the fume and the fret;
   You, and you,
5 Whom I never forget.

Safe from the frost and the snow,
   Safe from the storm and the sun,
Safe where the seeds wait to grow
   One by one
10 And to come back in blow.

"Is it well with the child?"

Lying a-dying.
Have done with vain sighing:
Life not lost but treasured,
God Almighty pleasured,
5 God's daughter fetched and carried,
Christ's bride betrothed and married.
Our tender little dove
Meek-eyed and simple,

Our love goes home to Love:
10   There shall she walk in white,
Where God shall be the Light,
And God the Temple.

Dear Angels and dear disembodied Saints
   Unseen around us, worshipping in rest,
May wonder that man's heart so often faints
   And his steps lag along the heavenly quest,
5   What while his foolish fancy moulds and paints
   A fonder hope than all they prove for best;
A lying hope which undermines and taints
   His soul, as sin and sloth make manifest.
Sloth, and a lie, and sin: shall these suffice
10   The unfathomable heart of craving man,
     That heart which being a deep calls to the deep?
   Behold how many like us rose and ran
     When Christ, life-giver, roused them from their sleep
To rise and run and rest in Paradise!

"To every seed his own body."

Bone to his bone, grain to his grain of dust:
   A numberless reunion shall make whole
   Each blessed body for its blessed soul,
Refashioning the aspects of the just.
5   Each saint who died must live afresh, and must
   Ascend resplendent in the aureole
   Of his own proper glory to his goal,
As seeds their proper bodies all upthrust.
Each with his own not with another's grace,
10   Each with his own not with another's heart,
Each with his own not with another's face,
Each dove-like soul mounts to his proper place:—
   O faces unforgotten! if to part
Wrung sore, what will it be to re-embrace?

"What good shall my life do me?"

Have dead men long to wait?—

There is a certain term
For their bodies to the worm
And their souls at heaven gate.
5 Dust to dust, clod to clod,
These precious things of God,
Trampled underfoot by man
And beast the appointed years.—

Their longest life was but a span
10 For change and smiles and tears.
Is it worth while to live,
Rejoice and grieve,
Hope, fear, and die?
Man with man, truth with lie,
15 The slow show dwindles by:
At last what shall we have
Besides a grave?—

Lies and shows no more,
No fear, no pain,
20 But after hope and sleep
Dear joys again.
Those who sowed shall reap:
Those who bore
The Cross shall wear the Crown:
25 Those who clomb the steep
There shall sit down.
The Shepherd of the sheep
Feeds His flock there,
In watered pastures fair
30 They rest and leap.
"Is it worth while to live?"
Be of good cheer:
Love casts out fear:
Rise up, achieve.

SONGS FOR STRANGERS
AND PILGRIMS.

"Her Seed; It shall bruise thy head."

Astonished Heaven looked on when man was made,
   When fallen man reproved seemed half forgiven;
Surely that oracle of hope first said,
   Astonished Heaven.

5   Even so while one by one lost souls are shriven,
A mighty multitude of quickened dead;
   Christ's love outnumbering ten times sevenfold seven.

Even so while man still tosses high his head,
   While still the All-Holy Spirit's strife is striven;—
10 Till one last trump shake earth, and undismayed
   Astonished Heaven.

"Judge nothing before the time."

Love understands the mystery, whereof
   We can but spell a surface history:
Love knows, remembers: let us trust in Love:
   Love understands the mystery.

5   Love weighs the event, the long pre-history,
Measures the depth beneath, the height above,
   The mystery, with the ante-mystery.

To love and to be grieved befits a dove
   Silently telling her bead-history:
10 Trust all to Love, be patient and approve:
   Love understands the mystery.

How great is little man!
   Sun, moon, and stars respond to him,
   Shine or grow dim
Harmonious with his span.

5   How little is great man!
          More changeable than changeful moon,
            Nor half in tune
      With Heaven's harmonious plan.

      Ah, rich man! ah, poor man!
10   Make ready for the testing day
            When wastes away
      What bears not fire or fan.

      Thou heir of all things, man,
          Pursue the saints by heavenward track:
15   They looked not back;
      Run thou, as erst they ran.

      Little and great is man:
          Great if he will, or if he will
            A pigmy still;
20   For what he will he can.

      Man's life is but a working day
          Whose tasks are set aright:
      A time to work, a time to pray,
          And then a quiet night.
5   And then, please God, a quiet night
      Where palms are green and robes are white;
      A long-drawn breath, a balm for sorrow,
      And all things lovely on the morrow.

      If not with hope of life,
          Begin with fear of death:
      Strive the tremendous life-long strife
            Breath after breath.
5   Bleed on beneath the rod;
          Weep on until thou see;
      Turn fear and hope to love of God
            Who loveth thee.

Turn all to love, poor soul;
10   Be love thy watch and ward;
Be love thy starting-point, thy goal,
    And thy reward.

"The day is at hand."

Watch yet a while,
Weep till that day shall dawn when thou shalt smile:
Watch till the day
When all save only Love shall pass away.
5 Then Love rejoicing shall forget to weep,
Shall hope or fear no more, or watch or sleep,
But only love and stint not, deep beyond deep.
Now we sow love in tears, but then shall reap.
Have patience as True Love's own flock of sheep:
10 Have patience with His Love
Who served for us, Who reigns for us above.

"Endure hardness."

A cold wind stirs the blackthorn
   To burgeon and to blow,
Besprinkling half-green hedges
   With flakes and sprays of snow.
5 Thro' coldness and thro' keenness,
   Dear hearts, take comfort so:
Somewhere or other doubtless
   These make the blackthorn blow.

"Whither the Tribes go up, even the Tribes of the
Lord."

Light is our sorrow for it ends tomorrow,
    Light is our death which cannot hold us fast;
So brief a sorrow can be scarcely sorrow,
    Or death be death so quickly past.

5   One night, no more, of pain that turns to pleasure,
    One night, no more, of weeping weeping sore;
And then the heaped-up measure beyond measure,
    In quietness for evermore.

Our face is set like flint against our trouble,
10   Yet many things there are which comfort us;
This bubble is a rainbow-coloured bubble,
    This bubble-life tumultuous.

Our sails are set to cross the tossing river,
    Our face is set to reach Jerusalem;
15   We toil awhile, but then we rest for ever,
    Sing with all Saints and rest with them.

Where never tempest heaveth,
Nor sorrow grieveth,
Nor death bereaveth,
Nor hope deceiveth,
5   Sleep.

Where never shame bewaileth,
Nor serpent traileth,
Nor death prevaileth,
Nor harvest faileth,
10   Reap.

Marvel of marvels, if I myself shall behold
With mine own eyes my King in His city of gold;
Where the least of lambs is spotless white in the fold,
Where the least and last of saints in spotless white is stoled,

5 Where the dimmest head beyond a moon is aureoled.
 O saints, my beloved, now mouldering to mould in the
   mould,
 Shall I see you lift your heads, see your cerements unrolled,
 See with these very eyes? who now in darkness and cold
 Tremble for the midnight cry, the rapture, the tale untold,
10 "The Bridegroom cometh, cometh, His Bride to enfold."

 Cold it is, my beloved, since your funeral bell was tolled:
 Cold it is, O my King, how cold alone on the wold.

"What is that to thee? follow thou me."

 Lie still, my restive heart, lie still:
 God's Word to thee saith, "Wait and bear."
 The good which He appoints is good,
 The good which He denies were ill:
5 Yea, subtle comfort is thy care,
 Thy hurt a help not understood.

 "Friend, go up higher," to one: to one,
 "Friend, enter thou My joy," He saith:
 To one, "Be faithful unto death."
10 For some a wilderness doth flower,
 Or day's work in one hour is done:—
 "But thou, could'st thou not watch one hour?"

 Lord, I had chosen another lot,
 But then I had not chosen well;
15 Thy choice and only Thine is good:
 No different lot, search heaven or hell,
 Had blessed me fully understood;
 None other, which Thou orderest not.

"Worship God."

 Lord, if Thy word had been "Worship Me not,
  For I than thou am holier: draw not near:"

We had besieged Thy Face with prayer and tear
And manifold abasement in our lot,
5   Our crooked ground, our thorned and thistled plot;
         Envious of flawless Angels in their sphere,
         Envious of brutes, and envious of the mere
Unliving and undying unbegot.
But now Thou hast said, "Worship Me, and give
10   Thy heart to Me, My child:" now therefore we
         Think twice before we stoop to worship Thee:
            We proffer half a heart while life is strong
And strung with hope; so sweet it is to live!
            Wilt Thou not wait? Yea, Thou hast waited long.

"Afterward he repented, and went."

Lord, when my heart was whole I kept it back
      And grudged to give it Thee.
Now then that it is broken, must I lack
      Thy kind word "Give it Me"?
5   Silence would be but just, and Thou art just.
Yet since I lie here shattered in the dust,
      With still an eye to lift to Thee,
A broken heart to give,
I think that Thou wilt bid me live,
10   And answer "Give it Me."

"Are they not all Ministering Spirits?"

Lord, whomsoever Thou shalt send to me,
Let that same be
      Mine Angel predilect:
Veiled or unveiled, benignant or austere,
5   Aloof or near;
      Thine, therefore mine, elect.

So may my soul nurse patience day by day,
Watch on and pray
      Obedient and at peace;

10   Living a lonely life in hope, in faith;
      Loving till death,
          When life, not love, shall cease.

    . . . . Lo, thou mine Angel with transfigured face
    Brimful of grace,
15   Brimful of love for me!
    Did I misdoubt thee all that weary while,
    Thee with a smile
         For me as I for thee?

    Our life is long. Not so, wise Angels say
    Who watch us waste it, trembling while they weigh
    Against eternity one squandered day.

    Our life is long. Not so, the Saints protest,
5   Filled full of consolation and of rest:
    "Short ill, long good, one long unending best."

    Our life is long. Christ's word sounds different:
    "Night cometh: no more work when day is spent.
    Repent and work today, work and repent."

10   Lord, make us like Thy Host who day nor night
    Rest not from adoration, their delight,
    Crying "Holy, Holy, Holy," in the height.

    Lord, make us like Thy Saints who wait and long
    Contented: bound in hope and freed from wrong
15   They speed (may be) their vigil with a song.

    Lord, make us like Thyself: for thirty-three
    Slow years of toil seemed not too long to Thee,
    That where Thou art, there Thy Beloved might be.

    Lord, what have I to offer? sickening fear
      And a heart-breaking loss.
    Are these the cross Thou givest me? then dear
      I will account this cross.

5   If this is all I have, accept even this
      Poor priceless offering,

A quaking heart with all that therein is,
   O Thou my thorn-crowned King.

Accept the whole, my God, accept my heart
10   And its own love within:
Wilt Thou accept us and not sift apart?
   —Only sift out my sin.

   Joy is but sorrow,
    While we know
   It ends tomorrow:—
    Even so!
5   Joy with lifted veil
   Shows a face as pale
As the fair changing moon so fair and frail.

   Pain is but pleasure,
    If we know
10   It heaps up treasure:—
    Even so!
   Turn, transfigured Pain,
   Sweetheart, turn again,
For fair thou art as moonrise after rain.

Can I know it?—Nay.—
Shall I know it?—Yea,
When all mists have cleared away
For ever and aye.—

5 Why not then today?—
Who hath said thee nay?
Lift a hopeful heart and pray
In a humble way.—

Other hearts are gay.—
10 Ask not joy today:
Toil today along thy way
Keeping grudge at bay.—

On a past May-day
Flowers pranked all the way;

15   Nightingales sang out their say
      On a night of May.—

      Dost thou covet May
      On an Autumn day?
      Foolish memory saith its say
20   Of sweets past away.—

      Gone the bloom of May,
      Autumn beareth bay:
      Flowerless wreath for head grown grey
      Seemly were today.—

25   Dost thou covet bay?
      Ask it not today:
      Rather for a palm-branch pray;
      None will say thee nay.

"When my heart is vexed I will complain."

      "The fields are white to harvest, look and see,
      Are white abundantly.
      The full-orbed harvest moon shines clear,
      The harvest time draws near,
5   Be of good cheer."

      "Ah, woe is me!
      I have no heart for harvest time,
      Grown sick with hope deferred from chime to chime."

      "But Christ can give thee heart Who loveth thee:
10   Can set thee in the eternal ecstasy
      Of His great jubilee:
      Can give thee dancing heart and shining face,
      And lips filled full of grace,
      And pleasures as the rivers and the sea.
15   Who knocketh at His door
      He welcomes evermore:

Kneel down before
That ever-open door
(The time is short) and smite
20   Thy breast, and pray with all thy might."

"What shall I say?"
                          "Nay, pray.
Tho' one but say 'Thy Will be done,'
He hath not lost his day
25   At set of sun."

"Praying always."

After midnight, in the dark
     The clock strikes one,
     New day has begun.
Look up and hark!
5   With singing heart forestall the carolling lark.

After mid-day, in the light
     The clock strikes one,
     Day-fall has begun.
Cast up, set right
10   The day's account against the on-coming night.

After noon and night, one day
     For ever one
     Ends not, once begun.
Whither away,
15   O brothers and O sisters? Pause and pray.

"As thy days, so shall thy strength be."

Day that hath no tinge of night,
     Night that hath no tinge of day,
These at last will come to sight
     Not to fade away.

5   This is twilight that we know,
     Scarcely night and scarcely day;

This hath been from long ago
   Shed around man's way:

Step by step to utter night,
10   Step by step to perfect day,
To the Left Hand or the Right
   Leading all away.

This is twilight: be it so;
   Suited to our strength our day:
15 Let us follow on to know,
   Patient by the way.

A heavy heart, if ever heart was heavy,
   I offer Thee this heavy heart of me.
Are such as this the hearts Thou art fain to levy
   To do and dare for Thee, to bleed for Thee?
5   Ah, blessed heaviness, if such they be!

Time was I bloomed with blossom and stood leafy
   How long before the fruit, if fruit there be:
Lord, if by bearing fruit my heart grows heavy,
   Leafless and bloomless yet accept of me
10   The stripped fruit-bearing heart I offer Thee.

Lifted to Thee my heart weighs not so heavy,
   It leaps and lightens lifted up to Thee;
It sings, it hopes to sing amid the bevy
   Of thousand thousand choirs that sing, and see
15   Thy Face, me loving, for Thou lovest me.

If love is not worth loving, then life is not worth living,
   Nor aught is worth remembering but well forgot;
For store is not worth storing and gifts are not worth
     giving,
   If love is not;
5   And idly cold is death-cold, and life-heat idly hot,
And vain is any offering and vainer our receiving,
   And vanity of vanities is all our lot.

Better than life's heaving heart is death's heart
    unheaving,
  Better than the opening leaves are the leaves that rot,
10 For there is nothing left worth achieving or retrieving,
    If love is not.

What is it Jesus saith unto the soul?
  "Take up the Cross, and come and follow Me."
  One word He saith to all men: none may be
Without a cross yet hope to touch the goal.
5 Then heave it bravely up, and brace thy whole
    Body to bear; it will not weigh on thee
    Past strength; or if it crush thee to thy knee
Take heart of grace, for grace shall be thy dole.
Give thanks today, and let tomorrow take
10   Heed to itself; today imports thee more,
      Tomorrow may not dawn like yesterday:
      Until that unknown morrow go thy way,
Suffer and work and strive for Jesus' sake:—
  Who tells thee what tomorrow keeps in store?

They lie at rest, our blessed dead;
The dews drop cool above their head,
They knew not when fleet summer fled.

Together all, yet each alone;
5 Each laid at rest beneath his own
Smooth turf or white allotted stone.

When shall our slumber sink so deep,
And eyes that wept and eyes that weep
Weep not in the sufficient sleep?

10 God be with you, our great and small,
Our loves, our best beloved of all,
Our own beyond the salt sea-wall.

"Ye that fear Him, both small and great."

Great or small below,
   Great or small above;
Be we Thine, whom Thou dost know
    And love:

5 First or last on earth,
   First or last in Heaven;
Only weighted with Thy worth,
    And shriven.

Wise or ignorant,
10   Strong or weak; Amen;
Sifted now, cast down, in want:—
    But then?

Then,—when sun nor moon,
   Time nor death, finds place,
15 Seeing in the eternal noon
    Thy Face:

Then,—when tears and sighing,
   Changes, sorrows, cease;
Living by Thy Life undying
20   In peace:

Then,—when all creation
   Keeps its jubilee,
Crowned amid Thy holy nation;
Crowned, discrowned, in adoration
25   Of Thee.

"Called to be Saints."

The lowest place. Ah, Lord, how steep and high
   That lowest place whereon a saint shall sit!
Which of us halting, trembling, pressing nigh,
    Shall quite attain to it?

5   Yet, Lord, Thou pressest nigh to hail and grace
       Some happy soul, it may be still unfit
  For Right Hand or for Left Hand, but whose place
       Waits there prepared for it.

The sinner's own fault? So it was.
    If every own fault found us out,
    Dogged us and hedged us round about,
What comfort should we take because
5   Not half our due we thus wrung out?

Clearly his own fault. Yet I think
    My fault in part, who did not pray
    But lagged and would not lead the way.
I, haply, proved his missing link.
10   God help us both to mend and pray.

Who cares for earthly bread tho' white?
    Nay, heavenly sheaf of harvest corn!
Who cares for earthly crown tonight?
    Nay, heavenly crown tomorrow morn!
5 I will not wander left or right,
    The straightest road is shortest too;
    And since we hold all hope in view
And triumph where is no more pain,
    Tonight I bid good night to you
10 And bid you meet me there again.

Laughing Life cries at the feast,—
    Craving Death cries at the door,—
"Fish, or fowl, or fatted beast?"
    "Come with me, thy feast is o'er."—
5 "Wreathe the violets."—"Watch them fade."—
"I am sunshine."—"I am shade:
I am the sun-burying west."—
"I am pleasure."—"I am rest:
Come with me, for I am best."

"The end is not yet."

Home by different ways. Yet all
   Homeward bound thro' prayer and praise,
Young with old, and great with small,
   Home by different ways.
5   Many nights and many days
Wind must bluster, rain must fall,
   Quake the quicksand, shift the haze.

Life hath called and death will call
   Saints who praying kneel at gaze,
10 Ford the flood or leap the wall,
   Home by different ways.

Who would wish back the Saints upon our rough
   Wearisome road?
     Wish back a breathless soul
     Just at the goal?
5   My soul, praise God
For all dear souls which have enough.

I would not fetch one back to hope with me
   A hope deferred,
     To taste a cup that slips
10   From thirsting lips:—
   Hath he not heard
And seen what was to hear and see?

How could I stand to answer the rebuke
   If one should say:
15   "O friend of little faith,
     Good was my death,
    And good my day
Of rest, and good the sleep I took"?

"That which hath been is named already, and it is known that it is Man."

"Eye hath not seen:"—yet man hath known and weighed
 A hundred thousand marvels that have been:
What is it which (the Word of Truth hath said)
  Eye hath not seen?

5 "Ear hath not heard:"—yet harpings of delight,
 Trumpets of triumph, song and spoken word,
Man knows them all: what lovelier, loftier might
  Hath ear not heard?

"Nor heart conceived:"—yet man hath now desired
10 Beyond all reach, beyond his hope believed,
Loved beyond death: what fire shall yet be fired
  No heart conceived?

"Deep calls to deep:"—man's depth would be despair
 But for God's deeper depth: we sow to reap,
15 Have patience, wait, betake ourselves to prayer:
  Deep answereth deep.

Of each sad word which is more sorrowful,
 "Sorrow" or "Disappointment"? I have heard
Subtle inflections baffling subtlest rule,
 Of each sad word.

5 Sorrow can mourn: and lo! a mourning bird
Sings sweetly to sweet echoes of its dule,
 While silent disappointment broods unstirred.

Yet both nurse hope, where Penitence keeps school
 Who makes fools wise and saints of them that erred:
10 Wise men shape stepping stone, or curb, or tool,
 Of each sad word.

"I see that all things come to an end."

I.

No more! while sun and planets fly,
   And wind and storm and seasons four,
And while we live and while we die,—
   No more.

5   Nevertheless old ocean's roar,
And wide earth's multitudinous cry,
   And echo's pent reverberant store

Shall hush to silence by and bye:
   Ah, rosy world gone cold and hoar!
10 Man opes no more a mortal eye,
   No more.

"But Thy Commandment is exceeding broad."

II.

Once again to wake, nor wish to sleep;
   Once again to feel, nor feel a pain!
Rouse thy soul to watch and pray and weep
   Once again.

5   Hope afresh, for hope shall not be vain:
Start afresh along the exceeding steep
   Road to glory, long and rough and plain.

Sow and reap: for while these moments creep,
   Time and earth and life are on the wane:
10 Now, in tears; tomorrow, laugh and reap
   Once again.

Sursum Corda.

"Lift up your hearts." "We lift them up." Ah me!
I cannot, Lord, lift up my heart to Thee:
Stoop, lift it up, that where Thou art I too may be.

"Give Me thy heart." I would not say Thee nay,
5   But have no power to keep or give away
My heart: stoop, Lord, and take it to Thyself today.

Stoop, Lord, as once before, now once anew
Stoop, Lord, and hearken, hearken, Lord, and do,
And take my will, and take my heart, and take me too.

O ye, who are not dead and fit
Like blasted tree beside the pit
But for the axe that levels it,

Living show life of love, whereof
5   The force wields earth and heaven above:
Who knows not love begetteth love?

Love poises earth in space, Love rolls
Wide worlds rejoicing on their poles,
And girds them round with aureoles.

10   Love lights the sun, Love thro' the dark
Lights the moon's evanescent arc,
Lights up the star, lights up the spark.

O ye who taste that love is sweet,
Set waymarks for all doubtful feet
15   That stumble on in search of it.

Sing notes of love: that some who hear
Far off inert may lend an ear,
Rise up and wonder and draw near.

Lead life of love: that others who
20   Behold your life, may kindle too
With love, and cast their lot with you.

Where shall I find a white rose blowing?—
   Out in the garden where all sweets be.—
But out in my garden the snow was snowing
   And never a white rose opened for me.
5   Nought but snow and a wind were blowing
     And snowing.

Where shall I find a blush rose blushing?—
   On the garden wall or the garden bed.—
But out in my garden the rain was rushing
10   And never a blush rose raised its head.
Nothing glowing, flushing or blushing:
      Rain rushing.

Where shall I find a red rose budding?—
   Out in the garden where all things grow.—
15 But out in my garden a flood was flooding
   And never a red rose began to blow.
Out in a flooding what should be budding?
      All flooding!

Now is winter and now is sorrow,
20   No roses but only thorns today:
Thorns will put on roses tomorrow,
   Winter and sorrow scudding away.
No more winter and no more sorrow
      Tomorrow.

"Redeeming the Time."

A life of hope deferred too often is
A life of wasted opportunities;
A life of perished hope too often is
A life of all-lost opportunities:
5 Yet hope is but the flower and not the root,
And hope is still the flower and not the fruit;—
Arise and sow and weed: a day shall come
When also thou shalt keep thy harvest home.

"Now they desire a Better Country."

Love said nay, while Hope kept saying
   All his sweetest say,
Hope so keen to start a-maying!—
   Love said nay.

5   Love was bent to watch and pray;
   Long the watching, long the praying;
    Hope grew drowsy, pale and grey.

   Hope in dreams set off a-straying,
    All his dream-world flushed by May;
10 While unslumbering, praying, weighing,
    Love said nay.

A CASTLE-BUILDER'S WORLD.
"The line of confusion, and the stones of emptiness."

Unripe harvest there hath none to reap it
  From the misty gusty place,
Unripe vineyard there hath none to keep it
  In unprofitable space.
5 Living men and women are not found there,
  Only masks in flocks and shoals;
Flesh-and-bloodless hazy masks surround there,
  Ever wavering orbs and poles;
Flesh-and-bloodless vapid masks abound there,
10 Shades of bodies without souls.

"These all wait upon Thee."

   Innocent eyes not ours
   Are made to look on flowers,
 Eyes of small birds and insects small:
   Morn after summer morn
5   The sweet rose on her thorn
 Opens her bosom to them all.
   The least and last of things
   That soar on quivering wings,
 Or crawl among the grass blades out of sight,
10 Have just as clear a right
 To their appointed portion of delight
   As Queens or Kings.

"Doeth well . . . doeth better."

My love whose heart is tender said to me,
    "A moon lacks light except her sun befriend her.
Let us keep tryst in heaven, dear Friend," said she,
    My love whose heart is tender.

5   From such a loftiness no words could bend her:
Yet still she spoke of "us" and spoke as "we,"
    Her hope substantial, while my hope grew slender.

Now keeps she tryst beyond earth's utmost sea,
    Wholly at rest, tho' storms should toss and rend her;
10 And still she keeps my heart and keeps its key,
    My love whose heart is tender.

Our heaven must be within ourselves,
    Our home and heaven the work of faith
All thro' this race of life which shelves
            Downward to death.

5   So faith shall build the boundary wall,
    And hope shall plant the secret bower,
That both may show magnifical
            With gem and flower.

While over all a dome must spread,
10   And love shall be that dome above;
And deep foundations must be laid,
            And these are love.

"Vanity of Vanities."

Of all the downfalls in the world,
    The flutter of an Autumn leaf
    Grows grievous by suggesting grief:
Who thought, when Spring was first unfurled,
5 Of this? The wide world lay empearled;
Who thought of frost that nips the world?
            Sigh on, my ditty.

There lurk a hundred subtle stings
　　To prick us in our daily walk:
10　　　An apple cankered on its stalk,
A robin snared for all his wings,
A voice that sang but never sings;
Yea, sight or sound or silence stings.
　　　　　　　　　　　Kind Lord, show pity.

The hills are tipped with sunshine, while I walk
　　In shadows dim and cold:
The unawakened rose sleeps on her stalk
　　In a bud's fold,
5　　　Until the sun flood all the world with gold.

The hills are crowned with glory, and the glow
　　Flows widening down apace:
Unto the sunny hill-tops I, set low,
　　Lift a tired face,—
10　　　Ah, happy rose, content to wait for grace!

How tired a face, how tired a brain, how tired
　　A heart I lift, who long
For something never felt but still desired;
　　Sunshine and song,
15　Song where the choirs of sunny heaven stand choired.

Scarce tolerable life, which all life long
　　Is dominated by one dread of death;
　　Is such life, life? if so, who pondereth
May call salt sweetness or call discord song.
5　Ah me, this solitude where swarms a throng!
　　Life slowly grows and dwindles breath by breath:
　　Death slowly grows on us; no word it saith,
Its cords all lengthened and its pillars strong.
Life dies apace, a life that but deceives:
10　　Death reigns as tho' it lived, and yet is dead:
Where is the life that dies not but that lives?
　　　The sweet long life, immortal, ever young,

True life that wooes us with a silver tongue
Of hope, much said and much more left unsaid.

All heaven is blazing yet
   With the meridian sun:
Make haste, unshadowing sun, make haste to set;
   O lifeless life, have done.
5 I choose what once I chose;
   What once I willed, I will:
Only the heart its own bereavement knows;
   O clamorous heart, lie still.

That which I chose, I choose;
10   That which I willed, I will;
That which I once refused, I still refuse:
   O hope deferred, be still.
That which I chose and choose
   And will is Jesus' Will:
15 He hath not lost his life who seems to lose:
   O hope deferred, hope still.

"Balm in Gilead."

Heartsease I found, where Love-lies-bleeding
   Empurpled all the ground:
Whatever flowers I missed unheeding,
   Heartsease I found.

5   Yet still my garden mound
Stood sore in need of watering, weeding,
   And binding growths unbound.

Ah, when shades fell to light succeeding
   I scarcely dared look round:
10 "Love-lies-bleeding" was all my pleading,
   Heartsease I found.

"In the day of his Espousals."

That Song of Songs which is Solomon's
   Sinks and rises, and loves and longs,
Thro' temperate zones and torrid zones,
   That Song of Songs.

5   Fair its floating moon with her prongs:
Love is laid for its paving stones:
   Right it sings without thought of wrongs.

Doves it hath with music of moans,
   Queens in throngs and damsels in throngs,
10 High tones and mysterious undertones,
   That Song of Songs.

"She came from the uttermost part of the earth."

"The half was not told me," said Sheba's Queen,
   Weighing that wealth of wisdom and of gold:
"Thy fame falls short of this that I have seen:
   The half was not told.

5   "Happy thy servants who stand to behold,
Stand to drink in thy gracious speech and mien;
   Happy, thrice happy, the flock of thy fold.

"As the darkened moon while a shadow between
   Her face and her kindling sun is rolled,
10 I depart; but my heart keeps memory green:
   The half was not told."

Alleluia! or Alas! my heart is crying:
So yours is sighing;
Or replying with content undying,
    Alleluia!

5 Alas! grieves overmuch for pain that is ending,
Hurt that is mending,
Life descending soon to be ascending,
    Alleluia!

The Passion Flower hath sprung up tall,
  Hath east and west its arms outspread;
  The heliotrope shoots up its head
To clear the shadow of the wall:
5   Down looks the Passion Flower,
  The heliotrope looks upward still,
    Hour by hour
  On the heavenward hill.

The Passion Flower blooms red or white,
10   A shadowed white, a cloudless red;
  Caressingly it droops its head,
Its leaves, its tendrils, from the light:
Because that lowlier flower
  Looks up, but mounts not half so high,
15   Hour by hour
  Tending toward the sky.

God's Acre.

Hail, garden of confident hope!
  Where sweet seeds are quickening in darkness and cold;
    For how sweet and how young will they be
  When they pierce thro' the mould.
5   Balm, myrtle, and heliotrope
  There watch and there wait out of sight for their Sun:
    While the Sun, which they see not, doth see
  Each and all one by one.

"The Flowers appear on the Earth."

Young girls wear flowers,
  Young brides a flowery wreath,
But next we plant them
  In garden plots of death.
5   Whose lot is best:

The maiden's curtained rest,
  Or bride's whose hoped-for sweet
  May yet outstrip her feet?
Ah! what are such as these
10 To death's sufficing ease?
He sleeps indeed who sleeps in peace
  Where night and morning meet.

Dear are the blossoms
  For bride's or maiden's head,
15 But dearer planted
  Around our blessed dead.
Those mind us of decay
And joys that fade away,
  These preach to us perfection,
20 Long love and resurrection.
We make our graveyards fair,
For spirit-like birds of air,
For Angels may be finding there
  Lost Eden's own delection.

"Thou knewest . . . thou oughtest therefore."

Behold in heaven a floating dazzling cloud,
  So dazzling that I could but cry Alas!
  Alas, because I felt how low I was;
Alas, within my spirit if not aloud,
5 Foreviewing my last breathless bed and shroud:
  Thus pondering, I glanced downward on the grass;
  And the grass bowed when airs of heaven would pass,
Lifting itself again when it had bowed.
That grass spake comfort; weak it was and low,
10 Yet strong enough and high enough to bend
    In homage at a message from the sky:
    As the grass did and prospered, so will I;
Tho' knowing little, doing what I know,
  And strong in patient weakness till the end.

"Go in Peace."

Can peach renew lost bloom,
Or violet lost perfume,
Or sullied snow turn white as overnight?
Man cannot compass it, yet never fear:
5   The leper Naaman
Shows what God will and can;
God Who worked there is working here;
Wherefore let shame, not gloom, betinge thy brow,
God Who worked then is working now.

"Half dead."

O Christ the Life, look on me where I lie
    Ready to die:
O Good Samaritan, nay, pass not by.

O Christ, my Life, pour in Thine oil and wine
5   To keep me Thine;
Me ever Thine, and Thee for ever mine.

Watch by Thy saints and sinners, watch by all
    Thy great and small:
Once Thou didst call us all,—O Lord, recall.

10   Think how Thy saints love sinners, how they pray
    And hope alway,
And thereby grow more like Thee day by day.

O Saint of saints, if those with prayer and vow
    Succour us now. . . .
15   It was not they died for us, it was Thou.

"One of the Soldiers with a Spear pierced His Side."

Ah, Lord, we all have pierced Thee: wilt Thou be
    Wroth with us all to slay us all?
Nay, Lord, be this thing far from Thee and me:
    By whom should we arise, for we are small,
5   By whom if not by Thee?

Lord, if of us who pierced Thee Thou spare one,
    Spare yet one more to love Thy Face,
And yet another of poor souls undone,
    Another, and another—God of grace,
10   Let mercy overrun.

Where love is, there comes sorrow
Today or else tomorrow:
Endure the mood,
Love only means our good.

5   Where love is, there comes pleasure
With or withouten measure,
Early or late
Cheering the sorriest state.

Where love is, all perfection
10   Is stored for heart's delection;
For where love is
Dwells every sort of bliss.

Who would not choose a sorrow
Love's self will cheer tomorrow?
15   One day of sorrow,
Then such a long tomorrow!

Bury Hope out of sight,
    No book for it and no bell;
It never could bear the light
    Even while growing and well:
5   Think if now it could bear

The light on its face of care
And grey scattered hair.

No grave for Hope in the earth,
   But deep in that silent soul
10 Which rang no bell for its birth
    And rings no funeral toll.
Cover its once bright head;
Nor odours nor tears be shed:
It lived once, it is dead.

15 Brief was the day of its power,
    The day of its grace how brief:
As the fading of a flower,
    As the falling of a leaf,
So brief its day and its hour;
20 No bud more and no bower
Or hint of a flower.

Shall many wail it? not so:
    Shall one bewail it? not one:
Thus it hath been from long ago,
25   Thus it shall be beneath the sun.
O fleet sun, make haste to flee;
O rivers, fill up the sea;
O Death, set the dying free.

The sun nor loiters nor speeds,
30   The rivers run as they ran,
Thro' clouds or thro' windy reeds
    All run as when all began.
Only Death turns at our cries:—
Lo, the Hope we buried with sighs
35 Alive in Death's eyes!

A Churchyard Song of Patient Hope.

All tears done away with the bitter unquiet sea,
    Death done away from among the living at last,
Man shall say of sorrow—Love grant it to thee and me!—
    At last, "It is past."

5   Shall I say of pain, "It is past," nor say it with thee,
      Thou heart of my heart, thou soul of my soul, my Friend?
    Shalt thou say of pain, "It is past," nor say it with me
      Beloved to the end?

    One woe is past. Come what come will
      Thus much is ended and made fast:
    Two woes may overhang us still;
      One woe is past.

5   As flowers when winter puffs its last
    Wake in the vale, trail up the hill,
      Nor wait for skies to overcast;

    So meek souls rally from the chill
    Of pain and fear and poisonous blast,
10   To lift their heads: come good, come ill,
      One woe is past.

"Take no thought for the morrow."

Who knows? God knows: and what He knows
    Is well and best.
The darkness hideth not from Him, but glows
Clear as the morning or the evening rose
5   Of east or west.

Wherefore man's strength is to sit still:
    Not wasting care
To antedate tomorrow's good or ill;
Yet watching meekly, watching with good will,
10   Watching to prayer.

Some rising or some setting ray
    From east or west,
If not today, why then another day
Will light each dove upon the homeward way
15   Safe to her nest.

"Consider the Lilies of the field."

Solomon most glorious in array
   Put not on his glories without care:—
Clothe us as Thy lilies of a day,
    As the lilies Thou accountest fair,
5   Lilies of Thy making,
      Of Thy love partaking,
   Filling with free fragrance earth and air:
Thou Who gatherest lilies, gather us and wear.

"Son, remember."

I laid beside thy gate, am Lazarus;
   See me or see me not I still am there,
   Hungry and thirsty, sore and sick and bare,
Dog-comforted and crumbs-solicitous:
5 While thou in all thy ways art sumptuous,
   Daintily clothed, with dainties for thy fare:
   Thus a world's wonder thou art quit of care,
And be I seen or not seen I am thus.
One day a worm for thee, a worm for me:
10   With my worm angel songs and trumpet burst
    And plenitude an end of all desire:
But what for thee, alas! but what for thee?
   Fire and an unextinguishable thirst,
    Thirst in an unextinguishable fire.

"Heaviness may endure for a night, but Joy cometh in the morning."

No thing is great on this side of the grave,
   Nor any thing of any stable worth:
   Whatso is born from earth returns to earth:
No thing we grasp proves half the thing we crave:

5   The tidal wave shrinks to the ebbing wave:
        Laughter is folly, madness lurks in mirth:
        Mankind sets off a-dying from the birth:
    Life is a losing game, with what to save?
    Thus I sat mourning like a mournful owl,
10   And like a doleful dragon made ado,
          Companion of all monsters of the dark:
    When lo! the light cast off its nightly cowl,
        And up to heaven flashed a carolling lark,
        And all creation sang its hymn anew.

15   While all creation sang its hymn anew
        What could I do but sing a stave in tune?
        Spectral on high hung pale the vanishing moon
    Where a last gleam of stars hung paling too.
    Lark's lay—a cockcrow—with a scattered few
20   Soft early chirpings—with a tender croon
        Of doves—a hundred thousand calls, and soon
    A hundred thousand answers sweet and true.
    These set me singing too at unawares:
        One note for all delights and charities,
25   One note for hope reviving with the light,
        One note for every lovely thing that is;
    Till while I sang my heart shook off its cares
        And revelled in the land of no more night.

"The Will of the Lord be done."

O Lord, fulfil Thy Will
Be the days few or many, good or ill:
Prolong them, to suffice
For offering up ourselves Thy sacrifice;
5   Shorten them if Thou wilt,
To make in righteousness an end of guilt.
Yea, they will not be long
To souls who learn to sing a patient song;
Yea, short they will not be

10   To souls on tiptoe to flee home to Thee.
    O Lord, fulfil Thy Will:
    Make Thy Will ours, and keep us patient still
    Be the days few or many, good or ill.

"Lay up for yourselves treasures in Heaven."

Treasure plies a feather,
    Pleasure spreadeth wings,
Taking flight together,—
    Ah! my cherished things.

5   Fly away, poor pleasure,
    That art so brief a thing:
Fly away, poor treasure,
    That hast so swift a wing.

Pleasure, to be pleasure,
10   Must come without a wing:
Treasure, to be treasure,
    Must be a stable thing.

Treasure without feather,
    Pleasure without wings,
15   Elsewhere dwell together
    And are heavenly things.

"Whom the Lord loveth He chasteneth."

"One sorrow more? I thought the tale complete."—
    He bore amiss who grudges what he bore:
Stretch out thy hands and urge thy feet to meet
    One sorrow more.

5   Yea, make thy count for two or three or four:
The kind Physician will not slack to treat
    His patient while there's rankling in the sore.

Bear up in anguish, ease will yet be sweet;
   Bear up all day, for night has rest in store:
10 Christ bears thy burden with thee, rise and greet
   One sorrow more.

"Then shall ye shout."

It seems an easy thing
Mayhap one day to sing
Yet the next day
We cannot sing or say.

5 Keep silence with good heart,
While silence fits our part:
Another day
We shall both sing and say.

Keep silence, counting time
10 To strike in at the chime:
Prepare to sound,—
Our part is coming round.

Can we not sing or say?
In silence let us pray,
15 And meditate
Our love-song while we wait.

Everything that is born must die;
   Everything that can sigh may sing;
Rocks in equal balance, low or high,
   Everything.

5   Honeycomb is weighed against a sting;
Hope and fear take turns to touch the sky;
   Height and depth respond alternating.

O my soul, spread wings of love to fly,
   Wings of dove that soars on home-bound wing:
10 Love trusts Love, till Love shall justify
   Everything.

Lord, grant us calm, if calm can set forth Thee;
   Or tempest, if a tempest set Thee forth;
   Wind from the east or west or south or north,
Or congelation of a silent sea,
5 With stillness of each tremulous aspen tree.

Still let fruit fall, or hang upon the tree;
   Still let the east and west, the south and north,
Curb in their winds, or plough a thundering sea;
   Still let the earth abide to set Thee forth,
10 Or vanish like a smoke to set forth Thee.

Changing Chimes.

It was not warning that our fathers lacked,
   It is not warning that we lack today.
The Voice that cried still cries: "Rise up and act:
   Watch alway,—watch and pray,—watch alway,—
              All men."

Alas, if aught was lacked goodwill was lacked;
   Alas, goodwill is what we lack today.
O gracious Voice, grant grace that all may act,
   Watch and act,—watch and pray,—watch alway.—
10   Amen.

"Thy Servant will go and fight with this Philistine."

Sorrow of saints is sorrow of a day,
   Gladness of saints is gladness evermore:
   Send on thy hope, send on thy will before
To chant God's praise along the narrow way.
5 Stir up His praises if the flesh would sway,
   Exalt His praises if the world press sore,
   Peal out His praises if black Satan roar
A hundred thousand lies to say them nay.

Devil and Death and Hades, threefold cord
10   Not quickly broken, front thee to thy face;
        Front thou them with a face of tenfold flint:
        Shout for the battle, David! never stint
    Body or breath or blood, but proof in grace
Die for thy Lord, as once for thee thy Lord.

Thro' burden and heat of the day
    How weary the hands and the feet
That labour with scarcely a stay,
    Thro' burden and heat!

5   Tired toiler whose sleep shall be sweet,
Kneel down, it will rest thee to pray:
    Then forward, for daylight is fleet.

Cool shadows show lengthening and grey,
    Cool twilight will soon be complete:
10 What matters this wearisome way
    Thro' burden and heat?

"Then I commended Mirth."

"A merry heart is a continual feast."
    Then take we life and all things in good part:
To fast grows festive while we keep at least
    A merry heart

5   Well pleased with nature and well pleased with art;
A merry heart makes cheer for man and beast,
    And fancies music in a creaking cart.

Some day, a restful heart whose toils have ceased,
    A heavenly heart gone home from earthly mart:
10 Today, blow wind from west or wind from east,
    A merry heart.

Sorrow hath a double voice,
    Sharp today but sweet tomorrow:
Wait in patience, hope, rejoice,
    Tried friends of sorrow.

5   Pleasure hath a double taste,
    Sweet today but sharp tomorrow:
Friends of pleasure, rise in haste,
    Make friends with sorrow.

Pleasure set aside today
10   Comes again to rule tomorrow:
Welcomed sorrow will not stay,
    Farewell to sorrow!

Shadows today, while shadows show God's Will.
    Light were not good except He sent us light.
    Shadows today, because this day is night
Whose marvels and whose mysteries fulfil
5   Their course and deep in darkness serve Him still.
    Thou dim aurora, on the extremest height
    Of airy summits wax not over-bright;
Refrain thy rose, refrain thy daffodil.
Until God's Word go forth to kindle thee
10   And garland thee and bid thee stoop to us,
      Blush in the heavenly choirs and glance not down:
      Today we race in darkness for a crown,
In darkness for beatitude to be,
    In darkness for the city luminous.

"Truly the Light is sweet."

Light colourless doth colour all things else:
Where light dwells pleasure dwells
And peace excels.
    Then rise and shine,
5   Thou shadowed soul of mine,
    And let a cheerful rainbow make thee fine.

Light, fountain of all beauty and delight,
Leads day forth from the night,
Turns blackness white.
10   Light waits for thee
     Where all have eyes to see:
     Oh, well is thee, and happy shalt thou be!

"Are ye not much better than they?"

The twig sprouteth,
The moth outeth,
The plant springeth,
The bird singeth:
5 Tho' little we sing today
Yet are we better than they;
Tho' growing with scarce a showing,
Yet, please God, we are growing.

The twig teacheth,
10 The moth preacheth,
The plant vaunteth,
The bird chanteth,
God's mercy overflowing
Merciful past man's knowing.
15 Please God to keep us growing
Till the awful day of mowing.

"Yea, the sparrow hath found her an house."

Wisest of sparrows that sparrow which sitteth alone
    Perched on the housetop, its own upper chamber, for
        nest;
Wisest of swallows that swallow which timely has flown
    Over the turbulent sea to the land of its rest:
5   Wisest of sparrows and swallows, if I were as wise!

Wisest of spirits that spirit which dwelleth apart
    Hid in the Presence of God for a chapel and nest,
Sending a wish and a will and a passionate heart
    Over the eddy of life to that Presence in rest:
10   Seated alone and in peace till God bids it arise.

"I am small and of no reputation."

The least, if so I am;
    If so, less than the least,
May I reach heaven to glorify the Lamb
    And sit down at the Feast.

5   I fear and I am small,
    Whence am I of good cheer;
For I who hear Thy call, have heard Thee call
    To Thee the small who fear.

O Christ my God Who seest the unseen,
    O Christ my God Who knowest the unknown,
    Thy mighty Blood was poured forth to atone
For every sin that can be or hath been.

5   O Thou Who seest what I cannot see,
    Thou Who didst love us all so long ago,
    O Thou Who knowest what I must not know,
Remember all my hope, remember me.

Yea, if Thou wilt, Thou canst put up Thy sword;
    But what if Thou shouldst sheathe it to the hilt
Within the heart that sues to Thee, O Lord?
    Yea, if Thou wilt.

5   For if Thou wilt Thou canst purge out the guilt
Of all, of any, even the most abhorred:
    Thou canst pluck down, rebuild, build up the unbuilt.

Who wanders, canst Thou gather by love's cord?
    Who sinks, uplift from the under-sucking silt

10   To set him on Thy rock within Thy ward?
        Yea, if Thou wilt.

Sweetness of rest when Thou sheddest rest,
    Sweetness of patience till then;
Only the Will of our God is best
    For all the millions of men.

5   For all the millions on earth today,
        On earth and under the earth;
Waiting for earth to vanish away,
        Waiting to come to the birth.

O foolish Soul! to make thy count
    For languid falls and much forgiven,
When like a flame thou mightest mount
        To storm and carry heaven.

5   A life so faint,—is this to live?
        A goal so mean,—is this a goal?
Christ love thee, remedy, forgive,
        Save thee, O foolish Soul.

Before the beginning Thou hast foreknown the end,
    Before the birthday the death-bed was seen of Thee:
Cleanse what I cannot cleanse, mend what I cannot mend,
    O Lord All-Merciful, be merciful to me.

5   While the end is drawing near I know not mine end;
    Birth I recall not, my death I cannot foresee:
O God, arise to defend, arise to befriend,
    O Lord All-Merciful, be merciful to me.

The goal in sight! Look up and sing,
    Set faces full against the light,
Welcome with rapturous welcoming
    The goal in sight.

5 Let be the left, let be the right:
  Straight forward make your footsteps ring
   A loud alarum thro' the night.

  Death hunts you, yea, but reft of sting;
   Your bed is green, your shroud is white:
10 Hail! Life and Death and all that bring
   The goal in sight.

  Looking back along life's trodden way
   Gleams and greenness linger on the track;
  Distance melts and mellows all today,
    Looking back.

5 Rose and purple and a silvery grey,
   Is that cloud the cloud we called so black?
  Evening harmonizes all today,
    Looking back.

  Foolish feet so prone to halt or stray,
10   Foolish heart so restive on the rack!
  Yesterday we sighed, but not today
    Looking back.

Separately Published Poems

DEATH'S CHILL BETWEEN.

Chide not; let me breathe a little,
  For I shall not mourn him long.
Tho' the life-cord was so brittle
  The love-cord was very strong.
5   I would wake a little space
    Till I find a sleeping-place.

You can go, I shall not weep;
  You can go unto your rest;
My heart-ache is all too deep,
10   And too sore my throbbing breast.
Can sobs be, or angry tears,
Where are neither hopes nor fears?

Tho' with you I am alone,
  And must be so everywhere,
15 I will make no useless moan;
    None shall say: "She could not bear;"
While life lasts I will be strong,
But I shall not struggle long.

Listen, listen! everywhere
20   A low voice is calling me,
And a step is on the stair,
    And one comes ye do not see.
Listen, listen! evermore
A dim hand knocks at the door.

25 Hear me: he is come again;
    My own dearest is come back.

Bring him in from the cold rain;
   Bring wine, and let nothing lack.
Thou and I will rest together,
30 Love, until the sunny weather.

I will shelter thee from harm,
   Hide thee from all heaviness;
Come to me, and keep thee warm
   By my side in quietness.
35 I will lull thee to thy sleep
With sweet songs; we will not weep.

Who hath talked of weeping? yet
   There is something at my heart
Gnawing, I would fain forget,
40   And an aching and a smart—
Ah my Mother, 'tis in vain,
For he is not come again.

HEART'S CHILL BETWEEN.

I did not chide him, tho' I knew
   That he was false to me:
Chide the exhaling of the dew,
   The ebbing of the sea,
5 The fading of a rosy hue,
   But not inconstancy.

Why strive for love when love is o'er?
   Why bind a restive heart?
He never knew the pain I bore
10   In saying: "We must part;
Let us be friends, and nothing more":—
   Oh woman's shallow art!

But it is over, it is done;
   I hardly heed it now;
15 So many weary years have run
   Since then, I think not how
Things might have been; but greet each one
   With an unruffled brow.

What time I am where others be
20   My heart seems very calm,
Stone calm; but if all go from me
  There comes a vague alarm,
A shrinking in the memory
  From some forgotten harm.

25 And often thro' the long long night
  Waking when none are near,
I feel my heart beat fast with fright,
  Yet know not what I fear.
Oh how I long to see the light
30   And the sweet birds to hear!

To have the sun upon my face,
  To look up through the trees,
To walk forth in the open space,
  And listen to the breeze,
35 And not to dream the burial place
  Is clogging my weak knees.

Sometimes I can nor weep nor pray,
  But am half stupified;
And then all those who see me say
40   Mine eyes are opened wide,
And that my wits seem gone away:—
  Ah would that I had died!

Would I could die and be at peace,
  Or living could forget;
45 My grief nor grows nor doth decrease,
  But ever is:—and yet
Methinks now that all this shall cease
  Before the sun shall set.

Repining.

She sat alway thro' the long day
Spinning the weary thread away;
And ever said in undertone:
"Come; that I be no more alone."

5   From early dawn to set of sun
       Working, her task was still undone;
       And the long thread seemed to increase
       Even while she spun and did not cease.
       She heard the gentle turtle dove
10   Tell to its mate a tale of love;
       She saw the glancing swallows fly,
       Ever a social company;
       She knew each bird upon its nest
       Had cheering songs to bring it rest;
15   None lived alone, save only she;
       The wheel went round more wearily;
       She wept, and said in undertone:
       "Come; that I be no more alone."

       Day followed day; and still she sighed
20   For love, and was not satisfied;
       Until one night, when the moon-light
       Turned all the trees to silver white,
       She heard, what ne'er she heard before,
       A steady hand undo the door.
25   The nightingale since set of sun
       Her throbbing music had not done,
       And she had listened silently;
       But now the wind had changed, and she
       Heard the sweet song no more, but heard
30   Beside her bed a whispered word:
       "Damsel, rise up; be not afraid,
       "For I am come at last;" it said.

       She trembled tho' the voice was mild,
       She trembled like a frightened child,
35   Till she looked up, and then she saw
       The unknown speaker without awe.
       He seemed a fair young man, his eyes
       Beaming with serious charities;
       His cheek was white, but hardly pale;
40   And a dim glory, like a veil,
       Hovered about his head, and shone

Thro' the whole room, till night was gone.

So her fear fled; and then she said,
Leaning upon her quiet bed:
45 "Now thou art come I prithee stay,
"That I may see thee in the day,
"And learn to know thy voice, and hear
"It evermore calling me near."
He answered: "Rise, and follow me."
50 But she looked upwards wonderingly:
"And whither would'st thou go friend? stay
"Until the dawning of the day."
But he said: "The wind ceaseth, Maid;
"Of chill nor damp be thou afraid."
55 She bound her hair up from the floor,
And passed in silence from the door.

So they went forth together, he
Helping her forward tenderly.
The hedges bowed beneath his hand;
60 Forth from the streams came the dry land
As they passed over; evermore
The pallid moonbeams shone before,
And the wind hushed, and nothing stirred;
Not even a solitary bird
65 Scared by their footsteps fluttered by,
Where aspen trees stood steadily.

As they went on, at length a sound
Came trembling on the air around;
The undistinguishable hum
70 Of life; voices that go and come
Of busy men and the child's sweet
High laugh, and noise of trampling feet.

Then he said: "Wilt thou go and see?"
And she made answer joyfully:
75 "The noise of life, of human life,
"Of dear communion without strife,
"Of converse held 'twixt friend and friend,
"Is it not here our path shall end?"

He led her on a little way
80 Until they reached a hillock: "Stay."

It was a village in a plain.
High mountains screened it from the rain
And stormy wind; and nigh at hand
A bubbling streamlet flowed, o'er sand
85 Pebbly and fine; and sent life up
Green succous stalk and flower cup.

Gradually, day's harbinger,
A chilly wind began to stir.
It seemed a gentle powerless breeze
90 That scarcely rustled thro' the trees;
And yet it touched the mountain's head,
And the paths man might never tread.
But hearken! in the quiet weather
Do all the streams flow down together?
95 No, 'tis a sound more terrible
Than tho' a thousand rivers fell.
The everlasting ice and snow
Were loosened then, but not to flow;
With a loud crash like solid thunder
100 The avalanche came, burying under
The village; turning life and breath
And rest and joy and plans to death.

"Oh let us fly, for pity fly,
"Let us go hence friend, thou and I.
105 "There must be many regions yet
"Where these things make not desolate."

He looked upon her seriously;
Then said: "Arise, and follow me."
The path that lay before them was
110 Nigh covered over with long grass,
And many slimy things and slow
Trailed on between the roots below.
The moon looked dimmer than before;
And shadowy cloudlets floating o'er

115   Its face, sometimes quite hid its light,
       And filled the skies with deeper night.

       At last, as they went on, the noise
       Was heard of the sea's mighty voice;
       And soon the ocean could be seen
120   In its long restlessness serene.
       Upon its breast a vessel rode
       That drowsily appeared to nod
       As the great billows rose and fell,
       And swelled to sink, and sank to swell.

125   Meanwhile the strong wind had come forth
       From the chill regions of the North;
       The mighty wind invisible.
       And the low waves began to swell;
       And the sky darkened overhead;
130   And the moon once looked forth, then fled
       Behind dark clouds; while here and there
       The lightning shone out in the air;
       And the approaching thunder rolled
       With angry pealings manifold.

135   How many vows were made; and prayers
       That in safe times were cold and scarce.
       Still all availed not; and at length
       The waves arose in all their strength,
       And fought against the ship, and filled
140   The ship; then were the clouds unsealed,
       And the rains hurried forth and beat
       On every side and over it.

       Some clung together; and some kept
       A long stern silence; and some wept.
145   Many, half crazed, looked on in wonder
       As the strong timbers rent asunder;
       Friends forgot friends; foes fled to foes;
       And still the water rose and rose.

       "Ah woe is me! whom I have seen
150   "Are now as tho' they had not been.

"In the earth there is room for birth,
"And there are graves enough in earth;
"Why should the cold sea, tempest torn,
"Bury those whom it hath not borne?"

155   He answered not, and they went on.
The glory of the heavens was gone;
The moon gleamed not, nor any Star;
Cold winds were rustling near and far;
And from the trees the dry leaves fell
160   With a sad sound unspeakable.

The air was cold; till from the South
A gust blew hot like sudden drouth
Into their faces, and a light
Glowing and red shone thro' the night.

165   A mighty city full of flame,
And death, and sounds without a name!
Amid the black and blinding smoke
The people, as one man, awoke.
Oh happy they who yesterday
170   On the long journey went away;
Whose pallid lips, smiling and chill,
While the flames scorch them smile on still;
Who murmur not, who tremble not
When the bier crackles fiery hot;
175   Who dying said in love's increase:
"Lord, let Thy servant part in peace."

Those in the town could see and hear
A shaded river flowing near.
The broad deep bed could hardly hold
180   Its plenteous waters calm and cold.
Was flame wrapped all the city wall,
The city gates were flame wrapped all.

What was man's strength, what puissance then?
Women were mighty as strong men.
185   Some knelt in prayer believing still,
Resigned unto a righteous will,
Bowing beneath the chastening rod,

Lost to the world, but found of God.
Some prayed for friend, for child, for wife;
190 Some prayed for faith; some prayed for life;
While some, proud even in death, hope gone,
Steadfast and still stood looking on.

"Death, death! oh let us fly from death,
"Where'er we go it followeth.
195 "All these are dead; and we alone
"Remain to weep for what is gone.
"What is this thing, thus hurriedly
"To pass into eternity?
"To leave the earth so full of mirth?
200 "To lose the profit of our birth?
"To die and be no more? to cease,
"Having numbness that is not peace?
"Let us go hence: and even if thus
"Death everywhere must go with us,
205 "Let us not see the change, but see
"Those who have been or still shall be."

He sighed, and they went on together.
Beneath their feet did the grass wither;
Across the heaven, high overhead,
210 Dark misty clouds floated and fled;
And in their bosom was the thunder;
And angry lightnings flashed out under,
Forkèd and red and menacing;
Far off the wind was muttering;
215 It seemed to tell, not understood,
Strange secrets to the listening wood.

Upon its wings it bore the scent
Of blood of a great armament;
Then saw they how on either side
220 Fields were downtrodden far and wide;
That morning at the break of day,
Two nations had gone forth to slay.

As a man soweth, so he reaps.
The field was full of bleeding heaps;

225   Ghastly corpses of men and horses
        That met death at a thousand sources;
        Cold limbs and putrifying flesh;
        Long love-locks clotted to a mesh
        That stifled; stiffened mouths beneath
230   Staring eyes that had looked on death.

        But these were dead; these felt no more
        The anguish of the wounds they bore.
        Behold; they shall not sigh again,
        Nor justly fear, nor hope in vain.
235   What if none wept above them; is
        The sleeper less at rest for this?
        Is not the young child's slumber sweet
        When no man watcheth over it?

        These had deep calm: but all around
240   There was a deadly smothered sound,
        The choking cry of agony
        From wounded men who could not die.
        Who watched the black wing of the raven
        Rise like a cloud 'twixt them and heaven,
245   And in the distance, flying fast,
        Beheld the eagle come at last.

        She knelt down in her agony:
        "O Lord, it is enough;" said she:
        "My heart's prayer putteth me to shame;
250   "Let me return to whence I came.
        "Thou, Who for love's sake didst reprove,
        "Forgive me, for the sake of love."

NEW ENIGMAS.

        Name any gentleman you spy,
        And there's a chance that he is I;
        Go out to angle, and you may
        Catch me a propitious day:
5   Booted and spurred, their journey ended,

The weary are by me befriended:
If roasted meat should be your wish,
I am more needful than a dish:
I am acknowledgedly poor:
10 Yet my resources are no fewer
Than all the trades; there is not one
But I profess, beneath the sun:
I bear a part in many a game;
My worth may change, I am the same.
15 Sometimes, by you expelled, I roam
Forth from the sanctuary of home.

CHARADES.

My *first* is no proof of my *second*,
    Though my second's a proof of my first:
If I were my *whole* I should tell you
    Quite freely my best and my worst.

5 One clue more: if you fail to discover
    My meaning, you're blind as a mole;
But if you will frankly confess it,
    You show yourself clearly my *whole*.

THE ROSE.

O Rose, thou flower of flowers, thou fragrant wonder,
    Who shall describe thee in thy ruddy prime;
    Thy perfect fulness in the summer time;
When the pale leaves blushingly part asunder
5 And show the warm red heart lies glowing under?
    Thou shouldst bloom surely in some sunny clime,
    Untouched by blights and chilly Winter's rime,
Where lightnings never flash, nor peals the thunder.
And yet in happier spheres they cannot need thee
10   So much as we do with our weight of woe;

Perhaps they would not tend, perhaps not heed thee,
   And thou wouldst lonely and neglected grow;
And He Who is All-Wise, He hath decreed thee
   To gladden earth and cheer all hearts below.

The Trees' Counselling.

I was strolling sorrowfully
   Thro' the corn fields and the meadows;
The stream sounded melancholy,
   And I walked among the shadows;
5   While the ancient forest trees
Talked together in the breeze;
In the breeze that waved and blew them,
With a strange weird rustle thro' them.

Said the oak unto the others
10   In a leafy voice and pleasant:
"Here we all are equal brothers,
   "Here we have nor lord nor peasant.
"Summer, Autumn, Winter, Spring,
"Pass in happy following.
15 "Little winds may whistle by us,
"Little birds may overfly us;

"But the sun still waits in heaven
   "To look down on us in splendour;
"When he goes the moon is given,
20   "Full of rays that he doth lend her:
"And tho' sometimes in the night
"Mists may hide her from our sight,
"She comes out in the calm weather,
"With the glorious stars together."

25 From the fruitage, from the blossom,
   From the trees came no denying;
Then my heart said in my bosom:
   "Wherefore art thou sad and sighing?
"Learn contentment from this wood

30   "That proclaimeth all states good;
      "Go not from it as it found thee;
      "Turn thyself and gaze around thee."

      And I turned: behold the shading
          But showed forth the light more clearly;
35   The wild bees were honey-lading;
          The stream sounded hushing merely,
      And the wind not murmuring
      Seemed, but gently whispering:
      "Get thee patience; and thy spirit
40   "Shall discern in all things merit."

"Behold, I stand at the door and knock."

      Who standeth at the gate?—A woman old,
          A widow from the husband of her love:
      "O Lady, stay; this wind is piercing cold,
          Oh look at the keen frosty moon above;
5   I have no home, am hungry, feeble, poor:"—
          "I'm really very sorry, but I can
          Do nothing for you, there's the clergyman,"—
      The Lady said, and shivering closed the door.

      Who standeth at the gate?—Way-worn and pale,
10   A grey-haired man asks charity again:
      "Kind Lady, I have journeyed far, and fail
          Thro' weariness; for I have begged in vain
      Some shelter, and can find no lodging-place:"—
          She answered: "There's the Workhouse very near,
15   Go, for they'll certainly receive you there:"—
      Then shut the door against his pleading face.

      Who standeth at the gate?—a stunted child,
          Her sunk eyes sharpened with precocious care:
      "O Lady, save me from a home defiled,
20   From shameful sights and sounds that taint the air.
      Take pity on me, teach me something good;"—
          "For shame, why don't you work instead of cry?—

I keep no young impostors here, not I;"—
She slammed the door, indignant where she stood.

25 Who standeth at the gate, and will be heard?—
        Arise, O woman, from thy comforts now:
    Go forth again to speak the careless word,
        The cruel word unjust, with hardened brow.
    But Who is This, That standeth not to pray
30   As once, but terrible to judge thy sin?
        This, Whom thou wouldst not succour, nor take in,
    Nor teach, but leave to perish by the way?—

    "Thou didst it not unto the least of these,
        And in them hast not done it unto Me.
35 Thou wast as a princess, rich and at ease,
        Now sit in dust and howl for poverty.
    Three times I stood beseeching at thy gate,
        Three times I came to bless thy soul and save:
        But now I come to judge for what I gave,
40 And now at length thy sorrow is too late."

Gianni my friend and I both strove to excel,
But, missing better, settled down in well.
Both fail, indeed; but not alike we fail—
My forte being Venus' face, and his a dragon's tail.

The Offering of the New Law, the One Oblation once Offered.

"Sacrifice and Offering Thou wouldest not, but a BODY hast Thou prepared Me."

    Once I thought to sit so high
    In the Palace of the sky;
    Now I thank God for His Grace,
If I may fill the lowest place.

5   Once I thought to scale so soon
    Heights above the changing moon;

Now I thank God for delay—
Today, it yet is called today.

While I stumble, halt and blind,
10   Lo! He waiteth to be kind;
Bless me soon, or bless me slow,
Except He bless, I let not go.

Once for earth I laid my plan,
Once I leaned on strength of man,
15   When my hope was swept aside,
I stayed my broken heart on pride:

Broken reed hath pierced my hand;
Fell my house I built on sand;
Roofless, wounded, maimed by sin,
20   Fightings without, and fears within:

Yet, a tree, He feeds my root;
Yet, a branch, He prunes for fruit;
Yet, a sheep, these eves and morns,
He seeks for me among the thorns.

25   With Thine Image stamped of old,
Find Thy coin more choice than gold;
Known to Thee by name, recall
To Thee Thy home-sick prodigal.

Sacrifice and Offering
30   None there is that I can bring;
None, save what is Thine alone:
I bring Thee, Lord, but of Thine Own—

Broken Body, Blood Outpoured,
These I bring, my God, my Lord;
35   Wine of Life, and Living Bread,
With these for me Thy Board is spread.

The eleventh hour.

Faint and worn and aged
   One stands knocking at a gate,

Tho' no light shines in the casement,
   Knocking tho' so late.
5   It has struck eleven
In the courts of Heaven,
   Yet he still doth knock and wait.

While no answer cometh
   From the heavenly hill,
10   Blessed Angels wonder
   At his earnest will.
Hope and fear but quicken
While the shadows thicken;
   He is knocking knocking still.

15   Grim the gate unopened
   Stands with bar and lock,
Yet within the unseen Porter
   Hearkens to the knock.
Doing and undoing,
20   Faint and yet pursuing,
   This man's feet are on the Rock.

With a cry unceasing
   Knocketh prayeth he:—
"Lord, have mercy on me
25   "When I cry to Thee."—
With a knock unceasing
And a cry increasing:—
   "O my Lord, remember me."

Still the Porter standeth,
30   Love-constrained He standeth near,
While the cry increaseth
   Of that love and fear:—
"Jesus look upon me;
"Christ hast Thou foregone me?
35   "If I must, I perish here."—

Faint the knocking ceases,
   Faint the cry and call:
Is he lost indeed for ever,

Shut without the wall?—
40 Mighty Arms surround him,
Arms that sought and found him,
   Held withheld and bore thro' all.—

O celestial mansion
   Open wide the door:
45 Crown and robes of whiteness,
   Stone inscribed before,
Flocking Angels bear them;
Stretch thy hand and wear them,
   Sit thou down for evermore.

I know you not.

O Christ the Vine with living Fruit,
The twelvefold fruited Tree of Life,
The Balm in Gilead after strife,
The valley Lily and the Rose:
5 Stronger than Lebanon, Thou Root,
Sweeter than clustered grapes, Thou Vine;
Oh Best, Thou Vineyard of red Wine
Keeping Thy best Wine till the close.

Pearl of great price Thyself alone
10 And ruddier than the ruby Thou,
Most precious lightening Jasper Stone,
Head of the corner spurned before;
Fair Gate of pearl, Thyself the Door,
Clear golden Street, Thyself the Way,
15 By Thee we journey toward Thee now
Thro' Thee shall enter Heaven one day.

I thirst for Thee, full Fount and Flood,
My heart calls Thine as deep to deep:
Dost Thou forget Thy sweat and pain,
20 Thy provocation on the Cross?
Heart pierced for me, vouchsafe to keep
The purchase of Thy lavished Blood;

The gain is Thine Lord if I gain,
Or if I lose Thine Own the loss.

25 At midnight, saith the parable,
A cry was made, the Bridegroom came:
Those who were ready entered in;
The rest shut out in death and shame
Strove all too late that feast to win
30 Their die was cast and fixed their lot,
A gulph divided heaven from hell,
The Bridegroom said, 'I know you not.'

But Who is This That shuts the door
And saith 'I know you not' to them?
35 I see the wounded Hands and Side,
The Brow thorn-tortured long ago:
Yea, This Who grieved and bled and died,
This Same is He Who must condemn;
He called, but they refused to know,
40 So now He hears their cry no more.

A Christmas Carol.

Before the paling of the stars
    Before the winter morn
Before the earliest cockcrow
    Jesus Christ was born:
5   Born in a stable
    Cradled in a manger,
In the world His Hands had made
    Born a Stranger.

Priest and King lay fast asleep
10   In Jerusalem,
Young and Old lay fast asleep
    In crowded Bethlehem:
Saint and Angel Ox and Ass
    Kept a watch together

15 Before the Christmas daybreak
   In the winter weather.

Jesus on His Mother's breast
   In the stable cold,
Spotless Lamb of God was He
20   Shepherd of the Fold:
Let us kneel with Mary Maid
   With Joseph bent and hoary
With Saint and Angel Ox and Ass
   To hail the King of Glory.

Easter Even.

There is nothing more that they can do
   For all their rage and boast;
Caiaphas with his blaspheming crew,
   Herod with his host,

5 Pontius Pilate in his judgment hall
   Judging their Judge and his,
Or he who led them all and passed them all
   Arch-Judas with his kiss.

The sepulchre made sure with ponderous stone
10   Seal that same stone, O priest;
It may be thou shalt block the Holy One
   From rising in the east:

Set a watch about the sepulchre
   To watch on pain of death;
15 They must hold fast the stone if One should stir
   And shake it from beneath.

God Almighty He can break a seal,
   And roll away a stone;
Can grind the proud in dust who would not kneel,
20   And crush the mighty one.

There is nothing more that they can do
    For all their passionate care,
Those who sit in dust, the blessed few,
    And weep and rend their hair.

25   Peter, Thomas, Mary Magdalen,
    The Virgin unreproved,
Joseph with Nicodemus foremost men,
    And John the well-beloved.

Bring your finest linen and your spice,
30   Swathe the Sacred Dead,
Bind with careful hands and piteous eyes
    The napkin round His Head;

Lay Him in the garden rock to rest;
    Rest you the Sabbath length:
35   The Sun That went down crimson in the west
    Shall rise renewed in strength.

God Almighty shall give joy for pain,
    Shall comfort him who grieves:
Lo, He with joy shall doubtless come again
40   And with Him bring His sheaves.

Come unto Me.

Oh for the time gone by when thought of Christ
    Made His yoke easy and His burden light;
    When my heart stirred within me at the sight
Of Altar spread for awful Eucharist;
5   When all my hopes His promises sufficed;
    When my soul watched for Him by day by night;
    When my lamp lightened, and my robe was white,
And all seemed loss except the Pearl unpriced.
Yet since He calls me still with tender call,
10   Since He remembers Whom I half forgot,
    I even will run my race and bear my lot:
    For Faith the walls of Jericho cast down,

And Hope to whoso runs holds forth a crown,
And Love is Christ, and Christ is All in all.

Ash Wednesday.

Jesus, do I love Thee?
Thou art far above me,
Seated out of sight
Hid in heavenly light
5   Of most highest height.
Martyred hosts implore Thee,
Seraphs fall before Thee,
Angels and Archangels,
Cherub throngs adore Thee;
10   Blessed she that bore Thee!—
All the Saints approve Thee,
All the Virgins love Thee.
I show as a blot
Blood hath cleansed not,
15   As a barren spot
In Thy fruitful lot.
I, figtree fruit-unbearing,
Thou, Righteous Judge unsparing:
What canst Thou do more to me
20   That shall not more undo me?
Thy Justice hath a sound:
"Why cumbereth it the ground?"
Thy Love with stirrings stronger
Pleads: "Give it one year longer."
25   Thou giv'st me time: but who
Save Thou, shall give me dew,
Shall feed my root with Blood
And stir my sap for good?—
Oh by Thy gifts that shame me
30   Give more lest they condemn me:
Good Lord, I ask much of Thee,
But most I ask to love Thee:

Kind Lord, be mindful of me,
Love me and make me love Thee.

SPRING FANCIES.

I.

Gone were but the Winter,
  Come were but the Spring,
I would go to a covert
  Where the birds sing
5   Ding ding, ding a ding.

Where in the whitethorn
  Singeth the thrush,
And the robin sings
  In a holly bush
10   With his breast ablush.

Full of fresh scents
  Are the budding boughs,
Arching high over
  A cool green house
15   Where doves coo the arouse.

There the sun shineth
  Most shadily;
There sounds an echo
  Of the far sea,
20   Tho' far off it be.

II.

All the world is out in leaf,
  Half the world in flower,
Faint the rainbow comes and goes
  In a sunny shower;
25 Earth has waited weeks and weeks
  For this special hour.

All the world is making love;
   Bird to bird in bushes,
Beast to beast in glades, and frog
30   To frog among the rushes:
Wake, O south wind sweet with spice
   Wake the rose to blushes.

All the world is full of change;
   Tomorrow may be dreary:
35 Life breaks forth, to right and left
   Pipe the woodnotes cheery—
Nevertheless there lie the dead
   Fast asleep and weary—

III.

If it's weary work to live,
40   It will rest us to lie dead,
With a stone at the tired feet
   And a stone at the tired head.

In the waxing April days
   Half the world will stir and sing,
45 But half the world will slug and rot
   For all the sap of spring.

"LAST NIGHT."

Where were you last night? I watched at the gate;
I went down early, I stayed down late.
   Were you snug at home, I should like to know,
Or were you in the coppice wheedling Kate?

5 She's a fine girl, with a fine clear skin;
Easy to woo, perhaps not hard to win.
   Speak up like a man and tell me the truth:
I'm not one to grow downhearted and thin.

If you love her best speak up like a man;
10 It's not I will stand in the light of your plan:

Some girls might cry and scold you a bit
And say they couldn't bear it; but I can.

Love was pleasant enough, and the days went fast;
Pleasant while it lasted, but it needn't last;
15   Awhile on the wax and awhile on the wane,
Now dropped away into the past.

Was it pleasant to you? to me it was;
Now clean gone as an image from glass,
    As a goodly rainbow that fades away,
20   As dew that steams upwards from the grass,

As the first spring day, or the last summer day,
As the sunset flush that leaves heaven grey,
    As a flame burnt out for lack of oil
Which no pains relight or ever may.

25   Good luck to Kate and good luck to you,
I guess she'll be kind when you come to woo;
    I wish her a pretty face that will last,
I wish her a husband steady and true.

Hate you? not I, my very good friend;
30   All things begin and all have an end.
    But let broken be broken; I put no faith
In quacks who set up to patch and mend.

Just my love and one word to Kate:
Not to let time slip if she means to mate;—
35   For even such a thing has been known
As to miss the chance while we weigh and wait.

PETER GRUMP / FORSS.

PETER GRUMP

If underneath the water
   You comb your golden hair
With a golden comb, my daughter,
   Oh, would that I were there.

5   If underneath the wave
You fill a slimy grave,
Would that I, who could not save,
    Might share.

FORSS.

If my love Hero queens it
10   In summer Fairyland,
What would I be
    But the ring on her hand?
Her cheek when she leans it
    Would lean on me:—
15   Or sweet, bitter-sweet,
    The flower that she wore
When we parted, to meet
    On the hither shore
    Anymore? nevermore.

Helen Grey.

Because one loves you, Helen Grey,
    Is that a reason you should pout
    And like a March wind veer about
And frown and say your shrewish say?
5   Don't strain the cord until it snaps,
    Don't split the sound heart with your wedge,
    Don't cut your fingers with the edge
Of your keen wit: you may perhaps.

Because you're handsome, Helen Grey,
10   Is that a reason to be proud?
    Your eyes are bold, your laugh is loud,
Your steps go mincing on their way:
But so you miss that modest charm
    Which is the surest charm of all;
15   Take heed; you yet may trip and fall,
And no man care to stretch his arm.

Stoop from your cold height, Helen Grey,
   Come down and take a lowlier place;
   Come down to fill it now with grace;
20 Come down you must perforce some day:
For years cannot be kept at bay,
   And fading years will make you old;
   Then in their turn will men seem cold,
When you yourself are nipped and grey.

If.

If he would come today today today,
   Oh what a day today would be;
But now he's away, miles and miles away
   From me across the sea.

5 O little bird flying flying flying
   To your nest in the warm west,
Tell him as you pass that I am dying,
   As you pass home to your nest.

I have a sister, I have a brother,
10   A faithful hound, a tame white dove;
But I had another, once I had another,
   And I miss him my love, my love.

In this weary world it is so cold so cold
   While I sit here all alone
15 I would not like to wait and to grow old
   But just to be dead and gone.

Make me fair when I lie dead on my bed,
   Fair where I am lying;
Perhaps he may come and look upon me dead
20   He for whom I am dying.

Dig my grave for two with a stone to show it
   And on the stone write my name:
If he never comes I shall never know it
   But sleep on all the same.

Seasons.

Oh the cheerful budding-time
   When thorn-hedges turn to green;
When new leaves of elm and lime
   Cleave and shed their winter screen:
5 Tender lambs are born and baa,
   North wind finds no snow to bring,
Vigorous nature laughs Haha
   In the miracle of spring.

Oh the gorgeous blossom-days
10   When broad flag-flowers drink and blow;
In and out in summer blaze
   Dragonflies flash to and fro:
Ashen branches hang out keys,
   Oaks put forth the rosy shoot,
15 Wandering herds wax sleek at ease,
   Lovely blossoms end in fruit.

Oh the shouting harvest-weeks:
   Mother Earth grown fat with sheaves;
Thrifty gleaner finds who seeks:
20   Russet golden pomp of leaves
Crowns the woods, to fall at length;
   Bracing winds are felt to stir,
Ocean gathers up her strength,
   Beasts renew their dwindled fur.

25 Oh the starving winter-lapse,
   Ice-bound, hunger-pinched and dim:
Dormant roots recal their saps,
   Empty nests show black and grim,
Short-lived sunshine gives no heat,
30   Undue buds are nipped by frost,
Snow sets forth a windingsheet
   And all hope of life seems lost.

HENRY HARDIMAN,
AGED 55.

Affliction sore long time he bore,
    Physicians were in vain,
Till God did please his soul release,
    And ease him of his pain.

Within the Veil.

She holds a lily in her hand,
Where long ranks of Angels stand;
A silver lily for her wand.

All her hair falls sweeping down,
5   Her hair that is a golden brown;
A crown beneath her golden crown.

Blooms a rose-bush at her knee,
Good to smell and good to see;
It bears a rose for her, for me:

10   Her rose a blossom richly grown,
My rose a bud not fully blown
But sure one day to be mine own.

Paradise: in a Symbol.

Golden-winged, silver-winged,
    Winged with flashing flame,
Such a flight of birds I saw,
    Birds without a name:
5   Singing songs in their own tongue
    (Song of songs) they came.

One to another calling,
    Each answering each,
One to another calling
10   In their proper speech:

High above my head they wheeled,
   Far out of reach.

On wings of flame they went and came
   With a cadenced clang,
15 Their silver wings tinkled,
   Their golden wings rang,
The wind it whistled thro' their wings
   Where in heaven they sang.

They flashed and they darted
20   Awhile before mine eyes,
Mounting mounting mounting still
   In haste to scale the skies,
Birds without a nest on earth,
   Birds of Paradise.

25 Where the moon riseth not
   Nor sun seeks the west,
There to sing their glory
   Which they sing at rest,
There to sing their love-song
30   When they sing their best:

Not in any garden
   That mortal foot hath trod,
Not in any flowering tree
   That springs from earthly sod,
35 But in the garden where they dwell
   The Paradise of God.

In July
No goodbye;
In Augùst
Part we must.

Love hath a name of Death:
He gives a breath
And takes away.

Lo we beneath his sway
5   Grow like a flower;
To bloom an hour,
To droop a day,
And fade away.

Tu scendi dalle stelle, O Re del Cielo,
E vieni in una grotta al freddo al gelo:
 O Bambino mio divino
 Io Ti voglio sempre amar!
5   O Dio beato
E quanto Ti costò l'avermi amato.

 Alas my Lord,
How should I wrestle all the livelong night
With Thee my God, my Strength and my Delight?

 How can it need
5   So agonized an effort and a strain
To make Thy Face of Mercy shine again?

 How can it need
Such wringing out of breathless prayer to move
Thee to Thy wonted Love, when Thou art Love?

10   Yet Abraham
So hung about Thine Arm outstretched and bared,
That for ten righteous Sodom had been spared.

 Yet Jacob did
So hold Thee by the clenched hand of prayer
15   That he prevailed, and Thou didst bless him there.

 Elias prayed,
And sealed the founts of Heaven; he prayed again
And lo, Thy Blessing fell in showers of rain.

 Gulped by the fish,
20   As by the pit, lost Jonah made his moan;
And Thou forgavest, waiting to atone.

All Nineveh
Fasting and girt in sackcloth raised a cry,
Which moved Thee ere the day of grace went by.

25   Thy Church prayed on
And on for blessed Peter in his strait,
Till opened of its own accord the gate.

Yea, Thou my God
Hast prayed all night, and in the garden prayed
30 Even while, like melting wax, Thy strength was made.

Alas for him
Who faints, despite Thy Pattern, King of Saints:
Alas, alas, for me, the one that faints.

Lord, give us strength
35 To hold Thee fast, until we hear Thy Voice
Which Thine own know, who hearing It rejoice.

Lord, give us strength
To hold Thee fast until we see Thy Face,
Full Fountain of all Rapture and all Grace.

40   But when our strength
Shall be made weakness, and our bodies clay,
Hold Thou us fast, and give us sleep till day.

AN ALPHABET.

A is the Alphabet, A at its head;
    A is an Antelope, agile to run.
B is the Baker Boy bringing the bread,
    Or black Bear and brown Bear, both begging for bun.

5 C is a Cornflower come with the corn;
    C is a Cat with a comical look.
D is a dinner which Dahlias adorn;
    D is a Duchess who dines with a Duke.

E is an elegant eloquent Earl;
10   E is an Egg whence an Eaglet emerges.

F is a Falcon, with feathers to furl;
   F is a Fountain of full foaming surges.

G is the Gander, the Gosling, the Goose;
   G is a Garnet in girdle of gold.
15 H is a Heartsease, harmonious of hues;
   H is a huge Hammer, heavy to hold.

I is an Idler who idles on ice;
   I am I—who will say I am not I?
J is a Jacinth, a jewel of price;
20   J is a Jay, full of joy in July.

K is a King, or a Kaiser still higher;
   K is a Kitten, or quaint Kangaroo.
L is a Lute or a lovely-toned Lyre;
   L is a Lily all laden with dew.

25 M is a Meadow where Meadowsweet blows;
   M is a Mountain made dim by a mist.
N is a Nut—in a nutshell it grows—
   Or a Nest full of Nightingales singing—oh list!

O is an Opal, with only one spark;
30   O is an Olive, with oil on its skin.
P is a Pony, a pet in a park;
   P is the Point of a Pen or a Pin.

Q is a Quail, quick-chirping at morn;
   Q is a Quince quite ripe and near dropping.
35 R is a Rose, rosy red on a thorn;
   R is a red-breasted Robin come hopping.

S is a Snow-storm that sweeps o'er the Sea;
   S is the Song that the swift Swallows sing.
T is the Tea-table set out for tea;
40   T is a Tiger with terrible spring.

U, the Umbrella, went up in a shower;
   Or Unit is useful with ten to unite.
V is a Violet veined in the flower;
   V is a Viper of venomous bite.

45   W stands for the water-bred Whale;
        Stands for the wonderful Wax-work so gay.
    X, or XX, or XXX is ale,
        Or Policeman X, exercised day after day.

    Y is a yellow Yacht, yellow its boat;
50   Y is the Yucca, the Yam, or the Yew.
    Z is a Zebra, zigzagged his coat,
        Or Zebu, or Zoöphyte, seen at the Zoo.

Husband and Wife.

"Oh kiss me once before I go,
    "To make amends for sorrow;
"Oh kiss me once before we part
    "Who shall not meet tomorrow.

5   "And I was wrong to urge your will,
    "And wrong to mar your life;
"But kiss me once before we part,
    "Because you are my wife."

She turned her head and tossed her head
10   And puckered up her brow:
"I never kissed you yet," said she,
    "And I'll not kiss you now.

"Tho' I'm your wife by might and right
    "And forsworn marriage vow,
15   "I never loved you yet," said she,
    "And I don't love you now."

So he went sailing on the sea,
    And she sat crossed and dumb
While he went sailing on the sea
20   Where the storm winds come.

He'd been away a month and day
    Counting from morn to morn:

And many buds had turned to leaves
   And many lambs were born

25 And many buds had turned to flowers
   For Spring was in a glow,
When she was laid upon her bed
   As white and cold as snow.

"Oh let me kiss my baby once,
30   "Once before I die;
"And bring it sometimes to my grave
   "To teach it where I lie.

"And tell my husband when he comes
   "Safe home from sea,
35 "To love the baby that I leave
   "If ever he loved me:

"And tell him, not for might or right
   "Or forsworn marriage vow
"But for the helpless baby's sake,
40   "I would have kissed him now."

MICHAEL F. M. ROSSETTI.
Born April 22nd, 1881; Died January 24th, 1883.

A holy Innocent gone home
Without so much as one sharp wounding word:
A blessed Michael in heaven's lofty dome
Without a sword.

─────────────

5 Brief dawn and noon and setting time!
Our rapid-rounding moon has fled:
A black eclipse before the prime
Has swallowed up that shining head.
Eternity holds up her lookingglass:—
10 The eclipse of Time will pass,
And all that lovely light return to sight.

─────────────

I watch the showers and think of flowers:
Alas, my flower that shows no fruit!
My snowdrop plucked, my daisy shoot
15   Plucked from the root.

Soon Spring will shower, the world will flower,
A world of buds will promise fruit,
Pear trees will shoot and apples shoot
   Sound at the root.

20 Bud of an hour, far off you flower;
My bud, far off you ripen fruit;
My prettiest bud, my straightest shoot
   Sweet at the root.

——————

The youngest bud of five,
25   The least lamb of the fold,—
Bud not to blossom, yet to thrive
   Away from cold.

Lamb which we shall not see
   Leap at its pretty pranks,
30 Our lamb at rest and full of glee
   On heavenly banks.

A SICK CHILD'S MEDITATION.

Pain and weariness, aching eyes and head,
   Pain and weariness all the day and night:
Yet the pillow's soft on my smooth soft bed,
   And fresh air blows in, and mother shades the light.

5 Thou, O Lord, in pain hadst no pillow soft,
   In Thy weary pain, in Thine agony:
But a cross of shame held Thee up aloft
   Where Thy very mother could do nought for Thee.

I would gaze on Thee, on Thy patient face;
10   Make me like Thyself, patient, sweet, at peace;

Make my days all love, and my nights all praise,
    Till all days and nights and patient sufferings cease.

Love is all happiness, love is all beauty,
    Love is the crown of flaxen heads and hoary,
Love is the only everlasting duty,
    And love is chronicled in endless story
5   And kindles endless glory.

A handy Mole who plied no shovel
To excavate his vaulted hovel,
While hard at work met in mid-furrow
An Earthworm boring out his burrow.
5 Our Mole had dined and must grow thinner
Before he gulped a second dinner,
And on no other terms cared he
To meet a worm of low degree.
The Mole turned on his blindest eye
10 Passing that base mechanic by;
The Worm entrenched in actual blindness
Ignored or kindness or unkindness;
Each wrought his own exclusive tunnel
To reach his own exclusive funnel.

15 A plough its flawless track pursuing
Involved them in one common ruin.
Where now the mine and countermine,
The dined-on and the one to dine?
The impartial ploughshare of extinction
20 Annulled them all without distinction.

"One swallow does not make a summer."

A Rose which spied one swallow
Made haste to blush and blow:
"Others are sure to follow:"
Ah no, not so!

5 The wandering clouds still owe
   A few fresh flakes of snow,
   Chill fog must fill the hollow,
   Before the bird-stream flow
   In flood across the main
10 And winter's woe
   End in glad summer come again.
   Then thousand flowers may blossom by the shore,
   But that Rose never more.

   Contemptuous of his home beyond
   The village and the village pond,
   A large-souled Frog who spurned each byeway,
   Hopped along the imperial highway.

5 Nor grunting pig nor barking dog
   Could disconcert so great a frog.
   The morning dew was lingering yet
   His sides to cool, his tongue to wet;
   The night dew when the night should come
10 A travelled frog would send him home.

   Not so, alas! the wayside grass
   Sees him no more:—not so, alas!

   A broadwheeled waggon unawares
   Ran him down, his joys, his cares.
15 From dying choke one feeble croak
   The Frog's perpetual silence broke:
   "Ye buoyant Frogs, ye great and small,
   Even I am mortal after all.
   My road to Fame turns out a wry way:
20 I perish on this hideous highway,—
   Oh for my old familiar byeway!"

   The choking Frog sobbed and was gone:
   The waggoner strode whistling on.

   Unconscious of the carnage done,
25 Whistling that waggoner strode on,
   Whistling (it may have happened so)

"A Froggy would a-wooing go:"
A hypothetic frog trolled he
Obtuse to a reality.

30 O rich and poor, O great and small,
Such oversights beset us all:
The mangled frog abides incog,
The uninteresting actual frog;
The hypothetic frog alone
35 Is the one frog we dwell upon.

A Word for the Dumb.

Pity the sorrows of a poor old Dog
    Who wags his tail a-begging in his need:
Despise not even the sorrows of a Frog,
    God's creature too, and that's enough to plead:
5 Spare Puss who trusts us purring on our hearth:
    Spare Bunny once so frisky and so free:
Spare all the harmless tenants of the earth:
    Spare, and be spared:—or who shall plead for thee?

CARDINAL NEWMAN.

"In the grave, whither thou goest."

O weary Champion of the Cross, lie still:
    Sleep thou at length the all-embracing sleep:
    Long was thy sowing day, rest now and reap:
Thy fast was long, feast now thy spirit's fill.
5 Yea, take thy fill of love, because thy will
    Chose love not in the shallows but the deep:
    Thy tides were springtides, set against the neap
Of calmer souls: thy flood rebuked their rill.
Now night has come to thee—please God, of rest:
10   So some time must it come to every man;

To first and last, where many last are first.
Now fixed and finished thine eternal plan,
    Thy best has done its best, thy worst its worst:
Thy best its best, please God, thy best its best.

An Echo from Willowwood.

"O ye, all ye that walk in Willowwood."
                    D. G. Rossetti.

Two gazed into a pool, he gazed and she,
    Not hand in hand, yet heart in heart, I think,
    Pale and reluctant on the water's brink,
As on the brink of parting which must be.
5   Each eyed the other's aspect, she and he,
    Each felt one hungering heart leap up and sink,
    Each tasted bitterness which both must drink,
There on the brink of life's dividing sea.
Lilies upon the surface, deep below
10   Two wistful faces craving each for each,
        Resolute and reluctant without speech:—
A sudden ripple made the faces flow
    One moment joined, to vanish out of reach:
        So those hearts joined, and ah! were parted so.

"YEA, I HAVE A GOODLY HERITAGE."

My vineyard that is mine I have to keep,
    Pruning for fruit the pleasant twigs and leaves.
Tend thou thy cornfield: one day thou shalt reap
    In joy thy ripened sheaves.

5   Or if thine be an orchard, graft and prop
    Food-bearing trees each watered in its place:
Or if a garden, let it yield for crop
    Sweet herbs and herb of grace.

But if my lot be sand where nothing grows?—
10   Nay, who hath said it? Tune a thankful psalm:
For tho' thy desert bloom not as the rose,
      It yet can rear thy palm.

A Death of a First-born.
JANUARY 14th, 1892.

One young life lost, two happy young lives blighted,
      With earthward eyes we see:
With eyes uplifted, keener, farther-sighted,
      We look, O Lord, to Thee.

5   Grief hears a funeral knell: hope hears the ringing
      Of birthday bells on high;
Faith, hope, and love make answer with soft singing,
      Half carol and half cry.

Stoop to console us, Christ, Sole Consolation,
10   While dust returns to dust;
Until that blessed day when all Thy Nation
      Shall rise up of the Just.

"FAINT, YET PURSUING."

1.

Beyond this shadow and this turbulent sea,
      Shadow of death and turbulent sea of death,
Lies all we long to have or long to be:—
      Take heart, tired man, toil on with lessening breath,
5   Lay violent hands on heaven's high treasury,
      Be what you long to be thro' life-long scathe:
A little while hope leans on charity,
      A little while charity heartens faith.
A little while: and then what further while?
10   One while that ends not and that wearies not,
      For ever new whilst evermore the same:
      All things made new bear each a sweet new name;

Man's lot of death has turned to life his lot,
And tearful charity to love's own smile.

2.

Press onward, quickened souls, who mounting move,
   Press onward, upward, fire with mounting fire;
   Gathering volume of untold desire
Press upward, homeward, dove with mounting dove.
5   Point me the excellent way that leads above;
   Woo me with sequent will, me too to aspire;
   With sequent heart to follow higher and higher,
To follow all who follow on to love.
Up the high steep, across the golden sill,
10   Up out of shadows into very light,
   Up out of dwindling life to life aglow,
I watch you, my beloved, out of sight;—
Sight fails me, and my heart is watching still:
   My heart fails, yet I follow on to know.

What will it be, O my soul, what will it be
To touch the long-raced-for goal, to handle and see,
To rest in the joy of joys, in the joy of the blest,
To rest and revive and rejoice, to rejoice and to rest!

Lord, Thou art fulness, I am emptiness:
Yet hear my heart speak in its speechlessness
Extolling Thine unuttered loveliness.

O Lord, I cannot plead my love of Thee:
I plead Thy love of me;—
The shallow conduit hails the unfathomed sea.

Faith and Hope are wings to Love,
Silver wings to golden dove.

A SORROWFUL SIGH OF A PRISONER.

Lord, comest Thou to me?
　　My heart is cold and dead:
Alas that such a heart should be
　　The place to lay Thy head!

"I sit a queen, and am no widow, and shall see no
　　　　　sorrow"—
Yea, scarlet woman, today: but not yea at all tomorrow.
Scarlet queen on a scarlet throne all today without sorrow,
Bethink thee: today must end; there is no end of
　　　　　tomorrow.

Passing away the bliss,
　　The anguish passing away:
Thus it is
　　　Today.

5　Clean past away the sorrow,
　　The pleasure brought back to stay:
Thus and this
　　　Tomorrow.

Love builds a nest on earth and waits for rest,
Love sends to heaven the warm heart from its breast,
Looks to be blest and is already blest,
And testifies: "God's Will is alway best."

Jesus alone:—if thus it were to me;
Yet thus it cannot be;
Lord, I have all things if I have but Thee.

Jesus and all:—precious His bounties are,
5　Yet He more precious far;
Day's-eyes are many, one the Morning Star.

Jesus my all:—so let me rest in love,
Thy peaceable poor dove,
Some time below till timeless time above.

The Way of the World.

A boat that sails upon the sea;
 Sails far and far and far away:
Who sail in her sing songs of glee,
  Or watch and pray.

5 A boat that drifts upon the sea
 Silent and void to sun and air:
Who sailed in her have ended glee
  And watch and prayer.

BOOKS IN THE RUNNING BROOKS.

"It is enough, enough," one said,
 At play among the flowers:
"I spy a rose upon the thorn,
 A rainbow in the showers;
5 I hear a merry chime of bells
 Ring out the passing hours."—
  Soft springs the fountain
   From the daisied ground:
  Softly falling on the moss
10   Without a sound.

"It is enough," she said, and fixed
 Calm eyes upon the sky:
"I watch a flitting tender cloud
 Just like a dove go by;
15 A lark is rising from the grass;
 A wren is building nigh."—
  Softly the fountain
   Threads its silver way,

Screened by the scented bloom
20   Of whitest may.

"Enough?" she whispered to herself,
    As doubting: "Is it so?
Enough to wear the roses fair?
    Oh sweetest flowers that blow:—
25 Oh yes, it surely is enough,
        My happy home below."—
            A shadow stretcheth
                From the hither shore:
            Those waters darken
30   More and more and more.

"It is enough," she says; but with
    A listless, weary moan:
"Enough," if mixing with her friends;
    "Enough," if left alone.
35 But to herself: "Not yet enough,
        This suffering, to atone?"—
            The cold black waters
                Seem to stagnate there;
            Without a single wave,
40   Or breath of air.

And now she says: "It is enough,"
    Half languid and half stirred:
"Enough," to silence and to sound,
    Thorn, blossom, soaring bird:
45 "Enough," she says; but with a lack
        Of something in the word.—
            Defiled and turbid
                See the waters pass;
            Half light, half shadow,
50   Struggling thro' the grass.

Ah, will it ever dawn, that day
    When calm for good or ill
Her heart shall say: "It is enough,
    For Thou art with me still;

55 It is enough, O Lord my God,
   Thine only blessed Will."—
    Then shall the fountain sing
     And flow to rest;
   Clear as the sun track
60   To the purple West.

GONE BEFORE.

She was most like a rose, when it flushes rarest;
She was most like a lily, when it blows fairest;
She was most like a violet, sweetest on the bank:
Now she's only like the snow cold and blank
5   After the sun sank.

She left us in the early days, she would not linger
For orange blossoms in her hair, or ring on finger:
Did she deem windy grass more good than these?
Now the turf that's between us and the hedging trees
10   Might as well be seas.

I had trained a branch she shelters not under,
I had reared a flower she snapped asunder:
In the bush and on the stately bough
Birds sing; she who watched them track the plough
15   Cannot hear them now.

Every bird has a nest hidden somewhere
For itself and its mate and joys that come there,
Tho' it soar to the clouds, finding there its rest:
You sang in the height, but no more with eager breast
20   Stoop to your own nest.

If I could win you back from heaven-gate lofty,
Perhaps you would but grieve returning softly:
Surely they would miss you in the blessed throng,
Miss your sweet voice in their sweetest song,
25   Reckon time too long.

Earth is not good enough for you, my sweet, my sweetest;
Life on earth seemed long to you tho' to me fleetest.
I would not wish you back if a wish would do:
Only love I long for heaven with you
30   Heart-pierced thro' and thro'.

Privately Printed Poems

THE DEAD CITY.

Once I rambled in a wood
With a careless hardihood,
Heeding not the tangled way;
Labyrinths around me lay,
5   But for them I never stood.

On, still on, I wandered on,
And the sun above me shone;
And the birds around me winging
With their everlasting singing
10   Made me feel not quite alone.

In the branches of the trees,
Murmured like the hum of bees
The low sound of happy breezes,
Whose sweet voice that never ceases
15   Lulls the heart to perfect ease.

Streamlets bubbled all around
On the green and fertile ground,
Thro' the rushes and the grass,
Like a sheet of liquid glass,
20   With a soft and trickling sound.

And I went, I went on faster,
Contemplating no disaster;
And I plucked ripe blackberries,
But the birds with envious eyes
25   Came and stole them from their master:

For the birds here were all tame;
Some with bodies like a flame,

Some that glanced the branches thro'
Pure and colourless as dew;
30   Fearlessly to me they came.

Before me no mortal stood
In the mazes of that wood;
Before me the birds had never
Seen a man, but dwelt for ever
35   In a happy solitude;

Happy solitude, and blest
With beatitude of rest;
Where the woods are ever vernal,
And the life and joy eternal,
40   Without Death's or Sorrow's test.

Oh most blessed solitude!
Oh most full beatitude!
Where are quiet without strife,
And imperishable life,
45   Nothing marred, and all things good.

And the bright sun, life begetting,
Never rising, never setting,
Shining warmly overhead,
Nor too pallid, nor too red,
50   Lulled me to a sweet forgetting,

Sweet forgetting of the time:
And I listened for no chime
Which might warn me to begone;
But I wandered on, still on,
55   'Neath the boughs of oak and lime.

Know I not how long I strayed
In the pleasant leafy shade;
But the trees had gradually
Grown more rare, the air more free,
60   The sun hotter overhead.

Soon the birds no more were seen
Glancing thro' the living green;

And a blight had passed upon
All the trees; and the pale sun
65   Shone with a strange lurid sheen.

Then a darkness spread around:
I saw nought, I heard no sound;
Solid darkness overhead,
With a trembling cautious tread
70   Passed I o'er the unseen ground.

But at length a pallid light
Broke upon my searching sight;
A pale solitary ray,
Like a star at dawn of day
75   Ere the sun is hot and bright.

Towards its faintly glimmering beam
I went on as in a dream;
A strange dream of hope and fear!
And I saw as I drew near
80   'Twas in truth no planet's gleam;

But a lamp above a gate
Shone in solitary state
O'er a desert drear and cold,
O'er a heap of ruins old,
85   O'er a scene most desolate.

By that gate I entered lone
A fair city of white stone;
And a lovely light to see
Dawned, and spread most gradually
90   Till the air grew warm and shone.

Thro' the splendid streets I strayed
In that radiance without shade,
Yet I heard no human sound;
All was still and silent round
95   As a city of the dead.

All the doors were open wide;
Lattices on every side

In the wind swung to and fro;
Wind that whispered very low:
100   Go and see the end of pride.

With a fixed determination
Entered I each habitation,
But they all were tenantless;
All was utter loneliness,
105   All was deathless desolation.

In the noiseless market-place
Was no care-worn busy face;
There were none to buy or sell,
None to listen or to tell,
110   In this silent emptiness.

Thro' the city on I went
Full of awe and wonderment;
Still the light around me shone,
And I wandered on, still on,
115   In my great astonishment,

Till at length I reached a place
Where amid an ample space
Rose a palace for a king;
Golden was the turreting,
120   And of solid gold the base.

The great porch was ivory,
And the steps were ebony;
Diamond and chrysoprase
Set the pillars in a blaze,
125   Capitalled with jewelry.

None was there to bar my way—
And the breezes seemed to say:
Touch not these, but pass them by,
Pressing onwards: therefore I
130   Entered in and made no stay.

All around was desolate:
I went on; a silent state

Reigned in each deserted room,
And I hastened thro' the gloom
135 Till I reached an outer gate.

Soon a shady avenue
Blossom-perfumed, met my view.
Here and there the sun-beams fell
On pure founts, whose sudden swell
140 Up from marble basins flew.

Every tree was fresh and green;
Not a withered leaf was seen
Thro' the veil of flowers and fruit;
Strong and sapful were the root,
145 The top boughs, and all between.

Vines were climbing everywhere
Full of purple grapes and fair:
And far off I saw the corn
With its heavy head down borne,
150 By the odour-laden air.

Who shall strip the bending vine?
Who shall tread the press for wine?
Who shall bring the harvest in
When the pallid ears begin
155 In the sun to glow and shine?

On I went, alone, alone,
Till I saw a tent that shone
With each bright and lustrous hue;
It was trimmed with jewels too,
160 And with flowers; not one was gone.

Then the breezes whispered me:
Enter in, and look, and see
How for luxury and pride
A great multitude have died:—
165 And I entered tremblingly.

Lo, a splendid banquet laid
In the cool and pleasant shade.

Mighty tables, every thing
Of sweet Nature's furnishing
170 That was rich and rare, displayed;

And each strange and luscious cate
Practised Art makes delicate;
With a thousand fair devices
Full of odours and of spices;
175 And a warm voluptuous state.

All the vessels were of gold
Set with gems of worth untold.
In the midst a fountain rose
Of pure milk, whose rippling flows
180 In a silver basin rolled.

In green emerald baskets were
Sun-red apples, streaked, and fair;
Here the nectarine and peach
And ripe plum lay, and on each
185 The bloom rested every where.

Grapes were hanging overhead,
Purple, pale, and ruby-red;
And in panniers all around
Yellow melons shone, fresh found,
190 With the dew upon them spread.

And the apricot and pear
And the pulpy fig were there;
Cherries and dark mulberries,
Bunchy currants, strawberries,
195 And the lemon wan and fair.

And unnumbered others too,
Fruits of every size and hue,
Juicy in their ripe perfection,
Cool beneath the cool reflection
200 Of the curtains' skyey blue.

All the floor was strewn with flowers
Fresh from sunshine and from showers,

Roses, lilies, jessamine;
And the ivy ran between
205 Like a thought in happy hours.

And this feast too lacked no guest
With its warm delicious rest;
With its couches softly sinking,
And its glow, not made for thinking,
210 But for careless joy at best.

Many banquetters were there,
Wrinkled age, the young, the fair;
In the splendid revelry
Flushing cheek and kindling eye
215 Told of gladness without care.

Yet no laughter rang around,
Yet they uttered forth no sound;
With the smile upon his face
Each sat moveless in his place,
220 Silently, as if spell-bound.

The low whispering voice was gone,
And I felt awed and alone.
In my great astonishment
To the feasters up I went—
225 Lo, they all were turned to stone.

Yea they all were statue-cold,
Men and women, young and old;
With the life-like look and smile
And the flush; and all the while
230 The hard fingers kept their hold.

Here a little child was sitting
With a merry glance, befitting
Happy age and heedless heart;
There a young man sat apart
235 With a forward look unweeting.

Nigh them was a maiden fair;
And the ringlets of her hair

Round her slender fingers twined;
And she blushed as she reclined,
240   Knowing that her love was there.

Here a dead man sat to sup,
In his hand a drinking cup;
Wine cup of the heavy gold,
Human hand stony and cold,
245   And no life-breath struggling up.

There a mother lay, and smiled
Down upon her infant child;
Happy child and happy mother
Laughing back to one another
250   With a gladness undefiled.

Here an old man slept, worn out
With the revelry and rout;
Here a strong man sat and gazed
On a girl, whose eyes upraised
255   No more wandered round about.

And none broke the stillness, none;
I was the sole living one.
And methought that silently
Many seemed to look on me
260   With strange stedfast eyes that shone.

Full of fear I would have fled;
Full of fear I bent my head,
Shutting out each stony guest:—
When I looked again the feast
265   And the tent had vanished.

Yes, once more I stood alone
Where the happy sunlight shone
And a gentle wind was sighing,
And the little birds were flying,
270   And the dreariness was gone.

All these things that I have said
Awed me, and made me afraid.

What was I that I should see
So much hidden mystery?
275 And I straightway knelt and prayed.

The Water Spirit's Song.

In the silent hour of even,
When the stars are in the heaven,
When in the azure cloudless sky
The moon beams forth all lustrously,
5 When over hill and over vale
Is wafted the sweet-scented gale,
When murmurs thro' the forest trees
The cool, refreshing, evening breeze,
When the nightingale's wild melody
10 Is waking herb and flower and tree,
From their perfumed and soft repose,
To list the praises of the rose;
When the ocean sleeps deceitfully,
When the waves are resting quietly,
15 I spread my bright wings, and fly far away
To my beautiful sister's mansion gay:
I leave behind me rock and mountain,
I leave behind me rill and fountain,
And I dive far down in the murmuring sea,
20 Where my fair sister welcomes me joyously;
For she's Queen of Ocean for ever and ever,
And I of each fountain and still lake and river.

She dwells in a palace of coral
  Of diamond and pearl;
25 And in each jewelled chamber the fishes
  Their scaly length unfurl;
And the sun can dart no light
  On the depths beneath the sea;
But the ruby there shines bright
30 And sparkles brilliantly;

No mortal e'er trod on the surface
   Of the adamantine floor;
No human being e'er passed the bound
   Of the pearl-encrusted door.
35 But the mermaidens sing plaintively
   Beneath the deep blue ocean,
And to their song the green fishes dance
   With undulating motion.
And the cold bright moon looks down on us
40   With her fixed unchanging smile;
'Neath her chilly glance the mermaids dance
   Upon each coral isle;
And her beams she laves in the briny waves
   With loving constancy;
45 And she never ceases with light caresses
   To soothe the swelling sea;
All night on us she softly shines
   With a fond and tender gaze,
Till the sun blushes red from his ocean bed
50   And sends forth his warming rays.
And then she flies to other skies
   Till the sun has run his race,
And again the day to the night's soft sway
   To the moon and stars gives place.

55 And when the bright sun doth arise,
To tinge with gold the vaulted skies,
When the nightingale no longer sings,
And the blush rose forth its odour flings,
When the breath of morn is rustling through
60 The trees, and kissing away the dew,
When the sea casts up its foam and spray,
And greets the fresh gale that speeds away,
I fly back to my home in the rushing cascade—
By the silvery streamlet my dark hair I braid,
65 And then when the sun once more sinks in the ocean,
I glide with a floating and passionless motion,
To my sister 'neath the boundless sea
And with her till morn dwell joyously.

The Song of the Star.

I am a star dwelling on high
In the azure of the vaulted sky.
I shine on the land and I shine on the sea,
And the little breezes talk to me.
5   The waves rise towards me every one
And forget the brightness of the sun:
The growing grass springs up towards me
And forgets the day's fertility.
My face is light, and my beam is life,
10   And my passionless being hath no strife.
In me no love is turned to hate,
No fulness is made desolate;
Here is no hope, no fear, no grief,
Here is no pain and no relief;
15   Nor birth nor death hath part in me,
But a profound tranquillity.
The blossoms that bloomed yesterday
Unaltered shall bloom on today,
And on the morrow shall not fade.
20   Within the everlasting shade
The fountain gushing up for ever
Flows on to the eternal river,
That, running by a reedy shore,
Bubbles, bubbles evermore.
25   The happy birds sing in the trees
To the music of the southern breeze;
And they fear no lack of food,
Chirping in the underwood;
For ripe seeds and berried bushes
30   Serve the finches and the thrushes,
And all feathered fowls that dwell
In that shade majestical.
Beyond all clouds and all mistiness
I float in the strength of my loveliness;
35   And I move round the sun with a measured motion
In the blue expanse of the skyey ocean;
And I hear the song of the Angel throng

In a river of extasy flow along,
Without a pausing, without a hushing,
40   Like an everlasting fountain's gushing
That of its own will bubbles up
From a white untainted cup.
Countless planets float round me
Differing all in majesty;
45   Smaller some, and some more great,
Amethystine, roseate,
Golden, silvery, glowing blue,
Hueless, and of every hue.
Each and all, both great and small,
50   With a cadence musical,
Shoot out rays of glowing praise,
Never ending, but always
Hymning the Creator's might
Who hath filled them full of light.
55   Pealing through eternity,
Filling out immensity,
Sun and moon and stars together,
In heights where is no cloudy weather;
Where is nor storm, nor mist, nor rain;
60   Where night goeth not to come again.
On, and on, and on for ever,
Never ceasing, sinking never,
Voiceless adorations rise
To the Heaven above the skies.
65   We all chant with a holy harmony,
No discord marreth our melody;
Here are no strifes nor envyings,
But each with love joyously sings,
For ever and ever floating free
70   In the azure light of infinity.

Summer.

Hark to the song of greeting! the tall trees
Murmur their welcome in the southern breeze.

Amid the thickest foliage many a bird
Sits singing, their shrill matins scarcely heard
5   One by one, but all together
Welcoming the sunny weather.
In every bower hums a bee
Fluttering melodiously.
Murmurs joy in every brook,
10   Rippling with a pleasant look.
What greet they with their guileless bliss?
What welcome with a song like this?

See in the south a radiant form,
    Her fair head crowned with roses;
15   From her bright foot-path flies the storm;
    Upon her breast reposes
Many an unconfinèd tress,
Golden, glossy, motionless.
Face and form are love and light,
20   Soft ineffably, yet bright.
All her path is strewn with flowers,
Round her float the laughing Hours,
Heaven and earth make joyful din,
Welcoming sweet Summer in.

25   And now she alights on the Earth
    To play with her children the flowers;
She touches the stems, and the buds have birth,
    And gently she trains them in bowers.
And the bees and the birds are glad,
30   And the wind catches warmth from her breath,
And around her is nothing sad,
    Nor any traces of death.
See now she lays her down
With roses for her crown,
35   With jessamine and myrtle
Forming her fragrant kirtle;
Conquered by softest slumbers
No more the hours she numbers,
The hours that intervene
40   Ere she may wing her flight

Far from this smiling scene
  With all her love and light,
And leave the flowers and the summer bowers
To wither in autumn and winter hours.

45 And must they wither then?
      Their life and their perfume
  Sinking so soon again
      Into their earthy tomb?
  Let us bind her as she lies
50 Ere the fleeting moment flies;
  Hand, and foot and arm and bosom,
  With a chain of bud and blossom;
  Twine red roses round her hands,
  Round her feet twine myrtle bands.
55 Heap up flowers higher, higher,
  Tulips like a glowing fire,
  Clematis of milky whiteness,
  Sweet geraniums' varied brightness,
  Honeysuckle, commeline,
60 Roses, myrtles, jessamine;
  Heap them higher, bloom on bloom,
  Bury her as in a tomb.

  But alas! they are withered all,
      And how can dead flowers bind her?
65 She pushes away her pall,
      And she leaves the dead behind her:
  And she flies across the seas
      To gladden for a time
  The blossoms and the bees
70   Of some far distant clime.

To my Mother on her Birthday.

Today's your natal day
  Sweet flowers I bring;
Mother accept I pray,
    My offering.

5   And may you happy live,
           And long us bless;
       Receiving as you give
           Great happiness.

The Ruined Cross.

She wreathed bright flower-wreaths in her hair,
    And all men smiled as she passed by:
And she smiled too, for now she knew
    That her last hour was nigh.

5   Soft radiance shone upon her path,
        Her step was fearless, free and light;
    Her cheek was flushed with burning red,
        Her azure eye was bright.

    On, on, still on, she hurried on,
10   For in the wind she heard a knell,
    And to her ear the water's splash
        Was as a dying bell.

    And in the flowers she saw decay,
        And saw decay in every tree;
15 And change was written on the sun,
        And change upon the sea.

    She might not pause upon the road,
        Lest Death should claim his promised bride
    Ere yet her longing was fulfilled,
20   Her young heart satisfied.

    The sun arose, the sun went down,
        The moonbeams on the waters shone
    How many times! yet paused she not,
        But ever journeyed on.

25 And still, tho' toilsome was the way,
        The colour flushed her sunken cheek;
    Nor dimmed the azure of her eye,
        Nor waxed her purpose weak.

At length she reached a lonely spot, . . .
30   Why trembled she? why turned she pale?
A ruined Cross stood in the midst
    Of a most quiet vale.

A Cross o'ergrown with moss and flowers,
    A cross fast sinking to decay;
35 The Cross she knew, the Cross she loved
    In childhood's happy day.

And she had journeyed many miles,
    Morning and eve untiringly,
To look again upon that Cross,
40   To look again and die.

She knelt within its sacred shade,
    And hung her garland on the stone;
Her azure eyes were bright with tears
    Of love and joy unknown.

45 And there she knelt, and there she prayed
    Until her heart was satisfied;—
The ancient Cross is standing yet,
    The youthful wanderer died.

Eva.

(From Maturin's "Woman.")

Yes, I loved him all too well,
    And my punishment is just,
But its greatness who can tell?
    Still I have a stedfast trust
5 That the sorrow shall not last,
And the trial shall be past,
And my faith shall anchor fast.

Lord, Thou knowest, I have said,
    All is good that comes from Thee;
10 Unto Thee I bow my head.
    I have not repented me.

Still, oh! still 'tis bitter ill;
Still I have a stubborn will,
And my heart is haughty still:

15   Haughty in its humbleness;
      Proud in its idolatry;
Let the loved heel gall and press
      On my neck: so it should be.
'Twas in madness that I spake it:
20   Let him leave my heart or take it,
Let him heal my heart or break it;

But it still shall be for him,
      It shall love him only still.—
Nay, it was no passing whim,
25   But a woman's stedfast will.
And this word is aye returning:
And I cannot quell the yearning
That in breast and brain is burning.

Tears of mine may quench it never,
30   Bitter tears shed all alone;
Dropping, dropping, dropping ever
      For the thought of him that's gone:
Dropping when none see or know.
Woe is me! they only flow
35   For the joys of long ago.

Foolish one, were it not fitter
      For thyself to mourn and pray?
Tho' thy Father's cup be bitter,
      Put it not from thee away.
40   It is good and meet and right.
Yea, if darksome be the night,
The day dawn shall be more bright.

Hast thou too much time, in sooth,
      For the work of penitence,
45   That thou wastest tears and youth
      Mourning one who is gone hence?
For thyself cry out and weep

    Ere that thou lie down and sleep,
    And for ever silence keep.

50   Humbly strive to enter in
      By the strait and narrow gate;
    Strive the courts of Heaven to win,
      Where nought maketh desolate;
    Where are none to come and go;
55   Where no tears may ever flow;
    Where nor death may be, nor woe.

    And in prayer think thou of him
      Who hath left thee sad and lone.
    Pray that earth's light may grow dim,
60   So to him Heaven's light be shown.
    Pray that, all thy sins forgiven,
    Pray that, from his errors shriven,
    Ye may meet at length in Heaven.

Love ephemeral.

    Love is sweet, and so are flowers
    Blooming in bright summer bowers;
    So are waters, clear and pure,
    In some hidden fountain's store;
5   So is the soft southern breeze
    Sighing low among the trees;
    So is the bright queen of heaven,
    Reigning in the quiet even:
    Yet the pallid moon may breed
10   Madness in man's feeble seed;
    And the wind's soft influence
    Often breathes the pestilence;
    And the waves may sullied be
    As they hurry to the sea;
15   Flowers soon must fade away—
    Love endures but for a day.

Burial Anthem.

Flesh of our flesh—bone of our bone—
  (For thou and we in Christ are one)
Thy soul unto its rest hath flown,
And thou has left us all alone
5   Our weary race to run
In doubt, and want, and sin, and pain,
Whilst thou wilt never sin again.
For us remaineth heaviness;
Thou never more shalt feel distress,
10   For thou hast found repose
Beside the bright eternal river
That clear and pure flows on for ever,
  And sings as on it flows.
And it is better far for thee
15   To reach at once thy rest,
Than share with us earth's misery,
  Or tainted joy at best;
Brother, we will not mourn for thee,
  Although our hearts be weary
20 Of struggling with our enemy,
  When all around is dreary.
But we will pray that still we may
Press onward in the narrow way
With a calm thankful resignation,
25 And joy in this our desolation.
And we will hope at length to be
With our Great Head, and, friend! with thee
  Beside that river blest.

Sappho.

I sigh at day-dawn, and I sigh
When the dull day is passing by.
I sigh at evening, and again
I sigh when night brings sleep to men.

5   Oh! it were better far to die
       Than thus for ever mourn and sigh,
       And in death's dreamless sleep to be
       Unconscious that none weep for me;
       Eased from my weight of heaviness,
10   Forgetful of forgetfulness,
       Resting from pain and care and sorrow
       Thro' the long night that knows no morrow;
       Living unloved, to die unknown,
       Unwept, untended and alone.

Tasso and Leonora.

A glorious vision hovers o'er his soul,
    Gilding the prison and the weary bed
    Though hard the pillow placed beneath his head;
Though brackish be the water in the bowl
5   Beside him; he can see the planets roll
    In glowing adoration, without dread;
    Knowing how, by unerring wisdom led,
They struggle not against the strong control.
When suddenly a star shoots from the skies,
10   Than all the other stars more purely bright,
Replete with heavenly loves and harmonies;
    He starts:—what meets his full awakening sight?
Lo! Leonora with large humid eyes,
    Gazing upon him in the misty light.

ON THE DEATH OF A CAT,
A Friend of Mine, Aged Ten Years and a Half.

Who shall tell the lady's grief
When her Cat was past relief?
Who shall number the hot tears
Shed o'er her, beloved for years?

5   Who shall say the dark dismay
     Which her dying caused that day?

     Come, ye Muses, one and all,
     Come obedient to my call.
     Come and mourn, with tuneful breath,
10   Each one for a separate death;
     And while you in numbers sigh,
     I will sing her elegy.

     Of a noble race she came,
     And Grimalkin was her name.
15   Young and old full many a mouse
     Felt the prowess of her house:
     Weak and strong full many a rat
     Cowered beneath her crushing pat:
     And the birds around the place
20   Shrank from her too close embrace.
     But one night, reft of her strength,
     She laid down and died at length:
     Lay a kitten by her side,
     In whose life the mother died.
25   Spare her line and lineage,
     Guard her kitten's tender age,
     And that kitten's name as wide
     Shall be known as her's that died.

     And whoever passes by
30   The poor grave where Puss doth lie,
     Softly, softly let him tread,
     Nor disturb her narrow bed.

Mother and Child.

     "What art thou thinking of," said the Mother,
         "What art thou thinking of my child?"
     "I was thinking of Heaven," he answered her,
         And looked up in her face and smiled.

5   "And what didst thou think of Heaven?" she said;
    "Tell me, my little one!"
   "Oh . . , I thought that there the flowers never fade,
    That there never sets the sun."

   "And wouldst thou love to go thither, my child?
10   Thither wouldst thou love to go?
And leave the pretty flowers that wither,
    And the sun that sets below?"

   "Oh, I would be glad to go there, mother,
    To go and live there now;
15 And I would pray for thy coming, mother,
    My mother, wouldst not thou?"

FAIR MARGARET.

"Fair Margaret sat in her bower window,
   Combing her yellow hair;
There she spied sweet William and his bride
   As they were a riding near."—*Old Ballad.*

———————

The faith of years is broken,
The fate of years is spoken,
    Years past, and years to come;
I pity and I scorn thee,
5 I would not now adorn me
    For thy false bridal home.

Yet thou, perfidious wooer,
Thou yet mayst be the ruer,
    For thou mayst meet with one
10 Who will not love thee really,
But cast kind glances merely
    That thou mayst be undone.

Soft eyes, and dark, and flashing,
Thy hopes may yet be dashing,
15   Thou yet mayst be deceived;
And then think on her sadly,

Whom once thou grievedst gladly,
 Ere thou thyself wast grieved.

And if despair should seize thee,
20 And urge thee to release thee
 From weariness and life,
Oh! think on her who'll languish,
Bearing the bitter anguish
 Of a heart's bitter strife.

25 For, though I may not love thee,
Though calm as heaven above me,
 My thoughts of thee must be,
I cannot break so lightly
The chain that bound me tightly,
30 *Once* bound my soul to thee.

Earth and Heaven.

Water calmly flowing,
Sun-light deeply glowing,
Swans some river riding,
That is gently gliding
5 By the fresh green rushes;
The sweet rose that blushes,
Hyacinths whose dow'r
Is both scent and flow'r,
Skylark's soaring motion,
10 Sun-rise from the ocean,
Jewels that lie sparkling
'Neath the waters darkling,
Sea-weed, coral, amber,
Flow'rs that climb and clamber,
15 Or more lowly flourish
Where the earth may nourish;
All these are beautiful,
Of beauty Earth is full:—
Say, to our promised Heaven
20 Can greater charms be given?

Yes; for aye in Heav'n doth dwell
Glowing, indestructible,
What here below finds tainted birth
In the corrupted sons of Earth;
25 For, filling there and satisfying
Man's soul unchanging and undying,
Earth's fleeting joys and beauties far above,
In Heaven is Love.

Love attacked.

Love is more sweet than flowers,
    But sooner dying;
Warmer than sunny hours,
    But faster flying;

5 Softer than music's whispers
    Springing with day
To murmur till the vespers,
    Then die away;

More kind than friendship's greeting,
10   But as untrue,
Brighter than hope, but fleeting
    More swiftly too;

Like breath of summer breezes
    Gently it sighs,
15 But soon, alas! one ceases,
    The other dies;

And like an inundation
    It leaves behind
An utter desolation
20   Of heart and mind.

Who then would court Love's presence,
    If here below
It can but be the essence
    Of restless woe?

25 Returned or unrequited
        'Tis still the same;
    The flame was never lighted,
        Or sinks the flame.

    Yet all, both fools and sages,
30   Have felt its power,
    In distant lands and ages,
        Here, at this hour.

    Then what from fear and weeping
        Shall give me rest?
35 Oh tell me, ye who sleeping
        At length are blest!

    In answer to my crying
        Sounds like incense
    Rose from the earth, replying,
40   Indifference.

Love defended.

    Who extols a wilderness?
        Who hath praised indifference?
    Foolish one, thy words are sweet,
        But devoid of sense.

5   As the man who ne'er hath seen,
        Or as he who cannot hear,
    Is the heart that hath no part
        In Love's hope and fear.

    True, the blind do not perceive
10   The unsightly things around;
    True, the deaf man trembleth not
        At an awful sound.

    But the face of Heaven and Earth,
        And the murmur of the main,
15 Surely are a recompense
        For a little pain.

So, tho' Love may not be free
   Always from a taint of grief,
If its sting is very sharp,
20   Great is its relief.

Divine and Human Pleading.

"I would the saints could hear our prayers!
   If such a thing might be,
O blessed Mary Magdalene,
   I would appeal to thee!

5 "For once in lowly penitence
   Thy head was bowed with shame;
But now thou hast a glorious place,
   And hast an unknown name."

So mused a trembling contrite man,
10   So mused he wearily;
By angels borne his thoughts appeared
   Before the Throne on high.

      *   *   *   *   *   *

The calm, still night was at its noon,
   And all men were at rest,
15 When came before the sleeper's eyes
   A vision of the blest.

A woman stood beside his bed,
   Her breath was fragrance all;
Round her the light was very bright,
20   The air was musical.

Her footsteps shone upon the stars,
   Her robe was spotless white;
Her breast was radiant with the Cross,
   Her head with living light.

25 Her eyes beamed with a sacred fire;
   And on her shoulders fair,

From underneath her golden crown
　　Clustered her golden hair.

Yet on her bosom her white hands
30　　Were folded quietly;
Yet was her glorious head bowed low
　　In deep humility.

Long time she looked upon the ground;
　　Then raising her bright eyes
35　Her voice came forth as sweet and soft
　　As music when it dies.

"O thou who in thy secret hour
　　Hast dared to think that aught
Is faulty in God's perfect plan,
40　　And perfect in thy thought!

"Thou who the pleadings would'st prefer
　　Of one sin-stained like me
To His Who is the Lord of Life,
　　To His Who died for thee!

45　"In mercy I am sent from Heaven:
　　Be timely wise, and learn
To seek His love Who waits for thee,
　　Inviting thy return.

"Well know I His long-suffering
50　　And intercession's worth;
My guilt was as a heavy chain
　　That bound me to the earth.

"It was a clog upon my feet,
　　To keep me from Life's path;
55　It was a stain upon my hands,
　　A curse upon my hearth.

"But there is mighty Power and Grace
　　Can loose the heavy chain,
Can free the feet, can cleanse the hands,
60　　Can purge the hearth again.

"Weeping I sought the Lord of Life,
   Bowed with my shame and sin;
And then unto my wondering heart
   Love's searching fire came in.

65   "It was with deep repentance,
    I knelt down at His Feet
Who can change the sorrow into joy,
   The bitter into sweet.

"I had cast away my jewels
70   And my rich attire;
And my breast was filled with a holy flame,
   And my heart with a holy fire.

"My tears were more precious
   Than my precious pearls;—
75   My tears that fell upon His Feet
   As I wiped Them with my curls.

"My youth and my beauty
   Were budding to their prime;
But I wept for the great transgression,
80   The sin of other time.

"Trembling betwixt hope and fear,
   I sought the King of Heaven;
Forsook the evil of my ways,
   Loved much, and was forgiven.

85   "In hope and fear I went to Him,
   He broke and healed my heart;
No man was there to intercede;
   As I was, so thou art."

TO MY FRIEND ELIZABETH.

with some Postage Stamps towards a collection.

Sweetest Elizabeth, accept I pray
These lowly stamps I send in homage true;

One hundred humble servants in their way
Are not to be despised, though poor to view.
5   Their livery of red and black, nor gay,
Nor sober all, is typical of you,
In whom are gravity and gladness mixed.
Thought here, smiles there; perfection lies betwixt.

AMORE E DOVERE.

Chiami il mio core
Crudele, altero,
No, non è vero,
   Crudel non è:
5   T'amo, t'amai,—
   E tu lo sai,—
Men del dovere,
   Ma più di me.

O ruscelletto,
10   Dì al Dio d'Amore
Che questo petto,
Che questo core,
A lui ricetto
   Più non darà.
15   L'alme tradisce
Senza rimorso;
Non compatisce,
Non dà soccorso,
E si nudrisce
20   Di crudeltà.

T'intendo, ti lagni,
   Mio povero core;
T'intendo, l'amore
   Si lagna di me.
25   Deh! placati alfine;
Mi pungon le spine
   Che vengon da te.

Amore e Dispetto.

O grande Amor possente
   Che reggi la mia mente,
   Odi l'umíl preghiera
   D'un tristo tuo fedel:
5 Deh fa che Lisa altiera
   Più non mi sia crudel.

Un giorno essendo stanco
   Posai sull' erba il fianco;
   Mesto pensando a quella
10   Che questo cor ferì,
Oh quanto sembò bella,
   Guardommi, e poi fuggì,

Quindì la vidi andare
   Con lievi passi al mare;
15   E parve sì pietosa
   Che dissi alfin: Chi sa!
Forse, non più sdegnosa,
   Verso di me sarà.

Timido allora io sorsi,
20   E ad incontrarla corsi;
   Mi vide, e gli occhi lenti
   Chinando, si arrossì;
Ed io sclamai: Deh senti,
   Lisa, pietà—così

25 Volea seguir; ma intanto
   Mi venne al ciglio il pianto;
   E mi confuse i detti
   Un tenero sospir;
Poi muto alquanto stetti,
30   Ed ella prese a dir:

Amar non voglio alcuno,
   E s'io volessi, l'uno
   Tu non saresti. E poi
   Tacendo, se ne andò.—

35   Se servo più mi vuoi,
       Amor, tu dei far ciò;

Spirar le devi in core
    Sensi d'un puro amore;
    Chè se ciò far non puoi,
40   O se non vuoi ciò far,
Io sprezzo i lacci tuoi,
    E più non voglio amar.

Love and Hope.

Love for ever dwells in Heaven,
    Hope entereth not there.
To despairing man Love's given,
    Hope dwells not with despair.
5   Love reigneth high, and reigneth low, and reigneth
        everywhere.

In the inmost heart Love dwelleth,
    It may not quenchèd be;
E'en when the life-blood welleth
    Its fond effects we see.
10   In the name that leaves the lips the last, fades last from
        memory.

And when we shall awaken
    Ascending to the sky,
Tho' Hope shall have forsaken,
    Sweet Love shall never die.
15   For perfect Love, and perfect bliss, shall be our lot on
        high.

Serenade.

Come, wander forth with me! the orange flowers
Breathe faintest perfume from the summer bowers.
Come, wander forth with me! the moon on high

Shines proudly in a flood of brilliancy.
5   Around her car each burning star
Gleams like a beacon from afar;
The night-wind scarce disturbs the sea
As it sighs forth so languidly,
Laden with sweetness like a bee;
10   And all is still, below, above,
Save murmurs of the turtle dove,
That murmurs ever of its love:
For now 'tis the hour, the balmy hour
When the strains of love have chiefly power;
15   When the maid looks forth from her latticed bower,
With a gentle yielding smile,
Donning her mantle all the while.
Now the moon beams down on high
From her halo brilliantly;
20   By the dark clouds unencumbered
That once o'er her pale face slumbered.
Far from her mild rays flutters Folly,
For on them floats calm Melancholy.
A passionless sadness without dread,
25   Like the thought of those we loved long dead,
Full of hope and chastened joy,
Heavenly without earth's alloy.
Listen, dearest! all is quiet,
Slumb'ring the world's toil and riot,
30   And all is fair in earth and sky and sea,
Come, wander forth with me!

The Rose.

Gentle, gentle river
    Hurrying along
With a sparkle ever,
    And a murmured song,
5   Pause in thine onward motion,
    Fast flowing toward the ocean,

And give this rose from me
To haughty Coralie.

Tell her that love's symbol,
10   The deep blushing rose,
Doth in all resemble
That it would disclose.
Untended, shortly thriving
There'll soon be no reviving;
15   But nursed with kindliness
'T will cheer life's wilderness.

Present and Future.

What is life that we should love it,
Cherishing it evermore,
Never prizing aught above it,
Ever loath to give it o'er?
5   Is it goodness? Is it gladness?
Nay, 'tis more of sin and sadness,
Nay, of weariness 'tis more.

Earthly joys are very fleeting—
Earthly sorrows very long;—
10   Parting ever follows meeting,
Night succeeds to even-song.
Storms may darken in the morning,
And eclipse the sun's bright dawning,
And the chilly gloom prolong.

15   But though clouds may screen and hide it
The sun shines for evermore;
Then bear grief in hope: abide it,
Knowing that it must give o'er:
And the darkness shall flee from us,
20   And the sun beam down upon us
Ever glowing more and more.

WILL THESE HANDS NE'ER BE CLEAN?

And who is this lies prostrate at thy feet?
And is he dead, thou man of wrath and pride?
    Yes, now thy vengeance is complete,
       Thy hate is satisfied.
5   What had he done to merit this of thee?
Who gave thee power to take away his life?
Oh deeply-rooted direful enmity
    That ended in long strife!
See where he grasped thy mantle as he fell,
10   Staining it with his blood; how terrible
Must be the payment due for this in hell!

And dost thou think to go and see no more
Thy bleeding victim, now the struggle's o'er?
    To find out peace in other lands,
15   And wash the red mark from thy hands?
    It shall not be; for everywhere
    He shall be with thee; and the air
    Shall smell of blood, and on the wind
    His groans pursue thee close behind.
20   When waking he shall stand before thee;
And when at length sleep shall come o'er thee,
    Powerless to move, alive to dream,
    So dreadful shall thy visions seem
    That thou shalt own them even to be
25   More hateful than reality
    What time thou stoopest down to drink
    Of limpid waters, thou shalt think
    It is thy foe's blood bubbles up
    From the polluted fountain's cup,
30   That stains thy lip, that cries to Heaven
    For vengeance—and it shall be given.

And when thy friends shall question thee,
"Why art thou changed so heavily?"
    Trembling and fearful thou shalt say
35   "I am not changed," and turn away;

For such an outcast shalt thou be
Thou wilt not dare ask sympathy.

And so thy life will pass, and day by day
The current of existence flow away;
40   And though to thee earth shall be hell, and breath
Vengeance, yet thou shalt tremble more at death.
And one by one thy friends will learn to fear thee,
And thou shalt live without a hope to cheer thee;
Lonely amid a thousand, chained though free,
45   The curse of memory shall cling to thee:
Ages may pass away, worlds rise and set—
    But thou shalt not forget.

SIR EUSTACE GREY.
SEE CRABBE.

When I die, oh lay me low
Where the greenest grasses grow;
Where the happy stream meanders;
Where the deer securely wanders;
5   Where the sweet birds sit and sing
In the branches quivering;
Where the violets spring to die,
And the breezes passing by,
Laden with their fragrant breath,
10   Scarcely seem to tell of death;
Where the sun can dart no ray
In the noon-tide of his day;
Where upon the fertile ground
    Broods an everlasting shade,
15   And a strange, mysterious sound
    By the rustling boughs is made,
And all's quiet, meet for one
Whose long, toilsome race is run.
O'er my grave the turf extend,
20   But beside me lay no friend,

And above me place no stone;
I would lie there all alone,
Unremembered or unknown.
Soon forgotten, none will taunt me;
25   Soon forgetting, none will haunt me
Of the ghosts of former pleasures
Meted out with scanty measures.
Resting from all human passion,
From earth's hate and its compassion,
30   From its hope and fear, from love
Stedfast as the stars above,
That shine clearly down for ever
On some cold, unglowing river;
By my faith and hope sure lighted
35   Through the darkness of the tomb;
And by Heavenly Love requited
For whatever love was slighted,
And whatever joy was blighted
        By earth's coldness and its gloom,
40   In the grave I'll rest secure
Till the appointed time is o'er,
And the work of love is done,
And the great sin; and the sun
Sets in night to rise no more.
45   What is life but toil and riot?
What is death but rest and quiet?
Life is but a dream of trouble,
        Death calm sleep from visions free;
Life is but a bursting bubble,
50   Death is immortality.

THE TIME OF WAITING.

Life is fleeting, joy is fleeting,
Coldness follows love and greeting,
Parting still succeeds to meeting.

If I say, "Rejoice today,"
5   Sorrow meets me in the way,
I cannot my will obey.

If I say, "My grief shall cease;
Now then I will live in peace:"
My cares instantly increase.

10   When I look up to the sky,
Thinking to see light on high,
Clouds my searching glance defy.

When I look upon the earth
For the flowers that should have birth,
15   I find dreariness and dearth.

And the wind sighs on for ever,
Murmurs still the flowing river,
On the graves the sun-beams quiver.

And destruction waxes bold,
20   And the earth is growing old,
And I tremble in the cold.

And my weariness increases
To an ache that never ceases,
And a pain that ne'er decreases.

25   And the times are turbulent,
And the Holy Church is rent,
And who tremble or repent?

And loud cries do ever rise
To the portals of the skies
30   From our earthly miseries;

From love slighted, not requited;
From high hope that should have lighted
All our path up, now benighted;

From the woes of human kind;
35   From the darkness of the mind;
From all anguish undefined;

From the heart that's crushed and sinking;
From the brain grown blank with thinking;
From the spirit sorrow drinking.

40   All cry out with pleading strong:
"Vengeance, Lord; how long, how long
Shall we suffer this great wrong?"

And the pleading and the cry
Of earth's sons are heard on high,
45   And are noted verily.

When this world shall be no more,
The Oppressors shall endure
The great Vengeance, which is sure.

And the sinful shall remain
50   To an endless death and pain;
But the good shall live again,

Never more to be oppressed;
Balm shall heal the bleeding breast,
And the weary be at rest.

55   All shall vanish of dejection,
Grief, and fear, and imperfection,
In that glorious Resurrection.

Heed not then a night of sorrow,
If the dawning of the morrow
60   From past grief fresh beams shall borrow.

Thankful for whate'er is given,
Strive we, as we ne'er have striven,
For love's sake to be forgiven.

Then, the dark clouds opening,
65   Ev'n to us the sun shall bring
Gladness; and sweet flowers shall spring.

For Christ's guiding Love alway,
For the everlasting Day,
For meek patience, let us pray.

Charity.

I praised the myrtle and the rose,
    At sunrise in their beauty vying;
I passed them at the short day's close,
    And both were dying.

5   The summer sun his rays was throwing
    Brightly; yet ere I sought my rest,
His last cold ray, more deeply glowing,
    Died in the west.

After this bleak world's stormy weather,
10   All, all, save Love alone, shall die;
For Faith and Hope shall merge together
    In Charity.

The Dead Bride.

There she lay so still and pale,
    With her bridal robes around her:
Joy is fleeting—life is frail—
    Death had found her.

5   Gone for ever: gone away
    From the love and light of earth;
Gone for ever: who shall say
    Where her second birth?

Had her life been good and kind?
10   Had her heart been meek and pure?
Was she of a lowly mind,
    Ready to endure?

Did she still console the sad,
    Soothe the widow's anguish wild,
15   Make the poor and needy glad,
    Tend the orphan child?

Who shall say what hope and fear
    Crowded in her short life's span?
If the love of God was dear,
20   Or the love of man?

Happy bride if single-hearted
    Her first love to God was given;
If from this world she departed
    But to dwell in Heaven;

25 If her faith on Heaven was fixed,
    And her hope; if love's pure worth
Made her rich indeed, unmixed
    With the dross of earth.

But alas! if tainted pleasure
30   Won her heart and held it here,
Where is now her failing treasure,
    All her gladness where? . . . . .

Hush, too curious questioner;
    Hush and think thine own sins o'er:
35 Little canst thou learn from her;
    For we know no more

Than that there she lies all pale
    With her bridal robes around her:
Joy is fleeting—life is frail—
40   Death hath found her.

LIFE OUT OF DEATH.

"Now I've said all I would, mother;
    My head is on thy breast,
And I feel I can die without a sigh,
    And sink into my rest.

5 "And if ever you weep o'er my grave, mother,
    Weep not for doubt or sadness;
I shall fall asleep in pain and in grief,
    But wake to perfect gladness."

Mourn not, thou mother of the dead,
10   That in her youth she died;
for He was with her then Who said:
    "Ye that in me abide,
Ask what ye will, it shall be given;
Faith, hope, and love on earth, and Love and Joy in
        Heaven."

The solitary Rose.

O happy Rose, red Rose, that bloomest lonely
    Where there are none to gather while they love thee;
That art perfumed by thine own fragrance only,
    Resting like incense round thee and above thee;—
5   Thou hearest nought save some pure stream that flows,
        O happy Rose.

What tho' for thee no nightingales are singing?
    They chant one eve, but hush them in the morning.
Near thee no little moths and bees are winging
10   To steal thy honey when the day is dawning;—
Thou keep'st thy sweetness till the twilight's close,
        O happy Rose.

Then rest in peace, thou lone and lovely flower;
    Yea be thou glad, knowing that none are near thee
15   To mar thy beauty in a wanton hour,
    And scatter all thy leaves, nor deign to wear thee.
Securely in thy solitude repose,
        O happy Rose.

Lady Isabella.

Lady Isabella,
    Thou art gone away,
Leaving earth's darksome trouble,
    To rest until the Day.

5   From thy youth and beauty,
      From each loving friend,
    Thou art gone to the land of sure repose,
      Where fears and sorrows end.

    Thou wert pure whilst with us;
10   Now, we trust, in Heaven,
    All thy tears are wiped away,
      All thy sins forgiven.

    Who would wish thee back again
      But to share our sorrow?
15   Who would grudge thine hour of rest,
      Ere the coming morrow?

    Let us rejoice the rather
      That thou hast reached that shore,
    Whilst yet thy soul was spotless,
20   And thy young spirit pure.

    And if thy crown be brighter
      By but one little ray,
    Why wish to dim its lustre? . .
      Oh! rather let us pray
25   That when we are most fitted
      We too may pass away.

THE DREAM.

    Rest, rest; the troubled breast
    Panteth evermore for rest:—
    Be it sleep, or be it death,
    Rest is all it coveteth.

5   Tell me, dost thou remember the old time
      We sat together by that sunny stream,
    And dreamed our happiness was too sublime
      Only to be a dream?

Gazing, till steadfast gazing made us blind,
10   We watched the fishes leaping at their play;
Thinking our love too tender and too kind
     Ever to pass away.

And some of all our thoughts were true at least
     What time we thought together by that stream;
15   THY happiness has evermore increased,—
     MY love was not a dream.

And now that thou art gone, I often sit
     On its green margin, for thou once wert there;
And see the clouds that, floating over it,
20   Darken the quiet air.

Yes, oftentimes I sit beside it now,
     Harkning the wavelets ripple o'er the sands;
Until again I hear thy whispered vow
     And feel thy pressing hands.

25   Then the bright sun seems to stand still in heaven,
     The stream sings gladly as it onward flows,
The rushes grow more green, the grass more even,
     Blossoms the budding rose.

I say: "It is a joy-dream; I will take it;
30   He is not gone; he will return to me."
What found'st thou in my heart that thou should'st break
          it?—
     How have I injured thee?

Oh! I am weary of life's passing show,—
     Its pageant and its pain.
35   I would I could lie down lone in my woe,
     Ne'er to rise up again;
I would I could lie down where none might know;
     For truly love is vain.
Truly love's vain; but oh! how vainer still
40   Is that which is not love, but seems;
Concealed indifference, a covered ill,
     A very dream of dreams.

The Dying Man to his Betrothed.

One word—'tis all I ask of thee;
   One word—and that is little now
That I have learned thy wrong of me;
   And thou too art unfaithful—thou!—
5   O thou sweet poison, sweetest death,
O honey between serpent's teeth,
Breathe on me with thy scorching breath!

The last poor hope is fleeting now,
   And with it life is ebbing fast;
10 I gaze upon thy cold white brow,
   And loathe and love thee to the last.
And still thou keepest silence—still
Thou look'st on me—for good or ill
Speak out, that I may know thy will.

15 Thou weepest, woman, and art pale!
   Weep not, for thou shalt soon be free;
My life is ending like a tale
   That was—but never more shall be.
O blessed moments, ye fleet fast,
20 And soon the latest shall be past,
And she will be content at last.

Nay, tremble not—I have not cursed
   Thy house or mine, or thee or me;
The moment that I saw thee first,
25   The moment that I first loved thee,
Curse them! alas!—I can but bless,
In this mine hour of heaviness;—
Nay, sob not so in thy distress!

I have been harsh, thou sayst of me;—
30   God knows my heart was never so;
It never could be so to thee—
   And now it is too late—I know
Thy grief—forgive me, love! 'tis o'er,
For I shall never trouble more
35 Thy life that was so calm before.

I pardon thee—mayst thou be blest!
   Say, wilt thou sometimes think of me?
Oh may I, from my happy rest,
   Still look with love on thine and thee,
40 And may I pray for thee alway,
And for thy Love still may I pray,
Waiting the everlasting Day.

Stoop over me—ah! this is death!
   I scarce can see thee at my side;
45 Stoop lower—let me feel thy breath,
   O thou, mine own, my promised bride!
Pardon me, love—I pardon thee,
And may our pardon sealèd be
Throughout the long eternity.

50 The pains of death my senses cover:—
   Oh! for His Sake Who died for men,
Be thou more true to this thy lover
   Than thou hast been to me—Amen!
And if he chide thee wrongfully,
55 One little moment think on me,
And thou wilt bear it patiently.

And now, O God, I turn to Thee:
   Thou Only, Father, canst not fail;
Lord, Thou hast tried and broken me,
60   And yet Thy Mercy shall prevail.
Saviour, through Thee I am forgiven—
Do Thou receive my soul, blood-shriven,
O Christ, Who art the Gate of Heaven!

The Martyr.

   See, the sun hath risen!
   Lead her from the prison;
She is young and tender, lead her tenderly:
   May no fear subdue her,
5   Lest the Saints be fewer,
Lest her place in Heaven be lost eternally.

Forth she came, not trembling,
No, nor yet dissembling
An o'erwhelming terror weighing her down—down;
10   Little, little heeding
Earth, but inly pleading
For the strength to triumph and to win a crown.

All her might was rallied
To her heart; not pallid
15 Was her cheek, but glowing with a glorious red,
Glorious red and saintly,
Never paling faintly,
But still flushing, kindling still, without thought of dread.

On she went, on faster,
20   Trusting in her Master,
Feeling that His Eye watched o'er her lovingly;
He would prove and try her,
But would not deny her,
When her soul had pass'd, for His sake, patiently.

25 "Christ," she said, "receive me,
Let no terrors grieve me,
Take my soul and guard it with Thy heavenly cares:
Take my soul and guard it,
Take it and reward it
30 With the Love Thou bearest for the love it bears."

Quickened with a fire
Of sublime desire,
She looked up to Heaven, and she cried aloud,
"Death, I do entreat thee,
35 Come! I go to meet thee;
Wrap me in the whiteness of a virgin shroud."

On she went, hope-laden;
Happy, happy maiden!
Never more to tremble, and to weep no more:
40 All her sins forgiven,
Straight the path to Heaven
Through the glowing fire lay her feet before.

On she went, on quickly,
　　And her breath came thickly,
45　With the longing to see God coming pantingly:
　　Now the fire is kindled,
　　And her flesh has dwindled
Unto dust;—her soul is mounting up on high:

　　Higher, higher mounting,
50　　The swift moments counting,
Fear is left beneath her, and the chastening rod:
　　Tears no more shall blind her,
　　Trouble lies behind her,
Satisfied with hopeful rest, and replete with God.

The End of Time.

　　Thou who art dreary
　　　With a cureless woe,
　　Thou who art weary
　　　Of all things below,
5　　Thou who art weeping
　　　By the loved sick-bed,
　　Thou who art keeping
　　　Watches o'er the dead,
Hope, hope! old Time flies fast upon his way,
10　And soon will cease the night, and soon will dawn the day.

　　The rose blooms brightly,
　　　But it fades ere night;
　　And youth flies lightly,
　　　Yet how sure its flight!
15　　And still the river
　　　Merges in the sea,
　　And death reigns ever
　　　Whilst old Time shall be;
Yet hope! old Time flies fast upon his way,
20　And soon will cease the night, and soon will dawn the day.

All we most cherish
   In this world below,
What tho' it perish?
   It has aye been so.
25   So thro' all ages
      It has ever been
   To fools and sages,
      Noble men and mean:
Yet hope, still hope! for Time flies on his way,
30   And soon will end the night, and soon will dawn the day.

All of each nation
   Shall that morning see
With exultation
   Or with misery:
35   From watery slumbers,
      From the opening sod,
   Shall rise up numbers
      To be judged by God.
Then hope and fear, for Time speeds on his way,
40   And soon must end the night, and soon must dawn the
      day.

Resurrection Eve.

He resteth: weep not!
The living sleep not
With so much calm:
He hears no chiding
5   And no deriding,
Hath joy for sorrow,
For night hath morrow,
For wounds hath balm,
For life's strange riot
10   Hath death and quiet.
Who would recall him
Of those that love him?

No fears appal him,
No ills befal him;
15 There's nought above him
Save turf and flowers
And pleasant grass.
Pass the swift hours,
How swiftly pass!
20 The hours of slumber
He doth not number;
Grey hours of morning
Ere the day's dawning:
Brightened by gleams
25 Of the sun-beams,
By the foreseeing
Of Resurrection,
Of glorious being,
Of full perfection,
30 Of sins forgiven
Before the face
Of men and spirits;
Of God in Heaven,
The Resting Place
35 That he inherits.

ZARA.

See Maturin's "Women."

Now the pain beginneth and the word is spoken;—
　　Hark unto the tolling of the churchyard chime!—
Once my heart was gladsome, now my heart is broken,—
　　Once my love was noble, now it is a crime.

5 But the fear is over; yea, what now shall pain me?
　　Arm thee in thy sorrow, O most Desolate!
Weariness and weakness, these shall now sustain me,—
　　Pride and bitter grieving, burning love and hate.

Yea, the fear is over, the strong fear and trembling;
10   I can doubt no longer, he is gone indeed.
Rend thy hair, lost woman, weep without dissembling;
    The heart torn forth from it, shall the breast not bleed?

Happy she who looketh on his beauty's glory!
    Happy she who listeneth to his gentle word!
15   Yet, O happy maiden, sorrow lies before thee;
    Greeting hath been given, parting must be heard.

He shall leave thee also, he who now hath left me,
    With a weary spirit and an aching heart;
Thou shalt be bereaved by him who hath bereft me;
20   Thou hast sucked the honey,—feel the stinging's smart.

Let the cold gaze on him, let the heartless hear him,
    For he shall not hurt them, they are safe in sooth:
But let loving women shun that man and fear him,
    Full of cruel kindness and devoid of ruth.

25   When ye call upon him, hope for no replying;
    When ye gaze upon him, think not he will look;
Hope not for his pity when your heart is sighing;
    Such another, waiting, weeping, he forsook.

Hath the Heaven no thunder wherewith to denounce
        him?
30   Hath the Heaven no lightning wherewith to chastise?
O my heart and spirit, O my soul, renounce him
    Who hath called for vengeance from the distant skies.

Vengeance which pursues thee, vengeance which shall
        find thee,
    Crushing thy false spirit, scathing thy fair limb:—
35   O ye thunders deafen, O ye lightnings blind me,
    Winds and storms from heaven, strike me but spare
        him.

I forgive thee, dearest, cruel, I forgive thee;—
    May thy cup of sorrow be poured out for me;
Though the dregs be bitter yet they shall not grieve me,
40   Knowing that I drink them, O my love, for thee.

Versi.

Figlia, la madre disse:
   Guardati dall' Amore;
   È crudo, è traditore,—
   Che vuoi saper di più?
5 Non fargli mai sperare
   D'entrare nel tuo petto;
   Chè chi gli diè ricetto
   Sempre tradito fu.

Colla sua benda al ciglio
10 È un bel fanciullo, è vero:
   Ma sempre è menzognero;
   Ma sempre tradirà.
Semplice tu se fidi
   Nel riso suo fallace;
15 Tu perderai la pace
   Nè mai ritornerà.

Ma vedo: già sei stanca
   Del mio parlar prudente;
   Già volgi nella mente
20 Il quando, il come, e il chi.
Odimi: i detti miei
   Già sai se son sinceri;
   E se son falsi o veri
   Saprai per prova un dì.

L'Incognita.

Nobil rosa ancor non crebbe
   Senza spine in sullo stelo:
Se vi fosse allor sarebbe
   Atta immagine di te.
5 È la luna in mezzo al cielo
   Bella è ver, ma passeggiera:
   Passa ancor la Primavera:
   Ah! l'immagin tua dov' è?

Purpurea rosa
Dolce, odorosa,
È molto bella,
Ma pur non è,
5   O mia Nigella,
Rival di te.

Donna nel velo,
Fior sullo stelo,
Ciascun l'amore
10   Reclama a se:
Ma passa il fiore,
Tu resti a me.

Soul rudderless, unbraced,
The Body's friend and guest,
Whither away today?
Unsuppled, pale, discased,
5   Dumb to thy wonted jest.

Animuccia, vagantuccia, morbiduccia,
    Oste del corpo e suora,
    Ove or farai dimora?
Palliduccia, irrigidita, svestituccia,
5   Non più scherzante or ora.

Unpublished Poems

Heaven.

1.

What is heaven? 'tis a country
   Far away from mortal ken;
'Tis a land, where, by God's bounty,
   After death live righteous men.

2.

5   That that blest land I may enter,
    Is my humble, earnest cry;
Lord! admit me to Thy presence,
    Lord! admit me, or I die.

Hymn.

To the God Who reigns on high,
To th'Eternal Majesty,
To the Blessed Trinity
    Glory on earth be giv'n;
5   In the sea, and in the sky,
    And in the highest heav'n.

Corydon's Lament and Resolution.

1.

I have wept and I have sighed;
   Chloe will not be my bride.

I have sighed and I have wept,
She hath not her promise kept.

2.

5   I have grieved and I have mourned;
She hath not my love returned.
I have mourned and I have grieved;
She hath not my pains relieved.

3.

But her pride I'll mortify,
10 For her love I will not die.
Amaryllis fair I'll wed,
Nor one tear for Chloe shed.

Rosalind.

She sat upon a mountain,
    And gazed upon the sea;
Beside her crouched a stag-hound,
    A boy stood at her knee.

5   She fixed upon the ocean
    An agonizèd stare—
The ship is fast receding—
    Her husband off they bear.

"Oh, robbers! take some pity
10   Upon my helpless state:
Restore him to my fond arms!
    Leave me not desolate!"

They heed not her entreaties,
    They list not to her prayer;
15 The ship is fast receding—
    Her husband off they bear.

"Oh Captain! take these jewels
　　That grace my hair of jet;
And ne'er in my devotion
20　　To bless thee I'll forget."

Then sudden cried the pirate,
　　"Lady, your prayers are vain;
When as my bride I sought you,
　　You heeded not my pain.

25　"Now for the grief I suffered
　　I'll compensated be"—
He said; and hurled her husband
　　Into the raging sea.

Upon her snow-white bosom
30　　Sank down that Lady's head;—
"I join thee, dearest Arthur"—
　　Fair Rosalind is dead.

Pitia a Damone.

Ah non chiamarlo pena,
　　È gioia quel ch'io sento;
　　Io morirò contento
　　Se morirò per te.
5　È fervido diletto
　　Quel che mi sta nel petto;
　　Per te la morte istessa
　　Terribile non è.

The Faithless Shepherdess.

1

There once was a time when I loved,
　　'Tis gone to return never more;
My shepherdess faithless has proved,
　　The maiden I once did adore.

2

5 And now we are parted for ever,
  And gone are my hopes and my fears,
 To forget Phillis false I'll endeavour,
  And arrest all these fast-flowing tears.

3

 Yet wherever I turn I must think
10 Of her who is faithless to me;
 I stand by the rivulet's brink,
  And the play of its waters I see.

4

 'Twas there I first told her my love,
  And she blushingly bade me hope still,
15 And the moon looking down from above
  Seemed to smile on the murmuring rill;

5

 On the rill that was murm'ring of love
  To its beautiful mistress in heaven,
 The moon seeming to speak far above
20 Of the rays that in token she'd given;

6

 In token of love never-ending,
  And pure as when first 'twas avowed,
 As long as that stream should be sending
  Soft sighs to its Queen in the cloud.

7

25 And false Phillis swore that she'd ever
  Keep faithful her pure heart to me,
 That she'd think of another love never,
  So long as the rill true should be.

8

The rill to its love true remains,
30   The moon still smiles on it from heaven,
But from you I've experienced sharp pains,
That the rill to the moon ne'er has given.

9

And now we are parted for ever,
    And gone are my hopes and my fears;
35 To forget Phillis false I'll endeavour,
    And arrest all these fast-flowing tears.

Ariadne to Theseus.

1

Sunlight to the river,
    Moonlight to the sea,
As false and as fleeting
    Thou hast been to me.

2

5 And I've been like the lily
    That to the summer clings,
Or like the nightingale
    That to the sweet rose sings:

3

That wooing never ceases
10   For her indifference,
And never his beloved flower
    Reproaching will incense.

4

But thou more cruel than the rose
    Hast left me faithlessly,

15   To mourn for ever and alone
         Over thy perfidy.

                    5

      Soft breezes! waft him not
         Across the wide wide sea;
      Ingulph, just waves of Ocean!
20   The wretch who flies from me.

                    6

      Ah no! 'tis vain! Affection
         For my false love still remains:
      Blow, breezes! Peace, ye waters!
         Revenge not ye my pains!

                    7

25   May happiness attend thee,
         Who hast ta'en from me all joy!
      Be thine unmixèd pleasure;
         Be mine the sad alloy!

On Albina.

The roses lingered in her cheeks,
   When fair Albina fainted;
Oh! gentle Reader, could it be
   That fair Albina painted?

A Hymn for Christmas Day.

The Shepherds watch their flocks by night,
Beneath the moon's unclouded light,
All around is calm and still,
Save the murm'ring of the rill:

5   When lo! a form of light appears,
     And on the awe-struck Shepherds' ears
     Are words, of peace and comfort flowing
     From lips with love celestial glowing.
     Spiritual forms are breaking
10   Through the gloom, their voices taking
     Part in the adoring song
     Of the bright angelic throng.
     Wondering the Shepherds bend
     Their steps to Bethlehem, and wend
15   To a poor and crowded inn:—
     Tremblingly their way they win
     To the stable, where they find
     The Redeemer of mankind,
     Just born into this world of danger,
20   Lying in an humble manger.
     And they spread abroad each word
     Which that joyful night they'd heard,
     And they glorified the name
     Of their gracious God, Who came
25   Himself to save from endless woe
     The offspring of this world below.

Love and Death.

     "Our bark's on the water; come down, come down,
     I'll weave for thy fair head a leafy crown,
     And in it I'll blend the roses bright,
     With asphodel woven of faint sunlight.
5   But more precious than these I'll twine the pearls
     In the flowing locks of thy chestnut curls;
     And the gem and the flow'r from wave and from tree
     Shall form a bright diadem, Bianca, for thee.
     The sea is calm, and I will guard thee;
10   Oh what, sweet love, should thus retard thee?
     Descend, fairest maiden, descend to the sea,
     And sail o'er the motionless waters with me."
     The sound of his last words was scarcely o'er,

When beside him she stood on the ocean shore.
15   Lightly she entered the gondola,
      And gaily her lover followed her—
      But for them it had been happier
      Had they quietly lain in their beds all night,
      Nor sailed forth 'neath the moonbeam's deceitful light.
20   Smoothly, swiftly the gondolier rowed along,
      The splash of his oars keeping time to his song;
      'Twas an old tale of hope and of fear and of danger,
      Of the loves of a noble princess and a stranger;
      How they fled, and were married one fine summer night,
25   And their days glided on in one stream of delight.
      But oh! wherefore trembles that lady fair?
      The lightning gleams forth through the heavy air;
      The thunder peals loudly, the low wind is wailing,
      And the heart of the lady for terror is failing.
30   But Gonsalvo around her his left arm clasped tightly,
      And he fought with the sea that was foaming so whitely;
      All vain are his struggles—the billows rise higher,
      The thunder is pealing, the sky seems on fire,
      The wild wind is howling, the lightning ne'er ceases—
35   He still clasps his love, but his strength fast decreases—
      Fair Bianca has fainted; she hears not the wind,
      Nor the splash of the rain; to the lightning she's blind—
      She knows not that down to the depths of the sea
      She's dragging her love irresistibly:
40   Gonsalvo's efforts have fainter grown,
      And she hangs on his arm like a heavy stone;—
      And now o'er them rolls each mighty wave—
      In the sea they have found a common grave.

Despair.

1

Up rose the moon in glory,
    And glittered on the sea;
Up rose the stars around her,
    Making the darkness flee.

2

5   The nightingale's wild warbling
      Rang in the far-off wood;
    When in his Father's castle
      A mournful figure stood.

3

    His heart was almost bursting,
10   He madly beat his breast;
    As, in low plaintive accents,
      His grief he thus exprest.

4

    "Stars, shroud yourselves in darkness!
      Pale moon, withdraw thy light!
15   Let darkness hide the ocean
      For ever from my sight;

5

    "Hide cottage, town and city;—
      Appear no more, thou Sun!
    But let in foreign countries
20   Thy cheering race be run.

6

    "For I have lost my loved one!
      Low lies she in her grave!
    Speak not to me of pleasure,
      For her I could not save.

7

25   "Hark to the distant murmur
      As waves break on the shore"—
    When lo! a light came flashing
      Along the corridor.

8

The mystic form that bore it
30   He scarcely could discern;
Its flowing robe was blackness—
    Higher the flame doth burn—

9

He cried, "What art thou, Spirit
    So luminous and bright?"
35 A voice said, "I'm the maid, Sir,
    A bringing in the light."

Forget Me Not.

1

"Forget me not! Forget me not!"
    The maiden once did say,
When to some far-off battle-field
    Her lover sped away.

2

5 "Forget me not! Forget me not!"
    Says now the chamber-maid
When the traveller on his journey
    No more will be delayed.

Easter Morning.

1

The sun arises from the sea,
    And all around his rays is flinging,
The flowers are opening on the lea,
    The merry birds are singing.

2

5   The summer breeze is rustling past,
      Sweet scents are gathering around it,
    The rivulet is flowing fast,
      Beside the banks that bound it.

3

    All nature seemeth to rejoice,
10   In the returning summer weather;
    Let us with nature raise our voice,
      And harmonise together.

4

    But not alone for summer skies
      Shall praise unto our God be given:
15   This day our Saviour did arise,
      And oped the gate of heaven.

5

    To sinful man, if only he
      His errings will confess with sorrow,
    Then, after earth's night-misery,
20   Shall dawn a glorious morrow:

6

    A blissful bright eternity
      Bought by the rising of the Giver,
    To Whom all praise, all honour be,
      For ever and for ever.

A Tirsi.

Chiami il mio core
Crudele, altero;

No, non è vero,
   Crudel non è.
5 T'amo, t'amai,
   E tu lo sai,
  Men del dovere,
   Ma più di me.

The Last Words of St. Telemachus.

There is a sound of weeping; wherefore weep
   That I should sleep?
Oh! wherefore mourn that I at last should be
   At liberty?
5 One only grief yet lingers at my heart—
   That we must part:
Part—! and perchance we never more may meet
   In converse sweet!
The memory of all thy gentle ways,
10   Kind without praise—
And of thy loving acts, scarce seen before,
   Now numbered o'er,
Weigh me to earth clinging about my heart—
   And must we part?
15 Yet still my trust in God shall stedfast be—
   By faith I see
Through the long vista of eternal years,
   Free from all fears,
Thee by my side in calm unchanging rest,
20   For ever blest!

Lord Thomas and fair Margaret.

1

Fair Marg'ret sat in her bower,
   Unbraiding of her hair,
When entered in Lord Thomas' ghost,
   And gave her greeting fair.

2

5 "Oh how pale thou art, my love," she said,
   "Oh how pale thou art to see!
Once thine eye was bright, and thy cheek was red;
   Why comest thou so to me?"

3

"Oh fair Marg'ret, oh sweet Marg'ret,
10   I murderèd have been—
They have ta'en my body for love of thee,
   And cast it in a stream.

4

"Oh fair Marg'ret, oh sweet Marg'ret,
   We aye maun parted be,
15 If thou wilt not bind up thy yellow hair,
   And quickly follow me."

5

Up and ris fair Marg'ret,
   And quickly followed him;
As the moon was the colour of his face,
20   And the colour of his limb.

6

The ghost he fled, the ghost he sped,
   The ghost he ran and glided,
And still fair Margaret pursued,
   Though never to be brided.

7

25 The ghost he sped, the ghost he fled,
   Ploughed land and hillocks over,
And still fair Margaret pursued
   After her flying lover.

8

Away, away "without stop or stay,"
30   Till they came to waters running,
"I canna stay, I maun away,
    For fast the day is coming.

9

"Oh fair Marg'ret, oh sweet Marg'ret,
    We now maun parted be,
35   If in the last trail thou shalt go through
    Thy heart should fail in thee."

10

On glided the ghost, while the starry host
    Glittered down on the sleeping stream;
O'er the waves glided he impalpably,
40   Then vanished like a dream.

11

Fair Margaret still followed him,
    Till she sank amid the wave;
Thus died for each other these lovers true,
    And were joinèd in the grave.

Lines to my Grandfather.

Dear Grandpapa,
        To be obedient,
    I'll try and write a letter;
Which (as I hope you'll deem expedient)
5   Must serve for lack of better.

My muse of late was not prolific,
    And sometimes I must feel

To make a verse a task terrific
  Rather of woe than weal.

10 As I have met with no adventure
      Of wonder and refulgence,
    I must write plain things at a venture
      And trust to your indulgence.

    The apple-tree is showing
15   Its blossom of bright red
    With a soft colour glowing
      Upon its leafy bed.

    The pear-tree's pure white blossom
      Like stainless snow is seen;
20 And all earth's genial bosom
      Is clothed with varied green.

    The fragrant may is blooming,
      The yellow cowslip blows;
    Among its leaves entombing
25   Peeps forth the pale primrose.

    The kingcup flowers and daisies
      Are opening hard by;
    And many another raises
      Its head, to please and die.

30 I love the gay wild flowers
      Waving in fresh spring air;
    Give me uncultured bowers
      Before the bright parterre!

    And now my letter is concluded,
35   To do well I have striven;
    And though news is well-nigh excluded,
      I hope to be forgiven.

    With love to all the beautiful,
      And those who cannot slaughter,
40 I sign myself,
                    your dutiful,
            Affectionate Granddaughter.

Charade.

My first may be the firstborn,
　　The second child may be;
My second is a texture light
　　And elegant to see:
5　My whole do those too often write
　　Who are from talent free.

Hope in Grief.

Tell me not that death of grief
Is the only sure relief.
Tell me not that hope when dead
Leaves a void that nought can fill,
5　Gnawings that may not be fed.
Tell me not there is no skill
That can bind the breaking heart,
That can soothe the bitter smart,
When we find ourselves betrayed,
10　When we find ourselves forsaken,
By those for whom we would have laid
Our young lives down, nor wished to waken.
Say not that life is to all
But a gaily coloured pall,
15　Hiding with its deceitful glow
The hearts that break beneath it,
Engulphing as they anguished flow
The scalding tears that seethe it.
Say not, vain this world's turmoil,
20　Vain its trouble and its toil,
All its hopes and fears are vain,
Long, unmitigated pain.
What though we should be deceived
By the friend that we love best?
25　All in this world have been grieved,
Yet many have found rest.
Our present life is as the night,

Our future as the morning light:
Surely the night will pass away,
30   And surely will uprise the day.

Lisetta all' Amante.

Perdona al primo eccesso
   D'un tenero dolore;
   A te promisi il core,
     E vo' serbarlo a te.
5   Ma dimmi, e mi consola:
    M'ami tu ancor, cor mio?
    Se a te fedel son io,
     Sarai fedele a me?

Chè se nell' alma ingrata
10   Pensi ad abbandonarmi,
    Anch'io saprò scordarmi
     D'un amator crudel.
    Ma crederlo non voglio;
    Ma non lo vo' pensare;
15   Chè nol potrei lasciare,
     Chè gli sarei fedel.

Song.

I saw her; she was lovely,
   And bright her eyes of blue,
Whilst merrily her white white hands
   Over the harp-strings flew.
5   I saw her and I loved her,
   I loved her for my pain,
For her heart was given to another
   Not to return again.

Again I saw her pacing
10   Down the cathedral aisle;
The bridal wreath was in her hair,

And on her lips a smile;
   A quiet smile and holy,
   Meet for a holy place,
15 A smile of certain happiness
   That lighted up her face.

And once, once more I saw her,
   Kneeling beside a bed;
The bright sun's rays were shining there,
20   And shone upon the dead;
From the body of her husband
   Earth's gloom they chased away,
And she gazed on him without a tear,
   And hailed the coming day.

Praise of Love.

And shall Love cease? Ask thine own heart, O Woman,
   Thy heart that beats restlessly on for ever!
All earthly things shall pass away and human,
But Love's divine: annihilated never,
5   It binds and nought shall sever.

Oh! it is Love makes the world habitable,
   Love is a foretaste of our promised Heaven;
Though sometimes robed in white, sometimes in sable,
   It still is Love, and still some joy is given,
10   Although the heart be riven.

And who would give Love's joy to 'scape its paining?
   Yea, who would lose its sorrow and its gladness?
Then let us bear its griefs without complaining:—
   This only earthly passion is not madness,
15   Nor leads to dearth and sadness.

Love is all happiness, Love is all beauty,
   Love is the crown of flaxen heads and hoary,
Love is the only everlasting duty,
   And Love is chronicled in endless story,
20   And leads to endless glory.

"I have fought a good fight."

"Who art thou that comest with a stedfast face
Thro' the hushed arena to the burying-place?"
"I am one whose footprints marked upon the sand
Cry in blood for vengeance on a guilty land."

5   "How are these thy garments white as whitest snow
Tho' thy blood hath touched them in its overflow?"
"My blood cannot stain them, nor my tears make white;
One than I more mighty, He hath made them bright."

"Say, do thy wounds pain thee open every one,
10   Wounds that now are glowing clearer than the sun?"
"Nay, they are my gladness unalloyed by grief;
Like a desert fountain, or a long relief."

"When the lion had thee in his deadly clasp,
Was there then no terror in thy stifled gasp?"
15   "Tho' I felt the crushing, and the grinding teeth,
He was with me ever, He Who comforteth."

"Didst thou hear the shouting, as of a great flood,
Crying out for vengeance, crying out for blood?"
"I heard it in silence, and was not afraid,
20   While for the mad people silently I prayed."

"Did their hate not move thee? art thou heedless then
Of the fear of children and the curse of men?"
"God looked down upon me from the Heaven above,
And I did not tremble, happy in His Love."

Wishes:
Sonnet.

Oh! would that I were very far away
    Among the lanes, with hedges all around,
    Happily listening to the dreamy sound
Of distant sheep-bells, smelling the new hay
5   And all the wild-flowers scattered in my way:

    Or would that I were lying on some mound
     Where shade and butterflies and thyme abound,
Beneath the trees, upon a sunny day:
Or would I strolled beside the mighty sea,
10   The sea before, and the tall cliffs behind;
While winds from the warm south might tell to me
     How health and joy for all men are designed:—
But be I where I may, would I had thee,
     And heard thy gentle voice, my Mother kind.

Eleanor.

Cherry-red her mouth was,
    Morning-blue her eye,
Lady-slim her little waist
    Rounded prettily;
5 And her sweet smile of gladness
    Made every heart rejoice;
But sweeter even than her smile
    The tones were of her voice.

Sometimes she spoke, sometimes she sang;
10   And evermore the sound
Floated, a dreamy melody,
    Upon the air around;
As tho' a wind were singing
    Far up beside the sun,
15 Till sound and warmth and glory
    Were blended all in one.

Her hair was long and golden,
    And clustered unconfined
Over a forehead high and white
20   That spoke a noble mind.
Her little hand, her little foot
    Were ready evermore
To hurry forth to meet a friend;
    She smiling at the door.

25 But if she sang, or if she spoke,
    'Twas music soft and grand,
As tho' a distant singing sea
    Broke on a tuneful strand;
As tho' a blessed Angel
30   Were singing a glad song,
Half way between the earth and Heaven
    Joyfully borne along.

Isidora.

/See Maturin's "Melmoth."/

Love, whom I have loved too well,
    Turn thy face away from me;
For I heed nor Heaven nor Hell
    While mine eyes can look on thee.
5 Do not answer, do not speak,
For thy voice can make me weak.

I must choose 'twixt God and man,
    And I dare not hesitate:
Oh how little is life's span,
10   And Eternity how great!
Go out from me; for I fear
Mine own strength while thou art here.

Husband, leave me; but know this:
    I would gladly give my soul
15 So that thine might dwell in bliss
    Free from the accursed control,
So that thou mightest go hence
In a hopeful penitence.

Yea, from Hell I would look up,
20   And behold thee in thy place,
Drinking of the living cup,
    With the joy-look on thy face,
And the Light that shines alone
From the Glory of the Throne.

25   But how could my endless loss
       Be thine everlasting gain?
    Shall thy palm grow from my cross?
       Shall thine ease be in my pain?
    Yea, thine own soul witnesseth
30   Thy life is not in my death.

    It were vain that I should die;
       That we thus should perish both;
    Thou would'st gain no peace thereby;
       And in truth I should be loath
35   By the loss of my salvation
    To increase thy condemnation.

    Little infant, his and mine,
       Would that I were as thou art;
    Nothing breaks that sleep of thine,
40   And ah! nothing breaks thy heart;
    And thou knowest nought of strife,
    The heart's death for the soul's life.

    None misdoubt thee; none misdeem
       Of thy wishes and thy will.
45   All thy thoughts are what they seem,
       Very pure and very still;
    And thou fearest not the voice
    That once made thy heart rejoice.

    Oh how calm thou art, my child!
50   I could almost envy thee.
    Thou hast neither wept nor smiled,
       Thou that sleepest quietly.
    Would I also were at rest
    With the one that I love best.

55   Husband, go. I dare not hearken
       To thy words, or look upon
    Those despairing eyes that darken
       Down on me—but he is gone.
    Nay, come back; and be my fate
60   As thou wilt—it is too late.

I have conquered; it is done;
   Yea, the death-struggle is o'er,
And the hopeless quiet won!—
   I shall see his face no more!—
65 And mine eyes are waxing dim
Now they cannot look on him.

And my heart-pulses are growing
   Very weak; and thro' my whole
Life-blood a slow chill is going:—
70   Blessed Saviour, take my soul
To Thy Paradise and care;—
Paradise, will he be there?

The Novice.

I love one, and he loveth me:
Who sayeth this? who deemeth this?
And is this thought a cause of bliss,
   Or source of misery?

5 The loved may die, or he may change:
And if he die thou art bereft;
Or if he alter, nought is left
   Save life that seemeth strange.

A weary life, a hopeless life,
10 Full of all ill and fear-oppressed;
A weary life that looks for rest
   Alone after death's strife.

And love's joy hath no quiet even;
It evermore is variable.
15 Its gladness is like war in Hell,
   More than repose in Heaven.

Yea, it is as a poison cup
That holds one quick fire-draught within;
For when the life seems to begin
20   The slow death looketh up.

Then bring me to a solitude
Where love may neither come nor go;
Where very peaceful waters flow,
   And roots are found for food;

25 Where the wild honey-bee booms by;
And trees and bushes freely give
Ripe fruit and nuts; there I would live,
   And there I fain would die.

There Autumn leaves may make my grave,
30 And little birds sing over it;
And there cool twilight winds may flit
   And shadowy branches wave.

Immalee:

/See Maturin's "Melmoth."/

Sonnet.

I gather thyme upon the sunny hills,
   And its pure fragrance ever gladdens me,
   And in my mind having tranquillity
I smile to see how my green basket fills.
5 And by clear streams I gather daffodils;
   And in dim woods find out the cherry-tree,
   And take its fruit, and the wild strawberry,
And nuts, and honey; and live free from ills.
I dwell on the green earth, 'neath the blue sky,
10 Birds are my friends, and leaves my rustling roof;
The deer are not afraid of me, and I
   Hear the wild goat, and hail its hastening hoof;
The squirrels sit perked as I pass them by,
   And even the watchful hare stands not aloof.

Lady Isabella.

Heart warm as Summer, fresh as Spring,
Gracious as Autumn's harvesting,
Pure as the Winter snows; as white

A hand as lilies in sun-light;
5 Eyes glorious as a midnight star;
Hair shining as the chestnuts are;
A step firm and majestical;
A voice singing and musical;
A soft expression, kind address;
10 Tears for another's heaviness;
Bright looks; an action full of grace;
A perfect form, a perfect face;
All these become a woman well,
And these had Lady Isabelle.

Night and Death.

Now the sun-lit hours are o'er,
Rise up from thy shadowy shore,
Happy Night, whom Chaos bore.

Better is the peaceful treasure
5 Of thy musings without measure,
Than the day's unquiet pleasure.

Bring the holy moon; so pale
She herself seems but a veil
For the sun, where no clouds sail.

10 Bring the stars, thy progeny;
Each a little lamp on high
To light up an azure sky.

Sounds incomprehensible
In the shining planets dwell
15 Of thy sister Queen to tell.

Of that sister Nature saith,
She hath power o'er life and breath;
And her name is written Death.

She is fairer far than thou;
20 Grief her head can never bow,
Joy is stamped upon her brow.

She is full of gentleness,
And of faith and hope; distress
Finds in her forgetfulness.

25 In her arms who lieth down
Never more is seen to frown,
Tho' he wore a thorny crown.

Whoso sigheth in unrest
If his head lean on her breast
30 Witnesseth she is the best.

All the riches of the earth
Weighed by her are nothing worth;
She is the eternal birth.

In her treasure-house are found
35 Stored abundantly around
Almsdeeds done without a sound;

Long forbearance; patient will;
Fortitude in midst of ill;
Hope, when even fear grew still;

40 Kindness given again for hate;
Hearts resigned tho' desolate;
Meekness, which is truly great;

Bitter tears of penitence;
Changeless love's omnipotence:—
45 And nought lacketh recompense.

In her house no tainted thing
Winneth any entering;
There the poor have comforting.

There they wait a little time
50 Till the angel-uttered chime
Sound the eternal matin-prime.

Then, upraised in joyfulness,
They shall know her; and confess
She is blessed and doth bless.

55   When earth's fleeting day is flown
      All created things shall own,
      Death is Life, and Death alone.

      "Young men aye were fickle found
      Since summer trees were leafy."

      Go in peace my Beloved; tho' never again
      Shall I feel in thy presence strange joy and sweet pain;
      Go in peace my Beloved; perhaps thou may'st yet
      Find a young heart to love thee that need not forget.

5   In glory and beauty and smiles thou shalt go,
      And I shall remain in my wearisome woe.
      Oh! thine is the rose on a bright summer morn
      Full of perfume and blushes;—and mine is the thorn.

      And thine is the sun-light, and mine is the cloud;
10   And thine is the feasting, and mine is the shroud.
      And thou shalt have gladness and honour's increase;
      And I in my cool silent grave shall have peace.

      But so it is fitting, and so let it be;
      The praise be thy portion, the shame be for me.
15   Ah! why should I chide thee and struggle in vain?
      For love, once recalled, is not given again.

      Thy word is forgotten, and broken thy vow;
      If I pray or reproach thee thou heedest not now.
      I would I could hate thee, false love; but in truth
20   How can I abhor the delight of my youth?

      Oh! happy the maiden whose beautiful strength
      Shall win thy proud heart and subdue it at length!
      Yet tho' she be true, what hath she more than I?
      She may live but for thee, and for thee I shall die.

25   The faith which endures and is mighty in death
      Is more real, to my thinking, than words which are
                  breath.

There are many fair women will court thee and live;
But who, broken-hearted, will die and forgive?

By the love that I bear thee, the hopes that are flown,
30   The heart that lies bleeding, the life left alone,—
Remember, remember the dear vanished time,
In thy far-distant country and sun-gladdened clime.

The Lotus-Eaters:
Ulysses to Penelope.

In a far-distant land they dwell,
     Incomprehensible,
Who love the shadow more than light,
     More than the sun the moon,
5   Cool evening more than noon,
Pale silver more than gold that glitters bright.
A dark cloud overhangs their land
     Like a mighty hand,
Never moving from above it;
10   A cool shade and moist and dim,
With a twilight-purple rim,
     And they love it.
And sometimes it giveth rain,
But soon it ceaseth as before,
15   And earth drieth up again;
Then the dews rise more and more,
Till it filleth, dropping o'er;
But no forked lightnings flit,
And no thunders roll in it.
20   Thro' the land a river flows;
With a sleepy sound it goes;
Such a drowsy noise, in sooth,
Those who will not listen, hear not;
But if one is wakeful, fear not;
25   It shall lull him to repose,
Bringing back the dream's of youth.
Hemlock groweth, poppy bloweth

In the fields where no man moweth;
And the vine is full of wine
30 And are full of milk the kine,
And the hares are all secure,
And the birds are wild no more,
And the forest-trees wax old,
And winds stir, or hot, or cold,
35 And yet no man taketh care,
All things resting everywhere.

Sonnet
from the Psalms.

All thro' the livelong night I lay awake
    Watering my couch with tears of heaviness.
    None stood beside me in my sore distress;—
Then cried I to my heart: If thou wilt, break,
5 But be thou still; no moaning will I make,
    Nor ask man's help, nor kneel that he may bless.
    So I kept silence in my haughtiness,
Till lo! the fire was kindled, and I spake
Saying: Oh that I had wings like to a dove,
10   Then would I flee away and be at rest:
I would not pray for friends, or hope, or love,
    But still the weary throbbing of my breast;
And, gazing on the changeless heavens above,
    Witness that such a quietness is best.

Song.

The stream moaneth as it floweth,
The wind sigheth as it bloweth,
Leaves are falling, Autumn goeth,
    Winter cometh back again;
5 And the air is very chilly,
And the country rough and hilly,
    And I shiver in the rain.

Who will help me? Who will love me?
Heaven sets forth no light above me;
10   Ancient memories reprove me,
Long-forgotten feelings move me,
    I am full of heaviness.
Earth is cold, too cold the sea;
Whither shall I turn and flee?
15   Is there any hope for me?
Any ease for my heart-aching?
Any sleep that hath no waking?
Any night without day-breaking?
    Any rest from weariness?
20   Hark! the wind is answering:
    Hark! the running stream replieth:
    There is rest for him that dieth;
    In the grave whoever lieth
Nevermore hath sorrowing.
25   Holy slumber, holy quiet,
Close the eyes and still the riot;
And the brain forgets its thought,
    And the heart forgets its beating.—
    Earth and earthly things are fleeting,
30   There is what all men have sought;
Long, unchangeable repose,
Lulling us from many woes.

A Counsel.

Oh weep for the glory departed
    That comes not again;
And weep for the friends hollow-hearted
    Ye cared for in vain;
5   And weep for the roses that perished
    Ere Summer had fled;
For hopes that ye vainly have cherished;—
    But not for the dead.

Nay mourn not for them: they have ended
10   All labours and woes;
Their hopes now of glory are blended
     With perfect repose.
And tell me, this thing that is given,
     Shall it not suffice?
15   They wait for the gladness of Heaven,
     And have Paradise.

The World's Harmonies.

Oh listen, listen; for the Earth
     Hath silent melody;
Green grasses are her lively chords,
     And blossoms; and each tree,
5   Chestnut and oak and sycamore,
     Makes solemn harmony.

Oh listen, listen; for the Sea
     Is calling unto us;
Her notes are the broad liquid waves
10   Mighty and glorious.
Lo, the first man and the last man
     Hath heard, shall hearken thus.

The Sun on which men cannot look
     Its splendour is so strong;
15   Which wakeneth life and giveth life
     Rolling in light along,
From day-dawn to dim eventide
     Sings the eternal song.

And the Moon taketh up the hymn,
20   And the Stars answer all;
And all the Clouds and all the Winds
     And all the Dews that fall
And Frost and fertilizing Rain
     Are mutely musical.

25 Fishes and Beasts and feathered Fowl
        Swell the eternal chant,
    That riseth through the lower air,
        Over the rainbow slant,
    Up through the unseen palace-gates,
30   Fearlessly jubilant.

    Before the everlasting Throne
        It is acceptable;
    It hath no pause or faltering;
        The Angels know it well;
35 Yea, in the highest heaven of heavens
        Its sound is audible.

    Yet than the voice of the whole World
        There is a sweeter voice,
    That maketh all the Cherubim
40   And Seraphim rejoice;
    That all the blessèd Spirits hail
        With undivided choice;

    That crieth at the golden door
        And gaineth entrance in;
45 That the palm-branch and radiant crown
        And glorious throne may win;—
    The lowly prayer of a poor man
        Who turneth from his sin.

Lines
given with a Penwiper.

    I have compassion on the carpeting,
        And on your back I have compassion too.
    The splendid Brussels web is suffering
        In the dimmed lustre of each glowing hue;
5   And you the everlasting altering
        Of your position with strange aches must rue.
    Behold, I come the carpet to preserve,
    And save your spine from a continual curve.

The last Answer.

She turned round to me with her steadfast eyes:
   "I tell you I have looked upon the dead;
   "Have kissed the brow and the cold lips;" she said;
"Have called upon the sleeper to arise;
5   "He loved me, yet he stirred not; on this wise,
    "Not bowing in weak agony my head,
    "But all too sure of what life is, to dread,
"Learned I that love and hope are fallacies."
She gazed quite calmly on me; and I felt
10   Awed and astonished and almost afraid:
      For what was I to have admonished her?
Then, being full of doubt and fear, I knelt,
    And tears came to my eyes even as I prayed:
      But she, meanwhile, only grew statelier.

One of the Dead.

Paler, not quite so fair as in her life,
   She lies upon the bed, perfectly still;
   Her little hands clasped with a patient will
Upon her bosom, swelling without strife;
5   An honoured virgin, a most blameless wife.
    The roses lean upon the window sill,
    That she trained once; their sweets the hot air fill,
And make the death-apartment odour-rife.
Her meek white hands folded upon her breast,
10   Her gentle eyes closed in the long last sleep,
She lieth down in her unbroken rest;
    Her kin, kneeling around, a vigil keep,
Venting their grief in low sobs unrepressed:—
    Friends, she but slumbers, wherefore do ye weep?

"The whole head is sick, and the whole heart faint."

Woe for the young who say that life is long,
   Who turn from the sun-rising to the west,

    Who feel no pleasure and can find no rest,
    Who in the morning sigh for evensong.
5   Their hearts weary because of this world's wrong,
        Yearn with a thousand longings unexpressed;
        They have a wound no mortal ever drest,
    An ill than all earth's remedies more strong.
    For them the fount of gladness hath run dry,
10   And in all nature is no pleasant thing;
    For them there is no glory in the sky,
        No sweetness in the breezes' murmuring;
    They say: The peace of heaven is placed too high,
        And this earth changeth and is perishing.

"I do set My bow in the cloud."

    The roses bloom too late for me;
    The violets I shall not see;
    Even the snowdrops will not come
    Till I have passed from home to home;
5   From home on earth to home in heaven,
    Here penitent and there forgiven.

    Mourn not, my Father, that I seek
    One Who is strong when I am weak.
    Through the dark passage, verily,
10   His rod and staff shall comfort me;
    He shall support me in the strife
    Of death, that dieth into life;
    He shall support me; He receive
    My soul when I begin to live,
15   And more than I can ask for give.

    He from the heaven-gates built above
    Hath looked on me in perfect love.
    From the heaven-walls to me He calls
    To come and dwell within those walls;
20   With Cherubim and Seraphim
    And Angels; yea, beholding Him.

His care for me is more than mine,
Father; His love is more than thine.
Sickness and death I have from thee,
25   From Him have immortality.
He giveth gladness where He will,
Yet chasteneth His belovèd still.

Then tell me; is it not enough
To feel that when the path is rough,
30   And the sky dark, and the rain cold,
His promise standeth as of old?
When heaven and earth have passed away,
Only His righteous word shall stay,
And we shall know His will is best.
35   Behold; He is a Haven Rest,
A Sheltering Rock, a Hiding Place,
For runners steadfast in the race;
Who, toiling for a little space,
Had light through faith when sight grew dim,
40   And offered all their world to Him.

"O Death where is thy Sting?"

She sleepeth: would ye wake her if ye could?
   Is her face sad that ye should pity her?
   Did Death come to her like a messenger
From a far land where is not any good?
5   I tell ye nay: but, having understood
   That God is Love, Death was her harbinger

[The rest of the manuscript is missing from the notebook.]

Undine.

She did not answer him again
   But walked straight to the door;
Her hand nor trembled on the lock,

Nor her foot on the floor,
5   But as she stood up steadily
        She turned, and looked once more.

She turned, and looked on him once more:
        Her face was very pale;
And from her forehead her long hair
10   Fell back like a thick veil;
But, though her lips grew white, the fire
        Of her eyes did not fail.

Then as she fixed her eyes on him
        Old thoughts came back again
15   Of the dear rambles long ago
        Through meadow-land and lane,
When all the woods were full of flowers,
        And all the fields of grain.

When all the birds were full of song
20   Except the turtle dove;
And that sat cooing tenderly
        In the green boughs above;
When they hoped the same hopes, and when
        He told her of his love.

25   Old memories came back to her
        Of what once made her glad,
Till her heart seemed to stand quite still,
        And every pulse she had:
Then the blood rose up to her brain
30   And she was almost mad.

Yet still she stood there steadily
        And looked him in the face;
There was no tear upon her cheek;
        Upon her brow no trace
35   Of the agonizing strife within,
        The shame and the disgrace.

And so she stayed a little while
        Until she turned once more,

Without a single sob or sigh;
40   But her heart felt quite sore:
The spirit had been broken, and
     The hope of life was o'er.

Lady Montrevor.

(See Maturin's "Wild Irish Boy.")

I do not look for love that is a dream:
     I only seek for courage to be still;
     To bear my grief with an unbending will,
And when I am a-weary not to seem.
5 Let the round world roll on; let the sun beam;
     Let the wind blow, and let the rivers fill
     The everlasting sea; and on the hill
The palms almost touch heaven, as children deem.
And though young Spring and Summer pass away,
10   And Autumn and cold Winter come again;
     And though my soul, being tired of its pain,
Pass from the ancient earth; and though my clay
     Return to dust; my tongue shall not complain:
No man shall mock me after this my day.

Floral Teaching.

O ye red-blushing summer roses, ye
     Who are like queens, crowned with a rich perfume,
     In whose deep heart there is no shade of gloom,
Who are a pasture for the honey-bee;
5 Surely your days and nights pass happily:
     And when the earth, your mother, doth resume
     Your little lives, do ye not think the tomb
Is full of soft leaves and looks pleasantly?
So be it with me: through life so may I deem
10   That this world's course is ordered well, and give
My help to others and my loving heed.

Then when the day comes that it is decreed
   I am to die, may I not cease to live,
But rest awhile waiting the morning beam.

"Death is swallowed up in Victory."

"Tell me: doth it not grieve thee to lie here,
   And see the cornfields waving not for thee,
   Just in the waxing Summer of the year?"

"I fade from earth; and lo! along with me
5   The season that I love will fade away:
   How should I look for Autumn longingly?"

"Yet Autumn beareth fruit whilst day by day
   The leaves grow browner with a mellow hue,
   Declining to a beautiful decay."

10 "Decay is death, with which I have to do,
   And see it near; behold, it is more good
   Than length of days and length of sorrow too."

"But thy heart hath not dwelt in solitude:
   Many have loved and love thee; dost not heed
15 Free love, for which in vain have others sued?"

"I thirst for love, love is mine only need,
   Love such as none hath borne me, nor can bear,
   True love that prompteth thought and word and deed."

"Here it is not: why seek it otherwhere?
20 Nay, bow thy head, and own that on this earth
   Are many goodly things, and sweet, and fair."

"There are tears in man's laughter; in his mirth
   There is a fearful forward look; and lo!
   An infant's cry gives token of its birth."

25 "I mark the ocean of Time ebb and flow:
   He who hath care one day, and is perplext
   Tomorrow may have joy in place of woe."

"Evil becomes good; and to this annext
   Good becomes evil; speak of it no more;
30   My heart is wearied and my spirit vext."

"Is there no place it grieves thee to give o'er?
   Is there no home thou lov'st, and so wouldst fain
   Tarry a little longer at the door?"

"I must go hence and not return again;
35   But the friends whom I have shall come to me,
   And dwell together with me safe from pain."

"Where is that mansion mortals cannot see?
   Behold the tombs are full of worms; shalt thou
   Rise thence and soar up skywards gloriously?"

40   "Even as the planets shine we know not how,
   We shall be raised then; changed, yet still the same;
   Being made like Christ; yea, being as He is now."

"Thither thou goest whence no man ever came:
   Death's voyagers return not; and in Death
45   There is no room for speech or sigh or fame."

"There is room for repose that comforteth;
   There weariness is not; and there content
   Broodeth for ever, and hope hovereth."

"When the stars fall, and when the graves are rent,
50   Shalt thou have safety? shalt thou look for life
   When the great light of the broad sun is spent?"

"These elements shall consummate their strife,
   This heaven and earth shall shrivel like a scroll
   And then be re-created, beauty-rife."

55   "Who shall abide it when from pole to pole
   The world's foundations shall be overthrown?
   Who shall abide to scan the perfect whole?"

"He who hath strength given to him, not his own;
   He who hath faith in that which is not seen,
60   And patient hope; who trusts in love alone."

"Yet thou! the death-struggle must intervene
  Ere thou win rest; think better of it; think
  Of all that is and shall be, and hath been."

"The cup my Father giveth me to drink,
65   Shall I not take it meekly? though my heart
  Tremble a moment, it shall never shrink."

"Satan will wrestle with thee, when thou art
  In the last agony; and Death will bring
  Sins to remembrance ere thy spirit part."

70   "In that great hour of unknown suffering
  God shall be with me, and His arm made bare
  Shall fight for me: yea, underneath His wing
I shall lie safe at rest and freed from care."

Death.

"The grave-worm revels now"
Upon the pure white brow,
And on the eyes so dead and dim,
And on each putrifying limb,
5   And on the neck 'neath the long hair;
Now from the rosy lips
He damp corruption sips,
Banquetting everywhere.
Creeping up and down through the silken tresses
10   That once were smoothed by her husband's caresses,
In her mouth, and on her breast
Where the babe might never rest
In giving birth to whom she lost her life;
She gave all and she gave in vain,
15   Nor saw the purchase of her pain,
Poor mother and poor wife.

Was she too young to die?
Nay, young in sorrow and in years,
Her heart was old in faith and love;

20   Her eyes were ever fixed above,
       They were not dimmed by tears.
       And as the time went swiftly by
       She was even as a stately palm
       Beside still waters, where a dove
25   Broodeth in perfect calm.
       Yea, she was as a gentle breeze
       To which a thousand tones are given;
       To tell of freshness to the trees,
       Of roses to the honey-bees,
30   Of Summer to the distant seas,
       And unto all of Heaven.

       They rest together in one grave,
       The mother and her infant child,
       The holy and the undefiled:
35   Let none weep that ye could not save
       So much of beauty from the earth;
       It is not death ye see, though they
       Pass into foulness and decay;
       It is the second birth.

A Hopeless Case.
(Nydia.)

       All night I dream of that which cannot be:
         And early in the morning I awake
         My whole heart saddened for a vision's sake.
       I in my sleep have joy; but woe is me!
5   Thro' the long day the shadowy pleasures flee
         And are not: wherefore I would gladly take
         Some warm and poppied potion that might make
       My slumbers long which pass so pleasantly.
       And if I slept and never woke again,
10   But dreamed on with a happy consciousness
       Of grass and flowers and perfect rest from pain,
       I would leave hope a thousand times found vain,

And own a twilight solitude doth bless
Shut in from cold and wind and storm of rain.

Ellen Middleton.

Raise me; undraw the curtain; that is well.
    Put up the casement; I would see once more
    The golden sun-set flooding sea and shore;
And hearken to the solemn evening-bell
5   That ringeth out my spirit like a knell.
    The tree of love a bitter fruitage bore,
    Sweet at the rind but rotten at the core,
Pointing to heaven and bringing down to hell.
I will not name His name, lest the young life
10   That dieth at my heart should live again;
Strengthening me to renew the weary strife
    That ceaseth,—is this death? It is not pain.
Write on my grave: Here lieth a lone wife
    Whose faith was hidden and whose love was vain.

St. Andrew's Church.

    I listen to the holy antheming
That riseth in thy walls continually,
What while the organ pealeth solemnly
    And white-robed men and boys stand up to sing.
5   I ask my heart with a sad questioning:
"What lov'st thou here?" and my heart answers me:
"Within the shadows of this sanctuary
    To watch and pray is a most blessed thing."
To watch and pray, false heart? it is not so:
10   Vanity enters with thee, and thy love
Soars not to Heaven, but grovelleth below.
    Vanity keepeth guard, lest good should reach
        Thy hardness; not the echoes from above
Can rule thy stubborn feelings or can teach.

Grown Cold.
Sonnet.

An old man asked me: What is Love? I turned
   In mirth away, and would not answer him;
   He filled a cup of wine up to the brim,
And yet no sparkling in its depths discerned.
5 Methought a death fire in his weak eyes burned
   While he beholding brightness called it dim;
   He sat and chuckled: 'twas a ghastly whim
In one whose spirit had so little learned.
So shall it be with me; but so not I
10 Shall question: certainly the blessèd thought
Of Love shall linger, when itself is gone.
Oh nest of thorns for dove to brood upon!
   Oh painful throbbings of a heart untaught
To rest when all its gladness goeth by!

Zara.
(see Maturin's "Women.")

The pale sad face of her I wronged
   Upbraids and follows me for ever:
The silent mouth grows many-tongued
   To chide me; like some solemn river
5 Whose every wave hath found a tone
To reason of one truth alone.

She loved and was beloved again:
   Why did I spoil her paradise?
Oh fleeting joy and lasting pain!
10 Oh folly of the heart and eyes!
I loved him more than all; and he,
He also hath forsaken me.

How have I wearied thee false friend?
   Answer me, wherein have I erred
15 That so our happy loves should end?

Was it in thought, or deed, or word?
My soul lay bare to thee; disclose
The hidden fountain of my woes.

The Lady Moon is all too bright
20   Loftily seated in the skies.
They say that love once dimmed her light,
    But surely such are poets' lies.
Who knoweth that she ever shone
On rosy cheeked Endymion?

25 Narcissus looked on his own shade,
    And sickened for its loveliness.
Grasping, he saw its beauties fade
    And stretch out into nothingness.
He died, rejecting his own good,
30 And Echo mourned in solitude.

But wherefore am I left alone?
    What was my sin, to merit this?
Of all my friends there is not one
    I slighted in my happiness,
35 My joyful days—oh, very white
One face pursues me day and night.

She loved him even as I love,
    For she is dying for his sake.
Oh happy hope that looks above!
40   Oh happy heart that still can break!
I cannot die, though hope is dead;
He spurned me, and my heart but bled.

Therefore because she did not speak,
    Being strong to die and make no sign;
45 Because her courage waxed not weak,
    Strengthened with love as with new wine;
Because she stooped not while she bore,
He will return to her once more.

Perhaps he still may bring her health,
50   May call her colour back again;
While I shall pine in fame and wealth,

Owning that such as these are vain,
And envying her happier fate:—
And yet methinks it is too late.

55 Thou doubly false to her and me,
      Boast of her death and my despair.
    Boast if thou canst: on land, on sea,
      I will be with thee everywhere;
    My soul, let loose by mine own deed,
60 Shall make thee fear who would'st not heed.

    Come, thou glad hour of vengeance, come,
      When I may dog him evermore,
    May track him to his distant home:
      Yea, though he flee from shore to shore
65 I will be there, the pallid ghost
    Of love and hope for ever lost.

    Old memories shall make him sad,
      And thin his hair and change his mien;
    He shall remember what he had,
70   And dream of what he might have been,
    Till he shall long for death; yet shrink
    From the cold cup that I shall drink.

    Who drinketh of that potent draught
      May never set it down again.
75 What matter if one wept or laughed?
      It killeth joy and numbeth pain:
    It hath sleep for the sorrowful,
    And for the sick a perfect lull.

    A drowsy lull, a heavy sleep:
80   Haply it may give such to me:
    And if my grave place were dug deep
      Beneath the cold earth, verily
    Such quietness I would not break,
    Not for my cherished vengeance' sake.

85 Bring me the cup: behold, I choose
      For all my portion nothingness.
    Bring me the cup: I would not lose

One drop of its forgetfulness.
On the grave brink I turn and think
90 Of thee, before I stoop to drink.

When the glad Summer time is past
   Shalt thou not weary of thy life
And turn to seek that home at last
   Where never enters fear nor strife?
95 Yea, at length, in the Autumn weather,
Shall not we twain repose together?

Ruin.

Amid the shade of a deserted hall
   I stand and think on much that hath been lost.
   How long it is since other step has cross'd
This time-worn floor; that tapestry is all
5 Worm-eaten; and those columns rise up tall
   Yet crumbling to decay; where banners toss'd
   Thin spiders' webs hang now; and bitter frost
Has even killed the flowers upon the wall.
Yet once this was a home brim full of life,
10   Full of the hopes and fears and love of youth,
      Full of love's language speaking without sound:
Here honour was enshrined and kindly truth;
   Hither the young lord brought his blushing wife,
      And here her bridal garlands were unbound.

I sit among green shady valleys oft
   Listening to echo-winds sighing of woe;
   The grass and flowers are strong and sweet below,
Yea, I am tired and the smooth turf is soft.
5 I sit and think and never look aloft
   Save to the tops of a tall poplar row
   That glisten in the wind, whispering low
Of sudden sorrow reaching those who laughed.

A very drowsy fountain bubbles near
10   Catching pale sunbeams o'er it wandering;
Its waters are so clear the stones look through:—
Then sitting by its lazy stream I hear
    Silence more loud than any other thing,
What time the trees weep o'er me honeydew.

Listen, and I will tell you of a face
    Not lovely, but made beautiful by mind;
    Lighted up with dark eyes in which you find
All womanly affections have their place;
5   Upon her even brow there is no trace
    Of passion; many fragrant blossoms bind
    Her hair glossy and golden; like a blind
It shadows her round cheeks blush full of grace.
I know now how it *is*, but it *was* so:
10   And when I think upon her bosom heaving,
And her full glistening eyes looking on me
When the poor bird was struggling; I still see
The throbbing tenderness, the virgin glow,
    And dream on, not at rest and yet believing.

Wouldst thou give me a heavy jewelled crown
    And purple mantle and embroidered vest?
    Dear Child, the colours of the glorious west
Are far more gorgeous when the sun sinks down.
5   The diadem would only make me frown
    With its own weight; nay, give me for my crest
    Pale violets dreaming in perfect rest,
Or rather leaves withered to Autumn brown.
A purple flowing mantle would but hinder
10   My careless walk, and an embroidered robe
Would shame me: what is the best man who stepped
On earth, more than the naked worm that crept
Over its surface? Earth shall be a cinder;
    Where shall be then the beauty of the globe?

I said within myself: I am a fool
   To sigh ever for that which being gone
   Cannot return: the sun shines as it shone;
Rejoice:—but who can be made glad by rule?
5 My heart and soul and spirit are no tool
   To play with and direct; my cheek is wan
   With memory; and ever and anon
I weep feeling life is a weary school.
There is much noise and bustle in the street;
10   It used to be so, and it is so now;
All are the same, and will be many a year.
   Spirit, that canst not break and wilt not bow,
Fear not the cold, thou who hast borne the heat;—
Die if thou wilt; but what hast thou to fear?

Methinks the ills of life I fain would shun;
   But then I must shun life which is a blank:
   Even in my childhood oft my spirit sank
Thinking of all that had still to be done.
5 Among my many friends there is not one
   Like her with whom I sat upon the bank
   Willow-o'er-shadowed; from whose lips I drank
A love more pure than streams that sing and run.
But many times that joy has cost a sigh;
10   And many times I in my heart have sought
For the old comfort, and not found it yet:
Surely in that calm day when I shall die
   The painful thought will be a blessed thought,
And I shall sorrow that I must forget.

Strange voices sing among the planets which
   Move on for ever; in the old sea's foam
   There is a prophecy; in Heaven's blue dome
Great beacon fires are lighted; black as pitch
5 Is night, and yet star jewels make it rich;
   And if the moon lights up her cloudy home
   The darkness flees, and forth strange gleamings roam

Lighting up hill and vale and mound and ditch.
Earth is full of all questions that all ask;
10   And she alone of heavy silence full
Answereth not: what is it severeth
Us from the spirits that we would be with?
    Or is it that our fleshly ear is dull,
And our own shadow hides light with a mask?

"Sleep, sleep, happy child;
  "All creation slept and smiled."
               Blake.

Sleep, sleep, happy one;
Thy night is but just begun.
Sleep in peace; still angels keep
Holy watches o'er thy sleep.

5   Softest breasts are pillowing,
Softest wings are shadowing
Thy calm slumber; little child,
Sleep in thy white robes undefiled.

There is no more aching now
10   In thy heart or in thy brow.
The red blood upon thy breast
Cannot scare away thy rest.

Though thy hands are clasped as when
A man thou prayedst among men,
15   Thy pains are lulled, thy tears are dried,
And thy wants are satisfied.

Sleep, sleep; what quietness
After the world's noise is this!
Sleep on, where the hush and shade
20   Like a veil are round thee laid.

At thy head a cross is hewn
Whereon shines the Advent moon:
Through all the hours of the night
Its shadow rests on thee aright.

25   In temptation thou wert firm;
        Now have patience with the worm.
        Yet a little while, and he
        And death and sin shall bow to thee.

        Yet a little while, and thou
30   Shalt have a crown upon thy brow,
        And a palm branch in thy hand
        Where the holy angels stand.

        Sleep, sleep, till the chime
        Sound of the last matin prime:
35   Sleep on until the morn
        Of another Advent dawn.

What Sappho would have said had her leap cured instead of killing her.

        Love, Love, that having found a heart
            And left it, leav'st it desolate;—
            Love, Love, that art more strong than Hate,
        More lasting and more full of art;—
5   O blessèd Love, return, return,
        Brighten the flame that needs must burn.

        Among the stately lilies pale,
            Among the roses flushing red,
            I seek a flower meet for my head,
10   A wreath wherewith to bind my veil:
        I seek in vain; a shadow-pain
        Lies on my heart; and all in vain.

        The rose hath too much life in it;
            The lily is too much at rest.
15   Surely a blighted rose were best,
        Or cankered lily flower more fit;
        Or purple violet, withering
        While yet the year is in its spring.

I walk down by the river side
20   Where the low willows touch the stream;
        Beneath the ripple and sun-gleam
The slippery cold fishes glide,
Where flags and reeds and rushes lave
Their roots in the unsullied wave.

25   Methinks this is a drowsy place:
        Disturb me not; I fain would sleep:
        The very winds and waters keep
Their voices under; and the race
Of Time seems to stand still, for here
30   Is night or twilight all the year.

A very holy hushedness
        Broods here for ever: like a dove
        That, having built its nest above
A quiet place, feels the excess
35   Of calm sufficient, and would fain
Not wake, but drowse on without pain.

And slumbering on its mossy nest
        Haply hath dreams of pleasant Spring;
        And in its vision prunes its wing
40   And takes swift flight, yet is at rest.
Yea, is at rest: and still the calm
Is wrapped around it like a charm.

I would have quiet too in truth,
        And here will sojourn for a while.
45   Lo; I have wandered many a mile,
Till I am foot-sore in my youth.
I will lie down; and quite forget
The doubts and fears that haunt me yet.

My pillow underneath my head
50   Shall be green grass; thick fragrant leaves
        My canopy; the spider weaves
Meet curtains for my narrow bed;
And the dew can but cool my brow
That is so dry and burning now.

55   Ah, would that it could reach my heart,
          And fill the void that is so dry
          And aches and aches;—but what am I
      To shrink from my self-purchased part?
      It is in vain; is all in vain;
60   I must go forth and bear my pain.

      Must bear my pain, till Love shall turn
          To me in pity and come back.
          His footsteps left a smouldering track
      When he went forth, that still doth burn.
65   Oh come again, thou pain divine,
      Fill me and make me wholly thine.

On Keats.

      A garden in a garden: a green spot
          Where all is green: most fitting slumber-place
          For the strong man grown weary of a race
      Soon over. Unto him a goodly lot
5   Hath fallen in fertile ground; there thorns are not,
          But his own daisies: silence, full of grace,
          Surely hath shed a quiet on his face:
      His earth is but sweet leaves that fall and rot.
      What was his record of himself, ere he
10   Went from us? *Here lies one whose name was writ
          In water:* while the chilly shadows flit
              Of sweet Saint Agnes' Eve; while basil springs,
              His name, in every humble heart that sings,
      Shall be a fountain of love, verily.

Have Patience.

      The goblets all are broken,
          The pleasant wine is spilt,
          The songs cease; if thou wilt,
      Listen, and hear truth spoken.

5   We take thought for the morrow,
          And know not we shall see it;
       We look on death with sorrow,
          And cannot flee it.
       Youth passes like the lightning,
10   Not to return again;
       Just for a little bright'ning
          The confines of a plain;
       Gilding the spires, and whitening
          The grave-stones and the slain.

15   Youth passes like the odour
          From the white rose's cup,
          When the hot sun drinks up
       The dew that overflowed her:
       Then life forsakes the petals
20   That had been very fair;
          No beauty lingers there,
             And no bee settles.
       But when the rose is dead,
          And the leaves fallen;
25   And when the earth has spread
          A snow-white pall on;
       The thorn remains, once hidden
          By the green growth above it;
       A darksome guest unbidden,
30   With none to love it.
       Manhood is turbulent,
          And old age tires;
       That, hath no still content,
          This, no desires.
35   The present hath even less
          Joy than the past,
             And more cares fret it:—
       Life is a weariness
          From first to last:—
40   Let us forget it.
       Fill high and deep:—but how?
          The goblets all are broken.

Nay then, have patience now:
   For this is but a token
45 We soon shall have no need
   Of such to cheer us:
The palm-branches, decreed,
And crowns, to be our meed,
   Are very near us.

To Lalla, reading my verses topsy-turvy.

Darling little Cousin,
   With your thoughtful look
Reading topsy-turvy
   From a printed book

5 English hieroglyphics,
   More mysterious
To you, than Egyptian
   Ones would be to us;—

Leave off for a minute
10   Studying, and say
What is the impression
   That those marks convey?

Only solemn silence,
   And a wondering smile:
15 But your eyes are lifted
   Unto mine the while.

In their gaze so steady
   I can surely trace
That a happy spirit
20   Lighteth up your face.

Tender, happy spirit,
   Innocent and pure;
Teaching more than science,
   And than learning more.

25   How should I give answer
       To that asking look?
    Darling little Cousin
       Go back to your book.

    Read on: if you knew it,
30   You have cause to boast:—
    You are much the wisest,
       Though I know the most.

Sonnet.

Some say that love and joy are one: and so
    They are indeed in heaven, but not on earth.
    Our hearts are made too narrow for the girth
Of love, which is infinity; below
5   The portion we can compass may bring woe;
    Of this the Church bears witness from her birth:
    And though a throne in heaven be more than worth
Tears, it *is* pain that makes them overflow.
Think of the utter grief that fell on them
10   Who knew that they should see his face no more,
    When, strong in faith and love, he went before,
Bound in the spirit, to Jerusalem,
    And yet the bitter parting scarcely bore,
Though burning for a martyr's diadem.

The last *Complaint.*

Woe is me! an old man said
Stretched upon his dying bed:
Woe is me! for life is short;
And one hour cannot be bought
5   With great treasure or long thought.
What have all my days been worth?

Weary labour without gain,
Pleasure ending in much pain,
Planting that brought forth no fruit,
10 Tree of life struck at the root,
Were my portion from my birth:
But my cold heart sickeneth
Shrinking from the touch of death;
And I fain would have again
15 Toil and weariness and pain
For a short time more on earth.
Yet the time was troublesome,
And the days lagged slowly on;
Surely it is better so:
20 And I cannot grieve to go
Hence. How fast the shadows come:—
Light and darkness both grow wan:—
Is that fire? it is not heat.
Cover up my face and feet;
25 Stand back; do not speak to me:
I would think how it will be
When the sun is blotted from
My existence, and the worm
Dwells with me as friend with friend
30 For a certain measured term.
But his term will have an end:
Then I shall be quite alone,
Quite alone without a sound;
For no wind beneath the ground
35 Can come jarring bone with bone.
Without eyes I shall behold
Darkness, and shall feel the cold
Without nerves, or brain, or flesh;—
Oh sweet air that blowest fresh;
40 Oh sweet stars that glimmer through
The dim casement;—I shall soon
Have a sod instead of you.
Draw the curtains, while I wake
Who shall sleep; and let me lie

45   In the blackness, till I die;
       For I cannot bear to take
       My last look of the clear moon.

Have you forgotten?

Have you forgotten how one Summer night
    We wandered forth together with the moon,
    While warm winds hummed to us a sleepy tune?
Have you forgotten how you praised both light
5   And darkness; not embarrassed yet not quite
    At ease? and how you said the glare of noon
    Less pleased you than the stars? but very soon
You blushed, and seemed to doubt if you were right.
We wandered far and took no note of time;
10   Till on the air there came the distant call
Of church bells: we turned hastily, and yet
Ere we reached home sounded a second chime.
    But what; have you indeed forgotten all?
Ah how then is it I cannot forget?

A Christmas Carol,
(on the stroke of Midnight.)

Thank God, thank God, we do believe,
Thank God that this is Christmas Eve.
Even as we kneel upon this day,
Even so the ancient legends say
5 Nearly two thousand years ago
The stalled ox knelt, and even so
The ass knelt full of praise which they
Could not express, while we can pray.
Thank God, thank God, for Christ was born
10 Ages ago, as on this morn:
In the snow-season undefiled

God came to earth a little Child;
He put His ancient glory by
To live for us, and then to die.

15   How shall we thank God? how shall we
Thank Him and praise Him worthily?
What will He have Who loved us thus,
What presents will He take from us?
Will He take gold, or precious heap
20   Of gems, or shall we rather steep
The air with incense, or bring myrrh?
What man will be our messenger
To go to Him and ask His Will?
Which having learned we will fulfil
25   Tho' He choose all we most prefer:—
What man will be our messenger?

Thank God, thank God, the Man is found,
Sure-footed, knowing well the ground:
He knows the road, for this the way
30   He travelled once, as on this day.
He is our Messenger; beside,
He is our Door, and Path, and Guide;
He also is our Offering,
He is the Gift that we must bring.
35   Let us kneel down with one accord
And render thanks unto the Lord:
For unto us a Child is born
Upon this happy Christmas morn;
For unto us a Son is given,
40   Firstborn of God and Heir of Heaven.

For Advent.

Sweet sweet sound of distant waters falling
    On a parched and thirsty plain;
Sweet sweet song of soaring skylark, calling
    On the sun to shine again;

5   Perfume of the rose, only the fresher
        For past fertilizing rain;
Pearls amid the sea, a hidden treasure
        For some daring hand to gain;—
        Better, dearer than all these
10   Is the earth beneath the trees:
        Of a much more priceless worth
        Is the old, brown, common earth.

Little snow-white lamb piteously bleating
        For thy mother far away;
15   Saddest, sweetest nightingale retreating
        With thy sorrow from the day;
Weary fawn whom night has overtaken,
        From the herd gone quite astray;
Dove whose nest was rifled and forsaken
20   In the budding month of May;—
        Roost upon the leafy trees;
        Lie on earth and take your ease:
        Death is better far than birth,
        You shall turn again to earth.

25   Listen to the never pausing murmur
        Of the waves that fret the shore:
See the ancient pine that stands the firmer
        For the storm-shock that it bore;
And the moon her silver chalice filling
30   With light from the great sun's store;
And the stars which deck our temple's ceiling
        As the flowers deck its floor;
        Look and hearken while you may,
        For these things shall pass away:
35   All these things shall fail and cease;
        Let us wait the end in peace.

Let us wait the end in peace; for truly
        That shall cease which was before:
Let us see our lamps are lighted, duly
40   Fed with oil, nor wanting more:
Let us pray while yet the Lord will hear us,

For the time is almost o'er;
Yea, the end of all is very near us;
Yea, the Judge is at the door.
45   Let us pray now while we may;
It will be too late to pray
When the quick and dead shall all
Rise at the last trumpet call.

Two Pursuits.

A voice said: "Follow, follow:" and I rose
And followed far into the dreamy night,
Turning my back upon the pleasant light.
It led me where the bluest water flows,
5   And would not let me drink; where the corn grows
I dared not pause, but went uncheered by sight
Or touch; until at length in evil plight
It left me, wearied out with many woes.
Some time I sat as one bereft of sense:
10   But soon another voice from very far
Called: "Follow, follow:" and I rose again.
Now on my night has dawned a blessèd star;
Kind, steady hands my sinking steps sustain,
And will not leave me till I shall go hence.

Looking forward.

Sleep, let me sleep, for I am sick of care;
Sleep, let me sleep, for my pain wearies me.
Shut out the light; thicken the heavy air
With drowsy incense; let a distant stream
5   Of music lull me, languid as a dream,
Soft as the whisper of a Summer sea.

Pluck me no rose that groweth on a thorn,
Nor myrtle white and cold as snow in June,

Fit for a virgin on her marriage morn:
10 But bring me poppies brimmed with sleepy death,
 And ivy choking what it garlandeth,
And primroses that open to the moon.

 Listen, the music swells into a song,
A simple song I loved in days of yore;
15 The echoes take it up and up along
 The hills, and the wind blows it back again.—
 Peace, peace, there is a memory in that strain
Of happy days that shall return no more.

 Oh peace, your music wakeneth old thought,
20 But not old hope that made my life so sweet,
  Only the longing that must end in nought.
 Have patience with me, friends, a little while:
 For soon where you shall dance and sing and smile,
My quickened dust may blossom at your feet.

25 Sweet thought that I may yet live and grow green,
That leaves may yet spring from the withered root,
  And buds and flowers and berries half unseen;
 Then if you haply muse upon the past,
 Say this: Poor child, she hath her wish at last;
30 Barren through life, but in death bearing fruit.

Life hidden.

Roses and lilies grow above the place
 Where she sleeps the long sleep that doth not dream.
If we could look upon her hidden face
 Nor shadow would be there nor garish gleam
5 Of light: her life is lapsing like a stream
That makes no noise but floweth on apace
 Seawards; while many a shade and shady beam
Vary the ripples in their gliding chase.
She doth not see, but knows: she doth not feel,
10 And yet is sensible: she hears no sound,

Yet counts the flight of time and doth not err.
Peace far and near; peace to ourselves and her:
   Her body is at peace in holy ground,
Her spirit is at peace where Angels kneel.

Queen Rose.

The jessamine shows like a star;
   The lilies sway like sceptres slim;
Fair clematis from near and far
   Sets forth its wayward tangled whim;
5   Curved meadowsweet blooms rich and dim;—
But yet a rose is fairer far.

The jessamine is odorous; so
   Maid lilies are, and clematis;
And where tall meadowsweet flowers grow
10   A rare and subtle perfume is;—
   What can there be more choice than these?—
A rose when it doth bud and blow.

Let others choose sweet jessamine,
   Or weave their lily crown aright,
15 And let who love it pluck and twine
   Loose clematis; or draw delight
   From meadowsweet's clustry downy white;—
The rose, the perfect rose be mine.

How one chose.

"Beyond the sea, in a green land
   Where only rivers are;—
Beyond the clouds, in the clear sky
   Close by some quiet star;—
5 Could you not fancy there might be
A home Beloved for you and me?"

"If there were such a home my Friend
   Truly prepared for us
Full of palm branches or of crowns
10   Sun-gemmed and glorious,
How should we reach it? let us cease
From longing; let us be at peace."

"The nightingale sang yestereve;
   A sweet song singeth she:
15 Most sad and without any hope
   And full of memory;
But still methought it seemed to speak
To me of home, and bid me seek."

"The nightingale ceased ere the morn:
20   Her heart could not contain
The passion of her song, but burst
   With the loud throbbing pain.
Now she hath rest which is the best,
And now I too would be at rest."

25 "Last night I watched the mounting moon:
   Her glory was too pale
To shine thro' the black heavy clouds
   That wrapped her like a veil;
And yet with patience she passed thro'
30 The mists and reached the depths of blue."

"And when the road was travelled o'er
   And when the goal was won
A little while and all her light
   Was swallowed by the sun:
35 The weary moon must seek again;
Even so our search would be in vain."

"Yet seek with me. And if our way
   Be long and troublesome,
And if our noon be hot until
40   The chilly shadows come
Of evening;—till those shadows flee
In dawn, think Love it is with me."

"Nay seek alone: I am no mate
   For such as you, in truth:
45 My heart is old before its time;
   Yours yet is in its youth:
This home with pleasures girt about
Seek you, for I am wearied out."

Seeking rest.

My Mother said: The child is changed
   That used to be so still;
All the day long she sings, and sings,
   And seems to think no ill;
5 She laughs as if some inward joy
   Her heart would overfill.

My Sisters said: Now prithee tell
   Thy secret unto us:
Let us rejoice with thee; for all
10   Is surely prosperous,
Thou art so merry: tell us Sweet:
   We had not used thee thus.

My Mother says: What ails the child
   Lately so blythe of cheer?
15 Art sick or sorry? nay, it is
   The Winter of the year;
Wait till the Spring time comes again
   And the sweet flowers appear.

My Sisters say: Come, sit with us,
20   That we may weep with thee:
Show us thy grief that we may grieve:
   Yea, haply, if we see
Thy sorrow, we may ease it; but
   Shall share it certainly.

25 How should I share my pain, who kept
   My pleasure all my own?

My Spring will never come again;
  My pretty flowers have blown
For the last time; I can but sit
30   And think and weep alone.

A Year Afterwards.

Things are so changed since last we met:
Come; I will show you where she lies.
Doubtless the old look fills her eyes,
And the old patient smile is set
5 Upon her mouth: it was even so
When last I saw her stretched and still,
So pale and calm I could not weep:
The steady sweetness did not go
Thro' the long week she lay asleep,
10 Until the dust was heaped on her.
Now many-feathered grasses grow
Above her bosom: come; I will
Show you all this, and we can talk
Going; it is a pleasant walk
15 And the wind makes it pleasanter.

This is the very path that she
So often trod with eager feet
Tho' weary. The dusk branches meet
Above, making green fretted work,
20 The screen between my saint and me.
There, where the softest sunbeams lurk,
Cannot you fancy she may be
Leaning down to me from her rest;
And shaking her long golden hair
25 Thro' the thick branches to my face,
That I may feel she still is mine?—
Is not this wood a pleasant place?
To me the faintest breath of air
Seems here to whisper tenderly
30 That she, mine own, will not forget.

It may be selfishness; and yet
I like to think her joy may not
Be perfected, although divine
In all the glory of the blest,

35 Without me: that the greenest spot
And shadiest, would not suffice,
Without me, even in Paradise.

But we must leave the wood to go
Across the sunny fields of wheat;

40 I used to fancy that the grass
And daisies loved to touch her feet.
This was the way we used to pass
Together; rain nor wind nor snow
Could hinder her, until her strength

45 Failed utterly; and when at length
She was too weak, they put her bed
Close to the window; there she lay
Counting the Church chimes one by one
For many weeks: at last a day

50 Came when her patient watch was done,
And some one told me she was dead.

Now we can see the Church tower; look,
Where the old flaky yew trees stand.
There is a certain shady nook

55 Among them, where she used to sit
When weary: I have held her hand
So often there: one day she said
That sometimes, when we sat so, she
Could fancy what being dead must be,

60 And long for it if shared by me:—
She had no cause for dreading it,
And never once conceived my dread.

This path leads to the Western door
Where the sun casts his latest beam,

65 And hard beside it is her grave.
I sowed those grasses there that wave
Like down, but would sow nothing more,

No flowers, as if her resting place
Could want for sweetness; where she is
70   Is sweetest of all sweetnesses.
If you look closely, you can trace
A Cross formed by the grass, above
Her head: and sometimes I could dream
She sees the Cross, and feels the love
75   That planted it; and prays that I
May come and share her hidden rest;
May even lie where she doth lie,
With the same turf above my breast,
And the same stars and silent sky.

Two thoughts of Death.

1.

Her heart that loved me once is rottenness
   Now and corruption; and her life is dead
   That was to have been one with mine she said.
The earth must lie with such a cruel stress
5   On her eyes where the white lids used to press;
   Foul worms fill up her mouth so sweet and red;
   Foul worms are underneath her graceful head.
Yet these, being born of her from nothingness
These worms are certainly flesh of her flesh.—
10   How is it that the grass is rank and green,
And the dew dropping rose is brave and fresh
Above what was so sweeter far than they?
Even as her beauty hath passed quite away
   Their's too shall be as tho' it had not been.

2.

15   So I said underneath the dusky trees:
   But because I still loved her memory
   I stooped to pluck a pale anemone
And lo! my hand lighted upon heartsease

Not fully blown: while with new life from these
20   Fluttered a starry moth that rapidly
         Rose toward the sun: sunlighted flashed on me
Its wings that seemed to throb like heart pulses.
Far far away it flew far out of sight,
         From earth and flowers of earth it passed away
25   As tho' it flew straight up into the light.
         Then my heart answered me: Thou fool to say
         That she is dead whose night is turned to day,
And whose day shall no more turn back to night.

Three Moments.

The Child said: "Pretty bird
"Come back and play with me."
The bird said: "It is in vain,
"For I am free.
5   "I am free, I will not stay,
"But will fly far away,
"In the woods to sing and play,
"Far away, far away."
The Child sought her Mother:
10   "I have lost my bird;" said she
Weeping bitterly:
But the Mother made her answer,
Half sighing pityingly,
Half smiling cheerily:
15   "Tho' thy bird come nevermore
"Do not weep;
"Find another playfellow
"Child, and keep
"Tears for future pain more deep."

20   "Sweet rose do not wither,"
The Girl said.
But a blight had touched its heart
And it drooped its crimson head.
In the morning it had opened

25   Full of life and bloom,
       But the leaves fell one by one
       Till the twilight gloom.
       One by one the leaves fell
       By summer winds blown from their stem;
30   They fell upon the dewy earth
       Which nourished once now tainted them.
       Again the young Girl wept
       And sought her Mother's ear:
       "My rose is dead so full of grace,
35   "The very rose I meant to place
       "In the wreath that I wear."
       "Nay, never weep for such as this;"
       The Mother answered her:
       "But weave another crown, less fair
40   "Perhaps, but fitter for thy hair.
       "And keep thy tears," the Mother said:
       "For something heavier."

       The Woman knelt; but did not pray
       Nor weep nor cry; she only said:
45   "Not this, not this:" and clasped her hands
       Against her heart and bowed her head
       While the great struggle shook the bed.
       "Not this, not this:" tears did not fall:
       "Not this:" it was all
50   She could say; no sobs would come;
       The mortal grief was almost dumb.—
       At length when it was over, when
       She knew it was and would be so,
       She cried: "Oh Mother, where are they,
55   "The tears that used to flow
       "So easily? one single drop
       "Might save my reason now, or stop
       "My heart from breaking. Blessed tears
       "Wasted in former years!"
60   Then the grave Mother made reply:
       "Oh Daughter mine be of good cheer,
       "Rejoicing thou canst shed no tear.

"Thy pain is almost over now.
"Once more thy heart shall throb with pain,
65 "But then shall never throb again.
"Oh happy thou who canst not weep,
"Oh happy thou!"

Once.

She was whiter than the ermine
      That half shadowed neck and hand,
And her tresses were more golden
      Than their golden band;
5   Snowy ostrich plumes she wore
Yet I almost loved her more
In the simple time before.

Then she plucked the stately lilies
      Knowing not she was more fair,
10 And she listened to the skylark
      In the morning air.
Then, a kerchief all her crown,
She looked for the acorns brown,
Bent their bough and shook them down.

15 Then she thought of Christmas holly
      And of maybloom in sweet May;
Then she loved to pick the cherries
      And to turn the hay.
She was humble then and meek,
20 And the blush upon her cheek
Told of much she could not speak.

Now she is a noble lady,
      With calm voice not overloud;
Very courteous in her action,
25   Yet you think her proud;
Much too haughty to affect;
Too indifferent to direct,
Or be angry, or suspect;
Doing all from self-respect.

Three Nuns.

1.

"Sospira questo core
  E non so dir perchè."

Shadow, shadow on the wall
  Spread thy shelter over me;
Wrap me with a heavy pall,
  With the dark that none may see.
5   Fold thyself around me; come:
Shut out all the troublesome
Noise of life; I would be dumb.

Shadow thou hast reached my feet,
  Rise and cover up my head;
10 Be my stainless winding sheet,
  Buried before I am dead.
Lay thy cool upon my breast:
Once I thought that joy was best,
Now I only care for rest.

15 By the grating of my cell
  Sings a solitary bird;
Sweeter than the vesper bell,
  Sweetest song was ever heard.*
Sing upon thy living tree:
20 Happy echoes answer thee,
Happy songster, sing to me.

When my yellow hair was curled
  Though men saw and called me fair,
I was weary in the world
25   Full of vanity and care.
Gold was left behind, curls shorn
When I came here; that same morn
Made a bride no gems adorn.

Here wrapped in my spotless veil,
30   Curtained from intruding eyes,

*"Sweetest eyes were ever seen." E. B. Browning.

I whom prayers and fasts turn pale
    Wait the flush of Paradise.
But the vigil is so long
My heart sickens:—sing thy song,
35   Blithe bird that canst do no wrong.

Sing on, making me forget
    Present sorrow and past sin.
Sing a little longer yet:
    Soon the matins will begin;
40   And I must turn back again
To that aching worse than pain
I must bear and not complain.

Sing, that in thy song I may
    Dream myself once more a child
45   In the green woods far away
    Plucking clematis and wild
Hyacinths, till pleasure grew
Tired, yet so was pleasure too,
Resting with no work to do.

50   In the thickest of the wood,
    I remember, long ago
How a stately oak tree stood,
    With a sluggish pool below
Almost shadowed out of sight.
55   On the waters dark as night,
Water-lilies lay like light.

There, while yet a child, I thought
    I could live as in a dream,
Secret, neither found nor sought:
60   Till the lilies on the stream,
Pure as virgin purity,
Would seem scarce too pure for me:—
Ah, but that can never be.

2.

"Sospirerà d'amore,
Ma non lo dice a me."

I loved him, yes, where was the sin?
65   I loved him with my heart and soul.
           But I pressed forward to no goal,
There was no prize I strove to win.
Show me my sin that I may see:—
Throw the first stone, thou Pharisee.

70   I loved him, but I never sought
           That he should know that I was fair.
           I prayed for him; was my sin prayer?
I sacrificed, he never bought.
He nothing gave, he nothing took;
75   We never bartered look for look.

My voice rose in the sacred choir,
           The choir of Nuns; do you condemn
           Even if, when kneeling among them,
Faith, zeal and love kindled a fire
80   And I prayed for his happiness
Who knew not? was my error this?

I only prayed that in the end
           His trust and hope may not be vain.
           I prayed not we may meet again:
85   I would not let our names ascend,
No, not to Heaven, in the same breath;
Nor will I join the two in death.

Oh sweet is death; for I am weak
           And weary, and it giveth rest.
90   The Crucifix lies on my breast,
And all night long it seems to speak
Of rest; I hear it through my sleep,
And the great comfort makes me weep.

Oh sweet is death that bindeth up
95   The broken and the bleeding heart.
           The draught chilled, but a cordial part

Lurked at the bottom of the cup;
And for my patience will my Lord
Give an exceeding great reward.

100 Yea, the reward is almost won,
         A crown of glory and a palm.
         Soon I shall sing the unknown psalm;
Soon gaze on light, not on the sun;
And soon, with surer faith, shall pray
105 For him, and cease not night nor day.

My life is breaking like a cloud;
         God judgeth not as man doth judge.—
         Nay, bear with me; you need not grudge
This peace; the vows that I have vowed
110 Have all been kept: Eternal Strength
Holds me, though mine own fails at length.

Bury me in the Convent ground
         Among the flowers that are so sweet;
         And lay a green turf at my feet,
115 Where thick trees cast a gloom around.
At my head let a Cross be, white
Through the long blackness of the night.

Now kneel and pray beside my bed
         That I may sleep being free from pain:
120   And pray that I may wake again
After His Likeness, Who hath said
(Faithful is He Who promiseth,)
We shall be satisfied Therewith.

3.

"Rispondimi, cor mio,
    Perchè sospiri tu?
Risponde: Voglio Iddio,
    Sospiro per Gesù."

My heart is as a freeborn bird
125   Caged in my cruel breast,
That flutters, flutters evermore,

Nor sings, nor is at rest.
But beats against the prison bars,
   As knowing its own nest
130 Far off beyond the clouded West.

My soul is as a hidden fount
   Shut in by clammy clay,
That struggles with an upward moan;
   Striving to force its way
135 Up through the turf, over the grass,
   Up, up into the day,
Where twilight no more turneth grey.

Oh for the grapes of the True Vine
   Growing in Paradise,
140 Whose tendrils join the Tree of Life
   To that which maketh wise.
Growing beside the Living Well
   Whose sweetest waters rise
Where tears are wiped from tearful eyes.

145 Oh for the waters of that Well
   Round which the Angels stand.
Oh for the Shadow of the Rock
   On my heart's weary land.
Oh for the Voice to guide me when
150   I turn to either hand,
Guiding me till I reach Heaven's strand.

Thou World from which I am come out,
   Keep all thy gems and gold;
Keep thy delights and precious things,
155   Thou that art waxing old.
My heart shall beat with a new life,
   When thine is dead and cold:
When thou dost fear I shall be bold.

When Earth shall pass away with all
160   Her pride and pomp of sin,
The City builded without hands
   Shall safely shut me in.

All the rest is but vanity
    Which others strive to win:
165 Where their hopes end my joys begin.

I will not look upon a rose
    Though it is fair to see:
The flowers planted in Paradise
    Are budding now for me.
170 Red roses like love visible
    Are blowing on their tree,
Or white like virgin purity.

I will not look unto the sun
    Which setteth night by night:
175 In the untrodden courts of Heaven
    My crown shall be more bright.
Lo, in the New Jerusalem
    Founded and built aright
My very feet shall tread on light.

180 With foolish riches of this World
    I have bought treasure, where
Nought perisheth: for this white veil
    I gave my golden hair;
I gave the beauty of my face
185   For vigils, fasts and prayer;
I gave all for this Cross I bear.

My heart trembled when first I took
    The vows which must be kept;
At first it was a weariness
190   To watch when once I slept.
The path was rough and sharp with thorns;
    My feet bled as I stepped;
The Cross was heavy and I wept.

While still the names rang in mine ears
195   Of daughter, sister, wife;
The outside world still looked so fair
    To my weak eyes, and rife

With beauty; my heart almost failed;
    Then in the desperate strife
200 I prayed, as one who prays for life,

Until I grew to love what once
    Had been so burdensome.
So now when I am faint, because
    Hope deferred seems to numb
205 My heart, I yet can plead; and say
    Although my lips are dumb:
"The Spirit and the Bride say, Come."

Song.

We buried her among the flowers
    At falling of the leaf,
And choked back all our tears; her joy
    Could never be our grief.

5 She lies among the living flowers
    And grass, the only thing
That perishes;—or is it that
    Our Autumn was her Spring?

Doubtless, if we could see her face,
10   The smile is settled there
Which almost broke our hearts, when last
    We knelt by her in prayer.

When with tired eyes and failing breath
    And hands crossed on her breast
15 Perhaps she saw her Guardian spread
    His wings above her rest.

So she sleeps hidden in the flowers:
    But yet a little while
And we shall see her wake, and rise
20   Fair, with the selfsame smile.

The Watchers.

She fell asleep among the flowers
In the sober Autumn hours.

Three there are about her bed,
At her side and feet and head.

5   At her head standeth the Cross
For which all else she counted loss:

Still and steadfast at her feet
Doth her Guardian Angel sit:

Prayers of truest love abide
10   Wrapping her on every side.

The Holy Cross standeth alone,
Beneath the white moon, whitest stone.

Evil spirits come not near
Its shadow, shielding from all fear;

15   Once she bore it in her breast,
Now it certifies her rest.

Humble violets grow around
Its base, sweetening the grassy ground,

Leaf-hidden; so she hid from praise
20   Of men her pious holy ways.

Higher about it, twining close,
Clingeth a crimson thorny rose;

So from her heart's good seed of love
Thorns sprang below, flowers spring above.

25   Tho' yet his vigil doth not cease,
Her Angel sits in perfect peace,

With white folded wings; for she
He watches, now is pure as he.

He watches with his loving eyes
30   For the day when she shall rise;

When full of glory and of grace
She shall behold him face to face.

Tho' she is safe for ever, yet
Human love doth not forget;

35　But prays that in her deep
Grave she may sleep a blessed sleep,

Till when time and the world are past
She may find mercy at the last.

So these three do hedge her in
40　From sorrow as death does from sin.

So freed from earthly taint and pain
May they all meet in Heaven.　Amen.

Annie.

Annie is fairer than her kith
　And kinder than her kin;
Her eyes are like the open heaven
　Holy and pure from sin;
5　Her heart is like an ordered house
　Good fairies harbour in;
Oh happy he who wins the love
　That I can never win.

Her sisters stand as hyacinths
10　　Around the perfect rose:
They bloom and open to the full,
　My bud will scarce unclose;
They are for every butterfly
　That comes and sips and goes,
15　My bud hides in the tender green
　Most sweet and hardly shows.

Oh cruel kindness in soft eyes
　That are no more than kind,
On which I gaze my heart away
20　　Till the tears make me blind.

How is it others find the way
    That I can never find
To make her laugh that sweetest laugh
    Which leaves all else behind?

25 Her hair is like the golden corn
    A low wind breathes upon;
Or like the golden harvest moon
    When all the mists are gone;
Or like a stream with golden sands
30   On which the sun has shone
Day after day in summer time
    Ere autumn leaves are wan.

I will not tell her that I love
    Lest she should turn away
35 With sorrow in her tender heart
    Which now is light and gay.
I will not tell her that I love
    Lest she should turn and say
That we must meet no more again
40   For many a weary day.

A Dirge.

She was as sweet as violets in the Spring,
    As fair as any rose in Summer time:
      But frail are roses in their prime
    And violets in their blossoming.
5 Even so was she:
    And now she lies,
      The earth upon her fast closed eyes,
Dead in the darkness silently.

The sweet Spring violets never bud again,
10   The roses bloom and perish in a morn:
      They see no second quickening lying lorn;
    Their beauty dies as tho' in vain.
Must she die so
    For evermore,

15   Cold as the sand upon the shore,
        As passionless for joy and woe?—

      Nay, she is worth much more than flowers that fade
        And yet shall be made fair with purple fruit;
          Branch of the Living Vine, Whose Root
20   From all eternity is laid.
      Another Sun
        Than this of our's,
        Has withered up indeed her flowers
      But ripened her grapes every one.

Song.

      It is not for her even brow
        And shining yellow hair,
      But it is for her tender eyes
        I think my love so fair;
5   Her telltale eyes that smile and weep
      As frankly as they wake and sleep.

      It is not for her rounded cheek
        I love and fain would win,
      But it is for the blush that comes
10   Straight from the heart within;
      The honest blush of maiden shame
      That blushes without thought of blame.

      So in my dreams I never hear
        Her song, although she sings
15   As if a choir of spirits swept
        From earth with throbbing wings;
      I only hear the simple voice
      Whose love makes many hearts rejoice.

A Dream.

      Oh for my love, my only love,
        Oh for my lost love far away!—

Oh that the grass were green above
   Her head or mine this weary day:—
5   The grass green in the morning grey.

She lies down in a foreign land
   And in a foreign land doth rise.
I cannot hold her by the hand;
   I cannot read her speaking eyes
10   That turned mere spoken words to lies.

This is the bough she leaned upon
   And watched the rose deep western sky,
For the last sun rays almost gone:
   I did not hear the wind pass by,
15   Nor stream; I only heard her sigh.

I saw the tears that did not fall,
   I saw the blush upon her cheek,
The trembling hand so white and small:
   She did not speak, I could not speak:—
20   Oh that strong love should make us weak.

Therefore we parted as we met,
   She on her way, and I on mine.
I think her tender heart was set
   On holier things and more Divine:—
25   We parted thus and gave no sign.

Oh that the grass were green above
   Her head or mine; so I could pray
In certain faith for her my love,
   Unchanging, all the night and day:
30   Most near altho' most far away.

"A fair World tho' a fallen."———

You tell me that the world is fair, in spite
   Of the old fall; and that I should not turn
   So to the grave, and let my spirit yearn
After the quiet of the long last night.

5 Have I then shut mine eyes against the light,
    Grief-deafened lest my spirit should discern?
    Yet how could I keep silence when I burn?
And who can give me comfort?—hear the right.
Have patience with the weak and sick at heart:
10   Bind up the wounded with a tender touch.
      Comfort the sad, tear-blinded as they go:—
For tho' I failed to choose the better part,
    Were it a less unutterable woe
If we should come to love this world too much?—

Advent.

"Come," Thou dost say to Angels,
    To blessed Spirits, "Come";
"Come," to the Lambs of Thine Own flock,
    Thy little Ones, "Come home."

5 "Come," from the many-mansioned house
    The gracious word is sent,
"Come," from the ivory palaces
    Unto the Penitent.

O Lord, restore us deaf and blind,
10   Unclose our lips tho' dumb;
Then say to us, "I come with speed,"
    And we will answer, "Come."

All Saints.

They have brought gold and spices to my King,
    Incense and precious stuffs and ivory;
O holy Mother mine, what can I bring
    That so my Lord may deign to look on me?
5 They sing a sweeter song than I can sing,
    All crowned and glorified exceedingly;
I, bound on earth, weep for my trespassing,
    They sing the song of love in Heaven, set free.

Then answered me my Mother, and her voice,
10   Spake to my heart, yea, answered in my heart:
Sing, saith He, to the Heavens, to Earth, rejoice;
Thou, also, lift thy heart to Him above;
    He seeks not thine, but thee, such as thou art,
For lo! His banner over thee is Love.

"Eye hath not seen."

Our feet shall tread upon the stars
    Less bright than we.
The everlasting shore shall bound
    A fairer sea
5   Than that which cold
Now glitters in the sun like gold.

Oh good, oh blest: but who shall say
    How fair, how fair,
Is the Light-region where no cloud
10   Darkens the air,
    Where weary eyes
Rest on the green of Paradise?

There cometh not the wind, nor rain,
    Nor sun, nor snow;
15 The trees of Knowledge and of Life
    Bud there and blow,
    Their leaves and fruit
Fed from an undecaying root.

There Angels flying to and fro
20   Are not more white
Than Penitents some while ago,
    Now Saints in Light:
    Once soiled and sad;
Cleansed now and crowned, fulfilled and glad.

25 Now yearning thro' the perfect rest
    Perhaps they gaze
Earthwards upon their best beloved

In all earth's ways:
   Longing, but not
30 With pain, as used to be their lot.

The hush of that beatitude
   Is ages long,
Sufficing Virgins, Prophets, Saints,
   Till the new song
35   Shall be sent up
From lips which drained the bitter cup.

If but the thought of Paradise
   Gives joy on earth,
What shall it be to enter there
40   Thro' second birth?
   To find once more
Our dearest treasure gone before?

To find the Shepherd of the Sheep,
   The Lamb once slain,
45 Who leads His Own by living streams.
   Never again
   To thirst, or need
Aught in green pastures where they feed.

But from the Altar comes a cry
50   Awful and strong
From martyred Saints: How long, they say,
   O Lord, how long
   Holy and True,
Shall vengeance for our blood be due?

55 Then the Lord gives them robes of white;
   And bids them stay
In patience till the time be full
   For the last day:
   The day of dread
60 When the last sentence shall be said.

When heaven and earth shall flee away;
   And the great deep
Shall render up her dead, and earth

Her sons that sleep;
65   And day of grace
Be hid for ever from Thy Face.

Oh hide us till Thy wrath be past,
Our grief, our shame,
With Peter and with Magdalene
70   And him whose name
No record tells
Who by Thy promise with Thee dwells.

St. Elizabeth of Hungary.

When if ever life is sweet,
Save in heart in all a child,
A fair virgin undefiled
Knelt she at her Saviour's feet;
5   While she laid her royal crown,
Thinking it too mean a thing
For a solemn offering,
Careless on the cushions down.

Fair she was as any rose,
10   But more pale than lilies white,
Her eyes full of deep repose
Seemed to see beyond our sight.
Hush, she is a holy thing:
Hush, her soul is in her eyes
15   Seeking far in Paradise
For her Light, her Love, her King.

Moonshine.

Fair the sun riseth,
Bright as bright can be,
Fair the sun shineth
On a fair fair sea.

5 "Across the water
   "Wilt thou come with me,
  "Miles and long miles, love,
   "Over the salt sea?"—

  "If thou wilt hold me
10   "Truly by the hand,
  "I will go with thee
   "Over sea and sand.

  "If thou wilt hold me
   "That I shall not fall,
15 "I will go with thee,
   "Love, in spite of all."

  Fair the moon riseth
   On her heavenly way
  Making the waters
20   Fairer than by day.

  A little vessel
   Rocks upon the sea,
  Where stands a maiden
   Fair as fair can be.

25 Her smile rejoices
   Though her mouth is mute,
  She treads the vessel
   With her little foot.

  Truly he holds her
30   Faithful to his pledge,
  Guiding the vessel
   From the water's edge.

  Fair the moon saileth
   With her pale fair light,
35 Fair the girl gazeth
   Out into the night.

  Saith she: "Like silver
   "Shines thy hair, not gold;"—

Saith she: "I shiver
40   "In thy steady hold.

"Love," she saith weeping,
    "Loose thy hold awhile,
"My heart is freezing
    "In thy freezing smile."

45 The moon is hidden
    By a silver cloud,
Fair as a halo
    Or a maiden's shroud.

No more beseeching,
50   Ever on they go:
The vessel rocketh
    Softly to and fro;

And still he holds her
    That she shall not fall,
55 Till pale mists whiten
    Dimly over all.

Onward and onward,
    Far across the sea;
Onward and onward,
60   Pale as pale can be;

Onward and onward,
    Ever hand in hand,
From sun and moon light
    To another land.

"The Summer is ended."

Wreathe no more lilies in my hair,
For I am dying, Sister sweet:
Or if you will for the last time
    Indeed, why make me fair
5   Once for my windingsheet.

Pluck no more roses for my breast,
For I like them fade in my prime:
Or if you will, why pluck them still
    That they may share my rest
10   Once more, for the last time.

Weep not for me when I am gone,
Dear tender one, but hope and smile:
Or if you cannot choose but weep
    A little while, weep on
15   Only a little while.

"I look for the Lord."

Our wealth has wasted all away,
    Our pleasures have found wings;
The night is long until the day,
    Lord, give us better things:
5 A ray of light in thirsty night
    And secret water springs.

Our love is dead, or sleeps, or else
    Is hidden from our eyes:
Our silent love, while no man tells
10   Or if it lives or dies.
Oh give us love, O Lord, above
    In changeless Paradise.

Our house is left us desolate,
    Even as Thy word hath said.
15 Before our face the way is great,
    Around us are the dead:
Oh guide us, save us from the grave,
    As Thou Thy saints hast led.

Lead us where pleasures evermore
20   And wealth indeed are placed,
And home on an eternal shore,
    And love that cannot waste;

Where Joy Thou art unto the heart,
    And Sweetness to the taste.

Song.

I have loved you for long long years Ellen,
    On you has my heart been set;
I have loved you for long patient years,
    But you do not love me yet.

5   Oh that the sun that rose that day
    Had never and never set,
When I wooed and you did not turn away,
    Tho' you could not love me yet.

I lay lands and gold at your feet Ellen,
10   At your feet a coronet,
I lay a true heart at your feet Ellen,
    But you do not love me yet.

Oh when I too lie dead at your feet,
    And in death my heart is set,
15   Will you love me then, cold proud Ellen,
    Tho' you will not love me yet?—

A Discovery.

"I thought your search was over."—"So I thought."—
    "But you are seeking still."—"Yes, even so:
    Still seeking in mine own despite below
That which in Heaven alone is found unsought;
5 Still spending for that thing which is not bought."—
    "Then chase no more this shifting empty show."—
    "Amen: so bid a drowning man forego
The straw he clutches; will he so be taught?
You have a home where peace broods like a dove
10   Screened from the weary world's loud discontent,

You have home here, you wait for home above:
    I must unlearn the pleasant ways I went,
Must learn another hope, another love,
    And sigh indeed for home in banishment."—

From the Antique.

The wind shall lull us yet,
    The flowers shall spring above us;
And those who hate forget,
    And those forget who love us.

5   The pulse of hope shall cease,
    Of joy and of regretting:
We twain shall sleep in peace,
    Forgotten and forgetting.

For us no sun shall rise,
10   Nor wind rejoice, nor river,
Where we with fast closed eyes
    Shall sleep and sleep for ever.

"The heart knoweth its own bitterness."

Weep yet a while
Weep till that day shall dawn when thou shalt smile
Watch till the day
When all save only Love shall pass away.

5   Weep, sick and lonely,
    Bow thy heart to tears,
For none shall guess the secret
    Of thy griefs and fears.
Weep, till the day dawn,
10   Refreshing dew:
Weep till the spring;
For genial showers

Bring up the flowers,
And thou shalt sing
15   In summer time of blossoming.

Heart sick and silent,
    Weep and watch in pain.
Weep for hope perished,
    Not to live again;
20   Weep for love's hope and fear
    And passion vain.
Watch till the day
When all save only love shall pass away.

Then love rejoicing
25   Shall forget to weep;
Shall hope or fear no more,
    Or watch, or sleep,
But only love and cease not,
    Deep beyond deep.
30   Now we sow love in tears,
    But then shall reap:
Have patience as the Lord's Own flock of sheep:
Have patience with His Love,
Who died below, Who lives for thee above.

"To what purpose is this waste?"

A windy shell singing upon the shore:
A lily budding in a desert place;
Blooming alone
With no companion
5   To praise its perfect perfume and its grace:
A rose crimson and blushing at the core,
Hedged in with thorns behind it and before:
A fountain in the grass,
Whose shadowy waters pass
10   Only to nourish birds and furnish food
For squirrels of the wood:

An oak deep in the forest's heart, the house
Of black-eyed tiny mouse;
Its strong roots fit for fuel roofing in
15 The hoarded nuts, acorns and grains of wheat;
Shutting them from the wind and scorching heat,
And sheltering them when the rains begin:

A precious pearl deep buried in the sea
Where none save fishes be:
20 The fullest merriest note
For which the skylark strains his silver throat,
Heard only in the sky
By other birds that fitfully
Chase one another as they fly:
25 The ripest plum down tumbled to the ground
By southern winds most musical of sound,
But by no thirsty traveller found:
Honey of wild bees in their ordered cells
Stored, not for human mouths to taste:—
30 I said, smiling superior down: What waste
Of good, where no man dwells.

This I said on a pleasant day in June
Before the sun had set, tho' a white moon
Already flaked the quiet blue
35 Which not a star looked thro.'
But still the air was warm, and drowsily
It blew into my face:
So since that same day I had wandered deep
Into the country, I sought out a place
40 For rest beneath a tree,
And very soon forgot myself in sleep:
Not so mine own words had forgotten me.
Mine eyes were opened to behold
All hidden things,
45 And mine ears heard all secret whisperings:
So my proud tongue that had been bold
To carp and to reprove,
Was silenced by the force of utter Love.

All voices of all things inanimate
50 Join with the song of Angels and the song
Of blessed Spirits, chiming with
Their Hallelujahs. One wind wakeneth
Across the sleeping sea, crisping along
The waves, and brushes thro' the great
55 Forests and tangled hedges, and calls out
Of rivers a clear sound,
And makes the ripe corn rustle on the ground,
And murmurs in a shell;
Till all their voices swell
60 Above the clouds in one loud hymn
Joining the song of Seraphim,
Or like pure incense circle round about
The walls of Heaven, or like a well-spring rise
In shady Paradise.

65 A lily blossoming unseen
Holds honey in its silver cup
Whereon a bee may sup,
Till being full she takes the rest
And stores it in her waxen nest:
70 While the fair blossom lifted up
On its one stately stem of green
Is type of her, the Undefiled,
Arrayed in white, whose eyes are mild
As a white dove's, whose garment is
75 Blood-cleansed from all impurities
And earthly taints,
Her robe the righteousness of Saints.

And other eyes than our's
Were made to look on flowers,
80 Eyes of small birds and insects small:
The deep sun-blushing rose
Round which the prickles close
Opens her bosom to them all.
The tiniest living thing
85 That soars on feathered wing,

Or crawls among the long grass out of sight,
Has just as good a right
To its appointed portion of delight
As any King.

90   Why should we grudge a hidden water stream
To birds and squirrels while we have enough?
As if a nightingale should cease to sing
Lest we should hear, or finch leafed out of sight
Warbling its fill in summer light;
95   As if sweet violets in the spring
Should cease to blow, for fear our path should seem
Less weary or less rough.

So every oak that stands a house
For skilful mouse,
100   And year by year renews its strength,
Shakes acorns from a hundred boughs
Which shall be oaks at length.

Who hath weighed the waters and shall say
What is hidden in the depths from day?
105   Pearls and precious stones and golden sands,
Wondrous weeds and blossoms rare,
Kept back from human hands,
But good and fair,
A silent praise as pain is silent prayer.
110   A hymn, an incense rising toward the skies,
As our whole life should rise;
An offering without stint from earth below,
Which Love accepteth so.

Thus is it with a warbling bird,
115   With fruit bloom-ripe and full of seed,
With honey which the wild bees draw
From flowers, and store for future need
By a perpetual law.
We want the faith that hath not seen
120   Indeed, but hath believed His truth
Who witnessed that His work was good:

So we pass cold to age from youth.
Alas for us: for we have heard
And known, but have not understood.

125 O earth, earth, earth, thou yet shalt bow
Who art so fair and lifted up,
Thou yet shalt drain the bitter cup.
Men's eyes that wait upon thee now,
All eyes shall see thee lost and mean,
130 Exposed and valued at thy worth,
While thou shalt stand ashamed and dumb.—
Ah, when the Son of Man shall come,
Shall He find faith upon the earth?—

Next of Kin.

The shadows gather round me, while you are in the sun;
My day is almost ended, but yours is just begun:
The winds are singing to us both and the streams are
                singing still,
And they fill your heart with music, but mine they cannot
                fill.

5   Your home is built in sunlight, mine in another day;
Your home is close at hand, sweet friend, but mine is far
                away:
Your bark is in the haven where you fain would be;
I must launch out into the deep, across the unknown sea.

You, white as dove or lily or spirit of the light;
10   I, stained and cold and glad to hide in the cold dark night:
You, joy to many a loving heart and light to many eyes;
I, lonely in the knowledge earth is full of vanities.

Yet when your day is over, as mine is nearly done,
And when your race is finished, as mine is almost run,
15   You, like me, shall cross your hands and bow your graceful
                head;
Yea, we twain shall sleep together in an equal bed.

"Let them rejoice in their beds."

The winds sing to us where we lie,
They sing to us a pleasant song;
Sweeter than song of mortal mouth,
Spice laden from the sunny south.
5   They say: This is not death you die;
This slumber shall not hold you long.

The north winds stir around our rest,
Their whispers speak to us and say:
Sleep yet awhile secure and deep,
10   A little while the blessed sleep;
For your inheritance is best,
And night shall yet bring forth the day.

The western winds are whispering too
Of love, with faith and hope as yet,
15   Of consummation that shall be,
Of fulness as the unfathomed sea,
When all creation shall be new
And day arise that shall not set.

But from the east a word is sent
20   To which all other words are dumb:
Lo, I come quickly, saith the Lord,
Myself thy exceeding great Reward:—
While we with thirsty hearts intent
Answer: Yea, come, Lord Jesus, come.

Portraits.

An easy lazy length of limb,
   Dark eyes and features from the south,
A short-legged meditative pipe
   Set in a supercilious mouth;
5   Ink and a pen and papers laid
   Down on a table for the night,

Beside a semi-dozing man
  Who wakes to go to bed by light.

A pair of brothers brotherly,
10   Unlike and yet how much the same
In heart and high-toned intellect,
    In face and bearing, hope and aim:
Friends of the selfsame treasured friends
    And of one home the dear delight,
15 Beloved of many a loving heart
    And cherished both in mine, good night.

Whitsun Eve.

The white dove cooeth in her downy nest,
Keeping her young ones warm beneath her breast:
The white moon saileth thro' the cool clear sky,
Screened by a tender mist in passing by:
5   The white rose buds, with thorns upon its stem,
All the more precious and more dear for them:
The stream shines silver in the tufted grass,
The white clouds scarcely dim it as they pass:
Deep in the valleys lily cups are white,
10 They send up incense all the holy night:
Our souls are white, made clean in Blood once shed:
White blessed Angels watch around our bed:—
O spotless Lamb of God, still keep us so,
Thou Who wert born for us in time of snow.

What?

Strengthening as secret manna,
Fostering as clouds above,
Kind as a hovering dove,
Full as a plenteous river,

5   Our glory and our banner
       For ever and for ever.

       Dear as a dying cadence
       Of music in the drowsy night;
       Fair as the flowers which maidens
10   Pluck for an hour's delight,
       And then forget them quite.

       Gay as a cowslip meadow
       Fresh opening to the sun
       When new day is begun;
15   Soft as a sunny shadow
       When day is almost done.

       Glorious as purple twilight,
       Pleasant as budding tree,
       Untouched as any islet
20   Shrined in an unknown sea;
       Sweet as a fragrant rose amid the dew;—
       As sweet, as fruitless too.

       A bitter dream to wake from,
       But oh how pleasant while we dream;
25   A poisoned fount to take from,
       But oh how sweet the stream.

A Pause.

       They made the chamber sweet with flowers and leaves,
           And the bed sweet with flowers on which I lay;
           While my soul, love-bound, loitered on its way.
       I did not hear the birds about the eaves,
5   Nor hear the reapers talk among the sheaves:
           Only my soul kept watch from day to day,
           My thirsty soul kept watch for one away:—
       Perhaps he loves, I thought, remembers, grieves.
       At length there came the step upon the stair,
10   Upon the lock the old familiar hand:

Then first my spirit seemed to scent the air
　　Of Paradise; then first the tardy sand
Of time ran golden; and I felt my hair
　　Put on a glory, and my soul expand.

Holy Innocents.

Sleep, little Baby, sleep,
　　The holy Angels love thee,
And guard thy bed and keep
　　A blessed watch above thee.
5　No spirit can come near
　　Nor evil beast to harm thee;
Sleep, Sweet, devoid of fear
　　Where nothing need alarm thee.

The Love Which doth not sleep,
10　　The eternal Arms surround thee;
The Shepherd of the sheep
　　In perfect love hath found thee.
Sleep thro' the holy night
　　Christ-kept from snare and sorrow
15　Until thou wake to light
　　And love and warmth tomorrow.

"There remaineth therefore a rest for the people of God."

1.

"Ye have forgotten the exhortation"—

Come blessed sleep, most full, most perfect, come;
　　Come sleep, if so I may forget the whole;
　　Forget my body and forget my soul,
Forget how long life is and troublesome.
5　Come happy sleep to soothe my heart or numb,
　　Arrest my weary spirit or control;
　　Till light be dark to me from pole to pole,

And winds and echoes and low songs be dumb.
Come sleep and lap me into perfect calm,
10   Lap me from all the world and weariness:
Come secret sleep that hidest us from harm,
    Safe sheltered in a hidden cool recess:
    Come heavy dreamless sleep, and close and press
Upon mine eyes thy fingers dropping balm.

2.
"Which speaketh unto you as unto children."

15   Art thou so weary then, poor thirsty soul?
    Have patience, in due season thou shalt sleep.
    Mount yet a little while, the path is steep;
Strain yet a little while to reach the goal;
Do battle with thyself, achieve, control:
20   Till night come down with blessed slumber, deep
    As love, and seal thine eyes no more to weep
Thro' long tired vigils while the planets roll.
Have patience, for thou too shalt sleep at length,
    Lapped in the pleasant shade of Paradise.
25   My Hands That bled for thee shall close thine eyes,
    My Heart That bled for thee shall be thy Rest:
I will sustain with everlasting Strength,
    And thou, with John, shalt lie upon my Breast.

Annie.

It's not for earthly bread, Annie,
    And it's not for earthly wine,
And it's not for all thou art, Annie,
    Nor for any gift of thine:
5   It's for other food and other love
    And other gifts I pine.

I long all night and day, Annie,
    In this glorious month of June,
Tho' the roses all are blossoming
10   And the birds are all in tune:

I dream and long all night, Annie,
    Beneath the tender moon.

There is a dearer home than this
    In a land that's far away,
15 And a better crown than cankered gold,
    Or withering leaves of bay:
There's a richer love than thine, Annie,
    Must fill an endless day.

I long to be alone indeed,
20   I long to sleep at last;
To know the lifelong fever
    And sick weariness are past;
To feel the night is come indeed,
    And the gate secure and fast.

25 Oh gate of death, of the blessed night,
    That shall open not again
On this world of shame and sorrow,
    Where slow ages wax and wane,
Where are signs and seasons, days and nights,
30   And mighty winds and rain.

I long to dwell in silence,
    In twilight cool and dim:
It may be sometimes seeing
    Soft gleams of Seraphim;
35 It may be sometimes catching
    Faint echoes of their hymn.

I am tired of all the shows
    And of all the songs of earth;
I am sick of the cold sky overhead,
40   And the cold land of my birth;
I am sick for the home-land of delight
    And love and endless worth.

Is the day wearing toward the west?—
    Far off cool shadows pass,
45 A visible refreshment
    Across the sultry grass;

Far off low mists are mustering,
    A broken shifting mass.

I know there comes a struggle
50   Before the utter calm,
And a searching pain like fire
    Before the healing balm;—
But the pain shall cease, and the struggle cease,
    And we shall take no harm.

55 Doubtless the Angels wonder
    That we can live at ease
While all around is full of change,
    Yea, full of vanities:
They wonder we can think to fill
60   Our hearts with such as these.

Still in the deepest knowledge
    Some depth is left unknown;
Still in the merriest music lurks
    A plaintive undertone;
65 Still with the closest friend some throb
    Of life is felt alone.

But vain it were to linger
    On the race we have to run,
For that which was must be again
70   Till time itself is done;
Yea, there is nothing new we know
    At all beneath the sun.

I am sick for love, and moan
    Like a solitary dove:
75 Love is as deep as hell, Annie,
    And as high as heaven above;
There's nothing in all the world, Annie,
    That can compete with love.

Time's summer breath is sweet, his sands
80   Ebb sparkling as they flow,
Yet some are sick that this should end
    Which is from long ago:—

Are not the fields already white
  To harvest in the glow?—

85 God puts the sickle to the corn
    And reaps it when He will
  From every watered valley
    And from every fruitful hill:
  He holdeth time in His Right Hand,
90   To check or to fulfil.

  There shall come another harvest
    Than was in days of yore:
  The reapers shall be Angels,
    Our God shall purge the floor:—
95 No more seed-time, no more harvest,
    Then for evermore.

  Come, let us kneel together
    Once again love, I and thou;
  We have prayed apart and wept apart,
100   But may weep together now:
  Once we looked back together
    With our hands upon the plough.

  A little while, and we must part
    Again, as on that day:
105 My spirit shall go forth alone
    To tread the untried way;
  Then thou shalt watch alone once more,
    And kneel alone to pray.

  When the shadows thicken round me
110   And the silence grows apace,
  And I cannot hear thy voice, Annie,
    Nor look upon thy face,
  Wilt thou kneel for me and plead for me
    Before the Throne of Grace?—

115 So surely if my spirit
    Hath knowledge while it lies
  In the outer courts of Heaven,
    It shall watch with longing eyes

And pray that thou mayest also come
120   To dwell in Paradise.

Seasons.

In spring time when the leaves are young,
Clear dewdrops gleam like jewels, hung
On boughs the fair birds roost among.

When summer comes with sweet unrest,
5   Birds weary of their mother's breast,
And look abroad and leave the nest.

In autumn ere the waters freeze,
The swallows fly across the seas:—
If we could fly away with these!—

10 In winter when the birds are gone,
The sun himself looks starved and wan,
And starved the snow he shines upon.

Thou sleepest where the lilies fade,
   Thou dwellest where the lilies fade not;
Sweet, when thy earthly part decayed
   Thy heavenly part decayed not.

5   Thou dwellest where the roses blow,
   The crimson roses bud and blossom;
While on thine eyes is heaped the snow,
   The snow upon thy bosom.

I wish I were a little bird
   That out of sight doth soar,
I wish I were a song once heard
   But often pondered o'er,
5   Or shadow of a lily stirred
   By wind upon the floor,
Or echo of a loving word

Worth all that went before,
Or memory of a hope deferred
10   That springs again no more.

(Two parted.)

"Sing of a love lost and forgotten,
   "Sing of a joy finished and o'er,
"Sing of a heart core-cold and rotten,
   "Sing of a hope springing no more."—
5   —"Sigh for a heart aching and sore."—

"I was most true and my own love betrayed me,
   "I was most true and she would none of me.
"Was it the cry of the world that dismayed thee?
   "Love, I had bearded the wide world for thee."
10   —"Hark to the sorrowful sound of the sea."—

"Still in my dreams she comes tender and gracious,
   "Still in my dreams love looks out of her eyes:
"Oh that the love of a dream were veracious,
   "Or that thus dreaming I might not arise!"
15   —"Oh for the silence that stilleth all sighs."—

All night I dream you love me well,
   All day I dream that you are cold:
Which is the dream? ah, who can tell,
   Ah would that it were told.

5 So I should know my certain doom,
   Know all the gladness or the pain;
So pass into the dreamless tomb,
   Or never doubt again.

(For Rosaline's Album.)

Do you hear the low winds singing,
   And streams singing on their bed?—

Very distant bells are ringing
   In a chapel for the dead:—
5   Death-pale better than life-red.

Mother, come to me in rest,
   And bring little May to see.—
Shall I bid no other guest?—
Seven slow nights have passed away
10   Over my forgotten clay:
     None must come save you and she.

Care flieth,
   Hope and fear together,
Love dieth
In the Autumn weather.

5   For a friend
     Even care is pleasant;
When fear doth end
     Hope is no more present:
Autumn silences the turtle dove;—
10   In blank Autumn who could speak of love?

(Epitaph.)

A slave yet wearing on my head a crown,
A captive from whose eyes no tears ran down,
Bound with no chain, compelled to do no work,
I fell a victim to the jealous Turk.

The P.R.B.

The P.R.B. is in its decadence:—
for Woolner in Australia cooks his chops;
And Hunt is yearning for the land of Cheops;
D. G. Rossetti shuns the vulgar optic;
5   While William M. Rossetti merely lops

His B.s in English disesteemed as Coptic;
Calm Stephens in the twilight smokes his pipe
But long the dawning of his public day;
And he at last, the champion, great Millais
10   Attaining academic opulence
Winds up his signature with A.R.A.:—
So rivers merge in the perpetual sea,
So luscious fruit must fall when over ripe,
And so the consummated P.R.B.

Seasons.

Crocuses and snowdrops wither,
Violets primroses together,
Fading with the fading spring
Before a fuller blossoming.

5   O sweet summer pass not soon,
Stay awhile the harvest moon;
O sweetest summer do not go,
For autumn's next and next the snow.

When autumn comes the days are drear,
10   It is the downfall of the year:
We heed the wind and falling leaf
More than the withered harvest sheaf.

Dreary winter come at last,
Come quickly, so be quickly past;
15   Dusk and sluggish winter wane
Till spring and sunlight dawn again.

"Who have a form of godliness."

When I am sick and tired it is God's will;
    Also, God's will alone is sure and best:—
    So in my weariness I find my rest,
And so in poverty I take my fill:

5   Therefore I see my good in midst of ill,
      Therefore in loneliness I build my nest;
       And thro' hot noon pant toward the shady west,
    And hope in sickening disappointment still.
    So when the times of restitution come,
10   The sweet times of refreshing come at last,
    My God shall fill my longings to the brim:
    Therefore I wait and look and long for Him;
    Not wearied tho' the work is wearisome,
      Nor fainting tho' the time be almost past.

Ballad.

Soft white lamb in the daisy meadow,
    Come hither and play with me,
For I am lonesome and I am tired
    Underneath the apple tree.

5   There's your husband if you're lonesome, lady,
      And your bed if you want for rest,
And your baby for a playfellow
    With a soft hand for your breast.

Fair white dove in the sunshine,
10   Perched on the ashen bough,
Come and perch by me and coo to me
    While the buds are blowing now.

I must keep my nestlings warm, lady,
    Underneath my downy breast;
15   There's your baby to coo and crow to you
    While I brood upon my nest.

Faint white rose come lie on my heart,
    Come lie there with your thorn;
    For I'll be dead at the vesper bell
20   And buried the morrow morn.

There's blood on your lily breast, lady,
    Like roses when they blow,

And there's blood upon your little hand
    That should be white as snow;
25 I will stay amid my fellows
    Where the lilies grow.

But its oh my own own little babe
    That I had you here to kiss,
And to comfort me in the strange next world
30   Tho' I slighted you so in this.

You shall kiss both cheek and chin, mother,
    And kiss me between the eyes,
Or ever the moon is on her way
    And the pleasant stars arise;
35 You shall kiss and kiss your fill, mother,
    In the nest of Paradise.

A Study. (A Soul.)

She stands as pale as Parian statues stand;
    Like Cleopatra when she turned at bay,
    And felt her strength above the Roman sway,
And felt the aspic writhing in her hand.
5 Her face is steadfast toward the shadowy land,
    For dim beyond it looms the land of day;
    Her feet are steadfast; all the arduous way
That foot-track hath not wavered on the sand.
She stands there like a beacon thro' the night,
10   A pale clear beacon where the storm-drift is;
She stands alone, a wonder deathly white;
She stands there patient, nerved with inner might,
    Indomitable in her feebleness,
Her face and will athirst against the light.

"There remaineth therefore a rest."

Very cool that bed must be
    Where our last sleep shall be slept:

     There for weary vigils kept,
     There for tears that we have wept,
5   Is our guerdon certainly.

     Underneath the growing grass,
       Underneath the living flowers,
       Deeper than the sound of showers;—
       There we shall not count the hours
10   By the shadows as they pass.

     No more struggling then at length,
       Only slumber everywhere;
       Nothing more to do or bear:
       We shall rest, and resting there
15   Eagle-like renew our strength.

     In the grave will be no space
       For the purple of the proud,
       They must mingle with the crowd;
       In the wrappings of a shroud
20   Jewels would be out of place.

     Youth and health will be but vain,
       Courage reckoned of no worth;
       There a very little girth
       Shall hold round what once the earth
25   Seemed too narrow to contain.

     High and low and rich and poor,
       All will fare alike at last:
       The old promise standeth fast:
       None shall care then if the past
30   Held more joys for him or fewer.

     There no laughter shall be heard,
       Nor the heavy sound of sighs;
       Sleep shall seal the aching eyes;
       All the ancient and the wise
35   There shall utter not a word.

     Yet it may be we shall hear
       How the mounting skylark sings

And the bell for matins rings;
   Or perhaps the whisperings
40 Of white Angels sweet and clear.

Sun or moon hath never shone
   In that hidden depth of night;
   But the souls there washed and white
   Are more fair than fairest light
45 Mortal eye hath looked upon.

The die cast whose throw is life—
   Rest complete; not one in seven—
   Souls love-perfected and shriven
   Waiting at the door of heaven,
50 Perfected from fear of strife.

What a calm when all is done,
   Wearing vigil, prayer and fast:—
   All fulfilled from first to last:—
   All the length of time gone past
55 And eternity begun.

Fear and hope and chastening rod
   Urge us on the narrow way:
   Bear we still as best we may
   Heat and burden of the day,
60 Struggling panting up to God.

"Ye have forgotten the exhortation."

Angel
Bury thy dead, dear friend,
Between the night and day;
Where depths of summer shade are cool,
And murmurs of a summer pool
5 And windy murmurs stray:—

Soul
Ah, gone away,
Ah, dear and lost delight,
Gone from me and for ever out of sight.

Angel

Bury thy dead, dear love,
10   And make his bed most fair above;
The latest buds shall still
Blow there, and the first violets too,
And there a turtle dove
Shall brood and coo:—

Soul

15   I cannot make the nest
So warm, but he may find it chill
In solitary rest.

Angel

Bury thy dead heart-deep;
Take patience till the sun be set;
20   There are no tears for him to weep,
No doubts to haunt him yet:
Take comfort, he will not forget:—

Soul

Then I will watch beside his sleep;
Will watch alone,
25   And make my moan
Because the harvest is so long to reap.

Angel

The fields are white to harvest, look and see,
Are white abundantly.
The harvest moon shines full and clear,
30   The harvest time is near,
Be of good cheer:—

Soul

Ah, woe is me;
I have no heart for harvest time,
Grown sick with hope deferred from chime to chime.

Angel

35   But One can give thee heart, thy Lord and his,
Can raise both thee and him
To shine with Seraphim

And pasture where the eternal fountain is.
Can give thee of that tree
40   Whose leaves are health for thee;
Can give thee robes made clean and white,
And love, and all delight,
And beauty where the day turns not to night.
Who knocketh at His door
45   And presseth in, goes out no more.
Kneel as thou hast not knelt before—
The time is short—and smite
Upon thy breast and pray with all thy might:—

                    Soul
O Lord, my heart is broken for my sin:
50   Yet hasten Thine Own day
And come away.
Is not time full? Oh put the sickle in,
O Lord, begin.

Guesses.

Was it a chance that made her pause
     One moment at the opened door,
     Pale where she stood so flushed before
As one a spirit overawes:—
5   Or might it rather be because
She felt the grave was at our feet,
And felt that we should no more meet
     Upon its hither side no more?

Was it a chance that made her turn
10   Once toward the window passing by,
     One moment with a shrinking eye
Wherein her spirit seemed to yearn:—
Or did her soul then first discern
How long and rough the pathway is
15   That leads us home from vanities,
     And how it will be good to die?

There was a hill she had to pass;
 And while I watched her up the hill
 She stooped one moment hurrying still,
20 But left a rose upon the grass:
Was it mere idleness:—or was
Herself with her own self at strife
Till while she chose the better life
 She felt this life has power to kill?

25 Perhaps she did it carelessly,
 Perhaps it was an idle thought;
 Or else it was the grace unbought,
A pledge to all eternity:
I know not yet how this may be;
30 But I shall know when face to face
In Paradise we find a place
 And love with love that endeth not.

From the Antique.

It's a weary life, it is; she said:—
 Doubly blank in a woman's lot:
I wish and I wish I were a man;
 Or, better than any being, were not:

5 Were nothing at all in all the world,
 Not a body and not a soul;
Not so much as a grain of dust
 Or drop of water from pole to pole.

Still the world would wag on the same,
10 Still the seasons go and come;
Blossoms bloom as in days of old,
 Cherries ripen and wild bees hum.

None would miss me in all the world,
 How much less would care or weep:
15 I should be nothing; while all the rest
 Would wake and weary and fall asleep.

Three Stages.

1.

I looked for that which is not, nor can be,
    And hope deferred made my heart sick in truth;
    But years must pass before a hope of youth
        Is resigned utterly.

5 I watched and waited with a steadfast will:
    And though the object seemed to flee away
    That I so longed for; ever, day by day,
        I watched and waited still.

Sometimes I said: This thing shall be no more:
10   My expectation wearies and shall cease;
    I will resign it now and be at peace:—
        Yet never gave it o'er.

Sometimes I said: It is an empty name
    I long for; to a name why should I give
15   The peace of all the days I have to live?—
        Yet gave it all the same.

Alas, thou foolish one! alike unfit
    For healthy joy and salutary pain;
    Thou knowest the chase useless, and again
20   Turnest to follow it.

2.

My happy happy dream is finished with,
    My dream in which alone I lived so long.
My heart slept—woe is me, it wakeneth;
    Was weak—I thought it strong.

5 Oh weary wakening from a life-true dream:
    Oh pleasant dream from which I wake in pain:
I rested all my trust on things that seem,
    And all my trust is vain.

I must pull down my palace that I built,
10   Dig up the pleasure-gardens of my soul;
Must change my laughter to sad tears for guilt,
   My freedom to control.

Now all the cherished secrets of my heart,
   Now all my hidden hopes are turned to sin:
15 Part of my life is dead, part sick, and part
   Is all on fire within.

The fruitless thought of what I might have been
   Haunting me ever will not let me rest:
A cold north wind has withered all my green,
20   My sun is in the west.

But where my palace stood, with the same stone,
   I will uprear a shady hermitage;
And there my spirit shall keep house alone,
   Accomplishing its age:

25 There other garden beds shall lie around
   Full of sweet-briar and incense-bearing thyme;
There I will sit, and listen for the sound
   Of the last lingering chime.

3.

I thought to deal the death-stroke at a blow,
   To give all, once for all, but nevermore;—
Then sit to hear the low waves fret the shore,
   Or watch the silent snow.

5 "Oh rest," I thought, "in silence and the dark;
   Oh rest, if nothing else, from head to feet:
Though I may see no more the poppied wheat,
   Or sunny soaring lark.

"These chimes are slow, but surely strike at last;
10   This sand is slow, but surely droppeth thro';
And much there is to suffer, much to do,
   Before the time be past.

"So will I labour, but will not rejoice:
  Will do and bear, but will not hope again;
15   Gone dead alike to pulses of quick pain,
    And pleasure's counterpoise:"

I said so in my heart, and so I thought
  My life would lapse, a tedious monotone:
  I thought to shut myself, and dwell alone
20   Unseeking and unsought.

But first I tired, and then my care grew slack;
  Till my heart slumbered, may-be wandered too:—
  I felt the sunshine glow again, and knew
    The swallow on its track;

25 All birds awoke to building in the leaves,
  All buds awoke to fulness and sweet scent,
  Ah, too, my heart woke unawares, intent
    On fruitful harvest sheaves.

Full pulse of life, that I had deemed was dead,
30 Full throb of youth, that I had deemed at rest,—
  Alas, I cannot build myself a nest,
    I cannot crown my head

With royal purple blossoms for the feast,
  Nor flush with laughter, nor exult in song;—
35   These joys may drift, as time now drifts along;
    And cease, as once they ceased.

I may pursue, and yet may not attain,
  Athirst and panting all the days I live:
  Or seem to hold, yet nerve myself to give
40   What once I gave, again.

Long looked for.

When the eye hardly sees,
  And the pulse hardly stirs,
And the heart would scarcely quicken

Though the voice were hers:
5   Then the longing wasting fever
    Will be almost past;
Sleep indeed come back again,
    And peace at last.

Not till then, dear friends,
10   Not till then, most like, most dear,
The dove will fold its wings
    To settle here.
Then to all her coldness
    I also shall be cold,
15 Then I also have forgotten
    Our happy love of old.

Close mine eyes with care,
    Cross my hands upon my breast,
Let shadows and full silence
20   Tell of rest:
For she yet may look upon me
    Too proud to speak, but know
One heart less loves her in the world
    Than loved her long ago.

25 Strew flowers upon the bed
    And flowers upon the floor,
Let all be sweet and comely
    When she stands at the door:
Fair as a bridal chamber
30   For her to come into,
When the sunny day is over
    At falling of the dew.

If she comes, watch her not
    But careless turn aside;
35 She may weep if left alone
    With her beauty and her pride:
She may pluck a leaf perhaps
    Or a languid violet
When life and love are finished
40   And even I forget.

Listening.

She listened like a cushat dove
   That listens to its mate alone;
She listened like a cushat dove
   That loves but only one.

5   Not fair as men would reckon fair,
   Nor noble as they count the line;
Only as graceful as a bough
   And tendrils of the vine;
Only as noble as sweet Eve
10   Your ancestress and mine.

And downcast were her dovelike eyes,
   And downcast was her tender cheek,
Her pulses fluttered like a dove
   To hear him speak.

Zara

(see Maturin's *Women.*)

I dreamed that loving me he would love on
   Thro' life and death into eternity:
   I dreamed that love would be and be and be
As surely as the sun shines that once shone.
5   Now even that my dream is killed and gone,
   It sometimes even now returns to me;
   Not what it was, but half being memory,
And half the pain that wears my cheek so wan.
Oh bitter pain, what drug will lull the pain?
10   Oh lying memory, when shall I forget?
For why should I remember him in vain
Who hath forgotten and rejoiceth still?
   Oh bitter memory, while my heart is set
On love that gnaws and gnaws and cannot kill.

The last look.

Her face was like an opening rose,
   So bright to look upon;
But now it is like fallen snows,
   As cold, as dead, as wan.
5   Heaven lit with stars is more like her
   Than is this empty crust;
Deaf, dumb and blind it cannot stir
   But crumbles back to dust.

No flower be taken from her bed
10   For me, no lock be shorn;
I give her up, the early dead,
   The dead, the newly born:
If I remember her, no need
   Of formal tokens set;
15   Of hollow token lies, indeed,
   No need, if I forget.

"I have a message unto thee."
(written in sickness.)

Green sprout the grasses,
   Red blooms the mossy rose,
Blue nods the harebell
   Where purple heather blows;
5   The water lily, silver white,
Is living—fair as light;
   Sweet jasmine branches trail
   A dusky starry veil:
Each goodly is to see,
10   Comely in its degree;
I, only I, alas that this should be,
   Am ruinously pale.

New year renews the grasses,
   The crimson rose renews,

15   Brings up the breezy bluebell,
          Refreshes heath with dews;
      Then water lilies ever
      Bud fresh upon the river;
          Then jasmine lights its star
20   And spreads its arms afar:
      I only in my spring
      Can neither bud nor sing;
      I find not honey but a sting
          Though fair the blossoms are.

25   For me no downy grasses,
          For me no blossoms pluck;
      But leave them for the breezes,
          For honey bees to suck,
      For childish hands to pull
30   And pile their baskets full:
          I will not have a crown
          That soon must be laid down;
      Trust me: I cannot care
      A withering crown to wear,
35   I who may be immortally made fair
          Where autumn turns not brown.

      Spring, summer, autumn,
          Winter, all will pass,
      With tender blossoms
40   And with fruitful grass.
      Sweet days of yore
      Will pass to come no more,
          Sweet perfumes fly,
          Buds languish and go by:
45   Oh bloom that cannot last,
      Oh blossoms quite gone past,
      I yet shall feast when you shall fast,
          And live when you shall die.

      Your workday fully ended,
50   Your pleasant task being done,
      You shall finish with the stars,

The moon and setting sun.
You and these and time
Shall end with the last chime;
55 For earthly solace given,
But needed not in heaven.
    Needed not perhaps
    Thro' the eternal lapse:
Or else, all signs fulfilled,
60 What you foreshow may yield
Delights thro' heaven's own harvest field
    With undecaying saps.

Young girls wear flowers,
    Young brides a flowery wreath;
65 But next we plant them
    In garden plots of death.
Whose sleep is best?—
The maiden's curtained rest,
    Or bride's whose hoped for sweet
70   May yet outstrip her feet?—
Ah, what are such as these
To death's sufficing ease—
How long and deep that slumber is
    Where night and morning meet.

75 Dear are the blossoms
    For bride's or maiden's head,
But dearer planted
    Around our happy dead.
Those mind us of decay
80 And joys that slip away;
    These preach to us perfection
    And endless resurrection.
We make our graveyards fair
For spirit-like birds of air;
85 For Angels, may be, finding there
    Lost Eden's own delection.

A blessing on the flowers
    That God has made so good,

From crops of jealous gardens
90   To wildlings of a wood.
They show us symbols deep
Of how to sow and reap;
        They teach us lessons plain
        Of patient harvest gain.
95 They still are telling of
God's unimagined love:—
"Oh gift," they say, "all gifts above,
    "Shall it be given in vain?—

"Better you had not seen us
100   "But shared the blind man's night,
"Better you had not scented
    "Our incense of delight,
"Than only plucked to scorn
"The rosebud for its thorn:
105 "Not so the instinctive thrush
"Hymns in a holly bush.
    "Be wise betimes, and with the bee
    "Suck sweets from prickly tree
"To last when earth's are flown;
110 "So God well pleased will own
"Your work, and bless not time alone
    "But ripe eternity."

Cobwebs.

It is a land with neither night nor day,
    Nor heat nor cold, nor any wind, nor rain,
    Nor hills nor valleys; but one even plain
Stretches thro' long unbroken miles away:
5   While thro' the sluggish air a twilight grey
    Broodeth; no moons or seasons wax and wane,
    No ebb and flow are there along the main,
No bud-time no leaf-falling there for aye,
No ripple on the sea, no shifting sand,
10   No beat of wings to stir the stagnant space,

No pulse of life thro' all the loveless land:
And loveless sea; no trace of days before,
   No guarded home, no toil-won restingplace
No future hope no fear for evermore.

Unforgotten.

   Oh unforgotten!
How long ago? one spirit saith:
As long as life even unto death,
The passage of a poor frail breath.

5   Oh unforgotten:
An unforgotten load of love,
A load of grief all griefs above,
A blank blank nest without its dove.

   As long as time is—
10 No longer? time is but a span
The dalliance space of empty man;
And is this all immortals can?—

   Ever and ever,
Beyond all time, beyond all space;—
15 *Now,* shadow darkening heart and face,—
Then, glory in a glorious place.

   Sad heart and spirit
Bowed now yea broken for a while,
Lagging and toiling mile by mile
20 Yet pressing toward the eternal smile.

   Oh joy eternal!—
Oh youth eternal without flaw!—
Thee not the blessed angels saw
Rapt in august adoring awe.

25   Not the dead have thee,
Not yet O all surpassing peace;
Not till this veiling world shall cease
And harvest yield its whole increase.

    Not the dead know thee,
30 Not dead nor living nor unborn:
    Who in the new sown field at morn
    Can measure out the harvest corn?—

    Yet they shall know thee;
    And we with them, and unborn men
35 With us, shall know and have thee when
    The single grain shall wax to ten.

An Afterthought.

    Oh lost garden Paradise:—
    Were the roses redder there
    Than they blossom otherwhere?
    Was the night's delicious shade
5 More intensely star inlaid?
    Who can tell what memories
    Of lost beloved Paradise
    Saddened Eve with sleepless eyes?—

    Fair first mother lulled to rest
10 In a choicer garden nest,
    Curtained with a softer shading
    Than thy tenderest child is laid in,
    Was the sundawn brighter far
    Than our daily sundawns are?
15 Was that love, first love of all
    Warmer, deeper, better worth
    Than has warmed poor hearts of earth
    Since the utter ruinous fall?—

    Ah supremely happy once,
20 Ah supremely broken hearted
    When her tender feet departed
    From the accustomed paths of peace:
    Catching Angel orisons
    For the last last time of all,
25 Shedding tears that would not cease
    For the bitter bitter fall.

Yet the accustomed hand for leading,
Yet the accustomed heart for love;
Sure she kept one part of Eden
30   Angels could not strip her of.
Sure the fiery messenger
Kindling for his outraged Lord,
Willing with the perfect Will,
Yet rejoiced the flaming sword
35   Chastening sore but sparing still
Shut her treasure out with her.

What became of Paradise?
Did the cedars droop at all
(Springtide hastening to the fall)
40   Missing the beloved hand—
Or did their green perfection stand
Unmoved beneath the perfect skies?—
Paradise was rapt on high,
It lies before the gate of Heaven:—
45   Eve now slumbers there forgiven,
Slumbers Rachel comforted,
Slumber all the blessed dead
Of days and months and years gone by,
A solemn swelling company.

50   They wait for us beneath the trees
Of Paradise that lap of ease:
They wait for us, till God shall please.
Oh come the day of death, that day
Of rest which cannot pass away:
55   When the last work is wrought, the last
Pang of pain is felt and past
And the blessed door made fast.

To the end.

There are lilies for her sisters—
   (Who so cold as they?)—
And heartsease for one I must not name

When I am far away.
5 I shall pluck the lady lilies
And fancy all the rest;
I shall pluck the bright eyed heartsease
For her sake I love the best,
As I wander on with weary feet
10 Toward the twilight shadowy west.

Oh bird that fliest eastward
Unto that sunny land
Oh wilt thou 'light on lilies white
Beside her whiter hand?
15 Soft summer wind that breathest
Of perfumes and sweet spice,
Ah tell her what I dare not tell
Of watchful waiting eyes
Of love that yet may meet again
20 In distant Paradise.

I go from earth to Heaven
A dim uncertain road,
A houseless pilgrim thro' the world
Unto a sure abode:
25 While evermore an Angel
Goes with me day and night,
A ministering spirit
From the land of light,
My holy fellow servant sent
30 To guide my steps aright.

I wonder if the Angels
Love with such love as our's,
If for each other's sake they pluck
And keep eternal flowers.
35 Alone I am and weary,
Alone yet not alone:
Her soul talks with me by the way
From tedious stone to stone,
A blessed Angel treads with me
40 The awful paths unknown.

When will the long road end in rest,
   The sick bird perch and brood?
When will my Guardian fold his wings
   At rest in the finished good?—
45 Lulling lulling me off to sleep:
   While death's strong hand doth roll
My sins behind His back,
   And my life up like a scroll,
Till thro' sleep I hear kind Angels
50   Rejoicing at the goal.

If her spirit went before me
   Up from night to day,
It would pass me like the lightning
   That kindles on its way.
55 I should feel it like the lightning
   Flashing fresh from Heaven:
I should long for Heaven sevenfold more,
   Yea and sevenfold seven;
Should pray as I have not prayed before,
60   And strive as I have not striven.

She will learn new love in Heaven
   Who is so full of love,
She will learn new depths of tenderness
   Who is tender like a dove.
65 Her heart will no more sorrow,
   Her eyes will weep no more:
Yet it may be she will yearn
   And look back from far before:
Lingering on the golden threshold
70   And leaning from the door.

"Zion said."

O Slain for love of me, canst Thou be cold,
   Be cold and far away in my distress:
   Is Thy love also changed growing less and less
That carried me thro' all the days of old?—

5   O Slain for love of me, O Love untold,
          See how I flag and fail thro' weariness:
          I flag, while sleepless foes dog me and press
       On me; behold O Lord, O Love behold.
       I am sick for home, the home of love indeed;
10   I am sick for Love, that dearest name for Thee:
       Thou Who hast bled, see how my heart doth bleed;
       Open Thy bleeding Side and let me in;
       Oh hide me in Thy Heart from doubt and sin,
          Oh take me to Thyself and comfort me.

May.

       Sweet Life is dead.—
                          Not so:
          I meet him day by day,
       Where bluest fountains flow
5   And trees are white as snow
          For it is time of May.
       Even now from long ago
          He will not say me nay;
          He is most fair to see;
10   And if I wander forth, I know
          He wanders forth with me.

       But Life is dead to me;
          The worn-out year was failing
          West winds took up a wailing
15   To watch his funeral:
       Bare poplars shivered tall
       And lank vines stretched to see;
          'Twixt him and me a wall
       Was frozen of earth like stone
20   With brambles overgrown;
          Chill darkness wrapped him like a pall
       And I am left alone.

       How can you call him dead?
          He buds out everywhere:

25   In every hedgerow rank,
      On every mossgrown bank
         I find him here and there.
      He crowns my willing head
      With may flowers white and red,
30   He rears my tender heartsease bed;
         He makes my branch to bud and bear,
      And blossoms where I tread.

River Thames (?).

There are rivers lapsing down
   Lily-laden to the sea;
Every lily is a boat
   For bees, one, two, or three:
5 I wish there were a fairy boat
   For you, my friend, and me.

We would rock upon the river,
   Scarcely floating by;
Rocking rocking like the lilies,
10   You, my friend, and I;
Rocking like the stately lilies
   Beneath the statelier sky.

But ah, where is that river
   Whose hyacinth banks descend
15 Down to the sweeter lilies,
   Till soft their shadows blend
Into a watery twilight?—
   And ah, where is my friend?—

A chilly night.

I rose at the dead of night
   And went to the lattice alone
To look for my Mother's ghost
   Where the ghostly moonlight shone.

5   My friends had failed one by one,
        Middleaged, young, and old,
    Till the ghosts were warmer to me
        Than my friends that had grown cold.

    I looked and I saw the ghosts
10   Dotting plain and mound:
    They stood in the blank moonlight
        But no shadow lay on the ground;
    They spoke without a voice
        And they leapt without a sound.

15 I called: "O my Mother dear,"—
        I sobbed: "O my Mother kind,
    Make a lonely bed for me
        And shelter it from the wind:

    "Tell the others not to come
20   To see me night or day;
    But I need not tell my friends
        To be sure to keep away."

    My Mother raised her eyes,
        They were blank and could not see;
25 Yet they held me with their stare
        While they seemed to look at me.

    She opened her mouth and spoke,
        I could not hear a word
    While my flesh crept on my bones
30   And every hair was stirred.

    She knew that I could not hear
        The message that she told
    Whether I had long to wait
        Or soon should sleep in the mould:
35 I saw her toss her shadowless hair
        And wring her hands in the cold.

    I strained to catch her words
        And she strained to make me hear,
    But never a sound of words
40   Fell on my straining ear.

From midnight to the cockcrow
  I kept my watch in pain
While the subtle ghosts grew subtler
  In the sad night on the wane.

45   From midnight to the cockcrow
  I watched till all were gone,
Some to sleep in the shifting sea
  And some under turf and stone:
Living had failed and dead had failed
50   And I was indeed alone.

"Let patience have her perfect work."

I saw a bird alone,
In its nest it sat alone,
For its mate was dead or flown
  Tho' it was early spring.
5   Hard by were buds half blown,
With cornfields freshly sown;
It could only perch and moan
  That used to sing:
Droop in sorrow left alone
10   A sad sad thing.

I saw a star alone,
In blue heaven it hung alone,
A solitary throne
  In the waste of space:
15   Where no moon glories are,
Where not a second star
Beams thro' night from near or far
  To that lone place.
Its beauties all unknown,
20   Its glories all alone
  Sad in heaven's face.

Doth the bird desire a mate,
Pine for a second mate
Whose first joy was so great

25   With its own dove?
  Doth the star supreme in night
  Desire a second light
  To make it seem less bright
  In the shrine of heavenly height
30   That is above?—
  Ah, better wait alone,
  In nest or heaven alone,
  Forsaken or unknown;
  Till time being past and gone
35 Full eternity rolls on,
  While patience reaps what it has sown
   In the harvest land of love.

A Martyr.

 It is over the horrible pain,
  All is over the struggle and doubt,
 She's asleep tho' her friends stand and weep,
  She's asleep while the multitudes shout,
5 Not to wake to her anguish again
  Not to wake until death is cast out.

 Stoop, look at the beautiful face,
  See the smile on the satisfied mouth,
 The hands crost—she hath conquered not lost,
10 She hath drunk who was fevered with drouth.
 She shall sleep in her safe restingplace
  While the hawk spreads her wings toward the south.

 She shall sleep while slow seasons are given,
  While daylight and darkness go round;
15 Her heart is at rest in its nest;
  Her body at rest in the ground:
 She has travelled the long road to heaven,
  She sought it and now she has found.

 Will you follow the track that she trod,
20 Will you tread in her footsteps, my friend?

That pathway is rough but enough
    Are the light and the balm that attend.
Do I tread in her steps, O my God,
    Shall I joy with her joy in the end?

In the Lane.

When my love came home to me
    Pleasant Summer bringing
Every tree was out in leaf
    Every bird was singing
5   Every red rose burst the bud
    On its bramble springing.

There I met her in the lane
    By those waters gleamy,
Met her toward the fall of day
10   Warm and dear and dreamy;
Did I loiter in the lane?
    None was there to see me.

Only roses in the hedge
    Lilies on the river
15   Saw our greeting fast and fond,
    Counted gift and giver,
Saw me take her to my home
    Take her home for ever.

Acme.

Sleep, unforgotten sorrow, sleep awhile;
    Make even awhile as tho' I might forget,
    Let the wound staunch thy tedious fingers fret
Till once again I look abroad and smile
5   Warmed in the sunlight: let no tears defile
    This hour's content, no conscious thorns beset
    My path; O sorrow slumber, slumber yet
A moment, rouse not yet the smouldering pile.

So shalt thou wake again with added strength
10   O unforgotten sorrow, stir again
        The slackening fire, refine the lulling pain
        To quickened torture and a subtler edge:
        The wrung cord snaps at last; beneath the wedge
The toughest oak groans long but rends at length.

A bed of Forget-me-nots.

Is love so prone to change and rot
We are fain to rear forget-me-not
By measure in a garden plot?—

I love its growth at large and free
5   By untrod path and unlopped tree,
Or nodding by the unpruned hedge,
Or on the water's dangerous edge
Where flags and meadowsweet blow rank
With rushes on the quaking bank.

10   Love is not taught in learning's school,
Love is not parcelled out by rule;
Hath curb or call an answer got?—
So free must be forget-me-not.
Give me the flame no dampness dulls,
15   The passion of the instinctive pulse,
Love steadfast as a fixèd star,
Tender as doves with nestlings are,
More large than time, more strong than death:
This all creation travails of—
20   She groans not for a passing breath—
This is forget-me-not and love.

The Chiefest among ten thousand.

When sick of life and all the world,
How sick of all the earth but Thee,
I lift mine eyes up to the hills,

Eyes of my heart that truly see:
5   I see beyond all death and ills
Refreshing green for heart and eyes;
The golden streets and gateways pearled,
The living trees of paradise.

Oh that a dove's white wings I had
10 To flee away from this distress
For Thou art in the wilderness
Drawing and leading Thine Own love:
Wherefore it blossoms like a rose,
The solitary place is glad;
15 There sounds the soft voice of the dove
And there the spicy south wind blows.

Draw us, we will run after Thee;
Call us by name, the name we know;
Call her beloved who was not so,
20 Beulah and blessed Hepzibah:
That where Thou art I too may be
Bride of the Bridegroom heart to heart;
Thou God, my Love, the Fairest art
Where all things fair and lovely are.

25 From north and south from east and west
Thy sons and daughters all shall flock
Who built their house upon the Rock
And eagle-like renew their strength:
How glad and glorious is their rest
30 Whom Thou hast purged from fleshly scum,—
The long-desired is come at length,
The fulness of the time is come.

Then the new heavens and earth shall be
Where righteousness shall dwell indeed:
35 There shall be no more blight nor need
Nor barrier of the tossing sea;
No sun and moon alternating
For God shall be the Light thereof,
No sorrow more no death no sting
40 For God shall reign and God is Love.

"Look on this picture and on this."

I wish we once were wedded,—then I must be true;
You should hold my will in yours to do or to undo:
But now I hate myself Eva when I look at you.

You have seen her hazel eyes, her warm dark skin,
5   Dark hair—but oh those hazel eyes a devil is dancing in:—
You my saint lead up to heaven she lures down to sin.

Listen Eva I repent, indeed I do my love:
How should I choose a peacock and leave and grieve a
        dove?—
If I could turn my back on her and follow you above.

10   No it's not her beauty bloomed like an autumn peach,
Not her pomp of beauty too high for me to reach;
It's her eyes, her witching manner—ah the lore they teach

You are winning, well I know it, who should know but I?
You constrain me, I must yield or else must hasten by:—
15   But she, she fascinates me, I can neither fight nor fly.

She's so redundant, stately;—in truth now have you seen
Ever anywhere such beauty, such a stature, such a mien?
She may be queen of devils but she's every inch a queen.

If you sing to me, I hear her subtler sweeter still
20   Whispering in each tender cadence strangely sweet to fill
All that lacks in music all my soul and sense and will.

If you dance, tho' mine eyes follow where my hand I gave
I only see her presence like a sunny wave
I only feel her presence like a wind too strong to rave.

25   If we talk: I love you, do you love me again?—
Tho' your lips speak it's her voice I flush to hear so plain
Say: Love you? yes I love you, love can neither change
        nor wane.

But, you ask, "why struggle? I have given you up:
Take again your pledges, snap the cord and break the cup:
30   Feast you with your temptation for I in heaven will sup."—

Can I bear to think upon you strong to break not bend,
Pale with inner intense passion silent to the end,
Bear to leave you, bear to grieve you, O my dove my friend?

One short pang and you would rise a light in heaven
35   While we grovelled in the darkness mean and unforgiven
Tho' our cup of love brimmed sevenfold crowns of love
          were seven.

What shall I choose, what can I choose for you and her and me;
With you the haven of rest, with her the tossing miry sea;
Time's love with her, or choose with you love's all eternity.—

40   Nay, you answer coldly yet with a quivering voice:
That is over, doubt and struggle, we have sealed our choice;
Leave me to my contentment vivid with fresh hopes
          and joys.

Listening so, I hide mine eyes and fancy years to come:
You cherished in another home with no cares burdensome;
45   You straitened in a windingsheet pulseless at peace
          and dumb.

So I fancy—The new love has driven the old away;
She has found a dearer shelter a dearer stronger stay;
Perhaps now she would thank me for the freedom of
          that day.

Open house and heart barred to me alone the door;
50   Children bound to meet her, babies crow before;—
Blessed wife and blessed mother whom I may see no more.

Or I fancy—In the grave her comely body lies;
She is 'tiring for the Bridegroom till the morning star
          shall rise,
Then to shine a glory in the nuptials of the skies.

55   No more yearning tenderness, no more pale regret,
She will not look for me when the marriage guests are set,
She joys with joy eternal as we had never met.

I would that one of us were dead, were gone no more
          to meet,

Or she and I were dead together stretched here at
      your feet,
60   That she and I were strained together in one windingsheet:

Hidden away from all the world upon this bitter morn;
Hidden from all the scornful world, from all your keener
      scorn;
Secure and secret in the dark as blessed babe unborn.

A pitiless fiend is in your eyes to tempt me and to taunt:
65   If you were dead I verily believe that you would haunt
The home you loved, the man you loved, you said you
      loved—avaunt.

Why do you face me with those eyes so calm they drive
      me mad,
Too proud to droop before me and own that you are sad?
Why have you a lofty angel made me mean and cursed
      and bad?

70   How have you the heart to face me with that passion in
      your stare
Deathly silent? weep before me, rave at me in your
      despair—
If you keep patience wings will spring and a halo from
      your hair.

Yet what matters—yea what matters? your frenzy can
      but mock:
You do not hold my heart's life key to lock and to unlock,
75   The door will not unclose to you tho' long you wait
      and knock.

Have I wronged you? nay not I nor she in deed or will:
You it is alone that mingle the venomous cup and fill;
Why are you so little lovely that I cannot love you still?—

One pulse, one tone, one ringlet of her's outweighs
      the whole
80   Of you, your puny graces puny body puny soul:
You but a taste of sweetness, she an overrunning bowl.

Did I make you, that you blame me because you are not
        the best?
Not so, be wise, take patience, turn away and be at rest:
Shall I not know her lovelier who is far loveliest?—

85   See now how proud you are, like us after all, no saint;
Not so upright but that you are bowed with the old bent;
White at white-heat, tainted with the devil's special taint.

Sit you still and wring the cup drop after loathsome drop:
You have let loose a torrent it is not you can stop;
90   You have sowed a noisome field-ful, now reap the
        stinging crop.

Did you think to sit in safety, to watch me torn and tost
Struggling like a mad dog, watch her tempting
        doubly lost?
Howl you, you wretched woman, for your flimsy hopes
        are crost.

Be still, tho' you may writhe you shall hear the branding
        truth:
95   You who thought to sit in judgment on our souls forsooth,
To sit in frigid judgment on our ripe luxuriant youth.

Did I love you? never from the first cold day to this;
You are not sufficient for my aim of life, my bliss;
You are not sufficient, but I found the one that is.

100   The wine of love that warms me from this life's mortal
        chill:
Drunk with love I drink again, a thirst I drink my fill;
Lapped in love I care not doth it make alive or kill.

Then did I never love you?—ah the sting struck home
        at last;
You are drooping, fainting, dying—the worst of death
        is past;
105   A light is on your face from the nearing heaven forecast.

Never?—yes I loved you then; I loved: the word still
        charms:—

For the first time last time lie here in my heart my arms,
For the first last time as if I shielded you from harms.

I trampled you, poor dove, to death; you clung to me, I
        spurned;
110 I taunted you, I tortured you, while you sat still and
           yearned:—
Oh lesson taught in anguish but in double anguish
           learned.

For after all I loved you, loved you then, I love you yet.
Listen love I love you: see, the seal of truth is set
On my face in tears—you cannot see? then feel them wet.

115 Pause at heaven's dear gate, look back, one moment back
           to grieve;
You go home thro' death to life; but I, I still must live:
On the threshold of heaven's love, O love can you forgive?—

Fully freely fondly, with heart truth above an oath,
With eager utter pardon given unasked and nothing loth,
120 Heaping coals of fire upon our heads forgiving both.

One word more—not one: one look more—too late
           too late:—
Lapped in love she sleeps who was lashed with scorn
           and hate;
Nestling in the lap of love the dove has found a mate.

Night has come, the night of rest; day will come, that day:
125 To her glad dawn of glory kindled from the deathless ray;
To us a searching fire and strict balances to weigh.

The tearless tender eyes are closed, the tender lips
           are dumb:
I shall not see or hear them more until that day
           shall come:
Then they must speak, what will they say—what then will
           be the sum?—

130 Shall we stand upon the left and she upon the right—
We smirched with endless death and shame, she glorified
           in white:

Will she sound our accusation in intolerable light?

Be open-armed to us in love—type of another Love—
As she forgave us once below will she forgive above,
135 Enthroned to all eternity our sister friend and dove?—

"Now they desire."

There is a sleep we have not slept
    Safe in a bed unknown;
There hearts are staunched that long have wept
    Alone, or bled alone:
5 Sweet sleep that dreams not, or whose dream
    Is foretaste of the truth;
Sweet sleep whose sweets are what they seem
    Refreshing more than youth.

There is a sea whose waters clear
10   Are never tempest tost;
There is a home whose children dear
    Are saved, not one is lost:
There Cherubim and Seraphim
    And Angels dwell with Saints,
15 Whose lustre no more dwindleth dim,
    Whose ardour never faints.

There is a Love Which fills desire
    And can our love requite;
Like fire It draws our lesser fire,
20   Like greater light our light:
For It we agonize in strife
    We yearn we famish thus—
Lo, in the far off land of life
    Doth It not yearn for us?—

25 "Oh fair oh fair Jerusalem,"
    How fair how far away,
When shall we see thy Jasper Gem
    That gives thee light for day?
Thy sea of glass like fire, thy streets

30   Of glass like virgin gold,
      Thy royal Elders on their seats,
        Thy four Beasts manifold?—

      Fair city of delights, the bride
        In raiment white and clean,
35   When shall we see thee loving eyed,
        Sun girdled, happy Queen?
      Without a wrinkle or a spot,
        Blood cleansed, blood purchased once:
      In how fair ground is fallen the lot
40   Of all thy happy sons.

      Dove's eyes beneath thy parted lock,
        A dove's soft voice is thine;
      Thy nest is safe within the Rock,
        Safe in the Very Vine;
45   Thy walls salvation buildeth them
        And all thy gates are praise
      Oh fair oh fair Jerusalem
        In sevenfold day of days.

A Christmas Carol, for my Godchildren.

      The shepherds had an angel,
        The wise men had a star,
      But what have I, a little child,
        To guide me home from far,
5   Where glad stars sing together
        And singing angels are?—

      Lord Jesus is my Guardian,
        So I can nothing lack:
      The lambs lie in His Bosom
10   Along life's dangerous track;
      The wilful lambs that go astray
        He bleeding fetches back.

Lord Jesus is my Guiding Star,
  My Beacon Light in heaven:
15 He leads me step by step along
  The path of life uneven;
He, True Light, leads me to that land
  Whose day shall be as seven.

Those shepherds thro' the lonely night
20   Sat watching by their sheep,
Until they saw the heavenly host
  Who neither tire nor sleep
All singing 'Glory glory'
  In festival they keep.

25 Christ watches me His little lamb,
  Cares for me day and night,
That I may be His Own in heaven:
  So angels clad in white
Shall sing their 'Glory, glory'
30   For my sake in the height.

The wise men left their country
  To journey morn by morn
With gold and frankincense and myrrh
  Because the Lord was born:
35 God sent a star to guide them
  And sent a dream to warn.

My life is like their journey,
  Their star is like God's Book,
I must be like those good wise men
40   With heavenward heart and look:
But shall I give no gifts to God?—
  What precious gifts they took.

Lord I will give my love to Thee,
  Than gold much costlier,
45 Sweeter to Thee than frankincense,
  More prized than choicest myrrh:
Lord make me dearer day by day,
  Day by day holier.

Nearer and dearer day by day:
50   Till I my voice unite
And sing my 'Glory, glory'
    With angels clad in white,
All 'Glory, glory' given to Thee
    Thro' all the heavenly height.

"Not yours but you."

He died for me: what can I offer Him?
    Toward Him swells incense of perpetual prayer;
    His court wear crowns and aureoles round their hair;
His ministers are subtle cherubim,
5   Ring within ring, white intense seraphim
    Leap like immortal lightnings thro' the air:
    What shall I offer Him? defiled and bare
My spirit broken and my brightness dim.—
Give Me thy youth;—I yield it to Thy rod
10   As Thou didst yield Thy prime of youth for me:—
Give Me thy life;—I give it breath by breath
    As Thou didst give Thy life so give I Thee:—
Give Me thy love;—So be it, my God, my God,
As Thou hast loved me even to bitter death.

An Answer.

[The first page of the MS is missing from the notebook.]

To make it glad with a goodly crop:
    Even so One Wiser deals with me:—
Amen, say I: if He choose to lop
    Branch after branch of my leafèd tree,
5   In its own ripe season more fruit shall be.

Tenfold fruit in the time of fruit,
    In the time of corn and wine and oil,
Sound at the core, firm at the root;

Repaying the years and years of toil,
10   Repaying the blood that fed the soil.

Sir Winter.

Sir Winter is coming across the wide sea,
With his blustering companions, so wild and so free:
He speeds on his way, like some bold buccaneer,
And Day flies before him with faltering and fear.

5   In the front of the battle new trophies to reap,
Mid the howl of the tempest, the roar of the deep,
Lo, he comes* with his noiseless-shod legions of snow
And nips the last buds that were lingering to blow.

Sweet blackbird is silenced with chaffinch and thrush,
10   Only waistcoated robin still chirps in the bush:
Soft sun-loving swallows have mustered in force
And winged to the spice-teaming southlands their course.

Plump housekeeper dormouse has tucked himself neat,
Just a brown ball in moss with a morsel to eat;
15   Armed hedgehog has huddled him into the hedge
While frogs miss freezing deep down in the sedge.

So sturdy Sir Winter has conquered us quite,
He has ravaged our country to left and to right:
Since we must bear his yoke for a season, we'd best
20   Try to lighten its weight on ourselves and the rest.

Soft swallows have left us alone in the lurch,
But robin sits whistling to us from his perch:
If I were red robin, I'd pipe you a tune
Would make you despise all the beauties of June.

25   But since that cannot be, let us draw round the fire,
Munch chestnuts, tell stories, and stir the blaze higher:

---

* Down to the * these verses are written by Mr. Jervis.

We'll comfort pinched robin with crumbs, little man,
Till he sings us the very best song that he can.

In an Artist's Studio.

One face looks out from all his canvasses,
    One selfsame figure sits or walks or leans;
    We found her hidden just behind those screens,
That mirror gave back all her loveliness.
5   A queen in opal or in ruby dress,
    A nameless girl in freshest summer greens,
    A saint, an angel;—every canvass means
The same one meaning, neither more nor less.
He feeds upon her face by day and night,
10   And she with true kind eyes looks back on him
Fair as the moon and joyful as the light:
    Not wan with waiting, not with sorrow dim;
Not as she is, but was when hope shone bright;
    Not as she is, but as she fills his dream.

Introspective.

I wish it were over the terrible pain,
Pang after pang again and again;
First the shattering ruining blow,
Then the probing steady and slow.

5   Did I wince? I did not faint:
My soul broke but was not bent;
Up I stand like a blasted tree
By the shore of the shivering sea.

On my boughs neither leaf nor fruit,
10   No sap in my uttermost root,
Brooding in an anguish dumb
On the short past and the long to come.

Dumb I was when the ruin fell,
Dumb I remain and will never tell:

15   O my soul I talk with thee
      But not another the sight must see.

      I did not start when the torture stung,
      I did not faint when the torture wrung;
      Let it come tenfold if come it must
20   But I will not groan when I bite the dust.

"The heart knoweth its own bitterness."

      When all the over-work of life
         Is finished once, and fast asleep
      We swerve no more beneath the knife
         But taste that silence cool and deep;
5   Forgetful of the highways rough,
         Forgetful of the thorny scourge,
         Forgetful of the tossing surge,
      Then shall we find it is enough?—

      How can we say 'enough' on earth;
10   'Enough' with such a craving heart:
      I have not found it since my birth
         But still have bartered part for part.
      I have not held and hugged the whole,
         But paid the old to gain the new;
15   Much have I paid, yet much is due,
      Till I am beggared sense and soul.

      I used to labour, used to strive
         For pleasure with a restless will:
      Now if I save my soul alive
20   All else what matters, good or ill?
      I used to dream alone, to plan
         Unspoken hopes and days to come:—
         Of all my past this is the sum:
      I will not lean on child of man.

25   To give, to give, not to receive,
         I long to pour myself, my soul,
      Not to keep back or count or leave

But king with king to give the whole:
   I long for one to stir my deep—
30   I have had enough of help and gift—
    I long for one to search and sift
Myself, to take myself and keep.

You scratch my surface with your pin;
   You stroke me smooth with hushing breath;—
35 Nay pierce, nay probe, nay dig within,
   Probe my quick core and sound my depth.
You call me with a puny call,
   You talk, you smile, you nothing do;
   How should I spend my heart on you,
40 My heart that so outweighs you all?

Your vessels are by much too strait;
   Were I to pour you could not hold,
Bear with me: I must bear to wait
   A fountain sealed thro' heat and cold.
45 Bear with me days or months or years;
   Deep must call deep until the end
   When friend shall no more envy friend
Nor vex his friend at unawares.

Not in this world of hope deferred,
50   This world of perishable stuff;—
Eye hath not seen, nor ear hath heard,
   Nor heart conceived that full 'enough':
Here moans the separating sea,
   Here harvests fail, here breaks the heart;
55   There God shall join and no man part,
I full of Christ and Christ of me.

"Reflection".

Gazing thro' her chamber window
   Sits my soul's dear soul;
Looking northward, looking southward,

Looking to the goal,
5   Looking back without control.—

I have strewn thy path, beloved,
    With plumed meadowsweet,
Iris and pale perfumed lilies,
    Roses most complete:
10   Wherefore pause on listless feet?—

But she sits and never answers;
    Gazing gazing still
On swift fountain, shadowed valley,
    Cedared sunlit hill:
15   Who can guess or read her will?

Who can guess or read the spirit
    Shrined within her eyes,
Part a longing, part a languor,
    Part a mere surprize,
20   While slow mists do rise and rise?—

Is it love she looks and longs for;
    Is it rest or peace;
Is it slumber self-forgetful
    In its utter ease;
25   Is it one or all of these?

So she sits and doth not answer
    With her dreaming eyes,
With her languid look delicious
    Almost Paradise,
30   Less than happy, over wise.

Answer me, O self-forgetful—
    Or of what beside?—
Is it day dream of a maiden,
    Vision of a bride,
35   Is it knowledge, love, or pride?

Cold she sits thro' all my kindling,
    Deaf to all I pray:
I have wasted might and wisdom,

Wasted night and day:
40   Deaf she dreams to all I say.

Now if I could guess her secret
    Were it worth the guess?—
Time is lessening, hope is lessening,
    Love grows less and less:
45   What care I for *no* or *yes?*—

I will give her stately burial,
    Tho', when she lies dead:
For dear memory of the past time,
    Of her royal head,
50   Of the much I strove and said.

I will give her stately burial,
    Willow branches bent;
Have her carved in alabaster,
    As she dreamed and leant
55   While I wondered what she meant.

A Coast-Nightmare.

I have a friend in ghostland—
    Early found, ah me, how early lost!—
Blood-red seaweeds drip along that coastland
    By the strong sea wrenched and tossed.
5   In every creek there slopes a dead man's islet,
    And such an one in every bay;
All unripened in the unended twilight:
    For there comes neither night nor day.

Unripe harvest there hath none to reap it
10   From the watery misty place;
Unripe vineyard there hath none to keep it
    In unprofitable space.
Living flocks and herds are nowhere found there;
    Only ghosts in flocks and shoals:
15   Indistinguished hazy ghosts surround there

Meteors whirling on their poles;
Indistinguished hazy ghosts abound there;
   Troops, yea swarms, of dead men's souls.—

Have they towns to live in?—
20   They have towers and towns from sea to sea;
Of each town the gates are seven;
   Of one of these each ghost is free.
Civilians, soldiers, seamen,
   Of one town each ghost is free:
25 They are ghastly men those ghostly freemen:
   Such a sight may you not see.—

How know you that your lover
   Of death's tideless waters stoops to drink?—
Me by night doth mouldy darkness cover,
30   It makes me quake to think:
All night long I feel his presence hover
   Thro' the darkness black as ink.

Without a voice he tells me
   The wordless secrets of death's deep:
35 If I sleep, his trumpet voice compels me
   To stalk forth in my sleep:
If I wake, he hunts me like a nightmare;
   I feel my hair stand up, my body creep:
Without light I see a blasting sight there,
40   See a secret I must keep.

'For one Sake.'

One passed me like a flash of lightning by
   To ring clear bells of heaven beyond the stars:
   Then said I: Wars and rumours of your wars
Are dull with din of what and where and why;
5 My heart is where these troubles draw not nigh:
   Let me alone till heaven shall burst its bars,
   Break up its fountains, roll its flashing cars

Earthwards with fire to test and purify.
Let me alone tonight, and one night more
10   Of which I shall not count the eventide;
Its morrow will not be as days before:
Let me alone to dream, perhaps to weep;
    To dream of her the imperishable bride,
Dream while I wake and dream on while I sleep.

My old Friends.

They lie at rest asleep and dead,
The dew drops cool above their head,
They knew not when past summer fled—
                              Amen.

5   They lie at rest and quite forget
The hopes and fears that wring us yet;
Their eyes are set, their heart is set—
                              Amen.

They lie with us, yet gone away
10   Hear nothing that we sob or say
Beneath the thorn of wintry may—
                              Miserere.

Together all yet each alone,
Each laid at rest beneath his own
15   Smooth turf or white appointed stone—
                              Amen.

When shall our slumbers be so deep,
And bleeding heart and eyes that weep
Lie lapped in the sufficient sleep?—
20   *Miserere.*

We dream of them: and who shall say
They never dream while far away
Of us between the night and day?—
                              Sursum corda.

25   Gone far away: or it may be
        They lean toward us and hear and see
        Yea and remember more than we—
                                    Amen.

        For wherefore should we deem them far
30   Who know not where those spirits are
        That shall outshine both moon and star?—
                                    Hallelujah.

        Where check or change can never rise
        Deep in recovered Paradise
35   They rest world-wearied heart and eyes—
                                    Jubilate.

        We hope and love with throbbing breast,
        They hope and love and are at rest:
        And yet we question which is best—
40   *Miserere.*

        Oh what is earth, that we should build
        Brief houses here, and seek concealed
        Poor treasure, and add field to field

        And heap to heap and store to store,
45   Still grasping, ever grasping more,
        While death stands knocking at our door?—
                                    Cui bono?

        But one will answer: Changed and pale
        And starved at heart, I thirst I fail
50   For love, I thirst without avail—
                                    Miserrima.

        Sweet love, a fountain sealed to me:
        Mere love, the sole sufficiency
        For every longing that can be—
55   *Amen.*

        Oh happy those alone whose lot
        Is love: I search from spot to spot;
        In life, in death, I find it not—
                                    Miserrima.

60   Not found in life: nay, verily.
       I too have sought: come sit with me
       And grief for grief shall answer thee—
                              Miserrima.

       Sit with me where the sapless leaves
65   Are fallen and sere: to one who grieves
       What cheer have last year's harvest sheaves?—
                              Cui bono?

       Not found in life: yet found in death.
       I sought life as but a breath
70   There is a nest of love beneath

       The sod, a home prepared before;
       Our brethren whom one mother bore
       Live there, and toil and ache no more—
                              Hallelujah.

75   Dear friends and kinsfolk great and small;
       Not lost but saved both one and all:
       They watch across the parting wall

       (Do they not watch?) and count the creep
       Of time, and sound the shallowing deep,
80   Till we in port shall also sleep—
                              Hallelujah, Amen.

"Yet a little while".

       These days are long before I die:
           To sit alone upon a thorn
           Is what the nightingale forlorn
       Does night by night continually;
5   She swells her heart to extasy
       Until it bursts and she can die.

       These days are long that wane and wax:
           Waxeth and wanes the ghostly moon
           Achill and pale in cordial June;

10 What is it that she wandering lacks?
    She seems as one that aches and aches
    Most sick to wane most sick to wax.

    Of all the sad sights in the world
        The downfall of an Autumn leaf
15   Is grievous and suggesteth grief:
    Who thought when Spring was fresh unfurled
    Of this? when Spring twigs gleamed impearled
    Who thought of frost that nips the world?

    There are a hundred subtle stings
20   To prick us in our daily walk:
        A young fruit cankered on its stalk,
    A strong bird snared for all his wings,
    A nest that sang but never sings;
    Yea sight and sound and silence stings.

25 There is a lack in solitude,
        There is a load in throng of life;
        One with another genders strife,
    To be alone yet is not good:
    I know but of one neighbourhood
30 At peace and full; death's solitude.

    Sleep soundly, dears, who lulled at last
        Forget the bird and all her pains,
        Forget the moon that waxes, wanes,
    The leaf, the sting, the frostful blast;
35 Forget the troublous years that past
    In strife or ache did end at last.

    We have clear call of daily bells,
        A dimness where the anthems are,
        A chancel vault of sky and star,
40 A thunder if the organ swells:
    Alas our daily life—what else?—
    Is not in tune with daily bells.

    You have deep pause betwixt the chimes
        Of earth and heaven, a patient pause

45   Yet glad with rest by certain laws:
You look and long; while oftentimes
Precursive flush of morning climbs
And air vibrates with coming chimes.

"Only believe."

I stood by weeping
Yet a sorrowful silence keeping
While an Angel smote my love
As she lay sleeping.—

5   Is there a bed above
More fragrant than these violets
That are white like death?

White like a dove
Flowers in the blessed islets
10   Breathe sweeter breath
All fair morns and twilights.

Is the gold there
More golden than these tresses?

There heads are aureoled
15   And crowned like gold
With light most rare.

Are the bowers of Heaven
More choice than these?

To them are given
20   All odorous shady trees.
Earth's bowers are wildernesses
Compared with the recesses
Made soft there now
Nest-like twixt bough and bough.

25   Who shall live in such a nest?

Heart with heart at rest:
All they whose troubles cease

In peace:
Souls that wrestled
30 Now are nestled
There at ease:
Throng from east and west
From north and south
To plenty from the land of drouth.

35 How long must they wait?

There is a certain term
For their bodies to the worm
And their souls at Heaven-gate.
Dust to dust, clod to clod
40 These precious things of God;
Trampled underfoot by man
And beast the appointed years.

Their longest life was but a span
For birth, death, laughter, tears:
45 Is it worth while to live,
Rejoice and grieve,
Hope, fear and die?
Man with man, lie with lie,
The slow show dwindles by:
50 At last what shall we have
Besides a grave?

Lies and shows no more,
No fear, no pain,
But after hope and sleep
55 Dear joys again.
Those who sowed shall reap:
Those who bore
The cross shall wear the crown:
Those who clomb the steep
60 There shall sit down.
The Shepherd of the sheep
Feeds His flock there;

[The rest of the poem is missing from the notebook.]

"Rivals."
A Shadow of Saint Dorothea.

"Golden haired, lily white,
    "Will you pluck me lilies;
"Or will you show me where they grow,
    "Show where the summer rill is?
5   "But is your hair of gold or light,
    "And is your foot of flake or fire,
"And have you wings rolled up from sight,
    "And joy to slake desire?"—

"I pluck young flowers of Paradise,
10   "Lilies and roses red;
"A sceptre for my hand,
    "A crown to crown my golden head.
"Love makes me wise:
"I sing, I stand,
15 "I pluck palm branches in the sheltered land."—

"Is there a path to Heaven
    "My heavy foot may tread;
"And will you show that way to go,
    "That rose and lily bed?
20 "Which day of all these seven
    "Will lighten my heart of lead,
"Will purge mine eyes and make me wise
    "Alive or dead?"—

"There is a Heavenward stair—
25   "Mount, strain upwards, strain and strain—
"Each step will crumble to your foot
    "That never shall descend again.
"There grows a tree from ancient root,
"With healing leaves and twelvefold fruit,
30 "In musical Heaven air:
"Feast with me there."—

"I have a home on earth I cannot leave,
"I have a friend on earth I cannot grieve:
    "Come down to me, I cannot mount to you."—

35   "Nay choose between us both,
       "Choose as you are lief or loath:
          "You cannot keep these things and have me too."—

A Yawn.

    I grow so weary: is it death
       This awful woful weariness?
    It is a weight to heave my breath,
       A weight to wake, a weight to sleep;
5   I have no heart to work or weep.

    The sunshine teazes and the dark;
       Only the twilight dulls my grief:
    Is this the Ark, the strong safe Ark,
       Or the tempestuous drowning sea
10   · Whose crested coursers foam for me?

    Why does the sea moan evermore?
       Shut out from Heaven it makes its moan,
    It frets against the boundary shore:
       All earth's full rivers cannot fill
15   The sea, that drinking thirsteth still.

    Sheer miracles of loveliness
       Lie hid in its unlooked-on bed:
    Salt passionless anemones
       Blow flower-like; just enough alive
20   To blow and propagate and thrive.

    Shells quaint with curve or spot or spike,
       Encrusted live things argus-eyed,
    All fair alike yet all unlike,
       Are born without a pang and die
25   Without a pang and so pass by.

    I would I lived without a pang:
       Oh happy they who day by day
    Quiescent neither sobbed nor sang;
       Unburdened with a what or why
30   They live and die and so pass by.

For H. P.

On the land and on the sea,
Jesus keep both you and me:

Going out and coming in,
Christ keep us both from shame and sin:

5 In this world, in the world to come,
Keep us safe and lead us home:

Today in toil, tonight in rest,
Be Best Beloved and love us best.

"Then they that feared the Lord spake often one to another."

Friend I commend to thee the narrow way:
Not because I, please God, will walk therein,
But rather for the love-feast of that day
    The exceeding prize which whoso will may win.
5 This world is old and rotting at the core
Here death's heads mock us with a toothless grin
    Here heartiest laughter leaves us spent and sore.
We heap up treasures for the fretting moth,
Our children heap our fathers heaped before,
10   But what shall profit us the cumbrous growth?
It cannot journey with us, cannot save,
Stripped in that darkness be we lief or loth
    Stripped bare to what we are from all we have,
Naked we came, naked we must return
15 To one obscure inevitable grave.
    If this the lesson is which we must learn
Taught by God's discipline of love or wrath
(To brand or purify His fire must burn)—
    Friend I commend to thee the narrow path
20 That thou and I, please God, may walk therein,

May taste and see how good is God Who hath
   Loved us while hating even to death our sin.

"What good shall my life do me?"

No hope in life; yet is there hope
In death, the threshold of man's scope:
Man yearneth (as the heliotrope

For ever seeks the sun) thro' light
5   Thro' dark for Love: all read aright
Is Love for Love is infinite.

Shall not this infinite Love suffice
To feed thy dearth? Lift heart and eyes
Up to the hills, grow glad and wise.

10   The hills are glad because the sun
Kisses their round tops every one
Where silver fountains laugh and run:

Smooth pebbles shine beneath; beside
The grass, mere green, grows myriad-eyed
15   With pomp of blossoms veined or pied.

So every nest is glad whereon
The sun in tender strength has shone;
So every fruit he glows upon;

So every valley depth, whose herds
20   At pasture praise him without words;
So the winged extasies of birds.

If there be any such thing, what
Is there by sunlight betters not?—
Nothing except dead things that rot.

25   Thou then who art not dead and fit
Like blasted tree beside the pit
But for the axe that levels it,

Living show life of Love, whereof
The force wields earth and heaven above:
30   Who knows not Love begetteth Love?—

Love in the gracious rain distils;
Love moves the subtle fountain rills
To fertilize uplifted hills

And seedful vallies fertilize;
35   Love stills the hungry lion's cries
And the young raven satisfies;

Love hangs this earth in space; Love rolls
Fair worlds rejoicing on their poles
And girds them round with aureoles;

40   Love lights the sun; Love thro' the dark
Lights the moon's evanescent arc;
Same Love lights up the glow-worm's spark;

Love rears the great; Love tends the small;
Breaks off the yoke, breaks down the wall;
45   Accepteth all, fulfilleth all.

O ye who taste that Love is sweet,
Set waymarks for the doubtful feet
That stumble on in search of it.

Sing hymns of Love, that those who hear
50   Far off in pain may lend an ear
Rise up and wonder and draw near.

Lead lives of Love, that others who
Behold your lives may kindle too
With Love and cast their lots with you.

The Massacre of Perugia.

A trumpet pealed thro' France. Then Italy
Stirred, shook, from sea to sea.
Then many cities broke

Their lawful yoke.
5   Then in an evil hour
Perugia on her fort-crowned hill

[The rest of the poem is missing from the notebook.]

I have done with hope;
Have done with lies from sea to sea:
How should I lie beneath the cope
Of Heaven's star-blazoned verity?

5   I will not wear your crown tonight,
But mine own crown tomorrow morn:

[The lines of the poem preceding and following the above are missing from the notebook.]

Promises like Piecrust.

Promise me no promises,
   So will I not promise you;
Keep we both our liberties,
   Never false and never true:
5   Let us hold the die uncast,
   Free to come as free to go;
For I cannot know your past,
   And of mine what can you know?

You, so warm, may once have been
10   Warmer towards another one;
I, so cold, may once have seen
   Sunlight, once have felt the sun:
Who shall show us if it was
   Thus indeed in time of old?
15   Fades the image from the glass
   And the fortune is not told.

If you promised, you might grieve
   For lost liberty again;

If I promised, I believe
20   I should fret to break the chain:
Let us be the friends we were,
   Nothing more but nothing less;
Many thrive on frugal fare
   Who would perish of excess.

By the waters of Babylon.

By the waters of Babylon
   We sit down and weep,
Far from the pleasant land
   Where our fathers sleep;
5   Far from our Holy Place
   From which the Glory is gone;
We sit in dust and weep
   By the waters of Babylon.

By the waters of Babylon
10   The willow trees grow rank:
We hang our harps thereon
   Silent upon the bank.
Before us the days are dark,
   And dark the days that are gone;
15   We grope in the very dark
   By the waters of Babylon.

By the waters of Babylon
   We thirst for Jordan yet,
We pine for Jerusalem
20   Whereon our hearts are set:
Our priests defiled and slain,
   Our princes ashamed and gone,
Oh how should we forget
   By the waters of Babylon?

25   By the waters of Babylon
   Tho' the wicked grind the just,
Our seed shall yet strike root

And shall shoot up from the dust:
The captive shall lead captive,
30   The slave rise up and begone,
And thou too shalt sit in dust
    O daughter of Babylon.

Better so.

Fast asleep, mine own familiar friend,
    Fast asleep at last:
        Tho' the pain was strong,
        Tho' the struggle long,
5   It is past;
All thy pangs are at an end.

Whilst I weep, whilst death bells toll,
    Thou art fast asleep,
        With idle hands upon thy breast
10   And heart at rest:
        Whilst I weep
Angels sing around thy singing soul.

Who would wish thee back upon the rough
    Wearisome dangerous road?
15   Wish back thy toil-spent soul
        Just at the goal?
        My soul, praise God
For one dear soul which hath enough.

I would not fetch thee back to hope with me
20   A sickening hope deferred,
        To taste the cup that slips
        From thirsty lips:
        Hast thou not heard
What was to hear, and seen what was to see?

25 I would not speak the word if I could raise
        My dead to life:
            I would not speak
            If I could flush thy cheek

      And rouse thy pulses' strife
30   And send thy feet on the once-trodden ways.

How could I meet the dear rebuke
    If thou should'st say:
      "O friend of little faith,
      Good was my lot of death,
35   And good my day
Of rest, and good the sleep I took"—?

Our widowed Queen.

The Husband of the widow care for her,
    The Father of the fatherless:
The faithful Friend, the abiding Comforter,
    Watch over her to bless.

5   Full twenty years of blameless married faith,
    Of love and honour questioned not,
Joys, griefs imparted: for the first time Death
    Sunders the common lot.

Christ help the desolate Queen upon her throne,
10   Strengthen her hands, confirm her heart:
For she henceforth must bear a load alone
    Borne until now in part.

Christ help the desolate Woman in her home,
    Broken of heart, indeed bereft;
15   Shrinking from solitary days to come,
    Beggared tho' much is left.

Rise up, O Sons and Daughters of the Dead,
    Weep with your Mother where she weeps;
Yet not as sorrowing without hope be shed
20   Your tears: he only sleeps.

Rise up, O Sons and Daughters of the realm,
    In pale reflected sorrow move;
Revere the widowed hand that holds the helm,
    Love her with double love.

25   In royal patience of her soul possess'd
           May she fulfill her length of days:
       Then may her children rise and call her bless'd,
           Then may her husband praise.

In progress.

Ten years ago it seemed impossible
    That she should ever grow so calm as this,
    With self-remembrance in her warmest kiss
And dim dried eyes like an exhausted well.
5 Slow-speaking when she has some fact to tell,
    Silent with long-unbroken silences,
    Centred in self yet not unpleased to please,
Gravely monotonous like a passing bell.
Mindful of drudging daily common things,
10   Patient at pastime, patient at her work,
Wearied perhaps but strenuous certainly.
Sometimes I fancy we may one day see
    Her head shoot forth seven stars from where they lurk
And her eyes lightnings and her shoulders wings.

"Out of the deep."

Have mercy, Thou my God; mercy, my God;
    For I can hardly bear life day by day:
    Be I here or there I fret myself away:
Lo for Thy staff I have but felt Thy rod
5 Along this tedious desert path long trod.
    When will Thy judgement judge me, Yea or Nay?
    I pray for grace; but then my sins unpray
My prayer: on holy ground I fool stand shod.
While still Thou haunts't me, faint upon the cross,
10   A sorrow beyond sorrow in Thy look,
Unutterable craving for my soul.
All faithful Thou, Lord: I, not Thou, forsook
    Myself; I traitor slunk back from the goal:
Lord, I repent; help Thou my helpless loss.

For a Mercy received.

Thank God Who spared me what I feared!
   Once more I gird myself to run.
   Thy promise stands, Thou Faithful One.
Horror of darkness disappeared
5   At length; once more I see the sun,

And dare to wait in hope for Spring,
   To face and bear the Winter's cold:
   The dead cocoon shall yet unfold
And give to light the living wing;
10   There's hidden sap beneath the mould.

My God, how could my courage flag
   So long as Thou art still the same?
   For what were labour, failure, shame,
Whilst Thy sure promise doth not lag
15   And Thou dost shield me with Thy Name?

Yet am I weak, my faith is weak,
   My heart is weak that pleads with Thee:
   O Thou That art not far to seek
Turn to me, hearken when I speak,
20   Stretch forth Thy Hand to succour me.

Thro' many perils have I pass'd,
   Deaths, plagues, and wonders, have I seen:
   Till now Thy Hand hath held me fast:
Lord help me, hold me, to the last;
25   Still be what Thou hast always been.

Open Thy Heart of Love to me,
   Give me Thyself, keep nothing back
Even as I give myself to Thee.
   Love paid by Love doth nothing lack,
30   And Love to pay Love is not slack.

Love doth so grace and dignify
   That beggars sue as King with King
Before the Throne of Grace on high:

         My God, be gracious to my cry;
35   My God, accept what gift I bring:

         A heart that loves; tho' soiled and bruised,
            Yet chosen by Thee in time of yore:
         Who ever came and was refused
         By Thee? Do, Lord, as Thou art used
40   To do, and make me love Thee more.

Summer.

         Come, cuckoo, come;
            Come again, swift swallow;
         Come and welcome; where you come
            Summer's sure to follow.
5   June, the month of months,
            Flowers and fruitage brings too;
         When green trees spread shadiest boughs,
            When each wild bird sings too.

         May is scant and crude,
10   Generous June is riper;
         Birds fall silent in July,
            June has its woodland piper:
         Rocks upon the maple-top
            Homely-hearted linnet,
15   Full in hearing of his nest
            And the dear ones in it.

         If the year would stand
            Still at June for ever,
         With no further growth on land
20   Nor further flow of river,
         If all nights were shortest nights
            And longest days were all the seven,—
         This might be a merrier world
            To my mind to live in.

A Dumb Friend.

I planted a young tree when I was young;
   But now the tree is grown and I am old:
   There wintry robin shelters from the cold
     And tunes his silver tongue.

5 A green and living tree I planted it,
   A glossy-foliaged tree of evergreen:
   All thro' the noontide heat it spread a screen
     Whereunder I might sit.

But now I only watch it where it towers:
10   I, sitting at my window, watch it tossed
   By rattling gale, or silvered by the frost;
     Or, when sweet summer flowers,

Wagging its round green head with stately grace
   In tender winds that kiss it and go by:
15   It shows a green full age; and what show I?
     A faded wrinkled face.

So often have I watched it, till mine eyes
   Have filled with tears and I have ceased to see;
   That now it seems a very friend to me
20   In all my secrets wise.

A faithful pleasant friend, who year by year
   Grew with my growth and strengthened with my
        strength,
   But whose green lifetime shows a longer length:
     When I shall not sit here

25 It still will bud in spring, and shed rare leaves
   In autumn, and in summer heat give shade,
   And warmth in winter; when my bed is made
     In shade the cypress weaves.

Margery.

What shall we do with Margery?
　　She lies and cries upon her bed,
　　All lily-pale from foot to head,
Her heart is sore as sore can be;
5　　Poor guileless shamefaced Margery.

A foolish girl, to love a man
　　And let him know she loved him so!
She should have tried a different plan;
　　Have loved, but not have let him know:
10　　Then he perhaps had loved her so.

What can we do with Margery
　　Who has no relish for her food?
We'd take her with us to the sea—
　　Across the sea—but where's the good?
15　She'd fret alike on land and sea.

Yes, what the neighbours say is true:
　　Girls should not make themselves so cheap.
But now it's done what can we do?
　　I hear her moaning in her sleep,
20　　Moaning and sobbing in her sleep.

I think—and I'm of flesh and blood—
　　Were I that man for whom she cares
　　I would not cost her tears and prayers
To leave her just alone like mud,
25　　Fretting her simple heart with cares.

A year ago she was a child,
　　Now she's a woman in her grief;
　　The year's now at the falling leaf,
At budding of the leaves she smiled;
30　Poor foolish harmless foolish child.

It was her own fault? so it was.
　　If every own fault found us out
　　Dogged us and snared us round about,

What comfort should we take because
35   Not half our due we thus wrung out?

At any rate the question stands:
    What now to do with Margery,
A weak poor creature on our hands?
    Something we must do: I'll not see
40   Her blossom fade, sweet Margery.

Perhaps a change may after all
    Prove best for her: to leave behind
    These home-sights seen time out of mind;
To get beyond the narrow wall
45   Of home, and learn home is not all.

Perhaps this way she may forget,
    Not all at once, but in a while;
May come to wonder how she set
    Her heart on this slight thing, and smile
50   At her own folly, in a while.

Yet this I say and I maintain:
    Were I the man she's fretting for
    I should my very self abhor
If I could leave her to her pain,
55   Uncomforted to tears and pain.

In Patience.

I will not faint, but trust in God
    Who this my lot hath given;
He leads me by the thorny road
    Which is the road to heaven.
5 Tho' sad my day that lasts so long,
At evening I shall have a song;
Tho' dim my day until the night,
At evening time there shall be light.

My life is but a working day
10   Whose tasks are set aright:

A while to work, a while to pray,
   And then a quiet night.
And then, please God, a quiet night
Where Saints and Angels walk in white:
15 One dreamless sleep from work and sorrow,
But re-awakening on the morrow.

Sunshine.

"There's little sunshine in my heart
   Slack to spring, lead to sink;
There's little sunshine in the world
         I think."—

5 "There's glow of sunshine in my heart
   (Cool wind, cool the glow);
There's flood of sunshine in the world
         I know."—

Now if of these one spoke the truth,
10   One spoke more or less:
But which was which I will not tell;—
         You, guess.

Meeting.

If we shall live, we live;
   If we shall die, we die;
If we live, we shall meet again;
   But tonight, good bye.
5 One word, let but one be heard—
What, not one word?

If we sleep, we shall wake again
   And see tomorrow's light;
If we wake, we shall meet again;
10   But tonight, good night.
Good night, my lost and found—
   Still not a sound?

If we live, we must part;
   If we die, we part in pain;
15 If we die, we shall part
   Only to meet again.
By those tears on either cheek,
Tomorrow you will speak.

To meet, worth living for;
20   Worth dying for, to meet;
To meet, worth parting for;
   Bitter forgot in sweet.
To meet, worth parting before
Never to part more.

"None with Him."

My God, to live: how didst Thou bear to live
   Preaching and teaching, toiling to and fro;
Few men accepting what Thou hadst to give,
     Few men prepared to know
5   Thy Face, to see the truth Thou camest to show?

My God, to die: how didst Thou bear to die
   That long slow death in weariness of pain;
A curse and an astonishment, passed by,
     Pointed at, mocked again,
10   By men for whom Thy Blood was shed in vain?

Whilst I do hardly bear my easy life,
   And hardly face my easy-coming death:
I turn to flee before the tug of strife;
     And shrink with troubled breath
15   From sleep, that is not death Thy Spirit saith.

Under Willows.

Under willows among the graves
   One was walking, ah welladay!
Where each willow her green boughs waves

Come April prime, come May.
5   Under willows among the graves
    She met her lost love, ah welladay!
Where in Autumn each wild wind raves
    And whirls sere leaves away.

He looked at her with a smile,
10   She looked at him with a sigh,
Both paused to look awhile;
    Then he passed by,
Passed by and whistled a tune;
    She stood silent and still:
15   It was the sunniest day in June,
    Yet one felt a chill.

Under willows among the graves
    I know a certain black black pool
Scarce wrinkled when Autumn raves;
20   Under the turf is cool;
Under the water it must be cold;
    Winter comes cold when Summer's past;
Though she live to be old, so old,
    She shall die at last.

A Sketch.

The blindest buzzard that I know
    Does not wear wings to spread and stir,
    Nor does my special mole wear fur
And grub among the roots below;
5   He sports a tail indeed, but then
    It's to a coat; he's man with men;
      His quill is cut to a pen.

In other points our friend's a mole,
    A buzzard, beyond scope of speech:
10   He sees not what's within his reach,
Misreads the part, ignores the whole.
    Misreads the part so reads in vain,

Ignores the whole tho' patent plain,
    Misreads both parts again.

15 My blindest buzzard that I know,
    My special mole, when will you see?
    Oh no, you must not look at me,
There's nothing hid for me to show.
    I might show facts as plain as day;
20   But since your eyes are blind, you'd say:
      Where? What? and turn away.

If I had Words.

If I had words, if I had words
    At least to vent my misery:—
But muter than the speechless herds
    I have no voice wherewith to cry.
5 I have no strength to lift my hands,
    I have no heart to lift mine eye,
My soul is bound with brazen bands,
    My soul is crushed and like to die.
My thoughts that wander here and there,
10   That wander wander listlessly,
Bring nothing back to cheer my care,
    Nothing that I may live thereby.
My heart is broken in my breast,
    My breath is but a broken sigh—
15 Oh if there be a land of rest
    It is far off, it is not nigh.
If I had wings as hath a dove,
    If I had wings that I might fly,
I yet would seek the land of love
20   Where fountains run which run not dry;
Tho' there be none that road to tell,
    And long that road is verily:
Then if I lived I should do well,
    And if I died I should but die.
25 If I had wings as hath a dove
    I would not sift the what and why,

I would make haste to find out love,
   If not to find at least to try.
I would make haste to love, my rest;
30   To love, my truth that doth not lie:
Then if I lived it might be best,
   Or if I died I could but die.

What to do?

Oh my love and my own own deary!
What shall I do? my love is weary.
Sleep, O friend, on soft downy pillow,
Pass, O friend, as wind or as billow,
5   And I'll wear the willow.

No stone at his head be set,
A swelling turf be his coverlet
Bound round with a graveyard wattle;
Hedged round from the trampling cattle
10   And the children's prattle.

I myself, instead of a stone,
Will sit by him to dwindle and moan;
Sit and weep with a bitter weeping,
Sit and weep where my love lies sleeping
15   While my life goes creeping.

Young Death.

Lying adying—
Such sweet things untasted,
Such rare beauties wasted:
Her hair a hidden treasure,
5   Her voice a lost pleasure;
Her soul made void of passion;
Her body going to nothing
Though long it took to fashion,
Soon to be a loathing:
10   Her road hath no turning,

Her light is burning burning
With last feeble flashes;
Dying from the birth:
Dust to dust, earth to earth,
15 Ashes to ashes.

Lying adying—
Have done with vain sighing:
Life not lost but treasured,
God Almighty pleasured,
20 God's daughter fetched and carried,
Christ's bride betrothed and married.
Lo, in the Room, the Upper,
She shall sit down to supper,
New bathed from head to feet
25 And on Christ gazing;
Her mouth kept clean and sweet
Shall laugh and sing, God praising:
Then shall be no more weeping,
Or fear, or sorrow,
30 Or waking more, or sleeping,
Or night, or morrow,
Or cadence in the song
Of songs, or thirst, or hunger;
The strong shall rise more strong
35 And the young younger.
Our tender little dove
Meek-eyed and simple,
Our love goes home to Love;
There shall she walk in white
40 Where God shall be the Light
And God the Temple.

In a certain place.

I found Love in a certain place
Asleep and cold—or cold and dead?—
All ivory-white upon his bed

All ivory-white his face.
5   His hands were folded
On his quiet breast,
To his figure laid at rest
Chilly bed was moulded.

His hair hung lax about his brow,
10   I had not seen his face before;
Or if I saw it once, it wore
Another aspect now.
No trace of last night's sorrow,
No shadow of tomorrow;
15   All at peace (thus all sorrows cease),
All at peace.

I wondered: Were his eyes
Soft or falcon-clear?
I wondered: As he lies
20   Does he feel me near?
In silence my heart spoke
And wondered: If he woke
And found me sitting nigh him
And felt me sitting by him,
25   If life flushed to his cheek,
He living man with men,
Then if I heard him speak
Oh should I know him then?

"Cannot sweeten."

If that's water you wash your hands in
    Why is it black as ink is black?—
Because my hands are foul with my folly:
    Oh the lost time that comes not back!—

5   If that's water you bathe your feet in
    Why is it red as wine is red?—
Because my feet sought blood in their goings;
    Red red is the track they tread.—

      Slew you mother or slew you father
10   That your foulness passeth not by?—
      Not father and oh not mother:
       I slew my love with an evil eye.—

      Slew you sister or slew you brother
       That in peace you have not a part?—
15   Not brother and oh not sister:
       I slew my love with a hardened heart.

      He loved me because he loved me,
       Not for grace or beauty I had;
      He loved me because he loved me;
20   For his loving me I was glad.

      Yet I loved him not for his loving
       While I played with his love and truth,
      Not loving him for his loving,
       Wasting his joy, wasting his youth.

25   I ate his life as a banquet,
       I drank his life as new wine,
      I fattened upon his leanness,
       Mine to flourish and his to pine.

      So his life fled as running water,
30   So it perished as water spilt:
      If black my hands and my feet as scarlet,
       Blacker redder my heart of guilt.

      Cold as a stone, as hard, as heavy;
       All my sighs ease it no whit,
35   All my tears make it no cleaner
       Dropping dropping dropping on it.

Of my life.

      I weary of my life
       Thro' the long sultry day,
       While happy creatures play

Their harmless lives away:—
5   What is my life?

I weary of my life
   Thro' the slow tedious night,
   While earth and heaven's delight
   The moon walks forth in white:—
10   What is my life?

If I might I would die;
   My soul should flee away
   To day that is not day
   Where sweet souls sing and say.—
15   If I might die!

If I might I would die;
   My body out of sight,
   All night that is not night
   My soul should walk in white—
20   If I might die!

      Yes, I too could face death and never shrink:
   But it is harder to bear hated life;
   To strive with hands and knees weary of strife;
      To drag the heavy chain whose every link
5   Galls to the bone; to stand upon the brink
Of the deep grave, nor drowse, though it be rife
With sleep; to hold with steady hand the knife
      Nor strike home: this is courage as I think.
Surely to suffer is more than to do:
10   To do is quickly done; to suffer is
      Longer and fuller of heart-sicknesses:
      Each day's experience testifies of this:
Good deeds are many, but good lives are few;
      Thousands taste the full cup; who drains the lees?—

      Would that I were a turnip white,
   Or raven black,

Or miserable hack
    Dragging a cab from left to right;
5   Or would I were the showman of a sight,
Or weary donkey with a laden back,
Or racer in a sack,
    Or freezing traveller on an Alpine height;
Or would I were straw catching as I drown,
10   (A wretched landsman I who cannot swim,)
  Or watching a lone vessel sink,
  Rather than writing: I would change my pink
Gauze for a hideous yellow satin gown
    With deep-cut scolloped edges and a rim.

I fancy the good fairies dressed in white,
Glancing like moon-beams through the shadows black;
Without much work to do for king or hack.
    Training perhaps some twisted branch aright;
5   Or sweeping faded Autumn leaves from sight
To foster embryo life; or binding back
Stray tendrils; or in ample bean-pod sack
    Bringing wild honey from the rocky height;
Or fishing for a fly lest it should drown;
10   Or teaching water-lily heads to swim,
  Fearful that sudden rain might make them sink;
  Or dyeing the pale rose a warmer pink;
Or wrapping lilies in their leafy gown,
    Yet letting the white peep beyond the rim.—

Some ladies dress in muslin full and white,
Some gentlemen in cloth succinct and black;
Some patronise a dog-cart, some a hack,
    Some think a painted clarence only right.
5   Youth is not always such a pleasing sight,
Witness a man with tassels on his back;
Or woman in a great-coat like a sack
    Towering above her sex with horrid height.

    If all the world were water fit to drown
10   There are some whom you would not teach to swim,
    Rather enjoying if you saw them sink;
    Certain old ladies dressed in girlish pink,
With roses and geraniums on their gown:—
      Go to the Bason, poke them o'er the rim.—

Autumn.

Fade tender lily,
    Fade O crimson rose,
Fade every flower
    Sweetest flower that blows.

5   Go chilly Autumn,
    Come O Winter cold;
Let the green things die away
    Into common mould.

Birth follows hard on death,
10   Life on withering:
Hasten, we shall come the sooner
    Back to pleasant Spring.

Il rosseggiar dell' Oriente
Canzoniere
"All' Amico Contano"—.

1.
Amor dormente?

Addio, diletto amico;
    A me non lece amore,
    Chè già m'uccise il core
      Amato amante.

5 Eppur per l'altra vita
    Consacro a te speranze;
    Per questa, rimembranze
      Tante e poi tante.

2.
Amor Si sveglia?

In nuova primavera
    Rinasce il genio antico;
Amor t'insinua "Spera"—
    Pur io nol dico.

5 S' "Ama"—ti dice Amore;
    S'ei t'incoraggia, amico,
Giurando "È tuo quel core"—
    Pur io nol dico.

Anzi, quel cor davvero
10   Chi sa se valga un fico?
Lo credo, almen lo spero;
    Ma pur nol dico.

3.
Si rimanda la tocca-caldaja.

Lungi da me il pensiere
    D'ereditar l'oggetto
    Ch'una fiata in petto
      Destar ti seppe amor.
5 Se più l'usar non vuoi,
    Se pur fumar nol puoi,
    Dolce ti sia dovere
      Il conservarlo ognor.

4.

"Blumine" risponde:

S'io t'incontrassi nell'eterna pace,
   Pace non più, per me saria diletto;
   S'io t'incontrassi in cerchio maledetto
Te più di me lamenterei verace.
5   Per te mia vita mezzo morta giace,
   Per te le notti veglio e bagno il letto:
   Eppur di rivederti un dì m'aspetto
In secol che riman, non che in fugace.
E perciò "Fuggi" io dico al tempo, e omai
10   "Passa pur" dico al vanitoso mondo:
Mentre mi sogno quel che dici e fai
   Ripeto in me "Doman sarà giocondo,
"Doman sarem"—ma s'ami tu lo sai,
   E se non ami a che mostrarti il fondo?—

5.

"Lassù fia caro il rivederci"—.

Dolce cor mio perduto e non perduto,
   Dolce mia vita che mi lasci in morte,
   Amico e più che amico, ti saluto.
Ricordati di me; che cieche e corte
5   Fur le speranze mie, ma furon tue:
   Non disprezzar questa mia dura sorte.
Lascia ch'io dica "Le speranze sue
   "Come le mie languiro in questo inverno"—
   Pur mi rassegnerò, quel che fue fue.
10   Lascia ch'io dica ancor "Con lui discerno
   "Giorno che spunta da gelata sera,
   "Lungo cielo al di là di breve inferno,
   "Al di là dell'inverno primavera."

6.

"Non son io la rosa ma vi stetti appresso."

Casa felice ove più volte omai
   Siede il mio ben parlando e ancor ridendo,
   Donna felice che con lui sedendo
Lo allegri pur con quanto dici e fai,
5 Giardin felice dove passeggiai
   Pensando a lui, pensando e non dicendo,
   Giorno felice fia quand'io mi rendo
Laddove passeggiando a lui pensai.
Ma s'egli vi sarà quand'io vi torno,
10 S'egli m'accoglie col suo dolce riso,
Ogni uccelletto canterà dintorno,
   La rosa arrossirà nel vago viso—
Iddio ci dia in eternità quel giorno,
   Ci dia per quel giardino il paradiso.

7.

"Lassuso il caro Fiore"—.

Se t'insegnasse Iddio
   Il proprio Amor così,
Ti cederei, cor mio,
   Al caro Fiore.
5 Il caro Fior ti chiama
   "Fammi felice un dì"—
Il caro Fior che t'ama
   Ti chiede amore.

Quel Fiore in paradiso
10 Fiorisce ognor per te;
Sì, rivedrai quel viso,
   Sarai contento:
Intorno al duol ch'è stato
   Domanderai "Dov'è?"—
15 Chè passerà il passato
   In un momento.

Ed io per tanta vista
   In tutta eternità,
Io qual Giovan Battista
20   Loderò Dio:
L'Amata tanto amata
   Tuo guiderdon sarà,
E l'alma tua salvata
    Sarammi il mio.

8.

Sapessi pure!

Che fai lontan da me,
   Che fai, cor mio?
    Quel che facc'io
È ch'ognor penso a te.

5 Pensando a te sorrido,
   Sospiro a te:
    E tu lontan da me
Tu pur sei fido?

9.

Iddio c'illumini!

Quando il tempo avverrà che partiremo
   Ciascun di noi per separata via,
Momento che verrà, momento estremo
    Quando che fia:

5 Calcando l'uno inusitata traccia,
   Seguendo l'altro il solito suo corso,
Non ci nasca in quel dì vergogna in faccia
    Nè in sen rimorso.

Sia che tu vada pria forte soletto,
10   O sia ch'io ti preceda in quel sentiero,

Deh ricordiamci allor d'averci detto
    Pur sempre il vero.

Quanto t'amavo e quanto! e non dovea
    Esprimer quell'amor che ti portavo:
15 Più ma assai più di quel che non dicea
    Nel cuor ti amavo.

Più di felicità, più di speranza;
    Di vita non dirò, chè è poca cosa:
Dolce-amaro tu fosti in rimembranza
20   A me gelosa.

Ma a me tu preferisti la virtude,
    La veritade, amico: e non saprai
Chi amasti alfin? Soltanto il fior si schiude
    D'un sole ai rai.

25 Se più di me la Veritade amasti,
    Gesù fu quel tuo sconosciuto Amore:—
Gesù, Che sconosciuto a lui parlasti,
    Vincigli il core.

       10.

Amicizia:

"Sirocchia son d'Amor"—.

Venga Amicizia e sia la benvenuta,
    Venga, ma non perciò sen parta Amore:
    Abitan l'uno e l'altra in gentil core
Che albergo ai pellegrini non rifiuta.
5 Ancella questa docile e compiuta,
    E quei tiranno no ma pio signore:
    Regni egli occulto nè si mostri fuore,
Essa si sveli in umiltà dovuta.
Oggi ed ancor doman per l'amicizia,
10   E posdomani ancor se pur si vuole,
    Chè dolci cose apporta e non amare:
    E venga poi, ma non con luna o sole,

Giorno d'amor, giorno di gran delizia,
   Giorno che spunta non per tramontare.

11.

"Luscious and sorrowful"—.*

Uccello-delle rose e del dolore,
   Uccel d'amore,
Felice ed infelice, quel tuo canto
   È riso o pianto?
5 Fido all'infido, tieni in freddo lido
   Spina per nido.

12.

"Oh forza irresistibile
Dell'umile preghiera"—.

Che Ti darò Gesù Signor mio buono?
Ah quello ch'amo più, quello Ti dono:
Accettalo Signor Gesù mio Dio,
Il sol mio dolce amor, anzi il cor mio;
5 Accettalo per Te, siati prezioso;
Accettalo per me, salva il mio sposo.
Non ho che lui, Signor, nol disprezzare,
Caro tienlo nel cor fra cose care.
Ricordati del dì che sulla croce
10 Pregavi Iddio così, con flebil voce,
Con anelante cor: "Questo che fanno
"Padre perdona lor, ch'essi non sanno"—:
Ei pur, Signor, non sa Quello che sdegna,
Ei pure T'amerà s'uno gl'insegna.
15 Se tutto quanto appar, che a Te non piace,
Fugace spuma in mar, nebbia fugace;
Successo o avversità, contento o duolo,

* "Did she perch thee on hand or shoulder?—"

Se tutto è vanità fuorchè Tu solo;
Se chi non prega Te nel vuoto chiama;
20 Se amore amor non è che Te non ama;—
Dona Te stesso a noi, ricchi saremo;
Poi nega quanto vuoi, chè tutto avremo:
Di mel più dolce Tu, che ben ci basti;
D'amore amabil più, Tu che ci amasti.

13.

Finestra mia orientale.
[In malattia.]

Volgo la faccia verso l'oriente,
    Verso il meriggio, ove colui dimora:—
    Ben fai che vivi ai lati dell'Aurora;
Chi teco vive par felice gente.
5 Volgo verso di te l'occhio languente,
    Lo spirito che teme e spera ancora;
    Volgiti verso quella che ti onora,
T'ama, ti brama, in core e colla mente.
Debole e stanca verso te mi volgo:
10   Che sarà mai questo che sento, amico?
Ogni cara memoria tua raccolgo
    Quanto dirti vorrei! ma pur nol dico.
Lungi da te dei giorni me ne dolgo:
    Fossimo insieme in bel paese aprico!

15   Fossimo insieme!
                Che importerebbe
            U'si facesse
                Il nostro nido?
            Cielo sarebbe
20   Quasi quel lido.

            Ah fossi teco,
                Col cor ben certo
            D'essere amato
                Come vorrebbe!

25   Sì che il deserto
        S'infiorirebbe.

14.
[Eppure allora venivi.]

Oh tempo tardo e amaro!—
    Quando verrai, cor mio,
      Quando, ma quando?
Siccome a me sei caro
5   Se cara a te foss'io
      Ti andrei cercando?

15.
Per Preferenza.

Felice la tua madre,
    Le suore tue felici,
    Che senton quanto dici,
      Che vivono con te,
5   Che t'amano di dritto
    D'amor contento e saggio:
    Pur questo lor vantaggio
      Non lo vorrei per me.

Quel grave aspetto tuo
10   Veder da quando in quando,
    Frattanto andar pensando
      "Un giorno riverrà";
    Ripeter nel mio core
    (Qual rosa è senza spine?)
15   "Ei sa che l'amo alfine—
      M'ama egli ancor?" Chi sa!

È questo assai più dolce
    Dell'altro, al parer mio:
    Essere in ver desio

20   O tutto o nulla* a te,
   Nè troppo vo'lagnarmi
     Ch'or stai da me diviso,
     Se un giorno in Paradiso
      Festeggerai con me.

   * Ma no; se non amante siimi amico:
Quel ch'io sarò per te, non tel predico.

16.

Oggi

Possibil non sarebbe
   Ch'io non t'amassi, o caro:
Chi mai si scorderebbe
    Del proprio core?
5 Se amaro il dolce fai,
   Dolce mi fai l'amaro;
Se qualche amor mi dài,
    Ti do l'amore.

17.

[Se fossi andata a Hastings.]

Ti do l'addio,
Amico mio,
Per settimane
   Che paion lunghe:
5 Ti raccomando
Da quando in quando
Circoli quadri,
   Idee bislunghe.

18.

Ripetizione.

Credea di rivederti e ancor ti aspetto;
   Di giorno in giorno ognor ti vo bramando:
Quando ti rivedrò, cor mio diletto,
    Quando ma quando?
5   Dissi e ridissi con perenne sete,
   E lo ridico e vo'ridirlo ancora,
Qual usignol che canta e si ripete
    Fino all'aurora.

19.

"Amico e più che amico mio"—.

Cor mio a cui si volge l'altro mio core
   Qual calamita al polo, e non ti trova,
   La nascita della mia vita nuova
Con pianto fu, con grida e con dolore.
5   Ma l'aspro duolo fummi precursore
   Di speranza gentil che canta e cova;
   Sì, chi non prova pena amor non prova,
E quei non vive che non prova amore.
O tu che in Dio mi sei, ma dopo Iddio,
10   Tutta la terra mia ed assai del cielo,
   Pensa se non m'è duol disotto a un velo
    Parlati e non ti dir mai che ti bramo:—
Dillo tu stesso a te, dolce cor mio,
   Se pur tu m'ami dillo a te ch'io t'amo.

20.

"Nostre voluntà quieti Virtù di carità"—.

Vento gentil che verso il mezzodì
   Soffiando vai, deh porta un mio sospir,
   Dicendo ad Un quel che non debbo dir,

Con un sospir dicendogli così:
5   Quella che diede un 'No' volendo un 'Sì'
     (Volendo e non volendo—a che ridir?),
      Quella ti manda: È vanità il fiorir
Di questa vita che meniam costì.
Odi che dice e piange: È vanità
10   Questo che nasce e muore amor mondan;
      Deh leva gli occhi, io gli occhi vo'levar
     Verso il reame dove non in van
      Amasi Iddio quanto ognun possa amar
Ed il creato tutto in carità.

21.

[Se così fosse.]

Io più ti amai che non mi amasti tu:—
    Amen, se così volle Iddio Signor;
    Amen, quantunque mi si spezzi il cor,
     Signor Gesù.

5   Ma Tu che Ti ricordi e tutto sai,
    Tu che moristi per virtù d'amor,
    Nell'altro mondo donami quel cor
     Che tanto amai.

By way of Remembrance.

Remember, if I claim too much of you,
    I claim it of my brother and my friend:
    Have patience with me till the hidden end,
Bitter or sweet, in mercy shut from view.
5   Pay me my due; though I to pay your due
    Am all too poor and past what will can mend:
    Thus of your bounty you must give and lend
Still unrepaid by aught I look to do.

Still unrepaid by aught of mine on earth:
10 But overpaid, please God, when recompense
Beyond the mystic Jordan and new birth
   Is dealt to virtue as to innocence;
When Angels singing praises in their mirth
   Have borne you in their arms and fetched you hence.

Will you be there? my yearning heart has cried:
   Ah me, my love, my love, shall I be there,
   To sit down in your glory and to share
Your gladness, glowing as a virgin bride?
5 Or will another dearer, fairer-eyed,
   Sit nigher to you in your jubilee;
   And mindful one of other will you be
Borne higher and higher on joy's ebbless tide?
—Yea, if I love I will not grudge you this:
10 I too shall float upon that heavenly sea
   And sing my joyful praises without ache;
   Your overflow of joy shall gladden me,
   My whole heart shall sing praises for your sake
And find its own fulfilment in your bliss.

In resurrection is it awfuller
   That rising of the All or of the Each:
   Of all kins of all nations of all speech,
Or one by one of him and him and her?
5 When dust reanimate begins to stir
   Here, there, beyond, beyond, reach beyond reach;
   While every wave disgorges on its beach
Alive or dead-in-life some seafarer.
In resurrection, on the day of days,
10 That day of mourning throughout all the earth,
   In resurrection may we meet again:
   No more with stricken hearts to part in twain;
   As once in sorrow one, now one in mirth,
One in our resurrection songs of praise.

I love you and you know it—this at least,
   This comfort is mine own in all my pain:
   You know it and can never doubt again,
And love's mere self is a continual feast.
5 Not oath of mine nor blessing-word of priest
   Could make my love more certain or more plain:—
   Life as a rolling moon doth wax and wane
O weary moon, still rounding, still decreased!
Life wanes: and when love folds his wings above
10 Tired joy, and less we feel his conscious pulse,
    Let us go fall asleep, dear Friend, in peace;—
    A little while, and age and sorrow cease;
   A little while, and love reborn annuls
Loss and decay and death—and all is love.

Valentines from C.G.R.

Fairer than younger beauties, more beloved
   Than many a wife,—
By stress of Time's vicissitudes unmoved
   From settled calm of life,—

5 Endearing rectitude to those who watch
   The verdict of your face,
Raising & making gracious those who catch
   A semblance of your grace:—

With kindly lips of welcome, & with pleased
10 Propitious eyes benign,
Accept a kiss of homage from your least
   Last Valentine.

A Valentine, 1877.

Own Mother dear,
We all rejoicing here
Wait for each other,

Daughter for Mother,
5   Sister for Brother,
Till each dear face appear
Transfigured by Love's flame
Yet still the same,—
The same yet new,—
10   My face to you,
Your face to me,
Made lovelier by Love's flame
But still the same;
Most dear to see
15   In halo of Love's flame,
Because the same.

1878.

Blessed Dear & heart's Delight,
Companion, Friend, & Mother mine
Round whom my fears & love entwine,—
With whom I hope to stand & sing
5   Where Angels form the outer ring
Round singing Saints who, clad in white,
Know no more of day or night
Or death or any changeful thing,
Or anything that is not love,
10   Human love & love Divine,—
Bid me to that tryst above,
Bless your Valentine.

1879.

Mother mine
Whom every year
Doth endear,
Before sweet Spring
5   (That sweetest thing
Brimfull of bliss)

Sets all the throng
Of birds a-wooing
Billing & cooing,—
10   Your Valentine
Sings you a song,
Gives you a kiss.

1880.

More shower than shine
Brings sweet St. Valentine;
Warm shine, warm shower,
Bring up sweet flower on flower:
5   Thro' shower & shine
Loves you your Valentine,
Thro' shine, thro' shower,
Thro' summer's flush, thro' Autumn's fading hour.

St. Valentine's Day
1881.

Too cold almost for hope of Spring
   Or firstfruits from the realm of flowers,
Your dauntless Valentine, I bring
   One sprig of love, and sing
5   "Love has no Winter hours"—.

If even in this world love is love
   (This wintry world which felt the Fall),
What must it be in Heaven above
   Where love to great and small
10   Is all in all?

A Valentine
1882.

My blessed Mother dozing in her chair
   On Christmas Day seemed an embodied Love,
A comfortable Love with soft brown hair
   Softened and silvered to a tint of dove,
5   A better sort of Venus with an air
   Angelical from thoughts that dwell above,
A wiser Pallas in whose body fair
   Enshrined a blessed soul looks out thereof.
Winter brought Holly then; now Spring has brought
10   Paler and frailer Snowdrops shivering;
And I have brought a simple humble thought
   —I her devoted duteous Valentine—,
A lifelong thought which thrills this song I sing,
   A lifelong love to this dear Saint of mine.

February 14. 1883.

A world of change & loss, a world of death,
Of heart & eyes that fail, of labouring breath,
Of pains to bear & painful deeds to do:—
Nevertheless a world of life to come
5   And love; where you're at home, while in our home
Your Valentine rejoices having you.

1884.

Another year of joy & grief,
   Another year of hope & fear:
O Mother, is life long or brief?
   We hasten while we linger here.

5   But since we linger, love me still
   And bless me still, O Mother mine,
While hand in hand we scale life's hill,
   You Guide, & I your Valentine.

1885.
St. Valentine's Day.

All the Robin Redbreasts
   Have lived the winter thro',
Jenny Wrens have pecked their fill
   And found a work to do,
5 Families of Sparrows
   Have weathered wind & storm
With Rabbit on the stony hill
   And Hare upon her form.

You & I, my Mother,
10 Have lived the winter thro',
And still we play our daily parts
   And still find work to do:
And still the cornfields flourish,
   The olive & the vine,
15 And still you reign my Queen of Hearts
   And I'm your Valentine.

1886
St. Valentine's Day.

Winter's latest snowflake is the snowdrop flower,
   Yellow crocus kindles the first flame of the Spring,
At that time appointed, at that day and hour
   When life reawakens and hope in everything.
5 Such a tender snowflake in the wintry weather,
   Such a feeble flamelet for chilled St. Valentine,—
But blest be any weather which finds us still together,
   My pleasure and my treasure O blessed Mother mine.

Ah welladay and wherefore am I here?
I sit alone all day I sit & think—

I watch the sun arise, I watch it sink
And feel no soul-light tho the day is clear
5   Surely it is a folly; it is mere
Madness to stand for ever on the brink
Of dark despair & yet not break the link
That makes me scorned who cannot be held dear.
I will have done with it; I will not stand
10   And fear on without hope & tremble thus
Look for the break of day & miss it ever
Although my heart be broken they shall never
Say: She was glad to sojourn among us
Thankful if one would take her by the hand.

Along the highroad the way is too long
Let us walk where the oak trees rise up thick
I take a crab-, you take a cherry stick
Let us go from among men to the throng
5   Of belted bees: the wild roses smell strong
And sweet; & my old dog is fain to lick
My hand: best so in good truth I am sick
Of the world; & hear silence as a song
And you I think are changed friend you who once
10   Would dance thro' the long night; a something called
From your heart; into your hid brain it sunk;
Oh listen silence maketh the air drunk
I would not give these shades that have not palled
On me, for the broad light of many suns.

And is this August weather? nay not so
With the long rain the cornfield waxeth dark.
How the cold rain comes pouring down & hark
To the chill wind whose measured pace & slow
5   Seems still to linger being loth to go.
I cannot stand beside the sea and mark
Its grandeur; it's too wet for that: no lark
In this drear season cares to sing or show.

And since its name is August all men find
10   Fire not allowable; Winter foregone
Had more of sunlight & of glad warmth more
I shall be fain to run upon the shore
And mark the rain. Hath the sun ever shone
Cheer up there can be nothing worse to mind.

From early dawn until the flush of noon
And from hot noon unto the hushèd night
I look around beholding all things bright
From the deep sun unto the silver moon
5   My heart & soul & spirit are in tune.
My sense is gladdened with an inward light.
The very clouds above my head are white
And glorious radiance shall disperse them soon.
All trees & bushes fruits & flowers bear,
10   The sea is full of life & beauty, how
The grand waves leap up—as tho' full of sense,
A better day was not I think & ne'er
Was I so full of joy as I am now.
Surely a chill shall come & this go hence

I seek among the living & I seek
Among the dead for some to love; but few
I find at last & these have quite run through
Their store of love & friendship is too weak
5   And cold for me; yet will I never speak
Telling my heart want to cold listeners who
Will wonder smiling; I can bear & do
No tears shall sully my unfurrowed cheek
So when my dust shall mix with other dust
10   When I shall have found quiet in decay
And lie at ease & cease to be & rot
Those whom I love thinking of me shall not
Grieve with a measure, saying: Now we must
Weep for a little ere we go & play.

O glorious sea that in each climbing wave
Bearest great thoughts as in a wondrous book
The ends of earth oft at thy presence shook
And not denied when thou hast stooped to crave.
5 Sometimes the mighty winds have dared to brave
Thy potency; but with a single look
Raising thy head forth from its ancient nook
Thou hast recalled the quiet thou wouldst have.
What is a ship save many a fragile stick?
10 How should it brave thy terrors when they wear
The lightning crest that maketh substance wither
Yea though the planks be seasoned well & thick
Thine anger is too hard a thing to bear:—
Thou sayest to men: go back & come not hither.

Oh thou who tell'st me that all hope is over
With lazy limbs that heavily recline
On the soft cushions; flushed & fair with wine
Scarce seeming conscious of the scents that hover
5 Round & above thee: can thy heart recover
So soon its quiet, while mine own shall pine?
Thou who canst love & not o'erstep the line
Of comfort, art thou in good truth a lover
O take away from me those chill calm glances
10 As thou hast ta'en thy heart away; & give
My heart again that must forget to wander
Thy words were worse than silence they were lances
To poison all the life I have to live
Stagnate the streams of life that should meander

Surely there is an aching void within
Man's spirit unto other men unknown
And which were it unveiled and freely shown
Would open to the sight so much of sin
5 And folly & a cry that at the din
His overbearing pride & overblown

Would quite shrink down & seem as it had grown
Humble, content to lose & not to win.
Oh that we so could hide the grief of years
10   From our own selves yea the whole guilt & trouble
And in our secret spirit look on grace;
Yet death for ever sendeth messengers
Before it conscience pricks, & were these double
They were not equal to our sin-stained face.

The spring is come again not as at first
For then it was my spring; & now a brood
Of bitter memories haunt me, & my mood
Is much changed from the time when I was nursed
5   In the still country. Oh! my heart could burst
Thinking upon the long ago: the crude
Hopes all unrealised; the flowers that strewed
My path, now changed to painful thorns & curst.
And though I know the kingcups are as fine
10   As they were then, my spirit cannot soar
As it did once: when shadows of a wood
Or thinking of a blossom that soon should
Unfold & fill the air with scent, would pour
Peace on my brow now marked with many a line.

Who shall my wandering thoughts steady & fix
When I go forth into the world and gaze
Around me, thinking on mens evil ways
I wonder in myself to see how mix
5   Evil & good; beyond the Sleepy Styx
All things shall be unravelled whoso lays
These things to heart after the settled days
Shall know all. Even as a dog that licks
Your hand whom tears chide not away nor laughter
10   So to your souls clingeth the taint of crime
Shall it be ever so? & if not why?
The river bed is full of filthy slime

And so our heart is lined with wonder: die
And having died thou shalt see all things after.

You who look on passed ages as a glass
To shadow forth the future, in your home
Peacefully dwelling little heeding some
But loving many; as the visions pass
5   Turn from them for a moment to the grass
And solemn sun & blue o'erarching dome
And in the hush of nature think on Rome
Not as it is now but as it once was.
As of the mighty dead think without hope
10   But if you will indulge a hopeful pile
Yea if you will write about it in rhyme
For if it once had a too mighty scope
To be all as the sun fails not to smile
It shall be nothing to the end of time.

Angeli al capo, al piede:
  E qual ricciuto agnello
Dormir fra lor si vede
  Il bel mio bambinello.

Amami, t'amo,
  Figliolin mio:
Cantisi, suonisi,
  Con tintinnio.
5   Mamma t'abbraccia,
  Cor suo ti chiama:
Suonisi, cantisi,
  Ama chi t'ama.

E babbo e mamma ha il nostro figliolino,
  Ricco bambino:

Ma ne conosco un altro senza padre
   E senza madre—
5   Il poverino!

S'addormentò la nostra figliolina;
   Nè si risveglierà
Per giorni e giorni assai sera o mattina:
   Ma poi si sveglierà,
5   E con cara ridente bocchettina
   Ribacerà Mammà.

Cuccurucù! cuccurucù!
   All'alba il gallo canta:
Chiccherichì! chiccherichì!
   Di rose il ciel si ammanta.
5   Cuccurucù! cuccurucù!
   Comincia un gorgheggiare:
Chiccherichì! chiccherichì!
   Risalta il sol dal mare.

Oibò, piccina
   Tutto atterrita;
La medicina
   Bever si de':—
5   Uno, due, tre,—
   Ed è finita!

Otto ore suonano:
Picchia il postino!
Ben cinque lettere
Son per Papà;
5   Una per te,
Nulla per me;
E un bigliettino
V'è per Mammà.

Nel verno accanto al fuoco
  Mangio la mia minestra;
   E al pettirosso schiudo la finestra,
Ch'ei pur ne voule un poco.

5   <u>ovvero</u>:—
S'affaccia un pettirosso alla finestra:—
Vieni, vieni a gustar la mia minestra!
Lana ben foderata io porto addosso,
Ma tu non porti che un corpetto rosso.

Gran freddo è infuori, e dentro è freddo un poco:
Quanto è grata una zuppa accanto al fuoco!
Mi vesto di buon panno—
Ma i poveri non hanno
5   Zuppa da bere, o fuoco a cui sedere,
O tetto, o panni, in questo freddo intenso:
Ah mi si stringe il cor mentr'io ci penso!

Scavai la neve,—sì che scavai!
Ma fior nè foglia spuntava mai:
Scavai la rena con ansia lena,
Ma fior nè foglia spicca da rena.

5   O vento aprico, con fiato lieve
Sveglia i fioretti, sgela la neve!
Ma non soffiare su quella rena:
Chi soffia in rena perde la lena.

Sì che il fratello s'ha un falconcello,
  E tiene un fior la suora;
Ma chè, ma che riman per te,
  Il neonato or ora?
5   Vo' farti cocchio del mio ginocchio,
  Minor mio figliolino;
Da capo a piè ti stringo a me,
  Minimo piccino.

Udite, si dolgono mesti fringuelli:
Bel nido facemmo per cari gemelli,
Ma tre ragazzacci lo misero in stracci.
Fuggì primavera, s'imbruna la sera,
5   E tempo ci manca da fare un secondo
Niduncolo tondo.

Ahi culla vuota! ed ahi sepolcro pieno
   Ove le smunte foglie autunno getta!
Lo spirto aspetta in Paradiso ameno,
      Il corpo in terra aspetta.

Lugubre e vagabondo in terra e in mare,
O vento, O vento, a che non ti posare?
Ci trai la pioggia fin dall'occidente,
E la neve ci trai dal nord fremente.

Aura dolcissima, ma donde siete?—
Dinfra le mammole: non lo sapete?
Abbassi il viso ad adocchiar l'erbetta
Chi vuol trovar l'ascosa mammoletta.
5   La madreselva il dolce caldo aspetta:
Tu addolci un freddo mondo, O mammoletta.

Foss'io regina
   Tu re saresti:
   Davanti a te
      M'inchinerei.

5   Ah, foss'io re!
      Tu lo vedresti:
      Sì, che regina
         Mi ti farei.

Pesano rena e pena:
Oggi e doman son brevi:
La gioventude e un fior son cose lievi:
Ed han profondità
5   Mar magno e magna verità.

Basta una notte a maturare il fungo;
Un secol vuol la quercia, e non par lungo:
Anzi, il secolo breve e il vespro lungo:
Chè quercia è quercia, e fungo è sempre fungo.

Porco la zucca
Fitta in parrucca!. .
Che gli diresti mai?
M'inchinerei, l'ossequirei,
5   "Ser Porco, come stai?"

Ahi! guai! per caso mai
Se la coda andasse a male?. . .
Sta tranquillo:
Buon legale
10   Gli farebbe un codicillo.

Salta, ranocchio, e mostrati;
    Non celo pietra in mano:
Merletto in testa e verde vesta,
    Vattene salvo e sano.

5   Rospo lordo, deh non celarti:
Tutto il mondo può disprezzarti,
Ma mal non fai nè mal vo'farti.

Spunta la margherita
Qual astro in sullo stelo,
E l'erbetta infiorita
Rassembra un verde cielo.

Agnellina orfanellina
Giace in cima alla collina,
Fredda, sola, senza madre,—
Senza madre, oimè!
5 Io sarotti e madre e padre,
Io sarò tua pastorella;
Non tremar, diletta agnella,
Io ci penso a te.

Amico pesce, piover vorrà:
Prendi l'ombrella se vuoi star secco.
Ed ecco!
Domani senza fallo si vedrà
5 Lucertolon "zerbino"
Ripararsi dal sol coll'ombrellino.

Sposa velata,
Innanellata,
Mite e sommessa:
Sposo rapito,
5 Insuperbito,
Accanto ad essa:—
Amici, amori,
Cantando a coro,
Davanti a loro
10 Spargete fiori!

Cavalli marittimi
    Urtansi in guerra,
E meglio ci servono
    Quelli di terra.
5 Questi pacifici
Corrono o stanno:
Quei rotolandosi
Spumando vanno.

O marinaro che mi apporti tu?
Coralli rossi e bianchi tratti in su
Dal mar profondo.
Piante non son, nè si scavar da mina:
5   Minime creature in salsa brina
    Fecerne mondo.

Arrossisce la rosa: e perchè mai?
A cagione del sol: ma Sol, che fai?
E tu, Rosa, che t'hai
Che ti fai rosea sì se bene stai?

La rosa china il volto rosseggiato,
    E bene fa:
Il giglio innalza il viso immacolato,
    E ben gli sta.

O ciliegia infiorita,
La bianco rivestita
Dall'Aprile gradita,
Bella sei tu!
5   O ciliegia infruttata,
La verde inghirlandata
La rosso incoronata,
Bella sei tu!

"In tema e in pena addio;
    Addio ma in van, tu sai;
Per sempre addio, cor mio"—
    "E poi più mai."
5   "Oggi e domani addio,
    Nel secolo de'guai
A tutto tempo addio"—
    "E poi più mai."

D'un sonno profondissimo
    Dorme la suora mia:
Gli angeli bianchi aligeri
    Verranno a trarla via?
5 In sonno profondissimo
    Calma e contenta giace:
Un fiore in man lasciamole,
    Un bacio in fronte,—e pace!

Ninna nanna, ninna nanna!
Giace e dorme l'agnellina:
Ninna nanna, ninna nanna!
Monna Luna s'incammina:
5 Ninna nanna, ninna nanna!
Tace e dorme l'uccellino:
Ninna nanna, ninna nanna!
Dormi, dormi, O figliolino:
Ninna nanna, ninna nanna!

Capo che chinasi,—
Occhi che chiudonsi,—
A letto, a letto,
Sonnacchiosetto!
5   Dormi, carino,
Fino al mattino,
    Dormi, carino.

The Succession of Kings.

William the Norman was brave in the field;
And *Rufus,* his Son, in the chase was killed.
Henry the first early lost his dear Son;
And *Stephen's* battles were bravely won.
5 *Henry the second* his kingdom increased.
Richard the first led Crusades in the East.
John signed Magna Charta at Runnymede.

Henry the third put his seal to the deed.
Brave *Edward the first* the Welsh did subdue.
10 Weak *Edward the second* had foes not a few.
Edward the third to France did aspire,
Whose Son, the Black Prince, died before his Sire.
Richard the second to weakness was prone;
And *Henry the fourth* was placed on his throne.
15 *Fifth Henry* at Agincourt won the field.
Meek *Henry the sixth* was forced to yield,
To *Edward the fourth* who abused his power.
Edward the fifth found a grave in the Tower.
Richard the third was a treacherous friend;
20 By *Henry the seventh* he came to his end.
Henry the eighth had six wives in succession.
Edward the sixth was the hope of the nation;
For ten days reigned his Cousin the Lady Jane.
Queen Mary espoused King Philip of Spain.
25 A reign glorious and long was *Elizabeth's* lot.
James the first shrewdly guessed at the Gunpowder Plot.
Charles the first on a scaffold lost his head;
The Protector Cromwell ruled in his stead.
Richard Cromwell from ruling with joy did retire.
30 *Charles the second* beheld both the Plague and Fire.
For his faith *James the second* the crown did lose;
Which *third William and Mary* did not refuse.
Marlborough fought under good *Queen Anne*.
The Hanover Line with *first George* began.
35 *Second George* overcame the second Pretender.
In the reign of *third George* did Napoleon surrender.
George the fourth was long Regent, but King at last.
Under *William the fourth* the Reform Bill passed.
Good *Queen Victoria*, the last King's Niece,
40 Reigns over England beloved and at peace.

A true Story.   (continued.)

In this great city now the haunt,
    Of priest and friar and monk

Where reason sees her ill-starr'd bark,
  By superstition sunk;

5 Where nature's voice by force repress'd,
  Its energy declares,
In demon deeds of wickedness,
  When fear its dagger bares;

In Rome itself there lately dwelt
10 Two sister-maidens fair,
Affianced both to noble youths,
  Of form and virtue rare.

Preparing now for that great step,
  Of weal or woe the seal,
15 Before they joyful give their hands,
  Where purest love they feel;
                      (To be continued)

The two Rossettis (brothers they)
And Holman Hunt and John Millais,
With Stephens chivalrous and bland,
And Woolner in a distant land,
5 In these six men I awestruck see
Embodied the great P.R.B.
D. G. Rossetti offered two
Good pictures to the public view:
Unnumbered ones great John Millais,
10 And Holman more than I can say
*   *   *   *   *   *   *
William Rossetti calm and solemn
Cuts up his brethren by the column.

*   *   *   *   *   *   *

Imitated from the Arpa Evangelica: Page 121.

My Lord, my Love! in pleasant pain
  How often have I said:

Blessed that John, who on Thy Breast
    Laid down his head.
5 It was that contact all Divine
    Transformed him from above,
And made him amongst men the man
    To show forth holy love.

Yet shall I envy blessed John?
10   Nay, not so verily,
Now that Thou, Lord, both Man & God
    Dost dwell in me:
Upbuilding with Thy Manhood's might
    My frail humanity;
15 Yea, Thy Divinehood pouring forth
    In fulness filling me.

Me, Lord, Thy temple consecrate,
    Even me to Thee alone;
Lord reign upon my willing heart
20   Which is Thy throne:
To Thee the Seraphim fall down
    Adoring round Thy house;
For which of them hath tasted Thee,
    My Manna & my Spouse?

25 Now that Thy Life lives in my soul
    And sways & warms it thro',
I scarce seem lesser than the world,
    Thy temple too.
O God Who dwellest in my heart,
30   My God Who fillest me,
The broad immensity itself
    Hath not encompassed Thee.

"T'amo; e fra dolci affanni"—. p. 121.—

My Lord, my Love!—in love's unrest
35   How often have I said:
"Blessed that John who on Thy Breast
    Reclined his head."
Thy touch it was, Love's Pelican,
    Transformed him from above,

40   And made him amongst men the man
        To show forth holy love!

    Yet shall I envy blessèd John?
        Nay, not so verily,
    While Thou indwellest as Thine own
45   Me, even me:
    Upbuilding with Thy Manhood's worth
        My frail humanity;
    Yea, Thy Divinehood pouring forth,
        In fulness filling me.

50   Me, Lord, Thy temple consecrate,
        Me unto Thee alone;
    Within my heart set up Thy state
        And mount Thy throne:
    The Seraphim in ecstasy
55   Fall prone around Thy house,
    For which of them hath tasted Thee
        My Manna and my Spouse?

    Now Thou dost wear me for a robe
        And sway and warm me thro',
60   I scarce seem lesser than the globe,—
        Thy temple too:
    O God Who for Thy dwelling place
        Dost take delight in me,
    The ungirt immensity of space
65   Hath not encompassed Thee.

    Mr. and Mrs. Scott, and I,
    With Mr. Manson, Editor,
    And of the social Proctors four,
    Agreed the season to defy.

5   We mustered forces at the Rail,
    Struck hands and made our interests one:
    Alas for absent Annie Hayle
    Who should have shared the fare and fun.

Not neighbour Humble and her child
10 —Tho' well-disposed of doubtful force—
But Annie Hayle my verse deplores,
Behatted plump alert and mild.

From Newcastle to Sunderland
Upon a misty morn in June
15 We took the train: on either hand
Grimed streets were changed for meadows soon.

Umbrellas, tarts and sandwiches
Sustained our spirits' temperate flow,
With potted jam, and cold as snow
20 Rough-coated sun-burnt oranges.

1.

Gone to his rest
  Bright little Bouby!
Build green his nest
  Where sun and dew be,
5 Nor snails molest

2.

A cheerful sage,
  Simple, light-hearted:
In ripe old age
  He had departed
10 And ta'en his wage.

3.

Dear for himself;
  Dear for another
Past price of pelf;
  —(Ah, dearest Mother!)—
15 Song-singing elf.

4.

O daisies, grow
   Lightly above him,
Strike root, and blow:
   For some who love him
20 Would have it so.

O Uommibatto
Agil, giocondo,
Che ti sei fatto
Irsuto e tondo!
5   Deh non fuggire
Qual vagabondo,
Non disparire
Forando il mondo:
Pesa davvero
10 D'un emisfero
Non lieve il pondo.

Cor mio, cor mio,
Più non ti veggo, ma mi rammento
Del giorno spento,
   Cor mio.
5   Pur ti ricordi del lungo amore,
Cor del mio core,
   Cor mio?

I said "All's over"—& I made my
Thenceforward to keep silence &
From any hope or enterprise aga
But as one certain day the sap
5   Sun warmed & solaced in its f
So something stirred in me th
And all my hardness broke [illegible fragment]
And hope once more tended [illegible fragment]

I said good bye in hope:
But now we meet again
I have no hope at all
Of anything but pain,
5   Our parting & our meeting
Alike in vain.

Hope on thro' all your life
Until the end, dear Friend.
Live thro' your noble life
10   Where joy & promise blend:
I too will live my life
Until the end.

Long may your vine entwine,
Long may your figtree spread
15   Their paradise of shade
Above your cherished head:
My shelter was a gourd,
And it is dead.

Yet when out of a grave
20   We are gathered home at last,
Then may we own life spilt
No good worth holding fast:—
Death had its bitterness
But it is past.

My Mouse.

A Venus seems my Mouse
Come safe ashore from foaming seas,
Which in a small way & at ease
    Keeps house.

5   An Iris seems my Mouse,
Bright bow of that exhausted shower
Which made a world of sweet-herbs flower
    And boughs.

      A darling Mouse it is:—
10   Part hope not likely to take wing,
     Part memory, part anything
         You please.

      Venus-cum-Iris Mouse
     From shifting tides set safe apart,
15   In no mere bottle, in my heart
         Keep house.

     Had Fortune parted us
       Fortune is blind,
     Had Anger parted us
       Anger unkind—
5   But since God parts us
       Let us part humbly
     Bearing our burden
       Bravely & dumbly.

     And since there is but one
10   Heaven, not another,
     Let us not close that door
       Against each other.
     God's Love is higher than mine,
       Christ's tenfold proved,
15   Yet even I would die
       For thee Beloved.

Counterblast on Penny Trumpet.
"When raged the conflict, fierce & hot."

     If Mr. Bright retiring does not please
       And Mr. Gladstone staying gives offence,
     What can man do which is not one of these?
       Use your own common sense.

5   Yet he's a brave man who abjures his cause
       For conscience' sake: let byegones be byegones:

Not *this* among the makers of our laws
    The least & and last of Johns.

If all our byegones could be piled on shelves
10   High out of reach of penny-line Tyrtaeus!
If only all of us could see ourselves
    As others see us!

A roundel seems to fit a round of days
    Be they the days of upright man or scoundrel:
Allow me to construct then in your praise
    A roundel.
5   [This flower of wit turns out a weed like groundsel:
Yet deign to welcome it, as loftiest bays
    Grown on the shore of Girvan's ocean groundswell.]
Accept the love that underlies the lays;
    Condone the barbarous rhymes that will not sound well
10 In building up, all Poets to amaze,
    A roundel.

Heaven overarches earth and sea,
    Earth-sadness and sea-bitterness;
Heaven overarches you and me:
A little while, and we shall be
5 (Please God) where there is no more sea
    Or barren wilderness.

Heaven overarches you and me
    And all earth's gardens and her graves:
Look up with me, until we see
10 The day break and the shadows flee;
What tho' tonight wrecks you and me,
    If so tomorrow saves?

Sleeping at last, the trouble & tumult over,
Sleeping at last, the struggle & horror past,

Cold & white out of sight of friend & of lover
Sleeping at last.

5   No more a tired heart downcast or overcast,
No more pangs that wring or shifting fears that hover,
Sleeping at last in a dreamless sleep locked fast.

Fast asleep. Singing birds in their leafy cover
Cannot wake her, nor shake her the gusty blast.
10 Under the purple thyme & the purple clover
Sleeping at last.

4th May morning.

My carrier pigeon is a "fancy" pigeon,
Less tangible than widgeon;
A sympathetic love,—yet not a Cupid,
Not pert nor stupid.
5   Heart-warm & snug tho' May Day deal in zeroes,
A well-known Eros.
On windless wings by flight untired for ever
Outspeed the speeding river,
From Torrington remote to utmost Chelsea
10 (—Do what I tells ye!—)
Carry a heart of love & thanks & blisses,
A beak of kisses,
Past Piccadilly's hills & populous valleys,
Past every human head that more or less is
15 Begirt with tawny tresses,
Past every house, to sumptuous Bellevue Palace;
There greet the courteous Courtneys with politeness,
And the dear Scotts with an affectionate brightness,
And give a kiss to dark-locked Alice.

"Quanto a Lei grata io sono
L'umil dirà semplicità del dono."

THE CHINAMAN.

'Centre of Earth!' a Chinaman he said,
And bent over a map his pig-tailed head,—
That map in which, portrayed in colours bright,
China, all dazzling, burst upon the sight:
5   'Centre of Earth!' repeatedly he cries,
'Land of the brave, the beautiful, the wise!'
Thus he exclaimed; when lo his words arrested
Showed what sharp agony his head had tested.
He feels a tug—another, and another—
10   And quick exclaims, 'Hallo! what's now the bother?'
But soon alas perceives. And, 'Why, false night,
Why not from men shut out the hateful sight?
The faithless English have cut off my tail,
And left me my sad fortunes to bewail.
15   Now in the streets I can no more appear,
For all the other men a pig-tail wear.'
He said, and furious cast into the fire
His tail: those flames became its funeral-pyre.

'Come cheer up, my lads, 'tis to glory we steer!'
As the soldier remarked whose post lay in the rear.

THE PLAGUE

"Listen, the last stroke of death's noon has struck—
   The plague is come," a gnashing Madman said,
   And laid him down straightway upon his bed.
His writhèd hands did at the linen pluck;
5   Then all is over. With a careless chuck
   Among his fellows he is cast. How sped
   His spirit matters little: many dead
Make men hard-hearted.—"Place him on the truck.
Go forth into the burial-ground and find
10   Room at so much a pitful for so many.

One thing is to be done; one thing is clear:
Keep thou back from the hot unwholesome wind,
    That it infect not thee." Say, is there any
        Who mourneth for the multitude dead here?

How many authors are my first!
    And I shall be so too
Unless I finish speedily
    That which I have to do.

5   My second is a lofty tree
        And a delicious fruit;
    This in the hot-house flourishes—
        That amid rocks takes root.

    My whole is an immortal queen
10   Renowned in classic lore:
    Her a god won without her will,
        And her a goddess bore.

        Me you often meet
        In London's crowded street,
    And merry children's voices my resting-place proclaim.
        Pictures and prose and verse
5   Compose me—I rehearse
    Evil and good and folly, and call each by its name.
        I make men glad, and I
        Can bid their senses fly,
    And festive echoes know me of Isis and of Cam.
10   But give me to a friend,
        And amity will end,
    Though he may have the temper and meekness of a lamb.

    So I began my walk of life; no stop
    Was possible; or else my will was frail;
    Or is it that the first stumblings entail
    Weakness no after strength has power to prop?

5   The heart puts forth her boughs; and these we lop
For very wantonness; until the gale
Is rank with blood; then our life-portions fail
And we are fain to share another's sop.
At first my heart was true and my soul true,
10   And then the outside world believed me false.
Therefore my sweets grew bitter, and I thrust
Life back, till it stood still and turned to must.
Yet sometimes through the great stagnation calls
Of spirits reach me: is it so with you?

So I grew half delirious and quite sick,
And thro' the darkness saw strange faces grin
Of Monsters at me. One put forth a fin,
And touched me clammily: I could not pick
5   A quarrel with it: it began to lick
My hand, making meanwhile a piteous din
And shedding human tears: it would begin
To near me, then retreat. I heard the quick
Pulsation of my heart, I marked the fight
10   Of life and death within me; then sleep threw
Her veil around me; but this thing is true:
When I awoke the sun was at his height,
And I wept sadly, knowing that one new
Creature had love for me, and others spite.

On the note you do not send me
I have thought too long: adieu.
Hope and fear no longer rend me:—
Home is near: not news of you.

CHARON

In my cottage near the Styx
Co. and Charon still combine
Us to ferry o'er like bricks

In a boat of chaste design.
5 Cerberus, thou triple fair,
Distance doth thy charms impair:
Let the passage give to us
Charon, Co., and Cerberus.

CHORUS

Now the passage gives us to
10 Charon, Cerberus, and Co.

FROM METASTASIO

First, last, and dearest,
  My love, mine own,
Thee best beloved,
  Thee love alone,
5 Once and for ever
    So love I thee.

First as a suppliant
  Love makes his moan,
Then as a monarch
10 Sets up his throne:
Once and for ever—
  So love I thee.

CHIESA E SIGNORE

LA CHIESA

Vola, preghiera, e digli
  Perchè Ti stai lontano?
Passeggi Tu frai gigli
  Portando rosa in mano?
5 Non Ti fui giglio e rosa
  Quando mi amasti Tu?
Rivolgiti alla sposa,
  O mio Signor Gesù.

IL SIGNORE

Di te non mi scordai,
10   Sposa mia dolce e mesta:
Se Mi sei rosa il sai,
    Chè porto spine in testa.
Ti diedi e core e vita,
    Me tutto Io diedi a te,
15   Ed or ti porgo aita:
    Abbi fidanza in Me.

LA CHIESA

Vola, preghiera, a Lui,
    E grida: Ahi pazienza!
Te voglio e non altrui,
20   Te senza è tutto senza.
Fragrante più di giglio
    E rosa a me sei Tu,
Di Dio l' Eterno Figlio,
    O mio Signor Gesù.

GOLDEN HOLLY

Common Holly bears a berry
To make Christmas Robins merry:—
Golden Holly bears a rose,
Unfolding at October's close
5   To cheer an old Friend's eyes and nose.

I toiled on, but thou
Wast weary of the way,
And so we parted: now
Who shall say
5   Which is happier—I or thou?

I am weary now
On the solitary way:
But art thou rested, thou?

Who shall say
10   Which of us is calmer now?

Still my heart's love, thou,
In thy secret way,
Art still remembered now:
Who shall say—
15   Still rememberest thou?

COR MIO

Still sometimes in my secret heart of hearts
   I say "Cor mio" when I remember you,
   And thus I yield us both one tender due,
Welding one whole of two divided parts.
5 Ah Friend, too wise or unwise for such arts,
   Ah noble Friend, silent and strong and true,
   Would you have given me roses for the rue
For which I bartered roses in love's marts?
So late in autumn one forgets the spring,
10   Forgets the summer with its opulence,
The callow birds that long have found a wing,
   The swallows that more lately got them hence:
Will anything like spring, will anything
   Like summer, rouse one day the slumbering sense?

My old admiration before I was twenty,—
Is predilect still, now promoted to se'enty!
My own demi-century plus an odd one
   Some weight to my judgment may fairly impart.
5 Accept this faint flash of a smouldering fun,
   The fun of a heavy old heart.

TO MARY ROSSETTI

You were born in the Spring
When the pretty birds sing

In sunbeamy bowers:
Then dress like a Fairy,
5   Dear dumpling my Mary,
In green and in flowers.

Ne' sogni ti veggo,
Amante ed amico;
Ai piedi ti seggo,
Ti tengo tuttor.
5   Nè chiedi nè chieggo,
Nè dici nè dico,
L' amore ab antico
Che scaldaci il cor.
Ah voce se avessi
10   Me stessa a scoprire—
Ah esprimer sapessi
L' angoscia e l' amor!
Ah almen se potessi
A lungo dormire,
15   Nè pianger nè dire,
Mirandoti ognor!

TO MY FIOR-DI-LISA

The Rose is Love's own flower, and Love's no less
The Lily's tenderness.
Then half their dignity must Roses yield
To Lilies of the field?
5   Nay, diverse notes make up true harmony,
All-fashioned loves agree:
Love wears the Lily's whiteness, and Love glows
In the deep-hearted Rose.

Hail, noble face of noble friend!—
Hail, honoured master hand and dear!—
On you may Christmas good descend
And blessings of the unknown year

5	So soon to overtake us here.
	Unknown, yet well known: I portend
	Love starts the course, love seals the end.

NOTES

Most of the material within brackets at the beginning of the notes for each poem, and the textual variants, are taken from R. W. Crump's three-volume edition. Of the latter I have included significant published title variants and a few examples. An edition is usually referred to by its date of publication, or, for American editions, the date followed by 'a'. Where edition dates are identical, other abbreviations, listed below, distinguish the editions from each other. The italicized date in the bracketed material indicates the edition used for the basic text of a poem; otherwise, a manuscript is the source of the text.

To save space, I have used a conservative approach to the Notes and cross-referenced as many as possible. For example, I have provided Rossetti's commentary from *The Face of the Deep* only when it seems to have a direct reference to the poem in which it figures; and when a Bible verse is repeated, I refer the reader to the first note in which it appears. I generally omit notes such as 'date of composition unknown', and where publishing histories for the poems in a collection are identical, I note the editions only once, at the heading for the collection, e.g., for *Sing-Song*. Where poems appear in both English and American editions of *Time Flies* and *The Face of the Deep*, I note page numbers for the earliest edition only.

Unless otherwise noted, Traci Andrighetti is the translator for Rossetti's Italian poems. We have attempted to follow Rossetti's original lines as closely as possible in order to produce a literal translation, but have sometimes found it necessary to change word order and punctuation in order to convey the meaning in English.

Editions and Reprints

1847   *Verses: Dedicated to Her Mother*. London: privately printed at G. Polidori's.

1862   *Goblin Market and Other Poems*. London: Macmillan.

1865   *Goblin Market and Other Poems*, 2nd edn. London: Macmillan.

1866   *The Prince's Progress and Other Poems*. London: Macmillan.

1866a   *Poems*. Boston: Roberts Brothers.

1870   *Commonplace, and Other Short Stories*. London: F. S. Ellis.

1870a   *Commonplace, A Tale of To-day; and Other Stories*. Boston: Roberts Brothers.

1872a   *Poems*. Boston: Roberts Brothers.

1872   *Sing-Song: A Nursery Rhyme Book*. London: George Routledge and Sons.

1872aSS   *Sing-Song: A Nursery Rhyme Book.* Boston: Roberts Brothers.

1874   *Annus Domini: A Prayer for Each Day of the Year, Founded on a Text of Holy Scripture.* Oxford and London: James Parker and Co.

1874r   *Annus Domini: A Prayer for Each Day of the Year, Founded on a Text of Holy Scripture.* Oxford and London: James Parker and Co. (Contains Rossetti's holograph marginalia.)

1875   *Goblin Market, The Prince's Progress, and Other Poems.* London: Macmillan.

1876a   *Poems.* Boston: Roberts Brothers.

1881   *A Pageant and Other Poems.* London: Macmillan.

1881a   *A Pageant and Other Poems.* Boston: Roberts Brothers.

1881CS   *Called to be Saints: The Minor Festivals Devotionally Studied.* London: Society for Promoting Christian Knowledge.

1882a   *Poems.* Boston: Roberts Brothers.

1885   *Time Flies: A Reading Diary.* London: Society for Promoting Christian Knowledge.

1885r   *Time Flies: A Reading Diary.* London: Society for Promoting Christian Knowledge. (Contains Rossetti's holograph marginalia.)

1886a   *Time Flies: A Reading Diary.* Boston: Roberts Brothers.

1888a   *Poems.* Boston: Roberts Brothers, 231 pp.

1888a2   *Poems.* Boston: Roberts Brothers. 208 pp.

1890   *Poems, New and Enlarged Edition.* London and New York: Macmillan.

1891   *Poems, New and Enlarged Edition.* London and New York: Macmillan.

1892   *The Face of the Deep: A Devotional Commentary on the Apocalypse.* London: Society for Promoting Christian Knowledge; New York: E. and J. B. Young.

1892P   *Poems: New and Enlarged Edition.* London and New York: Macmillan.

1893   *Verses. Reprinted from "Called to be Saints," "Time Flies," "The Face of the Deep."* London: Society for Promoting Christian Knowledge; New York: E. and J. B. Young.

1893GM   *Goblin Market.* Illustrated by Laurence Housman. London: Macmillan.

1893SS   *Sing-Song: A Nursery Rhyme Book.* London and New York: Macmillan.

1893FD   *The Face of the Deep: A Devotional Commentary on the Apocalypse.* 2nd ed. London: Society for Promoting Christian Knowledge; New York: E. and J. B. Young.

1894   *Verses. Reprinted from "Called to be Saints," "Time Flies," "The Face of the Deep."* 6th edn. London: Society for Promoting Christian Knowledge; New York: E. and J. B. Young.

1895   *The Face of the Deep: A Devotional Commentary on the Apocalypse.* 3rd edn. London: Society for Promoting Christian Knowledge; New York: E. and J. B. Young.

1896   *New Poems, Hitherto Unpublished or Uncollected.* Edited by William Michael Rossetti. London and New York: Macmillan.

1896s   *New Poems, Hitherto Unpublished or Uncollected.* Edited by William Michael

Rossetti. London and New York: Macmillan. (Special edition of 100 large paper copies.)

1897   *Maude: A Story for Girls.* London: James Bowden.

1897a *Maude: Prose & Verse by Christina Rossetti; 1850.* Chicago: Herbert S. Stone.

1904   *The Poetical Works of Christina Georgina Rossetti, with Memoir and Notes by William Michael Rossetti.* London: Macmillan.

Secondary works cited in Further Reading are referred to in the Notes by the author's surname and a short title. Other abbreviations:

Names

CR   Christina Rossetti
DGR Dante Gabriel Rossetti
MR   Maria Rossetti
PRB Pre-Raphaelite Brotherhood
WR   William Rossetti

Manuscript Locations

BL   British Library, London
BodL Bodleian Library, Oxford
DU   Duke University Library, Durham, North Carolina
GD   Mrs Geoffrey Dennis
HL   Huntington Library, San Marino, California
ISD   Iowa State Department of History and Archives, Des Moines
PML Pierpont Morgan Library, New York City
PU   Princeton University Library, Princeton, New Jersey
RO   Mrs Roderic O'Conor
UBC University of British Columbia Library, Vancouver
UK   University of Kentucky Libraries, Lexington
UT   Harry Ransom Humanities Research Center, University of Texas at Austin
YU   Beinecke Rare Book and Manuscript Library, Yale University, New Haven, Connecticut

Editor Editorial intervention in this edition (Crump)

Rossetti's Works

Annus Domini
Commonplace
CS (for *Called to be Saints*)
FD (for *The Face of the Deep*)
Maude
SF (for *Seek and Find*)
TF (for *Time Flies*)

Other Works

CR   Jan Marsh, *Christina Rossetti: A Literary Biography* (Cape, 1994).
CR Poems *Christina Rossetti: Poems and Prose*, ed. Jan Marsh (Everyman, 1994).
FL   *The Family Letters of Christina Georgina Rossetti*, ed. William Michael Rossetti (Brown, Langham, 1908).
Germ   *The Germ: Thoughts Towards Nature in Poetry, Literature, and Art.*
Letters *The Collected Letters of Christina Rossetti*, ed. Antony H. Harrison, Vols. I–III (of IV) (University Press of Virginia, 1997–).
'Notes' WR's notes for CR's poems in 1904.

Goblin Market and Other Poems (1862)

GOBLIN MARKET

[Composed 27 April 1859. Editions: *1862*, 1865, 1866a, 1875, 1876a, 1893GM, 1904. In a copy of 1893GM (at ISD), CR wrote a note dated 7 December 1893:

"Goblin Market" first published in 1862 was written (subject of course to subsequent revision) as long ago as April 27. 1859, and in M.S. was inscribed to my dear only sister Maria Francesca Rossetti herself long afterwards the author of "A Shadow of Dante." In the first instance I named it "A Peep at the Goblins" in imitation of my cousin Mrs. Bray's "A Peep at the Pixies," but my brother Dante Gabriel Rossetti substituted the greatly improved title as it now stands. And here I like to acknowledge the general indebtedness of my first and second volumes to his suggestive wit and revising hand. Christina G. Rossetti.]

Illustration: CR's own marginal water-colour sketches of the goblins, in MS (GD), WR describes as 'all very slim agile figures in a close-fitting garb of blue; their faces, hands, and feet are sometimes human, sometimes brute-like, but of a scarcely definable type. The only exception is the "parrot-voiced" goblin who cried "Pretty goblin." He is a true parrot (such as Christina could draw one)' ('Notes' 460). Arthur Rackham was the illustrator for 1862.

CR's Florentine cousin, Teodorico Pietrocola-Rossetti, translated the poem, which was published in Florence in 1867 under the title *Il Mercat de Folletti*. Emanuel Aguilar composed a cantata using the words of the poem in 1872.

D. M. R. Bentley suggests that the poem was completed some time after CR had begun working with 'fallen women' at Highgate, arguing that the date of composition (27 April 1859) is in reality the date of its conception, 'chosen by Rossetti as much for its spiritual significance as for its temporal accuracy' – 27 April being the feast day of Saint Zita, the patroness of domestic servants, known for visiting the sick and those in jail ('The Meretricious and the Meritorious in *Goblin Market*: A Conjecture and an Analysis', in Kent, *Achievement* 59). 'Lizzie also typifies Christ in the Eucharist as the means of salvation, in a symbolic meal that reverses the taste of forbidden fruit. "For Christ's sake we love you, care for you, long to rescue you" were the words used by the Highgate Sisters, in an almost exact replication of rhythm' (*CR* 237).

Marsh notes that Mrs Bray's *A Peep at the Pixies* (1854) contains a story in which the heroine hears fairy music and later falls into a decline because of her desire to hear it again. Marsh also sees antecedents in the Revd Mr Bray's fairy-tale 'The Rural Sisters' in *Poetical Remains* (1859), which contains the theme of two sisters, and 'The Pixies' by Archibald Maclaren (1819–84) in *The Fairy Family* (1857); but she suspects 'that Christina's goblins came more directly from *Comus* [1637 – by John Milton (1608–74)], where the sorcerer's crew are "headed like sundry sorts of wild beasts but otherwise like men", and the action describes a similar contest between evil and innocence' (*CR* 230–31). Eliza Bray (1790–1833) was a cousin of CR's mother; her husband, the Revd Stothard Bray (1786–1854), was a Devonshire clergyman.

WR wrote: 'I have more than once heard Christina say that she did not mean anything profound by this fairy tale – it is not a moral apologue consistently carried out in detail. Still the incidents are such as to be at any rate suggestive' ('Notes' 459).

Goblin Market continues to be the most widely read and commented upon of all CR's poems. It helped to inspire Lewis Carroll's *Alice's Adventures in Wonderland* (1865) (*CR Poems* 303). Edith Sitwell thought that it was 'perhaps the most perfect poem written by a woman in the English language' (*English Women* (1942), p. 41; quoted in Packer, *CR* 161).

3 *fruits* traditionally associated with temptation, from the 'apple' of the Fall of Adam and Eve to the 'fruits that thy soul lusted after' (Rev. 18:14; verse 15 begins with 'The merchants of these things . . .'). CR would also have been familiar with the pear-stealing episode in St Augustine's *Confessions*.

4 *Come buy, come buy* 'every one that thirsteth, come ye to the waters, and he that hath no money; come ye, buy, and eat; yea, come, buy wine and milk without money and without price' (Isa 55:1).

10 *Swart-headed* dark-headed.

22 *bullaces* wild plums.

23 *greengages* green plums.

24 *Damsons* small black or purple plums.

  bilberries small blue-black berries.

27 *barberries* oblong red berries.

29 *Citrons* acid tree fruits with pale yellow rinds thicker than that of a lemon.

34–5 *Laura ... Lizzie* Bentley points out that Laura is associated with Petrarchan love and Lizzie with Saint Elizabeth of Hungary, 'whose renunciation of the world in favor of the cloister provided the subject for several artistic works' ('Meretricious and the Meritorious', in Kent, *Achievement* 72 n. 34); see headnote of 'A Portrait'. CR considered herself a descendant of Petrarch's Laura, whom she identified as the daughter of Audebert de Noves, syndic of Avignon, and the wife of Hugh, son of Paul de Sade (*CR* 212). Kathleen Vejvoda cites the chaste Sabrina in *Comus* as an influence on the characterization of Lizzie ('The Fruit of Charity: *Comus* and Christina Rossetti's 'Goblin Market', *Victorian Poetry* 38 no. 4 (2000)).

75 *wombat* burrowing marsupial native to South Australia, characterized by a thick, heavy body, short legs and a general resemblance to a small bear. DGR owned a wombat (as well as a ratel – see l. 76), but, as WR told Mackenzie Bell, only after the publication of *Goblin Market*: 'It was C[hristina] and I who jointly discovered the Wombat in the Zoological Gardens – From us (more especially myself) Gabriel, [Sir Edward] Burne-Jones, and other wombat enthusiasts, ensued . . .' (Bell, *CR* 209). See also 'O Uommibatto' and its headnote.

76 *ratel* honey badger, native to Africa and southern Asia.

83 *beck* brook, particularly one with a stony bed or rugged course.

120 *furze* spiny evergreen shrub with yellow flowers; also called gorse.

126 *clipped a precious golden lock* cf. Alexander Pope (1688–1744), *Rape of the Lock* (1714).

129 *honey from the rock* 'He made him ride on the high places of the earth, that he might eat the increase of the fields; and he made him to suck honey out of the rock, and oil out of the flinty rock' (Deut. 32:13).

147 *Jeanie* CR may have taken this name from DGR's poem about a young prostitute, 'Jenny', written in 1848, but 'mostly 1858–69' (note on table of contents of WR's edition of *The Works of DGR* (1911)), or perhaps also from Leigh Hunt (1784–1859), 'Rondeau' ('Jenny kiss'd me when we met') (1838).

179 *Pellucid* translucent.

220 *flags* plants with a bladed leaf, usually a kind of iris.

258 *succous* juicy.

300 *cankerous* corroding, or eating into the flesh; a canker is an insect that destroys the buds and leaves of plants – 'As killing as the canker to the rose' (Milton, 'Lycidas' (1637), l. 45).

345–9 *Chattering like . . . caressed her* Bentley points to a parallel in the description of the attendants of Circe in *Endymion* (1818) by John Keats (1795–1821): '. . . all around her shapes, wizard and brute, / Laughing, and wailing, grovelling, serpenting, / Shewing tooth, tusk, and venom-bag, and sting! / O such deformities!' (III, 500–503). This would suggest 'a possibility that permits the perception of the goblin men as the male equivalents of Dante Gabriel's *femmes fatales* of the 1850s and later' ('Meretricious and the Meritorious', in Kent, *Achievement* 74 n. 36).

351 *Panniers* baskets for carrying provisions, usually carried in pairs, one on each side, slung across the back.

353 *Russet* variety of eating apple marked with brownish spots and having a rough skin.

401 *Clawed with their nails* CR uses similar imagery about 'the world', which, by day, 'wooes' with ripe fruits, but at night, turns into a clawing monster ('The World', l. 11).

408–10 *White and golden . . . Like a lily . . . blue-veined stone* Marsh points out that Lizzie wears the Virgin's colours of white, blue and gold (*CR* 236). The lily is emblematic of faith, purity, the Virgin and the Resurrection. Cf. 'Faith is like a lily lifted high and white' ('Hope is like a harebell trembling from its birth', l. 3), and 'Shining lilies tall and straight, / For royal state' ('Roses blushing red and white', ll. 7–8). See also headnote of 'Queen Rose'.

412 *Like a beacon left alone* in her entry for 'Rogation Tuesday' in *TF*, CR speaks of a missionary standing 'steadfast upon his watchtower', who will eventually be raised up to sit in heavenly places with Jesus, from which 'exceedingly high mountain' he will 'estimate and despise the world, and the things of the world' (268).

418–19 *Like a royal virgin town / Topped with gilded dome and spire* a town with a cathedral built in honour of the Virgin (as, for example, the Cathedral of Notre Dame in Paris).

430 *uttered not a word* cf. Jesus' trial before his crucifixion when, having been scourged and mocked, he remained silent under questioning (Matt. 27; Mark 15; Luke 23; John 19).

471 *Eat me, drink me, love me* echo of the sacrament of the Eucharist – also called 'Communion' or 'The Lord's Supper' or the 'Love Feast' – in which Jesus' body and blood are offered in the form of bread and wine (Matt. 26:26–9; Mark 14:22–5; Luke 22:17–20).

480 *Must your light like mine be hidden* 'Neither do men light a candle, and put it under a bushel, but on a candlestick; and it giveth light unto all that are in the house. Let your light so shine before men, that they may see your good works, and glorify your Father which is in heaven' (Matt. 5:15–16).

491 *aguish* shivering, shaky, feverish.

494 *wormwood* bitter-tasting plant, sometimes used in medicine and for making vermouth and absinthe. It is also an emblem or type of what is grievous or bitter to the soul.

562–7 *"For there is no friend like a sister . . . one stands"* 'These lines are clearly connected with the original inscription of the poem, "To M. F. R." Christina, I have no doubt, had some particular occurrence in her mind, but what it was I know not' ('Notes' 460). CG did not set them off with quotation marks in MS.

IN THE ROUND TOWER AT JHANSI, JUNE 8, 1857

[Composed Sept. 1857. Editions: *1862*, 1865, 1866a, 1875, 1876a, 1904. First published (without central stanza) in *Once a Week* (1857) under the byline of 'Caroline G. Rossetti' (*Letters*, I, 162 n. 2a).]

Illustration: 'In that copy of the *Goblin Market* volume in which Christina drew a few coloured designs, she has put a head- and tail-piece to the Jhansi poem. The former is a flag displayed – pink field, with a device of two caressing doves. The latter is the same flag, drooping from its broken staff, and seen on the reverse side, besmeared with blood' ('Notes' 480).

The *Illustrated London News* (5 Sept. 1857) reported that in June, Indian mutineers had murdered all European men, women and children in Jhansi. Captain Skene, his wife and a few others managed to escape into a tower. While the men shot at the rebels, Mrs Skene loaded for them. Eventually, the rebels began taking the tower. Seeing that there was no hope left, Captain Skene 'nobly resolved to save his wife from the atrocities perpetrated by the savages upon every Englishwoman unhappy enough to fall into their hands' (p. 243, col. 1). He kissed his wife, shot her, and then himself. This account was later shown to be false – the prisoners, including Skene and his wife, had been marched to a garden, where they were all killed by the sword (*The Times*, 11 Sept. 1857, p. 7, cols. 1–2). In 1875, CR added the footnote.

DREAM-LAND

[Composed April 1849. Editions: *1862*, 1865, 1866a, 1875, 1876a, 1904. First published in *Germ*, no. 1 (Jan. 1850), 20.]

Illustration: 'Christina made three coloured designs to this lyric. In the first we see the "She" of the poem journeying to her bourne. She is a rather sepulchral-looking, white-clad figure, holding a cross; the "single star" and the "water-springs" are apparent, also a steep slope of purplish hill which she is leaving behind. The second design gives the nightingale singing on a thorny rose-bough. In the third, "She" is rising and ascending winged; her pinions are golden, of butterfly-form' ('Notes' 478). See headnote of *Goblin Market*.

The title and the illustration suggest that this poem owes something to the theological doctrine of 'soul sleep' – the state of the soul between death and Judgement Day in which the soul 'sleeps' and dreams of Paradise. The Order for the Burial of the Dead in the *Book of Common Prayer* characterizes Christ as the 'First-fruits of them that slept' (1 Cor. 15:20). CR refers to 'them which sleep in Jesus (I Thes. iv: 14)' (*SF* 319). 'We know that this mortal life is the sufficient period of our probation, we know that the life immortal is the sufficing period—If we may call eternity a period—of our reward: let us not fret our hearts by a too anxious curiosity as to that intermediate state which hides for the moment so many whom we love and whom we hope to rejoin, for even now we know that "the souls of the righteous are in the hand of God, and there shall no torment touch them" (Wisdom iii.1)' (*SF* 154–5). Harrison suggests that 'Dream-Land' is the poem CR alludes to as 'My dreary poem' in her letter to WR [25 Aug. 1849] (*Letters*, I, 18–19 n. 6).

5–6 *Led by a single star, / She came from very far* cf. the wise men who came from the East, guided by a star, to worship the infant Jesus (Matt. 2; Luke 2).

AT HOME

[Composed 28 June 1858. Editions: *1862*, 1865, 1866a, 1875, 1876a, 1904]

Illustration:

She illustrated *At Home* with two coloured designs . . . No. 1 shows the blanched form of the ghost in a sky lit with cresset flames. On one side the sky is bright blue, the flames golden; on the other side, dark twilight grey, and the flames red. No. 2 is the globe of the earth, rudely lined for latitude and longitude. The equator divides it into a green northern and a grey-purple southern hemisphere. Over the former flare sunbeams in a blue sky; below the latter the firmament is dimly dark, and the pallid moon grey towards extinction. ('Notes' 482)

See headnote of *Goblin Market*.

WR reports that the poem 'was written (as a pencil-note by the authoress says) "after a Newcastle picnic," which must no doubt have been held in company with the Bell Scotts. This, however, was a trivial title, to which my brother raised some objection. He considered this to be about the best of all Christina's poems . . .' ('Notes' 482). WR dates the composition as 29 June, saying that on the same day, CR also produced or completed 'Up-Hill' and 'To-day and To-morrow'.

William Bell Scott (1811–90) was a poet, painter, writer and close friend of the Rossettis. CR was also a friend of Bell Scott's wife, Letitia, and his lifelong friend Alice Boyd. According to Packer, Letitia – 'a garrulous, long-winded, but harmless chatterer of commonplaces' – was the original for one of the characters in CR's 'Commonplace' (Packer, *CR* 271). Packer's biography is largely based on the (now discredited) claim that Bell Scott was the object of CR's love poems.

A TRIAD

[Composed 18 Dec. 1856. Editions: *1862*, 1865, 1866a, 1896, 1904.]

LOVE FROM THE NORTH

[Composed 19 Dec. 1856. Editions: *1862*, 1865, 1866a, 1875, 1876a, 1904.]

'Besides being a deft variation on a single rhyme-word . . . [the poem] has antecedents in *Jane Eyre* and *Wuthering Heights* as well as that most powerful figure from [CR's] adolescent reading, the demonic lover Melmoth, while his Viking attributes come from the Northern mythologies that everyone was reading in the mid-1850s' (*CR* 186). (Novels by Charlotte and Emily Brontë, both published in 1847; see also note for l. 135 of 'The Convent Threshold'. For *Melmoth*, see headnote for 'Isidora'.) The title in MS (BL) is 'In the days of the Sea Kings. Kings.'

WINTER RAIN

[Composed 31 Jan. 1859. Editions: *1862*, 1865, 1866a, 1875, 1876a, 1904.]

Illustration: WR reports four colour illustrations by CR: 'These are the "bower of love for birds," and the "canopy above nest and egg and mother," and the "meadow-grass pied with broad-eyed daisies," and the lilies on land and water' ('Notes' 482). See headnote of *Goblin Market*.

20 *lea-crops* crops cultivated on a tract of grassland or open ground.

COUSIN KATE

[Composed 18 Nov. 1859. Editions: *1862*, 1865, 1866a, 1896, 1904.]

'. . . the poem was later suppressed by CR, presumably because of its endorsement of single motherhood' (*CR Poems* 435). The title is in DGR's hand in MS (GD).

NOBLE SISTERS

[Probably composed between 18 Nov. 1859 and 27 Mar. 1860. Editions: *1862*, 1865, 1866a, 1875, 1876a, 1904.]

12 *'frayed* frightened.

SPRING

[Composed 17 Aug. 1859. Editions: *1862*, 1865, 1866a, 1875, 1876a, 1904.]

Illustration: WR reports a colour illustration by CR that 'applies to the line "Life nursed in its grave by Death." We see Death, a white and sufficiently "bogyfied" personage, holding on her lap a motionless female form, with yellow hair and pink drapery. A markedly leafless tree rises above the group' ('Notes' 483). See headnote of *Goblin Market*.

25 *He spreads their table that they nothing lack* allusion to God feeding the Israelites in the wilderness after the Israelites complained, 'Can God furnish a table in the wilderness or provide a table for his people?' (Ps. 78:19–20). Also see Ps. 23:1, 5: 'The LORD is my shepherd; I shall not want . . . Thou preparest a table before me in the presence of mine enemies . . .'

THE LAMBS OF GRASMERE, 1860

[Composed 24 July 1860. Editions: *1862*, 1865, 1866a, 1875, 1876a, 1904.]

In the copy of 1875 in which CR made jottings, WR reports her as writing of the lambs: ' "Mrs. Ruxton talked about them." I still remember the occasion well. Mrs. Ruxton (the "Mary Minto" mentioned in a published letter of Mrs. [Elizabeth Barrett] Browning) was married to a retired captain in the army, and for a brief while they lived at Grasmere. She was a lady of very dignified character and aspect, whom my sister both liked and respected in no common degree' ('Notes' 483).

A BIRTHDAY

[Composed 18 Nov. 1857. Editions: *1862*, 1865, 1866a, 1875, 1876a, 1904. First published in *Macmillan's Magazine*, 3 (April 1861), 498.]

'I have more then [*sic*] once been asked whether I could account for the outburst of exuberant joy evidenced in this celebrated lyric; I am unable to do so' ('Notes' 481). WR included a parody that had appeared in 'some illustrated comic paper', saying that CR had pasted it into a copy of 1875. The parody – about the visit of a mother-in-law – begins, 'My heart is like one asked to dine / Whose evening dress is up the spout', and ends, 'Because the mother of my wife / Has come – and means to stay with me'.

1 *My heart is like a singing bird* cf. 'My heart is as a freeborn bird' ('Three Nuns', l. 124).
6 *halcyon* calm; from a bird in an ancient fable thought to breed during the winter solstice on a nest floating on the sea, which charmed the winds and waves so that the sea was especially calm during this time.
10 *vair* fur obtained from a black and white squirrel; one of the heraldic furs.
14 *fleurs-de-lys* heraldic lily borne upon the royal arms of France.

REMEMBER

[Composed 25 July 1849. Editions: *1862*, 1865, 1866a, 1875, 1876a, 1904.]

Cf. Shakespeare, Sonnet 71, 'No longer mourn for me' (*CR Poems* 431).

AFTER DEATH

[Composed 28 April 1849. Editions: *1862*, 1865, 1866a, 1875, 1876a, 1904.]

2 *rosemary* emblematic of remembrance. Cf. Ophelia: 'There's rosemary, that's for remembrance. Pray you, love, remember' (*Hamlet* IV.v.172).

AN END

[Composed 5 March 1849. Editions: *1862*, 1865, 1866a, 1875, 1876a, 1904. First published in *Germ*, no. 1 (Jan. 1850), 48; also published in William Allingham (ed.), *Nightingale Valley, A Collection of Choice Lyrics and Short Poems* (Bell and Daldy, 1859).]

1 *Love, strong as Death, is dead* 'for love is strong as death; jealousy is cruel as the grave' (Song of Sol. 8:6).

MY DREAM

[Composed 9 March 1855. Editions: *1862*, 1865, 1866a, 1875, 1876a, 1904.]

Illustration: 'I possess a little bit of paper, containing three illustrations of her own to *The Dream*, and bearing the date 16 March '55. There is (1) the dreamer slumbering under a tree, from which the monarch crocodile dangles; (2) the crocodile sleeping with "unstrung claw," as the "winged vessel" approaches; and (3) the crocodile as he reared up in front of the vessel, and "wrung his hands" ' ('Notes' 479).

. . . in a copy of her collected edition of 1875, I find that she has marked the piece 'not a real dream.' As it was not a real dream, and she chose nevertheless to give it verbal form, one seeks for a meaning in it, and I for one cannot find any that bears development. She certainly liked the poem . . . I may add that, for some reason as untraceable perhaps as that which guided Christina in the writing of *The Dream*, Dante Gabriel bestowed the name of 'the prudent crocodile' (from this poem) upon Mr. William Morris [1834–96], and the nickname found favour with some other members of our circle. ('Notes' 479)

In a letter to DGR [23 Dec. 1864], CR wrote: 'But I am so happy in my nest of crocodiles that I beg you will on no account purchase the Prudent to laud [*sic*] it over them . . .' (*Letters*, I, 208). WR identifies 'the nest of crocodiles' as a drawing by Griset (Ernest Griset, illustrator of children's books), given to CR by DGR, and 'the Prudent' as a separate large Griset, which DGR purchased for CR (*Letters*, I, 209 n. 1).

Marsh finds antecedents for the crocodile of this poem in Thomas de Quincey's *Confessions of an English Opium Eater* (1822) and in Thomas Beddoes's *A Crocodile* (1851) and 'Song by Isbrand' in *Death's Jest-Book* (1850), 'a Rossetti favourite' (*CR* 167; *CR Poems* 162). The Middle Eastern images Marsh sees as connected to events occurring at this time in CR's life: she went to a party wearing a Syrian costume brought back from the Middle East by Tom Seddon, the companion on that trip of William Holman Hunt (1827–1910), painter and member of the PRB. Seddon, soon after, held an exhibition of his Middle Eastern landscapes (*CR* 164–5).

3 *Euphrates* one of the four rivers of Paradise and the river on which Babylon was located.
4 *Jordan* river where Jesus was baptized.
26 *battened* fed gluttonously; grew fat. Cf. 'If Death were seen / At first as Death, Love had not been . . . / Or in his coarsest Satyr-shape / Had bruised the herb and crushed the grape, / And basked and battened in the woods' (Alfred, Lord Tennyson (1809–92), *In Memoriam* (1850), XXXV, 18–19, 22–4).
48 *shed appropriate tears* 'crocodile tears' are shed hypocritically.

SONG ['Oh roses for the flush of youth']

[Composed 6 Feb. 1849. Editions: *1862*, 1865, 1866a, 1875, 1876a, 1904. First published in *Germ*, no. 2 (Feb. 1850), 64.]

Cf. Ophelia's lines in *Hamlet* IV.v.172–93.

2 *laurel* along with bay, associated with Apollo, and used in crowns and garlands for victorious heroes and poets.

3 *ivy* emblem of immortality.

5 *violets* emblematic of faithfulness. In 'Roses blushing red and white', CR also associates violets with death: 'With violets of fragrant breath, / For death' (ll. 11–12). Cf. 'that Queen / Of secrecy, the violet' (Keats, 'Blue! – 'Tis the life of heaven – the domain' (1848), ll. 11–12).

THE HOUR AND THE GHOST

[Composed 11 Sept. 1856. Editions: *1862*, 1865, 1866a, 1875, 1876a, 1904.]

The poem appears to be influenced by the traditional ballad of the demon lover. In one version, a woman is engaged to marry a seaman, but when she hears that he has died, she marries a carpenter. Years later, her first lover returns as a spirit and persuades her to leave her husband and children and to go to sea with him. At sea, when she discovers 'his cloven foot' (XIII), the lover grows as tall as the ship, a storm comes up and he breaks 'that gallant ship in twain, / And sank her in the sea' (XIX) ('The Daemon Lover', Sir Walter Scott (1771–1832), *Minstrelsy of the Scottish Border* (1802–3)).

52 *harvest gathered in* allusion to death and judgement: see note for l. 47 of 'After This the Judgment'.

60–62 *While thou and I together . . . Toss and howl and spin* allusion to Paolo and Francesca, Dante's lovers in Canto V of the *Inferno*, who are blown about for eternity on stormy winds, wailing; Marsh points out that these lines also resemble those of DGR's translation of *Lenore* (written in 1844) (*CR* 191).

A SUMMER WISH

[Composed 21 June 1851. Editions: *1862*, 1865, 1866a, 1875, 1876a, 1904.]

9–10 *Glad soaring bird; / Sing out thy notes on high* cf. 'And singing still dost soar, and soaring ever singest' (Percy Bysshe Shelley (1792–1822), 'To a Skylark' (1820)).

AN APPLE-GATHERING

[Composed 23 Nov. 1857. Editions: *1862*, 1865, 1866a, 1875, 1876a, 1904. First published in *Macmillan's Magazine* 4 (Aug. 1861), 329.]

SONG ['Two doves upon the selfsame branch']

[Composed by Sept. 1853. Editions: *1862*, 1865, 1866a, 1875, 1876a, 1904.]

See headnote of 'Thou sleepest where the lilies fade'.

2 *Two lilies on a single stem* cf. 'Like two blossoms on one stem' (*Goblin Market*, l. 188).

MAUDE CLARE

[Probably composed between 8 Dec. 1857 and 14 April 1858. Editions: *1862*, 1865, 1866a, 1875, 1876a, 1904. First published in *Once a Week* 1 (5 Nov. 1859), 381–2.]

Illustration: 'It was first published . . . with a design by Millais' ('Notes' 481). (John Everett Millais (1829–96), painter, was an original member of the PRB who later became a member of the Royal Academy of Art.)

'This poem was originally much longer than it is now. It numbered forty-three stanzas or thereabouts (there is a gap in the MS. note-book just before its close)' ('Notes' 481). In this longer version, 'Narrative description . . . dominates over dialogue, and as a result, the poem lacks the dramatic intensity of the 1862 version' (Harrison, *CR in Context* 6).

ECHO

[Composed 18 Dec. 1854. Editions: *1862*, 1866a, 1875, 1876a, 1904.]

WINTER: MY SECRET

[Composed 23 Nov. 1857. Editions: *1862*, 1865, 1866a, 1875, 1876a, 1904.]

'This was at first named *Nonsense*; but, if there is method in some madness, there may be nous in some nonsense' ('Notes' 481).

Title MY SECRET. *1862, 1865, 1866a*.

ANOTHER SPRING

[Composed 15 Sept. 1857. Editions: *1862*, 1865, 1866a, 1875, 1876a, 1904.]

The title is in WR's hand in MS (BL).

4 *mezereons* low shrubs having purplish or rose-coloured flowers and red berries.

A PEAL OF BELLS

[Composed 7 July 1857. Editions: *1862*, 1865, 1866a, 1875, 1876a, 1904.]

9 *Heap my golden plates with fruit* cf. 'One heaved the golden weight / Of dish and fruit to offer her' (*Goblin Market*, ll. 102–3).
27–8 *His bowl that sparkled to the brim / Is drained, is broken* 'Or ever the silver cord be loosed, or the golden bowl be broken . . .' (Ecc. 12:6).

FATA MORGANA

[Composed 18 April 1857. Editions: *1862*, 1865, 1866a, 1875, 1876a, 1904.]

Title 'Fata' is 'fairy' in Italian. 'Fata morgana' is a kind of mirage involving a reflection on the sea and in the air – named for Morgan le Fay, the sorceress of the Arthurian legends.

"NO, THANK YOU, JOHN"

[Composed 27 March 1860. Editions: *1862*, 1865, 1866a, 1875, 1876a, 1904.]

In a letter of 14 Dec. 1875, CR wrote DGR that 'no such person [as John] existed or exists' (*FL* 55). But WR reports that 'In the copy of my sister's combined *Poems* (1879), in which she made a few jottings, I find this rather amusing entry: "The original John was obnoxious, because he never gave scope for 'No, thank you.' " I think I understand who John was; he dated, so far as my sister was affected, at a period some years prior to 1860' ('Notes' 483); and elsewhere WR identifies him as 'the marine painter John Brett, who (at a date long antecedent, say 1852) had appeared to be somewhat smitten by Christina' (*FL* 54). Marsh conjectures that Brett proposed to CR in the summer of 1857 (*CR* 202–8).

Title echoes the traditional English song 'Oh, No, John' (*CR Poems* 435).

MAY ['I cannot tell you how it was']

[Composed 20 Nov. 1855. Editions: *1862*, 1865, 1866a, 1875, 1876a, 1904.]

A PAUSE OF THOUGHT

[Composed 14 Feb. 1848. Editions: *1862*, 1865, 1866a, 1875, 1876a, 1904. First published in *Germ*, no. 2 (Feb. 1850), 57.]

Title THREE STAGES / 1.—A PAUSE OF THOUGHT *1904*.

In MS1 (BodL), the title is: 'Lines / In memory of Schiller's "Der Pilgrim." ' Friedrich Schiller (1759–1805), German dramatist, poet and literary theorist; his 'Der Pilgrim' (1803) tells of a youth who leaves his home to seek happiness and journeys until he comes to a river, which leads him to an ocean – and as the ocean rolls around him, he realizes that nothing will bring him nearer to his goal because earth and heaven can never meet.

2 *hope deferred made my heart sick* 'Hope deferred maketh the heart sick: but when the desire cometh, it is a tree of life' (Pro. 13:12). See Introduction, pp. xl–xli.

TWILIGHT CALM

[Composed 7 Feb. 1850. Editions: *1862*, 1865, 1866a, 1875, 1876a, 1904. First published in Mary Howitt (ed.), *The Dusseldorf Artist's Album* (Dusseldorf, Germany: Arnz and Comp, 1854), 7–8.]

Title A Summer Evening. *1854*.

WIFE TO HUSBAND

[Composed 9 June 1861. Editions: *1862*, 1865, 1866a, 1875, 1876a, 1904.]

WR speculated that if this poem had 'any individual application' it might be to 'my brother's wife, whose constant and severe ill-health permitted no expectation of her living long' ('Notes' 483).

THREE SEASONS

[Composed 9 Nov. 1853. Editions: *1862*, 1865, 1866a, 1875, 1876a, 1904.]

MIRAGE

[Composed 12 June 1860. Editions: *1862*, 1865, 1866a, 1875, 1876a, 1904.]

5–6 *I hang my harp upon a tree, / A weeping willow* 'We hanged our harps upon the willows in the midst thereof' (Ps. 137:2).

SHUT OUT

[Composed 21 Jan. 1856. Editions: *1862*, 1865, 1866a, 1875, 1876a, 1904.]
25 *A violet bed* see note for l. 5 of 'Song' ['Oh roses for the flush of youth'].

SOUND SLEEP

[Composed 13 Aug. 1849. Editions: *1862*, 1865, 1866a, 1875, 1876a, 1904.]
2 *She is sleeping* see headnote of 'Dream-Land'.

SONG ['She sat and sang alway']

[Composed 26 Nov. 1848. Editions: *1862*, 1865, 1866a, 1875, 1876a, 1904; also published 1897a.]

SONG ['When I am dead, my dearest']

[Composed 12 Dec. 1848. Editions: *1862*, 1865, 1866a, 1875, 1876a, 1904.]
WR reports eleven musical settings of this lyric ('Notes' 478).

4 *shady cypress* tree that symbolizes mourning (because of its dark hue) and death (because, once cut down, it cannot grow again).
15 *Haply* by chance (archaic).

DEAD BEFORE DEATH

[Composed 2 Dec. 1854. Editions: *1862*, 1865, 1866a, 1875, 1876a, 1904.]
8 *But it is over as a tale once told* 'we spend our years as a tale that is told' (Ps. 90:9).

BITTER FOR SWEET

[Composed 1 Dec. 1848. Editions: *1862*, 1865, 1866a, 1875, 1876a, 1904.]
Title 'Woe unto them . . . that put bitter for sweet, and sweet for bitter!' (Isa. 5:20).

SISTER MAUDE

[Editions: *1862*, 1865, 1866a, 1875, 1876a, 1896, 1904.]

WR claimed this poem 'seems to show a certain reminiscence from Tennyson's composition, *The Sisters*' ['We were two daughters of one race' (1832)] ('Notes' 483). Both poems may have been influenced by Scott's *Minstrelsy*, especially by 'The Cruel Sister' (see headnote of 'The Hour and the Ghost').

REST

[Composed 15 May 1849. Editions: *1862*, 1865, 1866a, 1875, 1876a, 1904.]

See headnote of 'Dream-Land'.

THE FIRST SPRING DAY

[Composed 1 March 1855. Editions: *1862*, 1865, 1866a, 1875, 1876a, 1904.]

'In a copy of her *Poems*, 1875, Christina made the following note: "I was walking in the Outer Circle, Regent's Park, when the impulse or thought came" ' ('Notes' 479).

THE CONVENT THRESHOLD

[Composed 9 July 1858. Editions: *1862*, 1865, 1866a, 1875, 1876a, 1904.]

WR felt that this poem combined 'something of the idea of an Heloise and Abelard with something of the idea of a Juliet and Romeo' ('Notes' 482). The story appears to be taken from Pope's *Eloisa to Abelard* (1717). Jerome Bump suggests that it also echoes Tennyson's 'St Agnes' Eve' (1836) ('Christina Rossetti and the Pre-Raphaelite Brotherhood', in Kent, *Achievement* 343). Marsh points out that this poem is 'reminiscent of Poe, Beddoes and romances by Barrett Browning about immured nuns' (*CR* 214).

6 *To city and to sea of glass* 'And I saw as it were a sea of glass mingled with fire: and them that had gotten the victory over the beast, and over his image, and over his mark, and over the number of his name, stand on the sea of glass, having the harps of God' (Rev. 15:2). In her comments on this biblical verse in *FD*, CR writes that fire is added to the sea 'to illuminate, flash, augment beauty' (372).

21 *mansions where the righteous sup* 'In my Father's house are many mansions . . . I go to prepare a place for you' (John 14:2).

24 *Cherubim* angels with two or four wings, in the second order of angels; in Genesis, guardians of the tree of life.

Seraphim angels with six wings, in the highest order of angels. See also note for ll. 19–20 of 'Christian and Jew. A Dialogue'.

42 *Flee to the mountain* 'Then let them which be in Judaea flee into the mountains' (Matt. 24:16).

59 *laves* bathes.

63–4 *Alas for joy that went before, / For joy that dies, for love that dies* 'These words recall Keats's "Ode on Melancholy" [1820], in which he makes clear that melancholy "dwells with Beauty – Beauty that must die; / And Joy, whose hand is ever at his lips / Bidding adieu" [ll. 21–32]' (Bump, 'CR and the PRB', in Kent, *Achievement* 343).

67 *Lent* the fast of forty days before Easter, a custom revived by the Tractarians in the nineteenth century.

73 *Have pity upon me, ye my friends* 'Have pity upon me, have pity upon me, O ye my friends; for the hand of God hath touched me' (Job 19:21).

82–4 *No gladder song . . . Than Angels sing when one repents* 'I say unto you, that likewise joy shall be in heaven over one sinner that repenteth, more than over ninety and nine just persons, which need no repentance' (Luke 15:7), from the parable of the lost sheep; see also note to l. 14 of 'Good Friday' ['Am I a stone and not a sheep'].

87 *clomb* climbed.

91 *cars* wheeled vehicles, such as the chariots in the archaic image of the sun, moon and stars, imagined to be riding in a kind of grand procession. See also note for l. 7 of 'Lord, make us all love all: that when we meet'.

101 *aureole crown* radiant circle of light; glorifying halo.

125 *but were not drunk with wine* 'Others mocking said, These men are full of new wine' (Acts 2:13); 'And be not drunk with wine . . . but be filled with the Spirit' (Eph. 5:18).

135 *And frozen blood was on the sill* cf. the scene in the beginning of Emily Brontë's *Wuthering Heights* in which the ghost-child Catherine's wrist is cut on the broken window pane – an image echoed in the end of the novel, when Heathcliff is found dead, his hand, grazed by the open lattice, resting on the sill.

139 *Gone before* 'and exalt us unto the same place whither our Saviour Christ is gone before' (Collect for the Sunday after Ascension-day, *Book of Common Prayer*).

UP-HILL

[Composed 29 June 1858. Editions: *1862*, 1865, 1866a, 1875, 1876a, 1904. First published in *Macmillan's Magazine* 3 (Feb. 1861), 325.]

'This was, I believe, the first poem by Christina which excited marked attention' ('Notes' 481). It enjoyed a very wide circulation: for example, when the young Vincent van Gogh was a lay preacher in London, he quoted the first stanza in a sermon (*CR* 417).

[Devotional Pieces]

"THE LOVE OF CHRIST WHICH PASSETH KNOWLEDGE"

[Composed 15 Oct. 1858. Editions: *1862*, 1865, 1866a, 1875, 1876a, 1904.]

Title 'And to know the love of Christ, which passeth knowledge, that ye might be filled with all the fulness of God' (Eph. 3:19).
4 *For three and thirty years* it is the tradition that Jesus was thirty-three when he was crucified.
11 *Much sweeter thou than honey to My mouth* 'And I took the little book out of the angel's hand, and ate it up; and it was in my mouth sweet as honey: and as soon as I had eaten it, my belly was bitter' (Rev. 10:10). CR's commentary on this Bible verse in *FD* stresses that 'bitterness may be to us safeguard not destroyer of sweetness', and that Christ's own suffering was 'bitter', even though his love makes the 'taste' of the sinner sweet (284).
13 *I bore thee on My shoulders and rejoiced* see note for l. 14 of 'Good Friday' ['Am I a stone and not a sheep'].
16 *wagged their heads in scorn* 'All they that see me laugh me to scorn: they shoot out the lip, they shake the head' (Ps. 22:7).
18 *Did thorns for frontlets stamp between Mine eyes* a frontlet is a phylactery, a capsule containing scriptural texts, which is worn on the forehead. Jiménez (*Bible and the Poetry* xi) points out that this line illustrates CR's characteristic technique of conflating Old and New Testament allusions – here the crown of thorns placed on Jesus' head before his crucifixion, in the New Testament, and the commandment in the Old: 'Therefore shall ye lay up these my words in your heart and in your soul, and bind them for a sign upon your hand, that they may be as frontlets between your eyes' (Deut. 11:18).

21 *A thief upon My right hand and My left* Jesus was crucified between two thieves (Mark 15:27; Luke 23:33; John 19:18).

23–4 *one smote My heart and cleft / A hiding-place for thee* Jiménez reads these lines as referring to the passage in John 19:34 in which 'one of the soldiers with a spear pierced his side, and forthwith came there out blood and water' (*Bible and the Poetry* 122); also see 'Rock of ages, cleft for me, / Let me hide myself in Thee' (hymn (1775), ll. 1–2).

"A BRUISED REED SHALL HE NOT BREAK"

[Composed 13 June 1852. Editions: *1862*, 1865, 1866a, 1875, 1876a, 1904.]

Title 'A bruised reed shall he not break, and the smoking flax shall he not quench: he shall bring forth judgement unto truth' (Isa. 42:3). A prayer in *TF* ends with a reference to Christ: 'Who broke not the bruised reed nor quenched the smoking flax' (187).

7 *Because thy will cleaves to the better part* 'Mary hath chosen that good part, which shall not be taken away from her' (Luke 10:42).

A BETTER RESURRECTION

[Composed 30 June 1857. Editions: *1862*, 1865, 1866a, 1875, 1876a, 1904.]

Title 'Women received their dead raised to life again: and others were tortured, not accepting deliverance; that they might obtain a better resurrection' (Heb. 11:35).

5–6 *I lift mine eyes, but dimmed with grief / No everlasting hills I see* 'I will lift up mine eyes unto the hills, from whence cometh my help' (Ps. 121:1); 'The blessings of thy father have prevailed above the blessings of my progenitors unto the utmost bound of the everlasting hills' (Gen. 49:26).

9 *My life is like a faded leaf* 'we all do fade as a leaf' (Isa. 64:6).

17 *My life is like a broken bowl* see note for ll. 27–8 of 'A Peal of Bells'.

ADVENT ['This Advent moon shines cold and clear']

[Composed 2 May 1858. Editions: *1862*, 1865, 1866a, 1875, 1876a, 1904.]

'In the annotated copy of her *Poems*, Christina wrote against this one: "Liked, I believe, at East Grinstead [Anglican Sisterhood]" – which one may well credit of the "Wise Virgins" of that establishment. The greater part was set to music for Christina's funeral service at Christ Church, Woburn Square, by the organist, Mr. Lowden' ('Notes' 473).

Title Advent consists of the four Sundays before Christmas. The first, Advent Sunday, is the beginning of the ecclesiastical year. Through its celebration of Christ's birth, Advent also foreshadows Jesus' Second Coming and the Day of Judgement.

3 *Our lamps have burned* Jesus tells the story of the wise and foolish virgins as a parable illustrating the need to be ready for the Second Coming. The kingdom of heaven is compared to ten virgins who took their lamps to meet the bridegroom. At midnight, there was a cry – 'Behold the bridegroom cometh . . .' The five wise virgins were ready with oil in their lamps, but the five foolish virgins had to go out to buy oil, and when they returned, the door (where the marriage was taking place) was shut against them. They said, 'Lord, Lord, open to us. But he answered and said, Verily I say unto you, I know you not' (Matt. 25:1–12). CR associated this parable with Advent: 'Advent bids us look forward and upward, for "Behold the Bridegroom cometh" ' (*TF* 277).

5 *Watchman, what of the night* Isa. 21:11.

6 *Heart-sick with hope deferred* see note for l. 2 of 'A Pause of Thought'.

9 *The Porter watches at the gate* 'For the Son of man is as a man taking a far journey, who left his house, and gave authority to his servants, and to every man his work, and commanded the porter to watch. Watch ye therefore: for ye know not when the master of the house cometh, at even, or at midnight, or at the cockcrowing, or in the morning: Lest coming suddenly he find you sleeping' (Mark 13:34–6).

32 *Sweeter than honeycomb* 'More to be desired are they than gold, yea, than much fine gold: sweeter also than honey and the honeycomb' (Ps. 19:10).

37–8 *Eye hath not seen, ear hath not heard, / Nor heart conceived* 'Eye hath not seen, nor ear heard, neither have entered into the heart of man, the things which God hath prepared for them that love him' (1 Cor. 2:9).

45 *Who wept* 'Jesus wept' (John 11:35).

49–51 *Weeping we hold Him fast . . . Till daybreak* Jacob wrestled with an angel until daybreak, saying: 'I will not let thee go, except thou bless me' (Gen. 32:26).

53–6 *Then figs shall bud . . . come away* 'For, lo, the winter is past, the rain is over and gone; The flowers appear on the earth; the time of the singing of birds is come, and the voice of the turtle[dove] is heard in our land; The fig tree putteth forth her green figs, and the vines with the tender grape give a good smell. Arise, my love, my fair one, and come away' (Song of Sol. 2:11–13).

THE THREE ENEMIES

[Composed 15 June 1851. Editions: *1862*, 1865, 1866a, 1875, 1876a, 1904.]

A prayer for the eighteenth Sunday after Trinity asks for 'grace to withstand the temptations of the world, the flesh and the devil' (*Book of Common Prayer*).

Kent notes in the form of this poem an echo of the stanzas with single rhymes of George Herbert's 'Trinitie Sunday' (1633) (' "By thought, word, and deed": George Herbert and Christina Rossetti', in Kent, *Achievement* 262 n. 39).

8 *The winepress of the wrath of God* 'And out of his mouth goeth a sharp sword, that with it he should smite the nations: and he shall rule them with a rod of iron: and he treadeth the winepress of the fierceness and wrath of Almighty God' (Rev. 19:15). CR's commentary on this Bible verse stresses the final judgement of God upon sinners (*FD* 450–51).

16 *His Heart once bled for mine indeed* see note for ll. 23–4 of ' "The Love of Christ Which Passeth Knowledge" '.

24 *A visage marred beyond compare* 'his visage was so marred more than any man' (Isa. 52:14); taken as a prophecy of Christ.

28 *lacked where to lay His Head* 'but the Son of man hath not where to lay his head' (Matt. 8:20; Luke 9:58).

35 *He drained the dregs from out my cup* 'thou hast drunken the dregs of the cup of trembling, and wrung them out' (Isa. 51:17).

46 *Get thee behind me* from Jesus' temptation in the wilderness: 'And Jesus answered and said unto him, Get thee behind me, Satan: for it is written, Thou shalt worship the Lord thy God, and him only shalt thou serve' (Luke 4:8); and cf. his rebuke of his disciple Peter: 'Get thee behind me, Satan: thou art an offence unto me: for thou savourest not the things that be of God, but those that be of men' (Matt. 16:23; see also Mark 8:33).

ONE CERTAINTY

[Composed 2 June 1849. Editions: *1862*, 1865, 1866a, 1875, 1876a, 1904; also published in 1897a.]

WR speculates that the poem was written 'during a period of illness' ('Notes' 467). Several of the poems that appear in CR's notebook MS at this time are in the handwriting of MR or CR's mother.

Title [untitled] *1897a*.
1 *Vanity of vanities, the Preacher saith* 'Vanity of vanities, saith the preacher, vanity of vanities; all is vanity' (Ecc. 1:2). In an extended discussion of this Bible verse in *SF*, CR wrote that it 'amounts to so exquisite a dirge over dead hope and paralysed effort that we are almost ready to fall in love with our own desolation; and seeing that "man walketh in a vain shadow" . . . to become vain as that shadow, and to drift through life without disquietude, because without either aim or aspiration' (272).
2–3 *The eye and ear / Cannot be filled with what they see and hear* 'the eye is not satisfied with seeing, nor the ear filled with hearing' (Ecc. 1:8).
5 *the grass that withereth* 'The grass withereth, the flower fadeth: because the

spirit of the LORD bloweth upon it: surely the people is grass. The grass withereth, the flower fadeth: but the word of our God shall stand for ever' (Isa. 40:7–8; see also 1 Pet. 1:24–5).

11 *there is nothing new under the sun* 'The thing that hath been, it is that which shall be; and that which is done is that which shall be done: and there is no new thing under the sun' (Ecc. 1:9).

CHRISTIAN AND JEW / A DIALOGUE

[Composed 9 July 1858. Editions: *1862*, 1865, 1866a, 1875, 1876a, 1904.]

19–20 *(I hear them sing) / One "Holy, Holy, Holy" to their King* 'Above it stood the seraphims: each one had six wings; with twain he covered his face, and with twain he covered his feet, and with twain he did fly. And one cried unto another, and said, Holy, holy, holy, is the LORD of hosts: the whole earth is full of his glory' (Isa. 6:2–3); 'And the four beasts had each of them six wings about him; and they were full of eyes within: and they rest not day and night, saying, Holy, holy, holy, Lord God Almighty, which was, and is, and is to come' (Rev. 4:8). Cf. also the Communion service in the *Book of Common Prayer*: 'Therefore with Angels and Archangels, and with all the company of heaven, we laud and magnify thy glorious Name; evermore praising thee, and saying, Holy, holy, holy, Lord God of Hosts, heaven and earth are full of thy glory . . .'

23 *Garden and goal and nest* in *TF*, CR talks about occupying rooms in 'the spiritual Ark', adding: 'Our room, as God builds and makes it for us, is likewise our nest: and a nest is surely the very homeliest idea of a home' (164). Following this concluding sentence for 25 Aug., she devotes all of the entry for 26 Aug. to the idea of 'nest', associating it with warmth, softness, shade, safety and 'an overhanging presence of love' (165).

28 *elect by grace* the elect are those saved by faith in God by the 'grace' of Jesus, who died for their sins.

29 *All tears are wiped for ever from their face* 'and the Lord God will wipe away tears from off all faces' (Isa. 25:8; see also note for l. 7 of 'Beloved, yield thy time to God, for He'); 'and God shall wipe away all tears from their eyes' (Rev. 7:17 – see also note for l. 12 of ' "So great a cloud of Witnesses" ' – and 21:4 – see also note for l. 7 of ' "Hark! the Alleluias of the great salvation" '). CR's commentary on Rev. 21:4 in *FD* begins with an allusion to the comfort of a mother and later: 'If I can scarcely forecast a wiping away of my own tears, I can trustfully contemplate that blessed consummation for all tears of some whom I have loved and revered . . .' (485).

33 *Boughs of the Living Vine* the 'Living Vine' is Jesus: 'I am the true vine, and my Father is the husbandman', and 'Abide in me, and I in you. As the branch cannot bear fruit of itself, except it abide in the vine; no more can ye, except ye abide in me' (John 15:1, 4). CR refers to this image in *SF*: 'Though fruitless branch after fruitless branch be broken off, though graft after graft prove barren, yet these bear not the root but the root these: wherefore the True Vine ceases not to flourish, even if sometimes it be as a root out of a dry ground (see Rom. xi. 17–24; St John xv. 1–8; Isa. liii. 2)'; and she discusses it at greater length, saying: 'Our Lord is revealed to us under a variety of similitudes culled from the family of "green things" ' (136, 262).

40–41 *For He hath not abhorred / Our low estate nor scorn'd our offering* 'Who remembered us in our low estate: for his mercy endureth for ever' (Ps. 136:23; see also Luke 1:48).

43–4 *But Zion said: / My Lord forgetteth me* 'the Lord hath comforted his people, and will have mercy upon his afflicted. But Zion said, The Lord hath forsaken me, and my Lord hath forgotten me' (Isa. 49:13–14). Zion is used in reference to the household of God, the Israelites, their religious system and their homeland, the Christian Church, heaven as the final home of believers and a place of worship. See also note for l. 16 of 'All Saints' ['They are flocking from the East'].

50–51 *her harpstrings cannot sound / In a strange land* allusion to the captivity of the Israelites in Babylon: 'How shall we sing the Lord's song in a strange land?' (Ps. 137:4).

53 *O drunken not with wine* see note for l. 125 of 'The Convent Threshold'.

56–7 *Arise, shine, / For thy light is come* 'Arise, shine; for thy light is come, and the glory of the Lord is risen upon thee' (Isa. 60:1).

58–9 *"Can these bones live?"— / "God knows* 'And he said unto me, Son of man, can these bones live? And I answered, O Lord God, thou knowest' (Eze. 37:3).

60–62 *The prophet saw ... shook and rose* Ezekiel raised an 'exceeding great army' by bringing together scattered bones and breathing life into them (Eze. 37:3–10) – see also note for title of ' "Behold a Shaking" '.

SWEET DEATH

[Composed 9 Feb. 1849. Editions: *1862*, 1865, 1866a, 1875, 1876a, 1904. First published in *Art and Poetry: Being Thoughts Towards Nature Conducted Principally by Artists* 3 (March 1850), 117.]

24 *glean with Ruth* see note for l. 14 of 'Autumn Violets'.

SYMBOLS

[Composed 7 Jan. 1849. Editions: *1862*, 1865, 1866a, 1875, 1876a, 1904; also published 1897a.]

Title [untitled] *1897a*.
5 *matin* morning prayer.
6 *evensong* in the Anglican tradition, a prayer said or sung at evening.

"CONSIDER THE LILIES OF THE FIELD"
['Flowers preach to us if we will hear']

[Composed 21 Oct. 1853. Editions: *1862*, 1865, 1866a, 1875, 1876a, 1904.]

Title Jesus instructed his disciples to 'Behold the fowls of the air: for they sow not, neither do they reap, nor gather into barns; yet your heavenly Father feedeth them. Are ye not much better than they? . . . And why take ye thought for raiment? Consider the lilies of the field, how they grow; they toil not, neither do they spin: And yet I say unto you, That even Solomon in all his glory was not arrayed like one of these' (Matt. 6:26, 28–9 – see also note for l. 91 of 'Maiden May'; see also Luke 12:27).

22–4 *who sends the dew . . . To nourish one small seed* 'For the seed shall be prosperous; the vine shall give her fruit, and the ground shall give her increase, and the heavens shall give their dew; and I will cause the remnant of this people to possess all these things' (Zec. 8:12).

THE WORLD

[Composed 27 June 1854. Editions: *1862*, 1865, 1866a, 1875, 1876a, 1904.]

This is one of Christina Rossetti's most energetic utterances, and a highly characteristic one. She had in fact a great horror of 'the world,' in the sense which that term bears in the New Testament; its power to blur all the great traits of character, to deaden all lofty aims, to clog all the impulses of the soul aspiring to unseen Truth. I recollect her once saying to me with marked emphasis, when my children were past their very earliest years, 'I hope they are not *worldly*' . . . The primary sense . . . appears to be that the world – like other devils, spectres, and hobgoblins – appears *in propria persona* in the night-hours only; it is then that she is recognized for the fiend she actually is.' ('Notes' 471)

Marsh points out that, as in CR's 'The Dead City', worldly desires are represented by fruits and flowers. She also connects the image of terror to 'the opposing figures' of Samuel Taylor Coleridge (1772–1834), *Christabel* (1816) (*CR* 154).

11 *clawed and clutching hands* cf. 'Clawed with their nails' (*Goblin Market*, l. 401).
14 *cloven too* i.e. like the devil's foot.

A TESTIMONY

[Composed 31 Aug. 1849. Editions: *1862*, 1865, 1866a, 1875, 1876a, 1904. First published in *Germ* no. 2 (Feb. 1850), 73–5.]

1–2 *I said of laughter: it is vain. / Of mirth I said: what profits it* 'I said of laughter, it is mad: and of mirth, What doeth it?' (Ecc. 2:2).

6 *vanity beneath the sun* 'Then I returned, and I saw vanity under the sun' (Ecc. 4:7).

7–8 *Man walks in a vain shadow; he / Disquieteth himself in vain* 'Surely every man walketh in a vain shew: surely they are disquieted in vain' (Ps. 39:6). See note for l. 1 of 'One Certainty'.

10–11 *The rivers do not fill the sea, / But turn back to their secret source* 'All the rivers run into the sea; yet the sea is not full; unto the place from whence the rivers come, thither they return again' (Ecc. 1:7). In a commentary on 'Seas and Floods' in *SF* (271–2), CR associates this biblical verse with Ps. 39:6 (see note for ll. 7–8, above).

13–14 *Our treasures moth and rust corrupt, / Or thieves break thro' and steal* 'Lay not up for yourselves treasures upon earth, where moth and rust doth corrupt, and where thieves break through and steal: But lay up for yourselves treasures in heaven, where neither moth nor rust doth corrupt, and where thieves do not break through nor steal' (Matt. 6:19–20; see also Luke 12:33).

16–18 *One man made merry as he supped . . . His soul would be required of him* see the parable of the rich man who stores up earthly treasures, as told in Luke 12:16–21: he would 'eat, drink, and be merry. But God said unto him, Thou fool, this night thy soul shall be required of thee: then whose shall those things be, which thou has provided?' (19–20).

19–23 *We build our houses on the sand . . . quickly overthrown* in one of the parables of the house built on a rock, Jesus says:

whosoever heareth these sayings of mine, and doeth them, I will liken him unto a wise man, which built his house upon a rock: And the rain descended, and the floods came, and the winds blew, and beat upon that house; and it fell not; for it was founded upon a rock. And everyone that heareth these sayings of mine, and doeth them not, shall be likened unto a foolish man, which built his house upon the sand: And the rain descended, and the floods came, and the winds blew, and beat upon that house; and it fell: and great was the fall of it. (Matt. 7:24–7; see also Luke 6:47–9)

A rock image also occurs in Job: 'She [the eagle] dwelleth and abideth on the rock, upon the crag of the rock, and the strong place' (39:28). Jesus said to Peter (whose name means 'rock'): 'thou art Peter, and upon this rock I will build my church' (Matt. 16:18). In *TF*, CR quotes a number of Bible verses about Jesus as a rock: ' "He is the Rock . . . a God of Truth, and without iniquity . . . The Rock of his salvation." – "Thou shalt smite the rock, and there shall come water out of it, that the people may drink." – "They drank of that spiritual Rock that followed them: and that Rock was Christ." – "Blessed be my Rock; and let the God of my salvation be exalted" ' (15). (See also *SF* 259–60.)

25 *All things are vanity* see note for l. 1 of 'One Certainty'.

27 *The rich man dies; and the poor dies* cf. 'And it came to pass, that the beggar died, and was carried by the angels into Abraham's bosom: the rich man also died, and was buried' (Luke 16:22). See also note for title of ' "Son, remember" '.

37 *Man flourishes as a green leaf* 'As for man, his days are as grass: as a flower of the field, so he flourisheth' (Ps. 103:15); and see note for l. 5 of 'One Certainty'.

43–5 *Our eyes cannot be satisfied . . . With hearing* see note for ll. 2–3 of 'One Certainty'.

45 *yet we plant and build* 'I made me great works; I builded me houses; I planted me vineyards' (Ecc. 2:4).

49–50 *Why should we hasten to arise / So early* see Ecc. 2:11, in which 'the preacher' wonders about the value of labour, given that all is vanity.

53–4 *Verily, we sow wind; and we / Shall reap the whirlwind, verily* 'For they have sown the wind, and they shall reap the whirlwind' (Hos. 8:7).

55–6 *He who hath little shall not lack; / He who hath plenty shall decay* allusion to the Israelites gathering manna in the wilderness – 'he that gathered much had nothing over, and he that gathered little had no lack . . . And Moses said, Let no man leave of it till the morning. Notwithstanding they hearkened not unto Moses; but some of them left of it until the morning, and it bred worms, and stank' (Ex. 16:18–20).

73–4 *A King dwelt in Jerusalem . . . the wisest man* the biblical King Solomon, supposed author of Ecclesiastes, prayed for – and received – wisdom (1 Kings 3:5–28).

SLEEP AT SEA

[Composed 17 Oct. 1853. Editions: *1862*, 1865, 1866a, 1875, 1876a, 1904.]

DGR felt that the essential motif was 'one with that of the "Ballad of Boding" ' (letter of 7 Sept. 1881 (no. 2551), in O. Doughty and J. Wahl (eds.), *Letters of DGR* 1965, vol. IV (1967), p. 1920). The MSS (BodL, YU) are titled 'Something like Truth'.

72 *Sick with hope deferred* see note for l. 2 of 'A Pause for Thought'.

74 *amain* without delay (literary).

85–6 *Vanity of vanities, / The Preacher says* see note for l. 1 of 'One Certainty'.

FROM HOUSE TO HOME

[Composed 19 Nov. 1858. Editions: *1862*, 1865, 1866a, 1875, 1876a, 1904.]

WR reports that DGR wrote on the MS notebook: ' "This is so good it cannot be omitted; but could not something be done to make it less like *Palace of Art*?" Christina, however, did nothing at all in that direction . . . The essence of the poem is the severance of a human heart from the joys and the loves of earth, to centre in the joys and the loves of heaven; that it is in part a personal utterance is a fact too plain to need exposition' ('Notes' 461); see also note for l. 6. After WR directs the reader's attention to several other poems written at the same period, he adds: 'If the reader cares to turn to these several poems, he will see in all of them evidence of a spirit sorely wrung, and clinging for dear life to a hope not of this world' ('Notes' 461).

Title in MS (BL), the title is: ' "Sorrow not as those who have no hope." ' 'But I would not have you to be ignorant, brethren, concerning them which are asleep, that ye sorrow not, even as others which have no hope' (1 Thes. 4:13).

6 *a pleasure-place within my soul* cf. the 'pleasure-dome' of Coleridge's 'Kubla Khan' (1816) as well as the opening line of Tennyson's 'The Palace of Art' (1832): 'I built my soul a lordly pleasure-house.'

17 *pleasaunce* pleasure-ground, usually attached to a mansion.

94 *I lit my candle, searched from room to room* allusion to Jesus' parable of the lost coin: 'what woman having ten pieces of silver, if she lose one piece, doth not light a candle, and sweep the house, and seek diligently till she find it?' (Luke 15:8).

141 *founded on the Rock* see note for l. 19 of 'A Testimony'.

145–6 *I saw a cup sent down and come to her / Brim full of loathing and of bitterness* 'And the woman was arrayed in purple and scarlet colour, and decked with gold and precious stones and pearls, having a golden cup in her hand full of abominations and filthiness of her fornication' (Rev. 17:4).

154 *My soul shall nothing want* see note for l. 25 of 'Spring'.

158 *The wilderness shall blossom as a rose* 'The wilderness and the solitary place shall be glad for them; and the desert shall rejoice and blossom as the rose' (Isa. 35:1).

159 *Rend the veil* allusion to the veil of the Temple in Jerusalem that hid the Holy of Holies and that was 'rent in twain from the top to the bottom' at the moment of Jesus' death (Matt. 27:51).

161–84 *Then earth and heaven . . . knew no end thereof* this description combines elements of the vision in Revelation and the depiction of Paradise in Dante's *Divine Comedy*.

161 *Then earth and heaven were rolled up like a scroll* 'And all the host of heaven shall be dissolved, and the heavens shall be rolled together as a scroll: and all their host shall fall down, as the leaf falleth off from the vine, and as a falling fig from the fig tree' (Isa. 34:4); 'And the heaven departed as a scroll when it is rolled together; and every mountain and island were moved out of their places' (Rev. 6:14). CR alludes to both verses in *SF*: 'Yet has the unchanging sky no final stability, but at its appointed hour it shall be rolled up as a scroll and shall pass away' (24).

169 *They sang a song, a new song* see headnote of ' "I will come and heal him" '.

172 *Lo, all things were made new* 'And he that sat upon the throne said, Behold, I make all things new' (Rev. 21:5). About this biblical verse, CR writes in *FD* that 'human instinct craves after something new', but that 'sanctified human instinct sets its hope above the sun . . .' (182).

176 *Their secret sacred names* 'to him that overcometh will I give to eat of the hidden manna, and will give him a white stone, and in the stone a new name written, which no man knoweth saving he that receiveth it' (Rev. 2:17).

179 *cast down their crowns* 'The four and twenty elders fall down before him that sat on the throne, and worship him that liveth for ever and ever, and cast their crowns before the throne' (Rev. 4:10). In her commentary on this Bible verse, CR writes: 'To sit on thrones is an exaltation, to wear crowns a dignity: to fall prostrate in worship is a loftier exaltation, to cast down tributary crowns an enhanced dignity . . . The self-surrenders of earth rehearse in their rapturous triumph the all-surrendering self-surrender of heaven' (*FD* 161).

204 *Cast down but not destroyed* 'Persecuted, but not forsaken; cast down, but not destroyed' (2 Cor. 4:9).

205 *in patience I possess my soul* 'In your patience possess ye your souls' (Luke 21:19).

206 *therefore as a flint I set my face* 'For the Lord GOD will help me; therefore shall I not be confounded: therefore have I set my face like a flint, and I know that I shall not be ashamed' (Isa. 50:7). In her entry for the Feast of St Agatha in *TF* (5 Feb.), CR describes the saint as setting 'her face as a flint' to endure torture, returning to prison to fall 'asleep' in Jesus (27).

211 *My face is steadfast toward Jerusalem* allusion to Jesus' decision to go to Jerusalem, even though he knew he would be crucified there. 'And it came to pass, when the time was come that he should be received up, he stedfastly set his face to go to Jerusalem' (Luke 9:51); 'Son of man, set thy face toward Jerusalem, and drop thy word toward the holy places, and prophesy against the land of Israel' (Eze. 21:2); 'They shall ask the way to Zion with their faces thitherward' (Jer. 50:5).

217–18 *Beauty for ashes, oil of joy for grief, / Garment of praise for spirit of heaviness* 'To appoint unto them that mourn in Zion, to give unto them beauty for ashes, the soil of joy for mourning, the garment of praise for the spirit of heaviness' (Isa. 61:3).

219 *I fade as doth a leaf* see note for l. 9 of 'A Better Resurrection'.

OLD AND NEW YEAR DITTIES

[Editions: *1862*, 1865, 1866a, 1875, 1876a, 1904.]

'In framing the sections of her *Devotional Poems*, 1875 and 1890, Christina used to put these *Ditties* last, followed only by *Amen* and *The Lowest Place*' ('Notes' 472).

1

[Composed 13 Dec. 1856.]

9 *scathe* hurt (archaic).

2

[Composed 31 Dec. 1858.]

1 *Watch with me* when Jesus went to the Garden of Gethsemane to pray before being arrested, he asked his disciples to 'watch with me'. When he returned, he found them asleep and said: 'What, could ye not watch with me one hour? Watch and pray, that ye enter not into temptation: the spirit indeed is willing, but the flesh is weak' (Matt. 26:38, 40–41; see also Mark 14:38). The phrase is also an allusion to the Last Judgement: 'Take ye heed, watch and pray: for ye know not when the time is' (Mark 13:33); see also note for Part 3, ll. 16–17.
8 *walk in white* see note for l. 12.
12 *And cry, "How long?"* repeated in many contexts in the Bible – but CR may have in mind Rev. 6:10–11: 'And they cried with a loud voice, saying, How long, O Lord, holy and true, dost Thou not judge and avenge our blood on them that dwell on the earth? And white robes were given unto every one of them; and it was said unto them, that they should rest yet for a little season, until their fellowservants also and their brethren, that should be killed as they were, should be fulfilled'; and 'My soul is also sore vexed: but thou, O LORD, how long?' (Ps. 6:3).
18 *I, Love, am Thine; Thou, Lord my God, art mine* cf. 'My beloved is mine, and I am his' (Song of Sol. 2:16).

3

[Composed 31 Dec. 1860.]

WR regarded this as 'the summit and mountain-top of Christina's work . . . The poem depends for its effect on nought save its feeling, sense, and sound; for the verses avoid regularity of the ordinary kind, and there is but one single rhyme throughout. The note is essentially one of triumph, though of triumph through the very grievousness of experience past and present' ('Notes' 472). WR added that this is the only poem CR wrote between 24 July 1860 and 23 March 1861.

5 *That hath won neither laurel nor bay* see note for l. 2 of 'Song' ['Oh roses for the flush of youth'].

7 *Thou, root-stricken, shalt not rebuild thy decay* cf. 'And now also the axe is laid unto the root of the trees: therefore every tree which bringeth not forth good fruit is hewn down, and cast into the fire' (Matt. 3:10).

13 *Rust in thy gold, a moth is in thine array* see note for ll. 13–14 of 'A Testimony'.

16–17 *Lo the bridegroom shall come . . . Watch thou and pray* see notes for l. 3 of 'Advent' ['This Advent moon shines cold and clear'], and for Part 2, l. 1; and 'And what I say unto you I say unto all, Watch' (Mark 13:38).

19–25 *Passing away . . . Me say* The images and language – new grapes, new figs, turtledoves, the lover calling 'My love' to 'Arise, come away' – follow closely Song of Sol. 2:11–13. See also note for ll. 53–6 of 'Advent' ['This Advent moon shines cold and clear'].

AMEN

[Composed 20 April 1856. Editions: *1862*, 1865, 1866a, 1875, 1876a, 1904.]

6 *It is finished* 'When Jesus therefore had received the vinegar, he said, It is finished: and he bowed his head, and gave up the ghost' (John 19:30).

The Prince's Progress and Other Poems (1866)

THE PRINCE'S PROGRESS

[Lines 481–540 composed 11 Oct. 1861; ll. 1–480 composed Jan. 1865. Editions: *1866*, 1866a, 1875, 1876a, 1904. Lines 481–540 first published in *Macmillan's Magazine* 7 (May 1863), 36.]

The nucleus, according to WR, was the 'dirge-song' beginning with l. 481: 'This was written in 1861, and entitled *The Prince who arrived too late*. When Christina Rossetti was looking up, in 1865, the material for a fresh poetical volume, it was, I believe, my brother who suggested to her to turn the dirge into a narrative poem of some length. She adopted the suggestion – almost the only instance in which she wrote anything so as to meet directly the views of another person' ('Notes' 461). In a letter to the poet Dora Greenwell (1821–82) [?Oct. 1863], CR refers to 'The Prince Who Arrived Too Late' as 'my reverse of the *Sleeping Beauty*: except in fairy land such reverses must often occur; yet I don't think it argues a sound or grateful spirit to dwell on them as predominantly as I have done' (*Letters*, I, 184). Marsh sees antecedents to this poem in John Bunyan's *Pilgrim's Progress* (1678) and DGR's *The Staff and Scrip* (1856) (*CR* 322).

Title THE FAIRY PRINCE WHO ARRIVED TOO LATE. *1863*.

40 *love is sweet* cf. 'all love is sweet' (Shelley, *Prometheus Unbound* (1820), II.v.39).

56 *milkmaid loitered* 'Obviously a denizen of the dusky glen of Goblin Market, [the milkmaid] resembles Coleridge's sinister enchantress in *Christabel*' (Packer, *CR* 198).

94 *serpent-coils* related to Satan in his guise as serpent.

100 *mavis and merle* song thrush and blackbird.

101 *hodden* rustic woollen cloth.

121–50 *The grass . . . fire beneath* the landscape of this section resembles that of Robert Browning (1812–89), ' "Childe Roland to the Dark Tower Came" ' (1855).

181 *atomy* skeleton.

197 *aught* anything.

269 *Let him sow, one day he shall reap* 'for whatsoever a man soweth, that shall he also reap. For he that soweth to his flesh shall of the flesh reap corruption; but he that soweth to the Spirit shall of the Spirit reap life everlasting' (Gal. 6:7–8).

291 *aftermath* originally, the new growth of grass that springs up after the early summer mowing.

497 *The frozen fountain would have leaped* echo of the fairy-tale 'The Sleeping Beauty', in which the arrival of the prince causes the birds to begin singing, the fountains to begin flowing and all the 'frozen' life to become animate again. Cf. the description in Tennyson's version, *The Day-Dream* (1842): 'A sudden hubbub shook the hall, / And sixty feet the fountain leapt' ('The Revival', ll. 7–8).

516 *Kirtle* skirt.

MAIDEN-SONG

[Composed 6 July 1863. Editions: *1866*, 1866a, 1875, 1876a, 1904.]

WR says this poem – 'a kind of cross between the tone of a fairy-tale and that of a nursery-song, each of them sweetened into poetry – was deservedly something of a favourite with its authoress' ('Notes' 461–2). William Ewart Gladstone (1809–98) – Prime Minister at various times 1868–94 – repeated it by heart at a social gathering (Packer, *CR* 168). CR defended her choice of names in a letter to DGR [?4 April 1865]: '*Meggan* and *Margaret* are, I suppose, the same name: but this does not disturb me. Do you think it need? *Meggan* was (proposed) suggested by Scotus [William Bell Scott – see headnote of 'At Home'] once to me, and comes out of a Welsh song-book. *May, Meggan, Margaret*, sound pretty and pleasant' (*Letters*, I, 242).

16 *flag-flower* see note for l. 220 of *Goblin Market*.

JESSIE CAMERON

[Composed Oct. 1864. Editions: *1866*, 1866a, 1875, 1876a, 1904.]

59 *unked* uncanny, unpleasant, unnatural, eerie. 'Our uncle Henry Polydore told us . . . that the old country-woman with whom he was lodging used to keep a brief diary; and he had noticed that the entry made it in for one night of unusual storm was, "Oh what an unkid [*sic*] night!" . . . The small anecdote amused us all in its way and the phrase became a sort of catchword among us, and, when the occasion offered, Christina enshrined the word in a poem' ('Notes' 485).

SPRING QUIET

[Composed 1847. Editions: *1866*, 1866a, 1875, 1876a, 1904. First published in *Macmillan's Magazine* 11 (April 1865), 460. *Macmillan's* text is divided into three sections: the first is stanzas 1, 2, 3 and 6; the second and third constitute a separate poem in MS1 (BodL; entitled 'Today and Tomorrow'). Part I of MS1 was published in 1896 and 1904 as 'Spring Fancies'.]

Title SPRING FANCIES. / I. *1865*.

THE POOR GHOST

[Composed 25 July 1863. Editions: *1866*, 1866a, 1875, 1876a, 1904.]

23 *violet* see note for l. 5 of 'Song' ['Oh roses for the flush of youth'].
36 *Let me sleep now till the Judgment Day* see headnote of 'Dream-Land'.

A PORTRAIT

[Part I composed 21 Nov. 1850; Part II composed 24 Feb. 1847. Editions: *1866*, 1866a, 1875, 1876a, 1904. Part II is included in 1847.]

This poem was apparently created out of two separate poems, as indicated by the titles of the two parts in the manuscripts: 'Saint Elizabeth of Hungary.' and 'Sonnet. / On Lady Isabella.' (both in BodL). The first was written originally about Saint Elizabeth of Hungary (1207–31), the elder, and inspired, according to WR, by *The Saint's Tragedy* (1848), a drama by Charles Kingsley (1819–75); the second was written three years earlier, in response to the death of Lady Isabella Howard, a pupil of CR's aunt Charlotte Polidori: 'My sister entertained an ardent admiration for the loveliness of character and person which marked this young lady, who died of a decline at the age of eighteen or thereabouts ... The name *A Portrait* is intended, I assume, to reidentify the brace of sonnets with Lady Isabella Howard. I question, however, whether some of the stronger expressions in the first sonnet are wholly applicable to this young lady' ('Notes' 467, 477). St Elizabeth was noted for her generosity to the poor and the harsh conditions in which she lived after the death of her husband, when she came under the influence of a notorious inquisitor. James Collinson, while he was engaged to CR, painted a picture of St Elizabeth, depicting the episode in which 'the saint refuses to remarry, throws down her crown before the effigy of Christ and symbolically consecrates her nuptial gown before entering a convent' (*CR* 114). Marsh characterizes St Elizabeth's renunciation as 'a sacrifice that might, from an English Protestant viewpoint, be regarded as dangerously threatening to state and family, and emblematic of Catholic aggression' (*CR* 104). In *The Saint's Tragedy*, this sacrifice was viewed as misguided, but Collinson and other members of the PRB disagreed with Kingsley, and St Elizabeth became the subject of sketches by Millais (see headnote of 'Maude Clare') and DGR. In *TF* (20), CR quotes by memory 'as best I may' a sonnet by 'a friend' (whom Marsh identifies as Collinson), which is a dialogue between Christ and the speaker, and echoes St Elizabeth's decision to give up earthly marriage for religious reasons. See note for ll. 34–5 of *Goblin Market*.

Title SONNET. / LADY ISABELLA. *1847.*
5 *ruth* compassion.
21 *The Bridegroom calls* see note for l. 3 of 'Advent' ['This Advent moon shines cold and clear'].
23 *lily* see note for ll. 408–10 of *Goblin Market*.

DREAM-LOVE

[Composed 19 May 1854. Editions: *1866*, 1866a, 1875, 1876a, 1904. First published in *A Welcome: Original Contributions in Poetry and Prose* (Emily Faithfull, 1863), 63–6.]

TWICE

[Composed June 1864. Editions: *1866*, 1866a, 1875, 1876a, 1904.]

SONGS IN A CORNFIELD

[Composed 26 Aug. 1864. Editions: *1866*, 1866a, 1875, 1876a, 1904. Lines deleted from MS version were later published as Part I of 'Twilight Night'.]

WR reported that this was set to music as a cantata, 'which was performed more than once' ('Notes' 484). In a letter to DGR [11 March 1865], CR wrote: ' "Songs in a Cornfield" is one of my own favorites, so I am specially gratified by your and Mr. Swinburne's praise' (*Letters*, I, 232) – Algernon Charles Swinburne (1837–1909). It echoes 'The Prince's Progress' in its theme of the dilatory lover who arrives too late. See also headnote of 'Twilight Night'.

A YEAR'S WINDFALLS

[Composed 26 Feb. 1863. Editions: *1866*, 1866a, 1875, 1876a, 1904.]

'A note written by my sister says, "This was written for the Portfolio Society." I have not any distinct recollection about this Society; possibly Mrs. Bell Scott had something to do with it' ('Notes' 484). The society was a gathering of poets and painters with which CR was loosely associated and in which themes were set for poems and paintings. (Mrs Bell Scott – see headnote of 'At Home' – was not involved.) See *CR* 252.

THE QUEEN OF HEARTS

[Composed 3 Jan. 1863. Editions: *1866*, 1866a, 1875, 1876a, 1904. First published in *Macmillan's Magazine* 8 (Oct. 1863), 457.]

In card games, each Rossetti child identified with a different suit: CR with diamonds, MR with clubs, DGR with hearts and WR with spades (Bell, *CR* 13).

13 *prepense* intentionally.

ONE DAY

[Composed 6 June 1857. Editions: *1866*, 1866a, 1875, 1876a, 1904. First published in *Macmillan's Magazine* 9 (Dec. 1863), 159.]

23 *Is it well* 'Run now, I pray thee, to meet her, and say unto her, Is it well with thee? is it well with thy husband? is it well with the child? And she answered, It is well' (2 Kings 4:26). From the story of the Shunammite whose son Elisha raises from the dead. Elisha instructs his servant to ask these questions, to which the woman answers 'It is well', until she reaches Elisha, whom she tells of the death of her son.

A BIRD'S-EYE VIEW

[Composed 4 March 1863. Editions: *1866*, 1866a, 1875, 1876a, 1904. First published in *Macmillan's Magazine* 8 (July 1863), 207.]

The 'fatal black bird' may owe something to Edgar Allan Poe's 'The Raven' (1845). The ballad-like poem also echoes the traditional folk ballads 'Sir Patrick Spens' and 'The Twa Corbies' (*CR Poems* 436).

LIGHT LOVE

[Composed 28 Oct. 1856. Editions: *1866*, 1866a, 1896, 1904. First published in *Macmillan's Magazine* 7 (Feb. 1863), 287.]

33 *Wrung with the pang of shame and pain* see note for l. 2 of 'A Pause of Thought'.

ON THE WING

[Composed 17 Dec. 1862. Editions: *1866*, 1866a, 1875, 1876a, 1904.]

Title A DREAM. / SONNET. *1866, 1866a.*

A RING POSY

[Composed 20 Feb. 1863. Editions: *1866*, 1866a, 1896, 1904.]

Title Jess and Jill. *1896.*

BEAUTY IS VAIN

[Composed 20 Jan. 1864. Editions: *1866*, 1866a, 1875, 1876a, 1904.]

MAGGIE A LADY

[Composed 23 Feb. 1865. Editions: *1866*, 1866a, 1875, 1876a, 1904.]

DGR suggested that CR must have been reading Barrett Browning's *Lady Geraldine's Courtship* (1844), an influence she later acknowledged (Marsh, *CR Poems* 438).

Title LADY MAGGIE. *1866, 1866a.*

WHAT WOULD I GIVE?

[Composed 28 Jan. 1864. Editions: *1866*, 1866a, 1875, 1876a, 1904.]

'*They Come unto Me*, though in a different metrical form, may almost be regarded as continuous with *What would I Give*' ('Notes' 484).

1–2 *What would I give for a heart of flesh . . . Instead of this heart of stone* 'and I will take the stony heart out of their flesh, and will give them an heart of flesh' (Eze. 11:19).
9 *ingrain* thoroughly dyed.

THE BOURNE

[Composed 17 Feb. 1854. Editions: *1866*, 1866a, 1875, 1876a, 1904. First published in *Macmillan's Magazine* 7 (March 1863), 382. Originally part of ' "There remaineth therefore a rest" ', which CR never published as such, but from which she also took ' "There remaineth therefore a Rest to the People of God" '.]

See headnote of 'Dream-Land'.

SUMMER ['Winter is cold-hearted']

[Composed 15 Jan. 1864. Editions: *1866*, 1866a, 1875, 1876a, 1904.]

AUTUMN ['I dwell alone—I dwell alone, alone']

[Composed 14 April 1858. Editions: *1866*, 1866a, 1875, 1876a, 1904.]

53 *Uplifted, like a beacon, on her tower* cf. Lizzie in *Goblin Market* who stands 'Like a beacon left alone' (l. 412).

THE GHOST'S PETITION

[Composed 7 April 1864. Editions: *1866*, 1866a, 1875, 1876a, 1904.]

The speaker waiting for her lover to come in the deep of the night and find the latch to her door is reminiscent of the Song of Solomon, in which the lover knocks on the door, saying, 'Open to me, my sister, my love' (5:2); see also note for l. 13 of 'Whitsun Tuesday'.

CR wrote to DGR: 'Please cut it short, as you suggest' (31 March [1865] in *Letters*, I, 239), and the last four stanzas in MS (BL) were dropped.

13 *Go to sleep, my sweet sister Jane* 'In a copy of Christina's *Poems*, 1875, I find that she has altered line 1 of stanza 5 thus – "Sleep, sister, and wake again"' ('Notes' 484).

40 *Feel not after my clasping hand* when Jesus appeared to Mary at the tomb, he told her: 'Touch me not; for I am not yet ascended to my Father: but go to my brethren, and say unto them, I ascend unto my Father, and your Father; and to my God, and your God' (John 20:17).

MEMORY

[Part I composed 8 Nov. 1857; Part II composed 17 Feb. 1865. Editions: *1866*, 1866a, 1875, 1876a, 1904.]

A ROYAL PRINCESS

[Composed 22 Oct. 1851. Editions: *1866*, 1866a, 1875, 1876a, 1904. First published in *Poems: An Offering to Lancashire. Printed and Published for the Art Exhibition for the Relief of Distress in the Cotton Districts.* (Emily Faithfull, 1863), 2–10.]

Although published as part of an effort to help mill workers who were suffering as a result of the interruption of cotton shipments from the USA during the Civil War, CR had written this poem long before the 'Cotton Famine' began ('Notes' 461). Marsh suggests that it may have been inspired by the 'strife and peace' theme set by the Portfolio Society, of which CR was a member. She also points out that the tone is reminiscent of Barrett Browning's *Curse for a Nation* (1860) (*CR* 275–6). In a letter to DGR [13 March 1865], in which CR discusses which poems should appear in *The Prince's Progress* volume, she writes: 'Don't you think we might advantageously eject "Royal Princess" also, which is rather a spite of mine?' (*Letters*, I, 234).

31–3 *Some to work . . . winter nips* apparently DGR had advised CR to cut this stanza; but in a letter to him [?4 April 1865], she writes that it 'is by so much one of the best stanzas that I am loath to sacrifice it. Is it so very like Keats? I doubt if I ever read the lines in question, never having read the *Isabella* through. I do not fight for the R.P.'s heroism; though it seems to me that the royal soldiers might yet have succeeded in averting *roasting*. A *yell* is one thing, and a *fait accompli* quite another' (*Letters*, I, 242). CR is referring to 'Isabella; or, The Pot of Basil' (1820).

62 *There are families out grazing like cattle in the park* during the Irish Famine (1845–

9, especially 1848), starving families were reported to have eaten grass to survive. Chris Morash, 'Literature, Memory, Atrocity', in *'Fearful Realities': New Perspectives on the Famine*, ed. Chris Morash and Richard Hayes (Irish Academic Press, 1996), p. 113, quoting from a newspaper account of an inquest held in 1848 (from 'Inquests' in *United Irishman* I, 14 (13 May 1848), p. 211): 'A poor man, whose name we could not learn . . . lay down on the roadside, where shortly after he was found dead, his face turned to the earth, and a portion of the grass and turf on which he lay masticated in his mouth.'

76 *After us the deluge 'Après nous le déluge'* – Marquise de Pompadour's comment to Louis XV after Frederick the Great's defeat of the French and Austrian armies (1757) – in effect, pointing towards the likelihood of a revolution while, at the same time, expressing lack of interest in anything that might happen after their lifetimes.

77 *If bread's the staff of life* Bread is referred to as the 'staff of life' throughout the Old Testament: e.g. 'I will break the staff of bread in Jerusalem' (Eze. 4:16).

104, 105, 108 *I, if I perish, perish* Esther tells the story of the Hebrew wife of a Persian king, who risked her own life by pleading with her husband to save her people from an edict condemning them to death – 'so will I go unto the king, which is not according to the law: and if I perish, I perish' (Esther 4:16). Esther's intercession is seen as prefiguring Mary's intercession with Christ for the souls of sinners. See Part 8, l. 1 of 'Monna Innominata'.

SHALL I FORGET?

[Composed 21 Feb. 1865. Editions: *1866*, 1866a, 1875, 1876a, 1904.]

4 *watch with him* see note for Part 2, l. 1 of 'Old and New Year Ditties'.

VANITY OF VANITIES ['Ah woe is me for pleasure that is vain']

[Editions: *1866*, 1866a, 1875, 1876a, 1904. First published in 1847.]

Title see note for l. 1 for 'One Certainty'.

1 *Ah woe is me for pleasure that is vain* 'I said in mine heart, Go to now, I will prove thee with mirth, therefore enjoy pleasure: and, behold, this also is vanity' (Ecc. 2:1). See also note for l. 1 of 'One Certainty'.

L. E. L.

[Composed 15 Feb. 1859. Editions: *1866*, 1866a, 1875, 1876a, 1904. First published in *Victoria Magazine* I (May 1863), 40–41.]

WR says the footnote ('L.E.L. by E.B.B.') in the MS (BL):

must refer to Mrs. Browning's poem named *L. E. L.'s Last Question* [1844]; but it is not entirely clear what relation Christina meant to indicate between that poem and her own *Spring.* Apparently she relied either upon L. E. L.'s phrase, which was, 'Do you think of me as I think of you?' – or else upon a phrase occurring in Mrs. Browning's lyric, 'One thirsty for a little love' [VI, 4]. It will be clear to most readers that Christina's poem *Spring* relates to herself, and not at all to the poetess L. E. L. (Letitia Elizabeth Landon) [1802–39] . . . The poem, as it stands in my sister's MS. note-book, has lines 1 and 3 of each stanza unrhymed, and she has pencilled a note thus: 'Gabriel fitted the double rhymes as printed, with a brotherly request that I would use them'; and elsewhere she adds, 'greatly improving the piece' . . . ('Notes' 483)

Elizabeth Barrett Browning's poem refers to a poem by Landon and also pays 'homage to Landon's mourning ode to Felicia Hemans [1793–1835] in saluting the "bay-crowned living one that o'er the bay-crowned dead art bowing"' (*CR* 246–7). Marsh points out that this poem also echoes Barrett Browning's 'The Mask' (1850) (*CR* 247) and indirectly alludes to Landon's 'Night at Sea' (1841) and Hemans's 'A Parting Song' (1839) (*CR Poems* 435).

Epigraph misquotation of a line from Barrett Browning's 'L. E. L.'s Last Question' (see headnote, above).
3 *I turn my face in silence to the wall* Hezekiah, told by the prophet Amos that he was going to die, 'turned his face to the wall, and prayed unto the Lord' (2 Kings 20:2; see also Isa. 38:2).

LIFE AND DEATH

[Composed 24 April 1863. Editions: *1866*, 1866a, 1875, 1876a, 1904.]
12 *To sleep meanwhile* see headnote of 'Dream-Land'.

BIRD OR BEAST?

[Composed 15 Aug. 1864. Editions: *1866*, 1866a, 1875, 1876a, 1904.]

In a letter to DGR [11 March 1865], CR refers to this poem and 'Eve' as 'the two *Eves*' (*Letters*, I, 232).

19–20 *The lamb and the dove / Were preachers sent from God* Jesus Christ (the lamb) and the Holy Spirit (the dove) thus complete the Holy Trinity (God the Father, God the Son, God the Holy Spirit).

EVE

[Composed 20 Jan. 1865. Editions: *1866*, 1866a, 1875, 1876a, 1904.]

A prayer in *FD* illustrates CR's characteristic attitude towards Eve: 'O God All-Wise, let us not be as our mother Eve who thought to hanker after good knowledge denied, when in truth she hankered after evil knowledge kept back' (16).

13–14 *Tree of Life . . . Tree twelvefold-fruited* the tree of life was in the 'midst' of the Garden of Eden (Gen. 2:9); and see 'In the midst of the street of it, and on either side of the river, was there the tree of life, which bare twelve manner of fruits, and yielded her fruit every month: and the leaves of the tree were for the healing of nations' (Rev. 22:2). CR associates the Tree of Life with Christ, and the twelve-fold fruits with the manna sent from heaven to feed the Israelites in the wilderness – which 'mysteriously adapted to the palate of each eater', just as the 'True Bread from Heaven' will satisfy every taste of 'the perfected Israel' (*FD* 524).

33 *Cain hath slain his brother* Eve's child Cain killed his younger brother Abel because God accepted Abel's sacrifice but not his (Gen. 4:3–8).

56 *conies* rabbits.

61 *deprecation* prayer.

GROWN AND FLOWN

[Composed 21 Dec. 1864. Editions: *1866*, 1866a, 1875, 1876a, 1904.]

A FARM WALK

[Lines 1–40 composed 11 July 1864; date of composition of ll. 41–68 unknown. Editions: *1866*, 1866a, 1875, 1876a, 1904.]

SOMEWHERE OR OTHER

[Composed Oct. 1863. Editions: *1866*, 1866a, 1875, 1876a, 1904.]

A CHILL

[Probably composed between Oct. 1863 and 15 Jan. 1864. Editions: *1866*, 1866a, 1876a, 1904.]

CHILD'S TALK IN APRIL

[Composed 8 March 1855. Editions: *1866*, 1866a, 1875, 1876a, 1904.]

GONE FOR EVER

[Composed 14 Oct. 1846. Editions: *1866*, 1866a, 1875, 1876a, 1904. First published in 1847.]

Illustration: WR describes CR's illustration for this poem as 'a moss-rose, not fully blown' ('Notes' 466).

"THE INIQUITY OF THE FATHERS UPON THE CHILDREN"

[Composed March 1865. Editions: *1866*, 1866a, 1875, 1876a, 1904.]

Probably influenced by CR's work at Highgate with 'fallen women' as well as by Barrett Browning's 'Bertha in the Lane' (1844) and *Aurora Leigh* (1856) (*CR* 330). In a letter to DGR [13 March 1865], CR wrote: 'I did hope U. the R. ["Under the Rose"] possessed a not un-Crabbed aspect', i.e. not unlike the verse tales of George Crabbe (1754–1832). When DGR objected to including it in 1866, CR defended it by saying that even if the poem were thrown 'overboard', she would 'include within the female range such an attempt at this', adding that 'I yet don't see why "the Poet mind" should be less able to construct her [the "fallen woman"] from its own inner consciousness than a hundred other unknown quantities' (*Letters*, I, 234).

Title UNDER THE ROSE. / 'The iniquity of the fathers upon the children.' *1866, Am. edns.*

From the verse in Exodus describing the first commandment forbidding 'graven images': 'Thou shalt not bow down thyself to them, nor serve them: for I the Lord thy God am a jealous God, visiting the iniquity of the fathers upon the children unto the third and fourth generation of them that hate me' (Ex. 20:5).

3 *Under the rose I was born* from *sub rosa* (Latin) – privately, in secret, in strict confidence; euphemistic for 'She bore me out of wedlock.'

535 *pelf* riches (used as a disparaging term).

[*Devotional Pieces*]

DESPISED AND REJECTED.

[Composed 10 Oct. 1864. Editions: *1866*, 1866a, 1875, 1876a, 1904.]

'. . . the poem bears some faint analogy (yet not the least resemblance) to *The Poet's Vow* of Mrs. Browning [1838]' ('Notes' 475).

Title from a verse in Isaiah taken to be a prophecy about Jesus: 'He is despised and rejected of men; a man of sorrows, and acquainted with grief: and we hid as it were our faces from him; he was despised, and we esteemed him not' (53:3).

8 *Friend, open to Me* 'Behold, I stand at the door, and knock: if any man hear my voice, and open the door, I will come in to him, and will sup with him, and he with me' (Rev. 3:20); Holman Hunt based his painting *The Light of the World* (1853), which depicts Jesus standing at a door, on this text, and CR served as one of the models for the face of Jesus (Bell, *CR* 19).

13–17 *what art thou indeed . . . Or stranger lodge thee here* 'For I was an hungred, and ye gave me meat: I was thirsty, and ye gave me drink: I was a stranger, and ye took me in' (Matt. 25:35).

25–6 *Open, lest I should pass thee by, and thou / One day entreat My Face* 'And I will set my face against them . . . and ye shall know that I am the LORD, when I set my face against them' (Eze. 15:7).

58 *The mark of blood* allusion to Passover, when God killed the firstborn children of the Egyptians, but spared the houses of the Israelites, who had been instructed to mark their doors with the blood of a sacrificial lamb – 'and when I see the blood, I will pass over you' (Ex. 12:13). For Christians, Jesus serves the same purpose because as the sacrificial Lamb of God, he gives his blood to save sinners from God's wrath.

LONG BARREN

[Composed 21 Feb. 1865. Editions: *1866*, 1866a, 1875, 1876a, 1904.]

1 *barren tree* the Cross – but also an allusion to Jesus' warning in Matt. 3:10 (see note for Part 3, l. 7 of 'Old and New Year Ditties').

6 *the crown of thorn* 'And when they had platted a crown of thorns, they put it upon his head' (Matt. 27:29; see also Mark 15:17 and John 19:2).

7 *Spitting and scorn* 'And they smote him on the head with a reed, and did spit upon him, and bowing their knees worshipped him' (Mark 15:19; see also Matt. 27:30).

11 *Rose of Sharon, Cedar of broad roots* 'I am the rose of Sharon, and the lily of the valleys' (Song of Sol. 2:1); 'I will be as the dew unto Israel: he shall grow as the lily, and cast forth his roots as Lebanon' (Hos. 14:5); 'he shall grow like a cedar in Lebanon' (Ps. 92:12).

12 *Vine of sweet fruits* see note for l. 33 of 'Christian and Jew. A Dialogue'.

14 *Of thousands Chief* 'My beloved is white and ruddy, the chiefest among ten thousand' (Song of Sol. 5:10).

IF ONLY

[Composed 20 Feb. 1865. Editions: *1866*, 1866a, 1875, 1876a, 1904.]

12 *who weepeth now shall smile* 'Blessed are ye that weep now: for ye shall laugh' (Luke 6:21).

DOST THOU NOT CARE?

[Composed 24 Dec. 1864. Editions: *1866*, 1866a, 1875, 1876a, 1904.]

Title 'But Martha was cumbered about much serving, and came to him, and said, Lord, dost thou not care that my sister hath left me to serve alone? bid her therefore that she help me' (Luke 10:40).

WEARY IN WELL-DOING

[Composed 22 Oct. 1864. Editions: *1866*, 1866a, 1875, 1876a, 1904.]

Title 'And let us not be weary in well doing: for in due season we shall reap, if we faint not' (Gal. 6:9; see also 2 Thes. 3:13).
12 *moil* work hard.

MARTYRS' SONG

[Composed 20 March 1863. Editions: *1866*, 1866a, 1875, 1876a, 1904. First published in Orby Shipley (ed.), *Lyra Mystica: Hymns and Verses on Sacred Subjects, Ancient and Modern* (Longman, Green, Longman, Roberts and Green, 1865), 427–9.]

WR characterizes 'the Rev. Orby Shipley' as one 'who edited more than one volume of devotional verse' ('Notes' 476).

5–6 *Be it furnace-fire voluminous, / One like God's Son will walk with us* allusion to King Nebuchadnezzar's throwing three youths into a fiery furnace; when the king looked into the furnace, he saw not three, but four men walking unhurt in the fire, and the 'form of the fourth is like the Son of God' (Dan. 3:25; see verses 19–25). See also note for l. 28 of 'An "Immurata" Sister'.

7–8 *What are these that glow from afar, / These that lean over the golden bar* cf. 'The blessed damozel leaned out / From the gold bar of Heaven' (DGR, 'The Blessed Damozel' (1850), ll. 1–2).

13 *Out of great tribulation they went* 'These are they which came out of great tribulation, and have washed their robes, and made them white in the blood of the Lamb' (Rev. 7:14). In her comments on the biblical verse in *FD*, CR writes: 'But presumably for most of us tribulation rather than ease constructs the safe road and the firm stepping-stone' (235).

29 *As a King with many crowns He stands* 'and on his head were many crowns' (Rev. 19:12).

30 *And our names are graven upon His hands* 'Behold, I have graven thee upon the palms of my hands' (Isa. 49:16).

33 *As the Lamb of God for sinners slain* 'Worthy is the Lamb that was slain' (Rev. 5:12); 'Behold the Lamb of God, which taketh away the sins of the world' (John 1:29). In being offered up as a sacrifice for the sins of the world, Jesus takes the place of the lambs sacrificed to God for the sins of his people. In *TF*, CR discusses this image of Jesus at length (154–5), pointing out that sacrifice is 'the lamb's office, not his essence' (154). Cf. also the Communion service in the *Book of Common Prayer*: 'Lamb of God, son of the Father, that takest away the sins of the world . . .'

35–6 *behold Him stand . . . at God's Right Hand* 'Behold, I see the heavens opened, and the Son of man standing on the right hand of God' (Acts 7:56).

42 *That we may drink of Jesus' cup* When Jesus prayed in the Garden of Gethsemane, he asked God to 'take this cup from me', meaning to take away the agony of the coming Crucifixion (Luke 22:42). It also alludes to the Eucharist: 'But Jesus said unto them, Ye know not what ye ask: can ye drink of the cup that I drink of? and be baptized with the baptism that I am baptized with? And they said unto him, We can. And Jesus said unto them, Ye shall indeed drink of the cup that I drink of; and with the baptism that I am baptized withal shall ye be baptized' (Mark 10:38–9; see also Matt. 20:22–3); see also note for l. 471 of *Goblin Market*.

45–6 *At His Word, Who hath led us hither, / The Red Sea must part hither and thither* see note for ll. 70–71 of 'By the Waters of Babylon. B.C. 570'.

52 *the Veil and the Ark* the veil separating the Holy of Holies from the rest of the temple at Jerusalem (see note for l. 159 of 'From House to Home'); and the Ark of the Covenant, a gold-covered chest containing the Ten Commandments, carried before the Israelites in their battles, and eventually placed in the temple.

AFTER THIS THE JUDGMENT

[Composed 12 Dec. 1856. Editions: *1866*, 1866a, 1875, 1876a, 1904. The MS lines omitted from 1866 appeared in 1904 as 'Downcast'.]

The MS version of 'Downcast' is as follows:

> These roses are as perfect as of old,
> > Those lilies wear their selfsame sunny white,
> > I, only I, am changed and sad and cold;
> The morning star still glorifies the night,
> > And musical that fountain in its swell
> > Casts as of old its waters to the light;
> Oh that I were a rose, so I might dwell
> > Contented in a garden on my thorn
> > Fulfilling mine appointed fragrance well;
> Or stainless lily in the summer morn
> > Tho' no man pluck it, yet the honey bee
> > Knows it for sweetness in its bosom born;
> Or that I were a star, from sea to sea
> > Guiding the seekers to their port of rest,
> > Guiding them till night's shuffling shadows flee;
> Or that I were a spring, to which opprest
> > With desert drought, some wearied wayfarer
> > Comes from the barren regions of the west;—
> Then should I stand at peace and should not err,
> > Or lighten and make beautiful the sky,
> > Or make more glad than frankincense and myrrh:
> But now it is not so; I, only I,
> > Am changed and sad and cold, while in my soul
> > The very fountain of delight is dry.

Title 'And as it is appointed unto men once to die, but after this the judgement' (Heb. 9:27).

5 *mansion of perpetual peace* see note for l. 21 of 'The Convent Threshold'.

7 *gate stands open of perennial ease* the twelve gates of the Heavenly Jerusalem are always open because there is no night in heaven: see Rev. 21:25.

12 *rouse me to the race and make me strong* 'Which is as a bridegroom coming out of his chamber, and rejoiceth as a strong man to run a race' (Ps. 19:5).

24 *Love that dost pass the tenfold seven times seven* 'Then came Peter to him, and said, Lord, how oft shall my brother sin against me, and I forgive him? till seven times? Jesus saith unto him, I say not unto thee, Until seven times: but, Until seventy times seven' (Matt. 18:21–2).

31–4 *Yea, more than mother loves her little one; / For, earthly, even a mother may forget*

. . . *But Thou, O Love of God, remember yet* 'Can a woman forget her sucking child, that she should not have compassion on the son of her womb? yea, they may forget, yet will I not forget thee' (Isa. 49:15).

36 *Great White Throne* 'And I saw a great white throne, and him that sat on it, from whose face the earth and the heaven fled away; and there was found no place for them' (Rev. 20:11). In her commentary on this Bible verse in *FD*, CR writes: 'The Church Militant exhibits a pale, ascetic face, because the pale forecast of the "Great White Throne" abides upon it' (472).

47 *shock* a group of sheaves of grain placed upright and supporting each other for the drying and ripening of the grain before being carried to storage. Cf. the biblical fields of souls ready to be 'harvested': 'I say unto you, Lift up your eyes, and look on the fields; for they are white already to harvest' (John 4:35).

55–6 *if greater love than this / Hath no man, that a man die for his friend* 'Greater love hath no man than this, that a man lay down his life for his friends' (John 15:13).

64 *When darkness hid from Thee Thy heavens above* when Jesus was crucified, 'there was darkness over all the land' and 'the earth did quake' (Matt. 27:45, 51; see also Mark 15:33 and Luke 23:44–5).

66 *The bitter cup of death* see note for l. 42 of 'Martyrs' Song'.

69 *Grown sick of love* 'Stay me with flagons, comfort me with apples: for I am sick of love', and 'I charge you, O daughters of Jerusalem, if ye find my beloved, that ye tell him, that I am sick of love' (Song of Sol. 2:5, 5:8).

70 *Thy Life then ransomed mine* 'Who gave himself a ransom for all, to be testified in due time' (1 Tim. 2:6).

GOOD FRIDAY ['Am I a stone and not a sheep']

[Composed 20 April 1862. Editions: *1866*, 1866a, 1875, 1876a, 1904. First published in Orby Shipley (ed.), *Lyra Messianica: Hymns and Verses on the Life of Christ, Ancient and Modern; with Other Poems* (Longman, Green, Longman, Roberts and Green, 1864), 236–7.]

Title from 'God's Friday' (middle English): a day of fasting and prayer in commemoration of Christ's crucifixion.

5–6 *those women loved / Who with exceeding grief lamented Thee* 'And there followed him a great company of people, and of women, which also bewailed and lamented him' (Luke 23:27).

7 *Not so fallen Peter weeping bitterly* on the night of Jesus' arrest, his disciple Peter said he was willing to follow Jesus to prison and even to death. Jesus responded by saying that before the cock would crow, Peter would deny that he knew him. At the arrest, Peter fled, and later, when he was accused of being a follower of Jesus, he said, 'Man, I know not what thou sayest. And immediately, while he yet spake, the cock crew. And the Lord turned, and looked upon

Peter. And Peter remembered the word of the Lord, how he had said unto him, Before the cock crow, thou shalt deny me thrice. And Peter went out, and wept bitterly' (Luke 20:60–62; see also Mark 14:72; Matt. 26:74–5; and John 18:27).

8 *the thief was moved* when Jesus was dying on the cross, one of the thieves crucified next to him asked Jesus to 'remember me when thou comest into thy kingdom. And Jesus said unto him, Verily I say unto thee, To day shalt thou be with me in paradise' (Luke 23:42–3); see also l. 21 of ' "The Love of Christ Which Passeth Knowledge" '.

11 *darkness at broad noon* see l. 64 of 'After This the Judgment'.

14 *seek Thy sheep, true Shepherd* 'What man of you, having an hundred sheep, if he lose one of them, doth not leave the ninety and nine in the wilderness, and go after that which is lost, until he find it? And when he hath found it, he layeth it on his shoulders, rejoicing. And when he cometh home, he calleth together his friends and neighbours, saying unto them, Rejoice with me; for I have found my sheep which was lost' (Luke 15:4–6 – see also note to ll. 82–4 of 'The Convent Threshold'); and 'I am the good shepherd: the good shepherd giveth his life for the sheep' (John 10:11).

15–16 *Greater than Moses, turn and look once more / And smite a rock* 'Behold, I will stand before thee there upon the rock in Horeb; and thou shalt smite the rock, and there shall come water out of it, that the people may drink. And Moses did so in the sight of the elders of Israel' (Ex. 17:6).

THE LOWEST PLACE

[Composed 25 July 1863. Editions: *1866*, 1866a, 1875, 1876a, 1904.]

'As an expression of her permanent attitude of mind in the region of faith and hope, Christina evidently laid some stress on this little poem. She made it the concluding piece in the *Prince's Progress* volume, and also in the combined form of that volume with the *Goblin Market* one. Hence I thought the second stanza of this poem the most appropriate thing that I could get inscribed upon her tombstone in 1895' ('Notes' 475).

Title 'But when thou art bidden, go and sit down in the lowest room; that when he that bade thee cometh he may say unto thee, Friend, go up higher: then shalt thou have worship in the presence of them that sit at meat with thee' (Luke 14:10).

Poems Added in *Goblin Market, The Prince's Progress and Other Poems* (1875)

BY THE SEA

[Composed 11 Nov. 1858. Editions: *1875*, 1876a, 1904. First published in *A Round of Days Described in Original Poems by Some of Our Most Celebrated Poets, and in Pictures by Eminent Artists* (George Routledge and Sons, 1866), 68; also published in *Picture Posies: Poems Chiefly by Living Authors and Drawings by F. Walker et al.* (George Routledge and Sons, 1874). Originally part of 'A Yawn', which CR never published as such.]

4–5 *All earth's full rivers cannot fill / The sea, that drinking thirsteth still* see note for ll. 10–11 of 'A Testimony'.
12 *argus-eyed* extremely watchful or sharp-sighted; from a mythological monster fabled to have a hundred eyes.

FROM SUNSET TO STAR RISE

[Composed 23 Feb. 1865. Editions: *1875*, 1876a, 1904.]

'In the note-book containing the MS. of the sonnet I find a pencil note, "House of Charity," written against the title. The House of Charity was, I think, an Institution at Highgate for reclaiming "fallen" women; and it may perhaps be inferred that Christina wrote this sonnet as if it were an utterance of one of these women, not of herself' ('Notes' 485).

Title FROM SUNSET TO RISE STAR *1904*.
3 *benighted* overtaken by darkness of night.
7 *wold* elevated tract of open country.
11 *sedge* coarse, grassy, rush-like plants that grow in wet places.

DAYS OF VANITY

[Editions: *1875*, 1876a, 1904. First published in *Scribner's Monthly* 5 (Nov. 1872), 21.]

20 *Rust-eaten treasure* see note for ll. 13–14 of 'A Testimony'.

ONCE FOR ALL / (MARGARET)

[Composed 8 Jan. 1866. Editions: *1875*, 1876a, 1904. First published in Charles Rogers (ed.), *The Golden Sheaf: Poems Contributed by Living Authors* (Houlston and Rogers, 1868), 192.]

'The name Margaret was added when my sister printed this sonnet. The person whom she meant by it was the first Mrs. James Hannay – as I learn from a note pencilled in one of her editions. Presumably the sonnet was written when Mr. Hannay contracted a second marriage' ('Notes' 486). James Hannay (1827–73) was a writer and editor of the *Edinburgh Evening Courant*. Margaret Thompson, who married James Hannay in 1853, died in 1865; but Hannay did not remarry until 1868, two years after the sonnet was written.

ENRICA, 1865

[Composed 1 July 1865. Editions: *1875*, 1876a, 1904. First published in *A Round of Days Described in Original Poems* (1866), 6; also published in *Picture Posies* (1874).]

WR gives an extensive sketch of Signora Enrica Barile, called 'Signora Filopanti' (her husband had altered his name to 'Filopanti'): 'The general love of humankind which impelled him to rename himself as Filopanti was, unfortunately, unpropitious to a normal affection for his spouse; so after a while he gave her notice that she had better look out for some separate means of subsistence.' CR came to know her through Mrs Bell Scott (see headnote of 'At Home'). When Garibaldi visited London in 1864, Signora Filopanti 'delivered a brief and extemporized harangue to him in public, as he stood before a vast concourse *en route* from the railway station to the heart of London' ('Notes' 486). The MS (BL) is entitled 'E.F.'

Title AN ENGLISH DRAWING-ROOM. / 1865. *1866, 1874.*

AUTUMN VIOLETS

[Editions: *1875*, 1876a, 1904. First published in *Macmillan's Magazine* 19 (Nov. 1868), 84.]

Title see note for l. 5 of 'Song' ['Oh roses for the flush of youth'].
14 *A grateful Ruth tho' gleaning scanty corn* The widowed and destitute Ruth gleaned the grain left by reapers on a field belonging to Boaz, a kinsman she later married. After the first day, the corn was no longer 'scanty' because Boaz secretly ordered the reapers to leave extra grain for her to glean (Ruth 2:15–16).

A DIRGE ['Why were you born when the snow was falling?']

[Composed 21 Nov. 1865. Editions: *1875*, 1876a, 1904. First published in *Argosy* 17 (Jan. 1874), 25.]

"THEY DESIRE A BETTER COUNTRY"

[Editions: *1875*, 1876a, 1904. First published in *Macmillan's Magazine* 19 (March 1869), 422–3.]

Title 'But now they desire a better country, that is, an heavenly' (Heb. 11:16). In *SF*, CR writes: 'many entered the Holy Land and feasted on its milk and honey, who hungering and thirsting with a hunger and thirst which no earthly dainties could appease, still desired a better country, that is, a heavenly (Heb. xi. 16), still craved for the wine and milk which are priceless (Isa. lv. 1). If no trumpet from without, yet ever and anon an alarm from within, renewed the summons, "Arise ye, and depart; for this is not your rest" (Mic. ii. 10)' (145). (The earliest of numerous biblical references to a promised land flowing with milk and honey occurs in Ex. 3:8.)

11 *jubilee* occasion of general rejoicing; in Hebrew history, every fiftieth year was a 'jubilee' year, a time of rejoicing when the slaves were set free.

14 *Follow me here, rise up, and follow here* echoes Jesus' call to his disciple Matthew (Matt. 9:9; Mark 2:14; Luke 5:27) as well as the angel's call to Peter (Acts 12:7–8).

34 *serried* densely pressed together.

36 *And strengthening love almost to cast out fear* 'There is no fear in love; but perfect love casteth out fear' (1 John 4:18).

A GREEN CORNFIELD

[Editions: *1875*, 1876a, 1904.]

Epigraph see note for ll. 9–10 of 'A Summer Wish'.

A BRIDE SONG

[Editions: *1875*, 1876a, 1904. First published in *Argosy* 19 (Jan. 1875), 25.]

CONFLUENTS

[Editions: *1875*, 1876a, 1904.]

THE LOWEST ROOM

[Composed 30 Sept. 1856. Editions: *1875*, 1876a, 1904. First published in *Macmillan's Magazine* 9 (March 1864), 436–9.]

DGR criticized what he saw as the 'taint' of 'modern vicious style' in this poem, derived in part from Barrett Browning – 'what might be called a falsetto muscularity'. He said: 'Everything in which this tone appears is utterly foreign to your primary impulses . . .' CR ignored his advice to exclude from her writings everything 'so tainted' ('Notes' 460–61). Marsh sees the subject as deriving in part from MR's 'lifelong enthusiasm for the Homeric heroes, especially Achilles, despite her moral disapproval of his conduct. Other influences include [Thomas] Carlyle's [1795–1881] *On Heroes and Hero-Worship* (1841), and, indirectly, Tennyson's *The Princess* (1847), another debate on femininity' (*CR Poems* 442). In MS (BL), the title is 'A fight over the body of Homer'.

Title SIT DOWN IN THE LOWEST ROOM. *1864.*

22–3 *Hector . . . Aeacides* Hector and Achilles, two heroes of the Trojan War; 'Aeacides' is a patronymic from 'Aeacus', a hero and son of Zeus, and is given to various of Aeacus' descendants, including his grandson Achilles.

31 *Ajax' red right hand* in the Greek army during the Trojan War, Ajax was second only to Achilles as a fighter. CR associates Ajax with those who 'rank not first but second in their particular world' and who 'may be positively good, comparatively inferior' (*TF* 72). She adds that she cares 'more now for Ajax than for those who at some point excelled him', drawing from this the lesson that of 'ourselves likewise the comparative aspect will fade away, the positive will remain' (72). Cf. 'Should intermitted vengeance arm again / His red right hand to plague us' (Milton, *Paradise Lost* (1674), II, 173–4).

32 *grand like Juno's eyes* Juno's Greek counterpart, the goddess Hera, was often referred to as 'cow-eyed'.

54 *would not bend* 'from the Rossetti family motto "*frangas non flectas*" ' (*CR Poems* 442): 'Break, don't bend' (Latin).

63 *a slave* see note for ll. 127–8, below. Marsh also sees this as an allusion 'to the legal doctrine of coverture in English law, withholding legal status for married women, a focus of feminist debate at this time; cf. . . . *Subjection of Women* (1867)' by John Stuart Mill (1806–73) (*CR Poems* 442).

77 *dim Dian's face* Diana, the Roman counterpart of Artemis, virgin goddess of the woodland and the hunt, and also associated with the moon.

79–80 *holes / Amid that waste of white* needlework (see *CR Poems* 442).

111 *Sevenfold Sacred Fire* 'Moreover the light of the moon shall be as the light of the sun, and the light of the sun shall be sevenfold, as the light of seven days, in the day that the Lord bindeth up the breach of his people, and healeth the stroke of their wound' (Isa. 30:26).

124 *Diomed* a Greek hero of the Trojan War; King of Argos and friend of Odysseus.

127–8 *Achilles in his rage / And sloth* Homer's *Iliad* begins with 'the wrath of Achilles', an incident in which the great hero withdraws to sulk in his tent because his war prize, a slave woman, was taken away from him.

133–7 *He offered vengeance . . . Self-immolated to his friend* allusion to Achilles' grief at the death of Patroclus and his desire to avenge that death even if it meant death for himself.

174 *The wisest man* Solomon: see note for l. 200, below.

176 *Vanity of vanities* see note for l. 1 of 'One Certainty'.

177 *Beneath the sun there's nothing new* see note for l. 11 of 'One Certainty'.

187 *As the sea is not filled* see note for ll. 10–11 of 'A Testimony'.

200 *Greater than Solomon* 'The queen of the south shall rise up in the judgment with this generation, and shall condemn it: for she came from the uttermost parts of the earth to hear the wisdom of Solomon; and, behold, a greater than Solomon is here' (Matt. 12:42; see also Luke 11:31).

249 *She thrives, God's blessed husbandry* 'ye are God's husbandry, ye are God's building' (1 Cor. 3:9).

269–70 *So now in patience I possess / My soul* see note for l. 205 of 'From House to Home'.

271 *Content to take the lowest place* see note for title of 'The Lowest Place'.

275–6 *I lift mine eyes up to the hills / From whence my help shall come* see note for l. 5 of 'A Better Resurrection'.

280 *And many last be first* 'But many that are first shall be last; and the last shall be first' (Matt. 19:30; see also Mark 10:31; Luke 13:30; and Matt. 20:16).

DEAD HOPE

[Composed 15 March 1865. Editions: *1875*, 1876a, 1904. First published in *Macmillan's Magazine* 18 (May 1868), 86.]

A DAUGHTER OF EVE

[Composed 30 Sept. 1865. Editions: *1875*, 1876a, 1904.]

5 *A fool to snap my lily* see note for ll. 408–10 of *Goblin Market*.

SONG ['Oh what comes over the sea']

[Composed 11 June 1866. Editions: *1875*, 1876a, 1896, 1904.]
Title WHAT COMES? *1896*.

VENUS'S LOOKING-GLASS

[Composed Oct. 1872. Editions: *1875*, 1876a, 1904. First published in *Argosy* 15 (Jan. 1873), 31.]

Charles Cayley sent CR a MS poem called 'The Birth of Venus', and, later, a shorter poem on the same subject. On the latter, CR wrote: ' "The longer of these two poems was sent me first. Then I wrote one which the second rebuts. At last I wound up by my sonnet Venus's Looking-glass." In a copy of her collected *Poems* (1875), there is also the following note: "Perhaps 'Love-in-Idleness' would be a better title, with an eye to the next one" – *i.e.* to *Love Lies Bleeding* ('Notes' 487).

Title TWO SONNETS. / I. / VENUS'S LOOKING-GLASS. *1873*.
7 *white doves* the dove is sacred to Venus.

LOVE LIES BLEEDING

[Editions: *1875*, 1876a, 1904. First published in *Argosy* 15 (Jan. 1873), 31.]

'. . . Christina associated this sonnet with the preceding one, *Venus's Looking-glass*' ('Notes' 487).

Title TWO SONNETS. / II. / LOVES LIES BLEEDING. *1873*.

BIRD RAPTURES

[Editions: *1875*, 1876a, 1904.]

CR's contrast of lark and nightingale echoes Juliet: 'It was the nightingale, and not the lark' (*Romeo and Juliet* III.v.2). This pairing also appears in 'The summer nights are short' and 'When a mounting skylark sings'.

MY FRIEND

[Composed 8 Dec. 1857. Editions: *1875*, 1876a, 1904. First published in *Macmillan's Magazine* 11 (Dec. 1864), 155.]

WR, while certain that this poem 'refers to the death of some person known to and beloved by the writer', said that perhaps 'at one time I knew who it was, but do not now' ('Notes' 481).

TWILIGHT NIGHT

[Part I composed 26 Aug. 1864. Part II composed 25 June 1863. Editions: *1875*, 1876a, 1904. First published in *Argosy* 5 (1 Jan. 1868), 103. Part II is in 1896. Part I comprised lines deleted from MS version of 'Songs in a Cornfield'.]

The image of the clasped hands echoes Tennyson, *In Memoriam*: 'A hand that can be clasped no more' (VII, 5).

Title TO-MORROW *1896*.

A BIRD SONG

[Editions: *1875*, 1876a, 1904. First published in *Scribner's Monthly* 5 (Jan. 1873), 336.]

A SMILE AND A SIGH

[Composed 14 Feb. 1866. Editions: *1875*, 1876a, 1904. First published in *Macmillan's Magazine* 18 (May 1868), 86.]

The date of composition – Valentine's Day – highlights CR's frequent theme of the contrast between those fortunate and unfortunate in love.

AMOR MUNDI

[Composed 21 Feb. 1865. Editions: *1875*, 1876a, 1904. First published in *Shilling Magazine* 2 (June 1865), 193.]

Illustration: Frederick Sandys illustrated the poem for *Shilling Magazine*; later, Edward Hughes made it 'the subject of an oil-picture' ('Notes' 485).

WR reported having found in one of CR's editions her note on the poem: '"Gabriel remarked very truly, a reminiscence of *The Demon Lover*." This remark would refer more directly to stanza 3' ('Notes' 485). See headnote of 'The Hour and the Ghost'.

Title love of the world (Latin).

3 *The downhill path is easy* the uphill path is the strait and narrow way (Matt. 7:13–14 – see note to l. 46 of 'Paradise'); cf. 'Up-Hill': 'Does the road wind up-hill all the way? / Yes, to the very end.' (ll. 1–2).

13–14 *that glides quickly where velvet flowers grow . . . A scaled and hooded worm* reminiscent of Satan in serpent disguise coming towards Eve in the garden of Eden in Milton's *Paradise Lost* (IX, 494–531).

19 *nay, too late for cost-counting* Jiménez (*Bible and the Poetry* 103) points to a possible source: 'For which of you, intending to build a tower, sitteth not down first, and counteth the cost, whether he have sufficient to finish it?' (Luke 14:28).

THE GERMAN-FRENCH CAMPAIGN / 1870–1871

[Editions: *1875*, 1876a, 1904.]

The Franco-Prussian War (July 1870–Jan. 1871) ended with the defeat of France. 'The notice prefixed by the authoress to these two poems is no doubt correct in saying that they were not intended to express "political bias." It is none the less true that she had incomparably more general and native sympathy with the French nationality than with the German' ('Notes' 487). In 1871, DGR composed a poem on the same subject – 'After the German Subjugation of France, 1871' (1904).

1 "THY BROTHER'S BLOOD CRIETH"

Part title after Cain murdered Abel (see note for l. 33 of 'Eve'), God asked him where his brother was, and Cain answered: 'I know not: Am I my brother's keeper?' God responded: 'What hast thou done? the voice of thy brother's blood crieth unto me from the ground' (Gen. 4:9–10).

11–12 *Build barns, ye reapers, garner all aright, / Tho' your souls be called tonight* see note for ll. 16–18 of 'A Testimony'.

21 *As thou didst, men do to thee* 'Therefore all things whatsoever ye would that men should do to you, do ye even so to them: for this is the law and the prophets' (Matt. 7:12; see also Luke 6:31).

25 *O thou King* Marsh identifies the king as Napoleon III (Louis Napoleon, 1808–73, nephew of Napoleon I) (*CR Poems* 438); but given the warning addressed to him ('Art thou greater than great Babylon', l. 29), he may be the victorious Prussian King William I (1797–1888), who led the German armies in the Franco-Prussian War and was proclaimed German emperor in 1871 in the Hall of Mirrors at Versailles.

27–8 *Tho' he drink the last, the King of Sheshach, / Yet he shall drink at the last* 'And all the kings of the north, far and near, one with another, and all the kingdoms of the world, which are upon the face of the earth: and the king of Sheshach [Babylon] shall drink after them' (Jer. 25:26).

29–30 *Art thou greater than great Babylon, / Which lies overthrown* 'Babylon is fallen, is fallen; and all the graven images of her gods he hath broken unto the ground' (Isa. 21:9); 'Babylon is suddenly fallen and destroyed' (Jer. 51:8; see also Rev. 14:8). Biblical references to 'Babylon' refer to the period – roughly BC 597–538 – when a large number of Jews and their king were deported to Babylonia. Because of its polytheistic religion, 'Babylon' became associated not only with a place of exile from God, but also with sinfulness itself.

35 *"Vengeance is Mine, is Mine," thus saith the Lord* 'Vengeance is mine; I will repay, saith the Lord' (Rom. 12:19).

36 *O Man, put up thy sword* When Jesus was arrested in the Garden of Gethsemane, one of his disciples 'drew his sword, and struck a servant of the high priest's and smote off his ear. Then said Jesus unto him, Put up again thy sword into his place: for all they that take the sword shall perish with the sword' (Matt. 26:51–2).

2 "TODAY FOR ME"

'Dante Rossetti considered this to be among Christina's noblest productions' ('Notes' 487).

39 *Let us sit with thee weeping sore* echo of 'By the rivers of Babylon, there we sat down, yea, we wept, when we remembered Zion' (Ps. 137:1).

61 *A time there is for change and chance* 'To every thing there is a season, and a time to every purpose under the heaven' (Ecc. 3:1).

63 *And One abides can yet bind up* 'I will seek that which was lost, and bring again that which was driven away, and will bind up that which was broken, and will strengthen that which was sick: but I will destroy the fat and the strong; I will feed them with judgment' (Eze. 34:16).

66–7 *Who next shall drink the trembling cup, / Wring out its dregs and suck them up* see note for l. 35 of 'The Three Enemies'.

A CHRISTMAS CAROL ['In the bleak mid-winter']

[Editions: *1875*, 1876a, 1904. First published in *Scribner's Monthly* 3 (Jan. 1872), 278.]

This poem, in its musical setting by Gustav Holst (1874–1934), is a familiar carol. The details allude to the story of Jesus' birth as told in Luke 2:1–20.

CONSIDER

[Composed 7 May 1863. Editions: *1875*, 1876a, 1904. First published in *Macmillan's Magazine* 13 (Jan. 1866), 232.]

See note for title of ' "Consider the Lilies of the Field" '.

7 *sparrows of the air of small account* 'Are not two sparrows sold for a farthing? and one of them shall not fall on the ground without your Father [knowing]' (Matt. 10:29; see also Luke 12:6).

19–20 *Much more our Father seeks / To do us good* 'If then God so clothe the grass, which is today in the field, and tomorrow is cast into the oven; how much more will he clothe you, O ye of little faith?' (Luke 12:28; see also Matt. 6:30).

BY THE WATERS OF BABYLON / B.C. 570

[Composed 29 June 1864. Editions: *1875*, 1876a, 1904. First published in *Macmillan's Magazine* 14 (Oct. 1866), 424–6.]

Title see note for Part 2, l. 39 of 'The German-French Campaign. 1870–1871'. In the sixth century BC, the temple at Jerusalem was destroyed, and the Israelites were carried off to captivity in Babylon. In MS (BL), the title is 'In Captivity'.

1 *I waste to skin and bone* 'their skin cleaveth to their bones; it is withered, it is become like a stick' (Lam. 4:8).

9 *sore bestead* hard pressed.

10 *Sodom and Gomorrah* see note for Part 6, l. 4 of 'Monna Innominata'.

11 *As Jericho before God's trumpet-peal* 'So the people shouted when the priests blew with the trumpets; and it came to pass, when the people heard the sound of the trumpet, and the people shouted with a great shout, that the wall [of Jericho] fell down flat' (Jos. 6:20).

12 *elect* see note for l. 28 of 'Christian and Jew. A Dialogue'.

14 *With famished faces toward Jerusalem* see note for l. 211 of 'From House to Home'.

16–17 *His ears against our cry He shutteth them, / His hand He shorteneth that He will not save* 'Behold, the Lord's hand is not shortened, that it cannot save; neither his ear heavy, that it cannot hear' (Isa. 59:1).

22 *His Ark* see note for l. 52 of 'Martyrs' Song'.

36 *Where milk and honey flow* see note for title of 'They Desire a Better Country'.

38 *Under my fig-tree and my fruitful vine* see note for ll. 53–6 of 'Advent' ['This Advent moon shines cold and clear'].

40 *Now strangers press the olives that are mine* 'Our inheritance is turned to strangers, our houses to aliens' (Lam. 5:2).

47 *hip and thigh we smote* 'And he smote them hip and thigh with a great slaughter: and he went down and dwelt in the top of the rock Etam' (Jud. 15:8).

50 *Their daughters took we for a pleasant prey* 'They ravished the women in Zion, and the maids in the cities of Judah' (Lam. 5:11).

57 *gyves* leg shackles.

67 *His wrath came on us to the uttermost* 'for the wrath is come upon them to the uttermost' (1 Thes. 2:16).

70–71 *Who lit the Fiery Pillar in our path, / Who swept the Red Sea dry before our feet* when God led the Israelites out of Egypt, 'He divided the sea, and caused them to pass through; and he made the waters to stand as an heap. In the daytime also he led them with a cloud, and all the night with a light of fire' (Ps. 78:13–14). The 'pillar of a cloud' (Ex. 13:21) reappears in 'A Martyr', l. 7, and in ' "Slain from the foundation of the world" ', l. 9 and note. For Moses' parting of the Red Sea, which allowed them to escape from Pharaoh's army, see also ll. 45–6 of 'Martyrs' Song'.

73–4 *Sworn once to David: One shall fill thy seat / Born of thy body* 'The Lord hath sworn in truth unto David; he will not turn from it; Of the fruit of thy body will I set upon thy throne' (Ps. 132:11); by Christians this is taken as a prophecy of the coming of Jesus, a descendant of David.

77 *Ichabod* born prematurely when his mother hears of the capture of the Ark ('The glory is departed from Israel') and the death of her husband (1 Sam. 4:21).

82 *Thy Name will I remember, praising it* 'I will . . . praise thy name for thy lovingkindness and for thy truth; for thou hast magnified thy word above all thy name' (Ps. 138:2).

84 *And blot me from the Book which Thou hast writ* 'Yet now, if thou wilt forgive their sin –; and if not, blot me, I pray thee, out of thy book which thou hast written' (Ex. 32:32).

86 *Thy faithfulness of old* 'thy counsels of old are faithfulness and truth' (Isa. 25:1).

87 *Tho' as a weaver Thou cut off my days* 'I have cut off like a weaver my life' (Isa. 38:12).

88 *And end me as a tale ends that is told* see note for l. 8 of 'Dead Before Death'.

PARADISE

[Composed 28 Feb. 1854. Editions: *1875*, *1876a*, *1904*. First published in Orby Shipley (ed.), *Lyra Messianica: Hymns and Verses on the Life of Christ, Ancient and Modern; with Other Poems*, 2nd edn. (Longman, Green and Co., 1869), 365–6.]

'In a printed copy of her *Poems*, wherein Christina made a few jottings, she has here noted "Not a real dream" ' ('Notes' 471).

Title Easter Even. *MS (BodL and Yale)*. Paradise: in a Dream. *1869*.

5–7 *rose . . . lily . . . violet* the flowers most often repeated in CR's poetry: the rose usually emblematic of love, the lily of purity and faith, and the violet of faithfulness and humility. See also notes for ll. 408–10 of *Goblin Market* and for l. 5 of 'Song' ['Oh roses for the flush of youth'] and headnote of 'Queen Rose'.

17 *the fourfold River* 'And a river went out of Eden to water the garden; and from thence it was parted, and became into four heads' (Gen. 2:10).

25–9 *The Tree of Life stood . . . Its leaves are healing for the world* see note for ll. 13–14 of 'Eve'.

31–2 *Sweeter than honey to the taste / And balm indeed* 'How sweet are thy words unto my taste! yea, sweeter than honey to my mouth!' (Ps. 119:103); 'Is there no balm in Gilead; is there no physician there? why then is not the health of the daughter of my people recovered?' (Jer. 8:22).

33 *the gate called Beautiful* the gate in Jerusalem where Peter healed the lame man (Acts 3:10).

35–6 *I saw the golden streets begin, / And outskirts of the glassy pool* 'And the building of the wall of it was of jasper: and the city was pure gold, like unto clear glass' and 'the street of the city was pure gold, as it were transparent glass' (Rev. 21:18, 21). CR suggests that the ' "pure gold" of the city, inasmuch as it is "like unto clear glass," lets not nor hinders the universal permeation of light' and 'this supersensual gold is as precious metal with the virtue of glass superadded; not like poverty-stricken glass gilded over to simulate gold. Mere surface gilding belongs to earth not to heaven, and with earth it vanishes' (*FD* 507, 511–12). 'Jasper' is a kind of quartz, usually red, yellow or brown.

37–8 *harps . . . crowns . . . palm branches* all characteristics of the Heavenly Jerusalem. 'Christ of Whom it is mystically written: "I said, I will go up to the palm tree, I will take hold of the boughs thereof," – won all palms for all saints when on Calvary with His own right hand and with His holy arm He got Himself the victory. Christ it is Who triumphs in His triumphant redeemed: from Him they derive their victories, from Him their rewards. His Cross branched out into their crosses: His Cross, the one palm tree of victory, branches out into their palms' (*FD* 232). In *SF*, CR compares the oak ('of the earth earthy') and the palm ('heavenly'), although warning against 'pressing symbolism and our own guesses too far, for Jericho the accursed . . . was the City of Palm Trees' (101). The palm branch is also associated with Jesus' triumphant entry into Jerusalem the week before he was crucified, when crowds lined the streets waving palm branches as he passed.

39–40 *Eye hath not seen, nor ear hath heard, / Nor heart conceived* see note for ll. 37–8 of 'Advent' ['This Advent moon shines cold and clear'].

46 *For narrow way that once they trod* 'Because strait is the gate, and narrow is the way, which leadeth unto life, and few there be that find it' (Matt. 7:14; see also Luke 13:24).

MOTHER COUNTRY

[Composed 7 Feb. 1866. Editions: *1875*, 1876a, 1904. First published in *Macmillan's Magazine* 18 (March 1868), 403–4.]

71–2 *Vanity of vanities, / As the Preacher saith* see note for l. 1 of 'One Certainty'.

"I WILL LIFT UP MINE EYES UNTO THE HILLS" ['I am pale with sick desire']

[Composed 1 Feb. 1856. Editions: *1875*, 1876a, 1896, 1904. First published in Orby Shipley (ed.), *Lyra Eucharista: Hymns and Verses on the Holy Communion, Ancient and Modern; with Other Poems* (Longman, Green, Longman, Roberts and Green, 1863), 167–8; 2nd edn. (1864), 206–8.]

Both WR and Harrison identify this as the poem CR refers to as 'Come and See' in her letter to DGR [?4 April 1865]: 'could you re-consider your verdict on *Come & See*? It is, to own the truth, a special favourite of mine; and seems to me unlike any other in the volume, or indeed in G.M. I have moreover altered what you call the *queer rhyme*. In short, I should like particularly to put this piece in' (*Letters*, I, 243).

Title 'Now we [later 'they'] desire a better country', *MS (BodL)*; Conference between Christ, the Saints, and the Soul. / *Come up hither, and I will shew thee things which must be hereafter. 1863*; Conference between Christ, the Saints, and the Soul. *1864, 1896*.

See note for ll. 5–6 of 'A Better Resurrection'.

8 *the everlasting hills* see note for ll. 5–6 of 'A Better Resurrection'.

11 *We rest in Jesus* see headnote of 'Dream-Land'.

12 *Where is not day nor night* 'But it shall be one day which shall be known to the LORD, not day, nor night: but it shall come to pass, that at evening time it shall be light' (Zech. 14:7); 'Yea, the darkness hideth not from thee; but the night shineth as the day: the darkness and the light are both alike to thee' (Ps. 139:12); 'God is light, and in him is no darkness at all' (1 John 1.5); 'And there shall be no night there; and they need no candle, neither light of the sun; for the Lord God giveth them light: and they shall reign for ever and ever' (Rev. 22:5); 'And the gates of it shall not be shut at all by day: for there shall be no night there' (Rev. 21:25).

35 *We live in Jesus* in connection with 'We rest in Jesus' (l. 11), this is reminiscent of a hymn by Charles Wesley (1707–88): 'In Jesus we live, In Jesus we rest' (1745).

47 *Come and taste My sweets, saith Jesus* Jiménez points out that this line brings together two biblical passages: Psalm 34:8 ('O taste and see that the Lord is good') and John 6:53–7, where Jesus says that his followers must eat of his flesh and drink of his blood (the Eucharist) to attain eternal life (*Bible and the Poetry* xi–xii); see also note for l. 471 of *Goblin Market*. The line also echoes in *Goblin Market* both the goblins' cries ('Sweet to tongue and sound to eye; / Come buy, come buy' – ll. 30–31) and Lizzie's invitation to Laura to 'suck my juices / Squeezed from goblin fruits for you' (ll. 468–9).

48 *Be with Me where I am* 'Father, I will that they also, whom thou hast given me, be with me where I am' (John 17:24).

"THE MASTER IS COME, AND CALLETH FOR THEE"

[Editions: *1875*, 1876a, 1904.]

'In the annotated copy of Christina's poem I find a note as follows: "Dr. Littledale wanted a hymn – for a 'Profession,' I think; so I wrote this. But I think it was not adopted" ' ('Notes' 476). Richard Frederick Littledale (1830–90) was a noted Anglican priest and writer and CR's confessor. A 'profession' is an entry into a religious order or the vow made to enter such an order.

Title After Lazarus had died, Jesus went to visit Lazarus' sisters, Mary and Martha. Martha ran out to greet Jesus, and after a conversation with him, 'she went her way, and called Mary her sister secretly, saying, The Master is come, and calleth for thee' (John 11:28).

4 *Trims thy lamp* see note for l. 3 of 'Advent' ['This Advent moon shines cold and clear'].

15 *He is jealous, thy God almighty* Ex. 20:5 (see note for title of ' "The Iniquity of the Fathers Upon the Children" ') and elsewhere.

WHO SHALL DELIVER ME?

[Composed 1 March 1864. Editions: *1875*, 1876a, 1904. First published in *Argosy* 1 (Feb. 1866), 288. Originally part of MS (BL) of ' "What is that to thee? Follow thou me" '.]

Title 'O wretched man that I am! who shall deliver me from the body of this death?' (Rom. 7:24).

11–12 *the race / That all must run* 'Know ye not they which run in a race run all, but one receiveth the prize? So run, that ye may obtain. And every man that striveth for the mastery is temperate in all things. Now they do it to obtain a corruptible crown; but we an incorruptible' (1 Cor. 9:24–5); 'Wherefore seeing we also are compassed about with so great a cloud of witnesses, let us lay aside every weight, and the sin which doth so easily beset us, and let us run with patience the race that is set before us' (Heb. 12:1). In *TF*, CR writes:

'sloth runs no race', adding that 'a race is the one thing set before us. We are not summoned to pose picturesquely in *tableaux vivants*, or die away gracefully like dissolving views' (40).

24 *Break off the yoke and set me free* 'Stand fast therefore in the liberty wherewith Christ hath made us free, and be not entangled again with the yoke of bondage' (Gal. 5:1).

"WHEN MY HEART IS VEXED, I WILL COMPLAIN"
['"O Lord, how canst Thou say Thou lovest me?']

[Editions: *1875*, 1876a, 1904.]

Title cf. Job 7:11: 'Therefore I will not refrain my mouth; I will speak in the anguish of my spirit; I will complain in the bitterness of my soul.'

7 *I came from Edom* the figure from Edom, a territory near the Red Sea, is asked 'Wherefore art thou red in thine apparel, and thy garments like him that treadeth in the winefat?' (Isa. 63:2) – a passage often connected to Rev. 19:13: 'And he was clothed with a vesture dipped in blood: and his name is called The Word of God.'

11–12 *trod / The winepress all alone* 'I have trodden the winepress alone; and of the people there was none with me: for I will tread them in mine anger, and trample them in my fury' (Isa. 63:3).

14–15 *For Thou art strong to comfort: and could I / But comfort one I love* 'Who comforteth us in all our tribulation, that we may be able to comfort them which are in any trouble, by the comfort wherewith we ourselves are comforted of God' (2 Cor. 1:4).

20 *For thee I thirsted with the dying thirst* 'After this, Jesus knowing that all things were now accomplished that the scripture might be fulfilled, saith, I thirst' (John 19:28).

27 *Thy love is better than new wine* 'Let him kiss me with the kisses of his mouth: for thy love is better than wine' (Song of Sol. 1:2).

28 *And I am sick of love in loving Thee* see note for l. 69 of 'After this the Judgment'.

30 *For jealousy is cruel as the grave* see note for l. 1 of 'An End'.

32 *deep answers deep* 'Deep calleth unto deep' (Ps. 42:7).

33 *I give to My beloved sleep* 'It is vain for you to rise up early, to sit up late, to eat the bread of sorrows: for so he giveth his beloved sleep' (Ps. 127:2).

34 *for love is strong as death* see note for l. 1 of 'An End'.

36 *thou shalt wake in Paradise with Me* see note for l. 8 of 'Good Friday' ['Am I a stone and not a sheep'].

AFTER COMMUNION

[Composed 23 Feb. 1866. Editions: *1875*, 1876a, 1904. First published in Robert H. Baynes (ed.), *The Illustrated Book of Sacred Poems* (Cassell, Petter and Galpin, [1867]), 8.]

Title see note for l. 471 of *Goblin Market*.

5 *Lo, now Thy banner over me is love* 'He brought me to the banqueting house, and his banner over me was love' (Song of Sol. 2:4).

8 *Made me a nest for dwelling of Thy Dove* 'dwell in the rock, and be like the dove that maketh her nest in the sides of the hole's mouth' (Jer. 48:28); and Job 39:28 (see note for ll. 19–23 of 'A Testimony').

9–10 *What wilt Thou call me in our home above, / Who now hast called me friend* 'Henceforth I call you not servants; for the servant knoweth not what his lord doeth: but I have called you friends' (John 15:15).

10–11 *how will it be / When Thou for good wine settest forth the best* Jesus' first miracle was to turn water into wine. When it was tasted, the bridegroom was told: 'Every man at the beginning doth set forth good wine; and when men have well drunk, then that which is worse: but thou hast kept the good wine until now' (John 2:10).

13 *lean upon Thy breast* during the Passover meal on the night Jesus was arrested, 'Now there was leaning on Jesus' bosom one of his disciples, whom Jesus loved' (John 13:23). The disciple has traditionally been identified as John.

SAINTS AND ANGELS

[Editions: *1875*, 1876a, 1904.]

'On this poem Christina made a rather quaint note, personal to myself: "William aptly remarked that this contains nothing about angels"' ('Notes' 476).

7 *raiment white* 'He that overcometh, the same shall be clothed in white raiment and I will not blot out his name out of the book of life, but I will confess his name before my Father, and before his angels' (Rev. 3:5); see note for l. 13 of 'Martyrs' Song' and l. 9 of ' "Before the Throne, and before the Lamb" '.

8 *crown of gold* see note for l. 11 of 'Easter Day'.

9 *the fourfold river* see note for l. 17 of 'Paradise'.

11 *Fair are the gold and bdellium and the onyx stone* 'And the gold of that land is good: there is bdellium and the onyx stone' (Gen. 2:12). Bdellium is gum resin resembling myrrh, used in medicine and as a perfume. The land is Havilah, near one of the rivers (Pison) that watered the garden of Eden.

13–14 *O my love, my dove, lift up your eyes / Toward the eastern gate like an opening rose* cf. CR's Italian sonnet sequence 'The Reddening of the East'.

22 *'Vanity of vanities:'* see note for l. 1 of 'One Certainty'.

31 *Altho' there be nothing new beneath the sun* see note for l. 11 of 'One Certainty'.

38 *a strait gate* see note for l. 46 of 'Paradise'.

39 *The loves that meet in Paradise shall cast out fear* see note for l. 36 of ' "They Desire a Better Country" '.

A ROSE PLANT IN JERICHO

[Editions: *1875*, 1876a, 1904. Published in F. G. Lee (ed.), *Lyrics of Light and Life* (Basil Montagu Pickering, [1875]), 11–12.]

WR reports that the poem 'stands annotated by Christina thus: "Written once when Mr. Shipley wanted something" ' ('Notes' 476). For Shipley, see headnote of 'Martyrs' Song'.

Title allusion to the 'rose of Jericho', also called 'Resurrection Plant'.

Sing-Song. A Nursery Rhyme Book (1872)

RHYMES DEDICATED WITHOUT PERMISSION TO THE BABY WHO SUGGESTED THEM

[Editions: *1872*, 1872a, 1893, 1904.]

Illustration: 'In the MS. of *Sing-song* Christina made a series of pen-and-ink sketches – slight and primitive of course, but not without suggestiveness' ('Notes' 492).

WR identifies the child as the baby son of Arthur Cayley, a Cambridge mathematician (and Charles Cayley's brother) ('Notes' 492). Teodoro Pietrocola-Rossetti (see headnote of *Goblin Market*) translated *Sing-Song* into Italian, calling it *Ninna-Nanna*. 'Privately Christina told Gabriel that she liked some of her own translations better than her cousin's though "his No. 5 [presumably ' "Kookoorookoo kookoorookoo!" '] beats me hollow" ' (Packer, *CR* 327). See headnote to ['Ninna-Nanna'].

['Kookoorookoo! kookoorookoo!']

CR's 'earliest memory was of her father crowing like a cock to wake his children' (*CR* 3).

['There's snow on the fields']

4 *pottage* thick soup or stew.

['A city plum is not a plum']

1 *plum* 'plumb' is someone who possesses £100,000 (slang, now rare).
3 *party rat* politician who deserts his party.
4 *sailor's cat* part of the mechanism by which anchor is raised.
5 *soldier's frog* 'frog' is an ornamental fastening for the front of a military coat or cloak; also, a device attached to a soldier's belt for carrying a weapon, such as a sword.

['Your brother has a falcon']

3 *mannikin* little man.

['Hop-o'-my-thumb and little Jack Horner']

1 *Hop-o'-my-thumb and little Jack Horner* 'Hop-O'-My-Thumb' is a tiny boy in a children's story, and 'Little Jack Horner' is in a familiar Mother Goose rhyme about a boy who put his thumb into a Christmas pie.
3 *Trot* the name and character of the dog perhaps echo those of 'John Trot' in a William Blake poem that appears in a Blake MS that DGR owned (now referred to as the 'Rossetti MS'): 'Here lies John Trot, the Friend of all mankind: / He has not left one enemy behind' ('Another' [under 'An Epitaph'], [written *c.* 1807–9]).

['The summer nights are short']

See headnote of 'Bird Raptures'.

['Margaret has a milking-pail']

4 *betimes* early in the morning.

['In the meadow—what in the meadow?']

3 *fairy rings* circular bands of grass differing in colour from the grass around them; caused by the growth of certain fungi, but sometimes said to be produced by fairies when dancing.
7 *Love-lies-bleeding* garden plant having a long, drooping, purplish-red spike of bloom.
　All-heal name applied to various plants thought to heal all maladies.

['Rosy maiden Winifred']

6 *shepherd's-weatherglass* scarlet pimpernel, called 'weatherglass' because of its sensitivity to changes in the weather.

[' "Ferry me across the water" ']

1 *Ferry me across the water* in classical mythology and in Dante's *Divine Comedy*, the souls of the dead are ferried by Charon across the River Styx to Hades.
3 *If you've a penny in your purse* dead souls must pay Charon to ferry them across the Styx.

['When a mounting skylark sings']

See headnote of 'Bird Raptures'.

['The lily has a smooth stalk']

1 *The lily has a smooth stalk* see note for ll. 408–10 of *Goblin Market*.
3 *the rose* CR identified herself with the rose: in l. 2 of 'Roses blushing red and white', she characterizes the roses as 'for delight'. See also note for ll. 5–7 of 'Paradise'.

['Wee wee husband']

1 *wee husband* echoes folk-tale characters such as Tom Thumb.
3 *comfits* sweetmeats made of fruit preserved with sugar, such as sugar-plums.

['The rose that blushes rosy red']

1 *The rose* see note for l. 3 of 'The lily has a smooth stalk'.
3–4 *The lily that blows spotless white, / She may stand upright* see note for ll. 408–10 of *Goblin Market*.

['Clever little Willie wee']

7 *cons* studies so as to commit to memory.

['Baby lies so fast asleep']

7 *snowdrop* early-flowering plant having a white pendent flower; emblem of the Virgin Mary.

Poems Added in *Sing-Song. A Nursery Rhyme Book* (1893)

[Editions: *1893*, 1904.]

['Playing at bob cherry']

11 *cherry bob* two cherries with stalks attached, used by children for earrings and in games.

A Pageant and Other Poems (1881)

[Except where noted, the dates of composition are unknown. Editions, except where noted: *1881*, 1881a, 1890, 1904.]

DGR reported to CR that 'Swinburne's delight with the *Pageant* amounted to a dancing and screaming ecstasy' (letter of 7 Sept. 1881 (no. 2551), in O. Doughty and J. Wahl (eds.), *Letters of DGR*, vol. IV (1967), p. 1920).

['Sonnets are full of love, and this my tome']

CR used this sonnet for the dedication inscription to 1881. WR used it to open 1904 because, as he said: 'Christina Rossetti's books were, with few exceptions, dedicated to her mother; therefore the present inscription can very properly be removed from the position which it would occupy in order of date, and may form the dedication to the entire body of her poems' ('Notes' 459). After the poem (on the back of the page) in MS3 (UT), CR wrote: 'To my Mother / I offer / love / reverence / and / this little volume'.

Title DEDICATORY SONNET *1904*.
8 *loadstar* star that shows the way, especially the polestar.

THE KEY-NOTE

[Editions: *1881*, 1881a, 1890, 1896, 1904.]
Title LINES *1896*.

THE MONTHS: / A PAGEANT

Of this masque in a letter to DGR (9 Aug. 1881), CR writes: 'It had its rise in one of the All Saints Sisters asking me whether I could concoct something performable by her sister's family; and, though the result was on too grand a scale for the applicant, yet it was that hint which first set me off. The piece was, in the main, written at Seaford two summers ago' (*FL* 96). WR says that it was performed in girls' schools in America as well as England ('Notes' 462), and 'once on quite a striking scale, in the Albert Hall, Kensington' (*FL* 98).

11 *hunch* hunk or lump.
274–6 *Here comes my youngest sister, looking dim / And grim, / With dismal ways* self-parody, as CR wrote to DGR (5 Sept. 1881): 'I have had a quiet grin over

October's remark which ushers in November, as connecting it with my own brothers and myself! Pray appreciate the portrait' (*FL* 98). WR also reports that CR quoted these lines 'sometimes as a telling self-description' ('Notes' 462).

285 *cars* see note for l. 91 of 'The Convent Threshold'.

310 *privet* shrub used for garden hedges.

"ITALIA, IO TI SALUTO!"

In 1865, CR, her mother and WR took a trip to the continent which included a visit to Italy.

Title 'Italy, I salute you!' (Italian).

MIRRORS OF LIFE AND DEATH

[Lines 6–135 were first published in *Athenaeum*, no. 2577 (17 March 1877), 350.]

3 *Darkly as in a glass* 'For now we see through a glass, darkly; but then face to face: now I know in part; but then shall I know even as also I am known' (1 Cor. 13:12).

A BALLAD OF BODING

Uffelman suggests that CR may be alluding to chapters 12–13 of Revelation, where St Michael battles the dragons 'as well as a number of horned beasts which rise from the sea and land' ('Christina Rossetti's *A Pageant and Other Poems*', 145). Marsh points out that this poem draws 'on a famous ode translated by Spenser as *The Visions of Petrarch* [1590]' (*CR* 458).

See headnote of 'Sleep at Sea'.

8 *sackcloth* coarse clothing indicating poverty or humility; penitential garb; the material of mourning.

78–9 *In weariness . . . sore distress* allusion to St Paul's account of his sufferings and privations: 'In weariness and painfulness, in watchings often, in hunger and thirst, in fastings often, in cold and nakedness' (2 Cor. 11:27). See also headnote of 'Conversion of St. Paul'.

YET A LITTLE WHILE ['I dreamed and did not seek: today I seek']

Title 'Then Jesus said unto them, Yet a little while is the light with you. Walk while ye have the light, lest darkness come upon you: for he that walketh in darkness knoweth not whither he goeth' (John 12:35; see also John 14:19 and 16:16–20 – see note for l. 103 of 'Annie' ['It's not for earthly bread, Annie']).

MONNA INNOMINATA

CR insisted that this sequence of sonnets always be printed together and that one sonnet not be taken out of context and printed separately. (See William Whitla, 'Questioning the Convention: Christina Rossetti's Sonnet Sequence "*Monna Innominata*"', in Kent, *Achievement* 82–131; hereafter cited as 'Whitla'.) WR's note is frequently quoted:

> To any one to whom it was granted to be behind the scenes of Christina Rossetti's life – and to how few was this granted – it is not merely probable but certain that this 'sonnet of sonnets' was a personal utterance – an intensely personal one. The introductory prose-note, about 'many a lady sharing her lover's poetic aptitude,' etc., is a blind – not an untruthful blind, for it alleges nothing that is not reasonable, and on the surface correct, but still a blind interposed to draw off attention from the writer in her proper person. ('Notes' 462)

Translations of the epigraphs are by WR. The sources in Dante and Petrarch are noted by Uffelman ('CR's *A Pageant and Other Poems*') as well as by Whitla: 'The epigraphs' oblique references either involve a direct address by one of Dante's fellow poets or are spoken in the presence of those poets by Dante (or his persona) or allude to the invocation of the god of poetry ... Eight of the Petrarch epigraphs come from poems that refer directly or obliquely to writing poetry' (Whitla 103, 109).

Title 'unnamed lady' (Italian). Whitla points out that Charles Cayley refers to CR as 'dolce monna' (sweet lady) in a letter to her dated 6 Nov. 1881 (102 n. 25).

Prefatory note *altissimo poeta . . . cotanto amante* 'The "*altissimo poeta*" ("highest poet") appellation, here applied to Dante, is actually the greeting given Virgil by his fellow poets in *Inferno* IV, 80; and the second phrase, "with such a lover," refers to Lancelot in Francesca's story (*Inf.* V. 134). Rossetti used the first phrase, again referring to Dante, as an epigraph to her article "Dante, An English Classic" in *The Churchman's Shilling Magazine* 2, no. 8 (October 1867): 200–205' (Whitla 87 n. 10). Marsh claims that one source for the idea of the woman as the speaking subject came from Francis Hueffer's *The*

Troubadours (1878), 'which as well as noting the "scanty information" on the poets' objects of desire as individuals, also contained a chapter on "Lady Troubadours," identifying some "fourteen gifted women" – a "very modest figure seeing that the entire number of the troubadours is close on 400" – whose work had survived. Monna Innominata has, of course, fourteen sonnets' (*CR* 472). The meaning of CR's allusion to Elizabeth Barrett Browning's sonnets in the Prefatory note was often misunderstood, including by one of the poem's earliest reviewers. In a letter to DGR, CR writes:

I am much pleased with [Mr Caine's] *Academy* article, though sorry that he seems to have misapprehended my reference to the *Portuguese Sonnets*. Surely not only what I meant to say but what I do say is, not that the Lady of those sonnets is surpassable, but that a 'Donna innominata' by the same hand might well have been unsurpassable. The Lady in question, as she actually stands, I was not regarding as an 'innominata' at all, – because the latter type, according to the traditional figure I had in view, is surrounded by unlike circumstances. I rather wonder that no one (so far as I know) ever hit on my semi-historical argument before for such treatment, – it seems to me so full of poetic suggestiveness. (*FL* 98)

In commenting on this letter, WR says that CR's insistence

– that the speaker in her sonnets was not intended for an 'innominata at all' – is curious, and shows (what is every now and then apparent in her utterances) that her mind was conversant with very nice shades of distinction. It is indisputable that the real veritable speaker in these sonnets is Christina herself, giving expression to her love for Charles Cayley: but the prose heading would surely lead any reader to suppose that the *ostensible* speaker is one of those ladies, to whom it adverts, in the days of the troubadours. (*FL* 97; quoted by Whitla 91)

8 *less conspicuous poets; and in that land and that period* Provençal poets (troubadours) in Provence in the twelfth and early thirteenth centuries.

1

Epigraph 'The day that they have said adieu to their sweet friends' (*Purgatorio* 8.3).

'Love, with how great a stress dost thou vanquish me to-day!' (85.12).

2

Epigraph 'It was already the hour which turns back the desire' (*Purgatorio* 8.1).

'I recur to the time when I first saw thee' (20.3).

1–2 *I wish I could remember, that first day, / First hour, first moment of your meeting me* Marsh sees an echo of the opening lines of Cayley's translation (1879) of Petrarch's sonnet 285: 'Oh day and hour and moment of my cross!' (*CR* 472).

3

Epigraph 'Oh Shades, empty save in semblance!' (*Purgatorio* 2.79).

'An imaginary guide conducts her' (277.9).

14 *Tho' there be nothing new beneath the sun* see note for l. 11 of 'One Certainty'.

4

Epigraph 'A small spark fosters a great flame' (*Paradiso* 1.34).

'Every other thing, every thought, goes off, and love alone remains there with you' (72.44–5).

5

Epigraph 'Love, who exempts no loved one from loving' (*Inferno* 5.103).

'Love led me into such joyous hope' (56.11).

3 *leal* loyal.

4 *To Him whose noble service setteth free* see note for l. 24 of 'Who Shall Deliver Me?' Whitla sees an echo of the collect for peace at morning prayer in the *Book of Common Prayer* (121).

8 *perfect you as He would have you be* 'Be ye therefore perfect, even as your Father which is in heaven is perfect' (Matt. 5:48).

14 *Since woman is the helpmeet* 'And the Lord God said, it is not good that the man should be alone; I will make him an help meet for him' (Gen. 2:18).

6

Epigraph 'Now canst thou comprehend the quantity of the love which glows in me towards thee' (*Purgatorio* 21.133–34).

'I do not choose that Love should release me from such a tie' (59.17).

4 *Nor with Lot's wife cast back a faithless look* Lot and his wife were told not to look back at the burning Sodom and Gomorrah – cities of ancient Jordan, noted for their wickedness, which God destroyed by raining down fire and brimstone. 'But his wife looked back from behind him, and she became a pillar of salt' (Gen. 19:26). Orpheus, too, looked back at Eurydice as she came up from the Underworld and by doing this, lost her to Hades for ever. Whitla points out that this allusion to Lot's wife is 'a neat variation on the Eurydice figure that will be referred to later in sonnet 11 and its Dante epigraph' (121).

6 *having counted up the cost* see note for l. 19 of 'Amor Mundi'.

8 *The sorriest sheep Christ shepherds with His crook* see note for l. 14 of 'Good Friday' ['Am I a stone and not a sheep'].

9 *Yet while I love* 'In the sestet the persona moves from answering the rebuke to defending her position by an appeal to the expansiveness of love (the *volta* comes with "Yet") in the tradition of [John] Donne's "Valediction: Forbidding Mourning" [1633]' (Whitla 121).

13 *I cannot love you if I love not Him* Whitla says that this 'paradoxical conclusion is a more serious theological challenge to the beloved' than the idea to be found in Edmund Spenser (1552–99) *Amoretti* 68 (1595): 'So let us love, dear love, like as we ought: / Love is the lesson which the Lord us taught' (Whitla 121–2). Cf. also 'Let me not love thee, if I love thee not' (Herbert, 'Affliction (1)' ('When first thou didst entice to thee my heart') (1633), l. 1).

7

Epigraph 'Here always Spring and every fruit' (*Purgatorio* 28.143).

'Conversing with me, and I with him' (35.14).

4 *love, that knows not a dividing sea* Whitla sees an allusion to the myth of Hero and Leander, tragic lovers separated by the sea, a myth alluded to by Dante in ll. 71–4 'of the same canto that provides the epigraph' for this sonnet (122).

5 *Love builds the house on rock and not on sand* see note for ll. 19–23 of 'A Testimony'.

7 *love's citadel unmanned* 'For the conceit of the citadel besieged, see Petrarch (274), [Philip] Sidney (*Astrophel and Stella*, 12, 36) [1598], and Spenser (*Amoretti*, 14)' (Whitla 123 n. 43).

8 *held in bonds* 'for love's captivity in bonds and loss of liberty, see Petrarch (89), Sidney (2, 29), and [Barnabe] Barnes (*Parthenophil and Parthenophe* [1593], 65)' (Whitla 123 n. 43).

13–14 *Tho' jealousy be cruel as the grave, / And death be strong, yet love is strong as death* see note for l. 1 of 'An End'.

8

Epigraph 'As if he were to say to God, "I care for nought else"' (*Purgatorio* 8.12).

'I hope to find pity, and not only pardon' (1.8).

1 *I, if I perish, perish . . . Esther spake* see note for l. 104 of 'A Royal Princess'.

8 *Harmless as doves and subtle as a snake* 'Behold, I send you forth as sheep in the midst of wolves: be ye therefore wise as serpents, and harmless as doves' (Matt. 10:16).

9

Epigraph 'O dignified and pure conscience!' (*Purgatorio* 3.8).

'Spirit more lit with burning virtues' (283.3).

8 *Faithless and hopeless turning to the wall* see note for l. 3 of 'L. E. L.'

10–11 *love may toil all night, / But take at morning* in response to Jesus' instruction to Peter to 'Launch out into the deep, and let down your nets for a draught', Peter answered, 'Master, we have toiled all the night, and have taken nothing: nevertheless at thy word I will let down the net.' When 'they had this done, they inclosed a great multitude of fishes: and their net brake' (Luke 5:4–6).

11–12 *wrestle till the break / Of day* allusion to Jacob wrestling with an angel: 'And Jacob was left alone; and there wrestled a man with him until the breaking of the day.' Jacob said: 'I will not let thee go, except thou bless me' (Gen. 32:24, 26).

14 *Ready to spend and be spent for your sake* 'And I will very gladly spend and be spent for you; though the more abundantly I love you, the less I be loved' (2 Cor. 12:15).

10

'The sestet, with some variants and dated 1870, was from a sonnet "By Way of Remembrance" ("I love you and you know it . . ."), and was printed in facsimile in William Michael Rossetti's *Some Reminiscences*, II, opposite p. 312, where he says that it was dedicated to C. B. Cayley' (Whitla 126 n. 45).

Epigraph 'With better course and with better star' (*Paradiso* 1.40).
    'Life flees, and stays not an hour' (272.1).

11

Epigraph 'Come after me, and leave folk to talk' (*Purgatorio* 5.13).
    'Relating the casualties of our life' (285.12).

12

Epigraph 'Love, who speaks within my mind' (*Purgatorio* 2.112).
    'Love comes in the beautiful face of his lady' (13.2).

13

Epigraph 'And we will direct our eyes to the Primal Love' (*Paradiso* 32.142).
    'But I find a burden to which my arms suffice not' (20.5).
3 *Without Whose Will one lily doth not stand* 'Consider the lilies, how they grow' (Luke 12:27; and see note for title of ' "Consider the Lilies of the Field" ').
4 *Nor sparrow fall at his appointed date* see note for l. 7 of 'Consider'.
5 *Who numbereth the innumerable sand* 'If I should count them, they are more in number than the sand: when I awake, I am still with thee' (Ps. 139:18).
6 *Who weighs the wind and water with a weight* 'To make the weight for the winds; and he weigheth the waters by measure' (Job 28:25).

14

Epigraph 'And His will is our peace' (*Paradiso* 3.85).
    'Only with these thoughts, with different locks' (30.32).

"LUSCIOUS AND SORROWFUL" ['Beautiful, tender, wasting away for sorrow']

5 *jubilee* see note for l. 11 of ' "They Desire a Better Country" '.

DE PROFUNDIS

Title out of the depths (Latin). 'Out of the depths have I cried unto thee, O LORD' (Ps. 130:1).

TEMPUS FUGIT

Title time flies (Latin).

GOLDEN GLORIES

6 *gorsey* covered with gorse, a low spiny shrub with yellow flowers.

JOHNNY / FOUNDED ON AN ANECDOTE OF THE FIRST FRENCH REVOLUTION

'Christina got this pretty anecdote from a book in my possession ... *Recueil d'Actions Héroïques des Républicains Français* [1793], par Léonard Bourdon [1754–1807].' The story, as WR reports it, involves an eight-year-old boy who sold his 'fine head of hair' to a wig maker in order to earn money to give his dying mother. After she died, a soldier adopted the boy ('Notes' 488).

"HOLLOW-SOUNDING AND MYSTERIOUS"

Title 'Some readers will recognize this title as being a phrase applied to the sea in a poem by Mrs. Hemans' ('Notes' 488). The poem is probably 'The Treasures of the Deep' (1839), which contains the lines: 'What hidest thou in thy treasure-caves and cells? / Thou hollow-sounding and mysterious main! –' (ll. 1–2). For Hemans, see headnote of 'L. E. L.'

MAIDEN MAY

74 *Vanity of vanities* see note for l. 1 of 'One Certainty'.
91 *Let today suffice today* 'Take therefore no thought for the morrow: for the morrow shall take thought for the things of itself. Sufficient unto the day is the evil thereof' (Matt. 6:34).
95 *Watch and pray* Matt. 26:41. See note for Part 2, l. 1 of 'Old and New Year Ditties'.

BRANDONS BOTH

67 *The dead to the dead* 'But Jesus said unto him, Follow me; and let the dead bury their dead' (Matt. 8:22; see also Luke 9:60).

A LIFE'S PARALLELS

11 *Faint yet pursuing* 'And Gideon came to Jordan, and passed over, he, and the three hundred men that were with him, faint, yet pursuing them' (Jud. 8:4). This verse describes the march of Gideon's army from one battle to another, during which they crossed the River Jordan – emblematic of crossing from this life to the next in Christianity. Marsh suggests that this poem was probably written in mourning for MR, who died Nov. 1876 (*CR Poems* 439).

AT LAST

13 *that better part* see note for l. 7 of ' "A Bruised Reed Shall He Not Break" '.

IN THE WILLOW SHADE

13 *All things are vain* see note for l. 1 of 'One Certainty'.
52 *the unworking night* 'I must work the works of him that sent me, while it is day: the night cometh, when no man can work' (John 9:4). Cf. the *Book of Common Prayer*: 'take we heed betime, while the day of salvation lasteth; for the night cometh, when none can work'.

WHAT'S IN A NAME?

Title 'What's in a name? That which we call a rose / By any other name would smell as sweet' (*Romeo and Juliet* II.ii.43–4).

MARIANA

Cf. Tennyson's 'Mariana' (1830), which also tells the story of a woman yearning for an absent love; in 1851, Millais painted *Mariana*, based on it. (For Millais, see headnote of 'Maude Clare'.)

MEMENTO MORI

Title a reminder of death, such as a skull or other symbolic object; literally, 'Remember that you have to die' (Latin).

"ONE FOOT ON SEA, AND ONE ON SHORE"

Title 'Sigh no more, ladies, sigh no more, / Men were deceivers ever; / One foot in sea, and one on shore; / To one thing constant never' (*Much Ado About Nothing* II.iii.62–5).

BOY JOHNNY

1 *busk you* dress yourself.

FREAKS OF FASHION

WR reports this was first published in 'a so-called *Girls' Annual*, 1878' ('Notes' 488).

8 *hahas* sunken or trench-type boundaries to a garden.
52 *aurigerous* gilded.

AN OCTOBER GARDEN

[First published in *Athenaeum*, no. 2609 (17 Oct. 1877), 532.]

"SUMMER IS ENDED"

William Bell Scott (see headnote of 'At Home') wrote a reply to this poem which he sent to CR with dried rose leaves. She copied it on a blank end leaf of her mother's presentation copy of *A Pageant* (1881). Bell Scott's poem and CR's apparent appreciation of it are published in Packer's biography as an instance of what Packer supposed to be the 'past passion' between the two (Packer, *CR* 342).

Title 'The harvest is past, the summer is ended, and we are not saved' (Jer. 8:20).

PASSING AND GLASSING

22–4 *For there is nothing new beneath the sun . . . And that which shall be was* see note for l. 11 of 'One Certainty'.

"I WILL ARISE"

Title allusion to Jesus' parable of the Prodigal Son, who leaves his father's house and spends his inheritance in 'riotous living' (Luke 15:11–32). At the lowest point of his misery, he says: 'I will arise and go to my father, and will say unto him, Father, I have sinned against heaven, and before thee' (15:18). He decides to return as a hired servant, but his father receives him as an honoured guest. See also the following poem, 'A Prodigal Son'.

A PRODIGAL SON

Many of the details and much of the language come from the parable of the Prodigal Son: see note for title of ' "I Will Arise" ', above.

SOEUR LOUISE DE LA MISÉRICORDE / (1674)

The Duchesse de la Vallière, mistress of Louis XIV, entered a Carmelite Convent in 1674 and assumed the veil, becoming 'Soeur Louise' (Sister Louise) in 1675 ('Notes' 488).

Title *Miséricorde* compassion, mercy (French).
5 *vanity of vanities* see note for l. 1 of 'One Certainty'.

AN "IMMURATA" SISTER

[Lines 1–12 and 17–24 composed June 1865; date of composition of ll. 13–16 and 25–8 unknown.]

Title *IMMURATA* walled up, immured (Italian). An 'immured' sister is a nun belonging to an enclosed order.
4 These stanzas follow l. 4 in MS1 (BL), and were published in 1904 under the MS title 'En Route'.

Wherefore art thou strange, and not my mother?
  Thou has stolen my heart and broken it:
Would that I might call thy sons 'My brother',
  Call thy daughters 'Sister sweet';
Lying in thy lap not in another,
  Dying at thy feet.

Farewell land of love, Italy,
  Sister-land of Paradise;
With mine own feet I have trodden thee,
  Have seen with mine own eyes;
I remember, thou forgettest me,
  I remember thee.

Blessed be the land that warms my heart,
  And the kindly clime that cheers,
And the cordial faces clear from art,
  And the tongue sweet in mine ears:
Take my heart, its truest tenderest part,
  Dear land, take my tears.

WR noted that presumably the poem was written 'while my sister, along with my mother and myself, was making a flying visit to North Italy' in 1865 ('Notes' 485).

25 *Sparks fly upward toward their fount of fire* 'Yet man is born unto trouble, as the sparks fly upward' (Job 5:7).

28 *whole burnt-offering* this phrase had special significance for CR. In her entry in *TF* for 21 Jan. (Feast of St Agnes, Virgin Martyr), CR tells the story of St Agnes, who refused the marriage proposal of 'a youth of distinguished birth. But she, for spouse would have none save the Lamb of God: Who keeping her pure alike in body and in soul, accepted her as His whole burnt offering. Nevertheless the lighted pyre on which she prayed died out of itself: and unscathed by that death, and unshackled by man, she won her victory by submitting to the sword in the persecution under Diocletian' (17–18). In *SF*, CR writes about God as a jealous God, adding that 'the heart offered as a whole burnt-offering to Him becomes fuel not to His consuming jealousy but to His undying love' (51); and of the three youths placed in the fiery furnace, whose story is told in Daniel and celebrated in the apocryphal 'The Song of the Three Holy Children', she writes that they 'offered their own bodies to God as an acceptable whole burnt-sacrifice' (*SF* 164); see also note to ll. 5–6 of 'Martyrs' Song'. In her commentary on Rev. 8:4 ('And the smoke of the incense, which came with the prayers of the saints, ascended up before God out of the angel's hand'), she writes: 'the incense and smoke of the incense should kindle us to utmost adoration and love, by thus setting before us Christ

Who for our sakes made Himself once for all a whole Burnt Offering, an Offering and a sweet-smelling Savour to the Glory of God the Father . . .' (*FD* 245).

"IF THOU SAYEST, BEHOLD, WE KNEW IT NOT"

Title Pro. 24:12.

1

2 *My brother's blood* see note for Part 1, title of 'The German-French Campaign. 1870–1871'.

2

5 *Seek us and find us* 'Ask, and it shall be given you; seek, and ye shall find; knock, and it shall be opened unto you' (Matt. 7:7; Luke 11:9; see also John 16:23–4).

3

5 *Vanity of vanities* see note for l. 1 of 'One Certainty'.
12 *nard* aromatic balsam or ointment used by the ancients, derived from the plant of the same name.

THE THREAD OF LIFE

Packer, noting Coleridge's influence on this poem, calls it CR's equivalent of 'a Dejection ode [1802]' (Packer, *CR* 321).

2

14 *But what I was I am, I am even I* Packer (*CR* 323) points out that CR includes a prose statement of this theme in *FD*:

Concerning Himself, God Almighty proclaimed of old: 'I AM THAT I AM' [Ex. 3:14], and man's inherent feeling of personality seems in some sort to attest and correspond to this revelation: I who am myself cannot but be myself. I am what God has constituted me: so that however I may have modified myself, yet do I remain that same I; it is I who live, it is I who must die, it is I who must rise again at the last day. I rising out of my grave must carry on that very life which was mine before I died, and of which death itself could not altogether snap the thread. Who I was I am, who I am I am, who I am I must be for ever and ever.

I the sinner of to-day am the sinner of all the yesterdays of my life. I may loathe myself or be amazed at myself, but I cannot unself myself for ever and ever. (*FD* 47)

3

6 *sanative* curative healing; promoting moral or spiritual health.

9–10 *And this myself as king unto my King / I give* this image of the soul as king appears in CR's commentary on Rev. 1:6: 'each of us king with subject self to rule' (*FD* 16; quoted in Catherine Musello Cantalupo, 'Christina Rossetti: The Devotional Poet and the Rejection of Romantic Nature', in Kent, *Achievement* 291).

13–14 *He bids me sing: O death, where is thy sting? / And sing: O grave, where is thy victory* 'O death, where is thy sting? O grave, where is thy victory?' (1 Cor. 15:55).

AN OLD-WORLD THICKET

WR says this poem 'bears a certain analogy' to 'From House to Home', although the essence of the earlier poem is 'unison with the Church Triumphant, through self-abnegation', while this has more to do with 'the scheme of redemption, and the flock of Christ' ('Notes' 463). Packer says that in this poem 'the Wordsworthian concept of the healing power of nature provides the instrument for reconciliation' and calls it CR's 'equivalent of an Intimations ode' (Packer, *CR* 322, 321): William Wordsworth (1770–1850), 'Ode: Intimations of Immortality from Recollections of Early Childhood' (1807). Cantalupo points out that 'The "old-world thicket" is an ironic allusion to the Romantic landscape that is the unique and tangible medium of the poet's purgation – the Keatsian "thicket" of "Ode to a Nightingale" [1820]' ('CR: The Devotional Poet', in Kent, *Achievement* 293), and adds that 'Stanzas 21 to 28 are reminiscent of the *spiritus vertiginis* of St John of the Cross [1542–91], the spirit that destroys a person's capacity for private judgment because it "darkens their sense in such a way that it fills them with numerous scruples and perplexities" (*Dark Night of the Soul* [[1618]] trans. Allison Peers, 'Double Image' [1959], p. 88)' (297). Marsh sees the 'Old-World' as referring to 'the Covenant of the Old Law, before the coming of Christ, while the thicket is a reference to the story of Abraham and Isaac ("the ram caught in the thicket", Genesis 23:13) as a type of Christ's sacrifice' (*CR Poems* 446).

Epigraph a dark wood. Dante's *Divine Comedy* opens: 'Midway in our life's journey, I went astray / from the straight road and woke to find myself / alone in a dark wood' (trans. John Ciardi).

74–5 *but all creation / Moaning and groaning* 'For we know that the whole creation groaneth and travaileth in pain together until now' (Rom. 8:22).

86 *deep called to deep* see note for l. 32 of ' "When My Heart Is Vexed, I Will Complain" ' ['O Lord, how canst Thou say Thou lovest me?'].

87 *Out of the deep I called* see note for title of 'De Profundis'.

138 *With yearnings like a smouldering fire that burned* Cantalupo points out that this is an echo of St John of the Cross, who is ' "kindled in love with yearnings" ' ('CR: The Devotional Poet', in Kent, *Achievement* 297).

161–2 *Each twig was tipped with gold, each leaf was edged / And veined with gold from the gold-flooded west* Cantalupo suggests a source in Coleridge's 'Religious Musings' (1796), ll. 99–102: 'Touched by the enchantment of that sudden beam / Straight the black vapour melteth, and in globes / Of dewy glitter gems each plant and tree; / On every leaf, on every blade it hangs!' ('CR: The Devotional Poet', in Kent, *Achievement* 298).

"ALL THY WORKS PRAISE THEE, O LORD" / A PROCESSIONAL OF CREATION

'In 1897 Prebendary Glendinning Nash, the Incumbent of Christ Church, Woburn Square (the church frequented by Christina Rossetti in all her closing years), adapted a portion of this poem for a harvest festival under the name *A Processional of Creation*. It was set to music by Mr. Frank T. Lowden, and sung at the evening service in that church, 21 October' ('Notes' 463). Marsh argues that this poem must originally have been intended for *SF*, CR's study of the Benedicite (*CR* 464).

Title 'All thy works shall praise thee, O Lord; and thy saints shall bless thee' (Ps. 145:10).

23 *I flame His whole burnt-offering* see note for l. 28 of 'An "Immurata" Sister'.

24 *as a bridegroom I rejoice and sing* the image of the sun as a joyous bridegroom occurs in Ps. 19:4–5: 'a tabernacle for the sun, Which is as a bridegroom coming out of his chamber' (see also note for l. 12 of 'After This the Judgment').

44 *And God Who poised our weights and weighs our worth* see note for Part 13, l. 6 of 'Monna Innominata'.

47 *Ordained me image of His Jealousy* 'the whole land shall be devoured by the fire of his jealousy' (Zeph. 1:18). See also note for l. 28 of 'An "Immurata" Sister'.

146 *He the Lamb of lambs* see note for l. 33 of 'Martyrs' Song'.

180 *With milky mouths we praise God, from the breast* 'Out of the mouths of babes and sucklings thou hast perfected praise' (Matt. 21:16; see also Ps. 8:2).

185 *plenary beatitude* complete blessedness.

189–91 *Let everything that hath . . . breath . . . Praise God* 'Let every thing that hath breath praise the Lord' (Ps. 150:6).

LATER LIFE: A DOUBLE SONNET OF SONNETS

Marsh says that this sequence 'seems to draw on John Donne's nineteen *Holy Sonnets* [1633] with their alternation between despair, self-laceration and faithful hope.'

1

1–2 *Before the mountains were brought forth, before / Earth and the world were made, then God was God* 'Before the mountains were brought forth, or ever thou hadst formed the earth and the world, even from everlasting to everlasting, thou art God' (Ps. 90:2).

5–6 *His rod / Of righteous wrath* 'the rod of mine anger' (Isa. 10:5).

9 *For tho' He slay us we will trust in Him* 'Though he slay me, yet will I trust in him: but I will maintain mine own ways before him' (Job 13:15).

2

1 *Rend hearts and rend not garments* 'rend your heart, and not your garments' (Joel 2:13).

5 *the race* see note for ll. 11–12 of 'Who Shall Deliver Me?'

3

2 *Oh bear in mind our dust and nothingness* 'he remembereth that we are dust' (Ps. 103:14).

4

5 *watch or pray* see note for Part 2, l. 1 of 'Old and New Year Ditties'.

13–14 *Me now, as once the Thief in Paradise, / Even me, O Lord my Lord, remember me* see note for l. 8 of 'Good Friday' ['Am I a stone and not a sheep'].

6

10 *And all in vain to look to left or right* 'Turn not to the right hand nor to the left' (Pro. 4:27).

8

6 *Our life, our light, if once we turn to Thee* 'I am the light of the world: he that followeth me shall not walk in darkness, but shall have the light of life' (John 8:12).

10

10 *Thy dead thou shalt give up, nor hide thy slain* 'Thy dead men shall live, together with my dead body shall they arise. Awake and sing, ye that dwell in dust: for thy dew is as the dew of herbs, and the earth shall cast out the dead' (Isa. 26:19).

11–12 *Some who went weeping forth shall come again / Rejoicing* 'He that goeth forth and weepeth, bearing precious seed, shall doubtless come again with rejoicing, bringing his sheaves with him' (Ps. 126:6).

13 *As doves fly to their windows* 'Who are these that fly as a cloud, and as the doves to their windows?' (Isa. 60:8).

Footnote from Canto V of Dante's *Inferno*: 'As mating doves that love calls to their nest / glide through the air with motionless raised wings, / borne by the sweet desire that fills each breast –' (ll. 82–4, trans. John Ciardi). See note for ll. 60–62 of 'The Hour and the Ghost'.

13

4 *bruit* report.

11 *cautery* heated metallic instrument used for burning or searing organic tissue.

17

4 *Past certain cliffs, along one certain beach* WR identifies this as the beach of Hastings and St Leonard's ('Notes' 463). 'Between 1860 and 1884, [CR] made several trips to Hastings because of her precarious health. She was greatly pleased by the place and attempted to write about its fishermen in "The Waves of this Troublesome World," one of her stories included in *Commonplace*' (Uffelman, 'CR's *A Pageant and Other Poems*', 252).

18

[Lines 9–14 originally part of 'Cor Mio' ['Still sometimes in my secret heart of hearts'], which CR never published as such but which was printed in 1896.]

21

'The reference to foreign travel in this sonnet and its successor relates to the year 1865, when Christina, along with our mother, accompanied me to North Italy through Switzerland' ('Notes' 463). Uffelman adds that this poem refers to a night when CR and WR 'took a boat ride on Lake Como' ('CR's *A Pageant and Other Poems*', 256).

22

1–2 *The mountains in their overwhelming might / Moved me to sadness when I saw them first* CR comments on this experience in her entry for 10 June in *TF*, adding that she 'passed indoors, losing sight for a moment of the mountains'. Then, looking out of a window, she saw that 'the evening flush had turned snow to a rose, "and sorrow and sadness fled away"' (111).

9–14 *All Switzerland . . . its crown* this section apparently alludes to an experience recounted in *TF* for 14 June, where CR describes how she came upon a garden of forget-me-nots while ascending Mount St Gotthard. She draws in this a lesson, first about the allotment of gifts among 'the human family'. Then she asks: 'And what shall they do, who display neither loftiness nor loveliness? If "one member be honoured, all the members rejoice with it." ' In any case, even if 'this standard appears too exalted for frail flesh and blood to attain', then we can be reminded that the 'crowning summit of Mount St. Gotthard abides invested, not with flowers, but with perpetual snow'. Thus, in 'foresight of the grave, whither we all are hastening, is it worth while to envy any?' (113–14).

23

11 *we run a race* see note for ll. 11–12 of 'Who Shall Deliver Me?'

27

'This forecast of death came singularly true; for, if one had been writing a condensed account of Christina Rossetti's last days and hours in December 1894, one might have described them very nearly in these terms' ('Notes' 463).

13 *saint rejoicing on her bed* WR identifies this as a possible reference to MR, who was an Anglican nun at the time of her death ('Notes' 463).

UNTIL THE DAY BREAK

Title 'Until the day break, and the shadows flee away, turn, my beloved, and be thou like a roe or a young hart upon the mountains of Bether' (Song of Sol. 2:17); 'Until the day break, and the shadows flee away, I will get me to the mountain of myrrh, and to the hill of frankincense' (Song of Sol. 4:6).
5 *The Sower* CR echoes Jesus' parable of the sower in which some seed falls on barren ground and other seed falls on good ground and yields a good harvest (Mark 4:3–8; Matt. 13:3–8; Luke 8:5–8).
25 *Oh for the harvest* 'Pray ye therefore the Lord of the harvest, that he will send forth labourers into his harvest' (Matt. 9:38; see also Luke 10:2).

"OF HIM THAT WAS READY TO PERISH"

Title 'The blessing of him that was ready to perish came upon me' (Job 29:13).
3 *My wandering love hath not where to lay its head* see note for l. 28 of 'The Three Enemies'.
9 *How long, O Lord, how long* see note for Part 2, l. 12 of 'Old and New Year Ditties'.
17 *Come to Me and I will give thee rest* 'Come unto me, all ye that labour and are heavy laden, and I will give you rest' (Matt. 11:28).
18 *Take on thee My yoke and learn of Me* 'Take my yoke upon you, and learn of

me; for I am meek and lowly in heart: and ye shall find rest unto your souls'
(Matt. 11:29).

19 *Who calledst a little child to come to Thee* 'But Jesus said, Suffer little children,
and forbid them not, to come unto me: for of such is the kingdom of heaven'
(Matt. 19:14; see also Mark 10:14 and Luke 18:16).

20 *And pillowedst John on Thy breast* see note for l. 13 of 'After Communion'.

21 *Who spak'st to women that followed Thee sorrowing* 'But Jesus turning unto them
said, Daughters of Jerusalem, weep not for me, but weep for yourselves, and
for your children' (Luke 23:28). See note for ll. 5–6 of 'Good Friday' ['Am I a
stone and not a sheep'].

23 *Who didst welcome the outlaw adoring Thee all alone* see note for l. 8 of 'Good
Friday' ['Am I a stone and not a sheep'].

31 *Bid me also to Paradise* see note for l. 8 of 'Good Friday' ['Am I a stone and
not a sheep'].

''BEHOLD THE MAN!''

Title 'Then came Jesus forth, wearing the crown of thorns, and the purple
robe. And Pilate saith unto them, Behold the man!' (John 19:5).

13 *Not to send peace but send a sword He came* 'Think not that I am come to send
peace on earth: I came not to send peace, but a sword' (Matt. 10:34).

THE DESCENT FROM THE CROSS

5 *Yea, this defaced* see note for l. 24 of 'The Three Enemies'.

''IT IS FINISHED''

Title see note for l. 1 of 'Amen'.

46 *To Judgment when the Trump is blown* 'In a moment, in the twinkling of an
eye, at the last trump: for the trumpet shall sound, and the dead shall be raised
incorruptible, and we shall be changed' (1 Cor. 15:52); 'And I beheld, and
heard an angel flying through the midst of heaven, saying with a loud voice,
Woe, woe, woe, to the inhabiters of the earth by reason of the other voices of
the trumpet of the three angels, which are yet to sound!' (Rev. 8:13).

AN EASTER CAROL

4 *The rain is over and gone* see note for ll. 53–6 of 'Advent' ['This Advent moon shines cold and clear'].

"BEHOLD A SHAKING"

WR sees in the first of these two sonnets 'an evident recasting of the third sonnet in the series . . . named *By Way of Remembrance*' ('Notes' 476).

Title 'So I prophesied as I was commanded: and as I prophesied, there was a noise, and behold a shaking, and the bones came together, bone to his bone' (Eze. 37:7). See also note for ll. 60–62 of 'Christian and Jew. A Dialogue'.

I

3 *All kindreds of all nations of all speech* 'After this I beheld, and, lo, a great multitude, which no man could number, of all nations, and kindreds, and people, and tongues stood before the throne' (Rev. 7:9; see also Rev. 5:9).

ALL SAINTS ['They are flocking from the East']

16 *Zion* one of the hills of Jerusalem on which the city of David was built and which became the centre of Hebrew life and worship. See also note for ll. 43–4 of 'Christian and Jew. A Dialogue'.

"TAKE CARE OF HIM"

Title when a lawyer asked Jesus what he could do to inherit eternal life, Jesus asked him: 'What is written in the law?' The lawyer answered: 'Thou shalt love the Lord thy God with all thy heart and with all thy soul, and with all thy strength, and with all thy mind; and thy neighbour as thyself.' He then went on to ask: 'And who is my neighbour?' Jesus responded with the parable of the Good Samaritan, in which a man is attacked by thieves and left 'half dead', lying by the road. He is helped neither by the priest nor by the Levite, but by a despised Samaritan, who takes him to an inn and tells the host: 'Take care of him.' When Jesus asked, 'Which now of these three, thinkest thou, was neighbour unto him that fell among the thieves?', the lawyer answered, 'He that shewed mercy on him.' Jesus then said, 'Go, and do thou likewise' (Luke 10:25–37). A Levite was a member of the tribe of Levi and assisted priests in the temple of Jerusalem.

16 *what lack I yet* when a rich young ruler asked Jesus what he should do to have eternal life, Jesus told him to keep the commandments. 'The young man saith unto him, All these things have I kept from my youth up: what lack I yet?' (Matt. 19:20). When Jesus responded that he should sell his possessions and give to the poor and follow him (see note for ll. 17–19 of 'I, Lord, Thy foolish sinner low and small'), the young man walked away, 'for he had great possessions' (Matt. 19:22; see also Mark 10:17–22 and Luke 18:18–23).

32 *Thou diddest it to Me* at the Last Judgement, said Jesus, the King (God) will say to the righteous that they have fed and clothed him; and they will ask when did they do so. 'And the King shall answer and say unto them, Verily I say unto you, Inasmuch as ye have done it unto one of the least of these my brethren, ye have done it unto me' (Matt. 25:40).

A MARTYR / The Vigil Of The Feast

1–2 *without gnash of teeth / Or weeping* 'But the children of the kingdom shall be cast out into outer darkness: there shall be weeping and gnashing of teeth' (Matt. 8:12; see also Matt. 22:13).

3 *the Everlasting Arms* 'The eternal God is thy refuge, and underneath are the everlasting arms' (Deut. 33:27).

7 *thro' Thy darkened pillar* see notes for ll. 70–71 of 'By the Waters of Babylon. B.C. 570' and for l. 9 of ' "Slain from the foundation of the world" '.

17 *I am the Way, the Truth, the Life* 'Jesus saith unto him, I am the way, the truth, and the life: no man cometh unto the Father, but by me' (John 14:6).

32 *Chariot of fire and horses of sheer fire* Elijah (Elias), a prophet of the ninth century BC, was taken up to heaven in a whirlwind in a chariot of fire: 'behold, there appeared a chariot of fire, and horses of fire . . . and Elijah went up by a whirlwind into heaven' (2 Kings 2:11).

35 *Let not the waters close above my head* 'Let not the waterflood overflow me, neither let the deep swallow me up, and let not the pit shut her mouth upon me' (Ps. 69:15).

52 *Thy silly heartless dove* 'like a silly dove without heart' (Hos. 7:11).

57 *Thy fierce anger* the 'fierce anger of the Lord' is used throughout the Old Testament (e.g. Num. 25:4).

72 *As once by lonely Paul in his distress* most likely an allusion to Paul and other prisoners in a ship being tossed by a storm; an angel appeared saying: 'Fear not, Paul' (Acts 27:24). See also headnote of 'Conversion of St. Paul'.

75 *As one dove to an ark on shoreless sea* after the Flood, Noah sent out a dove to find dry land: 'But the dove found no rest for the sole of her foot, and she returned unto him into the ark, for the waters were on the face of the whole earth: then he put forth his hand, and took her, and pulled her in unto him into the ark' (Gen. 8:9).

93 *set Thou me up upon the rock* 'For in the time of trouble he shall hide me in his pavilion: in the secret of his tabernacle shall he hide me; he shall set me upon a rock' (Ps. 27:5).

119 *Ashes made ashes, earth becoming earth* when God cursed Adam, he said: 'In the sweat of thy face shalt thou eat bread, till thou return unto the ground; for out of it wast thou taken: for dust thou art, and unto dust shalt thou return' (Gen. 3:19). See also the Order for the Burial of the Dead in the *Book of Common Prayer*: 'we therefore commit *his* body to the ground; earth to earth, ashes to ashes, dust to dust'.

125 *I sit alone, my mouth is in the dust* 'He sitteth alone and keepeth silence, because he hath borne it upon him. He putteth his mouth in the dust; if so be there may be hope' (Lam. 3:28–9).

134–5 *The sun and moon grew dark for sympathy, / And earth cowered quaking* see note for l. 64 of 'After This the Judgment'.

139 *If trouble comes not from the south or north* the Old Testament prophets often warned of danger coming from the south or north – e.g. 'for evil appeareth out of the north, and great destruction' (Jer. 6:1).

145 *Shorten the race* see note for ll. 11–12 of 'Who Shall Deliver Me?'

WHY?

'It will be seen that this sonnet bears some relation to another sonnet, *If only* . . . and to the lyric, *When my heart is vexed I will complain*' ('Notes' 476).

"LOVE IS STRONG AS DEATH" [' "I have not sought Thee, I have not found Thee" ']

Title see note for l. 1 of 'An End'.
10 *the Everlasting Arms* see note for l. 3 of 'A Martyr. The Vigil Of the Feast'.

Poems Added in *Poems* (1888, 1890)

[Except where noted, dates of composition are unknown. Editions: 1888a, *1890*, 1904.]

BIRCHINGTON CHURCHYARD

[First published in *Athenaeum*, no. 2844 (29 April 1882), 538.]

Title WR identifies this as the 'churchyard in which Dante Gabriel Rossetti was buried in the same month when this sonnet was written' ('Notes' 488).

ONE SEA-SIDE GRAVE

[Composed 8 Feb. 1853. First published in *Century Magazine* 28 (May 1884), 134.]

'It would seem to most people that these lines also relate to Birchington; my belief, however, is that they relate to Hastings, where Charles Cayley lies buried' ('Notes' 488–9).

BROTHER BRUIN

'I think this may probably have been written in consequence of a letter I sent, enclosing for Christina a "history of a maltreated bear, from yesterday's *Daily News*"' ('Notes' 489).

9 *Pandean* of Pan.

"A HELPMEET FOR HIM"

[First published in *"New and Old:" For Seed-Time and Harvest* 16 (Jan. 1888), 22.]

Title allusion to the creation of Eve. See note for Part 5, l. 14 of 'Monna Innominata'.

A SONG OF FLIGHT

12 *To race for the promised prize* see note for ll. 11–12 of 'Who Shall Deliver Me?'

A WINTRY SONNET

[First published in *Macmillan's Magazine* 47 (April 1883), 498.]

8 *earth's rivers cannot fill the main* see note for ll. 10–11 of 'A Testimony'.

RESURGAM

[First published in *Athenaeum*, no. 2831 (28 Jan. 1882), 124.]

Title I shall rise again (Latin).
6 *wins the race* see note for ll. 11–12 of 'Who Shall Deliver Me?'

TODAY'S BURDEN

[First published in T. Hall Caine (ed.), *Sonnets of Three Centuries: A Selection, Including Many Examples Hitherto Unpublished* (Elliot Stock, 1882), 190.]

1 *Arise, depart, for this is not your rest* 'Arise ye, and depart; for this is not your rest: because it is polluted, it shall destroy you, even with a sore destruction' (Micah 2:10).

"THERE IS A BUDDING MORROW IN MIDNIGHT"

Title from Keats's sonnet 'To Homer' (1848), l. 11.

EXULTATE DEO

Title Rejoice in the Lord (Latin). The *Book of Common Prayer* prints this as the title for Psalm 81: 'Sing we merrily unto God our strength: make a cheerful noise unto the God of Jacob' (81:1).
11 *Deep unto deep* see note for l. 32 of ' "When My Heart Is Vexed, I Will Complain" ' ['O Lord, how canst Thou say Thou lovest me?'].

A HOPE CAROL

[First published in *Century Guild Hobby Horse*, no. 10 (April 1888), 41.]

CHRISTMAS CAROLS

1 ['Whoso hears a chiming for Christmas at the nighest']
[Editions: 1888a, *1890*, 1896, 1904. First published in *Century Guild Hobby Horse*, no. 5 (Jan. 1887), 1.]

Title A CHRISTMAS CAROL *1887, 1896*.

2 ['A holy, heavenly chime']

28–9 *That Voice which spake with might /* —*'Let there be light'* 'And God said, Let there be light: and there was light' (Gen. 1:3).
35 *Choosing the better part* see note for l. 7 of ' "A Bruised Reed Shall He Not Break" '.
39 *Haste we, make haste* 'And they came with haste, and found Mary, and Joseph, and the babe lying in a manger' (Luke 2:16).
43 *"Glory to God" they sing* the angels sing: 'Glory to God in the highest, and on earth peace, good will toward men' (Luke 2:14).

3 ['Lo! newborn Jesus']
25 *By staff and rod* 'thy rod and thy staff they comfort me' (Ps. 23:4).

A CANDLEMAS DIALOGUE

12 *The tree of life's own bough* complex image of Jesus (the tree of life) offering redemption through his crucifixion on a cross (the bough offered for the sinner to rest on, as a bird might rest on a tree branch). See notes for l. 2 of 'A Pause of Thought' and for ll. 13–14 of 'Eve'.
13 *Am I not Life and Resurrection now* 'Jesus said unto her, I am the resurrection, and the life: he that believeth in me, though he were dead, yet shall he live' (John 11:25).

MARY MAGDALENE AND THE OTHER MARY / A SONG FOR ALL MARIES

'Perhaps the authoress meant something special by the sub-title. She may have been thinking of her mother's second name Mary, and her sister's name Maria' ('Notes' 477).

Title 'In the end of the sabbath, as it began to dawn toward the first day of the week, came Mary Magdalene and the other Mary to see the sepulchre' (Matt. 28:1). Mary Magdalene is traditionally identified with the sinful woman who anointed Jesus's feet – hence the use of the term 'Magdalene' for a reformed prostitute. Along with Jesus' mother and her sister, Mary, the wife of Cleophas, Mary Magdalene was one of the 'three Marys' who stood at the foot of the cross when Jesus was crucified (John 19:25).
8 *Renew Thy youth, as eagle from the nest* 'Who satisfieth thy mouth with good things; so that thy youth is renewed like the eagle's' (Ps. 103:5).
9 *arise to reap* 'And he that sat on the cloud thrust in his sickle on the earth; and the earth was reaped' (Rev. 14:16). In her comments on Rev. 14:15 and 16, CR talks about the ripeness of the harvest and the postponement of

the harvesting of souls by Jesus: 'Imperfectly good people may feel such postponement a keen trial . . .' (*FD* 366).

PATIENCE OF HOPE

[Editions: 1888a, *1890*, 1896, 1904. First published in W. Walsham How, Ashton Oxenden and John Ellerton (eds.), *The Children's Hymn Book for Use in Children's Services, Sunday Schools and Families, Arranged in Order of the Church's Year* (Rivington's, (1881)), 212–13.]

WR reports that the words of the poem 'are set to be sung to the tune "Grasmere" by Mr. Cameron W. H. Brock' ('Notes' 476).

Title *"Thou art the same, and Thy years shall not fail." 1881*; THOU ART THE SAME AND THY YEARS SHALL NOT FAIL *1896*.
  'Remembering without ceasing your work of faith, and labour of love, and patience of hope in our Lord Jesus Christ, in the sight of God and our Father' (1 Thes. 1:3).

Verses (1893)

[For the most part, the poems were drawn from three earlier volumes of poetry and prose: *CS*, *TF* and *FD*. Except where noted, no dates of composition are known. Editions for poems from *CS*: 1881CS, *1893*, 1904. Editions for poems from *TF*: 1885, 1886a, *1893*, 1904. Editions for poems from *FD*: 1892, *1893*, 1904.]

"OUT OF THE DEEP HAVE I CALLED UNTO THEE, O LORD"

Section title see note for title of 'De Profundis'.

['Alone Lord God, in Whom our trust and peace']

FD (288) in CR's commentary on Rev. 11:1.

12 *Thy will be done in earth as heaven today* from the Lord's prayer: 'Thy kingdom come. Thy will be done in earth, as it is in heaven' (Matt. 6:10; see also Luke 11:2).

['Seven vials hold Thy wrath: but what can hold']

FD (377) in CR's commentary on Rev. 15:7: 'And one of the four beasts gave unto the seven angels seven golden vials full of the wrath of God, who liveth for ever and ever.'

Title see headnote, and also 'And I heard a great voice out of the temple saying to the seven angels, Go your ways, and pour out the vials of the wrath of God upon the earth' (Rev. 16:1). CR connects these seven vials with Jesus' answer to the question of how often we should forgive someone who has sinned against us (see note for l. 24 of 'After This the Judgment'). She attempts to justify God's wrath in the face of Jesus' words of forgiveness: 'Seven offences had not sufficed to draw down this sevenfold judgment, nay, nor seventy times seven, had man but turned and said, I repent. For certainly God All-Holy proposeth not to any a higher standard than His own' (*FD* 380).

7 *Heard of at Ephrata, found in the Wood* 'Lo, we heard of it at Ephratah: we found it in the fields of the wood' (Ps. 132:6). Ephrata is the ancient name for Bethlehem.

9–12 *that dove . . . Whom Noah's hand pulled in* see note for l. 75 of 'A Martyr. The Vigil Of The Feast'.

"Where neither rust nor moth doth corrupt"

FD (454) in CR's commentary on Rev. 19:17–18: 'And I saw an angel standing in the sun; and he cried with a loud voice, saying to all the fowls that fly in the midst of heaven, Come and gather yourselves together unto the supper of the great God; That ye may eat the flesh of kings, and the flesh of captains, and the flesh of mighty men, and the flesh of horses, and of them that sit on them, and the flesh of all men, both free and bond, both small and great.'

Title [untitled] *1892*.
    See note for ll. 13–14 of 'A Testimony'.

3 *world or flesh or devil* see headnote of 'The Three Enemies'.

9–10 *Not with the sparrow . . . But with the swallow tabernacling so* 'Yea, the sparrow hath found an house, and the swallow a nest for herself, where she may lay her young, even thine altars, O LORD of hosts, my King, and my God' (Ps. 84:3).

14 *the everlasting hills* see note for ll. 5–6 of 'A Better Resurrection'.

"As the sparks fly upwards"

FD (460) in CR's commentary on Rev. 20:2–3.

Title [untitled] *1892*.
   See note for l. 25 of 'An "Immurata" Sister'.
4–5 *Thy Name / Yesterday, this day, day by day the Same* 'Jesus Christ the same yesterday, and to day, and for ever' (Heb. 13:8).
10 *they have set their face* see note for l. 211 of 'From House to Home'.

['Lord, make us all love all: that when we meet']

FD (70–71) in CR's commentary on Rev. 2:15.

7 *flaming car* see note for l. 91 of 'The Convent Threshold'. In Milton's *Paradise Lost* Satan is described as crossing 'the car of Night' (IX.65). See also note for l. 32 of 'A Martyr. The Vigil Of The Feast'.
9 *if our brother's blood cry out at us* see note for Part 1, title of 'The German-French Campaign. 1870–1871'.
14 *the Vision Beatifical* a sight of the glories of Heaven, as, e.g. the vision granted to Dante's pilgrim at the end of *The Divine Comedy*. In *TF*, CR characterizes the 'Christian heaven of the Beatific Vision' as a 'heaven of music' (29).

['O Lord, I am ashamed to seek Thy Face']

FD (128) in CR's commentary on Rev. 3:12–13 (see headnote of ' "He shall go no more out" ').

10 *Call me Thy sinner unto penitence* 'I came not to call the righteous, but sinners to repentance' (Mark 2:17; Luke 5:32; see also Matt. 9:13).
12 *Set me above the waterfloods* see note for l. 35 of 'A Martyr. The Vigil Of The Feast'.
13 *Devil and shifting world and fleshly sense* see headnote of 'The Three Enemies'.

['It is not death, O Christ, to die for Thee']

FD (210) in CR's commentary on Rev. 6:9: 'And when he had opened the fifth seal, I saw under the altar the souls of them that were slain for the word of God, and for the testimony which they held.'

5 *Thyself who Wast and Art and Art to Be* 'And I heard the angel of the waters say, Thou art righteous, O Lord, which art, and wast, and shalt be, because thou hast judged thus' (Rev. 16:5).

13 *A handful of sun-courting heliotrope* cf. 'Roses blushing red and white', ll. 5–6: 'Dim sweet-scented heliotrope, / For hope'.

14 *Of myrrh a bundle* 'A bundle of myrrh is my well-beloved unto me; he shall lie all night betwixt my breasts' (Song of Sol. 1:13).

['Lord, grant us eyes to see and ears to hear']

FD (92) in CR's commentary on Rev. 3:4.

Title 'Yet the LORD hath not given you an heart to perceive, and eyes to see, and ears to hear, unto this day' (Deut. 29:4).

11 *Not as the world gives* 'Peace I leave with you, my peace I give unto you: not as the world giveth, give I unto you' (John 14:27).

13 *With walls of jasper and with streets of gold* see note for ll. 35–6 of 'Paradise'.

14 *And Thou Thyself, Lord Christ, for Corner Stone* 'Wherefore also it is contained in the scripture, Behold, I lay in Sion a chief corner stone, elect, precious: and he that believeth on him shall not be confounded' (1 Pet. 2:6). Jesus also referred to himself as the cornerstone (alluding to: 'The stone which the builders refused is become the head stone of the corner' (Ps. 118:22; see also Acts 4:11)): 'Jesus saith unto them, Did ye never read in the scriptures, The stone which the builders rejected, the same is become the head of the corner: this is the Lord's doing, and it is marvellous in our eyes?' (Matt. 21:42; see also Mark 12:10 and Luke 20:17).

"Cried out with Tears"

FD (388–9) in CR's commentary on Rev. 16:21.

Title When an epileptic child was brought to Jesus for healing, he said to the father that 'all things are possible to him that believeth. And straightway the father of the child cried out, and said with tears, Lord, I believe; help thou mine unbelief' (Mark 9:23–4).

3 *Hide not Thy Face from me* Ps. 102:2 and 143:7; see also Ps. 27:9.

5 *who worship with the thief* see note for l. 8 of 'Good Friday' ['Am I a stone and not a sheep'].

11 *Say "Come," say not "Depart"* allusion to the Last Judgement: 'Then shall the King say unto them on his right hand, Come, ye blessed of my Father, inherit the kingdom prepared for you from the foundation of the world ... Then shall he say also unto them on the left hand, Depart from me, ye cursed, into everlasting fire, prepared for the devil and his angels' (Matt. 25:34, 41), in the parable of the kingdom of heaven in which the redeemed (the 'sheep') are set on the right hand of God and the wicked (the 'goats') on the left (Matt. 25:32–46).

12–13 *out of the dust / I look to Thee* 'He raiseth up the poor out of the dust, and lifteth the needy out of the dunghill' (Ps. 113:7).

14 *Thou Face to face* see note for l. 3 of 'Mirrors of Life and Death'.

['O Lord, on Whom we gaze and dare not gaze']

FD (31) in CR's commentary on Rev. 1:12–16.

6 *Companion of the two or three* 'For where two or three are gathered together in my name, there am I in the midst of them' (Matt. 18:20).

8 *Lighten our darkness and amend our ways* 'the Lord my God, will lighten my darkness' (Ps. 18:28); 'Amend your ways . . .' (Jer. 7:3; see also Jer. 18:11 and 26:13); 'Lighten our darkness, we beseech Thee, O Lord' (3rd Collect for Evening Prayer, *Book of Common Prayer*); 'Amend your lives' (Exhortation, Communion, *Book of Common Prayer*).

10 *Our treasure and our heart may dwell at one* 'For where your treasure is, there will your heart be also' (Matt. 6:21; Luke 12:34).

"I will come and heal him"

FD (184) in CR's commentary on Rev. 5:9–10: 'And they sung a new song, saying, Thou art worthy to take the book, and to open the seals thereof: for thou wast slain, and hast redeemed us to God by thy blood out of every kindred, and tongue, and people, and nation; And hast made us unto our God kings and priests: and we shall reign on the earth.'

Title [untitled] *1892*.
'And when Jesus was entered into Capernaum, there came unto him a centurion, beseeching him, And saying, Lord, my servant lieth at home sick of the palsy, grievously tormented. And Jesus saith unto him, I will come and heal him.' But the centurion said: 'Lord, I am not worthy that thou shouldest come under my roof: but speak the word only, and my servant shall be healed. For I am a man under authority, having soldiers under me: and I say to this man, Go, and he goeth; and to another, Come, and he cometh; and to my servant, Do this, and he doeth it' (Matt. 8:5–7, 9–10; see also Luke 7:6–8).

8 *The spark that flies up* see note for l. 25 of 'An "Immurata" Sister'.

14 *No man hath greater love than thus to die* see note for ll. 55–6 of 'After This the Judgment'.

['Ah Lord, Lord, if my heart were right with Thine']

FD (163) in CR's commentary on Rev. 4:11.

5 *Then would Thy Love be more to me than wine* see note for l. 27 of ' "When My Heart Is Vexed, I Will Complain" ' ['O Lord, how canst Thou say Thou lovest me?'].
6 *Then should I seek being sure at length to find* see note for Part 2, l. 5 of ' "If Thou Sayest, Behold, We Knew It Not" '.
14 *long loved, and much forgiven* 'Her sins, which are many, are forgiven; for she loved much' (Luke 7:47).

"The gold of that land is good"

FD (137) in CR's commentary on Rev. 3:17–18.

Title [untitled] *1892*.
   See note for l. 11 of 'Saints and Angels'.

['Weigh all my faults and follies righteously']

[Composed 26 Feb. 1854.]

Entry for 6 April in *TF* (66).

4 *the Accuser* usually associated with Satan, although in *FD*, CR says that sins themselves can be a 'crying accusation' (324).
10 *Oh vanity my work* 'I have seen all the works that are done under the sun; and, behold, all is vanity and vexation of spirit' (Ecc. 1:14).

['Lord, grant me grace to love Thee in my pain']

Entry for 25 June in *TF* (121).

5 *A fading leaf* see note for l. 9 of 'A Better Resurrection'.

['Lord, make me one with Thine own faithful ones']

FD (47) in CR's commentary on Rev. 2:1.

7 *the crystal sea* see note for l. 6 of 'The Convent Threshold'.
10 *Who looked not back with hand upon the plough* 'And Jesus said unto him, No

man, having put his hand to the plough, and looking back, is fit for the kingdom of God' (Luke 9:62).

"Light of Light"

FD (266–7) in CR's commentary on Rev. 9:12 (see headnote of 'One woe is past. Come what come will').

Title [untitled] *1892.*
1 *O Christ our Light* see note for Part 8, l. 6 of 'Later Life'.
11 *What lack I yet* see note for l. 16 of ' "Take Care of Him" '.
13 *His wealth is not of earth* 'My kingdom is not of this world' (John 18:36).

CHRIST OUR ALL IN ALL

Section title 'Which is his body, the fulness of him that filleth all in all' (Eph. 1:23).

"The ransomed of the Lord"

FD (21) in CR's commentary on Rev. 1:7 (see headnote of ' "One of the Soldiers with a Spear pierced His Side" ').

Title [untitled] *1892.*
   'And the ransomed of the LORD shall return, and come to Zion with songs and everlasting joy upon their heads: they shall obtain joy and gladness, and sorrow and sighing shall flee away' (Isa. 35:10).

['Lord, we are rivers running to Thy sea']

FD (144) in CR's commentary on Rev. 3:21–2 (see headnote of 'Who sits with the King in His Throne? Not a slave but a Bride').

"An exceeding bitter cry"

FD (90) in CR's commentary on Rev. 3:3: 'Remember therefore how thou hast received and heard, and hold fast, and repent. If therefore thou shalt not watch, I will come on thee as a thief, and thou shalt not know what hour I will come upon thee.'

Title [untitled] *1892*.

Esau's younger brother Jacob tricked his father into giving him the blessing reserved for the firstborn, which rightfully belonged to Esau. When Esau discovered this: 'he cried with a great and exceeding bitter cry, and said unto his father, Bless me, even me also, O my father' (Gen. 27:34).

3 *Too late for rising from the dead* WR sees in this verse an allusion to Rev. 3:1, 'in which occur the words, "Thou hast a name that thou livest, and art dead"' ('Notes' 474–5).

17–18 *Surely a stone / Would raise Thy praises now* when Jesus made his triumphal entry into Jerusalem, the Pharisees (members of a sect that followed religious laws strictly and literally) told him to rebuke his disciples. Jesus replied that 'if these [my disciples] should hold their peace, the stones would immediately cry out' (Luke 19:40).

['O Lord, when Thou didst call me, didst Thou know']

FD (312–13) in CR's commentary on Rev. 12:2.

3 *Still hankering after Egypt* when the Israelites journeyed through the wilderness, they complained to Moses about the lack of food and expressed regret for having left Egypt: 'We remember the fish, which we did eat in Egypt freely; the cucumbers, and the melons, and the leeks, and the onions, and the garlick' (Num. 11:5).

"Thou, God, seest me"

FD (105–6) in CR's commentary on Rev. 3:7: 'And to the angel of the church in Philadelphia write; These things saith he that is holy, he that is true, he that hath the key of David, he that openeth, and no man shutteth; and shutteth, and no man openeth.'

Title God talked to Abraham and Sarah's slave girl Hagar, telling her she would bear a son, Ishmael: 'And she called the name of the LORD that spake unto her, Thou God seest me: for she said, Have I also here looked after him that seeth me?' (Gen. 16:13).

5 *Shulamite* young woman from the town of Shunem; alternatively, some scholars see this as the feminine form of 'Solomon', or a kind of feminine title for King Solomon. 'Return, return, O Shulamite; return, return, that we may look upon thee. What will ye see in the Shulamite? As it were the company of two armies' (Song of Sol. 6:13).

10 *the Roman spear* the spear that pierced the side of Jesus on the cross (see note for ll. 23–4 of ' "The Love of Christ Which Passeth Knowledge" ').

16 *My royal robe of righteousness* 'for he hath clothed me with the garments of salvation, he hath covered me with the robe of righteousness, as a bridegroom decketh himself with ornaments, and as a bride adorneth herself with her jewels' (Isa. 61:10).

['Lord Jesus, who would think that I am Thine?']

Entry for 8 Aug. in *TF* (152).

"The Name of Jesus"

Entry for 7 Aug. in *TF* (151).
Title FEAST OF THE NAME OF JESUS *1885*, *1886a*.

['Lord God of Hosts, most Holy and most High']

Entry for 1 July in *TF* (125–6).

['Lord, what have I that I may offer Thee?']

Entry for 22 Sept. in *TF* (183–4).

14 *I crave not thine, but thee* 'for I seek not yours, but you' (2 Cor. 12:14).

['If I should say "my heart is in my home" ']

Entry for 6 Sept. in *TF* (172–3).

2 *halidom* holy place.
4–5 *But with its treasure dwells / The heart* see note for l. 10 of 'O Lord, on Whom we gaze and dare not gaze'.

['Leaf from leaf Christ knows']

CS (494–5) in the chapter entitled 'St. Simon and St. Jude, Apostles'.

2 *Himself the Lily and the Rose* see note for l. 11 of 'Long Barren'.
4 *Himself the Shepherd* see note for l. 14 of 'Good Friday' ['Am I a stone and not a sheep'].

5 *Star and star He names* 'He telleth the number of the stars; he calleth them all by their names' (Ps. 147:4).
9–10 *He counts / The flood of ocean* see note for Part 13, l. 6 of 'Monna Innominata'.
11–12 *Grain by grain, His hand / Numbers the innumerable sand* 'Yet the number of the children of Israel shall be as the sand of the sea, which cannot be measured nor numbered' (Hos. 1:10).
16 *all dust* human flesh, or the body. See note for l. 119 of 'A Martyr. The Vigil Of The Feast'.

['Lord, carry me.—Nay, but I grant thee strength']

FD (79) in CR's commentary on Rev. 2:23.

11 *Lord, I believe; help Thou mine unbelief* see note for title of 'Cried Out with Tears'.
13 *The follower is not greater than the Chief* 'The servant is not greater than his lord; neither he that is sent greater than he that sent him' (John 13:16).

['Lord, I am here.—But, child, I look for thee']

FD (28) in CR's commentary on Rev. 1:8 (see headnote of 'Ascension Eve').

13 *Save, Lord, I perish* When Jesus' disciples were in a boat, he appeared to them, walking on the water. Peter began to walk on the water towards Jesus. 'But when he saw the wind boisterous, he was afraid; and beginning to sink, he cried, saying, Lord, save me' (Matt. 14:30). See also note for l. 8 of ' "Judge not according to the appearance" '.

['New creatures; the Creator still the Same']

FD (487) in CR's commentary on Rev. 21:5 (see note for l. 172 of 'From House to Home').

11 *To hold Thee fast and not to let Thee go* see note for ll. 49–51 of 'Advent' ['This Advent moon shines cold and clear'].

"King of kings and Lord of lords"

FD (453–4) in CR's commentary on Rev. 19:16: 'And he hath on his vesture and on his thigh a name written, KING OF KINGS, AND LORD OF LORDS.'

Title see headnote, above; also 1 Tim 6:15: 'Which in his times he shall shew, who is the blessed and only Potentate, the King of kings, and Lord of lords.' This phrase appears in the prayer for the ruler in the Collect for Evening Prayer in the *Book of Common Prayer*.

1–2 *that Name as ointment poured forth / For which the virgins love Thee* 'Because of the savour of thy good ointments thy name is as ointment poured forth, therefore do the virgins love thee' (Song of Sol. 1:3).

['Thy Name, O Christ, as incense streaming forth']

FD (100) in CR's commentary on Rev. 3:5–6 (see note for l. 7 of 'Saints and Angels').

1 *Thy Name, O Christ, as incense streaming forth* see note for ll. 1–2 of ' "King of kings and Lord of lords" ', above.
7 *Shepherd and Door, our Life and Truth and Way* see note for l. 14 of 'Good Friday' ['Am I a stone and not a sheep']; also 'I am the door: by me if any man enter in, he shall be saved, and shall go in and out, and find pasture' (John 10:9); see also note for l. 17 of 'A Martyr. The Vigil Of The Feast'.

"The Good Shepherd"

FD (50) in CR's commentary on Rev. 2:4.

Title [untitled] *1892*.
   See note for l. 14 of 'Good Friday' ['Am I a stone and not a sheep'].
7–8 *Is one worth seeking, when Thou hast of Thine / Ninety and nine* see note for l. 14 of 'Good Friday' ['Am I a stone and not a sheep'].
12 *Accounting gall and wormwood sweet* 'Remembering mine affliction and my misery, the wormwood and the gall' (Lam. 3:19).

"Rejoice with Me"

FD (44) in CR's commentary on Rev. 1:17–18.

Title [untitled] *1892*.
   Allusion to Jesus' parable of the lost sheep; see note for l. 14 of 'Good Friday' ['Am I a stone and not a sheep']. The other parable making the same point is of the woman who loses one of her ten pieces of silver: see note for l. 94 of 'From House to Home'.
1 *Little Lamb, who lost thee* cf. 'Little Lamb, who made thee?' (Blake, 'The Lamb' (1789)).

['Shall not the Judge of all the earth do right?']

Entry for 22 Dec. in *TF* (246).

1 *Shall not the Judge of all the earth do right* from Abraham's argument that it would not be just for God to destroy the wicked city of Sodom: 'That be far from thee to do after this manner, to slay the righteous with the wicked: and that the righteous should be as the wicked, that be far from thee: Shall not the Judge of all the earth do right?' (Gen. 18:25). Abraham's argument persuaded God that if there were ten righteous men in Sodom, it should be spared.
4 *altho' Thou slay* see note for Part 1, l. 9 of 'Later Life'.

['Me and my gift: kind Lord, behold']

FD (542) in CR's commentary on Rev. 22:17.

"He cannot deny Himself"

FD (193–4) in CR's commentary on Rev. 6:1: 'And I saw when the Lamb opened one of the seals, and I heard, as it were the noise of thunder, one of the four beasts saying, Come and see.'

Title [untitled] *1892*.
'If we believe not, yet he abideth faithful; he cannot deny himself' (2 Tim. 2:13).
11–12 *if He should say, / "Come," on that uttermost dread day* see note for l. 11 of ' "Cried out with Tears" '.

"Slain from the foundation of the world"

FD (339) in CR's commentary on Rev. 13:8: 'And all that dwell upon the earth shall worship him, whose names are not written in the book of life of the Lamb slain from the foundation of the world.' CR comments with a reference to Keats's epitaph ('Here lies one whose name was writ in water' (1821)): 'Once more, no neutral book, no neutral ground: no names "written in water," as one death-stricken man predicted of himself, presumably with reference to earthly fame' (338).

Title [untitled] *1892*.
1 *O Lamb of God* see note for l. 33 of 'Martyr's Song'.
5 *mark the race for indeed a crown* see note for ll. 11–12 of 'Who Shall Deliver Me?'
9 *Cloudy Pillar* 'And it came to pass, as Moses entered into the tabernacle, the

cloudy pillar descended, and stood at the door of the tabernacle, and the LORD talked with Moses' (Ex. 33:9). See also note for ll. 70–71 of 'By the Waters of Babylon. B.C. 570'.

['Lord Jesu, Thou art sweetness to my soul']

FD (519) in CR's commentary on Rev. 21:26.

['I, Lord, Thy foolish sinner low and small']

FD (121–2) in CR's commentary on Rev. 3:11 (see note for title of 'That no man take thy Crown').

4 *Who asked, What lack I yet* see note for l. 16 of ' "Take Care of Him" '.
17–19 *I loved that youth who little knew / The true / Width of his want, yet worshipped with goodwill* 'Then Jesus beholding him loved him, and said unto him, One thing thou lackest: go thy way, sell whatsoever thou hast, and give to the poor, and thou shalt have treasure in heaven: and come, take up the cross, and follow me' (Mark 10:21). See also note to l. 16 of ' "Take Care of Him" '.
28 *Not so: for what is that to thee* 'Jesus saith unto him, If I will that he tarry till I come, what is that to thee? follow thou me' (John 21:22).
31 *Keep patience, tho' I slay* see note for Part 1, l. 9 of 'Later Life'.

"Because He first loved us"

FD (202–3) in CR's commentary on Rev. 6:5.

Title 'We love him, because he first loved us' (1 John 4:19).
1 *I was hungry, and Thou feddest me* see note for ll. 13–17 of 'Despised and Rejected'.
5 *Feed My hungry brethren for My sake* Jesus asked Peter three times: 'Lovest thou me?' Each time, when Peter answered 'Yes', Jesus responded, 'Feed my sheep' or 'Feed my lambs' (John 21:15–17).
7 *Love them as I loved thee* 'This is my commandment, That ye love one another, as I have loved you' (John 15:12).

['Lord, hast Thou so loved us, and will not we']

FD (504) in CR's commentary on Rev. 21:15.

2 *Love Thee with heart and mind and strength and soul* 'And thou shalt love the Lord thy God with all thy heart, and with all thy soul, and with all thy mind, and with all thy strength' (Mark 12:30; see also Deut. 6:51, 10:12, 11:13, 30:6; Matt. 22:37; and Luke 10:27).

8 *Ninety and nine unwandering family* see note for ll. 7–8 of '"The Good Shepherd"'.

9 *Souls in green pastures* echo of Ps. 23:1–3: 'The LORD is my shepherd; I shall not want. He maketh me to lie down in green pastures: he leadeth me beside the still waters. He restoreth my soul.'

['As the dove which found no rest']

FD (245–6) in CR's commentary on Rev. 8:5.

1 *As the dove which found no rest* see note for l. 75 of 'A Martyr. The Vigil Of The Feast'.

"Thou art Fairer than the children of men"

Entry for 12 June in *TF* (112).

Title [untitled] *1885, 1886a*.
'Thou art fairer than the children of men: grace is poured into thy lips: therefore God hath blessed thee for ever' (Ps. 45:2).
3–5 *Rose of Sharon . . . Lily of the Valley* see note for l. 11 of 'Long Barren'.

"As the Apple Tree among the trees of the wood"

FD (450) in CR's commentary on Rev. 19:14: 'And the armies which were in heaven followed him upon white horses, clothed in fine linen, white and clean.'

Title [untitled] *1892*.
'As the apple tree among the trees of the wood, so is my beloved among the sons. I sat down under his shadow with great delight, and his fruit was sweet to my taste' (Song of Sol. 2:3).

['None other Lamb, none other Name']

FD (176) in CR's commentary on Rev. 5:6: 'And I beheld, and, lo, in the midst of the throne and of the four beasts, and in the midst of the elders, stood a Lamb as it had been slain, having seven horns and seven eyes, which are the seven Spirits of God sent forth into all the earth.'

9 *Lord, Thou art Life* see note for l. 17 of 'A Martyr. The Vigil Of The Feast'.

"Thy Friend and thy Father's Friend forget not"

[Lines 1–8 composed 26 Aug. 1859; date of composition of ll. 9–16 unknown. Originally part of ' "Then they that feared the Lord spake often one to another" ', which CR never published as such.]

Entry for 18 June in *TF* (116).

Title [untitled] *1885, 1886a*.
    'Thine own friend, and thy father's friend, forsake not; neither go into thy brother's house in the day of thy calamity: for better is a neighbour that is near than a brother far off' (Pro. 27:10).
1 *the narrow way* see note for l. 46 of 'Paradise'.
3 *the Love Feast* see note for l. 471 of *Goblin Market*.

"Surely He hath borne our griefs"

[Lines 1–8 probably composed after 7 March and before 9 May 1853; date of composition of ll. 9–14 unknown.]

Entry for 22 March in *TF* (56).

Title [untitled] *1885, 1886a*.
    'Surely he hath borne our griefs, and carried our sorrows: yet we did esteem him stricken, smitten of God, and afflicted' (Isa. 53:4).
3 *He had no place wherein to lay His Head* see note for l. 28 of 'The Three Enemies'.
5 *The cup . . . He drank of* see note for l. 42 of 'Martyrs' Song'.
7 *He hungered Who the hungry thousands fed* allusion to the miracles of the feeding of thousands of people who had come to hear Jesus: see Matt. 14:21, 15:38; Mark 6:44, 8:9; Luke 9:16; and John 6:11.

"They toil not, neither do they spin"

FD (474) in CR's commentary on Rev. 20:13.

Title [untitled] *1892*.
    See note for title of ' "Consider the Lilies of the Field" ' ['Flowers preach to us if we will hear:—'].
1 *Feeder of the sparrow* see headnote of 'Consider'.
3 *Tho' Thou set me as a mark against Thine arrow* 'He hath bent his bow, and set me as a mark for the arrow' (Lam. 3:12).
5 *As a ploughed up field beneath Thy harrow* 'Thus saith the LORD of hosts; Zion shall be plowed like a field' (Jer. 26:18).

7 *Let that cord be love* 'I drew them with cords of a man, with bands of love: and I was to them as they that take off the yoke on their jaws, and I laid meat unto them' (Hos. 11:4).

['Darkness and light are both alike to Thee']

Entry for 2 Oct. in *TF* (191).

Title Ps. 139:12 (see note for l. 12 of ' "I Will Lift Up Mine Eyes Unto the Hills" ' ['I am pale with sick desire']).
6 *Remember me* see note for l. 8 of 'Good Friday' ['Am I a stone and not a sheep'].
7 *so I may run my race* see note for ll. 11–12 of 'Who Shall Deliver Me?'
8 *That where Thou art there may Thy servant be* 'If any man serve me, let him follow me; and where I am, there shall also my servant be: if any man serve me, him will my Father honour' (John 12:26).
12 *Seeking I find* see note for Part 2, l. 5 of ' "If Thou Sayest, Behold, We Knew It Not" '.
13–14 *oh! that I had wings as hath a dove, / Then would I flee away to rest with Thee* 'And I said, Oh that I had wings like a dove! for then would I fly away, and be at rest' (Ps. 55:6).

"And now why tarriest thou?"

FD (298–9) in CR's commentary on Rev. 11:12: 'And they heard a great voice from heaven saying unto them, Come up hither. And they ascended up to heaven in a cloud; and their enemies beheld them.'
 The poem was set to music and 'sung at Christina's funeral service' ('Notes' 475).

Title [untitled] *1892*.
 'And now why tarriest thou? arise, and be baptized, and wash away thy sins, calling on the name of the Lord' (Acts 22:16).
2 *nearer, my God, to Thee* cf. the hymn by Sarah Flower Adams (1805–48), 'Nearer, my God, to Thee' (1841).
13–14 *lest fainting by the way / We come not to Thee, we who come from far* 'And if I send them away fasting to their own houses, they will faint by the way: for divers of them came from far' (Mark 8:3).
18 *holyday* day set apart for religious observance – later, 'holiday'.

['Have I not striven, my God, and watched and prayed?']

[Composed 30 Sept. 1863.]

Entry for 16 July in *TF* (136).

2 *Have I not wrestled in mine agony* see note for Part 9, ll. 11–12 of 'Monna Innominata'.

4 *Is Thine Arm shortened that Thou canst not aid* see note for ll. 16–17 of 'By the Waters of Babylon. B.C. 570'.

"God is our Hope and Strength"

FD (308) in CR's commentary on Rev. 11:19: 'And the temple of God was opened in heaven, and there was seen in his temple the ark of his testament: and there were lightnings, and voices, and thunderings, and an earthquake, and great hail.'

Title [untitled] *1892*.

   'God is our refuge and strength, a very present help in trouble' (Ps. 46:1).

3 *and where is an Ark for the dove* see note for l. 75 of 'A Martyr. The Feast Of The Vigil'.

9 *Where sin hath abounded make grace to abound* 'Moreover the law entered, that the offence might abound. But where sin abounded, grace did much more abound' (Rom. 5:20).

10 *face unto Face* see note for l. 3 of 'Mirrors of Life and Death'.

['Day and night the Accuser makes no pause']

FD (325) in CR's commentary on Rev. 12:10–12: 'for the accuser of our brethren is cast down, which accused them before our God day and night' (10). See note for l. 4 of 'Weigh all my faults and follies righteously'.

['O mine enemy']

FD (277) in CR's commentary on Rev. 10:5.

7 *To a house prepared* see note for l. 21 of 'The Convent Threshold'.

['Lord, dost Thou look on me, and will not I']

FD (148) in CR's commentary on Rev. 4:1.

"Peace I leave with you"

FD (154) in CR's commentary on Rev. 4:5.

Title [untitled] *1892.*
    See note for l. 11 of ' "Lord, grant us eyes to see and ears to hear" '.
4 *ever the better part* see note for l. 7 of ' "A Bruised Reed Shall He Not Break" '.

['O Christ our All in each, our All in all!']

[Composed 28 Sept. 1862.]

Entry for 26 Jan. in *TF* (21).

8 *my flesh is weak* see note for Part 2, l. 7 of 'Old and New Year Ditties'.

['Because Thy Love hath sought me']

FD (183) in CR's commentary on Rev. 5:9–10 (see headnote of ' "I will come and heal him" '.)

['Thy fainting spouse, yet still Thy spouse']

FD (248) in CR's commentary on Rev. 8:6.

"Like as the hart desireth the water brooks"

FD (182–3) in CR's commentary on Rev. 5:9–10 (see headnote of ' "I will come and heal him" ').

Title [untitled] *1892.*
    'As the hart panteth after the water brooks, so panteth my soul after thee, O God' (Ps. 42:1).
6–8 *Turn, as once turning / Thou didst behold Thy Saint / In deadly extremity* see note for l. 7 of 'Good Friday' ['Am I a stone and not a sheep'].

"That where I am, there ye may be also"

FD (206–7) in CR's commentary on Rev. 6:8.

Title [untitled] *1892*.
   'And if I go and prepare a place for you, I will come again, and receive you unto myself; that where I am, there ye may be also' (John 14:3).

"Judge not according to the appearance"

FD (285) in CR's commentary on Rev. 10:11.

Title [untitled] *1892*.
   'Judge not according to the appearance, but judge righteous judgment' (John 7:24).
8 *Fear not: it is I* 'But he saith unto them, It is I; be not afraid' (John 6:20; see also Matt. 14:27; and Mark 6:50). See also note for l. 13 of 'Lord, I am here.—But, child, I look for thee'.

['My God, wilt Thou accept, and will not we']

FD (60) in CR's commentary on Rev. 2:9.

['A chill blank world. Yet over the utmost sea']

FD (505) in CR's commentary on Rev. 21:16.

9 *Dust to dust, ashes to ashes* see note for l. 119 of 'A Martyr. The Vigil Of The Feast'.

"The Chiefest among ten thousand" ['O Jesu, better than Thy gifts']

FD (149) in CR's commentary on Rev. 4:1.

Title [untitled] *1892*.
   See note for l. 14 of 'Long Barren'.

SOME FEASTS AND FASTS

This section follows the liturgical calendar, as did the popular book of verse *The Christian Year* (1827), by Oxford Movement poet John Keble (1792–1866).

ADVENT SUNDAY

Appendix of *TF* (254).

Title see note for title of 'Advent' ['This Advent moon shines cold and clear'].
1 *Behold, the Bridegroom cometh* see note for l. 3 of 'Advent' ['This Advent moon shines cold and clear'].
10 *Like pure Rebekah at the appointed place* see Gen. 24. The 'appointed place' was the well at which Rebekah met the servant who had been sent to find a wife for Isaac.
12–13 *Like great Queen Esther in her triumphing, / She triumphs in the Presence of her King* 'and the king held out to Esther the golden sceptre that was in his hand. So Esther drew near, and touched the top of the sceptre' (Esther 5:2). See note for l. 104 of 'A Royal Princess'.
14 *she's Dove-eyed* 'Behold, thou art fair, my love; behold, thou art fair; thou hast doves' eyes' (Song of Sol. 1:15; see also 4:1).

ADVENT ['Earth grown old, yet still so green']

Entry for 17 Dec. in *TF* (243).

Title [untitled] *1885, 1886a.*
  See note for title of 'Advent' ['This Advent moon shines cold and clear'].
7 *swathings* the swaddling clothes used to wrap an infant. The image is of the sleeping dead, lying like infants in the swaddling bands of the earth. Behind it is the theological doctrine of 'soul sleep'. See headnote of 'Dream-Land'.

['Sooner or later: yet at last']

CS (295–6) in the chapter entitled 'St. John, Baptist'.

2–6 *The Jordan must be past; / It may be he will overflow . . . up on a heap* allusion to an incident when the priests bearing the Ark of the Covenant crossed the river Jordan 'and the feet of the priests that bare the ark were dipped in the brim of the water, (for Jordan overfloweth all his banks all the time of harvest,)

That the waters which came down from above stood and rose up upon an heap' (Jos. 3:15–16).

10 *Pass veiled within the veil* 'And not as Moses, which put a vail over his face, that the children of Israel could not stedfastly look to the end of that which is abolished: But their minds were blinded . . . even unto this day, when Moses is read, the vail is upon their heart' (2 Cor. 3:13–15).

14 *suretyship* responsibility or obligation undertaken by one person on behalf of another.

30–32 *Then cause to bud Thy rod, / To bloom with blossoms, and to give / Almonds* allusion to Aaron's rod, which, through God's intervention, 'brought forth buds, and bloomed blossoms, and yielded almonds' (Num. 17:8).

CHRISTMAS EVE

Entry for 24 Dec. in *TF* (248).

CHRISTMAS DAY

Entry for 25 Dec. in *TF* (248).

5–7 *Lily of lilies He . . . Rose of roses* see note for l. 11 of 'Long Barren'.
12 *the Lamb of God* see note for l. 33 of 'Martyrs' Song'.

CHRISTMASTIDE

Entry for 29 Dec. in *TF* (251).

Title [untitled] *1885, 1886a.*
4 *Star and Angels gave the sign* the 'angel of the Lord' came to the shepherds 'and the glory of the Lord shone round about them'; after the angel gives the message of Jesus' birth, 'a multitude of the heavenly host praising God' appear (Luke 2:9, 13). See also note for title of 'Epiphany'.

ST. JOHN, APOSTLE

FD (27) in CR's commentary on Rev. 1:8.

Title [untitled] *1892.*
  St John was traditionally thought to be the most beloved of Jesus' disciples and the author of Revelation and the Gospel of John.

4 *Eagle and sun gaze at each other* the eagle is used as an emblem for St John (see Rev. 4:7 and note for l. 6 of 'St. Mark'), and the sun for Jesus.

7–8 *with chains for thy wages, / Strong thy rock* combining of two allusions: 'For this cause therefore have I called for you, to see you, and to speak with you: because that for the hope of Israel I am bound with this chain' (Acts 28:20), and Job 39:28 (see note for ll. 19–23 of 'A Testimony').

9 *Rock of Ages* 'that Rock was Christ' (1 Cor. 10:4); 'Rock of ages, cleft for me' (1775), by Augustus Toplady (1740–78), in *Anglican Hymn Book*.

[' "Beloved, let us love one another," says St. John']

Entry for 27 Dec. (Feast of St John, Apostle and Evangelist) in *TF* (250).

Title FEAST OF ST. JOHN, APOSTLE AND EVANGELIST. *1885, 1886a*.

1 *"Beloved, let us love one another," says St. John* 'Beloved, let us love one another: for love is of God; and every one that loveth is born of God, and knoweth God' (1 John 4:7); and see note for title of 'St. John, Apostle', above.

2 *Eagle of eagles* see note for l. 4 of 'St. John, Apostle', above.

6 *winter is past and gone* see note for ll. 53–6 of 'Advent' ['This Advent moon shines cold and clear'].

HOLY INNOCENTS ['They scarcely waked before they slept']

CS (109–10) in the chapter entitled 'Holy Innocents'.

Title [untitled] *1881CS*.

The Feast of the Holy Innocents is celebrated in late Dec. to commemorate the children whom Herod slaughtered in his vain attempt to find the infant Jesus. Cf. Keble, 'The Holy Innocents' (1827).

['Unspotted lambs to follow the one Lamb']

FD (353) in CR's commentary on Rev. 14:4–5: 'These are they which were not defiled with women; for they are virgins. These are they which follow the Lamb whithersoever he goeth. These were redeemed from among men, being the firstfruits unto God and to the Lamb. And in their mouth was found no guile: for they are without fault before the throne of God.'

EPIPHANY

Entry for 6 Jan. (Feast of the Epiphany) in *TF* (5–6).

Title FEAST OF THE EPIPHANY. *1885, 1886a.*
   From the Greek *epiphaneia* ('manifestation') – a Christian holiday celebrated on 6 January to commemorate the manifestation of Jesus to the Wise Men. The questioners in CR's poem are the wise men who came from the East following the Star of Bethlehem, which appeared to them when Jesus was born: 'And when they were come into the house, they saw the young child with Mary his mother, and fell down, and worshipped him: and when they had opened their treasures, they presented unto him gifts; gold, and frankincense, and myrrh' (Matt. 2:11).
7 *span* distance, with hand stretched, from the tip of the thumb to the tip of the little finger.

EPIPHANYTIDE

FD (108–9) in CR's commentary on Rev. 3:7 (see headnote of ' "Thou, God, seest me" ').

Title [untitled] *1892.*
   See note for title of 'Epiphany', above.
6 *stretch Thy sceptre to us* see note for ll. 12–13 of 'Advent Sunday'.

SEPTUAGESIMA

Entry for 27 Aug. in *TF* (165–6).

Title [untitled] *1885, 1886a.*
   Seventieth day (Latin), that is, the third Sunday before Lent, and the ninth Sunday before Easter.
Epigraph see note for ll. 11–12 of 'Who Shall Deliver Me?'

SEXAGESIMA

FD (296) in CR's commentary on Rev. 11:10.

Title [untitled] *1892.*
   Sixtieth day (Latin), that is, the second Sunday before Lent, and the eighth before Easter.
Epigraph 'And unto Adam he said, Because thou hast hearkened unto the

voice of thy wife, and hast eaten of the tree, of which I commanded thee, saying, Thou shalt not eat of it: cursed is the ground for thy sake; in sorrow shalt thou eat of it all the days of thy life' (Gen. 3:17).

1 *earth was very good* 'And God saw every thing that he had made, and, behold, it was very good' (Gen. 1:31).

11 *God's Acre* graveyard, waiting to be harvested at the Last Judgement.

11–12 *where the happy sleep / All night that is not night* see headnote of 'Dream-Land'.

13 *Earth may not pass till heaven shall pass away* see headnote of ' "Was Thy Wrath against the Sea?" '

['That Eden of earth's sunrise cannot vie']

FD (58) in CR's commentary on Rev. 2:7: 'He that hath an ear, let him hear what the Spirit saith unto the churches; To him that overcometh will I give to eat of the tree of life, which is in the midst of the paradise of God.'

4 *Four rivers watered Eden* see note for l. 17 of 'Paradise'.

7 *but Paradise hath gold* see note for ll. 35–6 of 'Paradise'.

11 *Lamb for light* 'And the city had no need of the sun, neither of the moon, to shine in it: for the glory of God did lighten it, and the Lamb is the light thereof' (Rev. 21:23). In her commentary on this verse in *FD*, CR writes: 'Look beyond sun and moon, and thou shalt see greater things than they. Stint bodily indulgence, and thou shalt enlarge spiritual capacity. Make a covenant with thine eyes, and thou shalt be full of light. Lean not to thine own understanding, and the Lord shall even now be thy Light, and the Lamb thy Light and thy salvation' (512).

19–20 *your children rise / And call you blessed* from Proverbs 31 on 'the good wife': 'Her children arise up, and call her blessed; her husband also, and he praiseth her' (31:28).

QUINQUAGESIMA

FD (332) in CR's commentary on Rev. 13:2.

Title [untitled] *1892*.

Fiftieth day (Latin), that is, the Sunday before Lent, and the seventh before Easter.

['Piteous my rhyme is']

Entry for 20 April in *TF* (75).

ASH WEDNESDAY ['My God, my God, have mercy on my sin']

Appendix of *TF* (257).

Title the day following Shrove Tuesday (or 'Fat Tuesday') and the beginning of Lent, the forty days of fasting before Easter. 'Ash' comes from the Roman Catholic custom of the priest sprinkling ashes over the heads of the penitents on this day.

['Good Lord, today']

FD (235–6) in CR's commentary on Rev. 7:14 (see note for l. 13 of 'Martyrs' Song').

LENT

Entry for 20 March in *TF* (55).

Title [untitled] *1885, 1886a.*
1 *It is good to be last not first* see note for l. 280 of 'The Lowest Room'.
3–4 *to hunger and thirst, / So it be for righteousness* 'Blessed are they which do hunger and thirst after righteousness: for they shall be filled' (Matt. 5:6; see also Luke 6:21).
6 *It is good to watch and to pray* see note for Part 2, l. 1 of 'Old and New Year Ditties'.

EMBERTIDE

FD (169–70) in CR's commentary on Rev. 5:5.

This poem . . . takes occasion from the passage of *The Apocalypse* – 'And one of the elders saith unto me, Weep not.' The prose comment on the passage contains the following; 'What we know with certainty of this beatified elder is not his name, but his Christlikeness. As once his Master on earth, so now he in heaven saith, Weep not. The one and only aspect high or low need desire to be known by is Christlikeness. Thus the saints are stamped, thereby they become recognizable.' And then follows the present poem. ('Notes' 470)

Title [untitled] *1892.*
Comprises the days of fasting and prayer following the first Sunday in Lent, Whitsunday, Holy Cross Day and St Lucia's Day. Ordinations usually take place on the Sundays following these days.

11 *Christ bade him, "Do thou likewise"* see note for title of ' "Take Care of Him" '.
15 *Lo, I, with the child God hath given to me* Hannah prayed for a child, and when God answered her prayer, she dedicated her son Samuel as a priest to God – 'the LORD hath given me my petition . . . Therefore also I have lent him to the Lord' (1 Sam. 1:27–8).

MID-LENT

Entry for 9 Dec. in *TF* (236–7).
   'This sonnet . . . is obviously based in some degree upon the other sonnet, *Who have a Form of Godliness* . . . which was not published by the authoress' ('Notes' 470).

Title [untitled] *1885, 1886a.*
   The fourth Sunday in Lent, sometimes known as 'Refreshment Sunday' because at this point in Lent the church pauses in its penitential exercises.
14 *Still faint yet still pursuing* see note for l. 11 of 'A Life's Parallels'.

PASSIONTIDE

[Editions: *1893,* 1904.]

Title the season immediately preceding Easter.
2 *sevenfold powers* see note for l. 111 of 'The Lowest Room'.
11 *Come, every one that thirsteth, come* see note for l. 4 of *Goblin Market*; also 'In the last day, that great day of the feast, Jesus stood and cried, saying, If any man thirst, let him come unto me, and drink' (John 7:37).

PALM SUNDAY

FD (452) in CR's commentary on Rev. 19:15 (see note for l. 8 of 'The Three Enemies' and epigraph, below).

Title "He treadeth the winepress of the fierceness and wrath of Almighty God." *1892.*
   The Sunday before Easter, so called because when Jesus made his triumphal entry into Jerusalem, his followers waved palm branches along the route he travelled.
Epigraph from Rev. 19:15.
3 *Athirst for my sake* see note for l. 20 of ' "When My Heart Is Vexed, I Will Complain" ' ['O Lord, how canst Thou say Thou lovest me?'].
26 *When Thou shalt sift the living from the dead* allusion to the Last Judgement: see

note for l. 11 of ' "Cried out with Tears" '; also 'Satan hath desired to have you, that he may sift you as wheat' (Luke 22:31).

28 *Judge not before that day* 'Therefore judge nothing before the time, until the Lord come, who both will bring to light the hidden things of darkness, and will make manifest the counsels of the hearts' (1 Cor. 4:5).

29 *Trust Me with all thy heart, even tho' I slay* see note for Part 1, l. 9 of 'Later Life'.

MONDAY IN HOLY WEEK

[Composed by Sept. 1853. Editions: 1885, 1886a, *1893*, 1896, 1904.]

Appendix of *TF* (260).

Title (For under a Crucifix) *1896*.
    Holy Week the week between Palm Sunday and Easter.
Epigraph 'The voice of my beloved! behold, he cometh leaping up the mountains, skipping upon the hills' (Song of Sol. 2:8).

TUESDAY IN HOLY WEEK

Appendix of *TF* (261).

5 *Thou Who thirsting on the Cross* see note for l. 20 of ' "When My Heart Is Vexed, I Will Complain" ' ['O Lord, how canst Thou say Thou lovest me?'].

WEDNESDAY IN HOLY WEEK

Entry for 2 May in *TF* (84).

Title [untitled] *1885, 1886a.*
9 *Pointed at, mocked* 'And they that passed by reviled him, wagging their heads' (Matt. 27:39; see also Mark 15:29 and Luke 23:35).

MAUNDY THURSDAY

Appendix of *TF* (262–3) under 'Thursday in Holy Week'.

Title Thursday in Holy Week. *1885, 1886a.*
    The day before Good Friday. 'Maundy' comes from 'commandment' and commemorates the Passover Feast – the 'Last Supper' – Jesus celebrated with his disciples, when he said: 'A new commandment I give unto you, that ye love one another' (John 13:34).

Epigraph Judges 9:13. In the original story, the vine refuses the request to be king. CR uses this verse out of context and in relation to the image of Jesus as the living vine. See note for l. 33 of 'Christian and Jew. A Dialogue'.
16 *a death which hath lost the sting* see note for Part 3, ll. 13–14 of 'The Thread of Life'.

GOOD FRIDAY MORNING

[Editions: *1893*, 1904.]

'This is the only piece which the authoress added to the volume *Verses*, consisting otherwise of reprints from previous volumes' ('Notes' 470).

Title on the Friday after Passover, Jesus was forced to carry the cross upon which he was to be crucified to Golgotha. See also note for title of 'Good Friday' ['Am I a stone and not a sheep'].
Epigraph 'And he bearing his cross went forth into a place called the place of a skull, which is called in the Hebrew Golgotha' (John 19:17).

GOOD FRIDAY ['Lord Jesus Christ']

Appendix of *TF* (263).

Title see note for title of 'Good Friday' ['Am I a stone and not a sheep'].
6 *darkened heaven and earth that shook* see l. 64 of 'After This the Judgment'.

GOOD FRIDAY EVENING

FD (245) in CR's commentary on Rev. 8:3–4 (see note for l. 28 of 'An "Immurata" Sister').

Title "OUT OF THE ANGEL'S HAND". *1892.*
    See note for title of 'Good Friday' ['Am I a stone and not a sheep'].
Epigraph allusion to the piercing of Jesus' side with a spear while he was dying on the cross (John 19:34 – see note for ll. 23–4 of ' "The Love of Christ Which Passeth Knowledge" ').

"A bundle of myrrh is my Well-beloved unto me"

FD (232) in CR's commentary on Rev. 7:9 (see note for Part 1, l. 3 of ' "Behold a Shaking" ').

Title [untitled] *1892*.

See note for l. 14 of 'It is not death, O Christ, to die for thee'. In *SF*, CR writes: 'Frankincense and myrrh, Divine communion and Divine suffering: verily the Hills and Mountains of Christ's earthly life "smell as Lebanon" (Hos. xiv. 6)' (252).

1 *cruciferous* bearing flowers with four parts, like a cross.

8 *deep calls deep* see note for l. 32 of ' "When My Heart Is Vexed, I Will Complain" ' ['O Lord, how canst Thou say Thou lovest me?'].

9 *emulous* emulating or imitating. The faithful on earth, in bearing their cross (suffering), are emulating Jesus in his suffering on the cross; hence, 'cross calls Cross'.

10 *Remember us with him who shared Thy gall* when Jesus was dying on the cross, he was given vinegar and gall to drink (Matt. 27:34), and see note for l. 8 of 'Good Friday' ['Am I a stone and not a sheep'].

EASTER EVEN ['The tempest over and gone, the calm begun']

Appendix of *TF* (263–4).

2 *it is finished* see note for l. 6 of 'Amen'.

6 *a virgin cave and entrance stone* Joseph of Arimathea buried Jesus 'in his own new tomb, which he had hewn out in the rock: and he rolled a great stone to the door of the sepulchre and departed' (Matt. 27:60; see also Mark 15:46 and Luke 23:53).

7–10 *a garden full of Angels . . . who cry "Holy, Holy, Holy," . . . Veiling their faces* see note for ll. 19–20 of 'Christian and Jew. A Dialogue'.

14 *more strong than death* see note for l. 1 of 'An End'.

15 *Until the day break and the shadows flee* see note for title of 'Until the Day Break'.

16 *The Shaking and the Breath* see note for title of ' "Behold a Shaking" '; also 'For in my jealousy and in the fire of my wrath have I spoken, Surely in that day there shall be a great shaking in the land of Israel' (Eze. 38:19).

Our Church Palms are budding willow twigs

FD (18) in CR's commentary on Rev. 1:4–6.

1 *the widowed world* Jesus as the Bridegroom leaves the world widowed when he dies on the cross.

EASTER DAY

Appendix of *TF* (264–5).

3 *keep jubilee* see note for l. 11 of ' "They Desire a Better Country" '.
6 *Set your lamps burning* see note for l. 3 of 'Advent' ['This Advent moon shines cold and clear'].
11 *Christ the Chief Reaper* 'And I looked, and behold a white cloud, and upon the cloud one sat like unto the Son of man, having on his head a golden crown, and in his hand a sharp sickle. And another angel came out of the temple, crying with a loud voice to him that sat on the cloud, Thrust in thy sickle, and reap: for the time is come for thee to reap; for the harvest of the earth is ripe. And he that sat on the cloud thrust in his sickle on the earth; and the earth was reaped' (Rev. 14:14–16). See also note for l. 47 of 'After This the Judgment'.
17 *man's spousal day* on the day of the Last Judgement, the souls of the righteous shall be united with Christ, the 'bridegroom' of the Church.

EASTER MONDAY

[Composed 4 April 1864.]

Appendix of *TF* (265–6).

Title Easter Tuesday *1885, 1886a.*
5 *harvest* of souls. See note for l. 11 of 'Easter Day'.

EASTER TUESDAY

FD (484) in CR's commentary on Rev. 21:4.

Title [untitled] *1892.*
6 *Jesus Christ our Way* see note for l. 17 of 'A Martyr. The Vigil Of The Feast'.
7 *Jesus Christ the Same for ever, the Same today* see note for ll. 4–5 of ' "As the sparks fly upwards" '.
8–9 *Five Virgins replenish with oil their lamps, being wise, / Five Virgins awaiting the Bridegroom* see note for l. 3 of 'Advent' ['This Advent moon shines cold and clear'].

ROGATIONTIDE

Entry for 7 Feb. in *TF* (28).

Title [untitled] *1885, 1886a.*
From Latin *rogare* (to beseech) – the three days before Ascension Day in the Anglican calendar.

1 *Who scatters tares shall reap no wheat* 'But while men slept, his enemy came and sowed tares [weeds] among the wheat, and went his way. But when the blade was sprung up, and brought forth fruit, then appeared the tares also' (Matt. 13:25–6).

3 *sows the wind* see note for ll. 53–4 of 'A Testimony'.

ASCENSION EVE

FD (25) in CR's commentary on Rev. 1:8: 'I am Alpha and Omega, the beginning and the ending, saith the Lord, which is, and which was, and which is to come, the Almighty.'

Title [untitled] *1892.*
The evening before the celebration of the Ascension of Jesus into Heaven.

5–6 *ears to hear . . . eyes to see* see note for title of 'Lord, grant us eyes to see and ears to hear'.

7 *for Thou Thyself art meek* see note for l. 19 of ' "Of Him That Was Ready to Perish" '.

9 *O Thou the Life* see note for l. 17 of 'A Martyr. The Vigil Of The Feast'.

13 *Still gazing off from earth and up at heaven* 'And while they looked stedfastly toward heaven as he went up, behold, two men stood by them in white apparel' (Acts 1:10).

ASCENSION DAY

Appendix of *TF* (270).

Title the day Jesus ascended into Heaven; traditionally, the fortieth day after his resurrection.

Epigraph 'And when he had spoken these things, while they beheld, he was taken up; and a cloud received him out of their sight' (Acts 1:9; see also Luke 24:51).

25–6 *they beyond seven times seven / Forgive* see note for l. 24 of 'After This the Judgment'.

WHITSUN EVE [' "As many as I love."—Ah, Lord, Who lovest all']

FD (141) in CR's commentary on Rev. 3:19: 'As many as I love, I rebuke and chasten: be zealous therefore, and repent.'

Title [untitled] *1892*.
  The eve before Whitsunday ('White Sunday' or Pentecost), which is the Sunday fifty days after Easter that commemorates the descent of the Holy Spirit on the Apostles.
5 *Whom sin and sorrow make their worn reluctant thrall* 'Jesus answered them, Verily, verily, I say unto you, Whosoever committeth sin is the servant of sin' (John 8:34).
6 *Who fain would flee away but lack the wings of dove* see note for ll. 13–14 of 'Darkness and light are both alike to Thee'.

WHITSUN DAY

Appendix of *TF* (271).

Title see note for title of 'Whitsun Eve', above.
Epigraph 'And when the day of Pentecost was fully come, they were all with one accord in one place' (Acts 2:1).
1 *At sound as of rushing wind, and sight as of fire* 'And suddenly there came a sound from heaven as of a rushing mighty wind, and it filled all the house where they were sitting. And there appeared unto them cloven tongues like as of fire, and it sat upon each of them' (Acts 2:2–3).
7 *love that is strong as death* see note for l. 1 of 'An End'.

WHITSUN MONDAY

FD (523) in CR's commentary on Rev. 22:1: 'And he shewed me a pure river of water of life, clear as crystal, proceeding out of the throne of God and of the Lamb.'

Title [untitled] *1892*.
  The day after Whitsunday; see note for title of 'Whitsun Eve'.
Epigraph see headnote, above.
9–10 *Pure gold is the bed of that River / (The gold of that land is the best)* see notes for l. 11 of 'Saints and Angels' and for ll. 35–6 of 'Paradise'.
18 *The Tree of Life* see note for ll. 13–14 of 'Eve'.

WHITSUN TUESDAY

Appendix of *TF* (272–3).

Title the Tuesday after Whitsunday; see note for title of 'Whitsun Eve'.
7 *dove-eyed* see note for l. 14 of 'Advent Sunday'.
10 *wings of silver and of gold* 'Though ye have lien among the pots, yet shall ye be as the wings of a dove covered with silver, and her feathers with yellow gold' (Ps. 68:13). In *SF*, CR writes that if we obey the rule to 'Lay not up for yourselves treasures upon earth . . .' (Matt. 6:19), 'our possessions and our hearts together will unfold wings as "of a dove covered . . ."' (284). See also note for ll. 13–14 of 'A Testimony'.
12 *Winter is past and gone* see note for ll. 53–6 of 'Advent' ['This Advent moon shines cold and clear'].
13 *Spouse, sister, love and dove* 'I sleep, but my heart waketh: it is the voice of my beloved that knocketh, saying, Open to me, my sister, my love, my dove, my undefiled: for my head is filled with dew, and my locks with the drops of the night' (Song of Sol. 5:2); see also headnote of 'The Ghost's Petition'.

TRINITY SUNDAY

FD (15–16) in CR's commentary on Rev. 1:4–6.

Title [untitled] *1892*.
   The Sunday immediately following Whitsunday, in which the Trinity is honoured.
5 *O Christ the Lamb, O Holy Ghost the Dove* these phrases echo the description of the baptism of Jesus by John the Baptist: John 1:29 (see note for l. 33 of 'Martyrs' Song'); also 'And the Holy Ghost descended in a bodily shape like a dove upon him, and a voice came from heaven, which said, Thou art my beloved Son; in thee I am well pleased' (Luke 3:22; see also Matt. 3:16 and Mark 1:10).
6 *Reveal the Almighty Father unto us* 'Philip saith unto him, Lord, shew us the Father, and it sufficeth us' (John 14:8).
8 *our God is Love* 'He that loveth not knoweth not God; for God is love' (1 John 4:8).
12–13 *We change, but Thou remainest* 'They shall perish; but thou remainest' (Heb. 1:11).

CONVERSION OF ST. PAUL

Entry for 25 Jan. in *TF* (21).

Saul of Tarsus (later St Paul), who at the time was a persecutor of Christians, was on the road to Damascus, when he was suddenly blinded by a bright light and heard the voice of Jesus asking: 'Saul, Saul, why persecutest thou me?' (Acts 9:4).

Title FEAST OF THE CONVERSION OF ST. PAUL IN THE YEAR 35. *1885, 1886a*.

5 *thy outrunning race* see note for ll. 11–12 of 'Who Shall Deliver Me?'
6 *Christ shows the splendour of His Face* 'And as he journeyed, he came near Damascus: and suddenly there shined round about him a light from heaven' (Acts 9:3).

['In weariness and painfulness St. Paul']

Entry for 16 Sept. in *TF* (178).

Title see note for ll. 78–9 of 'A Ballad of Boding' and headnote for 'Conversion of St. Paul', above.

VIGIL OF THE PRESENTATION

FD (17) in CR's commentary on Rev. 1:4–6.

Title [untitled] *1892*.

The presentation of the infant Jesus at the temple, as was required by the law of Moses for all firstborn sons. At this time, both Simeon and Anna prophesied that Jesus would be the redeemer (Luke 2:21–38).

FEAST OF THE PRESENTATION

CS (149–50) in the chapter entitled 'The Presentation of Christ in the Temple, and Purification of St. Mary the Virgin'.

Title [untitled] *1881CS*.

See note on title of 'Vigil of the Presentation', above.
1 *Firstfruits of our grain* to be dedicated as a sacrifice to the Lord.
2 *Lamb appointed to be slain* see note for l. 33 of 'Martyrs' Song'.
3 *A Virgin and two doves were all Thy train* Jesus' mother, the Virgin Mary; see note for title of 'The Purification of St. Mary the Virgin', below.

4 *With one old man for state* Simeon, the old man who was 'waiting for the consolation of Israel' and who prophesied that Jesus would be 'a light to lighten the Gentiles, and the glory of thy people Israel' (Luke 2:25, 32).
5 *Thy Father's gate* the temple at Jerusalem.
13 *Gold, frankincense and myrrh* see note for title of 'Epiphany'.
20 *A bruised reed* see note for title of ' "A Bruised Reed Shall He Not Break" '.

THE PURIFICATION OF ST. MARY THE VIRGIN

Entry for 2 Feb. in *TF* (25).

Title FEAST OF THE PRESENTATION OF CHRIST IN THE TEMPLE, COMMONLY CALLED, THE PURIFICATION OF ST. MARY THE VIRGIN. *1885, 1886a.*
   'And when the days of her purification according to the law of Moses were accomplished, they brought him to Jerusalem to present him to the Lord . . . And to offer a sacrifice according to that which is said in the law of the Lord, A pair of turtledoves, or two young pigeons' (Luke 2:22, 24).
8 *The Lamb that indwelt by the Dove* see note for l. 5 of 'Trinity Sunday'.

VIGIL OF THE ANNUNCIATION

FD (37) in CR's commentary on Rev. 1:12–16.

Title [untitled] *1892.*
   The announcement to Mary by the angel Gabriel that she would bear Jesus. CR posed as Mary for a painting by DGR of the Annunciation (*Ecce Ancilla* (1850)).
14 *watch and pray* see note for Part 2, l. 1 of 'Old and New Year Ditties'.

FEAST OF THE ANNUNCIATION

Entry for 8 Sept. in *TF* (174).

Title FEAST OF THE NATIVITY OF THE BLESSED VIRGIN MARY. *1885, 1886a.*
   Celebrated on March 25. See headnote to 'Vigil of the Annunciation', above.
2 *Fruitful shoot from Jesse's root graciously emerging* 'And there shall come forth a rod out of the stem of Jesse, and a Branch shall grow out of his roots' (Isa. 11:1). Because Jesus was of the house of Jesse (which also included David), Christians read this passage as foretelling Jesus' coming. The 'Branch' also

alludes to his saying: 'I am the vine, ye are the branches: He that abideth in me, and I in him, the same bringeth forth much fruit: for without me ye can do nothing' (John 15:5).

7–8 *"Blessed among women, highly favoured," thus / Glorious Gabriel hailed her* 'And the angel came in unto her, and said, Hail, thou that art highly favoured, the Lord is with thee: blessed art thou among women' (Luke 1:28).

['Herself a rose, who bore the Rose']

CS (193) in the chapter entitled 'The Annunciation of the Blessed Virgin Mary'.

1, 6–7 *Herself a rose, who bore the Rose . . . Lily herself, she bore the one / Fair lily* the Virgin Mary is associated with both the rose and the lily. See also note for l. 11 of 'Long Barren'.

9 *The Sun of Righteousness her Son* 'But unto you that fear my name shall the Sun of righteousness arise with healing in his wings' (Mal. 4:2).

10 *She was His morning star* 'I Jesus have sent mine angel to testify unto you these things in the churches. I am the root and the offspring of David, and the bright and morning star' (Rev. 22:16). See note for l. 2 of 'Feast of the Annunciation', above.

18 *By hope and love and faith* 'And now abideth faith, hope, charity, these three; but the greatest of these is charity' (1 Cor. 13:13).

19–20 *"Dove, / Spouse, Sister, Mother," Jesus saith* see note for l. 13 of 'Whitsun Tuesday'.

ST. MARK

CS (214–15) in the chapter entitled 'St. Mark, Evangelist'.

Title [untitled] *1881CS*.
  One of Jesus' disciples, whose name was given to the earliest gospel.

1 *Once like a broken bow Mark sprang aside* when Jesus was arrested, a young man fled from the scene, leaving behind the linen cloth that had covered his naked body (Mark 14:51–2); he is usually taken to be Mark.

6 *Hath for his sign a Lion* the traditional symbol for St Mark. 'And the first beast was like a lion, and the second beast like a calf, and the third beast had a face as a man, and the fourth beast was like a flying eagle' (Rev. 4:7). In her comments on this verse, CR writes: 'St. Mark's lion may remind us how he alone notices that it was "with the wild beasts" that our Lord sojourned during Forty Days in the wilderness' (*FD* 156–7).

ST. BARNABAS

CS (267) in the chapter entitled 'St. Barnabas, Apostle'.

Title [untitled] *1881 CS*.

Barnabas was an early Christian known chiefly for his work in Antioch and his association with St Paul (see headnote for 'Conversion of St. Paul'). The quarrel between Barnabas and Paul over whether John Mark should be taken on a voyage with them is found in Acts 15:36–41.

3 *That chosen Vessel* St Paul.

5 *Divided while united* 'And the contention was so sharp between them, that they departed asunder one from the other' (Acts 15:39) – although both continued preaching the gospel.

VIGIL OF ST. PETER

FD (33) in CR's commentary on Rev. 1:12–16.

Title [untitled] *1892*.

3 *That look which pierced St. Peter's heart* see note for l. 7 of 'Good Friday' ['Am I a stone and not a sheep'].

ST. PETER

FD (326) in CR's commentary on Rev. 12:10–12.

Title [untitled] *1892*.

1 *Launch out into the deep* see note for Part 9, ll. 10–11 of 'Monna Innominata'.

5 *Prescience* knowledge of things before they happen.

['St. Peter once: "Lord, dost Thou wash my feet?" ']

FD (143) in the commentary on Rev. 3:20 (see note for l. 8 of 'Despised and Rejected').

1 *Lord, dost Thou wash my feet* when Jesus began washing the feet of his disciples before the Last Supper, Peter protested: 'Lord, dost Thou wash my feet?' (John 13:6), adding 'Thou shalt never wash my feet.' But when Jesus answered, 'If I wash thee not, thou hast no part with me,' Peter responded, 'Lord, not my feet only, but also my hands and my head' (8–9).

2 *Lord, dost thou stand and knock* see note for l. 8 of 'Despised and Rejected'.

7–8 *I have heard the crowing of the cock / And have not wept* see note for l. 7 of 'Good Friday' ['Am I a stone and not a sheep'].

['I followed Thee, my God, I followed Thee']

CS (335–7) in the chapter entitled 'St. Peter, Apostle'.

1 *I followed Thee* see note for l. 7 of 'Good Friday' ['Am I a stone and not a sheep'], for the story on which this poem is based.
3 *Gethsemane* see note for Part 2, l. 1 of 'Old and New Year Ditties'.
17–18 *I disbelieved / Thy word of warning* Jesus had predicted that Peter would deny him.
21 *Once I had urged: "Lord, this be far from Thee"* when Jesus told his disciples that he would be killed, Peter 'began to rebuke him, saying, Be it far from thee, Lord: this shall not be unto thee' (Matt. 16:22).
28 *faithless slumberer in Gethsemane* see note for l. 1, above.
29–30 *who instantly / Put trust, but in a sword* see note for l. 36 of 'The German-French Campaign. 1870–1871'.
36–7 *who bore to think on Thee / And yet to lie* allusion to Peter's denial that he knew Jesus.
41 *No balm I find in Gilead* Jer. 8:22 (see note for ll. 31–2 of 'Paradise').
47 *Magdalene* see note for title of 'Mary Magdalene and the Other Mary'.
49 *blessed above women she* echo of Elizabeth's greeting to Mary, pregnant with Jesus: 'Blessed art thou among women, and blessed is the fruit of thy womb' (Luke 1:42).
51 *the scorned thief* see note for l. 8 of 'Good Friday' ['Am I a stone and not a sheep'].
56–7 *Like as the hart the water-brooks I Thee / Desire* see note for title of 'Like as the Hart Desireth the Water Brooks'.

VIGIL OF ST. BARTHOLOMEW

FD (439) in CR's commentary on Rev. 19:9: 'And he saith unto me, Write, Blessed are they which are called unto the marriage supper of the Lamb. And he saith unto me, These are the true sayings of God.'

Title [untitled] *1892*.
    Bartholomew was one of the twelve disciples of Jesus.
5 *With Virgins who keep vigil* see note for l. 3 of 'Advent' ['This Advent moon shines cold and clear'].
6 *To sow among all sowers who shall reap* 'They that sow in tears shall reap in joy' (Ps. 126:5); see notes for l. 269 of 'The Prince's Progress' and for l. 11 of 'Easter Day'.

7 *From out man's deep to call Thy vaster deep* see note for l. 32 of ' "When My Heart Is Vexed, I Will Complain" ' ['O Lord, how canst Thou say Thou lovest me?'].

14 *Transfiguring their aspects* perhaps an allusion to Dante's vision at the end of the *Divine Comedy*: 'as I grew worthier to see, / the more I looked, the more unchanging semblance / appeared to change with every change in me' (Canto XXXIII, 112–14, trans. John Ciardi).

ST. BARTHOLOMEW

Entry for 24 Aug. in *TF* (163).

Title FEAST OF ST. BARTHOLOMEW, APOSTLE. Tradition assigns to this Saint, martyrdom in one of its most appalling forms *1885, 1886a*.

1 *He bore an agony* St Bartholomew is believed to have been flayed alive, then beheaded.

ST. MICHAEL AND ALL ANGELS

CS (450) in the chapter entitled 'St. Michael and All Angels'.

Title [untitled] *1881CS*.

'And there was war in heaven: Michael and his angels fought against the dragon' (Rev. 12:7). The archangel Michael, often depicted with a sword, is the leader of the angels.

Epigraph 'Bless the LORD, ye his angels, that excel in strength, that do his commandments, hearkening unto the voice of his word' (Ps. 103:20).

2 *Seraphs . . . Cherubim* see note for l. 24 of 'The Convent Threshold'.

His Seraphs fires 'Who maketh his angels spirits; his ministers a flaming fire' (Ps. 104:4).

6 *Princes* angels or celestial beings of high rank.

Powers the sixth order of angels in the celestial hierarchy. Cf. Milton, *Paradise Lost*, V, 600–601: 'all ye angels, progeny of Light, / Thrones, Dominations, Princedoms, Virtues, Powers'.

16–18 *Wherefore with Angels, wherefore with Archangels, / With lofty Cherubs, loftier Seraphim, / We laud and magnify our God Almighty* cf. 'Therefore with Angels and Archangels, and with all the company of heaven, we laud and magnify Thy glorious Name' (Communion Liturgy, *Book of Common Prayer*).

19 *veil our faces* see note for ll. 19–20 of 'Christian and Jew. A Dialogue'.

VIGIL OF ALL SAINTS

Entry for 4 Feb. in *TF* (26).

Title [untitled] *1885, 1886a.*
 In the fourteenth century, the Church instituted two days to commemorate the dead: the Feast of All Saints was to be held on 1 Nov. to celebrate the saints in heaven, and 2 Nov. was to remember the souls in purgatory.

ALL SAINTS ['As grains of sand, as stars, as drops of dew']

Entry for 1 Nov. in *TF* (209).

Title FEAST OF ALL SAINTS *1885, 1886a.*
1 *As grains of sand, as stars, as drops of dew* see note for ll. 11–12 of 'Leaf from leaf Christ knows'.
4 *Where all things ... are new* see note for l. 172 of 'From House to Home'.
14 *for God is Love* see note for l. 8 of 'Trinity Sunday'.

ALL SAINTS: MARTYRS

FD (214) in CR's commentary on Rev. 6:11 (see note for Part 2, l. 12 of 'Old and New Year Ditties').

Title [untitled] *1892.*
5 *New Jerusalem* the redeemed who will join Christ in Paradise after the Last Judgement. 'And I John saw the holy city, new Jerusalem, coming down from God out of heaven, prepared as a bride adorned for her husband' (Rev. 21:2); 'And he carried me away in the spirit to a great and high mountain, and shewed me that great city, the holy Jerusalem, descending out of heaven from God' (Rev. 21:10). In *FD*, CR includes a long, lyrical passage describing the New Jerusalem being gathered 'stone by stone, soul by soul' to become the Bride of Christ (480–81).
6–9 *And cry "How long?" ... White robes* see note for Part 2, l. 12 of 'Old and New Year Ditties'.

"I gave a sweet smell"

Entry for 30 June in *TF* (125).

Title 'But I have all, and abound: I am full, having received of Epaphroditus the things which were sent from you, an odour of a sweet smell, a sacrifice acceptable, wellpleasing to God' (Phil. 4:18). See also note for l. 28 of 'An "Immurata" Sister'.

['Hark! the Alleluias of the great salvation']

FD (538) in CR's commentary on Rev. 22:14: 'Blessed are they that do his commandments, that they may have right to the tree of life, and may enter in through the gates into the city.'

4–5 *Open ye the gates, that the righteous nation / Which have kept the truth may enter in* 'Open ye the gates, that the righteous nation which keepeth the truth may enter in' (Isa. 26:2).

6 *ye pearls, on your twelvefold station* 'And the twelve gates were twelve pearls; every several gate was of one pearl' (Rev. 21:21). CR notes in her commentary on the biblical verse that the vanished sea in the heavenly city is represented by pearls, and that even in the heavenly world, pearls are not to be clung to: 'a gate is to be passed through, not resided in' (*FD* 511). A commentary in *SF* points out that since pearls are connected with disease, they are 'representative of the precious fruits of all worthily borne human suffering: and because they form gates of entrance – exit, thanks be to God, is not in question – they connect themselves vividly with that "great tribulation" out of which came the general assembly of the saints as St. John beheld them in a vision' (235). Later in *SF*, CR writes that 'If we be such women as adorn themselves in modest apparel, with shamefacedness and sobriety . . . then we shall at length attain to gaze upon the Bride in her beauty, the Lamb's wife, holy Jerusalem, whose twelve gates are twelve pearls' (279).

7 *No more deaths to die* 'And God shall wipe away all tears from their eyes; and there shall be no more death, neither sorrow, nor crying, neither shall there be any more pain: for the former things are passed away' (Rev. 21:4). See note for l. 29 of 'Christian and Jew. A Dialogue'.

8 *Lift your heads, ye gates* 'Lift up your heads, O ye gates; and be ye lift up, ye everlasting doors; and the King of glory shall come in' (Ps. 24:7; see also 24:9).

A SONG FOR THE LEAST OF ALL SAINTS

FD (529–30) in CR's commentary on Rev. 22:7.

5–8 *As three times to His Saint He saith . . . "Lovest thou Me* see note for l. 5 of ' "Because He first loved us" '.

11 *But love it is, is strong as death* see note for l. 1 of 'An End'.

SUNDAY BEFORE ADVENT

FD (457) in CR's commentary on Rev. 19:21.

Title [untitled] *1892*.
See note for title of 'Advent' ['The Advent moon shines cold and clear'].
1 *The end of all things is at hand* 'But the end of all things is at hand: be ye therefore sober, and watch unto prayer' (1 Pet. 4:7).
10 *And Heaven flings wide its gates* see note for l. 7 of 'After This the Judgment'.

GIFTS AND GRACES

['Love loveth Thee, and wisdom loveth Thee']

FD (161) in CR's commentary on Rev. 4:9.

3 *grows million-eyed* Rev. 4:8 (see note for ll. 19–20 of 'Christian and Jew. A Dialogue').
13 *Palm shall they have, and harp and aureole* see note for ll. 37–8 of 'Paradise'.

['Lord, give me love that I may love Thee much']

FD (398) in CR's commentary on Rev. 17:1–2.

6 *some day my wings to soar* 'But they that wait upon the LORD shall renew their strength; they shall mount up with wings as eagles' (Isa. 40:31).

"As a king, ... unto the King"

[Composed 13 Jan. 1863. Originally part of 'For a Mercy received', which CR never published as such.]

Entry for 3 July in *TF* (126–7).

Title [untitled] *1885, 1886a*.
King David bought a threshing floor from Araunah in order to set up an altar 'that the plague may be stayed from the people' (2 Sam 24:21). 'All these things did Araunah, as a king, give unto the king. And Araunah said unto the king, The LORD thy God accept thee' (23).

['O ye who love today']

Preface of *FD* (7).

['Life that was born today']

[In 1892, the first stanza (with variants) is repeated later in the book.]

FD (140–41) in CR's commentary on Rev. 3:17–18 and again in *FD* (273) in CR's commentary on Rev. 9:21.

"Perfect Love casteth out Fear"

FD (171) in CR's commentary on Rev. 5:5.

Title see note for l. 36 of ' "They Desire a Better Country" '.

['Hope is the counterpoise of fear']

FD (173–4) in CR's commentary on Rev. 5:5.

"Subject to like Passions as we are"

FD (180–81) in CR's commentary on Rev. 5:8: 'And when he had taken the book, the four beasts and four and twenty elders fell down before the Lamb, having every one of them harps, and golden vials full of odours, which are the prayers of saints.'

Title [untitled] *1892*.

'Elias was a man subject to like passions as we are, and he prayed earnestly that it might not rain' (James 5:17).

6 *the new man* 'And that ye put on the new man, which after God is created in righteousness and true holiness' (Eph. 4:24; see also Col. 3:10).

['Experience bows a sweet contented face']

FD (198) in CR's commentary on Rev. 6:2.

3 *Beneath the sun, she knows, is nothing new* see note for l. 11 of 'One Certainty'.

4 *All things that go return with measured pace* 'The wind goeth toward the south, and turneth about unto the north; it whirleth about continually, and the wind returneth again according to his circuits' (Ecc. 1:6).

5 *man's still recommencing race* see note for ll. 11–12 of 'Who Shall Deliver Me?'

9 *My God doth all things well* 'He hath done all things well' (Mark 7:37).

10 *for the morrow taketh little care* see note for l. 91 of 'Maiden May'.

"Charity never Faileth"

FD (201) in CR's commentary on Rev. 6:4.

Title 'Charity never faileth: but whether there be prophecies, they shall fail; whether there be tongues, they shall cease; whether there be knowledge, it shall vanish away' (1 Cor. 13:8).

8 *Dove-eyed Love* see note for l. 14 of 'Advent Sunday'.

   the Twelve-fruited Tree see note for ll. 13–14 of 'Eve'.

"The Greatest of these is Charity"

FD (255) in CR's commentary on Rev. 8:12: 'And the fourth angel sounded, and the third part of the sun was smitten, and the third part of the moon, and the third part of the stars; so as the third part of them was darkened, and the day shone not for a third part of it, and the night likewise.'

Title [untitled] *1892*.

   See note for l. 18 of 'Herself a rose, who bore the Rose'.

13 *New Jerusalem* see note for l. 5 of 'All Saints: Martyrs'.

14 *where the palm-tree blows* see note for ll. 37–8 of 'Paradise'.

['All beneath the sun hasteth']

FD (282) in CR's commentary on Rev. 10:7.

1 *beneath the sun* see note for l. 6 of 'A Testimony'.

['If thou be dead, forgive and thou shalt live']

FD (18) in CR's commentary on Rev. 1:4–6.

2 *If thou hast sinned, forgive and be forgiven* 'For if ye forgive men their trespasses, your heavenly Father will also forgive you' (Matt. 6:14).

6 *Set not thy face as flint* see note for l. 206 of 'From House to Home'.

"Let Patience have her perfect work" ['Can man rejoice who lives in hourly fear?']

FD (550–51) in CR's commentary on Rev. 22:20.

Title [untitled] *1892*.
  'But let patience have her perfect work, that ye may be perfect and entire, wanting nothing' (James 1:4).
12 *underneath the rod* see note for l. 8 of 'The Three Enemies'.

['Patience must dwell with Love, for Love and Sorrow']

FD (116–17) in CR's commentary on Rev. 3:10: 'Because thou hast kept the word of my patience, I also will keep thee from the hour of temptation, which shall come upon all the world, to try them that dwell upon the earth.'

1–2 *for Love and Sorrow / Have pitched their tent together* cf. 'For love and sorrow alway come together' (Philip James Bailey (1816–1902), *Festus* (1839; l. no. taken from 1889 edn.), l. 20058).

"Let everything that hath breath praise the Lord"

FD (99) in CR's commentary on Rev. 3:5–6.

Title [untitled] *1892*.
  See note for ll. 189–91 of ' "All Thy Works Praise Thee, O Lord" '.

['What is the beginning? Love. What the course? Love still']

FD (75) in CR's commentary on Rev. 2:19.

['Lord, make me pure']

FD (54) in CR's commentary on Rev. 2:6.

['Love, to be love, must walk Thy way']

FD (45) in CR's commentary on Rev. 1:19–20.

['Lord, I am feeble and of mean account']

FD (12) in CR's commentary on Rev. 1:3: 'Blessed is he that readeth, and they that hear the words of this prophecy, and keep those things which are written therein: for the time is at hand.'

['Tune me, O Lord, into one harmony']

FD (489) in CR's commentary on Rev. 21:6: 'And he said unto me, It is done. I am Alpha and Omega, the beginning and the end. I will give unto him that is athirst of the fountain of the water of life freely.'

1 *Tune me* Kent points out the echo in this poem of Herbert's 'Deniall' (1633): 'O cheer and tune my heartlesse breast' (l. 26) (' "By thought, word, and deed": George Herbert and Christina Rossetti', in Kent, *Achievement* 269).
8–9 *Devil and world . . . flesh* see headnote of 'The Three Enemies'.

"They shall be as white as snow"

FD (484) in CR's commentary on Rev. 21:3.

Title [untitled] *1892*.
    'Though your sins be as scarlet, they shall be as white as snow' (Isa. 1:18).

['Thy lilies drink the dew']

Entry for 15 March in *TF* (53).

4 *types, dear Lord, of Thee* a type, in the Old Testament, is a symbol of the revelation (antitype) to come in the New: for example, the lamb (l. 2) is a type of Christ.
9–10 *They leave tomorrow's cares / Until the morrow* see note for l. 91 of 'Maiden May'.
15 *Fragrant with love and praise* see notes for l. 28 of 'An "Immurata" Sister' and for title of ' "I gave a sweet smell" '.

"When I was in trouble I called upon the Lord"

Entry for 26 March in *TF* (59).

Title [untitled] *1885, 1886a*.
    'In the day of my trouble I will call upon thee: for thou wilt answer me' (Ps. 86:7).

14 *Be not extreme to sift* at the Last Judgement, the wheat is sifted and separated from the chaff, the righteous from the unrighteous. See note for l. 26 of 'Palm Sunday'.

['Grant us such grace that we may work Thy Will']

FD (443–4) in CR's commentary on Rev. 19:10 (see headnote of 'Worship God').

8 *As rivers seek a sea they cannot fill* see note for ll. 10–11 of 'A Testimony'.

"Who hath despised the day of small things?"

FD (440) in CR's commentary on Rev. 19:10.

Title [untitled] *1892*.
'For who hath despised the day of small things? for they shall rejoice . . . they are the eyes of the LORD, which run to and fro through the whole earth' (Zech. 4:10).

"Do this, and he doeth it"

FD (410) in CR's commentary on Rev. 17:18.

Title [untitled] *1892*.
See note for title of ' "I will come and heal him" '.

1 *Content to come, content to go* 'for I have learned, in whatsoever state I am, therewith to be content' (Phil. 4:11).

"That no man take thy Crown"

FD (64) in CR's commentary on Rev. 2:10 (see note for l. 4, below).

Title [untitled] *1892*.
'Behold, I come quickly: hold that fast which thou hast, that no man take thy crown' (Rev. 3:11). In an extended discussion of 'thy crown', CR writes that love is 'the only crowned virtue' because the other virtues, 'divorced from love, would not be virtues' (*FD* 123).
1 *Be faithful unto death* 'Fear none of those things which thou shalt suffer: behold, the devil shall cast some of you into prison, that ye may be tried; and ye shall have tribulation ten days: be thou faithful unto death, and I will give thee a

crown of life' (Rev. 2:10). In her commentary on this biblical verse, CR writes: 'Our Lord in His own Person was "faithful unto death," thereby winning the "Crown of Life" He weareth. Shall we bemoan ourselves because He bids us do as He once did, and be made like Him as He now is? . . . Let us not despise others or ourselves for a mere instinctive dread of death; while we observe that Christ who by experience knew the bitterness of death, here sets death as the test of man's faithfulness and limit of his endurance' (*FD* 63).

"Ye are come unto Mount Sion"

FD (392) in CR's commentary on Rev. 16:21.

Title [untitled] *1892*.
  'But ye are come unto mount Sion, and unto the city of the living God, the heavenly Jerusalem, and to an innumerable company of angels' (Heb. 12:22).
10 *By day they rest not, nor they rest by night* see note for ll. 19–20 of 'Christian and Jew. A Dialogue'.
15 *New Jerusalem* see note for l. 5 of 'All Saints: Martyrs'.

"Sit down in the lowest room"

FD (350) in CR's commentary on Rev. 13:18.

Title [untitled] *1892*.
  See note for title of 'The Lowest Place'.

"Lord, it is good for us to be here"

FD (341) in CR's commentary on Rev. 13:10.

Title [untitled] *1892*.
  'Then answered Peter, and said unto Jesus, Lord, it is good for us to be here: if thou wilt, let us make here three tabernacles; one for thee, and one for Moses, and one for Elias' (Matt. 17:4; see also Mark 9:5 and Luke 9:33).

['Lord, grant us grace to rest upon Thy word']

FD (328) in CR's commentary on Rev. 12:15–16.

10 *hope deferred* see note for l. 2 of 'A Pause of Thought'.

THE WORLD. SELF-DESTRUCTION

"A vain Shadow"

FD (189) in CR's commentary on Rev. 5:12.

Title [untitled] *1892.*
  See note for ll. 7–8 of 'A Testimony'.

"Lord, save us, we perish"

FD (77) in CR's commentary on Rev. 2:22.

Title [untitled] *1892.*
  Jesus was asleep in a ship when a dangerous storm arose. 'And his disciples
came to him, and awoke him, saying, Lord, save us: we perish' (Matt. 8:25).
Jesus 'rebuked the winds and the sea; and there was a great calm' (26).

['What is this above thy head']

FD (425) in CR's commentary on Rev. 18:21: 'And a mighty angel took up a
stone like a great millstone, and cast it into the sea, saying, Thus with violence
shall that great city Babylon be thrown down, and shall be found no more at
all.'

Babylon the Great

FD (406) in CR's commentary on Rev. 17:9.

Title [untitled] *1892.*
  'And upon her forehead was a name written, MYSTERY, BABYLON
THE GREAT, THE MOTHER OF HARLOTS AND ABOMINA-
TIONS OF THE EARTH' (Rev. 17:5). In her commentary on this biblical
verse, CR describes this woman as 'illustrating the particular foulness, degra-
dation, loathsomeness, to which a perverse rebellious woman because feminine
not masculine is liable' (*FD* 400). In Rev. 17:16 she is described as 'drunken
with the blood of the saints'.

"Standing afar off for the fear of her torment"

FD (418–19) in CR's commentary on Rev. 18:9–10.

Title 'Standing afar off for the fear of her torment, saying, Alas, alas, that great city Babylon, that mighty city! for in one hour is thy judgment come' (Rev. 18:10).

"O Lucifer, Son of the Morning!"

FD (257–8) in CR's commentary on Rev. 9:1: 'And the fifth angel sounded, and I saw a star fall from heaven unto the earth: and to him was given the key of the bottomless pit.'

Title [untitled] *1892*.
'How art thou fallen from heaven, O Lucifer, son of the morning! how art thou cut down to the ground, which didst weaken the nations!' (Isa. 14:12).
2 *A glory hurtled from its car* see note for l. 7 of 'Lord, make us all love all: that when we meet'.
5 *earth's utmost bar* the barrier between heaven and earth. Cf. DGR, 'The Blessed Damozel', ll. 1–2 (see note for ll. 7–8 of 'Martyrs' Song').
7 *nebular* relating to the hazy masses of dust and gas seen among the stars.

['Alas, alas! for the self-destroyed']

FD (526) in CR's commentary on Rev. 22:3–4.

[As froth on the face of the deep']

FD (88) in CR's commentary on Rev. 3:2.

1 *the face of the deep* 'And the earth was without form, and void; and darkness was upon the face of the deep. And the Spirit of God moved upon the face of the waters' (Gen. 1:2); 'The waters are hid as with a stone, and the face of the deep is frozen' (Job 38.30).
4 *As gourd of a day and a night* allusion to the story in which God causes a gourd to shade Jonah 'to deliver him from his grief. So Jonah was exceeding glad of the gourd. But God prepared a worm when the morning rose the next day, and it smote the gourd that it withered' (Jonah 4:6–7). In *SF*, CR writes that the gourd 'turns our eyes inward upon our own selves, our own brief life, our own inevitable death. The gourd born in a night perished in a night, and

became as though it had never been. Even so, and yet not so, we: born and cut off in time, we must none the less fulfil our eternity; once loaded with the responsibility of life we can never shift it off, never repudiate our identity, never force our way back into the nothingness whence we emerged' (102). Later, she adds that 'like the gourd', sin 'puts forth rapidity of growth' (219).

5-6 *As harvest that no man shall reap, / As vintage that never shall be* 'Thou shalt sow, but thou shalt not reap; thou shalt tread the olives, but thou shalt not anoint thee with oil; and sweet wine, but shalt not drink wine' (Mic. 6:15).

      "Where their worm dieth not, and the fire is not quenched"

FD (338) in CR's commentary on Rev. 13:7 (see headnote of 'Slain in their high places: fallen on rest').

Title 'And if thy hand offend thee, cut it off: it is better for thee to enter into life maimed, than having two hands to go into hell, into the fire that never shall be quenched: Where their worm dieth not, and the fire is not quenched' (Mark 9:43–4).

      ['Toll, bell, toll. For hope is flying']

FD (296) in CR's commentary on Rev. 11:10.

DIVERS WORLDS. TIME AND ETERNITY.

      ['Earth has clear call of daily bells']

[Composed 6 Aug. 1858. Originally part of ' "Yet a little while" ' ['These days are long before I die'], which CR never published as such, but from which she also took ' "Vanity of Vanities" ' ['Of all the downfalls in the world'], printed in 1893.]

Entry for 11 March in *TF* (50).

2 *chancel-vault* arched ceiling of the chancel, which is the space around the altar of a church, often enclosed, for the clergy and choir.

"Escape to the Mountain"

FD (413) in CR's commentary on Rev. 18:2.

Title [untitled] *1892*.
   'escape to the mountain, lest thou be consumed' (Gen. 19:17). See note for
Part 6, l. 4 of 'Monna Innominata'.
11 *Lord, Who has called them happy that endure* 'but he that shall endure unto the
end, the same shall be saved' (Mark 13:13).

['I lift mine eyes to see: earth vanisheth']

FD (429) in CR's commentary on Rev. 19:1–2 (see headnote of 'Alleluia! or
Alas! my heart is crying').

1 *I lift mine eyes to see: earth vanisheth* cf. 'I lift mine eyes, and what to see / But a
world happy and fair!' (Ingelow, 'Seven Times Five. Widowhood' (1888)). See
also ll. 5–6 of 'A Better Resurrection': 'I lift mine eyes, but dimmed with
grief / No everlasting hills I see', and note for l. 11 of 'Easter Day'.

"Yet a little while" ['Heaven is not far, tho' far the sky']

['First published in *Dublin University Magazine* 1, n.s. (1878), p. 104' (*Letters*, II,
150).]

First poem in *FD* (11), appearing in CR's commentary on Rev. 1:1–2.

Title [untitled] *1892*.
   See note for title of 'Yet a Little While' ['I dreamed and did not seek: today
I seek']. 'As to darling Maria [who had died in 1876], I do trust her gain is too
great for our great loss to be weighed against it: "yet a little while" –' (letter
to DGR, [? late December 1877]; *Letters*, II, 155).
5–6 *how long? . . . O Lord, how long* see note for Part 2, l. 12 of 'Old and New
Year Ditties'.

"Behold, it was very good"

FD (159) in CR's commentary on Rev. 4:8 (see note for ll. 19–20 of 'Christian
and Jew. A Dialogue').

Title [untitled] *1892*.
   See note for l. 1 of 'Sexagesima'.

"Whatsoever is right, that shall ye receive"

[Composed 27 Aug. 1857. Originally part of ' "The heart knoweth its own bitterness" ' ['When all the over-work of life'], which CR never published as such.]

Entry for 17 Aug. in *TF* (158–9).

Title Matt. 20:7. A reference to the parable in which Jesus compared the Kingdom of Heaven to a landowner who hired labourers to work in his vineyard. Although he hired them at different times of day (some in the morning, some in the evening), he paid them all the same wage.

11–12 *Eye hath not seen, nor ear hath heard, / Nor heart conceived* see note for l. 37 of 'Advent' ['This Advent moon shines cold and clear'].

['This near-at-hand land breeds pain by measure']

CS (xviii–xix) in the preface ('The Key to my Book').

31–3 *ease you . . . please you . . . Jesu* In this rhyme, Kent hears an echo of Herbert's reconstruction of 'JESU' ('Jesu' [1633]) into 'I ease you' (' "By thought, word, and deed": George Herbert and CR,' in Kent, *Achievement* 261).

"Was Thy Wrath against the Sea?"

FD (479) in CR's commentary on Rev. 21:1: 'And I saw a new heaven and a new earth: for the first heaven and the first earth were passed away; and there was no more sea.' See note for title of ' "And there was no more sea" ', below.

Title [untitled] *1892*.
   'Was the LORD displeased against the rivers? was thine anger against the rivers? was thy wrath against the sea, that thou didst ride upon thine horses and thy chariots of salvation?' (Hab. 3:8). 'These lines from *The Face of the Deep* relate to the text, "There was no more sea," after the creation of "a new heaven and a new earth." This text dwelt much in Christina's mind, and prompted various allusions in her writings' ('Notes' 473).

"And there was no more Sea"

FD (191) in CR's commentary on Rev. 5:13: 'And every creature which is in heaven, and on the earth, and under the earth, and such as are in the sea, and all that are in them, heard I saying, Blessing, and honour, and glory, and power, be unto him that sitteth upon the throne, and unto the Lamb for ever and ever.' Referring to this verse, WR writes: 'Notwithstanding the title which the present piece bears in the volume *Verses*, it comes in *The Face of the Deep* in connection with a very different passage of *The Apocalypse* . . .' ('Notes' 473).

Title [untitled] *1892*.
See headnote of ' "Was Thy Wrath against the Sea?" ', above. In her commentary for Rev. 21:1 in *FD*, CR asks: 'And wherefore not the sea?' (477). The sea, writes CR, is 'constituted as a passage, not as an abode . . . Thus it presents to us a picture of all which must be left behind' (478). In her extensive commentary on this Bible verse in *SF*, CR writes that at first reading: 'our heart sinks at foresight of the familiar sea expunged from earth and heaven; that sea to us so long and so inexhaustibly a field of wonder and delight'. But, she adds: 'The Inspired Volume seems written rather for our instruction as regards ourselves, and consequently as regards the visible creation in reference to ourselves, than from a more general purpose of enlarging our knowledge touching matters wholly extraneous', and concludes that the only thing lost is the 'barrier of separation', 'restless waters' and floods (106–10). Later in *SF*, CR returns to the same verse, saying, ' "No more sea" (xxx. 1) puzzles us: but we bridge over our non-sequence by exclaiming, "No more separation" ' (176). Se also note for l. 6 of ' "Hark! the Alleluias of the great salvation" '.

['Roses on a brier']

Entry for 9 June in *TF* (110).

8 *There shall be no more sea* see notes for titles of ' "Was Thy Wrath against the Sea?" ' and ' "And there was no more Sea" ', above.

['We are of those who tremble at Thy word']

FD (35) in CR's commentary on Rev. 1:12–16.

10 *hope deferred* see note for l. 2 of 'A Pause of Thought'.

"Awake, thou that sleepest"

FD (532) in CR's commentary on Rev. 22:10: 'And he saith unto me, Seal not the sayings of the prophecy of this book: for the time is at hand.'

Title [untitled] *1892*.
'Wherefore he saith, Awake thou that sleepest, and arise from the dead, and Christ shall give thee light' (Eph. 5:14).

1–3 *The night . . . the armour of light* Rom. 13:12.
12 *the day is at hand* see note for l. 1 of 'Sunday before Advent'.

['We know not when, we know not where']

Entry for 18 Nov. in *TF* (221).

11 *One day to see Him face to Face* see note for l. 3 of 'Mirrors of Life and Death'.

"I will lift up mine eyes unto the Hills." ['When sick of life and all the world']

[Composed 26 June 1856. Originally part of 'The Chiefest among ten thousand' ('When sick of life and all the world'), which CR never published as such, but from which she also took 'I know you not'.]

Entry for 26 April in *TF* (79–80).
    In MS2 (BL), DGR wrote: 'might be shortened'.

Title see note for ll. 5–6 of 'A Better Resurrection'.
7 *The golden streets* see note for ll. 35–6 of 'Paradise'.
    gateways pearled see note for l. 6 of ' "Hark! the Alleluias of the great salvation" '.
9 *There is a time for all things* see note for Part 2, l. 61 of 'The German-French Campaign. 1870–1871'.
10 *The Word of Truth, Thyself the Word* 'In the beginning was the Word, and the Word was with God, and the Word was God' (John 1:1).
12 *A time for hope deferred* see note for l. 2 of 'A Pause of Thought'.
16 *When Thou shalt wipe our tears* see note for l. 29 of 'Christian and Jew. A Dialogue'.
17 *Then the new Heavens and Earth shall be* 'For, behold, I create new heavens and a new earth: and the former shall not be remembered, nor come into mind' (Isa. 65:17).
20 *Nor barrier of the sea* see notes for titles of ' "Was Thy Wrath against the Sea"?' and ' "And there was no more sea" '.
22 *God shall be the Light* 1 John 1:5 and Rev. 22:5 (see note for l. 12 of ' "I will Lift Up Mine Eyes Unto the Hills" ' ['I am pale with sick desire']).
23 *no death, no sting* see note for Part 3, ll. 13–14 of 'The Thread of Life'.
24 *For God Who reigns is Love* see note for l. 8 of 'Trinity Sunday'.

"Then whose shall those things be?"

[Composed 16 July 1858. Originally part of 'My old friends', which CR never published as such, but from which she also took 'They lie at rest, our blessed dead', printed in 1893.]

Entry for 15 April in *TF* (71–2), in which CR talks about 'the courageous reverence with which one [MR] to whom a friend was exhibiting prints from the Book of Job, avowed herself afraid to look at a representation which went counter to the Second Commandment ["Thou shalt not make . . . any graven image" – Ex. 20:4], and looked not at it.'

Title [untitled] *1885, 1886a.*
 See note for ll. 16–18 of 'A Testimony'.
3 *Poor treasure* see note for l. 10 of 'O Lord, on Whom we gaze and dare not gaze'.
 add field to field 'Woe unto them that join house to house, that lay field to field, till there be no place, that they may be placed alone in the midst of the earth!' (Isa. 5:8).

"His Banner over me was Love"

Entry for 24 Nov. in *TF* (225).

Title [untitled] *1885, 1886a.*
 See note for l. 5 of 'After Communion'.
10 *no more sea* see notes for titles of ' "Was Thy Wrath against the Sea?" ' and ' "And there was no more Sea" '.

['Beloved, yield thy time to God, for He']

FD (81) in CR's commentary on Rev. 2:25.

7 *Till death be swallowed up in victory* 'He will swallow up death in victory' (Isa. 25:8; see also note for l. 29 of 'Christian and Jew. A Dialogue'); 'So when this corruptible shall have put on incorruption, and this mortal shall have put on immortality, then shall be brought to pass the saying that is written, Death is swallowed up in victory' (1 Cor. 15:54).
13 *lily, rose or violet* see note for ll. 5–7 of 'Paradise'.

['Time seems not short']

FD (278) in CR's commentary on Rev. 10:6: 'And sware by him that liveth for ever and ever, who created heaven, and the things that therein are, and the earth, and the things that therein are, and the sea, and the things which are therein, that there should be time no longer.'

4 *amort* dead (French).

['The half moon shows a face of plaintive sweetness']

FD (242) in CR's commentary on Rev. 8:1.

"As the Doves to their windows"

FD (186) in CR's commentary on Rev. 5:9–10 (see headnote of ' "I will come and heal him" '). The first stanza is reminiscent of the childhood dream CR once reported to DGR in which she 'thought she was "in Regent's Park at dawn," while, just as the sun rose, she seemed to see "a wave of yellow light sweep from the trees." It "was a multitude of canaries, thousands of them," all the canaries in London. They had met, and were going back to captivity' (Bell, *CR*, quoting William Sharp, 11).

Title [untitled] *1892*.
  See note for Part 10, l. 13 of 'Later Life'.

['Oh knell of a passing time']

FD (121) in CR's commentary on Rev. 3:11 (see note for title of ' "That no man take thy Crown" ').

3–4 *tedious sea / Will it never cease to be* see notes for titles of ' "Was Thy Wrath against the Sea?" ' and ' "And there was no more Sea" '.
5–6 *when night and when day, / Moon and sun, pass away* 'and the sun became black as sackcloth of hair, and the moon became as blood; And the stars of heaven fell unto the earth . . .' (Rev. 6:12–13).

['Time passeth away with its pleasure and pain']

FD (463) in CR's commentary on Rev. 20:4.

2 *garlands of cypress and bay* suggestive of mourning and of triumph, respectively; see notes for l. 4 of 'Song' ['When I am dead, my dearest'] and for l. 2 of 'Song' ['Oh roses for the flush of youth'].

"The Earth shall tremble at the Look of Him"

FD (384–5) in CR's commentary on Rev. 16:21.

Title [untitled] *1892*.
  'He looketh on the earth, and it trembleth: he toucheth the hills, and they smoke' (Ps. 104:32).
1 *Tremble . . . at the Presence of the Lord* 'Fear ye not me? saith the LORD: will ye not tremble at my presence' (Jer. 5:22).

['Time lengthening, in the lengthening seemeth long']

FD (375) in CR's commentary on Rev. 15:5–6.

4 *ran a rapid race* see note for ll. 11–12 of 'Who Shall Deliver Me?'
12 *everlasting hill* see note for ll. 5–6 of 'A Better Resurrection'.
15 *Eternity still rolling forth its car* see note for l. 91 of 'The Convent Threshold'.

"All Flesh is Grass"

FD (304–5) in CR's commentary on Rev. 11:18.

Title [untitled] *1892*.
  See note for l. 37 of 'A Testimony'.

['Heaven's chimes are slow, but sure to strike at last']

[Lines 1–4 were composed 25 July 1854; date for ll. 5–8 unknown. Lines 1–4 form Part 3, stanza 3 of 'Three Stages', which CR never published as such.]

Entry for 5 April in *TF* (65).

Title [untitled] *1885, 1886a*.

7 *A time to suffer, and a time to do* see note for Part 2, l. 61 of 'The German-French Campaign. 1870–1871'.

"There remaineth therefore a Rest to the People of God"

[Composed 17 Feb. 1854. Originally part of ' "There remaineth therefore a rest" ', which CR never published as such, but from which she also took 'The Bourne'.]

Entry for 9 April in *TF* (68).

    MS2 (BodL) is an example of the editorial collaboration of CR and her brothers: above the title is written in DGR's hand: 'Take 2 stanzas' – advice she apparently followed, using stanzas marked '1' and '2' in DGR's hand (the second and fifth stanzas) to form 'The Bourne'; and some of the stanzas have marginal notations in WR's hand.

Title [untitled] *1885, 1886a.*

    'There remaineth therefore a rest to the people of God' (Heb. 4:9). CR used a variation of this title for three poems.

['Parting after parting']

[Lines 1–10 composed 15 June 1858; ll. 11–16 composed 11 June 1864. In MS3 (BL), ll. 11–16 originally part of 'Meeting', which CR never published as such. In 1885 and 1886a presented as two separate poems: ll. 1–10 and ll. 11–16.]

Lines 1–10 form the entry for 30 May in *TF* (102); 'stanza 2 belongs to 10 August [153], and in *Time Flies* it relates to the parting and reunion of two martyrs – Laurence and Pope Sixtus' ('Notes' 473). WR identifies the occasion for the original poem from which stanza 1 was taken ('Goodbye' – the title in MS2 (BL)) as a parting from a visit to friends, the Bell Scotts (see headnote of 'At Home'): 'It will thus be seen that the intensity of feeling here expressed really originated in a very slight occurrence – the occurrence itself merely served the poet's turn as a suggestion of highly serious matters' (473).

8 *Without a sea* see notes for titles of ' "Was Thy Wrath against the Sea?" ' and ' "And there was no more Sea" '.

"They put their trust in Thee, and were not confounded"

Part I is the entry for 15 Oct. and Part II for 16 Oct. in *TF* (199).

Title 'They cried unto thee, and were delivered: they trusted in thee, and were not confounded' (Ps. 22:5).

II

2 *Blessed it is, believing, not to see* when Jesus appeared to his disciples after the Resurrection, 'Doubting' Thomas insisted on touching Jesus' wounds before he would believe. Jesus said: 'Thomas, because thou hast seen me, thou hast believed: blessed are they that have not seen, and yet have believed' (John 20:29).

['Short is time, and only time is bleak']

FD (505) in CR's commentary on Rev. 21:16.

For Each

Unlike the other poems in *FD*, this (551) and the next ('For All') do not appear in the verse commentary, but form a conclusion to the book as a whole.

1 *My harvest is done* see note for l. 11 of 'Easter Day'.
8 *the narrow way* see note for l. 46 of 'Paradise'.
10 *The scythe has fallen* see note for l. 9 of 'Mary Magdalene and the Other Mary'.

For All

FD (552) as the concluding poem; see headnote of 'For Each', above. See headnote of 'Dream-Land'.

1 *Man's harvest is past, his summer is ended* see note for title of ' "Summer Is Ended" '.

NEW JERUSALEM AND ITS CITIZENS

"The Holy City, New Jerusalem"

CS (90–91) in the chapter entitled 'St. John, Apostle and Evangelist'.

Title [untitled] *1881CS*.
    See note for l. 5 of 'All Saints: Martyrs'. In *1881CS*, the poem is preceded by: ' "He shewed me the holy Jerusalem".—*Revelation* xxi.10.'
1 *Jerusalem is built of gold* see note for ll. 35–6 of 'Paradise'.

18 *Which see not day or night* see note for l. 12 of ' "I Will Lift Up Mine Eyes Unto the Hills" ' ['I am pale with sick desire'].
20 *The Tree of Life* see note for ll. 13–14 of 'Eve'.

['When wickedness is broken as a tree']

FD (432) in CR's commentary on Rev. 19:6: 'And I heard as it were the voice of a great multitude, and as the voice of many waters, and as the voice of mighty thunderings, saying, Alleluia: for the Lord God omnipotent reigneth.'

1 *When wickedness is broken as a tree* 'The womb shall forget him; the worm shall feed sweetly on him; he shall be no more remembered; and wickedness shall be broken as a tree' (Job 24:20).
4 *banished with the sea* see notes for titles of ' "Was Thy Wrath against the Sea?" ' and ' "And there was no more Sea" '.

['Jerusalem of fire']

FD (372) in CR's commentary on Rev. 15:2 (see note for l. 6 of 'The Convent Threshold').

"She shall be brought unto the King"

FD (496–7) in CR's commentary on Rev. 21:10–11.

Title [untitled] *1892*.
   'The king's daughter is all glorious within: her clothing is of wrought gold. She shall be brought unto the king in raiment of needlework: the virgins her companions that follow her shall be brought unto thee' (Ps. 45:13–14).
6 *With tears wiped away* see note for l. 29 of 'Christian and Jew. A Dialogue'.

['Who is this that cometh up not alone']

Entry for 30 Oct. in *TF* (208).
   In the margin, in CR's hand (1885r): 'These lines were suggested by a sermon I heard from the Rev.—Marshall Turner in Christ Church, Woburn Square.'

['Who sits with the King in His Throne? Not a slave but a Bride']

FD (145) in CR's commentary on Rev. 3:21–2: 'To him that overcometh will I grant to sit with me in my throne, even as I also overcame, and am set down with my Father in his throne. He that hath an ear, let him hear what the Spirit saith unto the churches.'

6 *Leviathan's whirlpool and Dragon's dominion* 'In that day the LORD with his sore and great and strong sword shall punish leviathan the piercing serpent, even leviathan that crooked serpent; and he shall slay the dragon that is in the sea' (Isa. 27:1).

8 *dove-eyed* see notes for l. 14 of 'Advent Sunday' and l. 10 of 'Whitsun Tuesday'.

Antipas

FD (68–9) in CR's commentary on Rev. 2:13, in which Christ speaks to the church of Pergamos: 'I know thy works, and where thou dwellest, even where Satan's seat is: and thou holdest fast my name, and hast not denied my faith, even in those days wherein Antipas was my faithful martyr, who was slain among you, where Satan dwelleth.' Immediately preceding this poem, CR writes: ' "Antipas was My faithful martyr."—Men know him not now, how he lived or how he died. God alone knows him. Enough for blessed Antipas' (68). Antipas (d. *c.* 90), the bishop of Perganum in Asia Minor, was burned to death for his faith.

Title [untitled] *1892*.

"Beautiful for situation"

FD (482) in CR's commentary on Rev. 21:2 (see note for l. 5 of 'All Saints: Martyrs').

Title [untitled] *1892*.
   'Beautiful for situation, the joy of the whole earth, is mount Zion, on the sides of the north, the city of the great King' (Ps. 48:2).

6 *all doves on gold or silver wing* see note for l. 10 of 'Whitsun Tuesday'.

7 *thro' agate windows* 'And I will make thy windows of agates' (Isa. 54:12).

8 *where pearl gates wide open stand* see note for l. 6 of 'Hark! the Alleluias of the great salvation'.

13 *set our face and go* see note for l. 211 of 'From House to Home'.

14 *Faint yet pursuing* see note for l. 11 of 'A Life's Parallels'.

['Lord, by what inconceivable dim road']

FD (495–6) in CR's commentary on Rev. 21:9 (see headnote of ' "Are they not all Ministering Spirits?" ').

11 *hope deferred* see note for l. 2 of 'A Pause of Thought'.

"As cold waters to a thirsty soul, so is good news from a far country"

[Composed 11 Nov. 1858. Originally part of ' "Rivals" ', which CR never published as such.]

Entry for 2 June in *TF* (104).

Title Pro. 25:25.
21 *The path to Heaven is steep and straight* see note for l. 46 of 'Paradise'.

['Cast down but not destroyed, chastened not slain']

FD (61–2) in CR's commentary on Rev. 2:10 (see note for l. 4 of ' "That no man take thy Crown" ').

Title see note for l. 204 of 'From House to Home'; also 'As unknown, and yet well known; as dying, and, behold, we live; as chastened and not killed' (2 Cor. 6:9).
6 *as a shadow I am flitting by* 'Man is like to vanity: his days are as a shadow that passeth away' (Ps. 144:4; see also Job 14:2).

['Lift up thine eyes to seek the invisible']

FD (471) in CR's commentary on Rev. 20:11 (see note on l. 36 of 'After This the Judgment').

5 *it is well* see note for l. 23 of 'One Day'.
10–11 *Those glorious beauties unexperienced / By ear or eye or by heart hitherto* see note for ll. 37–8 of 'Advent' ['This Advent moon shines cold and clear'].
12 *I know Whom I have trusted* 'For the which cause I also suffer these things: nevertheless I am not ashamed; for I know whom I have believed, and am persuaded that he is able to keep that which I have committed unto him against that day' (2 Tim. 1:12).
14 *Golden Jerusalem* see note for ll. 35–6 of 'Paradise'.

"Love is strong as Death" ['As flames that consume the mountains, as winds that coerce the sea']

FD (493) in CR's commentary on Rev. 11:7: 'And when they shall have finished their testimony, the beast that ascendeth out of the bottomless pit shall make war against them, and shall overcome them, and kill them.'

Title see note for l. 1 of 'An End'.
3 *the Trump of the Jubilee* see note for l. 11 of ' "They Desire a Better Country" '.

"Let them rejoice in their beds" ['Crimson as the rubies, crimson as the roses']

FD (402) in CR's commentary on Rev. 17:6.

Title [untitled] *1892*.
   'Let the saints be joyful in glory: let them sing aloud upon their beds' (Ps. 149:5).
5 *the rosy east* cf. CR's *Il rosseggiar dell' Oriente* ('The Reddening of the East') for a similar image.
8 *his race is run* see note for ll. 11–12 of 'Who Shall Deliver Me?'

['Slain in their high places: fallen on rest']

FD (337) in CR's commentary on Rev. 13:7: 'And it was given unto him to make war with the saints, and to overcome them: and power was given him over all kindreds, and tongues, and nations.'

1 *Slain in their high places* 'The beauty of Israel is slain upon thy high places: how are the mighty fallen!' (2 Sam. 1:19).
8 *heaven's amaranth* flower said never to fade; emblematic of continuance, immortality and incorruptibility.

"What hath God wrought!"

FD (541) in CR's commentary on Rev. 22:16 (see note for l. 10 of 'Herself a rose, who bore the Rose').

Title [untitled] *1892*.
   'Surely there is no enchantment against Jacob, neither is there any divination against Israel: according to this time it shall be said of Jacob and of Israel, What hath God wrought!' (Num. 23:23).

"Before the Throne, and before the Lamb"

FD (352–3) in CR's commentary on Rev. 14:2–3: 'And I heard a voice from heaven, as the voice of many waters, and as the voice of a great thunder: and I heard the voice of harpers harping with their harps: And they sung as it were a new song before the throne, and before the four beasts, and the elders: and no man could learn that song but the hundred and forty and four thousand, which were redeemed from the earth.'

Title [untitled] *1892*.
   See note for Part I, l. 3 of ' "Behold a Shaking" '.
1 *As the voice of many waters* 'and his voice as the sound of many waters' (Rev. 1:15). In her extensive commentary on this biblical verse, CR writes: 'Still waters are silent; flowing waters find a voice. This "voice as the sound of many waters" seems to address man not from the eternal calm of Christ's Godhead; but rather from that veritable and accessible Humanity which He assumed' (*FD* 36).
5 *Circling round the rainbow of their perfect ring* 'and there was a rainbow round about the throne, in sight like unto an emerald' (Rev. 4:3). In her commentary on this biblical verse in *FD*, CR points out three associations with the rainbow: the Holy Spirit, the conveying of hope to Noah and a form of light that enables us to look at it without it blinding us (152).
8 *Where raiment is white of blood-steeped linen* see note for l. 13 of 'Martyrs' Song'.
9 *Where crowns are golden* 'And round about the throne were four and twenty seats: and upon the seats I saw four and twenty elders sitting, clothed in white raiment; and they had on their heads crowns of gold' (Rev. 4:4).

"He shall go no more out"

FD (125) in CR's commentary on Rev. 3:12: 'Him that overcometh will I make a pillar in the temple of my God, and he shall go no more out: and I will write upon him the name of my God, and the name of the city of my God, which is new Jerusalem, which cometh down out of heaven from my God: and I will write upon him my new name.'

Title [untitled] *1892*.
10 *who cast their crowns on Heaven's high floor* see note for l. 179 of 'From House to Home'.

['Yea, blessed and holy is he that hath part in the First Resurrection']

FD (466) in CR's commentary on Rev. 20:6: 'Blessed and holy is he that hath part in the first resurrection: on such the second death hath no power, but they shall be priests of God and of Christ, and shall reign with him a thousand years.' Her comments focus on the promise that those who give all in this life gain all in the next (*FD* 465).

8 *that worshipful stone of the Wise Master Builder's election* see note for l. 14 of 'Lord, grant us eyes to see and ears to hear'.

9 *all Hallows* all the holy ones, or saints.

10 *Jonathan of David's delection* 'And it came to pass, when he had made an end of speaking unto Saul, that the soul of Jonathan was knit with the soul of David, and Jonathan loved him as his own soul' (1 Sam. 18:1). 'Delection' is delight.

['The joy of Saints, like incense turned to fire']

FD (181) in CR's commentary on Rev. 5:8 (see headnote of ' "Subject to like Passions as we are" ').

9 *All robed in white and all with palm in hand* see note for ll. 37–8 of 'Paradise'.

10 *Crowns too they have of gold* see note for l. 9 of ' "Before the Throne, and before the Lamb" '.

11–12 *The street is golden . . . Or on a sea of glass and fire they stand* see notes for ll. 35–6 of 'Paradise' and for l. 6 of 'The Convent Threshold'.

['What are these lovely ones, yea, what are these?']

FD (500) in CR's commentary on Rev. 21:12.

6 *By golden streets* see note for ll. 35–6 of 'Paradise'.

thro' gates of pearl see note for l. 6 of 'Hark! the Alleluias of the great salvation'.

7 *They entered on the joys that will not cease* allusion to the parable of the talents, in which the servant who invests the master's money is praised (while those who did not are blamed): 'His lord said unto him, Well done, thou good and faithful servant: thou hast been faithful over a few things, I will make thee ruler over many things: enter thou into the joy of thy lord' (Matt. 25:21).

8 *And found again all firstfruits sacrificed* in this context, the first-fruits – the sacrifice of the 'first' and 'best' – are the saints: see headnote of 'Unspotted lambs to follow the one Lamb'.

9–10 *And wherefore . . . crowns, O ye who walk in white* CR has tied together three different descriptions from the Book of Revelation: see notes for headnote of

' "Subject to like Passions as we are" ' and for l. 9 of ' "Before the Throne, and before the Lamb" '. See also note for ll. 37–8 of 'Paradise'.

12 *Te Deum* from the opening words *Te Deum laudamus* ('Thee, God, we praise') in the *Book of Common Prayer*, an ancient Latin hymn sung as a psalm at Morning Prayer in the Church of England or as a thanksgiving on special occasions; any public utterance in praise of God.

14 *We cast our crowns* see note for l. 179 of 'From House to Home'.

"The General Assembly and Church of the Firstborn"

FD (515) in CR's commentary on Rev. 21:24: 'And the nations of them which are saved shall walk in the light of it: and the kings of the earth do bring their glory and honour into it.'

Title [untitled] *1892*.

'But ye are come . . . To the general assembly and church of the firstborn, which are written in heaven, and to God the Judge of all, and to the spirits of just men made perfect' (Heb. 12:22–3).

6 *the ransomed race* see note for title of ' "The ransomed of the Lord" '.

16 *Life-losers* cf. Jesus' saying: 'he that loseth his life for my sake shall find it' (Matt. 10:39; see also Matt. 16:25; Mark 8:35; and Luke 9:24).

17 *All blessed hungry and athirst sufficed* see note for ll. 3–4 of 'Lent'.

18 *All who bore crosses* 'Then said Jesus unto his disciples, If any man will come after me, let him deny himself, and take up his cross, and follow me' (Matt. 16:24; see also Matt. 10:38; Mark 8:34; and Luke 9:23).

19 *Friends, brethren, sisters, of Lord Jesus Christ* 'For whosoever shall do the will of my Father which is in heaven, the same is my brother, and sister, and mother' (Matt. 12:50).

"Every one that is perfect shall be as his master"

Entry for 19 Oct. in *TF* (201–2). It follows the Feast of St Luke, Evangelist – and mentions the other gospel writers – Matthew, Mark and John – but not Luke.

Title [untitled] *1885, 1886a*.

'The disciple is not above his master: but every one that is perfect shall be as his master' (Luke 6:40).

2–3 *like St. Paul, / Like St. John, or like St. Peter* John and Peter were among Jesus' original twelve disciples; Paul was converted after Jesus' death and became the central influence in the growth of Christianity (see headnote of 'Conversion of St. Paul').

[' "As dying, and behold we live!" ']

FD (43) in CR's commentary on Rev. 1:17–18.

1 *'As dying, and behold we live!'* 2 Cor. 6:9 (see note for title of 'Cast down but not destroyed, chastened not slain').
10 *The morrow to its day they leave* see note for l. 91 of 'Maiden May'.

"So great a cloud of Witnesses"

FD (305) in CR's commentary on Rev. 11:18.

Title [untitled] *1892*.
   Heb. 12:1 (see note for ll. 11–12 of 'Who Shall Deliver Me?').
1 *lift up mine eyes* see note for ll. 5–6 of 'A Better Resurrection'.
4 *their jubilee* see note for l. 11 of ' "They Desire a Better Country" '.
5 *As the sound of waters their voice* see note for l. 1 of ' "Before the Throne, and before the Lamb" '.
12 *the Lamb on the Throne* 'For the Lamb which is in the midst of the throne shall feed them, and shall lead them unto living fountains of waters: and God shall wipe away all tears from their eyes' (Rev. 7:17).

['Our Mothers, lovely women pitiful']

FD (401) in CR's commentary on Rev. 17:4–5 (see notes for ll. 145–6 of 'From House to Home' and for title of 'Babylon the Great').

7 *scathe* harm.
8 *dule* grief, sorrow, mourning; the word is often found in Scottish ballads.
13 *Ah, happy eyes! whose tears are wiped away* see note for l. 29 of 'Christian and Jew. A Dialogue'.

['Safe where I cannot lie yet']

FD (205) in CR's commentary on Rev. 6:7.

3 *fume* fretful irritation.
10 *in blow* blooming.

"Is it well with the child?"

[Composed 3 Nov. 1865. Originally part of 'Young Death', which CR never published as such.]

Entry (untitled) for 7 Oct. in *TF* (194). 'This small lyric appeared in *Time Flies*, as being related to the martyrdom of St. Faith (supposed to be "a noble maiden of Aquitain" in the third century). Her feast is 6 October' ('Notes' 474). WR adds that the poem is 'obviously relating to some very youthful person known to the authoress. Who this may have been I cannot now say' (474).

Title 2. *1885, 1886a.*
    See note for l. 23 of 'One Day'.

['Dear Angels and dear disembodied Saints']

FD (222) in CR's commentary on Rev. 7:1: 'And after these things I saw four angels standing on the four corners of the earth, holding the four winds of the earth, that the wind should not blow on the earth, nor on the sea, nor on any tree.'

11 *deep calls to the deep* see note for l. 32 of ' "When My Heart Is Vexed, I Will Complain" ' ['O Lord, how canst Thou say Thou lovest me?'].

"To every seed his own body"

FD (109) in CR's commentary on Rev. 3:7 (see headnote of ' "Thou, God, seest me" ').

Title [untitled] *1892.*
    'But God giveth it a body as it hath pleased him, and to every seed his own body' (1 Cor. 15:38).

"What good shall my life do me?" ['Have dead men long to wait?']

[Probably composed between 6 Aug. and 15 Oct. 1858. Originally part of ' "Only believe" ', which CR never published as such.]

Entry for 12 Dec. in *TF* (238–9).

Title [untitled] *1885, 1886a.*
    From the story in which Jacob was sent to the land of his mother Rebekah's

people so he wouldn't marry one of the local women, as Esau had done: 'And Rebekah said to Isaac [Jacob's father], I am weary of my life because of the daughters of Heth: if Jacob take a wife of the daughters of Heth, such as these which are of the daughters of the land, what good shall my life do me?' (Gen. 27:46).

5 *Dust to dust* see note for l. 119 of 'A Martyr. The Vigil Of the Feast'.

22 *Those who sowed shall reap* see note for l. 6 of 'Vigil of St. Bartholomew'.

29 *In watered pastures fair* see note for l. 9 of 'Lord, hast Thou so loved us, and will not we'.

33 *Love casts out fear* see note for l. 36 of ' "They Desire a Better Country" '.

SONGS FOR STRANGERS AND PILGRIMS.

"Her Seed; It shall bruise thy head"

FD (13) in CR's commentary on Rev. 1:3 (see headnote of 'Lord, I am feeble and of mean account'). In a note in *FD*, CR writes: 'This one dearest mamma heard and liked' ('Notes' 468).

Title [untitled] *1892*.

God cursed the snake, who tempted Adam and Eve in the Garden of Eden: 'And I will put enmity between thee and the woman, and between thy seed and her seed; it shall bruise thy head, and thou shalt bruise his heel' (Gen. 3:15).

5 *shriven* to be shriven is to have confessed to one's sins and to be absolved of them.

7 *ten times sevenfold seven* see note for l. 24 of 'After This the Judgment'.

"Judge nothing before the time"

Entry for 16 Jan. in *TF* (13). 'The lines . . . appear to be intended to be read as a sequel to the entry for the 15th, which is on the text, "In the beginning God created the heaven and the earth," followed by a reflection that "Adam's initial work of production (so far as we are told) was sin, death, hell, for himself and his posterity" ' ('Notes' 468).

Title [untitled] *1885, 1886a*.

See note for l. 28 of 'Palm Sunday'.

9 *telling her bead-history* presumably praying a series of prayers and keeping count of them by using a rosary.

['How great is little man!']

FD (254) in CR's commentary on Rev. 8:12 (see headnote of ' "The Greatest of these is Charity" ').

1 *How great is little man* 'When I consider thy heavens, the work of thy fingers, the moon and the stars, which thou hast ordained; What is man, that thou art mindful of him? and the son of man, that thou visitest him? For thou has made him a little lower than the angels, and hast crowned him with glory and honour' (Ps. 8:3–5; see also Heb. 2:6–8).
15 *They looked not back* see note for l. 10 of 'Lord, make me one with Thine own faithful ones'.

['Man's life is but a working day']

[Composed 19 March 1864. Originally part of 'In Patience', which CR never published as such.]

Entry for 7 July in *TF* (132).

3 *A time to work, a time to pray* see note for Part 2, l. 61 of 'The German-French Campaign. 1870–1871'.

['If not with hope of life']

FD (320) in CR's commentary on Rev. 12:7–9.

5 *beneath the rod* 'And I will cause you to pass under the rod, and I will bring you into the bond of the covenant' (Eze. 20:37).

"The day is at hand"

[Date of composition of ll. 1–4 unknown; ll. 5–11 composed 23 Dec. 1852. Originally part of ' "The heart knoweth its own bitterness" ' ['Weep yet a while'], which CR never published as such.]

Entry for 19 March in *TF* (55).

Title [untitled] *1885, 1886a.*
    See note for l. 1 of 'Sunday before Advent'.

1 *Watch yet a while* see note for Part 2, l. 1 of 'Old and New Year Ditties'.

8 *Now we sow love in tears, but then shall reap* see note for l. 6 of 'Vigil of St. Bartholomew'.

"Endure hardness"

Entry for 13 April in *TF* (70).

Title [untitled] *1885, 1886a*.
   'Thou therefore endure hardness, as a good soldier of Jesus Christ' (2 Tim. 2:3).

"Whither the Tribes go up, even the Tribes of the Lord"

CS (518–19) in the chapter entitled 'All Saints'.

Title [untitled] *1881CS*.
   'Whither the tribes go up, the tribes of the LORD, unto the testimony of Israel, to give thanks unto the name of the LORD' (Ps. 122:4).
7 *heaped-up measure beyond measure* 'Give, and it shall be given unto you; good measure, pressed down, and shaken together, and running over, shall men give into your bosom. For with the same measure that ye mete withal it shall be measured to you again' (Luke 6:38).
9 *Our face is set like flint* see note for l. 206 of 'From House to Home'.
14 *Our face is set to reach Jerusalem* see note for l. 211 of 'From House to Home'.

['Where never tempest heaveth']

FD (295) in CR's commentary on Rev. 11:8.

['Marvel of marvels, if I myself shall behold']

FD (302) in CR's commentary on Rev. 11:15: 'And the seventh angel sounded; and there were great voices in heaven, saying, The kingdoms of this world are become the kingdoms of our Lord, and of his Christ; and he shall reign for ever and ever.' WR points out that the poem, like 'Passing Away' [Part 3 of 'Old and New Year Ditties'], 'is made up of one sole rhyme-sound; I think it holds nearly as high a rank [as "Passing Away"] among the authoress's verses. Its principal reference is, no doubt, to the deaths of her sister and mother' ('Notes' 468).

7 *cerements* graveclothes, or shrouds.

10 *The Bridegroom cometh* see note for l. 3 of 'Advent' ['This Advent moon shines cold and clear'].
12 *wold* elevated tract of open country.

"What is that to thee? follow thou me"

[Lines 1–12 composed 6 May 1864; ll. 13–18 composed 1 March 1864. Originally included part of 'Who Shall Deliver Me?' in MS3 (BL), printed in 1875. In 1885 and 1886a presented as two separate poems (untitled): ll. 1–12 and ll. 13–18.]

Lines 1–12 entry for 29 March in *TF* (61), and ll. 13–18 for 22 April (77).

Title [untitled] *1885, 1886a.*
    See note for l. 28 of 'I, Lord, Thy foolish sinner low and small'.
7 *Friend, go up higher* see note for title of 'The Lowest Place'.
8 *enter thou My joy* see note for l. 7 of 'What are these lovely ones, yea, what are these?'
9 *Be faithful unto death* see note for l. 4 of ' "That no man take thy Crown" '.
10 *wilderness doth flower* see note for l. 158 of 'From House to Home'.
12 *But thou, could'st thou not watch one hour* see note for Part 2, l. 1 of 'Old and New Year Ditties'.

"Worship God"

FD (442) in CR's commentary on Rev. 19:10: 'And I fell at his feet to worship him. And he said unto me, see thou do it not: I am thy fellowservant, and of thy brethren that have the testimony of Jesus: worship God: for the testimony of Jesus is the spirit of prophecy.'

Title see headnote, above; also 'for I am thy fellowservant, and of thy brethren the prophets, and of them which keep the sayings of this book: worship God' (Rev. 22:9). In her commentary on this biblical verse, CR writes: 'To study the Apocalypse out of idle curiosity would turn it, so far as the student's self were concerned, into a branch of the Tree of the Knowledge of Good and Evil. And what came of Eve's curious investigation of the original Tree we all know' (531).
2 *draw not near* when God appeared to Moses in the burning bush, God said, 'Draw not nigh hither: put off thy shoes from off thy feet, for the place whereon thou standest is holy ground' (Ex. 3:5).
5 *thorned and thistled plot* when Adam is cast out of the Garden of Eden, God curses the ground: 'Thorns also and thistles shall it bring forth to thee' (Gen. 3:18).

9–10 *give / Thy heart to Me, My child* 'My son, give me thine heart, and let thine eyes observe my ways' (Pro. 23:26).

"Afterward he repented, and went"

Entry for 11 May in *TF* (90).

I do not remember that any salient event of Christina's life was associated with that particular day, but may mention that 12 May was the birthday of Dante Gabriel, and the prose entry for this latter day might, without much straining, be supposed to have a certain reference to him; he had died three years before *Time Flies* was published. It may be that the two entries were, in some degree, 'read together' in their author's mind, as having a relation to him. ('Notes' 468)

Title [untitled] *1885, 1886a*.
From a parable Jesus tells of a man who asked his son to work in the vineyard; 'He answered and said, I will not: but afterward he repented, and went' (Matt. 21:29). The second son said he would work, but did not. Jesus, asking the rhetorical question which of the sons did the will of the Father, makes the point that 'the publicans and the harlots go into the kingdom of God before you' (Matt. 21:31).
4 *Thy kind word "Give it Me"* see note for ll. 9–10 of ' "Worship God" '.

"Are they not all Ministering Spirits?"

FD (495) in CR's commentary on Rev. 21:9: 'And there came unto me one of the seven angels which had the seven vials full of the seven last plagues, and talked with me, saying, Come hither, I will shew thee the bride, the Lamb's wife.' 'The point specially raised in the prose comment, which leads up to the poem, is that this gracious and joyful message is delivered by one of those same angels who poured forth the plagues' ('Notes' 468–9).

Title [untitled] *1892*.
'Are they not all ministering spirits, sent forth to minister for them who shall be heirs of salvation?' (Heb. 1:14).
3 *predilect* chosen or favoured in preference to others.
8 *Watch on and pray* see notes for l. 3 of 'Advent' ['This Advent moon shines cold and clear'] and for Part 2, l. 1 of 'Old and New Year Ditties'.

['Our life is long. Not so, wise Angels say']

[Composed 14 April 1856. Editions: 1885, 1886a, *1893*, 1896, 1904.]

Entry for 28 Sept. in *TF* (187).

Title How long? *1896*.

8 *Night cometh: no more work* see note for l. 52 of 'In the Willow Shade'.

10–12 *Thy Host who day nor night / Rest not from adoration, their delight / Crying "Holy, Holy, Holy," in the height* see note for ll. 19–20 of 'Christian and Jew. A Dialogue'.

18 *That where Thou art, there Thy Beloved might be* see note for l. 8 of 'Darkness and light are both alike to Thee'.

['Lord, what have I to offer? sickening fear']

Entry for 24 April in *TF* (78). 'The reference to "a heart-breaking loss" seems to indicate that these lines refer to some particular event in my sister's life. They appear in *Time Flies*, under the date 24 April; I do not identify any such event with that day, but can easily conceive a relation in the poem to some different day' ('Notes' 469).

['Joy is but sorrow']

Entry for 19 Jan. in *TF* (16).

['Can I know it?—Nay.—']

FD (112) in CR's commentary on Rev. 3:8. 'This composition . . . forms a sort of meditation on the words addressed by Christ to the Church of Philadelphia. Amid those words comes the expression "Thou hast a little strength." On this the authoress comments (in prose) – "Why not much strength? God knoweth." And soon afterwards the poem ensues' ('Notes' 469).

14 *pranked* dressed up.

25–7 *Dost thou covet bay? . . . Rather for a palm-branch pray* see notes for l. 2 of 'Song' ['Oh roses for the flush of youth'] and for ll. 37–8 of 'Paradise'.

"When my heart is vexed I will complain" [' "The fields are white to harvest, look and see']

[Lines 1–20 composed 10 May 1854. Originally part of ' "Ye have forgotten the exhortation" ', which CR never published as such.]

Entry for 2 Aug. in *TF* (147–8).

Title A DIALOGUE *1885, 1886a*.
'My soul is weary of my life; I will leave my complaint upon myself; I will speak in the bitterness of my soul' (Job 10:1).
1 *The fields are white to harvest* see note for l. 11 of 'Easter Day'.
8 *Grown sick with hope deferred* see note for l. 2 of 'A Pause of Thought'.
11 *His great jubilee* see note for l. 11 of ' "They Desire a Better Country" '.
15 *Who knocketh at His door* see note for l. 8 of 'Despised and Rejected'.
23 *Thy Will be done* see note for l. 12 of 'Alone Lord God, in Whom our trust and peace'.

"Praying always"

Entry for 8 March in *TF* (48).

Title [untitled] *1885, 1886a*.
'Praying always with all prayer and supplication in the Spirit, and watching thereunto with all perseverance and supplication for all saints' (Eph. 6:18).

"As thy days, so shall thy strength be"

FD (517) in CR's commentary on Rev. 21:25 (see note for l. 12 of ' "I Will Lift Up Mine Eyes Unto the Hills" ' ['I am pale with sick desire']).

Title [untitled] *1892*.
'Thy shoes shall be iron and brass; and as thy days, so shall thy strength be' (Deut. 33:25).
11 *To the Left Hand or the Right* allusion to Judgement Day, when Jesus separates the 'sheep', who will 'inherit the kingdom', from the 'goats', who are thrown into 'everlasting fire' (Matt. 25:31–46). See note for l. 11 of ' "Cried out with Tears" '.

['A heavy heart, if ever heart was heavy']

Entry for 4 Jan. in *TF* (4).

3 *fain to levy* willing to require.

['If love is not worth loving, then life is not worth living']

Entry for 16 May in *TF* (93).

7 *vanity of vanities* see note for l. 1 of 'One Certainty'.

['What is it Jesus saith unto the soul?']

[Lines 1–7 composed 2 March 1850; date of composition of ll. 8–14 unknown. Also published in 1897 and 1897a.]

Entry for 17 March in *TF* (54).

2 *Take up the Cross, and come and follow Me* see note for l. 18 of 'The General Assembly and Church of the Firstborn'.
9–10 *let tomorrow take / Heed to itself* see note for l. 91 of 'Maiden May'.

['They lie at rest, our blessed dead']

[Composed 16 July 1858. Originally part of 'My old Friends', which CR never published as such, but from which she also took 'Then whose shall those things be?', printed in 1893.]

Entry for 28 May in *TF* (101–2).

9 *sufficient sleep* see headnote of 'Dream-Land'.

"Ye that fear Him, both small and great"

CS (242) in the chapter entitled 'St. Philip and St. James the Less, Apostles'.

Title [untitled] *1881CS*.
'And a voice came out of the throne, saying, Praise our God, all ye his servants, and ye that fear him, both small and great' (Rev. 19:5). In her commentary on this biblical verse, CR writes: 'A very dear and saintly person years ago called home, once in my hearing exulted at this appearance of the

small that fear God: viewing it as a vast encouragement. Even they will be there not on sufferance, but taken account of, brought forward, called upon to enhance the acceptable rapture' (*FD* 430).
22 *Keeps its jubilee* see note for l. 11 of ' "They Desire a Better Country" '.

"Called to be Saints"

CR's book of this title was published in 1881. The poem is the entry for 15 June in *TF* (114). The entries for the previous two days form a suggestive context, dealing with the subject of envy and with images suggested by crossing the Alps: 'Better be the last of eagles than the first of worms'; 'And what shall they do, who display neither loftiness nor loveliness? If "one member be honoured, all the members rejoice in it" '; 'In foresight of the grave, whither we are all hastening, is it worth while to envy any? . . . "Grudge not one against another, brethren, lest ye be condemned: behold, the Judge standeth before the door" ' (113–14).

Title [untitled] *1885, 1886a*.
    'to them that are sanctified in Christ Jesus, called to be saints' (1 Cor. 1:2).
1 *The lowest place* see note for title of 'The Lowest Place'.
7–8 *For Right Hand or for Left Hand, but whose place / Waits there prepared for it* 'But to sit on my right hand and on my left hand is not mine to give; but it shall be given to them for whom it is prepared' (Mark 10:40; see also Matt. 20:23).

['The sinner's own fault? So it was']

[Lines 1–5 composed 1 Oct. 1863. Lines 1–5 originally part of 'Margery', which CR never published as such.]

Entry for 21 July in *TF* (139).

['Who cares for earthly bread tho' white?']

Entry for 12 Jan. in *TF* (11).

['Laughing Life cries at the feast']

[Composed by Sept. 1853.]
Entry for 3 March in *TF* (44).

"The end is not yet"

Entry for 19 Feb. in *TF* (35).

Title [untitled] *1885, 1886a.*
   'And ye shall hear of wars and rumours of wars: see that ye be not troubled: for all these things must come to pass, but the end is not yet' (Matt. 24:6; see also Mark 13:7).

['Who would wish back the Saints upon our rough']

[Composed 13 Dec. 1861. Originally part of 'Better so', which CR never published as such.]

Entry for 23 July in *TF* (140).

8 *hope deferred* see note for l. 2 of 'A Pause of Thought'.

"That which hath been is named already, and it is known that it is Man"

Entry for 30 April in *TF* (82–3).

Title [untitled] *1885, 1886a.*
   'That which hath been is named already, and it is known that it is man: neither may he contend with him that is mightier than he' (Ecc. 6:10).
1, 5, 9 *Eye hath not seen . . . Ear hath not heard . . . Nor heart conceived* see note for ll. 37–8 of 'Advent' ['This Advent moon shines cold and clear'].
13 *Deep calls to deep* see note for l. 32 of ' "When My Heart Is Vexed, I Will Complain" ' ['O Lord, how canst Thou say Thou lovest me?'].
15 *betake* to take oneself to.

['Of each sad word which is more sorrowful']

Entry for 5 Aug. in *TF* (150).

"I see that all things come to an end"

Entry for 11 Feb. in *TF* (31).

Title see note for l. 1 of 'Sunday before Advent'.

"But Thy Commandment is exceeding broad"

Entry for 12 Feb. in *TF* (31).

Title 'I have seen an end of all perfection: but thy commandment is exceeding broad' (Ps. 119:96).
3 *Rouse thy soul to watch and pray* see notes for l. 3 of 'Advent' ['This Advent moon shines cold and clear'] and for Part 2, l. 1 of 'Old and New Year Ditties'.

Sursum Corda

Entry for 12 Nov. in *TF* (217).

Title [untitled] *1885, 1886a*.
    Lift up your hearts (Latin).
1 *Lift up your hearts . . . We lift them up* at the beginning of the Eucharistic prayer in the *Book of Common Prayer*, the priest says to the congregation, 'Lift up your hearts', and the congregation answers, 'We lift them up unto the Lord.'
3 *that where Thou art I too may be* see note for l. 8 of 'Darkness and light are both alike to Thee'.
4 *Give Me thy heart* see note for ll. 9–10 of ' "Worship God" '.

['O ye, who art not dead and fit']

Entry for 21 June in *TF* (117–18).

7–8 *Love poises earth in space, Love rolls / Wide worlds rejoicing on their poles* cf. the last words of Dante's *Divine Comedy*: 'the Love that moves the Sun and the other stars' (*Paradiso*, Canto XXXIII, 146 – trans. John Ciardi).

['Where shall I find a white rose blowing?']

[On a copy of a printing of the poem on a single sheet is added in WR's handwriting: 'Printed for Bazaar, June / 84, for Boys' Home at Barnet (Gillum)'.]

Entry for 5 March in *TF* (46).

Title ROSES AND ROSES. / BY CHRISTINA G. ROSSETTI. / *(Copyright of the Author.) 1884*.

"Redeeming the Time"

Entry for 29 Jan. in *TF* (23).

Title [untitled] *1885, 1886a*.
    'Redeeming the time, because the days are evil' (Eph. 5:16); 'Walk in wisdom toward them that are without, redeeming the time' (Col. 4:5).
1 *A life of hope deferred* see note for l. 2 of 'A Pause of Thought'.
8 *harvest home* the time of harvest is Judgement Day, after which the righteous will live in Paradise.

"Now they desire a Better Country"

Entry for 5 May in *TF* (86).
    In the margin, in CR's hand (1885r): 'My first roundel'.

Title [untitled] *1885, 1886a*.
    See note for title of ' "They Desire a Better Country" '.
5 *to watch and pray* see notes for l. 3 of 'Advent' ['This Advent moon shines cold and clear'] and for Part 3, l. 17 of 'Old and New Year Ditties'.

A CASTLE-BUILDER'S WORLD

Entry for 1 April in *TF* (63). The imagery may echo Tennyson's *In Memoriam*: 'And mix with hollow masks of night; / Cloud-towers by ghostly masons wrought' (LXX, 4–5).

Epigraph 'But the cormorant and the bittern shall possess it; the owl also and the raven shall dwell in it: and he shall stretch out upon it the line of confusion, and the stones of emptiness' (Isa. 34:11).

"These all wait upon Thee"

[Composed 22 Jan. 1853. Originally part of ' "To what purpose is this waste?" ' which CR never published as such.]

Entry for 5 July in *TF* (128). In the next day's entry, CR relates two childhood experiences with frogs, ending her account with the question: 'is it quite certain that no day will ever come when even the smallest, weakest, most grotesque, *wronged* creature will not in some fashion rise up in the Judgment with us to condemn us, and so frighten us effectually once for all?' (129).

Title [untitled] *1885, 1886a.*

'These wait all upon thee; that thou mayest give them their meat in due season' (Ps. 14:27).

"Doeth well . . . doeth better"

Entry for 15 Feb. in *TF* (33). 'As in Wordsworth's elegy "A slumber did my spirit seal," statements are validated in ways that are as surprising as unforeseen' (W. David Shaw, 'Poet of Mystery: The Art of Christina Rossetti', in Kent, *Achievement* 50). 'I consider that this poem relates to Maria Francesca Rossetti, who had died in 1876. Christina often called her playfully "Moon" or "Moony"' ('Notes' 469).

Title "Doeth well, . . . doeth better."—(I COR. vii. 38.) *1885, 1886a.*

'So then he that giveth her in marriage doeth well; but he that giveth her not in marriage doeth better' (1 Cor. 7:38). In *TF* (33), this verse is used as the epigraph for 'My love whose heart is tender said to me'.

['Our heaven must be within ourselves']

[Lines 1–4 composed 25 Jan. 1854; date of composition of ll. 5–12 unknown.]

Entry for 8 Nov. in *TF* (213–14).

1 *Our heaven must be within ourselves* 'Neither shall they say, Lo here! or, lo there! for, behold, the kingdom of God is within you' (Luke 17:21).
7 *magnifical* royally bountiful.
9 *over all a dome must spread* cf. 'I would build that dome in air' (Coleridge, 'Kubla Khan', (l. 46).

"Vanity of Vanities" ['Of all the downfalls in the world']

[Composed 6 Aug. 1858. Originally part of ' "Yet a little while" ' ['These days are long before I die'], which CR never published as such, but from which she also took 'Earth has clear call of daily bells', printed in 1893.]

Entry for 26 Oct. in *TF* (205–6).

Title [untitled] *1885, 1886a.*
See note for l. 1 of 'One Certainty'.

['The hills are tipped with sunshine, while I walk']

FD (423) in CR's commentary on Rev. 18:20.

['Scarce tolerable life, which all life long']

[Editions: 1885, 1886a, *1893*, 1896, 1904.]

Entry for 10 Nov. in *TF* (214–15). WR describes the rough draft of this poem as having been written on a scrap of paper with the date 'Easter Eve 1884' ('Notes' 469).

Title LIFE *1896*.

['All heaven is blazing yet']

[In 1885 and 1886a, presented as two separate poems (untitled): ll. 1–8 and ll. 9–16, numbered '1.' and '2.' respectively.]

Lines 1–8 form the entry for 10 Oct. in *TF* (196); ll. 9–16 for 11 Oct. (196).

12 *O hope deferred* see note for l. 2 of 'A Pause of Thought'.
15 *He hath not lost his life who seems to lose* see note for l. 16 of ' "The General Assembly and Church of the Firstborn" '.

"Balm in Gilead"

Entry for 6 June in *TF* (108).

Title [untitled] *1885, 1886a*.
    See note for ll. 31–2 of 'Paradise'.

"In the day of his Espousals"

Entry for 20 May in *TF* (96).

Title [untitled] *1885, 1886a*.
    'Go forth, O ye daughters of Zion, and behold king Solomon with the crown wherewith his mother crowned him in the day of his espousals, and in the day of the gladness of his heart' (Song of Sol. 3:11).
1 *Song of Songs* traditionally ascribed to King Solomon.

"She came from the uttermost part of the earth"

Entry for 21 May in *TF* (96).

Title [untitled] *1885, 1886a.*
  See note for l. 200 of 'The Lowest Room'.
1 *"The half was not told me," said Sheba's Queen* upon visiting King Solomon, the Queen of Sheba said: 'Howbeit I believed not the words, until I came, and mine eyes had seen it: and, behold, the half was not told me: thy wisdom and prosperity exceedeth the fame which I heard' (1 Kings 10:7).
5 *Happy thy servants* 'Happy are thy men, happy are these thy servants, which stand continually before thee, and that hear thy wisdom' (1 Kings 10:8).

['Alleluia! or Alas! my heart is crying']

FD (428–9) in CR's commentary on Rev. 19:1–2: 'And after these things I heard a great voice of much people in heaven, saying, Alleluia; Salvation, and glory, and honour, and power, unto the Lord our God: For true and righteous are his judgments: for he hath judged the great whore, which did corrupt the earth with her fornication, and hath avenged the blood of his servants at her hand.' The poem 'depends immediately upon those texts of *The Apocalypse* which purport that "the kings of the earth" were "saying Alas, alas, that great city Babylon!" on the same occasion when "much people in heaven" were "saying, Alleluia! Salvation and glory and honour and power unto the Lord our God." From this consideration the authoress proceeds to reflect upon the alternative in her own spiritual state' ('Notes' 469).

['The Passion Flower hath sprung up tall']

FD (373) in CR's commentary on Rev. 15:3.

1 *Passion Flower* type of climbing shrub with edible fruit, so called because the parts of the flower were thought to resemble the instruments of Jesus' Passion, or crucifixion.
3 *heliotrope* plant that turns its leaves and flowers towards the sun.

God's Acre

FD (343) in CR's commentary on Rev. 13:11.

Title [untitled] *1892.*

"The Flowers appear on the Earth"

[Composed 26 March 1855. Originally part of 'I have a message unto thee', which CR never published as such.]

Entry for 14 May in *TF* (91).

Title [untitled] *1885, 1886a*.
 See note for ll. 53–6 of 'Advent' ['This Advent moon shines cold and clear'].
11 *sleeps indeed* see headnote of 'Dream-Land'.
24 *delection* delight.

"Thou knewest . . . thou oughtest therefore"

FD (315–16) in CR's commentary on Rev. 12:4.

Title [untitled] *1892*.
 'His lord answered and said unto him, Thou wicked and slothful servant, thou knewest that I reap where I sowed not, and gather where I have not strawed: Thou oughtest therefore to have put my money to the exchangers, and then at my coming I should have received mine own with usury' (Matt. 25:26–7). On the parable of the talents, see note for l. 7 of 'What are these lovely ones, yea, what are these?'

"Go in Peace"

FD (354) in CR's commentary on Rev. 14:4–5 (see headnote of 'Unspotted lambs to follow the one Lamb').

Title [untitled] *1892*.
 'And he said to the woman, Thy faith hath saved thee; go in peace' (Luke 7:50; see also Mark 5:34); 'And the keeper of the prison told this saying to Paul, The magistrates have sent to let you go; now therefore depart, and go in peace' (Acts 16:36).
5 *The leper Naaman* following the prophet Elisha's instructions, Naaman dipped himself seven times in the Jordan and was healed of leprosy (2 Kings 5:14).

"Half dead"

FD (57) in CR's commentary on Rev. 2:7 (see headnote of 'That Eden of earth's sunrise cannot vie').

Title [untitled] *1892*.

For the story of the Good Samaritan, in which this phrase appears, see note for title of ' "Take Care of Him" '.

1 *Christ the Life* see note for l. 17 of 'A Martyr. The Vigil Of The Feast'.

"One of the Soldiers with a Spear pierced His Side"

FD (21) in CR's commentary on Rev. 1:7: 'Behold, he cometh with clouds; and every eye shall see him, and they also which pierced him: and all kindreds of the earth shall wail because of him. Even so, Amen.'

Title [untitled] *1892*.

See note for ll. 23–4 of ' "The Love of Christ Which Passeth Knowledge" '.

['Where love is, there comes sorrow']

Entry for 14 Jan. in *TF* (12).

['Bury Hope out of sight']

Entry for 5 Dec. in *TF* (232–3). WR points out that this 'was the authoress's birthday. I assume that it was purposely inserted in relation to that anniversary, and probably to the death of Charles Bagot Cayley on the same day' ('Notes' 469–70). Cayley had been a suitor of CR.

2 *No book for it and no bell* the ceremony of excommunication is performed with bell, book and candle. Cf. 'I shall curse you with book and bell and candle' (Malory, *Le Morte d' Arthur* (1485), Book XXI. 1).

A Churchyard Song of Patient Hope

FD (486) in CR's commentary on Rev. 21:4 (see note for l. 7 of 'Hark! The Alleluias of the great salvation'). 'Christina, in placing this poem in the *Verses* next after the last-named ["Bury Hope out of sight"], seems to have intended that the two should be read together. The original framework of the *Churchyard Song* was quite different: it formed in *Face of the Deep* part of the reflections upon the Apocalyptic text, "And God shall wipe away all tears from their eyes," etc.' ('Notes' 470). See also note for l. 29 of 'Christian and Jew. A Dialogue'.

['One woe is past. Come what come will']

FD (265) in CR's commentary on Rev. 9:12: 'One woe is past; and, behold, there come two woes more hereafter.' 'As arranged in the *Verses*, I think Christina intended it to be read in association with the preceding two compositions ["Bury Hope out of sight" and "A Churchyard Song of Patient Hope"]' ('Notes' 470). Introducing this poem in *FD*, CR writes: ' "One woe is past" shows that none need hesitate to call woe woe, even when short of the final woe: for man is not framed without nerves but with nerves, and many times an horrible dread overwhelmeth him' (265).

"Take no thought for the morrow"

FD (259–60) in CR's commentary on Rev. 9:2.

Title [untitled] *1892*.
    See note for l. 91 of 'Maiden May'.
10 *Watching to prayer* see notes for l. 3 of 'Advent' ['This Advent moon shines cold and clear'] and for Part 2, l. 1 of 'Old and New Year Ditties'.

"Consider the Lilies of the field" ['Solomon most glorious in array']

FD (391) in CR's commentary on Rev. 16:21.

Title [untitled] *1892*.
    See note for title of ' "Consider the Lilies of the Field" ' ['Flowers preach to us if we will hear'].

"Son, remember"

[First published in *"New and Old:" For Seed-Time and Harvest* 17 (Oct. 1889), 274.]

FD (480) in CR's commentary on Rev. 21:2 (see note for l. 5 of 'All Saints: Martyrs').

Title LAZARUS LOQUITUR *1889*; [untitled] *1892*.
    The title and images of the poem come from the story of Lazarus, the beggar who ate the crumbs from a rich man's table and whose sores were licked by dogs. At death, Lazarus went to heaven, and the rich man to hell, where he begged Father Abraham to send Lazarus down with water to relieve his torment. But Abraham said to the rich man: 'Son, remember that thou in thy lifetime receivedst thy good things, and likewise Lazarus evil things: but

now he is comforted, and thou art tormented' (Luke 16:25). See also note for l. 27 of 'A Testimony'.

"Heaviness may endure for a night, but Joy cometh in the morning"

[In 1885 and 1886a, presented as two separate poems (untitled): ll. 1–14 and 15–28, numbered '1.' and '2.' respectively.]

Lines 1–14 of this poem form the entry for 4 Oct. in *TF* (192); ll. 15–28 for 5 Oct. (193).

Title 'For his anger endureth but a moment; in his favour is life: weeping may endure for a night, but joy cometh in the morning' (Ps. 30:5).
3 *Whatso is born from earth returns to earth* see note for l. 119 of 'A Martyr. The Vigil Of The Feast'.
9–10 *Thus I sat mourning like a mournful owl, / And like a doleful dragon made ado* 'Therefore I will wail and howl, I will go stripped and naked: I will make a wailing like the dragons, and mourning as the owls' (Mic. 1:8).
16 *stave* stanza.

"The Will of the Lord be done"

FD (464) in CR's commentary on Rev. 20:4.

Title [untitled] *1892*.
When a prophetess predicted St Paul would be bound and handed over to the Gentiles if he went to Jerusalem, his companions tried to persuade him not to go. But he answered that he was ready not only to be bound but also to die. 'And when he would not be persuaded, we ceased, saying, The will of the Lord be done' (Acts 21:14). See also headnote of 'Conversion of St. Paul'.

"Lay up for yourselves treasures in Heaven"

Entry for 12 Sept. in *TF* (176).

Title [untitled] *1885, 1886a*.
See note for ll. 13–14 of 'A Testimony'.

"Whom the Lord loveth He chasteneth"

Entry for 25 Feb. in *TF* (39).

Title [untitled] *1885, 1886a.*
'For whom the Lord loveth he chasteneth, and scourgeth every son whom
he receiveth' (Heb. 12:6); see also headnote of 'Whitsun Eve'.

"Then shall ye shout"

Entry for 14 Nov. in *TF* (218).

Title [untitled] *1885, 1886a.*
'And Joshua had commanded the people, saying, Ye shall not shout, nor
make any noise with your voice, neither shall any word proceed out of your
mouth, until the day I bid you shout; then shall ye shout' (Jos. 6:10).

['Everything that is born must die']

Entry for 21 Nov. in *TF* (222–3).

['Lord, grant us calm, if calm can set forth Thee']

FD (222) in CR's commentary on Rev. 7:1 (see headnote of 'Dear Angels and
dear disembodied Saints').

4 *congelation* the action of congealing or freezing, i.e. the sea is so still as to
seem frozen.

Changing Chimes

FD (216) in CR's commentary on Rev. 6:13.

Title "THOU SHALT HEAR A VOICE BEHIND THEE." *1892.*
4 *watch and pray* see notes for l. 3 of 'Advent' ['This Advent moon shines cold
and clear'] and for Part 2, l. 1 of 'Old and New Year Ditties'.

"Thy Servant will go and fight with this Philistine"

FD (207–8) in CR's commentary on Rev. 6:8.

Title [untitled] *1892*.
   The youth David, speaking of the giant Goliath to King Saul, said: 'Let no man's heart fail because of him; thy servant will go and fight with this Philistine' (1 Sam. 17:32).
11 *face of tenfold flint* see note for l. 206 of 'From House to Home'.

['Thro' burden and heat of the day']

Entry for 29 July in *TF* (145).

1 *Thro' burden and heat of the day* 'These last have wrought but one hour, and thou hast made them equal unto us, which have borne the burden and heat of the day' (Matt. 20:12). See note for title of ' "Whatsoever is right, that shall ye receive" '.

"Then I commended Mirth"

Entry for 28 Nov. in *TF* (227).

Title [untitled] *1885, 1886a*.
   'Then I commended mirth, because a man hath no better thing under the sun, than to eat, and to drink, and to be merry: for that shall abide with him of his labour the days of his life, which God giveth him under the sun' (Ecc. 8:15).
1 *A merry heart is a continual feast* 'he that is of a merry heart hath a continual feast' (Pro. 15:15).

['Sorrow hath a double voice']

Entry for 25 Sept. in *TF* (185).

['Shadows today, while shadows show God's Will']

FD (166) in CR's commentary on Rev. 5:1.

12 *we race . . . for a crown* see note for ll. 11–12 of 'Who Shall Deliver Me?'

"Truly the Light is sweet"

FD (40–41) in CR's commentary on Rev. 1:12–16.

Title [untitled] *1892*.
  'Truly the light is sweet, and a pleasant thing it is for the eyes to behold the sun' (Ecc. 11:7).

"Are ye not much better than they?"

FD (42) in CR's commentary on Rev. 1:17–18.

Title [untitled] *1892*.
  See note for title of 'Consider'.
11 *vaunteth* 'charity vaunteth not itself, is not puffed up' (1 Cor. 13:4).
16 *the awful day of mowing* see note for l. 9 of 'Mary Magdalene and the Other Mary'.

"Yea, the sparrow hath found her an house"

FD (119–20) in CR's commentary on Rev. 3:10 (see headnote of 'Patience must dwell with Love, for Love and Sorrow').

Title [untitled] *1892*.
  See note for ll. 9–10 of ' "Where neither rust nor moth doth corrupt" '.

"I am small and of no reputation"

FD (431) in CR's commentary on Rev. 19:5 (see note for title of ' "Ye that fear Him, both small and great" ').

Title [untitled] *1892*.
  'I am small and despised; yet do not I forget thy precepts' (Ps. 119:141); 'But made himself of no reputation, and took upon him the form of a servant, and was made in the likeness of men' (Phil. 2:7).

['O Christ my God Who seest the unseen']

Entry for 4 June in *TF* (106). CR, telling a story of seeing a waxwork exhibition and feeling shy in the presence of the wax characters, writes: 'Things seen are as that waxwork, things unseen as those real people. Yet over and over again we are influenced and constrained by the hollow momentary world we behold in presence, while utterly obtuse as regards the substantial eternal world no less present around us though disregarded' (*TF* 36).

8 *remember me* see note for l. 8 of 'Good Friday' ['Am I a stone and not a sheep'].

['Yea, if Thou wilt, Thou canst put up Thy sword']

Entry for 9 Aug. in *TF* (152–3).

1 *Thou canst put up Thy sword* see note for Part 1, l. 36 of 'The German-French Campaign. 1870–1871'.
9–10 *uplift from the under-sucking silt / To set him on Thy rock* see note for ll. 19–23 of 'A Testimony'.

['Sweetness of rest when Thou sheddest rest']

FD (360) in CR's commentary on Rev. 14:12: 'Here is the patience of the saints: here are they that keep the commandments of God, and the faith of Jesus.'

1 *Sweetness of rest when Thou sheddest rest* see headnote of 'Dream-Land'.

['O foolish Soul! to make thy count']

FD (83) in CR's commentary on Rev. 2:26–7.

['Before the beginning Thou has foreknown the end']

FD (455) in CR's commentary on Rev. 19:17–18 (see headnote of ' "Where neither rust nor moth doth corrupt" ').

1 *Before the beginning Thou hast foreknown the end* see headnote of 'Tune me, O Lord, into one harmony'.

['The goal in sight! Look up and sing']

Entry for 16 Nov. in *TF* (219).

8 *reft of sting* see note for Part 3, ll. 13–14 of 'The Thread of Life'.

['Looking back along life's trodden way']

Entry for 31 Dec. (Feast of St Silvester) in *TF* (253).

Separately Published Poems

[Basic text: MS, unless otherwise stated.]

DEATH'S CHILL BETWEEN

[Composed 29 Sept. 1847. Edition: 1904. First published in *Athenaeum*, no. 1094 (14 Oct. 1848), 1032, and reprinted with revisions in *Beautiful Poetry* 1 (1853), 248–9. MS: BodL.]

This and 'Heart's Chill Between', below, were CR's first published poems. As the MS title ('Anne of Warwick') indicates, the poem is about 'the dolorous emotions and flitting frenzy of Anne, when widowed of her youthful husband, the Prince of Wales, slain after the battle of Tewkesbury. If I remember right, this poem was offered to *The Athenaeum* at the same time as *Heart's Chill between*; and my brother then substituted these titles for the original ones, so as to establish between the two a certain relation of contrast in similarity' ('Notes' 467).

Title A LAMENT *1853*.

HEART'S CHILL BETWEEN

[Composed 22 Sept. 1847. Edition: 1904. First published in *Athenaeum*, no. 1095 (21 Oct. 1848), 1056. MS: BodL.]

See note for 'Death's Chill Between', above. After these two poems were published in the *Athenaeum*, 'The editor, apparently, rejected further submissions on the grounds that they were "too infected with Tennysonian mannerisms"' (*CR* 88). The MS title is 'The Last Hope'.

Repining

[Composed Dec. 1847. Editions: 1896, 1904. First published in *Germ*, no. 2 (Feb. 1850), 111–17. MS: BodL.]

WR says that 'It is, of all the poems by Christina Rossetti which appeared in that short-lived magazine, the only one which she did not afterwards reprint.' He adds that it is 'to some extent modelled upon Parnell's *Hermit* [1721]. The moral, however, is different. Parnell aims to show that the dispensations of Providence, though often mysterious, are just. Christina's thesis might be summarized thus: Solitude is dreary, yet the life of man among his fellows may easily be drearier: therefore let not the solitary rebel' ('Notes' 460). (Thomas Parnell (1679–1718) was an Irish archdeacon and poet, and friend of Pope, who published Parnell's work in 1721.)

Barbara Fass has noted the influence of Keats's 'The Eve of St Agnes' (1820) on this poem ('Christina Rossetti and St Agnes' Eve', *Victorian Poetry* 14 (1976), 33–46).

1–2 *She sat alway thro' the long day / Spinning the weary thread away* cf. Part II, 1–2 of Tennyson's 'The Lady of Shalott' (1832): 'There she weaves by night and day / A magic web with colours gay'.
49 *He answered: "Rise, and follow me"* see note for l. 14 of ' "They Desire a Better Country" '.
86 *succous* juicy.
176 *Lord, let Thy servant part in peace* 'Lord, now lettest thou thy servant depart in peace, according to thy word' (Luke 2:29).
223 *As a man soweth, so he reaps* see note for l. 269 of *The Prince's Progress*.

NEW ENIGMAS

[Editions: 1896, 1904. First published in *Marshall's Ladies' Daily Remembrancer. For 1850* (R. and A. Suttaby and J. Toulmin, (1850), 135–6, as the seventh in a series of enigmas by various authors. CR's copy with her holograph revisions (1850r) is at PU. Basic text: 1850r.]

WR printed this together with another 'enigma' ('Me you often meet') under the title 'Two Enigmas', with this note: 'The answer to the first of these enigmas is "Jack" ' ('Notes' 491).

In 1850r CR wrote next to ll. 1–2: 'in honour of grammar'.

Title NEW ENIGMAS. *Editor* NEW ENIGMAS. / VII. BY C. *1850*; NEW ENIGMAS. / VII. BY Christina. *1850r*; TWO ENIGMAS / I *1896*, *1904*.

CHARADES

[Editions: 1896, 1904. First published in *Marshall's Ladies' Daily Remembrancer. For 1850*, p. 140, as the sixth in a series of charades by various authors. Basic text: 1850r (see headnote of 'New Enigmas', above).]

WR printed this together with 'How many authors are my first!', under the title 'Two Charades', writing: 'The first means "Candid" . . .' ('Notes' 491).

Title CHARADES. *Editor* CHARADES. / VI. BY C. *1850*; CHARADES. / VI. BY Christina. *1850r*; TWO CHARADES / I *1896, 1904*.

THE ROSE ['O Rose, thou flower of flowers, thou fragrant wonder']

[Composed 17 April 1847. Editions: 1896, 1904. First published in 1847, p. 29, and then in Mary Howitt (ed.), *Pictorial Calendar of the Seasons Exhibiting the Pleasures, Pursuits, and Characteristics of Country Life for Every Month in the Year and Embodying the Whole of Aikin's Calendar of Nature* (Henry G. Bohn, 1854), 305. MS: BodL.]

Title [untitled] *1854*.

The Trees' Counselling

[Composed 5 Dec. 1847. First published in Mary Howitt (ed.), *Midsummer Flowers. For the Young* (Lindsay and Blakiston, 1854), 202–3. MS: MS1 (BodL).]

"Behold, I stand at the door and knock"

[Composed 1 Dec. 1851. Editions: 1896, 1904. Published in *English Woman's Journal* 8:46 (1 Dec. 1861), p. 245 (*CR Poems* 431). MS: BodL.]

Title see note for l. 8 of 'Despised and Rejected'.
33–4 *Thou didst it not unto the least of these, / And in them hast not done it unto Me* 'Verily I say unto you, Inasmuch as ye did it not to one of the least of these, ye did it not to me' (Matt. 25:45).

['Gianni my friend and I both strove to excel']

[First published in *Crayon* 3 (1856), 200–202, as part of the short story 'The Lost Titian', and reprinted in 1870, p. 161, and 1870a. Basic text: 1870.]

In 'The Lost Titian', the poem is presented as an epigram written by Giann-uccione about another painter, Gianni; neither painter is as good as the third friend, Titian.

4 *My forte being Venus' face, and his a dragon's tail* Giannuccione has achieved his fame with the appearance of his first picture – 'Venus whipping Cupid with feathers plucked from his own wing'; Gianni has hidden the Titian masterpiece he won in a bet by painting it over with a dragon – 'flaming, clawed, preposterous' (1870, p. 146, and 1870a, p. 158).

The Offering of the New Law, the One Oblation once Offered

[Composed 23 May 1861. Editions: 1896, 1904. First published in Orby Shipley (ed.), *Lyra Eucharistica: Hymns and Verses on the Holy Communion, Ancient and Modern; with Other Poems* (Longman, Green, Longman, Roberts and Green, 1863), 48–9, and reprinted with revisions in the 2nd edn. (1864), 61–2. MS: MS2 (BodL).

Title a prayer in the Communion Service of the *Book of Common Prayer* refers to Jesus' death on the Cross, 'who made there (by his one oblation of himself once offered) a full, perfect, and sufficient sacrifice, oblation, and satisfaction, for the sins of the whole world'. 'Love transmutes bounden duty into freewill oblation' (*TF* 174). An 'oblation' is the offering of a sacrifice to God.
Epigraph 'Wherefore when he cometh into the world, he saith, Sacrifice and offering thou wouldest not, but a body hast thou prepared me' (Heb. 10:5).
4 *the lowest place* see note for title of 'The Lowest Place'.
12 *Except He bless, I let not go* see note for ll. 49–51 of 'Advent' ['This Advent moon shines cold and clear'].
17 *Broken reed* see note for title of 'A Bruised Reed Shall He Not Break'.
18 *house I built on sand* see note for ll. 19–23 of 'A Testimony'.
24 *He seeks for me* allusion to the parable of the Good Shepherd; see note for l. 14 of 'Good Friday' ['Am I a stone and not a sheep'].
28 *Thy home-sick prodigal* allusion to the parable of the Prodigal Son; see note for title of ' "I Will Arise" '.

"The eleventh hour"

[Composed 5 Sept. 1853. Editions: 1896, 1904. First published in *Victoria Magazine* 2 (Feb. 1864), 317–18. MS: BodL.]

Title see note for l. 20 of 'A Martyr. The Vigil Of The Feast'.
20 *Faint and yet pursuing* see note for l. 11 of 'A Life's Parallels'.
21 *This man's feet are on the Rock* see note for ll. 19–23 of 'A Testimony'.

28 *O my Lord, remember me* see note for l. 8 of 'Good Friday' ['Am I a stone and not a sheep'].

29 *Still the Porter standeth* see note for l. 9 of 'Advent' ['This Advent moon shines cold and clear'].

45 *Crown and robes of whiteness* see note for ll. 9–10 of 'What are these lovely ones, yea, what are these?'

    "I know you not"

[Composed 26 June 1856. Editions: 1896, 1904. First published in Shipley, *Lyra Messianica*, 28–9 (see headnote of 'Good Friday' ['Am I a stone and not a sheep']), and reprinted with revisions in the 2nd edn. (1869), 28–9. Originally part of 'The Chiefest among ten thousand' ['When sick of life and all the world'], which CR never published as such, but from which she also took 'I will lift up mine eyes unto the Hills' ['When sick of life and all the world']. MS: BL.]

Title allusion to the parable of the Wise and Foolish Virgins; see note for l. 3 of 'Advent' ['This Advent moon shines cold and clear']. See also ll. 26 and 32 of this poem.

1 *the Vine with living Fruit* see note for l. 33 of 'Christian and Jew. A Dialogue'.

2 *The twelvefold fruited Tree of Life* see note for ll. 13–14 of 'Eve'.

3 *The Balm in Gilead* see note for ll. 31–2 of 'Paradise'.

4–5 *The valley Lily and the Rose: / Stronger than Lebanon, Thou Root* see note for l. 11 of 'Long Barren'.

7 *Thou Vineyard of red Wine* 'In that day sing ye unto her, A vineyard of red wine' (Isa. 27:2).

8 *Keeping Thy best Wine till the close* see note for ll. 10–11 of 'After Communion'.

9 *Pearl of great price* allusion to the parable of a man 'Who, when he had found one pearl of great price, went and sold all that he had, and bought it' (Matt. 13:46). The pearl is the kingdom of heaven.

10 *And ruddier . . . Thou* see note for l. 14 of 'Long Barren'.

11 *Most precious . . . Jasper Stone* 'Having the glory of God: and her light was like unto a stone most precious, even like a jasper stone, clear as crystal' (Rev. 21:11). See note for ll. 35–6 of 'Paradise'.

12 *Head of the corner spurned before* see note for l. 14 of ' "Lord, grant us eyes to see and ears to hear" '.

13 *Fair Gate of pearl* see note for l. 6 of ' "Hark! the Alleluias of the great salvation" '.

    Thyself the Door see note for l. 7 of ' "Thy Name, O Christ, as incense streaming forth" '. See also l. 16.

14 *Clear golden Street* see note for ll. 35–6 of 'Paradise'.

    Thyself the Way see note for l. 17 of 'A Martyr. The Vigil Of The Feast'.

17 *I thirst for Thee* see note for l. 11 of 'Passiontide'.

18 *as deep to deep* see note for l. 32 of ' "When My Heart Is Vexed, I Will Complain" ' ['O Lord, how canst Thou say Thou lovest me?'].

20 *provocation* summons or invitation (obsolete).

21 *Heart pierced for me* see note for ll. 23–4 of ' "The Love of Christ Which Passeth Knowledge" '.

A Christmas Carol ['Before the paling of the stars']

[Composed 26 Aug. 1859. Editions: 1896, 1904. First published in Shipley (ed.), *Lyra Messianica* (1864), 63–4, and reprinted with revisions in the 2nd edn. (1869), 81. MS: GD.]

Title Before the paling of the Stars. *1864, 1869.*

6 *Cradled in a manger* 'And she brought forth her firstborn son, and wrapped him in swaddling clothes, and laid him in a manger; because there was no room for them in the inn' (Luke 2:7).

7 *In the world His Hands had made* refers to the doctrine that Jesus was present at the creation of the world. 'All things were made by him; and without him was not any thing made that was made' (John 1:3).

8 *Born a Stranger* 'He came unto his own, and his own received him not' (John 1:11).

16 *In the winter weather* cf. CR's more familiar Christmas carol, 'In the bleak mid-winter'.

19 *Spotless Lamb of God was He* see note for l. 33 of 'Martyrs' Song'.

24 *the King of Glory* see note for l. 8 of 'Hark! the Alleluias of the great salvation'.

Easter Even ['There is nothing more that they can do']

[Composed 23 March 1861. Editions: 1896, 1904. First published in Shipley (ed.), *Lyra Messianica* (1864), 251–2, and reprinted with revisions in the 2nd edn. (1869), 279–80. MS: BL.]

3 *Caiaphas* Jewish high priest who presided at the council that condemned Jesus to death.

4 *Herod* Roman ruler of Judea at the time of Jesus' crucifixion. 'And Herod with his men of war set him at nought, and mocked him, and arrayed him in a gorgeous robe, and sent him again to Pilate' (Luke 23:11).

5 *Pontius Pilate* Roman procurator of Judea under whom Jesus was tried and condemned to death.

8 *Arch-Judas with his kiss* Judas, one of Jesus' disciples, agreed to lead soldiers to Jesus, pointing him out to them with a kiss (Matt. 26:49; Mark 14:44; Luke 22:47) – hence, 'Arch-Judas', from 'arch-fiend' or 'arch-rebel', i.e. Satan.

9 *The sepulchre made sure* When the Romans buried Jesus, they sealed the door to the tomb and set a watch to be sure that no one stole the body (Matt. 27:66).
28 *John the well-beloved* see note for l. 13 of 'After Communion'.
29 *finest linen* 'And he bought fine linen, and took him down, and wrapped him in the linen, and laid him in a sepulchre' (Mark 15:46; also John 19:40).
33 *Lay Him in the garden rock* see note for l. 6 of 'Easter Even' ['The tempest over and gone, the calm begun'].
40 *bring His sheaves* see note for l. 47 of 'After This the Judgment'.

Come unto Me

[Composed 23 Feb. 1864. Editions: 1896, 1904. First published in Shipley (ed.), *Lyra Eucharistica*, 2nd edn. (1864), p. 5. MS: BL.]

Title Matt. 11.28 (see note on l. 17 of ' "Of Him That Was Ready to Perish" ').
2 *Made His yoke easy and His burden light* 'For my yoke is easy, and my burden is light' (Matt. 11:30).
4 *awful* awe-inducing.
    Eucharist see note for l. 471 of *Goblin Market*.
6 *When my soul watched for Him by day by night* see note for l. 9 of 'Advent' ['This Advent moon shines cold and clear']; see also Matt. 24:42.
7 *my lamp lightened* see note for l. 3 of 'Advent' ['This Advent moon shines cold and clear'].
8 *the Pearl unpriced* see note for l. 9 of ' "I know you not" '.
11 *I even will run my race* see note for ll. 11–12 of 'Who Shall Deliver Me?'
12 *For Faith the walls of Jericho cast down* 'By faith the walls of Jericho fell down, after they were compassed about seven days' (Heb. 11:30).
14 *Christ is All in all* see note for section title 'Christ Our All in All' (p. 982).

Ash Wednesday ['Jesus, do I love Thee?']

[Composed 21 March 1859. Editions: 1896, 1904. First published in Shipley (ed.), *Lyra Eucharistica*, 2nd edn., pp. 355–6. MS: GD.]

Title Jesus, do I love Thee? *1864*.
    See note for title of 'Ash Wednesday' ['My God, my God, have mercy on my sin'].
14 *Blood hath cleansed not* 'the blood of Jesus Christ his Son cleanseth us from all sin' (1 John 1:7).
17 *figtree fruit-unbearing* 'And when he saw a fig tree in the way, he came to it, and found nothing thereon, but leaves only, and said unto it, Let no fruit grow on thee henceforward for ever. And presently the fig tree withered away'

(Matt. 21:19; see also Mark 11:13, 20–21). 'The barren fig-tree mocked His hunger with leaves only' (*SF* 184).

'Every tree that is pleasant to the sight, and good for food' (Gen. ii. 9), grew in the Garden of Eden: but one only of those still accessible to us is named and this one, the fig tree, connects itself not with man's innocence, but with his fall (iii. 7). Subsequently however the same tree appears and reappears associated with plenty (Numb. xiii. 23), sweetness (Judges ix. 10, 11), security (I Kings iv. 25), hospitality (I Chron. xii. 40), reward (Prov. xxvii. 18), revival (Song of Sol. ii. 13), healing (Isa. xxxvii. 21); more frequently than with destruction or discriminative judgment (Isa. xxxiv. 4; Jer. xxiv; Hos. ii. 2; Nah, iii. 12). (*SF* 98).

22–4 *Why cumbereth it the ground . . . Give it one year longer* 'Then said he unto the dresser of his vineyard, Behold, these three years I come seeking fruit on this fig tree, and find none: cut it down; why cumbereth it the ground? And he answering said unto him, Lord, let it alone this year also, till I shall dig about it, and dung it' (Luke 13:7–8).

SPRING FANCIES

[Part I composed 1847; Parts II and III composed 29 June 1858. Editions: 1896, 1904 (Parts II and III only). First published in *Macmillan's Magazine* 11 (April 1865), 460. Part I is printed in 1866 as 'Spring Quiet'. MSS: Part I: MS2 (PU); Parts II and III: MS3 (BL).]

Title Today and Tomorrow. *1896, 1904.*

"LAST NIGHT"

[Probably composed between Oct. 1863 and 15 Jan. 1864. Editions: 1896, 1904. First published in *Macmillan's Magazine* 12 (May 1865), 48. Basic text: title, ll. 1–9 and 33–6: 1865; ll. 10–32: MS (BL).]

PETER GRUMP / FORSS

[Editions: 1896, 1904. First published in *Argosy* 1 (Jan. 1866), 164, as part of the short story 'Hero: A Metamorphosis', and reprinted in 1870, pp. 209–10, and 1870a. Basic text: 1870.]

In 'Hero', the poem is a 'boat-song' sung by Hero's father (Peter Grump) and lover (Forss), which Hero hears as she floats on the sea back towards her village.

Title FATHER AND LOVER *1896, 1904.*

Helen Grey

[Composed 23 Feb. 1863. Editions: 1896, 1904. First published in *Macmillan's Magazine* 13 (March 1866), 375. MS: BL.]

12 *Your steps go mincing* 'Because the daughters of Zion are haughty, and walk with stretched forth necks and wanton eyes, walking and mincing as they go, and making a tinkling with their feet: Therefore the Lord will smite with a scab the crown of the head of the daughters of Zion' (Isa. 3:16–17). The passage describes additional punishments for them, including 'instead of well set hair baldness' and 'burning instead of beauty' (24), and concluding: 'being desolate shall sit upon the ground' (26).

18 *Come down and take a lowlier place* cf. 'The Lowest Place'.

If

[Composed 12 April 1864. Editions: 1896, 1904. First published in *Argosy* 1 (March 1866), 366. MS: BL.]

Illustration: WR reports that Frederick A. Sandys illustrated the poem for *Argosy*, although the design was 'not in character with the poem' ('Notes' 484).

Title HOPING AGAINST HOPE. *1904.*

In 1904, WR writes that although the poem was originally titled 'If', it 'was afterwards reprinted with the title which I give, sanctioned (I presume) by my sister' ('Notes' 484). 'Hoping against Hope' refers to Abraham, who was told by God he would have a son in his old age: 'Who against hope believed in hope, that he might become the father of many nations; according to that which was spoken, So shall thy seed be' (Rom. 4:18).

Seasons ['Oh the cheerful budding-time']

[Composed 20 Jan. 1863. Editions: 1896, 1904. First published in *Macmillan's Magazine* 15 (Dec. 1866), 168–9. MS: BL.]

HENRY HARDIMAN

[First published in *Churchman's Shilling Magazine and Family Treasury* 1 (May 1867), 292, as part of the short story 'The Waves of this Troublesome World: a Tale of Hastings Ten Years Ago', and reprinted in 1870, p. 302, and 1870a. Basic text: 1870.]

In 'The Waves of this Troublesome World', the poem appears as a tombstone inscription. Hardiman's daughter, who is the presumed 'affliction', having married without his consent, 'did not perceive that these lines are doggrel [*sic*]; she only felt that they were true' (302–3).

Within the Veil

[Composed 13 Dec. 1861. Editions: 1896, 1904. First published in Shipley (ed.), *Lyra Messianica*, 2nd edn., p. 393. MS: BL.]

'These verses would seem to refer to the recent death of some religious and cherished young friend; I cannot say who it was' ('Notes' 475).
    MS is titled 'One Day'.

Paradise: in a Symbol

[Composed 14 Nov. 1864. Editions: 1896, 1904. First published in Shipley (ed.), *Lyra Messianica*, 2nd edn, pp. 417–18. MS: BL.]

The poem may have been inspired by one of CR's childhood dreams (Packer, *CR* 15): see headnote of 'As the Doves to their windows'.

Title Birds of Paradise. *1896, 1904.*
1 *Golden-winged, silver-winged* see note for l. 10 of 'Whitsun Tuesday'.

['In July']

[First published in 1870, p. 54, and 1870a, as part of the short story 'Commonplace'. MS: PU (dated April 1870).]

In 'Commonplace', the lines appear in a letter to the main character, Lucy Charlmont, from her sister Catherine, who is explaining why she is extending her holiday. She introduces the poem by writing: 'Mrs. Tyke presses us to remain with her through July, and Dr. Tyke is no less urgent. When I hinted that their hospitality had already been trespassed upon, the Doctor quoted Hone (as he said: I doubt if it is there):—' (54). 'Hone' refers to William Hone (1780–1842), author of *Every-Day Book* (1826–7) and *Table-Book* (1827–8).

['Love hath a name of Death']

[Editions: 1896, 1904. First published in 1870, p. 79, and 1870a, as part of the short story 'Commonplace'. MS: PU (dated April 1870).]

In 'Commonplace', the song is written by Dr Tyke and sung by six young ladies posing as 'English-Grecian' maidens in a charades processional.

Title LOVE'S NAME *1896, 1904*.

['Tu scendi dalle stelle, O Re del Cielo']

[First published in 1870, p. 230, and 1870a, as part of the short story 'Vanna's Twins'. Basic text: 1870.]

In 'Vanna's Twins', the mother of the twins hums what the narrator calls 'the first words of a Christmas carol', describing these words as 'so pathetic in their devout simplicity' (229).

Translation You descend from the stars, O King of the Heavens, / And you come in a cold cave: / O my divine Child / I want to love You always! / O blessed Lord [5] / And how much it cost You having loved me.

['Alas my Lord']

[Edition: 1904. First published in 1874, pp. ix–xii. Basic text: 1874r (PU).]

Title WRESTLING *1904*.
2 *wrestle all the livelong night* see note for Part 9, ll. 11–12 of 'Monna Innominata'. See also l. 15, below, and note.
10–12 *Yet Abraham . . . for ten righteous Sodom had been spared* see notes for l. 1 of 'Shall not the Judge of all the earth do right?' and also for l. 10 of 'By the Waters of Babylon. B.C. 570' and for Part 6, l. 4 of 'Monna Innominata'.
15 *Thou didst bless him* see note for ll. 49–51 of 'Advent' ['This Advent moon shines cold and clear'].
16–18 *Elias prayed . . . showers of rain* 'Elias was a man subject to like passions as we are, and he prayed earnestly that it might not rain: and it rained not on the earth by the space of three years and six months. And he prayed again, and the heaven gave rain, and the earth brought forth her fruit' (James 5:17–18).
19–20 *Gulped by the fish . . . Jonah* 'Now the LORD had prepared a great fish to swallow up Jonah. And Jonah was in the belly of the fish three days and three nights' (Jon. 1:17).
22–4 *Nineveh . . . day of grace* 'But let man and beast be covered with sackcloth, and cry mightily unto God: yea, let them turn every one from his evil way, and from the violence that is in their hands' (Jon. 3:8). After this repentance, Nineveh was saved.
27 *opened of its own accord the gate* allusion to the story of St Peter being rescued from prison by an angel. When they 'were past the first and the second ward,

they came unto the iron gate that leadeth unto the city; which opened to them of his own accord: and they went out, and passed on through one street; and forthwith the angel departed from him' (Acts 12:10).

29 *in the garden prayed* Jesus in the Garden of Gethsemane: 'And being in an agony he prayed more earnestly: and his sweat was as it were great drops of blood falling down to the ground' (Luke 22:44); see also notes for l. 3 of 'Advent' ['This Advent moon shines cold and clear'] and for Part 2, l. 1 and Part 3, l. 17 of 'Old and New Year Ditties'.

35–6 *until we hear Thy Voice / Which Thine own know* 'And when he putteth forth his own sheep, he goeth before them, and the sheep follow him: for they know his voice' (John 10:4).

42 *sleep till day* see headnote of 'Dream-Land'.

AN ALPHABET

[Editions: 1896, 1904. Basic text: 1896.]

In 1896, WR notes: 'This was printed in 1875, with some woodcuts, in some magazine; the headline of the pages is *For Very Little Folks*, which may or may not be the title of the magazine itself. It must be an American publication, as the verses are headed *An Alphabet from England*' ('Notes' 384). It has not been located.

47 *X, or XX, or XXX is ale* 'X' identifies the strength of the ale: weak (X), medium (XX) or strong (XXX).
52 *Zebu* humped species of ox.
Zoöphyte general name for various animals, such as sponges, which were formerly classed as intermediate between plants and animals.

Husband and Wife

[Composed 12 July 1865. Editions: 1896, 1904. First published in *A Masque of Poets. Including Guy Vernon, A Novelette in Verse*, No Name Series (Roberts Brothers 1878), 42–3. MS: MS2 (PU).]

Title apparently, DGR proposed the title 'Grave-clothes and Baby-clothes' for this poem ('Notes' 486).

MICHAEL F. M. ROSSETTI

[Probably composed between 24 Jan. and 17 Feb. 1883. Editions: 1896, 1904. First published in *Athenaeum*, no. 2886 (17 Feb. 1883), 214. MS: GD.]

Title WR's youngest child, a twin, who died when he was two years old. CR baptized the child before he died.

3–4 *Michael . . . sword* see headnote for 'A Ballad of Boding' and for the title of 'St. Michael and All Angels'.

A SICK CHILD'S MEDITATION

[WR dates '*Circa* 1885'. Editions: 1904. Basic text: 1904.]

The poem 'comes from a little Church serial named *New and Old*' ('Notes' 476).

['Love is all happiness, love is all beauty']

[Composed 24 Feb. 1847. Editions: 1885, 1886a, 1904. Originally part of 'Praise and Love', which CR never published as such. Basic text: 1885r (UT).]

Entry for 17 Feb. in *TF* (34).

Title LOVE *1904*.

['A handy Mole who plied no shovel']

[Editions: 1885, 1886a, 1904. Basic text: 1885r (UT).]

Entry for 27 Feb. in *TF* (40–41).

Title MOLE AND EARTHWORM *1904*.

"One swallow does not make a summer"

[Editions: 1885, 1886a, 1904. Basic text: 1885r (UT).]

Entry for 4 May in *TF* (85).

Title Aristotle, *Nicomachean Ethics*, Bk. 1, Ch. 7.

['Contemptuous of his home beyond']

[Editions: 1885, 1886a, 1904. Basic text: 1885r (UT).]

Entry for 7 July in *TF* (129–30). In a letter to WR [14 Jan. 1850], CR writes of a 'splendid frog' she has 'met', adding: 'The trees, the deer, the scenery, and indeed everything here, seems to influence me but little, with two exceptions, the cold, and the frog. The cold can never fail to interest a well brought-up Englishwoman; and the frog possesses every claim on my sympathy. He appeared to be leading a calm and secluded life' (*Letters*, I, 31).

Title A FROG'S FATE *1904*.
27 *A Froggy would a-wooing go* popular song, sometimes appearing as 'Frog Went Courting'.
32 *incog* incognito, or disguised.

A Word for the Dumb

[Editions: 1885, 1886a, 1896, 1904. MS: UBC (from letter CR to DGR, undated).]

Entry for 19 July in *TF* (138). The entry for the day before is about animal rights: 'My sister was a very staunch supporter of the Anti-Vivisection Movement. In a letter to our brother (dated perhaps in 1879) she sent the present verses, with the following remarks:—"There has just been held a fancy sale at a house in Prince's gate for the Anti-Vivisection cause, and, having nothing else to contribute, I sent a dozen autographs as follows [then come the verses]. Of these, nine on the first day fetched 2s. 6d. or 3s., while one even brought in 10s.!"' ('Notes' 492).

Title [untitled] *1885, 1886a*; A Poor Old Dog *1896, 1904*.

CARDINAL NEWMAN

[Editions: 1896, 1904. First published in *Athenaeum*, no. 3276 (16 Aug. 1890), 225. Basic text: 1890.]

Title John Henry Newman (1801–90) was an influential Anglican leader of the Oxford Movement and later a Roman Catholic cardinal, author of *Tracts for the Times* and other works. His highly publicized conversion to Catholicism exacerbated the fears of many mid-Victorians that the Oxford Movement was essentially a step on the 'road to Rome'.
Epigraph 'Whatsoever thy hand findeth to do, do it with thy might; for there is no work, nor device, nor knowledge, nor wisdom, in the grave, whither thou goest' (Ecc. 9:10).
6 *Chose love not in the shallows but the deep* W. David Shaw reads in this a commendation of Newman's doctrine of reserve ('Poet of Mystery: The Art of CR', in Kent, *Achievement* 25).
7 *neap* a neaptide occurs at the time when the difference between low and high tide is smallest.

An Echo from Willowwood

[Editions: 1896, 1904. First published in *Magazine of Art* 13 (Sept. 1890), 385. MS: UT.]

In 1896, WR notes: 'The title indicates that this sonnet by Christina is based on those sonnets by our brother, named *Willow-wood*, which were first published in 1869. I incline to think that Christina's sonnet is intended to refer to the love and marriage of my brother and Miss Siddal, and to her early death in 1862' (383). In 1904, WR undercuts his conjecture by adding 'or it may (which I think far more probable) be intended for a wholly different train of events' ('Notes' 487). *Willowwood* is a four-sonnet sequence (49–52) in DGR's *The House of Life*.

Title WILLOWWOOD *1890*; FROM WILLOW-WOOD *1896, 1904*.
Epigraph first line of a song sung by Love (Sonnet 51, l. 1).
12 *A sudden ripple made the faces flow* in DGR's sonnet, the ripple in the water is created by the lover kissing the image of his beloved.

"YEA, I HAVE A GOODLY HERITAGE"

[Editions: 1896, 1904. First published in *Atalanta* 4 (Oct. 1890), 3. Basic text: 1890.]

Title 'The lines are fallen unto me in pleasant places; yea, I have a goodly heritage' (Ps. 16:6).
1 *My vineyard that is mine I have to keep* 'they made me the keeper of the vineyards; but mine own vineyard have I not kept' (Song of Sol. 1:6).
11 *thy desert bloom not as the rose* see note for l. 158 of 'From House to Home'.
12 *palm* tree associated with those in Paradise.

A Death of a First-born

[Composed 14 Jan. 1892. Editions: 1896, 1904. First published in *Literary Opinion* 7 (Feb. 1892), 277. Lines 5–8 are printed in E[leanor] V[ere] B[oyle] (ed.), *A Book of Heavenly Birthdays* (A. C. McClurg and Co., [1893], 23). Basic text: 1892.]

'Relates to the death of the Duke of Clarence and Avondale' ('Notes' 477). Albert Victor Christian Edward, Duke of Clarence and Avondale and Earl of Athlone (1864–92), was the eldest son of the Prince of Wales (later Edward VII) and was next to his father in direct line of succession to the throne. He died of pneumonia on 14 Jan. 1892. Cf. Tennyson's elegy 'The Death of the Duke of Clarence and Avondale' (1892).

Title [untitled] *1893*.
7 *Faith, hope, and love* see note for l. 18 of 'Herself a rose, who bore the Rose'.
10 *dust returns to dust* see note for l. 119 of 'A Martyr. The Vigil Of The Feast'.
11–12 *when all Thy Nation / Shall rise up of the Just* see headnote of 'The General Assembly and Church of the Firstborn'.

"FAINT, YET PURSUING"

[Editions: 1896, 1904. First published in *Literary Opinion* 2 (May 1892), 67. Basic text: facsimile of the proof of 1892, in Bell, *CR* 132.]

Title see note for l. 11 of 'A Life's Parallels'.

1

7 *A little while* see note for title of 'Yet a Little While' ['I dreamed and did not seek: today I seek'].
7–8 *hope leans on charity . . . charity heartens faith* see note for l. 18 of 'Herself a rose, who bore the Rose'.
12 *All things made new bear each a sweet new name* see notes for ll. 172 and 176 of 'From House to Home'; also 'and thou shalt be called by a new name, which the mouth of the LORD shall name' (Isa. 62:2).

2

6 *sequent* following from, or attendant.

['What will it be, O my soul, what will it be']

[Except where noted, no dates of composition are known for the poems published in *FD*. Edition: 1904. Basic text: 1892.]
FD (35) in CR's commentary on Rev. 1:12–16.

Title WHAT WILL IT BE? *1904*.

['Lord, Thou art fulness, I am emptiness']

FD (36) in CR's commentary on Rev. 1:12–16.

Title SPEECHLESS *1904*.

['O Lord, I cannot plead my love of Thee']

FD (84) in CR's commentary on Rev. 2:28–9.
Title PLEADING *1904*.

['Faith and Hope are wings to Love']

FD (198) in CR's commentary on Rev. 6:2.
2 *Silver wings to golden dove* see note for l. 10 of 'Whitsun Tuesday'.

A SORROWFUL SIGH OF A PRISONER

FD (224) in CR's commentary on Rev. 7:2.

[' "I sit a queen, and am no widow, and shall see no sorrow" ']

FD (417) in CR's commentary on Rev. 18:7–8: 'How much she hath glorified herself, and lived deliciously, so much torment and sorrow give her: for she saith in her heart, I sit a queen, and am no widow, and shall see no sorrow. Therefore shall her plagues come in one day, death, and mourning, and famine; and she shall be utterly burned with fire: for strong is the Lord God who judgeth her.'

Title SCARLET *1904*.
2 *scarlet woman* allusion to the 'great whore' described in Rev. 17:1–5; sometimes used as an abusive epithet for the Church of Rome. Cf. 'where a heated pulpiteer / Not preaching simple Christ to simple men, / Announced the coming doom, and fulminated / Against the scarlet woman and her creed' (Tennyson, 'Sea Dreams' (1860)).

['Passing away the bliss']

FD (448) in CR's commentary on Rev. 19:12.
Title TO-MORROW *1904*.

['Love builds a nest on earth and waits for rest']

FD (513) in CR's commentary on Rev. 21:23 (see note for l. 11 of 'That Eden of earth's sunrise cannot vie').

Title HOMEWARDS *1904*.

['Jesus alone:—if thus it were to me']

FD (549) in CR's commentary on Rev. 22:18–19.

Title ALL THINGS *1904*.
6 *one the Morning Star* see note for l. 10 of 'Herself a rose, who bore the Rose'.

The Way of the World

[Editions: 1896, 1904. First published in *Magazine of Art* 17 (July 1894), 304. MS: UT.]

WR identifies this poem as 'the latest printed of any verse compositions within my sister's lifetime' ('Notes' 489).

4 *watch and pray* see note for Part 2, l. 1 of 'Old and New Year Ditties'.

BOOKS IN THE RUNNING BROOKS

[Composed 26 Aug. 1852. Editions: 1896, 1904. MS: BodL.]

In 1896, WR states that the poem was published in 'some magazine; I know neither the name nor the date of the latter' (380).

Title 'And this our life, exempt from public haunt, / Finds tongues in trees, books in the running brooks, / Sermons in stones and good in every thing' (*As You Like It*, II.i.15–17). The MS title is 'After a picture in the Portland Gallery', and WR comments: 'What this picture may have been I cannot now say; not one by Dante Rossetti, who did not exhibit in that gallery after 1850' ('Notes' 479).
13 *I watch a flitting tender cloud* cf. Wordsworth's 'I Wandered Lonely as a Cloud' (1807).

GONE BEFORE

[Composed 12 July 1856. Editions: 1896, 1904. MS: BL.]

In 1896, WR writes that the poem was printed in a magazine, but 'I cannot now say which nor when' (382).

The title in MS was ' "Till thou return." '

7 *in her hair, or ring on finger* in MS, this line reads: 'on the bough or sweet syringa', and to the right is a pencil cross and, in DGR's hand, 'wont do'.

Privately Printed Poems

[Basic text: MS, unless otherwise stated.]

THE DEAD CITY

[Composed 9 April 1847. Editions: 1896, 1904. First published in 1847, pp. 1–10. MS: BodL.]

WR says the poem 'bears a certain relation to a story in *The Arabian Nights*, which was one of the comparatively few books that my sister, from a very early age, read frequently and with delight' ('Notes' 466). The fairy-tale 'Sleeping Beauty', with its castle of frozen life, is an obvious source as well. Packer suggests the poem was influenced by childhood visits to Madame Tussaud's waxwork exhibition, which was within walking distance of CR's home (Packer, *CR* 15). Marsh says that the 'opening passages recall the first pages of *Melmoth* [1820], where Immalee wanders through her paradise island, as well as Tennyson's version of the Sleeping Beauty, *The Day Dream* [1842], which likewise features a royal court arrested in mid-banquet' (*CR* 73). Lines 181–200 also resemble the descriptions of fruit in *Goblin Market*.

1 *Once I rambled in a wood* possible allusion to opening of Dante's *Divine Comedy*; see note for epigraph of 'An Old World Thicket'.
123 *chrysoprase* golden green gem that was thought to shine in the dark.
171 *cate* edible delicacy.
188 *panniers* see note for l. 351 of *Goblin Market*.

The Water Spirit's Song

[Composed 4 March 1844. First published in 1847, pp. 10–12. MS: BL.]

Marsh points out that this poem is 'inspired by Tennyson's mermaids and mermen, who frolic "merrily" all night ["The Merman", 1830], and by water-nymph stories such as *Undine*' (*CR* 44). For *Undine*, see headnote of 'Love and Death'.

The Song of the Star

[Composed 19 March 1847. Editions: 1896, 1904. First published in 1847, pp. 12–14. MS: BodL.]

46 *Amethystine* composed of the precious purple stone, amethyst.

Summer. ['Hark to the song of greeting! The tall trees']

[Composed 4 Dec. 1845. Editions: 1896, 1904. First published in 1847, pp. 15–17. MSS: ll. 1–10, 15–70: MS2 (BodL); ll. 11–14: MS1 (PU).]

36 *kirtle* skirt.
59 *commeline* plant with bright blue flowers. A gardener in CR's short story 'Hero' describes his niece as 'a peach-coloured damsel, with commeline eyes' (*Commonplace* 203).

To my Mother on her Birthday

[Composed 27 April 1842. Editions: 1896, 1904. First printed on a card by CR's grandfather, Gaetano Polidori (1842), and then published in 1847, p. 17. MS: MS1 (BL).]

Illustration: CR created coloured illustrations for 1847, and for this poem, the 'device' or 'emblem' was 'two sprigs of heartsease' ('Notes' 464).

This is the first poem CR wrote – she was eleven. Her mother stated on the flyleaf of CR's notebook containing this poem (MS2 (BL, in Frances Rossetti's hand)): 'These verses are truly and literally by my little daughter, who scrupulously rejected all assistance in her rhyming efforts, under the impression that in that case they would not be her own' ('Notes' 464).

Title TO MY MOTHER / ON THE ANNIVERSARY OF HER BIRTH. /April 27. 1842. *1842*; TO MY MOTHER. / WITH A

NOSEGAY. *1847*; TO MY MOTHER / ON THE ANNIVERSARY
OF HER BIRTH / (Presented with a Nosegay) *1896, 1904*.

The Ruined Cross

[Composed 22 April 1846. First published in 1847, pp. 18–19. MS: BodL.]

Eva

[Composed 18 March 1847. First published in 1847, pp. 20–22. MS: BodL.]

In Maturin's *Women; or, Pour et Contre* (1818), the hero loves two women: Zaira
(whom CR calls 'Zara'), a worldly actress, and Eva, a simple girl, raised by
Calvinists. Just before Zaira discovers that Eva is her long-lost daughter, Eva
dies, broken-hearted because her fiancé has left her for Zaira. He, meanwhile,
has left Zaira to be with the dying Eva. See also 'Zara' ['Now the pain
beginneth and the word is spoken'], 'Zara' ['The pale sad face of her I
wronged'], 'Zara' ['I dreamed that loving me he would love on'] and ' "Look
on this picture and on this" '.

40 *It is good and meet and right* 'It is meet and right' is found in the Communion
liturgy of the *Book of Common Prayer*.

Love ephemeral

[Composed 25 Feb. 1845. Editions: 1896, 1904. First published in 1847, p. 22.
MS: BL.]

Illustration: WR describes CR's illustration as 'the crescent moon, with a lunar
(more like a solar) rainbow' ('Notes' 465).

   Cantalupo sees Quarles's emblem poems as a model for this work ('CR:
The Devotional Poet', in Kent, *Achievement* 286 n. 17). (Francis Quarles (1592–
1644), poet, whose best-known work, *Emblems*, was published in 1635.)

Burial Anthem

[Composed 3 March 1845. Editions: 1896, 1904. First published in 1847, p. 23.
MS: BL.]

Illustration: CR's illustration was 'a sprig of blue and pink forget-me-not'
('Notes' 465).

'I have an impression that this was written in relation to the death of some young clergyman esteemed in our household . . .' ('Notes' 465).

1 *Flesh of our flesh* 'This is now bone of my bones, and flesh of my flesh' (Gen. 2:23) – a verse often quoted in marriage ceremonies.
5 *weary race to run* see note for ll. 11–12 of 'Who Shall Deliver Me?'
23 *the narrow way* see note for l. 46 of 'Paradise'.

Sappho

[Composed 11 Sept. 1846. First published in 1847, p. 24. MS: BodL.]

Title Sappho was a seventh-century Greek lyric poet whom Plato refers to as the 'tenth Muse' and who threw herself into the sea in despair because of an unrequited love. See 'What Sappho would have said had her leap cured instead of killing her'.

Tasso and Leonora

[Composed 19 Dec. 1846. Editions: 1896, 1904. First published in 1847, p. 24. MS: BodL.]

Illustration: CR's illustration is 'the shooting star in a female form' ('Notes' 466).
   The Italian poet Torquato Tasso (1544–95) was imprisoned by the Duke of Ferrara. Goethe's play, *Torquato Tasso* (1790), imagines him as having a forbidden love for the duke's sister Leonora.

ON THE DEATH OF A CAT, / A FRIEND OF MINE, AGED TEN YEARS AND A HALF

[Composed 14 March 1846. Editions: 1896, 1904. First published in 1847, pp. 25–6. MS: BodL.]

Illustration: CR's illustration is of 'a cat, in a rather sentimental attitude of languor, extending its right arm over a kitten. The cat is sandy and white, the kitten tabby' ('Notes' 465). The MS title identified it as Aunt Eliza's cat.

14 *Grimalkin* name given to a cat, especially an old she-cat; probably from 'grey' and 'malkin' (diminutive of 'Matilda'); sometimes used to denote a female spectre or demon. 'I come, Graymalkin!' says the witch in *Macbeth* I.i.9.

Mother and Child

[Composed 10 Jan. 1846. Editions: 1896, 1904. First published in 1847, p. 26. MS: BodL.]

Illustration: WR describes CR's illustration as 'some flowers of undefined genus, with sun-rays behind them' ('Notes' 465).

WR quotes an article by William Sharp published in the *Atlantic Monthly* (June 1895), in which Sharp says that DGR 'pointed out that Blake might have written the four verses called *Mother and Child*' ('Notes' 465).

Fair Margaret

[Composed 28 Dec. 1844. First published in 1847, pp. 27–8. MS: BL.]

In the original ballad 'Fair Margaret and Sweet William', Margaret dies 'for pure true love' and, as a ghost, appears to William on his wedding night. The next day he rides to her bower, finds her dead and dies 'for sorrow' (in Thomas Percy (1729–1811), *Reliques* (1765/1839)).

8 *ruer* the one who 'rues', that is, regrets.

Earth and Heaven

[Composed 28 Dec. 1844. Editions: 1896, 1904. First published in 1847, pp. 28–9. MS: BL.]

Love attacked

[Composed 21 April 1846. Editions: 1896, 1904. First published in 1847, pp. 30–31. MS: BodL.]

Love defended

[Composed 23 April 1846. Editions: 1896, 1904. First published in 1847, pp. 31–2. MS: BodL.]

Illustration: WR describes CR's illustration as 'a blind man (stanza 3) groping, with trees in the background' ('Notes' 466).

Divine and Human Pleading

[Lines 1–64, 85–8 composed 30 March 1846; ll. 65–84 composed 8 Feb. 1846. Edition: 1904 (ll. 65–84 only). First published in 1847, pp. 32–5. MSS: ll. 1–64, 85–8: MS2 (BodL); ll. 65–84: MS1 (BodL).]

In 1904, WR printed ll. 65–84 under the title 'Mary Magdalene' with the explanation: 'these simple and somewhat touching verses were written on 8 Feb. 1846. On 30 March Christina wrote a different poem, *Divine and Human Pleading* – of a slightly "preachy" kind, dissuading from the invocation of saints. Then, in the printed volume *Verses*, the two compositions, under the second title, were joined together. I am certain that the *Mary Magdalene* is better singly; and I so give it, omitting the *Divine and Human Pleading*' ('Notes' 465).

Title Mary Magdalene *1904*.
6 *Thy head was bowed with shame* See note for title of 'Mary Magdalene and the Other Mary'.
75–6 *My tears that fell upon His Feet / As I wiped Them with my curls* 'And stood at his feet behind him weeping, and began to wash his feet with tears, and did wipe them with the hairs of her head, and kissed his feet, and anointed them with the ointment' (Luke 7:38).
83–4 *Forsook the evil of my ways, / Loved much, and was forgiven* see note for l. 14 of ' "Ah, Lord, Lord, if my heart were right with Thine" '.

TO MY FRIEND ELIZABETH

[Composed 17 March 1846. Editions: 1904. First published in 1847, p. 36. MS: BodL.]

Illustration: 'The design to this trifle is a human personation of one of the stamps, bowing in the character of a "humble servant," and wearing the "livery of red and black," of a sort of mediaeval cut' ('Notes' 465).

WR identifies Elizabeth Read as 'a young lady under the tuition of our sister Maria: she is now Mrs. Bull, widow of a leading physician in Hereford. Christina had a most cordial liking for her' ('Notes' 465).

Title TO ELIZABETH READ *1904*.

AMORE E DOVERE

[Composed 15 Sept. 1845. Editions: 1896, 1904. Includes 'A Tirsi'. First published in 1847, p. 37. Basic text: 1847.]

WR says CR wrote to DGR that the second stanza should be cut, but 'She assigns no reason, and I think best to leave it in . . .' ('Notes' 465).

Translation LOVE AND DUTY // You call my heart / Cruel, scornful, / No, it is not true, / Cruel it is not: / I love you, I loved you, – [5] / And you know it, – / Less than duty, / But more than myself. // O little brook, / Tell the Lord of Love [10] / That this breast, / That this heart, / To him shelter / Will no longer give. // The soul betrays [15] / Without remorse; / It does not pity, / It gives no relief, / And it feeds / Upon cruelty. [20] // I understand you, you complain, / My poor heart; / I understand you, love / Complains about me. / Ah! Placated at last; [25] / The spines prick me / That come from you.

25 *Deh* (Ah) 'Although "Deh" is usually translated as "Ah" or "Oh", it is actually an exclamation used in prayer, often followed by "ascoltami" ("hear me" or "listen to me")' (Andrighetti).

Amore e Dispetto

[Composed 21 Aug. 1846. First published in 1847, pp. 38–9. MS: BodL.]

Translation Love and Spite // O great powerful Love / That holds my mind, / Hear the humble prayer / Of one of your sad faithful: / O make Lisa change [5] / So that she will no longer be cruel to me. // One day being tired / I lay my hip on the grass; / While thinking of the one / Who wounded this heart, [10] / O how she seemed beautiful, / She looked at me, and then she fled, // Then I saw her go / With gentle steps to the sea; / And she seemed so merciful [15] / That at the end I said: Who knows! / Maybe, no longer disdainful, / She will be toward me. // Timid, then I rose, / And ran to meet her; [20] / She saw me, and the bespectacled eyes / Lowering, she blushed; / And I exclaimed: Oh listen, / Lisa, pity – so // I wanted to proceed; but in the meantime [25] / Tears came to my eyes; / And it confused my words / A soft sigh; / Then quite silent I was, / And she began to say: [30] // I do not want to love anyone, / And if I did, the one / would not be / you. And then / Falling silent, she left. – / If you want me any longer to serve you, [35] / Love, you must do this; // You must blow into your heart / Senses of a pure love; / Because if this you cannot do, / Or if you do not want to do this, [40] / I scorn your snares, / And I no longer want to love.

7 *stanco* (tired) 'The descriptive adjectives in this poem indicate that the narrator is intended to be a male. For example, if this were a female narrator, CR would have used the feminine form of "tired" ("stanca") instead of the masculine ("stanco")' (Andrighetti).

26 *Mi venne al ciglio il pianto* (Tears came to my eyes) literally, 'the tear came to my lash'.

Love and Hope

[Composed 9 Oct. 1843. Editions: 1896, 1904. First published in 1847, pp. 39–40. MS: BL.]

Serenade

[Composed 4 Dec. 1845. Editions: 1896, 1904. First published in 1847, pp. 40–41. MS: BL.]

The Rose ['Gentle, gentle river']

[Composed 25 Feb. 1846. First published in 1847, pp. 41–2. MS: BodL.]

Present and Future

[Composed 5 Nov. 1846. Editions: 1896, 1904. First published in 1847, p. 42. MS: BodL.]

WILL THESE HANDS NE'ER BE CLEAN?

[Composed 16 Sept. 1846. Editions: 1896, 1904. First published in 1847, pp. 43–4. MS: BodL.]

The MS title is 'To a Murderer.'

Title 'What, will these hands ne'er be clean?' (*Macbeth* V.i.41.)

SIR EUSTACE GREY

[Composed 14 Oct. 1846. First published in 1847, pp. 45–6. MS: BodL.]

'Sir Eustace Grey' (1807) by Crabbe takes place in an insane asylum, where the patient (Grey) tells a doctor and a visitor the story of how he killed his best friend, who had become his wife's lover; the second half of Crabbe's poem describes the nightmarish visions that arise from Grey's guilty conscience.

18 *race is run* see note for ll. 11–12 of 'Who Shall Deliver Me?'

THE TIME OF WAITING

[Composed 16 Nov. 1846. Editions: 1896, 1904. First published in 1847, pp. 46–9. MS: BodL.]

Illustration: WR describes CR's illustration for this poem as 'a damsel on a steep green slope, stretching her arms up longingly; from the sky a black-hooded woman, or spectre, addresses her with an action of admonition. This seems to be apposite chiefly to triplet 2' ('Notes' 466).

41 *Lord; how long, how long* see note for Part 2, l. 12 of 'Old and New Year Ditties'.

Charity

[Composed 15 Sept. 1844. Editions: 1896, 1904. First published in 1847, p. 49. MS: BL.]

11–12 *For Faith and Hope shall merge together / In Charity* see note for l. 18 of 'Herself a rose, who bore the Rose'.
12 *Charity* MS is in MR's hand, and includes a note: 'The foregoing verses are imitated from that beautiful little poem '*Virtue*', by George Herbert.' Like Herbert in 'Vertue' (1633), CR mourns the passing of the day, the rose and the season (summer rather than spring, however). She diverges from the model in the last stanza: Herbert talks of a 'vertuous soul' where CR talks of charity.

The Dead Bride

[Composed 10 Sept. 1846. Editions: 1896, 1904. First published in 1847, pp. 50–51, and reprinted in *Our Paper, Being a Monthly Serial for Private Circulation*, no. 1 (Jan. 1855), 21. MS: BodL.]

LIFE OUT OF DEATH

[First published in 1847, pp. 51–2. Basic text: 1847.]

13 *Ask what ye will, it shall be given* see note for Part 2, l. 5 of 'If Thou Sayest, Behold, We Knew It Not'.
14 *Faith, hope, and love* see note for l. 18 of 'Herself a rose, who bore the Rose'.

The solitary Rose

[Composed 15 March 1847. Editions: 1896, 1904. First published in 1847, pp. 52–3. MS: BodL.]

CR adopted the rose as her emblem (*CR* 72).

Lady Isabella ['Lady Isabella']

[Composed 1 March 1846. First published in 1847, pp. 53–4. MS: BodL.]

CR wrote two poems with this title, the second in 1847. WR identifies the subject of the second ('Lady Isabella' ['Heart warm as Summer, fresh as Spring']) as 'Lady Isabella Howard, a daughter of the Earl of Wicklow; she was a pupil of my aunt, Charlotte Polidori. My sister entertained an ardent admiration for the loveliness of character and person which marked this young lady, who died of a decline at the age of eighteen or thereabouts' ('Notes' 467).

THE DREAM

[Editions: 1896, 1904. First published in 1847, pp. 55–6. Basic text: 1847.]

'I am not sure whether the first short quatrain here printed is an integral portion of the poem, or rather a quotation from some other writer; I fancy the latter' ('Notes' 466). If it is a quotation, the writer has not been identified.

The Dying Man to his Betrothed

[Composed 14 July 1846. Editions: 1896, 1904. First published in 1847, pp. 56–8. MS: BodL.]

Illustration: WR describes CR's illustration as 'a rosebush intertwined by a snake' ('Notes' 466).

6 *O honey between serpent's teeth* 'They have sharpened their tongues like a serpent; adders' poison is under their lips' (Ps. 140:3); 'But I fear, lest by any means, as the serpent beguiled Eve through his subtilty, so your minds should be corrupted from the simplicity that is in Christ' (2 Cor. 11:3).

62 *blood-shriven* see note for l. 5 of ' "Her Seed; It shall bruise thy head" '.

The Martyr

[Composed 24 May 1846. Editions: 1896, 1904. First published in 1847, pp. 59–61. MS: BodL.]

Illustration: WR describes CR's illustration as 'the soul of the martyr received into heaven by an angel. Between the angel's wings are a series of red and white curves, symbolizing (I suppose) the nine heavens, as in Dante' ('Notes', 466).

The End of Time

[Composed 9 Dec. 1845. Editions: 1896, 1904. First published in 1847, pp. 61–2. MS: BodL.]

Illustration: WR describes CR's illustration as 'a rose crossing a scythe; within the angle of the scythe, an hour-glass' ('Notes' 465).

Cantalupo sees Quarles's emblem poems as a model for this work ('CR: The Devotional Poet' in Kent, *Achievement*, 286 n. 17); see headnote of 'Love ephemeral.' Also cf. Blake's 'The Sick Rose' (1789).

Resurrection Eve

[Composed 8 April 1847. Editions: 1896, 1904. First published in 1847, pp. 63–4. MS: BodL.]

Illustration: WR describes CR's illustration as 'a white grave-cross, two palm-shrubs interlacing above it; in the sky, crescent moon and star' ('Notes' 466).

1 *He resteth* reference to 'soul sleep' – see headnote of 'Dream-Land'.

ZARA ['Now the pain beginneth and the word is spoken']

[Editions: 1896, 1904. First published in 1847, pp. 64–6. Basic text: 1847.]

Illustration: 'The device to *Zara* is a foxglove plant, with insects sucking its poison-honey' ('Notes' 467).

The poem is based on incidents in Maturin's novel *Women* in which 'Zara is the rival (she finally turns out to be the mother) of Eva; she is a shining leader of society . . .' ('Notes' 467). See headnote of 'Eva'. See also 'Zara' ['The pale sad face of her I wronged'].

Versi

[Composed 6 Oct. 1849. Editions: 1896, 1904. First published in *The Bouquet, Culled from Marylebone Gardens* no. 5 (printed at the 'Bouquet' Press for private circulation, Oct. 1851), 175. MS: BodL.]

In 1851, after this poem and after 'L'Incognita', below, is printed CR's Italian pen name: 'CALTA'. 'Perhaps created from "C" for "Christina" and "alta", the feminine form of "alto" (high above/heaven)' (Andrighetti).

Translation Verses // Daughter, the mother said: / Beware of Love; / He is crude, he is a traitor, – / What more do you want to know? / Do not ever hope to make him [5] / Enter into your breast; / Because she who gave him refuge / Was always betrayed. // With the ribbon at his brow / He is a handsome boy, it is true: [10] / But he is always mendacious; / But he will always betray. / You are simple if you trust / In his deceptive smile; / You will lose your peace [15] / It will never return. // But I see: already you are tired / Of my prudent speech; / Already your mind is turning / The when, the how, and the who. [20] / Hear me: my words / If they are sincere you already know; / And if they are false or true / You will know from experience one day.

L'Incognita

[Editions: 1896, 1904. First published in *The Bouquet, Culled from Marylebone Gardens*, no. 7 (printed at the 'Bouquet' Press for private circulation, Dec. 1851), 216. Basic text: 1851.]

See headnote of 'Versi', above.

Translation The Unknown // Noble rose still not grown / Without thorns on its stem: / If it were, then it would be / A suitable image of you. / It is the moon in the middle of the sky [5] / Beautiful it is true, but fleeting: / The Spring passes once more: / Ah! Your image where is it?

Title 'This could be translated as "The Puzzle" or "The Dark Horse" when referring to a person' (Andrighetti).

7 *Passa* (passes) 'This could also be translated as "comes" ' (Andrighetti).

['Purpurea rosa']

[Editions: 1896, 1904. First published in *The Bouquet, Culled from Marylebone Gardens*, no. 15 (printed at the 'Bouquet' Press for private circulation, Aug. 1852), 56, as a part of a series of letters in Italian entitled 'Corrispondenza Famigliare'. Basic text: 1852.]

Translation Crimson rose / Sweet, odorous, / And very beautiful, / But still it does not, / O my Nigella, [5] / Rival you. // Woman in a veil, / Flower on a stem, / Every love / Claims to be singular: [10] / But the flower passes, / You remain with me.

Title NIGELLA *1896, 1904.*
5 *Nigella* simply a proper name, 'although an unusual one' (Andrighetti).

['Soul rudderless, unbraced']

[Editions: 1896, 1904. First published in David Johnston (ed.), *Translations, Literal and Free, of the Dying Hadrian's Address to His Soul* (printed at the 'Chronicle' office, for private circulation only, 1876), MS: PU.]

Of the many translations of these lines, supposedly spoken by the Emperor Hadrian (75–138) as he was dying, see, for example, Byron, 'Adrian's Address to His Soul, When Dying' (1806) and Pope, '*Adriani morientis ad Animam, or, The Heathen to his departing Soul*' (1713).

Title XII. *1876*; HADRIAN'S DEATH-SONG TRANSLATED *1896, 1904.*

['Animuccia, vagantuccia, morbiduccia']

[Editions: 1896, 1904. First published in Johnston (ed.), *Translations, Literal and Free, of the Dying Hadrian's Address to His Soul* (1876), p. 49. Basic text: 1876.]

Translation Little soul, wandering, gentle, / Guest of the body and sister, / Where will you make your home now? / Pallid, rigid, naked, / No longer jesting. [5]

Title XIII. *1876*; ADRIANO *1896, 1904.*

Unpublished Poems [in Rossetti's lifetime]

[Basic text: MS, unless otherwise stated.]

Heaven

[Composed in 1842. MS: BL.]

Hymn ['To the God Who reigns on high']

[Composed 2 July 1843. Editions: 1896, 1904. MS: BL.]

Corydon's Lament and Resolution

[Composed July 1843. MS: BL.]

Title 'Corydon' is a generic proper name in pastoral poetry for a rustic. 'Amaryllis' and 'Chloe' (ll. 2, 11) are taken from a drama by John Fletcher (1579–1625), *The Faithful Shepherdess* (1609–10); see 'The Faithless Shepherdess'.

Rosalind

[Composed July 1843. MS: BL.]

Marsh states that this poem owes 'something to *Sir Hugh the Heron* [1843]' – a rendition of a ballad by the young DGR – 'as well as to Gottfried Bürger's *Lenore* (which the young Rossettis were reading with Dr Heimann [and which DGR translated in 1844])' (*CR* 40).

Pitia a Damone

[Composed 20 April 1844. MS: BL.]

Translation Pithius to Damon // Ah do not call it sorrow, / That which I feel is joy; / I will die content / If I die for you. / It is fervid beloved [5] / That which is in my breast; / For you death itself / Is not terrible.

Title Damon and Pithius were young Siracusans held up by tradition as the example of true friendship. Condemned to death by Dionysus the Younger,

Pithius obtained his freedom for one day, thanks to Damon, who consigned himself as his guarantor. Just when Damon was about to be executed, Pithius returned, and Dionysus, moved by his loyalty, pardoned him.

The Faithless Shepherdess

[Composed 17 June 1844. MS: BL.]

Title cf. Fletcher's *The Faithful Shepherdess* (see note for title of 'Corydon's Lament and Resolution').

Ariadne to Theseus

[Composed 18 June 1844. MS: BL.]

MS is in MR's hand, and includes a note: 'The reader may perhaps detect in these verses a resemblance to an idea in one of Metastasio's dramas.' Possibly the drama referred to is *La Didone abbandonata* ('Dido abandoned') (1724), which is characterized by the same theme, by Pietro Metastasio, Italian poet, dramatist and librettist (1698–1782).

Title Ariadne was a mythological Cretan princess who fell in love with the Greek hero Theseus and helped him find his way through the labyrinth to kill her half-brother, the Minotaur. Theseus later abandoned her on the island of Naxos.

On Albina

[Composed June 1844. Editions: 1896, 1904. MS: BL.]

Edward Jerningham (1737–1812) in 'Albina' (1806) tells what the poet claims to be the true story of a young woman led to her ruin by a false lover who pretends to marry her. The poet asks 'Genius' to bestow a 'vivid pencil to this hand' so that he can 'paint on the poetic page / Albina's elegance of frame' – including 'Her cheek – that wears a lively glow' (ll. 1–13).

A Hymn for Christmas Day

[Composed 30 June 1844. MS: BL.]

The poem follows closely the account of Jesus' birth in Luke 2.

Love and Death

[Composed 2 July 1844. MS: BL.]

Marsh points out that this poem owes something 'to the story of Undine by the German Romantic Fouqué (1777–1843) – '([Daniel] Maclise's painting [1844] of the water-spirit was the star of this year's Royal Academy, bought by the Queen for Prince Albert) but it also betrays the powerful influence of Gabriel's translation of *Lenore* [1844], in which a ghostly horseman returns to claim his wife' (*CR* 45). Fouqué's *Undine* (1811) tells of the tragic love between a knight and a water spirit. The story was set to music by Hoffmann.

Despair

[Composed 19 Aug. 1844. MS: BL.]

Forget Me Not

[Composed 19 Aug. 1844. Editions: 1896, 1904. MS: BL.]

Easter Morning

[Composed 15 Sept. 1844. MS: BL.]

A Tirsi

[Composed 25 Sept. 1845. Originally part of 'Amore e Dovere', printed in 1847. MS: BL.]

For translation, see notes to 'Amore e Dovere'.

Title To Tirsi (Italian). A masculine name. The noun 'tirso' (plural 'tirsi') refers to the thyrsus, the staff carried by Bacchus.

The Last Words of St. Telemachus

[Composed 1 March 1845. MS: BL.]

Title Telemachus, also known as Almachius (d. *c.* 400), was a Christian martyr in Rome, stoned to death as he tried to stop a gladiatorial contest.

Lord Thomas and fair Margaret.

[Composed 2 April 1845. MS: BL.]

Like 'The Hour and the Ghost', this poem seems to be influenced by the traditional folk-ballad motif of the demon lover (see headnote of 'The Hour and the Ghost').

MS is in MR's hand, and includes a note: 'This is imitated from the ballad of "Sweet William's Ghost," in Percy's "Reliques of Ancient English Poetry." ' See headnote of 'Fair Margaret'. It also contains elements of 'Fair Margaret and Sweet William', in which it is Margaret who appears as the ghost.

1–2 *Fair Marg'ret sat in her bower, / Unbraiding of her hair* cf. 'Fair Margaret sat in her bower-window, / Combing her yellow hair' ('Fair Margaret and Sweet William', ll. 9–10).
14 *maun* must.
31 *canna* cannot.

Lines to my Grandfather

[Composed 1 May 1845. Editions: 1904. MS: BL.]

CR's maternal grandfather, Gaetano Polidori, her first publisher, tutored her in Italian.
33 *parterre* ornamental arrangement of flower beds.

Charade ['My first may be the firstborn']

[Composed 3 Dec. 1845. MS: BL.]

MS is in MR's hand, and includes a note: 'Answer. Sonnet.'

Hope in Grief

[Composed 3 Dec. 1845. MS: MS1 (PU).]

Marsh notes echoes of the Tractarian writer Isaac Williams (1802–65) in this poem (*CR Poems* 429).

1–2 *Tell me not that death of grief / Is the only sure relief* 'Christina's desperate lines "Tell me not that death of grief" were clearly written in direct response to the . . . instruction contained in [John] Keble's *St John's Day* [1827] to trust in the Lord's "sure relief" ' (*CR* 56).

Lisetta all' Amante

[Composed 11 Aug. 1846. Editions: 1896, 1904. MS: BodL.]

Translation Lisetta to her Lover // Pardon the first excess / Of a tender pain; / I promised my heart to you, / And I want to save it for you. / But tell me, and it will comfort me: [5] / Do you still love me, my heart? / If I am faithful to you, / Will you be faithful to me? // Because if in your ungrateful soul / You are planning to abandon me, [10] / I will know I must forget / A cruel lover. / But I do not want to believe it; / But I do not want to think it; / Because I could not leave him, [15] / Because I would be faithful to him.

Song ['I saw her; she was lovely']

[Composed 27 Sept. 1846. MS: BodL.]

Praise of Love

[Composed 24 Feb. 1847. Editions: 1885, 1886a. Includes lines printed in *TF* as ' "Love is all happiness, love is all beauty" '. MS: BodL.]

"I have fought a good fight"

[Composed July 1847. Editions: 1896, 1904. MS: BodL.]

Title 'I have fought a good fight, I have finished my course, I have kept the faith' (2 Tim. 4:7).

Wishes:/Sonnet

[Composed 22 July 1847. Editions: 1896, 1904. MS: BodL.]

Eleanor

[Composed 30 July 1847. Editions: 1896, 1904. MS: BodL.]

WR writes: 'This may be a portrait from the life – I know not now of whom' ('Notes' 466).

Isidora

[Composed 9 Aug. 1847. Editions: 1896, 1904. MS: BodL.]

The story comes from Charles Maturin's romance, *Melmoth the Wanderer* (1820).

Melmoth is a personage who has made a compact with the Devil, thereby securing an enormous length of life (say at least a century and a half), and the power of flitting at will from land to land. At the end of the term, Melmoth's soul is to be forfeited, unless he can meanwhile induce some one else to take the compact off his hands. Melmoth makes numerous efforts in this direction, but all abortive. One of his intended victims is a beautiful girl named Immalee, a child of Nature in an Indian island – a second Miranda. She becomes deeply enamoured of Melmoth, but resists his tamperings with her soul. She is finally identified as the daughter of a Spanish Grandee, and is then baptized as Isidora. At one point of the story she espouses Melmoth, and bears him a child. Christina's poem is her deathbed scene. ('Notes' 466–7)

'While most of Melmoth's qualities derive from religious folklore, it appears that Maturin was directly energized in several of his tales by Polidori's *The Vampyre*, which appeared in 1819' (Dale Kramer, *Charles Robert Maturin* (Twayne Publishers, *c.* 1973) 98). Polidori, Byron's physician, was CR's maternal uncle, who committed suicide in 1820.

72 *Paradise, will he be there?* 'The last line is truly a fine stroke of pathos and of effect; but it is not Christina's – it comes *verbatim* out of Maturin' ('Notes' 467). *Melmoth* ends: ' "Paradise!" uttered Isidora, with her last breath – "*Will he be there?*" ' See also l. 1 of 'Will you be there? my yearning heart has cried'.

The Novice

[Composed 4 Sept. 1847. Editions: 1896, 1904. MS: BodL.]

Immalee

[Composed 21 Sept. 1847. Editions: 1896, 1904.]

Title character in Maturin's *Melmoth the Wanderer*: see headnote of 'Isidora'.

Lady Isabella ['Heart warm as Summer, fresh as Spring']

[Composed 27 Sept. 1847. Editions: 1896, 1904. MS: BodL.]

See headnote of 'Lady Isabella' ['Lady Isabella'].

Night and Death

[Composed 28 Sept. 1847. Editions: 1896, 1904. MS: BodL.]

WR surmises that this poem 'has some reference to the death of Lady Isabella Howard' ('Notes' 467). See headnote of 'Lady Isabella' ['Lady Isabella'].

3 *Happy Night, whom Chaos bore* 'In the beginning how the heavens and earth / Rose out of Chaos'; 'eldest Night / And Chaos, ancestors of Nature' (*Paradise Lost* I, 9–10; II, 894–5).
51 *matin-prime* first prayer of the morning.

"Young men aye were fickle found / Since summer trees were leafy"

[Composed 30 Sept. 1847. MS: BodL.]

Title 'For young men ever were fickle found, / Since summer trees were leafy' (anon. ballad, 'The Friar of Orders Gray', in Percy, *Reliques*, I, 71).
1 *Go in peace my Beloved* see note for title of ' "Go in Peace" '.

The Lotus-Eaters: / Ulysses to Penelope

[Composed 7 Oct. 1847. Editions: 1896, 1904. MS: BodL.]

MS is in MR's hand, and originally included a note (below the subtitle): '(an echo from Tennyson).' Cf. Tennyson, 'The Lotos-Eaters' (1832).

Sonnet / from the Psalms

[Composed 7 Nov. 1847. Editions: 1896, 1904. MS: BodL.]

1–2 *All thro' the livelong night I lay awake / Watering my couch with tears of heaviness* 'I am weary with my groaning; all the night make I my bed to swim; I water my couch with my tears' (Ps. 6:6).
9 *Oh that I had wings like to a dove* see note for ll. 13–14 of 'Darkness and light are both alike to Thee'.

Song ['The stream moaneth as it floweth']

[Composed 7 Nov. 1847. Editions: 1896, 1904. MS: BodL.]

A Counsel

[Composed 15 Nov. 1847. MS: BodL.]

The World's Harmonies.

[Composed 20 Nov. 1847. Editions: 1896, 1904. MS: BodL.]

Lines / given with a Penwiper

[Composed 20 Nov. 1847. MS: BodL.]

The last Answer

[Composed 2 Dec. 1847. Editions: 1896, 1904. MS: BodL.]

As subtitle to MS (in WR's hand), 1896 and 1904 is '(Written to Bouts-rimés)'. 'Bout-rimés' is a verse-making game in which given words must be used as end rhymes. CR's manuscript versions of such sonnets often end with a number (sometimes followed by the letter 'm') – apparently the number of minutes required to complete the verse.

One of the Dead

[Composed 4 Dec. 1847. MS: BodL.]

14 *Friends, she but slumbers, wherefore do ye weep* see headnote of 'Dream-Land'.

"The whole head is sick, and the whole heart faint"

[Composed 6 Dec. 1847. Editions: 1896, 1904. MS: MS2 (BodL).]

Title 'Why should ye be stricken any more? ye will revolt more and more: the whole head is sick, and the whole heart faint' (Isa. 1:5).

"I do set My bow in the cloud"

[Composed Dec. 1847. Editions: 1896, 1904. MS: BodL.]

Title after the Flood, God promised Noah and his sons that never again would He destroy the earth by flood: 'I do set my bow in the cloud, and it shall be for a token of a covenant between me and the earth' (Gen. 9:13).
10 *His rod and staff shall comfort me* see note for Part 3, l. 25 of 'Christmas Carols'.
27 *Yet chasteneth His belovèd still* see note for title of " 'Whom the Lord loveth He chasteneth' ".
32–3 *When heaven and earth have passed away, / Only His righteous word shall stay* 'Heaven and earth shall pass away: but my words shall not pass away' (Matt. 24:35; Mark 13:31; Luke 21:33).
35–6 *Behold; He is a Haven Rest, / A Sheltering Rock, a Hiding Place* 'And a man shall be as an hiding place from the wind, and a covert from the tempest; as rivers of water in a dry place, as the shadow of a great rock in a weary land' (Isa. 32:2).
37 *the race* see note for ll. 11–12 of 'Who Shall Deliver Me?'

"O Death where is thy Sting?"

[Probably composed between Dec. 1847 and 12 Jan. 1848. MS: BodL.]

Title see note for Part 3, ll. 13–14 of 'The Thread of Life'.
6 *God is Love* see note for l. 8 of 'Trinity Sunday'.

Undine

[Composed 12 Jan. 1848. MS: BodL.]

Title see headnote of 'Love and Death'.

Lady Montrevor

[Composed 18 Feb. 1848. Editions: 1896, 1904. MS: BodL.]

'This sonnet applies to a personage in Maturin's novel *The Wild Irish Boy* [1808]. Christina, as well as her brothers, was in early youth very fond of Maturin's novels, and more than one of her poems relate to these. Lady Montrevor is possibly now almost forgotten. She is a brilliant woman of the world who fascinates "the Wild Irish Boy," and leads both him and herself into grave dilemmas' ('Notes' 477).

6–7 *let the rivers fill / The everlasting sea* see note for ll. 10–11 of 'A Testimony'.

Floral Teaching

[Composed 19 Feb. 1848. MS: BodL.]

"Death is swallowed up in Victory"

[Composed 20 Feb. 1848. Editions: 1896, 1904. MS: BodL.]

Title see note for l. 7 of 'Beloved, yield thy time to God, for He'.
28 *annext* added.

30 *My heart is wearied and my spirit vext* see note for Part 2, l. 12 of 'Old and New Year Ditties'.

37 *Where is that mansion mortals cannot see* see note for l. 21 of 'The Convent Threshold'.

41 *We shall be raised then; changed, yet still the same* see note for l. 46 of ' "It is Finished" '.

43 *Thither thou goest whence no man ever came* 'I shall go the way whence I shall not return' (Job 16:22).

59 *He who hath faith in that which is not seen* see note for Part 2, l. 2 of ' "They put their trust in Thee, and were not confounded" '.

59–60 *faith . . . hope . . . love* see note for l. 18 of 'Herself a rose, who bore the Rose'.

64–5 *The cup my Father giveth me to drink, / Shall I not take it meekly* 'Then said Jesus unto Peter, Put up thy sword into the sheath: the cup which my Father hath given me, shall I not drink it?' (John 18:11).

71 *His arm made bare* 'The LORD hath made bare his holy arm in the eyes of all the nations; and all the ends of the earth shall see the salvation of our God' (Isa. 52:10).

72–3 *underneath His wing / I shall lie safe at rest* 'in the shadow of thy wings will I make my refuge' (Ps. 57:1).

Death

[Composed 12 April 1848. MS: BodL.]

39 *the second birth* spiritual birth. 'Jesus answered and said unto him, Verily, verily, I say unto thee, Except a man be born again, he cannot see the kingdom of God' (John 3:3; see also John 3:7 and 1 Pet. 1:23).

A Hopeless Case / (Nydia)

[Composed 24 April 1848. MS: MS2 (PU).]

Nydia is a slave girl in Bulwer-Lytton's *The Last Days of Pompeii* (1834).

Ellen Middleton

[Composed May 1848. MS: BodL.]

Title cf. Lady Georgiana Fullerton (1812–85), *Ellen Middleton* (1844).

St. Andrew's Church

[Composed 1 June 1848. First published in 1897a, p. 67. MS: MS2 (HL).]

Bell identifies the church as 'probably intended for St. Andrews, Wells Street, W.' (Bell, *CR* 20).

Title [untitled] *1897a*.
8 *watch and pray* see note for Part 2, l. 1 of 'Old and New Year Ditties'.
10–11 *thy love / Soars not to Heaven, but grovelleth below* cf. Claudius, also vainly trying to pray: 'My words fly up, my thoughts remain below' (*Hamlet* III.iii.96).

Grown Cold/Sonnet

[Composed 18 June 1848. MS: BodL.]

Zara ['The pale sad face of her I wronged']

[Composed 18 June 1848. MS: BodL.]

See headnote of 'Eva'. The poem refers to the hero's leaving Zara for Eva, who is dying. See also 'Zara' ['Now the pain beginneth and the word is spoken'].

24 *Endymion* in Greek myth, a shepherd who attracts the love of Selene, the goddess of the moon.
25 *Narcissus* in Greek myth, a beautiful youth who spurns the love of the nymph Echo and is made to fall in love with his own reflection.
30 *Echo mourned* in some versions of the Greek myth of Echo and Narcissus, Echo mourns for Narcissus until she becomes only a disembodied voice.

Ruin

[Composed 1848. Editions: 1896, 1904. MS: MS3 (PU).]

In the MS in BodL, this is the first in a series entitled 'Bouts rimés Sonnets'. The others are: 'I sit among green shady valleys oft', 'Listen, and I will tell you of a face', 'Wouldst thou give me a heavy jewelled crown', 'I said within myself: I am a fool', 'Methinks the ills of life I fain would shun' and 'Strange voices sing among the planets which'.

Title SONNETS / WRITTEN TO BOUTS-RIMÉS / I *1896, 1904*.
   See headnote of 'The last Answer'.

['I sit among green shady valleys oft']

[Composed 1848. Editions: 1896, 1904. MS: MS2 (BodL).]

See headnote of 'Ruin', above.

Title SONNETS / WRITTEN TO BOUTS-RIMÉS / II *1896, 1904*.
   See headnote of 'The last Answer'.

['Listen, and I will tell you of a face']

[Composed 1848. MS: MS2 (BodL).]

See headnote of 'Ruin' and of 'The last Answer'.

['Wouldst thou give me a heavy jewelled crown']

[Composed 1848. Editions: 1896, 1904. MS: MS2 (BodL).]

See headnote of 'Ruin'.

Title SONNETS / WRITTEN TO BOUTS-RIMÉS / III *1896, 1904*.
   See headnote of 'The last Answer'.

['I said within myself: I am a fool']

[Composed 1848. Editions: 1896,1904. MS: MS2 (BodL).]

See headnote of 'Ruin'.

Title SONNETS / WRITTEN TO BOUTS-RIMÉS / IV *1896, 1904.*
See headnote of 'The last Answer'.

['Methinks the ills of life I fain would shun']

[Composed 1848. Editions: 1896, 1904. MS: MS3 (BodL).]

In 1848, DGR said this sonnet was 'as good as anything she has written, and well worthy of revision' ('Notes' 490). Judging from the manuscript notes in his hand in MS1 (PU), he appears to have taken on part of the job himself, and his suggestions are given in the notes below. In MS2 (DU), a fair copy, CR signed and dated it '21st August 1848' with the place given as 'Brighton', and she noted '7 minutes', probably how long it took her to compose the poem.

See headnote of 'Ruin'.

Title SONNETS / WRITTEN TO BOUTS-RIMÉS / VIII *1896, 1904.*
1 *Methinks the ills of life I fain would* in DGR's hand: 'the ills of life for care I'.
2 *is* in DGR's hand: 'though'.
3 *Even in my childhood* in DGRs hand: 'Is life: even when a child'.
5 *my many* in DGR's hand: 'these other'.
7 *from whose lips* in DGR's hand: 'at whose soul'.
9 *But many times* in DGR's hand: 'many times since'.
10 *And many times I in my heart have* in DGR's hand: 'many times I in my spirit have'. CR revised this line in MS2 to read: 'And many times in my heart have I'.

['Strange voices sing among the planets which']

[Composed 1848. MS: BodL.]

See headnote of 'Ruin' and of 'The last Answer'.

"Sleep, sleep, happy child"

[Composed 12 Nov. 1848. MS: BodL.]

Epigraph from Blake's 'Cradle Song' (1789), ll. 17–18.
27, 29 *Yet a little while* see note for title of 'Yet a Little While' ['I dreamed and did not seek: today I seek'].

What Sappho would have said had her leap cured instead of killing her

[Composed 7 Dec. 1848. MSS: ll. 1–56: MS1 (BodL); ll. 57–66: MS2 (PML).]
Title see note for title of 'Sappho'.

On Keats

[Composed 18 Jan. 1849. Editions: 1896, 1904. MS: BodL.]

3 *grown weary of a race* see note for ll. 11–12 of 'Who Shall Deliver Me?'
6 *his own daisies* daisies appear in several of Keats's poems, especially in *Endymion*.
10–11 *Here lies one whose name was writ / In water* see headnote of ' "Slain from the foundation of the world" '.
12 *Saint Agnes' Eve* Keats's 'The Eve of St Agnes' was one of CR's favourite poems. She wrote 'For the Eve of Saint Agnes' at the end of this poem in MS.
      basil reminiscent of Keats's 'Isabella; or, The Pot of Basil'. See note for ll. 31–3 of 'A Royal Princess'.

Have Patience

[Composed 23 Jan. 1849. Editions: 1896, 1904. MS: BodL.]

5 *We take thought for the morrow* see note for l. 91 of 'Maiden May'.
47–8 *palm-branches . . . And crowns* see note for ll. 37–8 of 'Paradise'.

To Lalla, reading my verses topsy-turvy

[Composed 24 Jan. 1849. Editions: 1896, 1904. MS: BodL.]

'Lalla' was the pet name given to Henrietta Polydore, CR's cousin. 'The name was her own baby invention, I think. She became consumptive, and died in America in 1874, aged about twenty-eight' ('Notes' 491).

Sonnet ['Some say that love and joy are one: and so']

[Composed 6 Feb. 1849. MS: BodL.]

12 *Bound in the spirit, to Jerusalem* see note for l. 211 of 'From House to Home'.

The last *Complaint*

[Composed 7 Feb. 1849. MS: BodL.]

Have you forgotten?

[Composed 7 Feb. 1849. MS: BodL.]

MS has a note in WR's hand: 'must be Bouts rimés'.

A Christmas Carol, / (on the stroke of Midnight)

[Composed 7 March 1849. Editions: 1896, 1904; also published 1897a (77–9). MS: MS3 (PU).]

Title A CHRISTMAS CAROL *1896, 1904*; [untitled] *1897a*.
19–21 *gold . . . incense . . . myrrh* see headnote of 'Epiphany'.
32 *He is our Door, and Path, and Guide* cf. John 10:9: see note for l. 7 of 'Thy Name, O Christ, as incense streaming forth'.
37–9 *For unto us a Child is born . . . For unto us a Son is given* 'For unto us a child is born, unto us a son is given' (Isa. 9:6).

For Advent

[Composed 12 March 1849. Editions: 1896, 1904; also published in 1897a (49–51). MS: HL.]

Title [untitled] *1897a*.
34 *For these things shall pass away* see note for ll. 32–3 of ' "I do set My bow in the cloud" '.
39 *Let us see our lamps are lighted* see note for l. 3 of 'Advent' ['This Advent moon shines cold and clear'].
44 *the Judge is at the door* 'Grudge not one against another, brethren, lest ye be condemned: behold, the Judge standeth before the door' (*TF* 114). See headnote of 'Called to Be Saints' and note for l. 8 of 'Despised and Rejected'.
47–8 *When the quick and dead shall all / Rise at the last trumpet call* see notes for l. 46 of ' "It is Finished" ' and for l. 11 of 'By the Waters of Babylon. B.C. 570'.

Two Pursuits

[Composed 12 April 1849. Editions: 1896, 1904. MS: BodL.]

Looking forward

[Composed 8 June 1849. Editions: 1896, 1904; also published in 1897a (117–19). MS: MS2 (HL).]

WR, pointing out that MS1 (BodL) is in Frances Rossetti's handwriting, says that the 'tone of this lyric suggests that it was written in expectation of seemingly imminent death' ('Notes' 478).

Title [untitled] *1897a.*

Life hidden

[Composed 23 July 1849. Editions: 1896, 1904. MS: BodL.]
2 *Where she sleeps the long sleep* see headnote of 'Dream-Land'.

Queen Rose

[Composed 13 Aug. 1849. Editions: 1896, 1904. MS: BodL.]

'Christina sang often – possibly too often – the praises of the rose; she regarded it not merely in its own beauty, but as the symbol of love, whether construed as deep human affection or as union with the Divine. The lily stood with her (as with so many another) for faith' ('Notes' 478).

How one chose

[Composed 6 Oct. 1849. Editions: 1896, 1904. MS: BodL.]
9 *palm branches or of crowns* see note for ll. 37–8 of 'Paradise'.

Seeking rest

[Composed 10 Oct. 1849. Editions: 1896, 1904. MS: BodL.]
In MS, the poem has four opening stanzas, marked through and followed by

a note in what appears to be DGR's hand: 'Begin here'. W. David Shaw points out that CR's original opening lines – 'She knocked at the Earth's greeny door: / O Mother, let me in' – echo 'the old man's petition in "The Pardoner's Tale": "And on the ground which is my modres gate / I knokke . . . / and saye, 'Leve moder, leet me in"' (lines 442–3)' ('Poet of Mystery: The Art of Christina Rossetti' in Kent, *Achievement*, 31).

Title 'When the unclean spirit is gone out of a man, he walketh through dry places, seeking rest, and findeth none' (Matt. 12:43; see also Luke 11:24).

A Year Afterwards

[Composed 18 Feb. 1850. MS: BodL.]

23–4 *Leaning down to me from her rest; / And shaking her long golden hair* cf. DGR's 'The Blessed Damozel', ll. 1–2 (see note for ll. 7–8 of 'Martyrs' Song').

Two thoughts of Death

[Composed 16 March 1850. Editions: 1896, 1904. MS: BodL.]

Marsh calls this a 'Tennysonian monologue in response to [Poe's] *Annabel Lee* [1849], in which a modern paragon of piety lies in her grave' (*CR* 111). In a letter to WR [18 Jan. 1850], CR writes: 'Many thanks for *Annabel Lee*, which I do not like . . . Till your letter enlightened me I imagined the whole poem to be an imitation of Poe by Gabriel' (*Letters*, I, 31).

Three Moments

[Composed 23 March 1850. Editions: 1896, 1904. MS: BodL.]

10–11 *"I have lost my bird;" said she / Weeping bitterly* 'Maria's thrush cast a longer shadow than has been perceived' (Marsh, referring to MR's 'Epitaph on a Thrush', written when Maria was ten (*CR* 111)).

Once

[Probably composed between 23 March and 10 May 1850. MS: MS2 (YU).]

Title Is and was. *1896, 1904.*
29 *Doing all from self-respect*

Much about the time when the poem was written, a lady told my sister that the latter seemed to 'do all from self-respect,' not from fellow-feeling with others, or from kindly consideration for them. Christina mentioned the remark, with an admission that it hit a blot in her character, in which a certain amount of reserve and distance, not remote from *hauteur*, was certainly at that date perceptible. She laid the hint to heart, and, I think, never forgot it. A like phrase appears in a poem of much later date, July 1865, *Enrica*. ('Notes' 478–9)

Three Nuns

[Part 2 composed 12 Feb. 1849; Parts 1 and 3 composed 10 May 1850. Editions: 1896, 1904; also published in 1897a (93–105). MS: MS3 (HL).]

WR says the poem was originally 'inserted into the prose tale *Maude*, with the observation: "Pray read the mottoes [epigraphs]; put together, they form a most exquisite little song which the nuns sing in Italy." ' When *Maude* was published in England, 'Three Nuns' was excluded 'on copyright grounds' ('Notes' 460).

1

Epigraph 'This heart sighs, and I know not wherefore' (trans. WR, 'Notes' 460).

1 *Shadow, shadow on the wall* possible echo of 'Mirror, mirror on the wall' from the fairy-tale 'Snow White'.

3 *pall* velvet cloth for spreading over a coffin.

8–9 *Shadow thou hast reached my feet, / Rise and cover up my head* echoing Socrates' death, in which he covers his face while the poison numbs his feet, then his legs. The death of Falstaff is also described as a numbing beginning with the feet (*Henry V*, II.iii.9–25).

18 footnote from 'Catarina to Camoens: Dying in his absence abroad, and referring to the poem in which he recorded the sweetness of her eyes' [1838].

39 *matins* morning prayers.

2

Epigraph 'It may be sighing for love, but to me it says not so' (trans. WR, 'Notes' 460).

69 *Throw the first stone, thou Pharisee* Jesus saves the woman taken in adultery from being stoned to death when he says: 'He that is without sin among you, let him first cast a stone at her' (John 8:7).

98–9 *And for my patience will my Lord / Give an exceeding great reward* 'After these things the word of the Lord came unto Abram in a vision, saying, Fear not, Abram: I am thy shield, and thy exceeding great reward' (Gen. 15:1).

101 *A crown of glory and a palm* see note for ll. 37–8 of 'Paradise'.

122 *Faithful is He Who promiseth* 'Let us hold fast the profession of our faith without wavering (for he is faithful that promised;)' (Heb. 10:23).

3

Epigraph 'Answer me, my heart, wherefore sighest thou? It answers: I want God – I sigh for Jesus' (trans. WR, 'Notes' 460).

124 *My heart is as a freeborn bird* cf. 'My heart is like a singing bird' ('A Birthday', l. 1).

131–2 *My soul is as a hidden fount / Shut in by clammy clay* 'A garden inclosed is my sister, my spouse; a spring shut up, a fountain sealed' (Song of Sol. 4:12).

138 *the True Vine* see note for l. 33 of 'Christian and Jew. A Dialogue'.

140 *the Tree of Life* see note for ll. 13–14 of 'Eve'.

142 *the Living Well* in talking with the Samaritan woman at Jacob's Well, Jesus said: 'Whosoever drinketh of this water shall thirst again: But whosoever drinketh of the water that I shall give him shall never thirst; but the water that I shall give him shall be in him a well of water springing up into everlasting life' (John 4:13–14).

144 *Where tears are wiped from tearful eyes* see note for l. 29 of 'Christian and Jew. A Dialogue'.

147 *the Shadow of the Rock* see note for ll. 19–23 of 'A Testimony'.

159 *When Earth shall pass away* see notes for ll. 32–3 of 'I do set My bow in the cloud', and for ll. 5–6 of 'Oh knell of a passing time'.

161 *The City builded without hands* the heavenly city, the New Jerusalem; cf. 'we have a building of God, an house not made with hands, eternal in the heavens (2 Cor. 5:1).

177 *the New Jerusalem* see note for l. 5 of 'All Saints: Martyrs'.

181–2 *I have bought treasure, where / Nought perisheth* see note for ll. 13–14 of 'A Testimony'.

190 *To watch when once I slept* see note for Part 2, l. 1 of 'Old and New Year Ditties'.

204–5 *Hope deferred seems to numb / My heart* see note for l. 2 of 'A Pause of Thought'.

207 *The Spirit and the Bride say, Come* 'And the Spirit and the bride say, Come' (Rev. 22:17).

Song ['We buried her among the flowers']

[Composed 14 May 1850. Editions: 1896, 1904. MS: BodL.]

17–18 *she sleeps . . . But yet a little while* see headnote of 'Dream-Land', and see also note for title of 'Yet a Little While' ['I dreamed and did not seek: today I seek'].

The Watchers

[Composed 25 May 1850. Editions: 1896, 1904. MS: MS2 (YU).]

32 *She shall behold him face to face* see note for l. 3 of 'Mirrors of Life and Death'.
35–6 *But prays that in her deep / Grave she may sleep a blessed sleep* see headnote of 'Dream-land'.

Annie ['Annie is fairer than her kith']

[Composed 26 Sept. 1850. Editions: 1896, 1904. MS: BodL.]

'Christina, the most scrupulous of women and of writers, put to this lyric a note – "query Borrows" [in the MS]. She meant that there may, or possibly may not, be here some unconscious reminiscences from other poems' ('Notes' 479).

A Dirge ['She was as sweet as violets in the Spring']

[Composed 18 Jan. 1851. Editions: 1896, 1904. MS: BodL.]

1 *violets* see note for l. 5 of 'Song' ['Oh roses for the flush of youth'].
19 *Branch of the Living Vine* see note for l. 33 of 'Christian and Jew. A Dialogue'.

Song ['It is not for her even brow']

[Composed 1851. Editions: 1896, 1904. MS: BodL.]

A Dream

[Composed 14 May 1851. MS: BodL.]

"A fair World tho' a fallen" ————

[Composed 30 Aug. 1851. Editions: 1896, 1904. MS: BodL.]

12 *For tho' I failed to choose the better part* see note for l. 7 of ' "A Bruised Reed Shall He Not Break" '.

Advent [' "Come," Thou dost say to Angels']

[Composed 12 Dec. 1851. Editions: 1896, 1904. MS: BodL.]

Title see note for title of 'Advent' ['This Advent moon shines cold and clear'].
5 *The many-mansioned house* see note for l. 21 of 'The Convent Threshold'.

All Saints ['They have brought gold and spices to my King']

[Composed 20 Jan. 1852. Editions: 1896, 1904. MS: BodL.]

Title see headnote of 'Epiphany'.
13 *He seeks not thine, but thee* see note for l. 14 of 'Lord, what have I that I may offer Thee?'
14 *His banner over thee is Love* see note for l. 5 of 'After Communion'.

"Eye hath not seen"

[Composed 1 May 1852. Editions: 1885, 1886a, 1896, 1904. MS: BodL.]

Entry for 30 April in *TF* (82).

Title see note for ll. 37–8 of 'Advent' ['This Advent moon shines cold and clear'].
15 *The trees of Knowledge and of Life* see note for ll. 13–14 of 'Eve'.
36 *From lips which drained the bitter cup* see note for l. 42 of 'Martyrs' Song'.
40 *second birth* see note for l. 39 of 'Death'.
44 *The Lamb once slain* see note for l. 33 of 'Martyrs' Song'.
45 *living streams* see headnotes of 'Tune me, O Lord, into one harmony' and of 'Whitsun Monday'; also '. . . And let him that is athirst come. And whosoever will, let him take the water of life freely' (Rev. 22:17).
48 *green pastures* see note for l. 9 of 'Lord, hast Thou so loved us, and will not we'.
51–2 *How long . . . O Lord, how long* see note for Part 2, l. 12 of 'Old and New Year Ditties'.
68–9 *Our grief, our shame, / With Peter and with Magdalene* on Peter, see note for l. 7 of 'Good Friday' ['Am I a stone and not a sheep']; and on Mary Magdalene, see note for title of 'Mary Magdalene and the Other Mary'.
70–72 *him whose name / No record tells / Who by Thy promise with Thee dwells* see note for l. 8 of 'Good Friday' ['Am I a stone and not a sheep']. Cf. 'There lives no record of reply, / Which telling what it is to die' (Tennyson, *In Memoriam*, XXXI, 6–7).

St. Elizabeth of Hungary

[Composed 16 June 1852. Editions: 1896, 1904. MS: BodL.]

'I take it that the lyric received its immediate inspiration from the picture of like subject painted by [CR's fiancé] James Collinson' ('Notes' 470). See headnote of 'A Portrait'.

9–10 *rose . . . lilies* see note for ll. 5–7 of 'Paradise'.

Moonshine

[Composed 16 June 1852. Editions: 1896, 1904. MS: BodL.]

"The Summer is ended"

[Composed 11 Sept. 1852. Editions: 1896, 1904. MS: BodL.]

Title see note for title of 'Summer Is Ended'.
11–15 *Weep not . . . a little while* cf. 'Song' ['When I am dead, my dearest'].

"I look for the Lord"

[Composed 28 Sept. 1852. Editions: 1896, 1904. MS: BodL.]

Title The women who looked for Jesus' body in the tomb were greeted by an angel who said: 'Why seek ye the living among the dead?' (Luke 24:5). According to John 20:15, Mary Magdalene mistakes Jesus for the gardener, and asks: 'Sir, if thou have borne him hence, tell me where thou hast laid him, and I will take him away.'
13 *Our house is left us desolate* 'Behold, your house is left unto you desolate. For I say unto you, Ye shall not see me henceforth, till ye shall say, Blessed is he that cometh in the name of the Lord' (Matt. 23:38–9; Luke 13:35).

Song ['I have loved you for long long years Ellen']

[Composed 15 Oct. 1852. MS: BodL.]

Elements of this song echo Crabbe's poem 'Ellen' in *Tales of the Hall* (1819); it tells of a scholarly girl whose father allows her to study with her brothers' tutor. The tutor and Ellen fall in love, and he leaves abruptly. When he returns, she refuses to see him. She later regrets her refusal, but it is too late.

A Discovery

[Composed 24 Oct. 1852. Editions: 1896, 1904. MS: MS2 (PU).]

Title After all. *1896, 1904.*
9 *peace broods like a dove* cf. 'For peace broods quiet on her dovelike wings'
(Landon, *The Golden Violet* (1827), l. 2787).

From the Antique ['The wind shall lull us yet']

[Composed 10 Dec. 1852. Editions: 1896, 1904. MS: BodL.]

"The heart knoweth its own bitterness" ['Weep yet a while']

[Composed 23 Dec. 1852. Editions: 1896, 1904. Lines from MS poem were
published in 1893 as ' "The day is at hand" '. MS: BodL.]

Title see note for title of ' "Whatsoever is right, that shall ye receive" '.
30–31 *Now we sow love in tears, / But then shall reap* see note for l. 6 of 'Vigil of
St. Bartholomew'.

"To what purpose is this waste?"

[Composed 22 Jan. 1853. Editions: 1896, 1904. Lines from MS poem were
published in 1893 as ' "These all wait upon thee" '. MS: BodL.]

Title a woman poured precious ointment over the head of Jesus, 'But when
his disciples saw it, they had indignation, saying, To what purpose is this
waste?' (Matt. 26:8).
2 *lily* see note for ll. 408–10 of *Goblin Market*.
72 *Is type of her, the Undefiled* although this could be read as referring to the
Virgin Mary, given CR's aversion to Mariolatry and her deep immersion in
images from Revelation, the 'Undefiled' is probably the resurrected soul in
Paradise. The lily is the 'type' or model for which the 'Undefiled' robed
in white is the 'antitype' or fulfilment.
119–20 *We want the faith that hath not seen / Indeed, but hath believed His truth* see
note for Part II, l. 2 of ' "They put their trust in Thee, and were not
confounded" '.
127 *Thou yet shalt drain the bitter cup* see note for l. 42 of 'Martyrs' Song'.

Next of Kin

[Composed 21 Feb. 1853. Editions: 1896, 1904. MS: BodL.]

'This might appear to be a personal address to some very youthful relative; if so, it can only be intended for the "Lalla" [of "To Lalla"] . . . for Christina had no other relative younger than herself. But perhaps no personal reference is really intended' ('Notes' 479).

8 *I must launch out into the deep* see note for Part 9, ll. 10–11 of 'Monna Innominata'.
14 *And when your race is finished, as mine is almost run* see note for ll. 11–12 of 'Who Shall Deliver Me?'

"Let them rejoice in their beds" ['The winds sing to us where we lie']

[Composed 7 March 1853. MS: BodL.]

See headnote of 'Dream-Land'.

Title see note on title of ' "Let them rejoice in their beds" ' ['Crimson as the rubies, crimson as the roses'].
14 *love . . . faith . . . hope* see note for l. 18 of 'Herself a rose, who bore the Rose'.
21 *Lo, I come quickly, saith the Lord* see note for title of 'That No Man Take Thy Crown'.
22 *thy exceeding great Reward* see note for Part 2, ll. 98–9 of 'Three Nuns'.

Portraits

[Composed 9 May 1853. Editions: 1896, 1904. Lines 1–8: MS (BodL); ll. 9–16: 1896.]

Stanza 1 describes WR; the stanza below l. 8, describing DGR, according to WR, is missing from the MS, 'torn out [by DGR's] rather arbitrary hand, beyond a doubt' (1896).

Whitsun Eve ['The white dove cooeth in her downy nest']

[Composed 18 May 1853. Editions: 1896, 1904. MS: BodL.]

Title see note for title of 'Whitsun Eve' [' "As many as I love."—Ah, Lord, Who lovest all'].

What?

[Composed May 1853. Editions: 1896, 1904. MS: BodL.]

1 *Strengthening as secret manna* see notes for l. 176 of 'From House to Home' and for ll. 13–14 of 'Eve'.

A Pause

[Composed 10 June 1853. Editions: 1896, 1904. MS: BodL.]

9–10 *At length . . . the old familiar hand* cf. 'waiting for a hand / A hand that can be clasped no more' (Tennyson, *In Memoriam*, VII, 4–5).

Holy Innocents ['Sleep, little Baby, sleep']

[Composed 1 July 1853. Editions: 1896, 1904. MS: BodL.]

Title see note for title of 'Holy Innocents' ['They scarcely waked before they slept'].
10 *The eternal Arms* see note for l. 3 of 'A Martyr: The Vigil Of The Feast'.

"There remaineth therefore a rest for the people of God"

[Composed 1 July 1853. Editions: 1896, 1904. MS: BodL.]

Title see note for title of " 'There remaineth therefore a Rest to the People of God'".

1

Epigraph 'And ye have forgotten the exhortation which speaketh unto you as unto children, My son, despise not thou the chastening of the Lord, nor faint when thou art rebuked of him' (Heb. 12:5).

2

Epigraph see note for epigraph of Part 1, above.
28 *And thou, with John, shalt lie upon my Breast* see note for l. 13 of 'After Communion'.

Annie ['It's not for earthly bread, Annie']

[Composed 1 Aug. 1853. Editions: 1896, 1904. MS: BodL.]

'. . . possibly the poignantly pathetic lines of Edgar Poe, *For Annie* [1849], were partly in my sister's mind. At some later date she numbered five out of the twenty stanzas, evidently contemplating to retain those five alone. I follow her lead and supply a new title' ('Notes' 470). Thus WR published under his title 'A Harvest' (taken from ll. 83–4): ll. 25–30, 43–8, 61–6, 79–84 and 91–6.

Title A HARVEST *1896, 1904.*

21–2 *the lifelong fever / And sick weariness* cf. Poe, 'For Annie': 'The sickness . . . the fever called "Living" ', ll. 25–9.

58 *Yea, full of vanities* see note for l. 1 of 'One Certainty'.

68 *the race we have to run* see note for ll. 11–12 of 'Who Shall Deliver Me?'

71–2 *there is nothing new we know / At all beneath the sun* see note for l. 11 of 'One Certainty'.

73 *I am sick for love* see note for l. 69 of 'After This the Judgment'.

83–4 *Are not the fields already white / To harvest in the glow* see note for l. 11 of 'Easter Day'.

95 *No more seed-time, no more harvest* 'While the earth remaineth, seedtime and harvest, and cold and heat, and summer and winter, and day and night shall not cease' (Gen. 8:22).

101–2 *Once we looked back together / With our hands upon the plough* see note for l. 10 of 'Lord, make me one with Thine own faithful ones'.

103 *A little while, and we must part* 'A little while, and ye shall not see me: and again, a little while, and ye shall see me, because I go to the Father' (John 16:16); see also note for title of 'Yet a Little While' ['I dreamed and did not seek: today I seek'].

Seasons ['In spring time when the leaves are young']

[Composed Sept. 1853. Editions: 1896, 1904. MS: BodL.]

['Thou sleepest where the lilies fade']

[Composed by Sept. 1853. Editions: 1896, 1904. MS: BodL.]

Title BURIED *1896, 1904.*

MS has ten poems in a group entitled 'Odds and Ends', at the end of which is written: 'Copied, September 1853'. They are, in order: 'Monday in Holy Week', 'Thou sleepest where the lilies fade', 'Laughing Life cries at the feast',

'I wish I were a little bird', (Two parted), 'All night I dream you love me well', (For Rosaline's Album), 'Care flieth', (Epitaph) and SONG ['Two doves upon the selfsame branch'].

['I wish I were a little bird']

[Composed by Sept. 1853. Editions: 1896, 1904. MS: BodL.]

See headnote of 'Thou sleepest where the lilies fade'.

Title A WISH *1896, 1904*.
9 *a hope deferred* see note for l. 2 of 'A Pause of Thought'.

(Two parted)

[Composed by Sept. 1853. Editions: 1896, 1904. MS: BodL.]

See headnote of 'Thou sleepest where the lilies fade'.
9 *bearded* boldly opposed.

['All night I dream you love me well']

[Composed by Sept. 1853. MS: BodL.]

See headnote of 'Thou sleepest where the lilies fade'.

(For Rosaline's Album)

[Composed by Sept. 1853. Editions: 1896, 1904. MS: BodL.]

See headnote of 'Thou sleepest where the lilies fade'.
  'Rosaline was Miss Orme, who, not long after the date of these verses, married Professor David Masson, now King's Historiographer for Scotland. These sepulchral verses are perhaps not quite the staple for a very youthful (and I might add charming) lady's album' ('Notes' 479).

['Care flieth']

[Composed by Sept. 1853. Editions: 1896, 1904. MS: BodL.]

See headnote of 'Thou sleepest where the lilies fade'.

Title AUTUMN *1896, 1904*.

(Epitaph)

[Composed by Sept. 1853. Editions: 1896, 1904. MS: BodL.]

See headnote of 'Thou sleepest where the lilies fade'.

4 *I fell a victim to the jealous Turk* cf. 'Bear, like the Turk, no Brother near the throne' (Pope, 'An Epistle from Mr Pope, to Dr Arbuthnot' (1735), l. 198).

The P.R.B.

[Composed 10 Nov. 1853. Editions: 1904. First published in WR (ed.), *Dante Gabriel Rossetti: His Family-Letters with a Memoir*, 2 vols. (Ellis and Elvey, 1895), I, 138. MS: BodL.]

Title on the Pre-Raphaelite Brotherhood (PRB), see Introduction, p. xli. They disbanded by 1854, for reasons given in the poem.

2 *Woolner in Australia* Thomas Woolner (1825–92), sculptor and poet, left for the Australian gold-fields in 1852, inspiring Ford Madox Brown's famous picture *The Last of England*.

3 *Hunt is yearning for the land of Cheops* Hunt went for an extended visit to Egypt and the Holy Lands, a trip that inspired his painting *The Scapegoat*; see headnote of 'My Dream'.

4 *D. G. Rossetti shuns the vulgar optic* at this time, DGR was refusing to exhibit his paintings.

6 *B.s* Marsh identifies as 'Brothers' in the PRB (*CR Poems* 432).

7 *Calm Stephens* F. G. Stephens (1828–1907), art critic.

9–11 *great Millais / Attaining academic opulence / Winds up his signature with A.R.A.* Millais had recently been elected Associate of the Royal Academy of Art, which was founded by George III for the purpose of presenting an annual exhibition of the works of contemporary artists. Membership was a much coveted honour. For Millais, see headnote of 'Maude Clare'.

Seasons ['Crocuses and snowdrops wither']

[Composed 7 Dec. 1853. Editions: 1896, 1904. MS: BodL.]

"Who have a form of godliness"

[Composed 18 Dec. 1853. Editions: 1896, 1904. MS: BodL.]

Title Paul warned Timothy to turn away from those 'Having a form of godliness, but denying the power thereof' (2 Tim. 3:5). See also headnote of 'Conversion of St. Paul'.

Ballad

[Composed 7 Jan. 1854. Editions: 1896, 1904. MS: BodL.]

A Study. (A Soul)

[Composed 7 Feb. 1854. Editions: 1896, 1904. MS: MS2 (PW).]

Title A Soul *1896, 1904.*
1 *Parian statues* made of highly valued white marble from the island of Paros.
2–4 *Cleopatra when she turned at bay . . . And felt the aspic* the first-century-BC queen killed herself with an asp, a poisonous snake.
10 *A pale clear beacon where the storm-drift is* cf. description of Lizzie in *Goblin Market*: 'Like a beacon left alone / In a hoary roaring sea' (ll. 412–13).

"There remaineth therefore a rest"

[Composed 17 Feb. 1854. Editions: 1896, 1904. Some lines from MS poem were published in 1863 as 'The Bourne' and others in 1885 as ' "There remaineth therefore a Rest to the People of God" '. In 1896 and 1904, the poem consists of ll. 16–20, 31–40 and 51–60. MS: BodL.]

Title see note for title of ' "There remaineth therefore a Rest to the People of God" '.
2 *our last sleep* see headnote of 'Dream-Land'.
15 *Eagle-like renew our strength* see note for l. 8 of 'Mary Magdalene and the Other Mary'.
56 *chastening rod* see note for l. 5 of 'If not with hope of life'.
57 *on the narrow way* see note for l. 46 of 'Paradise'.
59 *Heat and burden of the day* see note for l. 1 of ' "Thro' burden and heat of the day" '.

"Ye have forgotten the exhortation"

[Composed 10 May 1854. Editions: 1896, 1904. Lines from MS poem were published in 1893 as ' "When my heart is vexed I will complain" ' [' "The fields are white to harvest, look and see']. MS: BodL.]

'Our father having died on 26 April 1854, it is not unnatural to think that this poem, dated 10 May 1854, bears some direct relation to that loss. There had been two other deaths in the family, April and December 1853 – those of our maternal grandparents; to her grandfather especially Christina was most warmly attached' ('Notes' 471).

Title see note for Part 1, epigraph of ' "There remaineth therefore a rest for the people of God" '.

27 *The fields are white to harvest* see note for l. 11 of 'Easter Day'.

34 *Grown sick with hope deferred* see note for l. 2 of 'A Pause of Thought'.

39–40 *that tree / Whose leaves are health* the tree of life in Revelation (22:2): see note for ll. 13–14 of 'Eve'.

44 *Who knocketh at His door* see note for Part 2, l. 5 of 'If Thou Sayest, Behold, We Knew It Not'.

Guesses

[Composed 27 June 1854. MS: BodL.]

From the Antique ['It's a weary life, it is; she said']

[Composed 28 June 1854. MS: BodL.]

1 *It's a weary life, it is; she said* cf. 'A weary lot is thine, fair maid, / A weary lot is thine!', the first line of a popular song, taken from a ballad that Scott used in Canto XXVIII of 'Rokeby' (1813), later reprinted as 'The Rover', ll. 1–2 (for Scott, see headnote of 'The Hour and the Ghost'). See also Felicia Hemans's 'Woman on the Field of Battle' (1830), in which the narrator says that some women come to a battlefield 'to fling away / A weary life' (ll. 47–8); and 'to free him from a weary life', from the translation of *The Odyssey of Homer* by William Cowper (1731–1800), Book XV, 429.

Three Stages

WR suggests that CR did not publish Parts 2 and 3 in her lifetime, not because 'she thought them below the mark, but because of their intimately personal character' ('Notes' 477).

1

[Composed 14 Feb. 1848. Edition: 1904. Published as 'A Pause of Thought' in 1862. MS: MS2 (BodL).]

Title THREE STAGES *1904*.
   See note for title of 'A Pause of Thought'.
2 *And hope deferred made my heart sick in truth* see note for l. 2 of 'A Pause of Thought'.

2

[Composed 18 April 1849. Editions: 1896, 1904. MS: MS2 (BodL).]

WR, while saying that the poem 'appears to be a personal utterance', adds that he feels 'no assurance' as to 'what condition of facts it was founded on ... "Tears for guilt" is, in reference to Christina, a very exaggerated phrase; or possibly nothing is implied beyond "original guilt" or "original sin"' (1896, p. 379).

Title THE END OF THE FIRST PART. *1896*.
9–10 *I must pull down my palace that I built, / Dig up the pleasure-gardens of my soul* see note for l. 6 of 'From House to Home'.

3

[Composed 25 July 1854. Lines from MS poem were published in 1893 as 'Heaven's chimes are slow, but sure to strike at last'. MS: BodL.]

Title *RESTIVE*. 1896.

Long looked for

[Composed 12 Aug. 1854. Editions: 1896, 1904. MS: BodL.]

Listening

[Composed Oct. 1854. Editions: 1896, 1904. MS: BodL.]

This poem is 'traditionally taken to have been inspired by Elizabeth Siddal,

with whom DGR was currently in love' (Marsh, *CR Poems* 432).
    The title in MS is 'Two choices.'

1 *cushat dove* wood pigeon or ring dove.

Zara ['I dreamed that loving me he would love on']

[Composed 8 Jan. 1855. MS: BodL.]
Title see headnote of 'Eva'.

The last look

[Composed 8 Jan. 1855. Editions: 1896, 1904. MS: BodL.]

"I have a message unto thee"

[Composed 26 March 1855. Editions: 1896, 1904. Lines from MS poem were published in 1893 as ' "The Flowers appear on the Earth" '. MS: BodL.]

Title 'I have a message from God unto thee' (Judges 3:20). In *TF* CR tells the story of thinking she was being called by a tap at her bedchamber door, but discovering the tapping was 'only of jackdaws or of starlings lodged in the turrets . . . How many fancied calls or omens are in fact no more significant than jackdaws or starlings? On the other hand: to him "that hath ears to hear," any good creature of God may convey a message' (62). Later, CR remarks on how we 'act eager, instantly, on telegrams' but not on those messages conveyed 'from the Creator to the human creature' (203).

Cobwebs

[Composed Oct. 1855. Editions: 1896, 1904. MS: BodL.]

This poem may owe something to Byron's 'Darkness' (1816) and to Browning's 'Childe Roland to the Dark Tower Came' (1855) (Ralph A. Bellas, *Christina Rossetti* 47).

Unforgotten

[Composed 20 Nov. 1855. Editions: 1896, 1904. MS: BodL.]

An Afterthought

[Composed 18 Dec. 1855. Editions: 1896, 1904. MS: BodL.]

31 *the fiery messenger* in *Paradise Lost*, Milton's version of the Fall, the fiery messenger, in charge of the cherubim who guard the gates of Eden, is Michael.
34 *the flaming sword* after driving Adam and Eve out of the Garden of Eden, God placed at the east of Eden 'a flaming sword which turned every way, to keep the way of the tree of life' (Gen. 3:24).
46 *Slumbers Rachel comforted* allusion to a prophecy later fulfilled when Herod slaughtered the innocents: 'Rachel weeping for her children, and would not be comforted, because they are not' (Matt. 2:18; Jer. 31:15).

To the end

[Composed 18 Dec. 1855. Editions: 1896, 1904. MS: BodL.]

'The last quatrain of this poem seems to present a certain reminiscence (yet far from being a plagiarism) from Dante Rossetti's early achievement, *The Blessed Damozel*' ('Notes' 480).

46-8 *roll . . . my life up like a scroll* see note for l. 161 of 'From House to Home'.
69–70 *Lingering on the golden threshold / And leaning from the door* cf. opening lines of DGR's 'The Blessed Damozel': see note for ll. 7–8 of 'Martyrs' Song'.

"Zion said"

[Composed 31 Dec. 1855. Editions: 1896, 1904. MS: BodL.]

Title see note for ll. 43–4 of 'Christian and Jew. A Dialogue'.
10 *I am sick for Love* see note for l. 69 of 'After This the Judgment'.

May ['Sweet Life is dead']

[Composed 31 Dec. 1855. Editions: 1896, 1904. MS: BodL.]

River Thames (?)

[Composed 7 Feb. 1856. Editions: 1896, 1904. MS: MS2 (PU).]
Title BY THE WATER *1896, 1904.*

A chilly night

[Composed 11 Feb. 1856. Editions: 1896, 1904. MS: BodL.]

"Let patience have her perfect work" ['I saw a bird alone']

[Composed 12 March 1856. Editions: 1896, 1904. MS: BodL.]

Title see note for title of ' "Let Patience have her perfect work" ' ['Can man rejoice who lives in hourly fear?'].
36 *While patience reaps what it has sown* see notes for title of 'Weary in Well-Doing' and for l. 269 of *The Prince's Progress*.

A Martyr

[Composed 23 April 1856. Editions: 1896, 1904. MS: BodL.]

12 *While the hawk spreads her wings toward the south* 'Doth the hawk fly by thy wisdom, and stretch her wings toward the south?' (Job 39:26).

In the Lane

[Composed 3 May 1856. Editions: 1896, 1904. MS: BodL.]

Acme

[Composed 9 May 1856. Editions: 1896, 1904. MS: BodL.]

'In point of sentiment, not at all in the form of treatment, this sonnet bears some analogy to one by Dante Rossetti, *A Superscription*. The latter was written in Jan. 1869, long after Christina's sonnet: the resemblance must be fortuitous' ('Notes' 480).

A bed of Forget-me-nots

[Composed 17 June 1856. Editions: 1896, 1904. MS: BL.]

18 *more strong than death* see note for l. 1 of 'An End'.
19 *This all creation travails of* see note for ll. 74–5 of 'An Old-World Thicket'.

The Chiefest among ten thousand ['When sick of life and all the world']

[Composed 26 June 1856. Some lines, including deleted lines, from the MS poem were published in 1893 as 'I will lift up mine eyes unto the Hills' ['When sick of life and all the world'], and other lines, also including deleted lines, were published in Shipley (ed.), *Lyra Messianica* as 'I know you not'. MS: BL.]

Title see note for l. 14 of 'Long Barren'.

3 *I lift mine eyes up to the hills* see note for l. 5 of 'A Better Resurrection'.

9 *Oh that a dove's white wings I had* see note for l. 13 of 'Darkness and light are both alike to Thee'.

13 *it blossoms like a rose* see note for l. 158 of 'From House to Home'.

20 *Beulah and blessed Hepzibah* 'Thou shalt no more be termed Forsaken; neither shall thy land any more be termed Desolate: but thou shalt be called Hephzibah, and thy land Beulah: for the LORD delighteth in thee, and thy land shall be married' (Isa. 62:4).

21 *That where Thou art I too may be* 'And Ruth said, Intreat me not to leave thee, or to return from following after thee: for whither thou goest, I will go; and where thou lodgest, I will lodge: thy people shall be my people, and thy God my God' (Ruth 1:16).

22 *Bride of the Bridegroom* the New Jerusalem: see note for l. 5 of 'All Saints: Martyrs'.

23 *Thou God . . . the Fairest art* cf. 'Fairest Lord Jesus, Ruler of all Nature' (anon. hymn, 'Fairest Lord Jesus' (1677)).

27 *Who built their house upon the Rock* see note for ll. 19–23 of 'A Testimony'.

28 *And eagle-like renew their strength* see note for l. 8 of 'Mary Magdalene and the Other Mary'.

32 *The fulness of the time is come* 'But when the fulness of the time was come, God sent forth his Son, made of a woman, made under the law' (Gal. 4:4).

33 *the new heavens and earth* see headnote of ' "Was Thy Wrath against the Sea?" '.

34 *Where righteousness shall dwell* 'Nevertheless we, according to his promise, look for new heavens and a new earth, wherein dwelleth righteousness' (2 Pet. 3:13).

36 *Nor barrier of the tossing sea* see notes for title of 'Was Thy Wrath against the Sea?' and for ' "And there was no more Sea" '.

38 *For God shall be the Light thereof* see note for l. 11 of 'That Eden of earth's sunrise cannot vie'.

39 *no death no sting* see note for Part 3, ll. 13–14 of 'The Thread of Life'.

40 *God is Love* see note for l. 8 of 'Trinity Sunday'.

"Look on this picture and on this"

[Composed 12 July 1856. Editions: 1896, 1904. MS: BL.]

In 1896, WR states: 'In my sister's MS, this poem is a rather long one, forty-six triplets; I have reduced it to twenty-three – omitting those passages which appear to me to be either in themselves inferior, or adapted rather for spinning out the theme than intensifying it' (382). 1896 omits: ll. 7–15, 22–7, 34–42, 46–8, 61–9, 73–84, 88–96, 100–102, 109–11 and 133–5.

'Were it not for the name "Eva," I should be embarrassed to guess what could have directed my sister's pen to so singular a subject and treatment; but that name satisfies me that she was here recurring to a favourite romancist of her girlhood, Maturin … In Maturin's novel entitled *Women* there is a personage Eva, and a situation which must certainly have prompted the present poem' ('Notes' 480). See headnote of 'Eva'.

Title Hamlet, comparing his father to his uncle, shows Gertrude two pictures and says: 'Look here upon this picture and on this, / The counterfeit presentment of two brothers' (III.iv.54–5). In Maturin's novel, a similar comparison might be made between the worldly Zaira and the saintly Eva.
6 *You my saint lead up to heaven she lures down to sin* perhaps an echo from *Hamlet*: 'My words fly up, my thoughts remain below. / Words without thoughts never to heaven go' (III.iii.97–8).
16 *redundant* superabundant. Perhaps an echo of Milton's description of the serpent: 'erect / Amidst his circling spires, that on the grass / Floated redundant' (*Paradise Lost*, IX, 501–3).
36 *sevenfold crowns* see note for l. 111 of 'The Lowest Room'.
120 *Heaping coals of fire upon our heads* 'Therefore if thine enemy hunger, feed him; if he thirst, give him drink: for in so doing thou shalt heap coals of fire on his head' (Rom. 12:20).
130 *Shall we stand upon the left and she upon the right* see note for l. 11 of ' "Cried out with Tears" '.

"Now they desire"

[Composed 13 Aug. 1856. Editions: 1896, 1904. MS: BL.]

Title see note for title of ' "They Desire a Better Country" '.
5 *Sweet sleep that dreams not* see headnote of 'Dream-Land'.
25 *Oh fair oh fair Jerusalem* 'O Jerusalem, Jerusalem, which killest the prophets, and stonest them that are sent unto thee; how often would I have gathered thy children together, as a hen doth gather her brood under her wings, and ye would not!' (Luke 13:34).

27–9 *thy Jasper Gem . . . Thy sea of glass* see note for ll. 35–6 of 'Paradise'.

31–2 *Thy royal Elders . . . Thy four Beasts* 'And the four and twenty elders and the four beasts fell down and worshipped God that sat on the throne, saying, Amen; Alleluia' (Rev. 19:4).

33–4 *the bride / In raiment white and clean* Rev. 21:2: see note for l. 5 of 'All Saints: Martyrs'.

37 *Without a wrinkle or a spot* 'That he might present it to himself a glorious church, not having spot, or wrinkle, or any such thing; but that it should be holy and without blemish' (Eph. 5:27).

38 *Blood cleansed, blood purchased* Rev. 7:14: see note for l. 13 of 'Martyrs' Song'.

41 *Dove's eyes beneath thy parted lock* 'thou hast doves' eyes within thy locks' (Song of Sol. 4:1). See also note for l. 14 of 'Advent Sunday'.

43 *Thy nest is safe within the Rock* 'And he looked on the Kenites, and took up his parable, and said, Strong is thy dwellingplace, and thou puttest thy nest in a rock' (Num. 24:21).

44 *the Very Vine* Jesus: see note for l. 33 of 'Christian and Jew. A Dialogue'.

48 *sevenfold day of days* see note for l. 111 of 'The Lowest Room'.

A Christmas Carol, / for my Godchildren

[Composed 6 Oct. 1856. Editions: 1896, 1904. MS: BL.]

'Christina, from time to time, acted as godmother to various children – mostly, I think, children of poor people in the neighbourhood of Christ Church, Albany Street, Regent's Park' ('Notes' 472).

1–2 *The shepherds had an angel, / The wise men had a star* CR follows closely the story of the birth of Jesus as told in Luke 2 and Matthew 2.

11–12 *The wilful lambs that go astray / He bleeding fetches back* see note for ll. 7–8 of ' "The Good Shepherd" '.

17–18 *that land / Whose day shall be as seven* see note for l. 111 of 'The Lowest Room'.

19–20 *Those shepherds . . . their sheep* 'And there were in the same country shepherds abiding in the field, keeping watch over their flock by night' (Luke 2:8).

23 *All singing 'Glory, glory'* combination of Luke 2:14 (see note for Part 2, l. 43 of 'Christmas Carols'), and the 'holy, holy, holy' sung by the heavenly hosts in Isaiah and Revelation. Cf. '(I hear them sing) / One "Holy, Holy, Holy" to their King' in 'Christian and Jew. A Dialogue', ll. 19–20 and note.

36 *a dream to warn* The dream warned the wise men not to visit King Herod on their return (Matt. 2:12).

"Not yours but you"

[Composed 27 Oct. 1856. Editions: 1896, 1904. MS: BL.]

Title see note for l. 14 of 'Lord, what have I that I may offer Thee?'

An Answer

[Composed 26 Nov. 1856. MS: BL.]

Sir Winter

[Composed 28 Nov. 1856. Editions: 1896, 1904. MS: BL.]

'Mr. Swynfen Jervis, a friendly acquaintance of our father, wrote a quatrain and a half entitled *Sir Winter*; and he appears to have got Christina to complete the little poem. Christina finished quatrain two, and wrote five others. The third of these five reverts to the idea of "*Sir* Winter"; so I omit it, as being extraneous to the character of her own composition: it has no poetical value' ('Notes' 491–2).

Title WINTER *1896, 1904.*

In an Artist's Studio

[Composed 24 Dec. 1856. Editions: 1896, 1904. MS: BL.]

'The reference is apparently to our brother's studio, and to his constantly-repeated heads of the lady whom he afterwards married, Miss Siddal' ('Notes' 480).

Introspective

[Composed 30 June 1857. Editions: 1896, 1904. MS: BL.]

"The heart knoweth its own bitterness" ['When all the over-work of life']

[Composed 27 Aug. 1857. Editions: 1896, 1904. Lines from MS poem were published in 1893 as ' "Whatsoever is right, that shall ye receive" '. MS: BL.]

'Few things written by Christina contain more of her innermost self than this' ('Notes' 472).

Title see note for title of ' "Whatsoever is right, that shall ye receive" '.

44 *A fountain sealed* see note for Part 3, ll. 131–2 of 'Three Nuns'.

46 *Deep must call deep* see note for l. 32 of ' "When My Heart Is Vexed, I Will Complain" ' ['O Lord, how canst Thou say Thou lovest me?'].

49 *hope deferred* see note for l. 2 of 'A Pause of Thought'.

51 *Eye hath not seen, nor ear hath heard* see note for ll. 37–8 of 'Advent' ['This Advent moon shines cold and clear'].

55 *There God shall join and no man part* 'What therefore God hath joined together, let not man put asunder' (Mark 10:9; Matt. 19:6). This phrase is often used as part of the Christian sacrament of marriage.

"Reflection"

[Composed 8 Sept. 1857. Editions: 1896, 1904. MS: MS2 (PU).]

Title DAY-DREAMS *1896, 1904*.

Marsh points out that this title was added in response to one of the Portfolio Society set themes – 'Reflection' (*CR* 286).

A Coast-Nightmare

[Composed 12 Sept. 1857. Editions: 1896, 1904. 1896 and 1904 consist of ll. 1–4 and 37–40. MS: MS2 (PU).]

Offered to the Portfolio Society in response to its theme – 'A Coast' (*CR* 297).

Title A NIGHTMARE / FRAGMENT *1896, 1904*.

'For one Sake'

[Composed 25 Oct. 1857. Editions: 1896, 1904. MS: BL.]

Barbara Fass has noted the influence of Keats's 'The Eve of St Agnes' on this poem ('Christina Rossetti and St. Agnes' Eve', *Victorian Poetry* 14 (1976), 33–46); Bump has also noted the influence of Tennyson's 'St Agnes' Eve' (1836) ('CR and the Pre-Raphaelite Brotherhood', in Kent, *Achievement* 343).

3 *Wars and rumours of your wars* see note for title of ' "The end is not yet" '. 'The war of the Indian Mutiny was then raging; and it may be that the writer intended to express the opinion – which she certainly entertained – that any such turmoil is a very little thing, in comparison with the question whether the human soul is to be saved or lost to all eternity' ('Notes' 481).

7 *its flashing cars* see notes for l. 91 of 'The Convent Threshold'.
12 *to dream, perhaps to weep* cf. 'To sleep, perchance to dream' (*Hamlet* III.i.64).

My old Friends

[Composed 16 July 1858. Editions: 1896, 1904. Some lines from MS poem were published in 1893 as 'They lie at rest, our blessed dead', and others in 1893 as ' "Then whose shall those things be?" '. MS: MS2 (PU).]

Title A BURDEN *1896, 1904*.
1 *They lie at rest asleep and dead* see headnote of 'Dream-Land'.
12 *Miserere* a cry of 'Have mercy.' Psalm 51 in the *Book of Common Prayer* is titled 'Miserere mei, Deus' ('Have mercy upon me, O God').
24 *Sursum corda* see notes for title and l. 1 of 'Sursum Corda'.
43 *add field to field* see note for l. 3 of ' "Then whose shall those things be?" '.
47 *Cui bono* from a Latin phrase attributed to Cicero, meaning 'Who profits by it?' Popularly used in English to mean 'To what use, or good purpose?'
51 *Miserrima* most miserable.
52 *Sweet love, a fountain sealed to me* see note for Part 3, ll. 131–2 of 'Three Nuns'.

"Yet a little while" ['These days are long before I die']

[Composed 6 Aug. 1858. Editions: 1896, 1904. Some lines from MS poem were published in 1893 as ' "Vanity of Vanities" ' ['Of all the downfalls in the world'], and others in 1893 as 'Earth has clear call of daily bells'. MS: BL.]

Title see note for title of 'Yet a Little While' ['I dreamed and did not seek: today I seek'].

"Only believe"

[Probably composed between 6 Aug. and 15 Oct. 1858. Editions: 1896, 1904. 1896 and 1904 consist of ll. 1–34. Lines from MS poem were published in 1893 as 'What good shall my life do to me?'. MS: BL.]

Title soon after the ruler of the synagogue asked Jesus to heal his daughter, word came that the daughter had died. 'As soon as Jesus heard the word that was spoken, he saith unto the ruler of the synagogue, Be not afraid, only believe' (Mark 5:36; Luke 8:50).

39 *Dust to dust* see note for l. 119 of 'A Martyr. The Vigil Of The Feast'.
56 *Those who sowed shall reap* see note for title of 'Weary in Well-Doing' and for l. 269 of *The Prince's Progress*.

"Rivals" / A Shadow of Saint Dorothea

[Composed 11 Nov. 1858. Editions: 1896, 1904. Includes ' "As cold waters to a thirsty soul, so is good news from a far country" ', printed in 1893. MS: MS2 (PU).]

'I cannot find in the legend of St. Dorothea any incident corresponding closely to this. I understand that, in the poem, the speaker is a human soul, not as yet confirmed in saintliness, appealing to the flower-bearing Angel of the legend, or rather indeed to the Saviour Christ' ('Notes' 474). St Dorothy, or Dorothea (d. 303), was mocked on the way to her execution by a young man, Theophilus, who had heard her say she would soon be in a garden. He asked her to send him fruits from her 'garden'. When Dorothea knelt to pray before her execution, an angel came with a basket of roses and apples, which Dorothea asked be sent to Theophilus. He was converted to Christianity and later became a martyr for his faith.

The question-and-answer format resembles 'Up-Hill', written five months earlier.

Title A SHADOW OF DOROTHEA *1896, 1904.*
28–9 *There grows a tree . . . twelvefold fruit* see note for ll. 13–14 of 'Eve'.

A Yawn

[Composed 11 Nov. 1858. Includes 'By the Sea', printed in 1875. MS: BL.]

14–15 *All earth's full rivers cannot fill / The sea, that drinking thirsteth still* see note for ll. 10–11 of 'A Testimony'.

For H. P.

[Composed 16 Jan. 1859. Editions: 1896, 1904. MS: BL.]

'H. P.' was Henrietta Polydore, CR's cousin. 'By a curious train of circumstances she was at one time, while still a child, in Salt Lake City with the Mormons. Her father recovered her thence, at a time when a military expedition was sent by the Federal Government to control affairs in the Territory of Utah; and the present lines were presumably written by Christina

when she heard that her youthful cousin was about to re-embark for England'
('Notes' 474).

Title FOR HENRIETTA POLYDORE *1896, 1904.*

"Then they that feared the Lord spake often one to another"

[Composed 26 Aug. 1859. Includes part of ' "Thy Friend and thy Father's
Friend forget not" ', printed in 1893. MS: GD.]

Title 'Then they that feared the LORD spake often one to another: and the
LORD hearkened, and heard it, and a book of remembrance was written
before him for them that feared the LORD, and that thought upon his name'
(Mal. 3:16).
1 *the narrow way* see note for l. 46 of 'Paradise'.
3 *love-feast* among the early Christians, a meal in token of brotherly love,
originally in connection with the Eucharistic celebration; see note for l. 471 of
Goblin Market.
4 *The exceeding prize* see note for ll. 11–12 of 'Who Shall Deliver Me?'
8 *We heap up treasures for the fretting moth* see note for ll. 13–14 of 'A Testimony'.
10 *But what shall profit us* 'For what shall profit a man, if he shall gain the whole
world, and lose his own soul?' (Mark 8:36).
14 *Naked we came, naked we must return* 'Naked came I out of my mother's womb,
and naked shall I return thither: the Lord gave, and the Lord hath taken
away; blessed be the name of the Lord' (Job 1:21).

"What good shall my life do me?" ['No hope in life; yet is there hope']

[Composed 27 Aug. 1859. Editions: 1896, 1904. MS: GD.]

Title see note for title of ' "What good shall my life do me?" ' ['Have dead
men long to wait?'].
8–9 *Lift heart and eyes / Up to the hills* see note for ll. 5–6 of 'A Better
Resurrection'.

The Massacre of Perugia

[Probably composed between 27 Aug. and 18 Nov. 1859. MS: GD.]

In commenting on the destruction of ten manuscript pages, that presumably
contained the rest of the poem, Marsh offers WR's 'surmise that it cast odium
on the Pope', thus causing CR to destroy it; or, Marsh suggests, perhaps it
was 'sent to *Once a Week* and rejected, in a way that soured Christina's relations

with the magazine' (*CR* 248). The poem refers to an incident in 1859 involving 'brutalities by Papal States troops against the citizens of Perugia, during a short insurrection' (*CR* 248). It was perhaps inspired by Milton's 'On the Late Massacre in Piedmont' (written in 1655) about an incident in which inhabitants who did not conform to the Catholic religion were massacred.

['I have done with hope']

[Probably composed between 27 Aug. and 18 Nov. 1859. MS: GD.]

Promises like Piecrust

[Composed 20 April 1861. Editions: 1896, 1904. MS: BL.]

Title from an old English proverb: 'Promises are like piecrust, made to be broken.'

By the waters of Babylon

[Composed 1 Dec. 1861. Editions: 1896, 1904. MS: BL.]

1–2 *By the waters of Babylon / We sit down and weep* see notes for Part 2, l. 39 of 'The German-French Campaign. 1870–1871', and for title of 'By the waters of Babylon. B.C. 570'.

10–11 *The willow trees grow rank: / We hang our harps thereon* see note for ll. 5–6 of 'Mirage'.

23 *Oh how should we forget* 'If I forget thee, O Jerusalem, let my right hand forget her cunning' (Ps. 137:5).

31–2 *And thou too shalt sit in dust / O daughter of Babylon* 'O daughter of Babylon, who art to be destroyed' (Ps. 137:8).

Better so

[Composed 13 Dec. 1861. Editions: 1896, 1904. 1904 consists of ll. 1–12 and 25–30. Lines from MS poem were published in 1893 as 'Who would wish back the Saints upon our rough'. MS: BL.]

'It might be possible (not, I think, probable) to suppose that Christina wrote the present lines as an appropriate utterance for "Our Widowed Queen." The Prince indeed died on 14 (not 13) December [1861], but on the 13th his death was clearly anticipated' ('Notes' 483).

20 *A sickening hope deferred* see note for l. 2 of 'A Pause of Thought'.
33 *O friend of little faith* see note for ll. 19–20 of 'Consider'.

Our widowed Queen

[Composed 16 Dec. 1861. Editions: 1896, 1904. MS: BL.]

See headnote of 'Better so', above.

3 *the abiding Comforter* 'And I will pray the Father, and he shall give you another Comforter, that he may abide with you for ever' (John 14:16).
25 *In royal patience of her soul possess'd* see note for l. 205 of 'From House to Home'.
27–8 *Then may her children rise and call her bless'd, / Then may her husband praise* see note for ll. 19–20 of 'That Eden of earth's sunrise cannot vie'.

In progress

[Composed 31 March 1862. Editions: 1896, 1904. MS: BL.]

'. . . I can think of two ladies not wholly unlike this touching portrait – one more especially whom Christina first knew in Newcastle-on-Tyne. But any such guess may be quite wrong' ('Notes' 483).

"Out of the deep"

[Composed 17 Dec. 1862. Editions: 1896, 1904. MS: BL.]

Title see note for title of 'De Profundis'.
8 *on holy ground I fool stand shod* see note for l. 2 of 'Worship God'.

For a Mercy received

[Composed 13 Jan. 1863. Editions: 1896, 1904. Lines from MS poem were published in 1893 as ' "As a king, . . . unto the King" '.

'I am unable to say what the "mercy" was' ('Notes' 475).

Summer ['Come, cuckoo, come']

[Composed 5 Feb. 1863. Editions: 1896, 1904. MS: MS2 (PU).]
Title JUNE *1896, 1904.*

A Dumb Friend

[Composed 24 March 1863. Editions: 1896, 1904. MS: BL.]

Margery

[Composed 1 Oct. 1863. Editions: 1896, 1904. Lines from MS poem were published in 1893 as part of 'The sinner's own fault? So it was'. MS: BL.]

In Patience

[Composed 19 March 1864. Editions: 1896, 1904. Lines from MS poem were published in 1893 as part of 'Man's life is but a working day'. MS: BL.]

15 *One dreamless sleep* see headnote of 'Dream-Land'.

Sunshine

[Composed 31 May 1864. Editions: 1896, 1904. MS: MS2 (PU).]

Meeting

[Composed 11 June 1864. Editions: 1896, 1904. Lines from MS poem were published in 1893 as part of 'Parting after parting'. MS: BL.]

"None with Him"

[Composed 14 June 1864. Editions: 1896, 1904. MS: BL.]

Title see note for ll. 11–12 of ' "When My Heart Is Vexed, I Will Complain" ' [' "O Lord, how canst Thou say Thou lovest me?" '].

Under Willows

[Composed 27 July 1864. Editions: 1896, 1904. MS: BL.]

A Sketch

[Composed 15 Aug. 1864. Editions: 1896, 1904. MS: BL.]

It is clear to me that the person here bantered was Charles Bagot Cayley, a man eminently unpractical in habit of mind, and abstracted and wool-gathering in demeanour. It is equally clear that, by the date when the verses were written, August 1864, Christina, though the least forward of women, had evinced towards him an amount of graciousness which a man of ordinary alertness would not have overlooked. This *Sketch* might apparently be interpolated, by a reader of *Ill Rosseggiar dell' Oriente*, between Nos. 2 and 3 of that series. ('Notes' 484)

If I had Words

[Composed 3 Sept. 1864. Editions: 1896, 1904. MS: BL.]

17 *If I had wings as hath a dove* see note for l. 13 of 'Darkness and light are both alike to Thee'.

What to do?

[Composed 4 Aug. 1865. Editions: 1896, 1904. MS: BL.]

8 *wattle* fence made of rods interwoven with twigs.

Young Death

[Composed 3 Nov. 1865. Edition: 1904. Lines from MS poem were published in 1893 as ' "Is it well with the child?" '.

14 *Dust to dust* see note for l. 119 of 'A Martyr. The Vigil Of The Feast'.
22–3 *in the Room, the Upper, / She shall sit down to supper* Jesus ate the Last Supper in an 'upper room': 'And he shall shew you a large upper room furnished: there make ready' (Luke 22:12; see also Mark 14:15).

In a certain place

[Composed 6 March 1866. Editions: 1896, 1904. MS: BL.]

"Cannot sweeten"

[Composed 8 March 1866. Editions: 1896, 1904. MS: BL.]

Title in the sleepwalking scene in *Macbeth*, Lady Macbeth says: 'Here's the smell of the blood still: all the perfumes of Arabia will not sweeten this little hand' (V.i.47–8). CR remembers 'will not' as 'cannot' again when she quotes the line in a letter of 29 July 1880 (*Letters*, II, 240).

Of my life

[Composed 15 May 1866. Editions: 1896, 1904. MS: BL.]

['Yes, I too could face death and never shrink']

[Edition: 1904; also published in 1897 and 1897a. MS: HL.]

WR characterizes this poem as 'a morbid effusion of "Maude"' ('Notes' 478).

Title ENDURANCE *1904*.

['Would that I were a turnip white']

[Editions: 1896, 1904; also published in 1897 and 1897a. MS: HL.]

This intentionally imperfect sonnet figures in an incident in *Maude* in which three girls compete in composing bout-rimés sonnets (the other sonnets being the two poems following this). On bout-rimés, see note on title of 'The last Answer'.

Title X*a 1896, 1904*.

['I fancy the good fairies dressed in white']

[Editions: 1896, 1904; also published in 1897 and 1897a. MS: HL.]

See headnote of 'Would that I were a turnip white', above.

Title X*b 1896, 1904*.

['Some ladies dress in muslin full and white']

[Editions: 1896, 1904; also published in 1897 and 1897a. MS: MS2 (HL).]

See note for 'Would that I were a turnip white'. This was written in '7M.' (MS1 (PU)).

Title X*c*—VANITY FAIR *1896, 1904*.
3 *dog-cart* open coach with two seats, back to back.
  hack coach for hire.
4 *clarence* four-wheeled carriage with seats for four inside.
6 *Witness a man with tassels on his back* in defending this detail of her poem, one of the characters in *Maude* says: 'I have literally seen a man in Regent Street wearing a sort of hooded cloak with one tassel' (1897, p. 23).
14 *Bason* variant of basin. 'Of course every one will understand the Bason to mean the one in St. James' Park' (1897, p. 23).

Autumn ['Fade tender lily']

[Editions: 1904. First published in 1897, p. 79, and 1897a. MS: MS2 (PU).]

Title [untitled] *1897, 1897a*; WITHERING *1904*.

Il rosseggiar dell' Oriente / Canzoniere

[Composed from Dec. 1862 to Aug. 1868. Editions: 1896, 1904. MS: BL.]

These poems were written in response to Charles Cayley's *The Purple of the West* (composed, 1862; published 1863), 'an ambitious production that gradually discloses itself as a love sequence addressed to a fair mistress' (*CR* 290). CR's poems were written within four years of the time when it is assumed Cayley proposed to CR (1866). 'The verses were kept by Christina in the jealous seclusion of her writing-desk, and I suppose no human eye had looked upon them until I found them there after her death' ('Notes' 493). Although WR published them, he did not translate them. In offering translations of nine of the series (*Antigonish Review* 2 (Summer 1971), 46–61), James A. Kohl describes the Italian of the poems as 'stylized rather than conversational in effect' (48).

Title 'The Reddening of the East / Poems'. Cf. CR's image of the sunrise in

'Saints and Angels': 'O my love, my dove, lift up your eyes / Toward the eastern gate like an opening rose' (ll. 13–14).
Epigraph They recite to a Friend

1. Amor dormente?

[Composed in Dec. 1862.]

Translation Love sleeps? // Good-bye, dear friend; / To me is forbidden the love / That has already killed my heart / Beloved lover. // And yet for the afterlife [5] / I consecrate hopes to you; / Because of memories – / So many and then so many.

Title see headnote of 'Dream-Land'.

2. Amor Si sveglia?

[Composed Jan. 1863.]

Translation Love awakens? // In new spring / The ancient spirit is reborn; / Love suggests 'Hope' – / Still I would not say it. // If Love says to you – 'Love'; [5] / If it encourages you, friend, / Swearing 'That heart is yours' – / Still I would not say it. // And yet, that heart indeed / Who knows, is it worth a fig? [10] / I believe so, at least I hope so; / But still I would not say it.

3. Si rimanda la tocca-caldaja

[Probably composed between Jan. 1863 and Jan. 1867.]

'The lines were written in reply to other lines by Cayley named *Si scusa la Tocca-caldaja* ["the steamer is being 'excused'"]. His final line contains the phrase, "S'ei mi fumma" ["If it smokes"], and hence Christina's words in reply' ('Notes' 493–4). Perhaps this 'steamer', or 'cauldron', or 'slow-boiler' is a cooking pot or maybe even a medicinal steamer for colds, much like a modern vaporizer.

Translation The steamer is being sent back. // Far be from me the thought / Of inheriting the object / That once was able to awaken / Love in your breast. / If you no longer want to use it, [5] / If you cannot even make it steam, / It is your sweet duty / To keep it always.

4. "Blumine" risponde:

[Composed Jan. 1867.]

'In "Blumine" the reader will recognize a name used by Carlyle in *Sartor Resartus* [1834]' ('Notes' 494).

Translation 'Blumine' responds: // If I met you in eternal peace, / It would no longer be peaceful for me, beloved; / If I met you in the cursed circle / I would truly lament you more than myself. / Because of you my life lies half-dead. [5] / For you I keep night vigil and bathe the bed [with tears]: / And yet I wait to see you again one day / In the long time that remains, not [in the time] that flies by / And so I say 'Fly' to time, and now / I say 'Pass as well' to the vain world: [10] / While I dream of that which you say and do / I repeat to myself 'Tomorrow will be joyous, / 'Tomorrow we will be' – but if you love me, you know it, / And if you do not love, why show you the depths [of my heart]? –

1 *If I met you in eternal peace* Marsh points out that this poem answers one of Cayley's sonnets, 'also in Italian, beginning "If I should meet her in the eternal peace", originally printed in *Psyche's Interludes* [1857] . . . She headed her own lines *Blumine replies*, in reference to Carlyle's imaginary Professor Teufelsdrockh, who in *Sartor Resartus* is enamoured of the lovely Blumine.' Cayley had 'prefaced one of his Dante volumes with a dedicatory poem addressed to Blumine' (*CR* 370).
3 *the cursed circle* 'By the cursed circle she probably means the second circle in the Inferno, where lovers are tempest-blown' (Packer, *CR* 237).

5. "Lassù fia caro il rivederci"—

[Composed Jan. 1867.]

Translation 'Let it be precious seeing each other again up above' –. // My sweet heart lost and not lost, / My sweet life, that leaves me in death, / Friend and more than friend, I say farewell to you. / Remember me; how blind and limited / Were my hopes, but they were also yours: [5] / Do not scorn this my hard lot. / Let me say 'His hopes' / 'Like mine languished in this winter' – / But I will resign myself – that which was, was. / Let me say once more 'With him I can see [10] / 'Day that breaks from frozen night, / 'Vast heaven beyond brief hell – / 'Beyond the winter, spring.'

6. "Non son io la rosa ma vi stetti appresso"

[Composed April 1867.]

Translation 'I am not the rose but I was in the presence of it.' // Happy house where many times now / My beloved sits speaking and [still] smiling, / Happy woman sitting with him / You cheer him with what you say and do, / Happy garden where I walked, [5] / Thinking of him, thinking and not speaking, / Happy day it will be when I return / Where walking, I thought of him. / And if he is there when I return, / If he welcomes me with his sweet smile, [10] / Every little bird around will sing, / The rose will blush its pretty face – / May God give us that day in eternity, / And in that garden, paradise.

7. "Lassuso il caro Fiore"—

[Composed April 1867.]

'The main topic in this little poem must have some relation to what is touched upon in No. 3 of the series' ('Notes' 494).

Translation 'The beloved, Flower up above' –. // If God were to teach you / True Love / I would surrender you, my heart, / to the beloved Flower. / The beloved Flower calls you [5] / 'Make me happy one day' – / The beloved Flower that loves you / Asks you for love. // That Flower in paradise / Blooms always for you; [10] / Yes, you will see that face again, / You will be content: / About the sorrow that has been / You will ask 'Where is it?' – / Because the past will pass [15] / In a moment. // And because of so much sight / In all eternity, / I like John the Baptist / Will praise God: [20] / The Beloved so beloved / Will be your guerdon, / And your saved soul / Will be mine.

Title 'The closest word for the unknown "lassuso" is "lussuoso" ("grand"). Perhaps "lassuso" is a play on words – "lassu" ("up above"), which refers to "heaven", and "-[o]so" (often the equivalent of the English "-ous" ending)' (Traci Andrighetti, trans.).

8. Sapessi pure!

[Composed May 1867.]

Translation If only I knew! // What are you doing far away from me, / What are you doing, my heart? / That which I do / Is that I always think of you. //

Thinking of you I smile, [5] / I long for you: / And you far away from me – / Are you also devoted?

9. Iddio c'illumini!

[Composed May 1867.]

Translation May God illuminate us! // When the time comes that we will part / Each of us a separate way, / Moment that will come, extreme moment, / Whenever it will be: // The one treading on the uncommon trail, [5] / The other following his usual course, / May there not be born on that day shame in our face / Nor in our breast, remorse. // Whether you go first so alone, / Or whether I precede you on that path, [10] / Ah let us remember then having told each other / In spite of it all, the truth. // How much I loved you and how much! and I should not have / Expressed that love I held for you: / But more, much more than that I was not saying: [15] / In my heart I loved you. // More than happiness, more than hope; / Of life I will not speak, because it is a small thing: / Bitter-sweet you were in remembrance / To a jealous me. [20] // But to me you preferred virtue, / And the truth, friend: and will you not know / Whom you loved at last? The flower opens only / To the rays of a sun. // If you loved Truth more than me, [25] / Jesus was your unknown Love: – / Jesus, although You spoke unbeknownst to him, / Conquer his heart.

10. Amicizia: / "Sirocchia son d'Amor"—

[Composed Aug. 1867.]

Marsh points out that this sonnet answers Charles Cayley's sonnet 'L'Amicizia', 'quoting his opening phrase as epigraph' (*CR* 371).

Translation Friendship: / 'I am Sirocchia of Love' –. // Come Friendship and be welcome, / Come – but let not Love depart: / Both reside in the gentle heart / That refuses not shelter to pilgrims. / This, a sweet and accomplished handmaid, [5] / And that, not a tyrant but a pious master: / May he rule hidden, may he not show himself outside, / May she reveal herself in proper humility. / Today and still tomorrow for friendship, / And still the day after tomorrow if you wish [10] / Because she brings sweet and not bitter things: / And come then, but not with moon or sun, / Day of love, day of great delight, / Day that dawns not to fade away.

Title 'Because *"amiciza"* ("friendship") is a feminine noun, it is the "she" or "handmaid" of this poem. The masculine noun "amore" ("love") is the "he" or "master" of the poem'. "Sirocchi" is probably a dialect form of "sirocco", the hot and dry wind that blows from Africa to the coasts of Southern Italy, sometimes used to mean a storm or tempest. "Sirocco" can also mean "South-East", so perhaps CR is making a play on "the reddening of the East" with a reference to the south-east. Another possibility is that "Sirocchia" may be idiolect for "sister" ' (Andrighetti).

5 *Ancella* ' "Ancella" ("handmaid") also means "sister" in the religious sense' (Andrighetti).

11. "Luscious and sorrowful"— ['Uccello-delle rose e del dolore']

[Composed Aug. 1867.]

Translation Bird of roses and sorrow, / Bird of love, / Happy and unhappy, that song of yours / Is it laughter or despair? / Devout to the irreverent, you have on cold shore [5] / Thorn for nest.

12. "Oh forza irresistibile / Dell'umile preghiera"—

[Composed Sept. 1867.]

Translation 'Oh irresistible force / Of the humble prayer' –. // What will I give You my good Lord Jesus? / Ah the one whom I love most, I present him to You: / Accept him Lord Jesus my God, / My only sweet love, also my heart; / Accept him for Yourself, may he be precious to You; [5] / Accept him for me, save my spouse. / I have nothing but him, Lord, do not scorn him, / Keep him in Your heart among things most dear. / Remember that day while on the cross / You were praying to God so, with feeble voice, [10] / With yearning heart: 'This that they do / 'Father pardon them, because they do not know' –: / He also, Lord, does not know that which he disdains, / He also will love You if one teaches him. / If everything You do not like is but [15] / Fleeting foam in the sea, fleeting mist, / Success or adversity, happiness or sorrow / If all is vanity except You alone; / If he who does not pray calls to You in the void; / If love that does not love You is not love; – [20] / Give Yourself to us, and we will be rich: / Then deny what You will, because we will have everything: / You sweeter than honey, are enough for us; / Worthiest of love, You who loved us.

11–12 *'This that they do / 'Father pardon them, for what they do not know'* Of his crucifiers, Jesus said: 'Father, forgive them; for they know not what they do' (Luke 23:34).

13. Finestra mia orientale

[Composed Oct. 1867.]

Translation My eastern window. / [In Illness.] // I turn my face towards the dawn, / Towards the south, where he dwells: – / You do well you who live at the sides of Aurora; / Those who live with you seem happy. / I turn my languishing eye towards you, [5] / The spirit that fears and hopes still; / Turn towards the one who worships you, / Who loves you, who desires you, in heart and in mind. / Weak and tired I turn myself towards you: / What will become of that which I feel, friend? [10] / Each dear memory of you I gather / How much I would like to tell you! But I never say it. / Far away from you I grieve for the days: / O that we were together in the beautiful, sunny countryside! // O that we were together! [15] / What would it matter / Where we make / Our nest? / The sky would be / Almost that shore. [20] // Ah that I were with thee, / With a heart well certain / Of being loved / How it would desire! / So that the desert [25] / Might bloom.

3 *Aurora* in Roman mythology, the Goddess of Dawn.
19 *Cielo* literally 'sky', but also 'heaven'.

14. [Eppure allora venivi]

[Composed Feb. 1868.]

Translation [And yet you were coming then.] // Oh slow and bitter time! – / When will you come, my heart, / When, oh when? / As dear as you are to me / If I were as dear to you [5] / Would I be searching for you?

15. Per Preferenza

[Composed March 1868.]

Translation By Preference. // Happy your mother, / Happy your sisters, / Who hear what you say, / Who live with you, / Who have a right to love you [5] / Of love content and wise: / Even this their advantage / I would not want for myself. // That grave expression of yours / To see that every so often, [10] / Meanwhile to go on thinking / 'One day he will return'; / To repeat in my heart / (What rose is without thorns?) / 'He knows that I love him at last – [15] / Does he love me still?' Who knows! // This is much more sweet / Than the other, in my opinion: / To be in true desire / Either all or nothing* to you, [20] / Nor do I want to complain too much / Since now that you are apart from me, / If one day in Paradise / You will celebrate with me. // [CR's footnote:] *But no, if not my lover you will be my friend: / That which I will be for you, I do not foretell to you.

16. Oggi

[Composed March 1868.]

Translation Today // It would be impossible / For me not to love you, O beloved: / Who would ever forget / His own heart? / Though you make the sweet bitter, [5] / For me, you make the bitter sweet. / If you give me a little love, / I will give love to you.

17. [Se fossi andata a Hastings]

[Composed March 1868.]

On several occasions, CR's health led her to spend time at Hastings, a seaside resort.

Translation [If I had gone to Hastings.] // I say farewell to you, / My friend, / For weeks / That seem long: / I commend to you [5] / Every so often / Square circles, / Oblong ideas.

Title [untitled] *1896, 1904*.

18. Ripetizione

[Composed June 1868.]

Translation Repetition. // I believed I would see you again, but still I await you; / From day to day I always want you, longing: / When will I see you again, my beloved heart, / When, oh when? // I said it and said it again with perpetual thirst, [5] / And I say it and I still want to say it again, / Like a nightingale that sings and repeats itself / Until the dawn.

1 *Credea* 'Rossetti often uses a particular style of verb conjugation that was used by Dante. In this instance, she uses "credea" to mean "I believed" from the verb "credere" ("to believe"). The modern conjugation for "I believed" is "cred*evo*". "Cred*ea*" has not been in use for centuries' (Andrighetti).

19. "Amico e più che amico mio"—

[Composed Aug. 1868.]

Translation 'Friend and more than my friend' –. // Heart of mine, to which my other heart turns / Like magnet to pole, and does not find you, / The birth of my new life / Was with sorrow, grief, and pain. / But the harsh pain was for me the precursor [5] / To lofty hope that sings and nurses; / Yes, without pain, love cannot be felt / And he who does not feel love does not live. / O you who in God are in me, but after God, / All my earth and much of heaven, [10] / Think of the pain for me, behind a veil, / Speak to yourself and do not ever say that I long for you – / Tell it to yourself, my sweet heart, / If you really love me tell yourself that I love you.

20. "Nostre volontà quieti Virtù di carità"—

[Composed Aug. 1868.]

The opening lines bear some resemblance to Petrarch's sonnet 122: 'Go, ye warm sighs, to reach a frozen heart' (Cayley's translation in *Qui Comincian le rime di M. F. Petrarca: The Sonnets and Stanzas of Petrarch* (1879)).

Translation 'May the Virtue of charity soothe our wills' –. // Gentle wind that towards the noon / Goes blowing, ah carry one of my sighs, / Saying to him that which I must not say, / With a sigh speaking to him thus: / She who said 'No' wishing 'Yes' [5] / (Wishing and not wishing – why tell it again?), / She sends you this: It is vanity the blossoming / Of this life that we lead there. / Hear what she says, weeping: It is vanity / This worldly love that is born and dies; [10] / Ah raise your eyes, as I want to raise mine / Towards the kingdom where not in vain / God loved as much as one can love / And all the creation in charity.

Title ' "*carità*" means "charity" or "alms" – but in poetry, it often means "love" ' (Andrighetti).

21. [Se così fosse]

[Composed Aug. 1868.]

Translation [If only it were so.] // I loved you more than you loved me: – / Amen, if Lord God wanted it this way; / Amen, even though You are breaking my heart, / Lord Jesus. // But You who remember and know all, [5] / You who died for virtue of love, / In the other world give me that heart / That I loved so much.

By way of Remembrance

[Basic text: MS, unless otherwise stated.]

Section title 'This second epistle, beloved, I now write unto you; in both which I stir up your pure minds by way of remembrance' (2 Pet. 3:1).

['Remember, if I claim too much of you']

[Composed 1870. Editions: 1896, 1904. MS: BL.]

Pointing out that this poem was never published by CR, Marsh says it is 'thought to be related to [CR's] "*Il Rosseggiar*"' (*CR Poems* 447).

Title BY WAY OF REMEMBRANCE *1896, 1904*.

['Will you be there? my yearning heart has cried']

[Composed 1870. Editions: 1896, 1904. MS: BL.]

See headnote of 'Isidora'.

1 *Will you be there* see note for l. 72 of 'Isidora'.
6 *jubilee* see note for l. 11 of ' "They Desire a Better Country" '.

['In resurrection is it awfuller']

[Composed 23 Oct. 1870. Editions: 1896, 1904. MS: MS2 (BL).]

3 *Of all kins of all nations of all speech* see note for Part 1, l. 3 of ' "Behold a Shaking" '.

['I love you and you know it—this at least']

[Composed 1870. Editions: 1896, 1904.]

Valentines from C.G.R.

[Composed from 1876 to 1886. Editions: 1896, 1904. MS: BL.]

In the MS, at the end of the series, CR wrote: 'These *Valentines* had their origin from my dearest Mother's remarking that she had never received one. I, her CGR, ever after supplied one on the day = & so far as I recollect it was a *surprise* every time, she having forgotten all about it in the interim.'

Section title VALENTINES TO MY MOTHER *1896, 1904.*

['Fairer than younger beauties, more beloved']

[Composed 1876.]

Title 1876 *1896, 1904.*

A Valentine, 1877

[Composed 1877.]

'The signature "C. G. for M. F. R." [at the end of MS] means that these verses are spoken as in the person of Maria Francesca (our elder sister) in heaven; she had died in November 1876' ('Notes' 488).

Title 1877 *1896, 1904.*

1878

[Composed 1878.]

'This is marked on the back [of MS] "To the Queen of Hearts," and the like with all the ensuing Valentines' ('Notes' 488). All the Valentine poems below are so labelled.

1879

[Composed 1879.]

1880

[Composed 1880.]

St. Valentine's Day / 1881

[Composed 1881.]
Title 1881 *1896, 1904.*

A Valentine / 1882

[Composed 1882.]
Title 1882 *1896, 1904.*
7 *Pallas* Athena, Greek goddess of wisdom.

February 14. 1883

[Composed 1883.]
'Here is an evident reminiscence as to the death of Dante Gabriel in April 1882; probably also as to the death of my infant son Michael in January 1883' ('Notes' 488).

Title 1883 *1896, 1904.*

1884

[Composed 1884.]

1885 / St. Valentine's Day.

[Composed 1885.]

1886 / St. Valentine's Day.

[Composed 1886.]

['Ah welladay and wherefore am I here?']

[Editions: 1896, 1904. MS: PU.]

This poem and all the others up to ['You who looked on passed ages as a glass'] are bouts-rimés (see note on headnote of 'The last Answer'). All have the number of minutes (5–9) to compose written on MS.

Title SONNETS / WRITTEN TO BOUTS-RIMÉS / VI *1896, 1904.*

['Along the highroad the way is too long']

[MS: PU.]

['And is this August weather? nay not so']

[Editions: 1896, 1904. MS: PU.]

Title SONNETS / WRITTEN TO BOUTS-RIMÉS / VII *1896, 1904.*

['From early dawn until the flush of noon']

[MS: PU.]

['I seek among the living & I seek']

[Editions: 1896, 1904. MS: PU.]

Title SONNETS / WRITTEN TO BOUTS-RIMÉS / V *1896, 1904.*
1 *I seek among the living & I seek* see note for title of ' "I Look for the Lord" '.

['O glorious sea that in each climbing wave']

[MS: PU.]

['Oh thou who tell'st me that all hope is over']

[MS: PU.]

['Surely there is an aching void within']

[MS: PU.]

['The spring is come again not as at first']

[MS: PU.]

['Who shall my wandering thoughts steady & fix']

[MS: PU.]

5 *the Sleepy Styx* see note for l. 1 of ' "Ferry me across the water" '.

['You who look on passed ages as a glass']

[MS: PU.]

[Ninna-Nanna]

[Dates of composition of the poems are unknown. Editions: 1896, 1904. MS: RO.]

Ninna-Nanna consists of CR's translations or paraphrases of some of the poems in *Sing-Song*. 'Our cousin Teodorico Pietrocola-Rossetti first made some translations from that book, whose title he rendered as *Ninna-nanna*; herein I follow his lead. His translations were felicitous. Inspired by his example,

Christina made other – and, I conceive, in poetic essentials still better –
translations' ('Notes' 494).

In 1896 and 1904, each poem was given the general title 'NINNA-
NANNA', a number and the first line of the original version. For example,
the first, 'Angeli al capo, al piede', is called 'NINNA-NANNA / I /
[ANGELS AT THE FOOT]'. These titles are not given here, but the first
line of the original English version is indicated.

['Angeli al capo, al piede']

Translation of 'Angels at the foot'.

['Amami, t'amo']

6 *Cor suo ti chiama* ('She calls you her heart') cf. CR's original English version:
'Her eyes above you', in 'Love me,—I love you'.

['E babbo e mamma ha il nostro figliolino']

4 *senza madre* in CR's original English version there follows a line omitted in
her Italian version: 'Forlorn as may be', in 'My baby has a father and a
mother'.

['S'addormentò la nostra figliolina']

In this version, the subject is a little girl; in CR's original English version,
'Our little baby fell asleep', it is a boy.

['Cuccurucù! cuccurucù!']

4 *Di rose il ciel si ammanta* ('The sky is covered with roses') cf. CR's original
English version: 'Roses in the east are born', in ' "Kookoorookoo!
kookoorookoo!" '
8 *Risalta il sol dal mare* ('The sun leaps out of the sea') cf. CR's original
English version: 'The day, the day, the day is springing', in ' "Kookoorookoo!
kookoorookoo!" '

['Oibò, piccina']

Translation of 'Baby cry'.

['Otto ore suonano']

4–8 *Son per Papà . . . V'è per Mammà* ('One for you, / None for me; / And there is a short little note / for Mamma') cf. ll. 4–6 of CR's original English version, 'Eight o'clock'.

['Nel verno acccanto al fuoco']

Translation In the winter near the fire / I eat my soup; / And I open the window to the robin, / Since he also wants a little of it. // <u>alternate</u>: – [5] / The robin looked into the window: – / Come, come taste <u>my soup!</u> / I am wearing well-lined wool, / But you are only wearing a little red body. (Cf. CR's original English version, 'Bread and milk for breakfast'.)

['Gran freddo è infuori, e dentro è freddo un poco']

Translation It is very cold out, it is a little cold inside: / How pleasing soup is near the fire! / I am wearing good cloth – / But the poor do not have / Soup to drink, or fire near which to sit, [5] / O roof, O cloth, in this intense cold: / Ah my heart aches when I think about it! (Cf. CR's original English version, 'There's snow on the fields'.)

['Scavai la neve,—sì che scavai!']

7–8 *Ma non . . . la lena* ('But do not blow in that sand: / He who blows in sand loses his breath') cf. CR's original English version: 'But all the winds from every land / Will rear no blossom from the sand', in 'I dug and dug amongst the snow'.

['Sì che il fratello s'ha un falconcello']

7 *Da capo a piè ti stringo a me* ('From head to foot I squeeze you to me') cf. CR's original English version: 'I'll rock you, rock you in my arms', in 'Your brother has a falcon'.

['Udite, si dolgono mesti fringuelli']

Translation Listen, while the chaffinches lament: / We made a beautiful nest for our dear twins, / But three naughty boys came and laid it to waste, / Spring fled, the evening grew dark, / And we lacked the time to make a second [5] / Little round nest. (Cf. CR's original English version, 'Hear what the mournful linnets say'.)

['Ahi culla vuota! ed ahi sepolcro pieno']

Translation of 'A baby's cradle with no baby in it'.

['Lugubre e vagabondo in terra e in mare']

Translation of 'O wind, why do you never rest'.

['Aura dolcissima, ma donde siete?']

6 *Tu addolci un freddo mondo, O mammoletta* ('You sweeten a cold world, O little violet') cf. CR's original English version: 'But violets in the chilly Spring / Make the turf so sweet', in 'O wind, where have you been'.

['Foss'io regina']

Translation of 'If I were a Queen'.

['Pesano rena e pena']

Translation of 'What are heavy? sea-sand and sorrow'.

['Basta una notte a maturare il fungo']

Translation Only one night is enough for the mushroom to mature; / The oak wants a century, and it does not seem long: / And yet, the brief century and the long evening: / Since the oak is an oak, but a mushroom is only a mushroom. (Cf. CR's original English version, 'A toadstool comes up in a night'.)

['Porco la zucca']

Translation Foolish Pig / Fitted in wig! .. / Whatever would you say to him? / I would kneel, I would pay my respects, / 'Good evening Pig, how are you?' [5] // Ah! Woe! If ever by chance / The tail were to go bad? ... / Keep calm: / Good lawyer / It would become a codicil. [10] (Cf. CR's original English version, 'If a pig wore a wig'.)

10 *codicillo* 'CR is playing on words: "coda" means "tail", but "codicillo" means "codicil" or "postscript"' (Traci Andrighetti, trans.).

['Salta, ranocchio, e mostrati']

6 *disprezzarti* in CR's original English version there follows a line omitted in her Italian version: 'But though you're lumpish, you're harmless too', in 'Hopping frog, hop here and be seen'.

['Spunta la margherita']

Translation of 'Where innocent bright-eyed daisies are'.

['Agnellina orfanellina']

Translation An orphaned little lamb [female] / lies at the top of a hill, / Cold, alone, without mother, – / Without mother, alas! / I will be both mother and father to you, [5] / I will be your shepherd girl; / Do not tremble, beloved lamb, / I am thinking of you. (Cf. CR's original English version, 'A motherless soft lambkin'.)

['Amico pesce, piover vorrà']

Translation of 'When fishes set umbrellas up'.

['Sposa velata']

The Italian version of CR's original English version, 'A ring upon her finger'.

Translation Veiled bride, / Curled, / Meek and submissive: / Entranced groom, / Proud, [5] / Next to her: – / Friends, lovers, / Singing at heart, / In front of them / Spread flowers! [10]

['Cavalli marittimi']

2 *Urtansi in guerra* ('Colliding in war') cf. CR's original English version: 'Rear a foaming crest', in 'The horses of the sea'.

6–8 *Corrono o ... Spumando vanno* ('Running or being: / Those [others] go rolling / Bubbling') cf. CR's original English version: 'Munch corn and clover, / While the foaming sea-horses / Toss and turn over', in 'The horses of the sea'. In a letter to DGR (17 Sept. 1878), CR writes: ' "Rotolandosi spumando vanno" ["Rolling, bubbling, they go"] gave, I thought, something of the accumulative on-come of the waves, mounting on each other's backs: otherwise *I* am not aware of any reason against "spumanti" ["foaming" or "frothing"] as you suggest; or one might obliterate the sound yet more by making it "spumosi" ["foamy" or "frothy"] ...] (*Letters*, II, 186).

['O marinaro che mi apporti tu?']

4–6 *Piante non ... Fecerne mondo* ('They are not plants, nor are they dug from a mine / Lesser creatures in brine / Made the world from it') cf. ll. 5–8 of CR's original English version, in 'O sailor, come ashore'.

['Arrossisce la rosa: e perchè mai?']

Translation The Italian version condenses the English version, 'The rose with such a bonny blush', into its first two lines, followed by: 'And you, Rose, what do you have / That makes you blush so if you are well?'

['La rosa china il volto rosseggiato']

Translation of 'The rose that blushes rosy red'.

['O ciliegia infiorita']

6–8 *La verde ... Bella sei tu* ('Wreathed in green / Crowned in red, / You are beautiful') cf. ll. 8–10 of CR's original English version, 'Oh fair to see'.

[' "In tema e in pena addio']

6 *Nel secolo de'guai* (In the century of woes) cf. CR's original English version: 'Goodbye till earth shall wane', in ' "Goodbye in fear, goodbye in sorrow'.

['D'un sonno profondissimo']

In the English version, 'Baby lies so fast asleep', 'baby' is the subject; in the Italian, 'my sister'.

5–8 *In sonno . . . e pace* ('In very profound sleep / Calm and content she lies / Leave a flower in her hand, / A kiss on her forehead, – and peace!') cf. CR's original English version, in 'Baby lies so fast asleep'.

['Ninna nanna, ninna nanna!']

2 *Giace e dorme l'agnellina* ('The little lamb lies and sleeps') cf. CR's original English version: 'Flowers are closed and lambs are sleeping', in 'Lullaby, oh lullaby!'
4 *Monna Luna s'incammina* ('Lady Moon gets going') cf. CR's original English version: 'Stars are up, the moon is peeping', in 'Lullaby, oh lullaby!'

['Capo che chinasi']

Translation 'Head that is lowering, – / Eyes that are closing, – / To bed, to bed, / Sleepy head! / Sleep, dear one, [boy] [5] / Until the morning, / Sleep, dear one.' (Cf. CR's original version, 'Lie a-bed'.)

The Succession of Kings

[MS: PU.]

In the upper right margin of the MS is a note in WR's hand: 'Unpublished / (very early)'.

A true Story. (continued.)

[MS: UK.]

On the reverse side of the MS, WR has written: 'These are early poems (say 1847) by Christina G. Rossetti. The handwriting . . . is my mother's.'

['The two Rossettis (brothers they)']

[Composed 19 Sept. 1853. Edition: 1904. MS: UBC.]

'These lines were sent to me in a letter from Christina (then settled with our parents at Frome, Somerset), saying: "This morning I commenced a remarkable doggerel on the P. R. B.," etc. And then, after copying out the lines, "You may guess that at this point of my letter I came to a stand, from the extra finish bestowed on the three last asterisks"' ('Notes' 491).

   Cf. 'The P.R.B.', written two months later; and its notes identifying PRB members mentioned in this poem.

Title THE P.R.B. / I *1904*.
1 *The two Rossettis* WR and DGR.
7–8 *D. G. Rossetti offered two / Good pictures The Girlhood of Mary Virgin* (1849) and *Ecce Ancilla* (1850). (In both CR posed as the model for Mary.)
11–12 *William Rossetti . . . Cuts up his brethren* alluding to WR's activities as a critic.

Imitated from the Arpa Evangelica: Page 121

[Editions: 1896, 1904. In 1896 and 1904, ll. 33–65 are presented as 'First Version', and ll. 1–32 afterwards as 'Second Version'. MSS: ll. 1–32: MS1 (PU); ll. 33–65: MS2 (BL).]

'In our father's volume of religious poems, *L'Arpa Evangelica* (1852), there is a composition named *Nell' Atto della Communione*, in three parts. The third begins with the words – "T'amo, e fra dolci affani," and is the one which Christina here translates in two separate versions. The date which I give is conjectural ['*Circa* 1855', 1904, p. 184]. I assume the translation to have been made not long after our father's death' ('Notes' 471).

Title HYMN AFTER GABRIELE ROSSETTI *1896, 1904*.
3 *Blessed that John, who on Thy Breast* see note for l. 13 of 'After Communion'.
24 *My Manna & my Spouse* Christ, as bridegroom of the redeemed, and, in himself, like the manna God provided to the Israelites when they wandered in the wilderness. See notes for l. 176 of 'From House to Home' and for ll. 13–14 of 'Eve'.
33 *'T'amo; e fra dolci affanni'* I love you; and within sweet doubts.
38 *Love's Pelican* according to tradition, the pelican wounds her breast to feed her young, and so becomes an image of Christ, sacrificing himself to save the world.

['Mr. and Mrs. Scott, and I']

[MS: PU.]

1 *Mr. and Mrs. Scott* see headnote of 'At Home'.
2 *Mr. Manson, Editor* unidentified.
3 *the social Proctors* possibly the family of Ellen Proctor (1837–1909), a close friend whom WR asked to write a biographical sketch of CR after her death. See Marsh on Ellen Proctor, *CR* 560–61.
7 *Annie Hayle* unidentified.

['Gone to his rest']

[MS: PU.]

On the MS, above the border enclosing the text, in an unknown hand, is written: 'Feb' 6, 1869'; below the border, 'On the death of AB's chaffinch Bouby.' 'AB' is most likely Alice Boyd (see headnote of 'At Home').

2 *Bouby* presumably the name of the chaffinch who died (see headnote, above).
13 *Past price of pelf* worth more than money.

['O Uommibatto']

[Editions: 1896, 1904. MS: PU.]

In the lower right margin of MS in WR's hand: 'Circa 1869'.

Christina took it upon her to Italianize in this form the name of the *Wombat*, which was a cherished pet animal of our brother. It will be understood that she is exhorting the Wombat not to follow (which he was much inclined to do) his inborn propensity for burrowing, and not to turn up in the Antipodes, his native Australia. As a motto to these verses Christina wrote an English distich: – 'When wombats do inspire, / I strike my disused lyre'. ('Notes' 494)

Translation O Wombat / Agile, joyful, / How you have grown / Hairy and round! / Ah do not flee [5] / Like a vagabond, / Do not vanish / Burrowing through the world: / It's really the weight of / a hemisphere [10] / Not a light burden.

Title L'UOMMIBATTO *1896, 1904.*

['Cor mio, cor mio']

[Editions: 1896, 1904. MS: PU.]

Below the poem in MS, in WR's hand: 'Circa 1870'.

Translation My heart, my heart, / I no longer see you, but I remember / The spent day, / My heart. / Do you even remember the long love, [5] / Heart of my heart, / My heart?

Title COR MIO *1896, 1904*.

['I said "All's over"—& I made my']

[MS: PU.]

The partial MS is written in pencil, and recopied over in ink – and then deleted.

['I said good bye in hope']

[Editions: 1896, 1904. MS: PU.]

Below the poem in MS, in WR's hand: 'C75 / Circa 1875'.

Title MEETING *1896, 1904*.
17–18 *My shelter was a gourd, / And it is dead* see note for l. 4 of 'As froth on the face of the deep'.

My Mouse

[Composed 1 Jan. 1877. Editions: 1896, 1904. MS: BL.]

'This was not a "mouse" in the ordinary sense, but a "*sea*-mouse." Mr. Cayley had picked it up on the seashore, and presented it to my sister, preserved in spirits. The sea-mouse was with her to the end, and may remain with me to the end; its brilliant iridescent hues are still vivid. The scientific name of this creature is *Aphrodita aculeata*; hence the allusion to "Venus"' ('Notes' 492).

5 *Iris* Greek goddess of the rainbow and messenger of the gods.

['Had Fortune parted us']

[Editions: 1896, 1904. MS: BL.]

Cayley's poem, 'Moor and Christian' (1880), expressed the emotion of 'a

Moslem woman severed from her Christian lover. Christina, using the same metre and number of lines, wrote the present composition – of course from a very diverse point of view' ('Notes' 488). On MS, CR wrote: 'Una replica / Lo vedesti, Cor mio.' ['A replica / You saw it, my Heart.']; WR annotated 'Circa 1880'.

Title PARTED *1896, 1904.*

Counterblast on Penny Trumpet

[Editions: 1896, 1904. MS: BL.]

WR, remarking on CR's note below the poem ('*see* St. James's Gazette / July 21. 1882'), 'infers' that the newspaper 'contained some effusion censuring Mr. Bright for having quitted the Ministry after the bombardment of Alexandria, and also censuring Mr. Gladstone for continuing in the Ministry. My sister knew and cared next to nothing about party politics (apart from questions having a religious bearing); in all her later years, however, her feeling leaned more towards the Conservative than the Liberal cause' ('Notes' 493). The 21 July issue of the *St James's Gazette* published a verse commentary on the resignation of John Bright (Marsh, *CR* 502).

Epigraph 'Then wax'd the skirmish fierce and hot' from Joanna Baillie (1762–1851), *The Phantom: A Musical Drama in Two Acts* (1836), l. 171.

1 *Mr. Bright retiring* John Bright (1811–89) was an English statesman and reform advocate who resigned over British intervention in Egypt.

2 *Mr. Gladstone staying* see headnote of 'Maiden-Song'.

10 *Tyrtaeus* seventh-century BC Greek poet whose songs were said to have inspired the Spartans to defeat the Messenians.

['A roundel seems to fit a round of days']

[MS: UBC.]

Below the poem in MS is a note: 'W.B.S. spurns the birthday (Sept. 12. 1887) tribute of CGR: *tableau* visible to the "fine frenzied" mental eye.' 'W.B.S.' probably refers to William Bell Scott (see headnote of 'At Home'); 'fine frenzied' comes from *A Midsummer' Night's Dream*: 'The poet's eye, in a fine frenzy rolling' (V.i.12).

1 *roundel* originally a synonym for 'rondeau' (a poetic form of three stanzas built on two rhymes), but used by Swinburne for a variant form consisting of eleven lines (two rhymes and a repeated refrain that is either the first word of the poem or some part of its first line). Swinburne popularized the form in *A Century of Roundels* (1883), dedicated to CR.

5 *groundsel* plant given as food to caged birds and sometimes used for medicinal purposes.
7 *Girvan's ocean groundswell* Girvan is a small seaport and holiday resort in Scotland.

['Heaven overarches earth and sea']

[MS: MS2 (BodL).]

Except for 'Good Friday Morning', and 'Sleeping at Last', this poem appears to be 'about the last lines produced by my sister' ('Notes' 477). On MS1 (PU), a rough draft, WR wrote: 'C93'.

Title HEAVEN OVERARCHES *1896, 1904*.
5 *no more sea* see notes for titles of ' "Was Thy Wrath against the Sea?" ' and 'And there was no more Sea'.

['Sleeping at last, the trouble & tumult over']

[Editions: 1896, 1904. MS: BL.]

On the back of the MS, in WR's hand: '13/2/95 – I found these verses at Christina's house, in a millboard-case containing some recent memoranda &c – nothing of old date – The verses must I think be the last that C. ever wrote – perhaps late in 1893, or early in 94/WMRossetti.' ('Millboard' is a kind of pressed pasteboard.)

Title SLEEPING AT LAST *1896, 1904*.

4th May morning

[MS: PU.]

2 *widgeon* a wild duck.
9 *From Torrington remote to utmost Chelsea* from CR's street (Torrington Square) to the neighbourhood of DGR and William Bell Scott (see headnote of 'At Home').
16 *Bellevue Palace* Bellevue House, home of Bell Scott.
17 *courteous Courtneys* relatives of Alice Boyd (see headnote of 'At Home'), who were frequent visitors to Bellevue House.
18 *dear Scotts* see headnote of 'At Home'.
19 *dark-locked Alice* Alice Boyd.

[' "Quanto a Lei grata io sono']

[MS: PU.]

Translation As for you I am grateful / Humility will express the simplicity of the gift.

THE CHINAMAN

[Edition: 1904. First published in WR (ed.), *DGR: His Family-Letters*, I, 79. Basic text: *DGR: His Family-Letters*.]

WR dates '1842' and identifies this poem as the second CR wrote. As a schoolboy, WR was asked to write a composition in verse on the Anglo-Chinese Opium War, and his younger sister, seeing him at work, 'chose to enter the poetic lists' and produced this poem ('Notes' 464).

[" 'Come cheer up, my lads, 'tis to glory we steer!' "]

[Edition: 1904. First published in WR (ed.), *DGR: His Family-Letters*, I, 78. Basic text: *DGR: His Family-Letters*.]

WR dates the poem '*Circa* 1845' and states it was an 'oral improvise' and that its first line comes from 'a well-known old-fashioned song' ('Notes' 465). The song is 'Hearts of Oak'.

Title COUPLET *1904*.

THE PLAGUE

[Editions: *1896*, 1904.]

WR dates the poem '*August* 1848' and quotes DGR as saying: 'I grinned tremendously over Christina's *Plague*, which however is forcible, and has something good in it' ('Notes' 490).

['How many authors are my first!']

[Editions: *1896*, 1904. WR notes that the charade was published in *Marshall's Ladies' Daily Remembrancer* (1850), but it has not been located there.]

WR dates the poem '*Spring* 1849'. The solution to this charade, according to him, is 'Proserpine' ('Notes' 491).

Title TWO CHARADES / II *1896, 1904*.

['Me you often meet']

[Editions: *1896*, 1904. WR notes that the enigma was published in *Marshall's Ladies' Daily Remembrancer* (1850), but it has not been located there.]

WR dates the poem '*Spring* 1849'. He identifies the enigma as ' "Punch," which was another of the subjects for the *Remembrancer* of 1850' (1896, p. 377).

Title TWO ENIGMAS / II *1896, 1904*.
9 *of Isis and of Cam* rivers – that flow through Oxford and through Cambridge, respectively.

['So I began my walk of life; no stop']

[Appended to a letter dated 31 Aug. 1849. First published in *FL*, p. 8. Basic text: *FL*.]

8 *sop* solid food used for dipping in liquid food.
12 *must* commenting on this word in a letter to WR [8 Sept. 1849], CR writes: 'The *must* to which my life has turned is the substantive. You cannot imagine the grief which filled me on learning that you could answer *Yes* to anything connected with my sonnet: yours is less bad, but also less uncommon' (*Letters*, I, 24).

['So I grew half delirious and quite sick']

[WMR's typescript letter containing the poem is dated 24 Sept. 1849. Edition: 1904. Basic text: TS (PU).]

Title A BOUTS-RIMÉS SONNET *1904*. (See note on title of 'The last Answer'.)

['On the note you do not send me']

[WR's typescript letter containing the poem is dated 18 Jan. 1850. Basic text, TS (PU).]

In the letter, which is addressed to WR, CR states: 'Will you recite to Gabriel the following admonitory stanza:—' Following the poem she adds: 'The last line is a little mystic. Never mind' (*Letters*, I, p. 32)]

CHARON

[Editions: *1896*, 1904.]

WR dates the poem '*June* 1853'. 'These sportive lines take their cue, of course, from the old song, "In my cottage near the wood." They tickled our sister Maria uncommonly. I had totally forgotten them; Christina on her deathbed (9 October 1894) happened to recite them to me . . . and I wrote them down from her lips' ('Notes' 491).

Title NEAR THE STYX *1896*.
In 1904, WR notes: 'When first published (1896), the verses were entitled by me *Near the Styx*; but I now gather that Christina's own name for them was *Charon*' ('Notes' 491). See note for l. 1 of ' "Ferry me across the water'.
5 *Cerberus, thou triple fair* three-headed dog who guards the entrance to the underworld.

FROM METASTASIO

[Editions: *1896*, 1904.]

WR dates the poem '1857 – or earlier rather than later' in 1896, and '1868 or rather earlier' in 1904. 'These lines form a paraphrastic translation from a lyric ("Amo te solo") in Metastasio's *Clemenza di Tito* [1734]. I found them as a scrap of MS., pencilled by Christina thus: "I must have done this for Traventi, who wanted English words set to music." Traventi was a Neapolitan musical composer and teacher' ('Notes' 486–7).

Title see headnote of 'Ariadne to Theseus'.

CHIESA E SIGNORE

[Editions: *1896*, 1904.]

WR dates the poem 'perhaps towards 1860'. 'These lines appear in a scrap of MS. which is thus inscribed: "Written out at Folkestone 6 Aug. 1871, but date of composition not recollected by C. G. R." ' ('Notes' 493).

Translation CHURCH AND LORD / THE CHURCH / Fly, prayer, and say to him / Why are You so far away? / Do You walk among the lilies / carrying a rose in hand? / Were You not lily and rose [5] / When You loved me? /

Turn to your bride, / O my Lord Jesus. // THE LORD / I will not forget you, / My sweet and melancholy bride: [10] / If you are the rose to me, you know it, / Because I wear thorns on my head. / I gave you heart and life, / All of myself I gave to you, / And now I offer you help: [15] / Have faith in Me. // THE CHURCH / Fly, prayer, to Him, / And cry: Be patient! / I want You and no other, / Without You all is without. [20] / More fragrant than lily / And rose to me You are, / The Eternal Son of God, / O my Lord Jesus'.

5 *Non Ti fui giglio e rosa* ('Were You not lily and rose') see note for l. 11 of 'Long Barren'.

GOLDEN HOLLY

[Editions: *1896*, 1904.]

WR dates the poem '*Circa* 1872'. He reports Swinburne as having pronounced this poem 'an excellent thing'; it was addressed

to Holman [Holly] Frederic Stephens, then a little boy, son of our constant friend, Frederic George Stephens (one of the seven members of the 'P.R.B.'). Tennyson once saw the child in the Isle of Wight, and pronounced him (not unreasonably) to be 'the most beautiful boy I have ever seen.' Mr. Stephens senior, in sending me the verses at my request, wrote that they refer 'to H. F. S.'s frequent pet name of "The Golden Holly," given because of the brightness of his long hair, as well as his birthday being on October 31. He had sent a tea-rose to C. G. R.' ('Notes' 492)

['I toiled on, but thou']

[Editions: *1896*, 1904.]

WR dates the poem '*Circa* 1875' in 1896, and '*Circa* 1884' in 1904. The rough draft was written on the back of the sonnet 'Scarce Tolerable Life' ('Notes' 489).

Title WHO SHALL SAY? *1896, 1904.*

COR MIO ['Still sometimes in my secret heart of hearts']

[Editions: *1896*, 1904.] Lines from MS poem were published in 1881 in Part 18 of 'Later Life'.

WR dates the poem '*Circa* 1875'.

Title My Heart (Italian).

7 *rue* plant with yellow flowers, but with the connotation of the verb 'rue' (to feel regret or sorrow).

['My old admiration before I was twenty']

[Edition: 1904. First published in William Bell Scott, *Autobiographical Notes of the Life of William Bell Scott*, 2 vols. (Harper and Brothers, 1892), I, 314. Basic text: Bell Scott, *Autobiographical Notes*.]

WR dates the poem '*Spring* 1882'. 'These verses were sent to Mr. Scott in acknowledgement of a copy of his volume, *A Poet's Harvest-Home*, issued in April 1882' ('Notes' 493). See headnote of 'At Home'.

Title TO WILLIAM BELL SCOTT *1904*.
2 *predilect* chosen or favoured.
6 *a heavy old heart* 'The reference to "a heavy old heart" has no doubt to do with the death of Dante Rossetti, 9 April 1882' ('Notes' 493).

TO MARY ROSSETTI

[Edition: 1904.]

WR dates the poem '*Circa* 1887'. 'These slight lines were addressed to my daughter Mary, probably when aged from five to six' ('Notes' 493).

['Ne' sogni ti veggo']

[Editions: *1896*, 1904.]

WR dates the poem '*Circa* 1890'.

Translation In my dreams I see you / Lover and friend; / At your feet I sit, / I hold you still. / Neither you nor I question, [5] / Neither you nor I express, / The ancient love / That inflames our hearts. / Ah if I had a voice / Myself to discover – [10] / Ah if I knew to tell / Of anguish and love! / Ah if only I could have / Slept at length, / Neither crying nor speaking, [15] / Gazing at you always!

Title SOGNANDO *1896*, *1904*.
   'I give this title ['Sognando' – 'Dreaming'] to two stanzas which I find written by Christina into a copy of our father's book of sacred poems – *Il Tempo, ovvero Dio e l' Uomo, Salterio* ['Time; or God and Man, Psalter'], 1843 . . . they would thus be the last Italian verses which my sister produced. She has signed them thus: "C. G. R., fired by papa's calling this metre difficult" – the

metre being the one adopted throughout the whole book *Il Tempo* in its original form' ('Notes' 494).

TO MY FIOR-DI-LISA

[Editions: *1896*, 1904.]

WR dates the poem '1892'. 'One of the friends who saw my sister most frequently and affectionately in her closing years was Miss Lisa Wilson. Christina sometimes called her Fior-di-lisa (which is the same as Fleur-de-lys). Miss Wilson . . . presented to Christina in 1892 a little illuminated book of poems by herself; my sister inserted into it the present lines of response' ('Notes' 489). See note on l. 14 of 'A Birthday'. Marsh identifies Wilson as 'Christina's close friend and companion' and 'an aspiring poet and artist of whom virtually nothing is known'. CR cast 'Lisa as a lily and herself as a rose – their respective flower emblems' (*CR* 538).

['Hail, noble face of noble friend!']

[Appended to a letter dated 19 Dec. 1885. First published in Packer, 'Christina Rossetti and Alice Boyd of Penkill Castle', *The Times Literary Supplement*, 26 June 1959, p. 389. Basic text: Packer, 'CR and Alice Boyd'.] For Boyd, see headnote of 'At Home'.

[The Crump three-volume edition ended with a poem ('Hymn') that she later concluded was by Theodore Monod rather than CR; it has been dropped from this edition.]

INDEX OF TITLES

The page numbers in italics refer to the relevant Notes for each poem.

INDEX OF FIRST LINES

The page numbers in italics refer to the relevant Notes for each poem.

THE STORY OF PENGUIN CLASSICS

Before 1946 …'Classics' are mainly the domain of academics and students, without readable editions for everyone else. This all changes when a little-known classicist, E. V. Rieu, presents Penguin founder Allen Lane with the translation of Homer's *Odyssey* that he has been working on and reading to his wife Nelly in his spare time.

1946 *The Odyssey* becomes the first Penguin Classic published, and promptly sells three million copies. Suddenly, classic books are no longer for the privileged few.

1950s Rieu, now series editor, turns to professional writers for the best modern, readable translations, including Dorothy L. Sayers's *Inferno* and Robert Graves's *The Twelve Caesars*, which revives the salacious original.

1960s The Classics are given the distinctive black jackets that have remained a constant throughout the series's various looks. Rieu retires in 1964, hailing the Penguin Classics list as 'the greatest educative force of the 20th century'.

1970s A new generation of translators arrives to swell the Penguin Classics ranks, and the list grows to encompass more philosophy, religion, science, history and politics.

1980s The Penguin American Library joins the Classics stable, with titles such as *The Last of the Mohicans* safeguarded. Penguin Classics now offers the most comprehensive library of world literature available.

1990s The launch of Penguin Audiobooks brings the classics to a listening audience for the first time, and in 1999 the launch of the Penguin Classics website takes them online to a larger global readership than ever before.

The 21st Century Penguin Classics are rejacketed for the first time in nearly twenty years. This world famous series now consists of more than 1300 titles, making the widest range of the best books ever written available to millions – and constantly redefining the meaning of what makes a 'classic'.

The Odyssey continues …

The best books ever written

PENGUIN 🐧 CLASSICS

SINCE 1946

Find out more at www.penguinclassics.com